Celebrate Everything!

Fun Ideas to Bring Your Parties to Life

WRITTEN AND ILLUSTRATED BY

DARCY MILLER

WILLIAM MORROW

An Imprint of HarperCollinsPublishers

ALSO BY
DARCY MILLER

Our Wedding Scrapbook

Celebrate Everything!

HarperCollins books may be purchased for
educational, business, or sales promotional use.
For information please e-mail the Special Markets
Department at SPsales@HarperCollins.com.

FIRST EDITION

Cover design by Lauren O'Neill
Cover photograph by Johnny Miller
Author photograph by Donna Newman

Library of Congress Cataloging-in-Publication Data
has been applied for.

ISBN 978-0-06-238875-9

16 17 18 19   [IMA]   10 9 8 7 6 5 4 3 2 1

for my family and friends
who make life worth celebrating
...every day!

celebrating Martha

At Martha's 70th birthday, I used old photos of her on coasters, wine bottles, and a memory book, and incorporated her most-loved things—Scrabble, gardening, animals—into food and décor. And my drawings of her appeared throughout the night. The favor? A tote with a map of her favorite spots in NYC.

FOREWORD

Martha, my daughter Daisy, me, and Martha's dog, Ghengis Khan.

Martha and me at my wedding.

My daughters and Martha at my parents' anniversary party.

FOR THOSE OF US who love to entertain, this charming book will come as an eye-opener. Can one person really and truly be this creative, this inspired, and this talented? Can Darcy Miller Nussbaum really make each party, party after party, so different? So fun? So colorful? And so beloved by all attendees? The answer is abundantly yes, and each celebration, so beautifully photographed in this book, clearly illustrates Darcy's ability to collect diverse ingredients and combine them into a cohesive, mind-boggling whole.

I have known Darcy and worked closely with her for more than twenty years. Darcy was fresh out of college when she came to *Martha Stewart Living* to work on a new initiative, *Martha Stewart Weddings*.

It was as clear then as it is now that Darcy has great organizational skills, a lively personality full of originality and whimsy, and a penchant for treating her friends and family to amazing celebratory events. Under her direction, birthdays, anniversaries, graduations, weddings, engagements, showers, and even weekend dinners or pool parties become ultra special, ultra exciting, and ultra enjoyable.

It is helpful that Darcy's personal living style is very like what you see photographed in this book. Darcy has opened her home and introduced her family, including her husband, Andy, her three daughters, Daisy, Ella, and Pippa, her sister and her family, and her parents and parents-in-law. Darcy's own wedding, which I attended and which graced the pages of *Martha Stewart Weddings*, was perhaps one of the most beautiful weddings I ever saw. The many children's birthdays have always been inventive and thoroughly enjoyable; crafting, sewing, swimming, cooking—all have been incorporated into colorful and detailed events at which all guests, kids and parents alike, are absorbed in the activities and thrilled to be busy and productive.

Darcy and Andy fêted me at their home on one of my birthdays and we were all amazed at the clever personal details, the lovely table settings, and the delicious foods, savory and sweet!

I suggest you use this book as inspiration first, then as instruction. Darcy's sources for paper, candy, crafts, decorations, and themes are generously shared, and her suggestions for photography, archiving, and "recording" celebrations are valuable reminders that making memories of celebrations and rites of passage is important in the preservation of the fine fabric of family life.

Congratulations, Darcy!

Martha Stewart

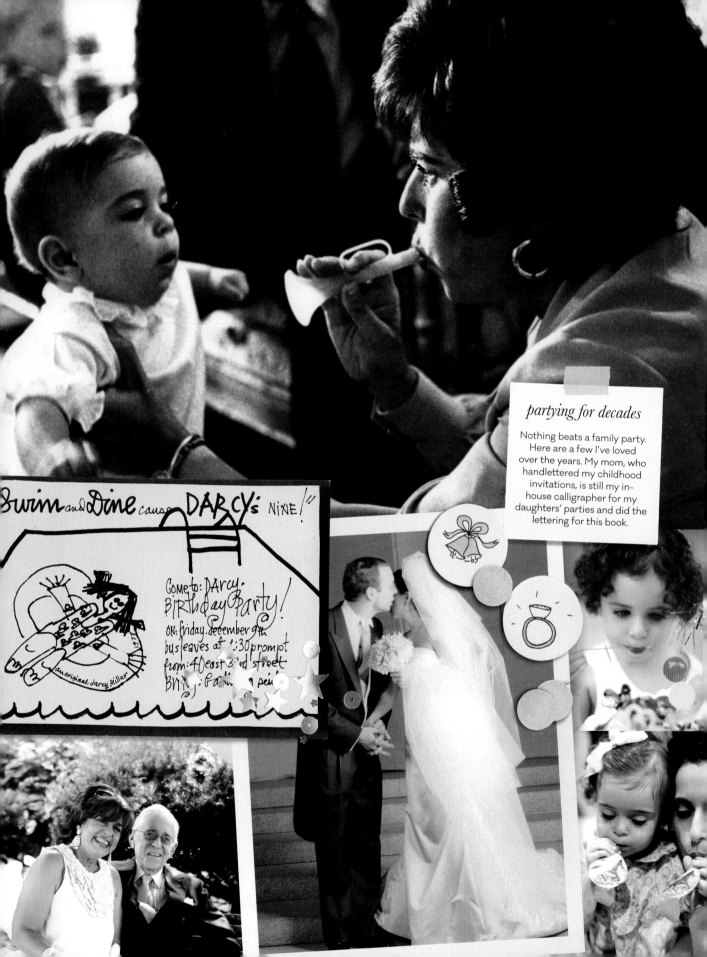

Swim and Dine cause DARCY's NiNE!"

Come to: DARCY'
BIRTHday Party!
ON: friday. december 9th
bus leaves at 4:30 prompt
from: 40 east 3rd street
BRING: a bathing suit

an original darcy miller

partying for decades

Nothing beats a family party.
Here are a few I've loved
over the years. My mom, who
handlettered my childhood
invitations, is still my in-
house calligrapher for my
daughters' parties and did the
lettering for this book.

INTRODUCTION

WHEN I WAS LITTLE, I loved celebrating—my friends, my family, milestones, and everyday moments. My mother always involved my sister, Jenny, and me in planning parties. She understood that including us made things more fun. I still have the invitation for my ninth birthday pool party, which read "Swim and Dine cause Darcy's Nine!" I did the drawing, and my mom did the writing. Decades later, we are still making our invitations together.

My love of drawing and celebrations grew along with me. When I was in college at the University of Pennsylvania, my friend Robin and I started a small business making customized party favors. After I graduated, I freelanced for New York City event planner Robert Isabell, doing things like taking a thousand votive candles out of boxes, arranging them throughout a massive event space, lighting them . . . then returning at one in the morning to blow out each one and pack them up. It was tiring, but when the lights dimmed, and the candles glowed, I was reminded how magical a party can be.

I've tried to convey that magic for over two decades as an editor working for Martha Stewart. Now, in this book, I'll show you how to focus your own vision for a celebration. I encourage you to take all the ideas offered on these pages and put your own spin on them.

Personally, the celebrations I love can take any number of forms: a full-blown party, but also balloons tied on a child's chair on their birthday, or even a note tucked into a briefcase on an anniversary. In our home, every birthday starts with a super festive breakfast table—banners and confetti included. Continuing my mother's tradition, I've chosen to involve my daughters, Daisy, Ella, and Pippa, in planning family celebrations, and my husband, Andy, also plays a part, decorating the breakfast table on Valentine's Day and leaving birthday notes in the girls' packed lunches. Even if we don't D.I.Y. everything, we *always* D.I.T. (Do-It-Together)!

I hope this book inspires you to start your own traditions, whether you go all out with dozens of details or pick one simple idea. You might craft, you might bake, you might do none of the above and simply stick a candle in a birthday doughnut (a favorite of mine!).

The point of a party is to gather people to enjoy one another's company, so host a celebration where you can enjoy your guests, rather than just appearing as a blur between the kitchen, the buffet table, and the bar. Enjoy the parties *and* the planning.

What I've learned from my parents, and what I hope I have passed on to my daughters, is that the most important thing about celebrating is doing something special for the people you love. It makes them feel good and that, in turn, makes you feel good.

So let's celebrate. Everything!

Darcy Miller

1

First...

WHAT ARE YOU CELEBRATING?

Anything can work as the jumping-off point for a party, but the options tend to fall into two groups: the time-honored occasions, like showers and holidays, and the more personal—even off-beat—reasons to celebrate. Here are some ideas to get you started.

IT'S A BIG DEAL!

BOUGHT A HOUSE

CLEAN BILL OF HEALTH

GAINED CITIZENSHIP

GOT A DRIVER'S LICENSE

GOT CAST OFF

RETIREMENT

TOOTH FAIRY'S FIRST VISIT

THE CLASSICS

ANNIVERSARY

BABY SHOWER

BACHELOR/BACHELORETTE

BIRTHDAY

BON VOYAGE

BRIDAL SHOWER

CULTURAL EVENT

ENGAGEMENT

GRADUATION

HOLIDAYS

HOMECOMING

HOUSEWARMING

REUNION

SWEET 16

WEDDING

PEOPLE & PROJECTS

BUSINESS LAUNCH

FUNDRAISER

MOMS'/DADS' NIGHT OUT

NEIGHBORHOOD WATCH

STAFF APPRECIATION

WE VOLUNTEERED

WELCOME HOME

IN SEASON

4TH OF JULY

APRIL FOOL'S DAY

CINCO DE MAYO

EARTH DAY

FATHER'S DAY

HALLOWEEN

LABOR DAY

MEMORIAL DAY

MOTHER'S DAY

NEW YEAR'S EVE

SCHOOL STARTS/ENDS

SNOW DAY

SOLSTICE

ST. PATRICK'S DAY

THANKSGIVING

VALENTINE'S DAY

YOU DID IT!

EXAMS ARE OVER

GOOD REPORT CARD

GOT INTO COLLEGE

JOB PROMOTION

NEW JOB

PAID OFF YOUR LOANS

SCHOOL AWARD

SCIENCE FAIR WIN

TEAM WIN

POP CULTURE & SPORTS

AWARD-SHOW VIEWING

BIG GAME

MARATHON VIEWING

OLYMPICS

OPENING DAY

SPORTING EVENT FINALS

SUPER BOWL

TV SHOW VIEWING

WHY NOT?

CHECK OUT MY HAIRCUT

HALF BIRTHDAY

JUST BECAUSE

NEW PET

OPEN THE GOOD WINE!

QUIT YOUR JOB

TGIF

WE'RE ALL SINGLE

Then ...

PICK A THEME

No one says a party has to have a theme. But choosing one can help focus your ideas, map out the details (food, drinks, activities), and make everything a little more fun. A theme doesn't have to be exhaustive—it could be as simple as your favorite color. Sometimes, the occasion is the theme. Why not throw a Super Bowl party with guests in jerseys, and serve snacks and décor in team colors? Here are some suggestions, along with ways to bring your party to life.

places

A favorite locale can turn your party into the place to be.

ENGLAND
flag décor • crowns • tea • Britpop soundtrack • jam, scones, clotted cream

FRANCE
berets • baguettes • flag palette • classic French sayings (*oh là là, c'est la vie, joie de vivre*) • crêpe-making station • portrait artist

HAWAIIAN LUAU
grass skirts • tiki torches • lei-making activity • fruity drinks with umbrellas • fruit salad served in carved-out melon

ITALY
Red, white, and green décor • pasta bar • biscotti and Amaretto dessert • olive oil favors

MEXICAN FIESTA
sombreros • Mexican flag banner • taco/margarita bar • piñata • maracas favors

NEW YORK CITY
Playbill invites • paper cutout skyline • neighborhood table names (SoHo, Chinatown) • Liberty crowns • pizza, bagel, cheesecake bar • black-and-white-cookie favors

music

Play up your playlist.

DISCO
disco balls • foil fringe doorway curtains • dance contest • disco ball cake pop favors

HIP-HOP
headphones • sneakers • microphones • graffiti • break dance contest

JAZZ
black-and-white-stripe décor • sheet music place mats • musical notes décor

ROCK STAR
ticket as invitation • blow-up instruments • all-access passes • fog machine • karaoke

iconic eras

Look back in time (or into the future!)
for great ideas.

STONE AGE
"bone" decorations •
faux animal skins •
dinosaur décor • candy
rocks • volcano cake

WILD WEST
"Most Wanted" invite
or photobooth • cowboy
hats/boots • cacti •
bandanas • sheriff's badges

ANCIENT ROME
togas • gladiator • sandals
• laurel leaf wreathes •
gold temporary tattoos

VICTORIAN
floral china • lace
doilies • teacups to hold
flowers • high tea

MEDIEVAL
stick horses • pigtail braids
• jousting competitions •
turkey drumsticks • goblets
• flower crowns

SOCK HOP
poodle skirts • cat's-eye
glasses • root beer
float station • record cake

FUTURE
come dressed as you see
the future • crystal balls •
tarot readings • 8-ball favors

food & drink

Let the menu be your muse.

BAKING/COOKING
decorate aprons • recipe swap
• top chef contest •
ingredients in a jar favors

BEER/WINE TASTING
food and drink
pairings • blind taste test
• decorate coasters

CANDY
candy buffet • make candy
bracelets • bubblegum blowing
contest • toothbrush favors

COCKTAILS
bartending contest • garnish-
your-drink bar • shaker favors

ICE CREAM
scoop décor • sundae bar •
ice cream scooper favors
See page 204 for more ideas.

PICNIC
gingham blankets • snacks in
baskets • Frisbee tag

PIZZA
checkered tablecloths •
garland with slice pennants
• toppings bar

pampering parties

Treat yourself—and your guests—
to a relaxing celebration.

PAJAMA
decorate pillowcases •
flashlight tag • tell
scary bedtime stories •
sleep masks • pancake
breakfast • personalized
slipper favors

SPA
cucumber slices • mani/
pedi station • bejeweling
mirrors • decorating robes

YOGA
yoga attire • follow
a yoga video or have an
instructor come • juice
bar • essential oils favor

fantasy

Let the party's theme supply some magic.

ALIEN/MONSTER
decorate masks • monster impersonation competition • monster juice • stick googly eyes on everything

MAD SCIENTIST
candy or flowers in beakers • goggles • drinks served in test tubes • make-your-own edible concoction

MAGIC
top hats • stuffed bunnies • playing cards décor • balloon animals • learn magic tricks • magic wand favors

MERMAID
seashells for placecards • snacks served in fish bowls • treasure chests with pearls • bubble favors • make shell necklaces

PIRATE
eye patches • a treasure chest to hold favors • red and white stripes • skull and crossbones temporary tattoos • pirate hat-making • walk the plank contest

SUPERHERO
POW and BAM signs • everyone has a super-power all night • cape decorating + design your own superhero insignia • "super food" station

TREASURE HUNT
treasure map invitation • messages in bottles • balloons • gold chocolate coins • treasures buried in a sand box

PRINCESS
tiaras • magic wands • feather boas and beads • decorate crowns with stick-on jewels • tea sandwiches

planes, trains, & autos

A mode of transport will get your party moving.

AIRPLANE
plane ticket invites • peanuts • mini drinks • paper airplane contest • wing pins

BULLDOZERS
construction signs • black paper tablecloth with neon tape stripes • toy dump truck races • orange cone party hats

CARS & TRUCKS
toy truck cake topper • remote-control car relay • stoplight games • chocolate doughnut "tires" • red, yellow, and green M&M's in brownies for traffic light

RACE CARS
a checkered flag banner • construction paper racetrack • Matchbox car cake toppers • food table "refueling station"

ROCKET SHIPS & OUTER SPACE
silver palette • glow-in-the-dark stars • hanging ball lanterns • freeze-dried space food

dress-up

It's not what you do, but what you wear.

BLACK TIE
tuxes • gowns • hors d'oeuvres on silver trays • martini glasses/champagne coupes

FASHIONISTA
makeshift runway (use tea-lights) • D.I.Y. paper dress competition • catwalk contest • mini "purse" favor bags

GLOW-IN-THE-DARK
dress in white • glow tape • glow markers/chalk • glow stick accessories • LED lights in balloons

MASQUERADE
candlelight • bow ties • elbow gloves • decorate masks with feathers and jewels

DOUBLE THE FUN

If your party has multiple guests of honor, or you can't decide on a theme, combine a few favorites.

ballplayers

+

ballet

princesses

+

pirates

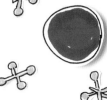

games

Make an activity your theme and it's play time!

CASINO
playing card garland • chocolate casino chips • roulette wheel cake • dice brownies • poker games

COPS & ROBBERS
eye masks • sheriff's badges • photo booth for taking "mug shots" • limbo with caution tape • hidden $$$ bags with prizes

POKER NIGHT
card décor • bubblegum cigars • chocolate coins • card-suit-shaped cookies, or mini sandwiches • Texas Hold 'em game

LEGO
D.I.Y. shoebox Legos for décor • Lego cupcake toppers • Lego-building competition • Lego brick cake (made with sliced cupcake tops)

MONOPOLY
Get Out of Jail Free invites • $ confetti • "GO" and a red arrow sign on front door • top hats, mustaches, and canes • Monopoly street table names • play Monopoly!

MURDER MYSTERY
magnifying glass invite • guests come as characters with a secret • chalk body outline • crime scene tape • fingerprint place cards • question mark cake

LASERTAG
glow sticks • glow-in-the-dark paint for D.I.Y. T-shirts • face paint • target decorated cookies

TWISTER
primary color palette • round stickers on everything • freeze dance to "The Twist" • play Twister! • cupcakes in Twister colors

numbers, letters, & colors

Everyone's got a favorite.

MILESTONE BIRTHDAY
play up the number
(1, 16, 18, 21, 65, etc.) • new
privileges (driving, voting)

SINGLE INITIAL
celebrate the honoree's
initial (for Jesse: serve
Jell-O • juice bar • jam
favors • guests dress in "J"
costumes like Jackie O.)

ALPHABET
alphabet soup • letters
on cupcakes • make letter
bead keychains • say
the alphabet backward
contest • who can
come up with the most
words for each letter •
letter rubber stamp favors

FAVORITE COLOR
have everything from
décor, crafts, food,
and favors be in your
chosen hue

RAINBOW PARTY
food and décor in
rainbow colors • clouds
(cotton, felt, or balloons)
• chocolate coins
For more, see page 184.

PICK A THEME COLOR

PIPPA'S PURPLE PARTY

*A single shade makes an instant
theme. When my daughter
Pippa turned 3, her favorite color
was a perfect starting point.*

IDEAS TO TRY

Sprinkle colored sanding
sugar on iced doughnuts.

Give guests colored
accessories.

Make wands out of on-
palette candy sticks by simply
taping on a paper star.

why not?

Cut out paper flowers and tape to the top of pixie sticks for dessert table décor.

Pippa

keep in mind

—

Stuffed animals make adorable décor and double as prizes for games or gifts for the baby's room.

PICK A THEME BOOKS

GOODNIGHT MOON BABY SHOWER

This party for my friend Anne included red balloons, bunnies, and cows jumping over the moon.

IDEAS TO TRY

Use drawings and mini clothespins to make garlands.

Serve moon cakes, kitten cookies, and "starry" milk.

Cut out a star-and-moon garland to wrap around cake stand.

books

Let classic books inspire the story of your party.

ALICE IN WONDERLAND
EAT ME and DRINK ME signs • mushrooms • top hats • mismatched teacups • pastel sweets • decks of cards as favors

BREAKFAST AT TIFFANY'S
blue boxes with white ribbons as centerpieces or to hold favors • long strands of pearls • black opera-length gloves • black sunglasses • coffee bar

CHARLIE AND THE CHOCOLATE FACTORY
golden ticket invites • "chocolate river" fondue • white suspenders • guess how many gumballs in a jar • movie viewing • LOTS of candy

CURIOUS GEORGE
monkey décor • yellow hats • city skyline décor • banana muffins • hidden monkey game • curious contest (guests guess things about each other)

ELOISE
pink, white, and black palette • hair ribbons • hide-and-seek • tea sandwiches • turtle-shaped treats

THE GREAT GATSBY
all-white dress code • green lights • jazz music • Charleston dance contest • mint juleps

THE WONDERFUL WIZARD OF OZ
ruby slippers • blue gingham napkins • rainbow candy • witch legs sticking out from couch • braiding station with blue ribbons • yellow brick road hopscotch

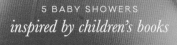

5 BABY SHOWERS
inspired by children's books

1
Corduroy: buttons + teddy bears

2
The Little Prince: stars + roses

3
Madeline: French pastries + Paris décor

4
Charlotte's Web: pigs + plastic spiders + string

5
The Very Hungry Caterpillar: caterpillars + butterflies

nature

Little kids (and the young at heart) love celebrating outdoors.

BUGS & CRITTERS
antennae headbands •
AstroTurf • make
dirt pudding with gummy
worms • caterpillar
sleeping bag race

BUTTERFLIES
decorate paper butterflies
• butterfly face painting
• paper butterflies as
straw toppers • butterfly-
shaped sandwiches

GARDEN
lots of flowers •
wheelbarrow as drink
cooler • crudité • decorate
pots • "dirt" cupcake
with crushed Oreos • seed
packet favor

JUNGLE
animal masks • animal
print balloons • vine
garlands • bamboo leaves
• animal crackers

CAMPING
woodland scavenger
hunt • trail mix • s'mores •
compass cookies • ghost
stories • survivial kit favors

PICK A THEME FLOWER

DAISY'S FIRST BIRTHDAY

*Flowers are great inspiration.
A daisy party was a natural for my
daughter Daisy's first birthday.*

IDEAS TO TRY

Choose a color palette inspired
by your flower.

Top cupcakes with flower-
shaped cookies; make a
hole in the middle to act as
a candle holder.

Mix and match real and paper
flowers in décor.

why not?
—
Top cupcakes with flower stickers on toothpicks.

movies

Whether it's an award-show viewing party or an entire night built around an iconic film, a big-screen bash is always a big hit.

MOVIE NIGHT
come dressed as a character from movie • ticket décor • movie projector • flavored popcorn bar • red-and-white cartons • movie trivia games

OSCARS
a red carpet for your guests • a formal dress code • Hollywood sign backdrop • ballot cards • rate outfits • awards for guests

SPY FILM
"Top Secret" invites • 007 décor • disguise props • fingerprints • magnifying glass favors

CARTOON
cartoon strip invites • come as a character • brightly colored decor • cartoon trivia contest

PICK A THEME HOLLYWOOD

EVERYONE'S A STAR

Movies are a blockbuster hit for a theme. This birthday party was inspired by Hollywood itself.

IDEAS TO TRY

Serve star-shaped Rice Krispies Treats.

Wrap a ticket roll around cake stands and trays.

Line up "Walk of Fame" removable decals for guests to sign and take home.

why not?

String garlands of Oscar statues, gold stars, and popcorn.

why not?

—

Cut ear shapes out of paper ahead of time. Day of, fill balloons, draw faces, and tape on ears.

PICK A THEME PUPPY

PUP PUP HOORAY

My daughter Pippa loves dogs, so we threw her "Pippa's Puppy Party." Pick an animal to make your party bark, chirp, or even roar.

IDEAS TO TRY

Cut faces out of colored paper and glue to paper favor bags or slip around party blowers.

Post a wall decal of your pet.

Line toy dogs down the table as a centerpiece/favors.

animals

Fill your fête with stuffed critters and decorate-your-own animal masks— guests will go wild!

FARM

hay bales • animal noses • bandanas • farm coloring pages • play "B-I-N-G-O"

DINOSAURS

toy dinos • dino egg hunt • make clay fossils • invent a new dinosaur

SAFARI

toy binoculars • toy Jeep cake topper • tracks in frosting • animal print décor

ZOO

balloon animals • zookeepers vs. animals as teams • animal crackers • make paper bag puppets

why not?
—
Hang paper snowflakes
from the ceiling
with monofilament.

MERINGUE
ANGEL CAKE

SUGAR-DUSTED
CANÉLLES

SNOWFLAKE
LOLLIPOP
TOPPERS

NUTCRACKER SUITE

The holidays always make me think of the Nutcracker ballet. A table filled with sugarplums is one way to celebrate the season.

IDEAS TO TRY

Cut doilies into sections and attach to edges of cake stand.

Display angel cake pops in Styrofoam covered with cotton batting "snow."

seasons

Any time is right to celebrate your favorite time of the year.

SPRING

daffodils • tulips • wheatgrass (as shakes or as décor) • decorate a birdhouse activity • make-your-own kites activity favor • butterfly-shaped tea sandwiches from cookie cutters • picnic-style lunch • lemonade • pastel candies • plant seeds

SUMMER

all-white dress code • sunglasses • flip-flops • beach balls • snacks served in sand pails • make-your-own popsicles • gummy fish • watermelon ice cubes • snow cones (boozy or not) • beach games (Frisbee, volleyball) • decorate water bottles

FALL

autumn leaves • pumpkins and gourds • mums • hay bales • cornucopias • heirloom corn • cider • candy apples

WINTER

silver tinsel • white lights/candles • white-and-silver décor • snowflakes • holiday classics such as *Frosty the Snowman*. For more ideas, see page 231.

MARZIPAN FRUITS

sports

An activity, a culture, a dress code and maybe even a menu—choose a sport or sporting event and your party is as good as planned.

BALLET
tutu attire • pink lemonade • ballerina cake topper • legwarmer favor

BASEBALL
wear team caps • pitching contest • wiffleball • hot dogs • Cracker Jacks

BOWLING
red, white, black palette • bowling shirts • funny team name contest • guests sign a pin

FOOTBALL
hosts dress as refs • tape "yard lines" on green place mats • touch football • football piñata • football cookies

ICE SKATING
glitter makeup • cocoa • make pom-poms • glove/ earmuff favors • rink cake

KENTUCKY DERBY
horse décor • fancy hats • roses • trophy center- piece • horse names as table names • mint juleps

SKATEBOARDING
Band-Aids • graffiti • learn a trick • guests sign host's skateboard or sneaker

OLYMPICS
flags banner • invent games • relay with paper torch • chocolate medals • international food • colored doughnuts as Olympic rings

PING PONG
globe string lights • decorate paddles • ping pong tournament • cup games

SOCCER
black, white, and green décor • whistles • dribble contest • take team photo • soccer ball cake

TENNIS
"tennis whites" attire • round-robin tournament • tennis ball cake pops • wristband favors

keep in mind

Don't forget to take a "team photo" of all the guests before the party's end.

ALL PLAY BALL

A sport theme is an instant activity, but you can also use it as inspiration for décor and treats to make a party a slam dunk.

IDEAS TO TRY

Use a black paint pen to turn orange balloons into basketballs.

Have guests sign a basketball for the birthday child to keep.

Arrange a "who can spin a ball on their finger the longest" contest.

crafts

Throw a party centered on making something and you've got an activity and a favor!

ARTS & CRAFTS

craft supplies • a D.I.Y. necklace station • color-your-own place mat • crayon-shaped candles on cake • decorate ceramics with oil-based pens

PHOTOGRAPHY

photo backdrops with props • decorate a frame • cookies printed with photos

SCRAPBOOKING / CARDMAKING

everyone brings photos with guest of honor • scrapbooking supplies • finger-food snacks • album favors

GLITTER

sequins • glitter makeup • glitter party hat/crown • a glitter manicure station • edible glitter on cake

PICK A THEME SEWING

A "SEW ELLA" PARTY

My daughter Ella loves crafts, so we threw a party stitched together with all things sewing.

IDEAS TO TRY

Create "spools" made with wafer cookies and a big marshmallow.

Make pin cushion sewing kit favors out of jam jars.

Pre-cut felt letters for name banners.

why not?

—

Stack two round cakes, frost, and sandwich between two foam core circles to create the spool cake shown opposite.

3

Take some time to ...

MAKE IT PERSONAL

If your party honors a person, spend time thinking about him or her to help you customize the celebration. I always sit down and answer a list of questions about the guests of honor to help develop the details. At my wedding, for example, the cake was inspired by Ladurée, a bakery my husband and I visited when we started dating.

PICK A THEME CANDY

SWEET EMOTION

What's my friend Dylan's obsession? Candy. For her engagement party, sweets inspired everything from invitations to cocktails.

IDEAS TO TRY

Showcase the couple's initials (here in a candy display using Lucite letters and trays).

Wrap a chocolate bar as an invitation.

Make custom swizzle sticks.

PLEASE JOIN ME FOR
CANDY COCKTAILS
BRIDE-TO-BE DYLAN LAUREN!

DYLAN LOVES PAUL

ask yourself...

Use the following questions as prompts that will lead to ideas about themes, venues, or certain details. A favorite color might become the theme or simply show up in the flower arrangements.

WHAT'S THE GUEST OF HONOR'S FAVORITE...

actor/actress

animal

artist

author

band

bar

board game

book

candy

cartoon

city

clothing brand

color

dance move

decade

dessert

drink

fashion trend

flower

food

fruit

hobby

holiday

ice cream flavor

location

movie

musician

newspaper

painting

pastime

pet

place to travel

professional sports team

quote

restaurant

singer

song

sport to play

subject in school

time of year

TV show

WHAT'S HIS OR HER...

birthstone

childhood dream job

guilty pleasure

heritage

hometown

nickname

profession

WHAT WAS HIS OR HER FIRST...

word

crush

kiss

job

award

WHERE DID HE OR SHE...

grow up

go to school/camp

study abroad

WHO'S HIS OR HER...

celebrity crush

fashion icon

role model

favorite athlete

DOES HE OR SHE...

collect (or hoard!) anything

have a lucky charm

speak any other languages

two's company

For an anniversary, shower, or any event celebrating a couple, use the previous prompts plus these for-two questions:

WHAT DO YOU KNOW ABOUT THEIR...

proposal

wedding

WHEN AND WHERE DID THEY...

meet

go on their first date

have their first kiss

realize they were in love

say "I love you"

first travel together

get engaged

WHAT'S THEIR FAVORITE...

activity to do together

date spot

dream retirement

place to vacation

restaurant or bar

song

tradition

4

And finally, let's...

GET REAL

Once you've come up with the ideas to personalize your party, it's time to devise a game plan for making it happen. Obviously it all depends on the size of the party—and of your budget—but even for a small gathering, the more organized you are, the better. From setting the guest list to planning how you'll invite people, here are some nitty gritty logistics to consider sooner rather than later in order to make realizing your vision, on your budget, easier, and to bring your party from your imagination into reality.

STEP 1
set the budget

Figure out your budget early on, since it will determine the shape your party takes. It's always smart to set the spending goal 20 percent below your absolute ceiling, because there are always unexpected expenses at the end (umbrellas if it rains). Building in that "cushion" will give you some wiggle room just in case. Budgets vary, but here are some general rules to keep in mind.

DECIDE WHERE TO SPLURGE (AND SAVE)

For your foodie husband's surprise birthday, you might opt for fancy passed hors d'oeuvres and rely on your own playlist rather than live music. At your sister's bachelorette, the finger food may matter less than a great champagne bar.

REMEMBER: PEOPLE ONLY SEE WHAT'S THERE

No one will know what you considered but cut, or that store-bought mini cupcakes replaced expensive petits fours— especially if you set them out in a beautiful way.

START EARLY

Pretend your party is two weeks before the actual date. You can shop around and look for best prices, and you'll avoid overnight shipping and unexpected costs, and having that extra time will save your sanity, too.

GET IT IN WRITING

If you're hiring outside help, or even just ordering a cake, be sure to get price quotes, fee agreements, or work hours in writing. For big-picture hires like a caterer, ask each vendor for an item-by-item (or hour-by-hour) breakdown, and request that they detail every charge you'll incur—overtime, delivery fees, taxes, tips, etc. Keep a copy for your records.

SUPER SAVERS: ON THE MONEY

If you can have your event in an off season, on an off day, or at an off time, you'll save on venue, food, and staff. Reconsider:

a prime-time slot

If you can host your dad's retirement party on a Tuesday evening rather than a Saturday, it's liable to cost less. And if you host a birthday party or shower that starts at 3 p.m., guests won't show up expecting a meal. Or, make it clear that your event is a cocktail party, rather than a full meal, by specifying that on the invite—an end time can do this very tactfully: "Please join us from 6 – 8 to celebrate . . ."

helping hands

If you feel overwhelmed with to-dos, ask friends to lend a hand. Just be strategic about how much you delegate and to whom. Does your sister have beautiful hand-writing? Perhaps she can address your envelopes! Have your buddies over to assemble favors. (You supply the wine and snacks!) Finally, don't forget that kids love to be included. Give them a fun job like greeting guests at the door or handing out favors to keep them involved.

don't forget
—
the best things in life are free, and the best things in life aren't things.

WHERE THE MONEY GOES

a sample list of expenses

Most celebrations entail only a fraction of these items (and major rituals such as weddings, baptisms, and bar/bat mitzvahs will require some special additions). But having this list of needs will help get you thinking.

STATIONERY	Calligrapher, save-the-dates, invitations, map, placecards, menus, postage
LOCATION	Venue, insurance, guest transportation, cleanup
RENTALS	Tents, tables and chairs, linens, tableware and glassware, kitchen equipment, AV equipment, HVAC/fans, generator
DÉCOR	Accents (balloons, garlands, wall hanging, backdrops), lighting (candles, string lights, strobes, professional setup), flowers
DRINKS	Bar (alcohol, corkage fee, mixers), nonalcoholic (soft drinks, bottled water, juices), coffee and tea service, ice
FOOD	Cost per head, caterer, hors d'oeuvres, meal, kids' menu, dessert, cake/cake-cutting fee
HELPERS	Planner, valet, coat check, bartenders, servers, cleanup, extras (tips, overtime, delivery charges)
ENTERTAIN-MENT	DJ/band, dance floor, photo booth and props, speakers (for an iPod if doing music yourself), miscellaneous (magician, petting zoo, psychics, sketch artists, etc.)
PHOTOGRAPHY	Montage/video played during event, photographer, videographer, prints

choose your location

Figuring out your venue is key to managing your overall budget, and will affect how much you spend on everything else. A gathering at home has its benefits (the space is free!) but moving the party to an event space has lots of perks, too (no spills on your furniture—and there won't be 40 people lining up to use your bathroom). Answer these questions to help determine which option is best for you:

STYLE OF SPACE

How do you want the party to feel? The bones of a room (furniture, the amount of light, even the architecture) will influence the look and vibe of your fête. A botanical garden, for instance, automatically sets the tone for a floral-inspired party, whereas you may have to rely more on your own decorations in a space with dark walls and heavy leather couches.

DÉCOR

How much control do you want over the space? Different venues have different rules. Some limit decorations (do you want to hang streamers from the ceiling?) or prohibit things like lit candles.

RAIN PLAN

Outdoor parties are beautiful, but if your back-up plan for bad weather doesn't have a decent indoor option, it probably shouldn't be an option. Assume it will rain on the day-of, and make sure you like your plan B.

RENTALS

What will you need to bring in? Do you have enough tables, chairs, and cutlery to serve dinner for 20? If not, it may be more cost-efficient to host in a restaurant or a rented space that is set up for catering. If you need to bring in rentals, generators, valets, etc., a home-based party can actually cost more than a venue that will provide all of these services.

STEP 2

make your guest list

The number of guests will help determine the size of your venue. Or, if you have a location in mind, that can limit your list. Budget plays a role, too—the same amount of money goes further with a smaller group. When making a list, the big questions are:

WHO ARE YOU INCLUDING?

Friends (from work, school, childhood)? Immediate or extended family? Make a list of people who you must have, and people who you'd like to have so you can figure out head count. Do your best, but know you cannot include everyone.

WHO CAN THEY BRING?

Before invites go out, think about add-ons. Will guests be offered plus-ones? For a kid's party, is it a drop-off or will parents stick around (and need refreshments as well)? Are siblings welcome?

STEP 4
set the scene

You want guests to be comfortable and excited from beginning to end of the party. Two key elements to help that happen are making sure your event flows nicely in your venue and creating a welcoming environment.

AVOID TRAFFIC JAMS

Do a mental walk-through of the space before setting up, imagining how guests will circulate. Steer clear of bottlenecks by setting up a main bar and providing an extra station or two—it could be as simple as an ice-filled bucket with serve-yourself bottles and cans. Plant a few snacks around the space to avoid one big cluster around a food table.

KEEP GUESTS COMFORTABLE

The temperature of your venue can make people eager to linger or to flee. Decide whether you'll need to bring in heaters or crank the AC. Also think about where you'll put coats in winter (will you need to track down a wheeled coat rack and hangers?). For outdoor parties, consider stocking a few buckets with shawls, bug spray, sunscreen, and any other necessities.

party countdown

Get excited! In my house, it's tradition for the kids to make a birthday paper chain countdown. Each morning a chain link is removed.

MOOD MUSIC

Every party needs a soundtrack, whether you hire a band or hook up an iPod. Here are tips on making a playlist from **DJ Lucy Wrubel,** who contributed playlists to match every celebration in The Party Playbook section of this book:

ask: how do i want guests to feel?

If you want them to snuggle, that's a chill, downtempo playlist. If you want them to dance on tables, that's upbeat. For the playlists in this book, I tried to set a vibe. For example, the baby shower is dreamy, precious, and magical.

set the tempo

Try starting with cocktail music, lowering the tempo for supper then upping the energy by raising the volume and lowering the lights—no one wants to dance in a bright room.

consider your crowd

If you have a variety of ages, you'll need a variety of music. It always helps to toss in some old school. People love to sing while they dance. Give the people what they want—songs they recognize!

STEP 5
extend your invitation

The main role of an invitation is to offer up the facts: who, what, when, and where you're celebrating. Since it's your guests' first glimpse of your party, the invite is also an opportunity to set the tone and style from the start. Parties are fun—so have fun inviting guests to yours!

GET CREATIVE

An unusual invite will get people excited, and it's always nice if it celebrates the theme. But it doesn't have to come in an envelope. Invitations can take many forms—if you can print on it, write on it, or order it from a website that customizes items, you can use it! Consider sending:

A DEFLATED BALLOON		that shows the info once the recipient blows it up
A LOLLIPOP, PACK OF CANDY, OR CHOCOLATE BAR		with the info on the wrapper or tied on with a tag (see page 158)
A HORN		proclaiming your party (see page 49)
PUZZLE PIECES		that spell out the info when assembled
A BOTTLE		with info on the label
ACCESSORIES		paper crown, eye patch, or sheriff's badge—whatever fits the theme
A PAPER AIRPLANE		fold it ahead of time or send it flat
A PARTY BLOWER		that unfurls to show the details
ART SUPPLIES		like a couple of crayons or colored pencils sent with a black-and-white invitation for guests to color

4 WAYS TO
amp up your invite

—

1
Custom postage: a personalized stamp, or, even simpler, a few regular ones that are pretty and/or on-theme

2
An envelope liner (pick a color, pattern, or photo)

3
Stickers, labels, or rubber stamps

4
Confetti inside the envelope

color, cut & place

pip pip hooray!

see it through

If your invite has extras like crayons and confetti, slip everything into a clear sleeve to keep it all together, and then mail in an envelope.

...pas 5th Birthday

...day, January 5th 3:30–5...

...street M...

...r.v.p. dar...ller

An accordion-style invitation let our story unfold.

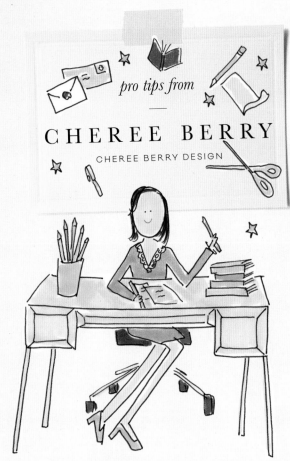

Cheree Berry is a paper fanatic I've been collaborating with for years. She comes up with surprising, fun invitations that are "outside of the envelope." Here's her advice on creating a mailing that's, well, inviting.

DO
BASE YOUR INVITES ON YOUR THEME

We always try to learn about the theme of the party first. If it's a wedding, what is the style of the couple—classic, preppy, bohemian? If it's a child's party, is it Disney mania or puppies galore? Is there a color palette or décor motif? The more we know about your vision, the better we can create an invitation that will truly set the tone and excite.

DO
PLAY WITH WORDS

If it's a wedding, we say, "All hail Emily Post" and keep it classic. As for other invites, have fun! We put as much emphasis on the copy as design. We've done "Truth or Pair" for a wine pairing party, and, for a 50th birthday invitation, we did a sticker paper doll, and guests were asked to "Assemble his ensemble to look his best for the fest!" Words and imagery should go together like peas and carrots.

DO
BE ORIGINAL

We love fun, unexpected formats. We once added a game spinner to a baby shower invitation to celebrate the crazy cravings of the expecting guest of honor, like ice cream and pickles. The game board was designed with colorful food illustrations and asked the recipient to spin and see what the mom-to-be's next meal will be.

DO
CHOOSE TYPOGRAPHY WISELY TO SET A MOOD

For a formal event, script is standard. For a more casual affair, mix up the fonts. Personally, I can't get enough of hand lettering these days.

We mailed these horn invitations in a box.

We packed this invite full of surprises: confetti, a notepad, and added interactive stamps.

DON'T
FEEL LIMITED TO STANDARD CARD SIZE

Bring on the surprises! For example, go small and think about the invitation like it's a Cracker Jack box, adding a tiny prize. It's so fun to fish out the mini tattoo or sticker. For an oversize Saratoga-based wedding invite, we tucked a mini "Dark and Stormy" drink ticket in the invite for a fun find.

DON'T
FEEL LIKE YOU HAVE TO SPEND BIG MONEY TO MAKE A BIG IMPACT

You can make invitations budget-friendly and fabulous. Try flat printing instead of letterpress, or choose a colored envelope in lieu of a more expensive envelope liner (the handwork involved with lining drives up the cost). If it's not a wedding, put RSVP info on the invite itself, instead of using a separate reply card. We also like to hide details in the designs—say, a monogram or a ladybug—or use creative copy to elevate the personalization. If the invitation design is a standout, you don't have to dip it in gold to make it sing.

BUT DO
SPLURGE ON WHAT FLOATS YOUR BOAT

Me, I'm a fool for gold foil.

D.Y.I.Y.
do your invite yourself

1
Think small: A limited number of invites can easily be done the D.I.Y. route.

2
Stamps make a statement; choose wisely!

3
Have fun with the envelope, too—paint the flap!

4
Cut it up: With so many paper options available in fun patterns and colors, grab your scissors and go!

...SE JOIN US F...

DÉCOR DETAILS

Visually, décor gives your party its magic and makes it personal. When I hosted my sister's birthday brunch, for example, I decorated the table with things from different cities she's lived in. Décor can be grand—covering the ceiling in balloons—but even a simple touch, like tying one balloon to a chair, makes the moment feel special.

D.I.Y.
(darcy it yourself)

Each element of your party
is another excuse to expand on
your theme. Here's how
to use décor to make a party
extra personal.

1
pick a palette

Color is key when it comes to pulling
a theme together. I start with a
palette and then it's easy to narrow down
the seemingly endless decor options.

2
find the focus

Think about where people spend time and
concentrate your efforts there. At a sit-
down dinner, you might make centerpieces
special; at a cocktail party, the buffet.
Keep in mind first and last impressions, like
something hanging in the door as guests
arrive or a favor table as they leave.

3
pack your table

Fill the table with lots of elements such
as place cards, napkin rings, and
fun extras—think mini paint palettes if the
guest of honor is artistic.

4
look to the little details

Extra touches make a party extra festive;
look for ways to add fun, like personalizing a
cake stand by wrapping the base
with paper hearts for Valentine's Day.

timeline centerpiece

Chronological photos
of my dad taped to glass
cylinders holding votive
candles lit up his birthday.

WHAT'S A
PARTY
WITHOUT
PARTY HATS?

*letters
or numbers
+
headband
=*
BIRTHDAY GIRL
HEADBAND

*gold paper
+
sticker number
=*
BIRTHDAY
CROWN

*white party hat
+
paint
+
pom pom
=*
1ST BIRTHDAY HAT

DESIGN YOUR DÉCOR
To make a party feel pulled together, repeat:

A LABEL
Print custom stickers
and stick on cups, bottles, plates,
balloons, trays, and favors.

A SHAPE
At a Hollywood-themed
party, have a star-shaped cake,
banner, and balloons.

AN OBJECT
For a sports-themed party, turn
plates, balloons, the cake—
anything round—into a basketball,
soccer ball, or baseball.

SIX EASY PIECES
Pick one or all to dress up your party.

FLOWERS
A floral touch makes any
event a special occasion,
whether you choose
fresh, silk, or paper; single
stems, floating blossoms,
or bunches of bouquets.

CONFETTI
Sprinkled on a table, or
tucked into an invitation
or favor bag, it's a fun,
colorful way to say "party"
that can be personalized
in so many different ways.

GARLANDS
They can dangle from the
ceiling, wrap around a
chair back, or hang from
wall to wall.

MOOD LIGHTING
Get the party glowing with
strings of lights or lots
of candles, and keep your
regular lamps dim.

BALLOONS
In bunches, scattered, or as
just one special stand-
out, these add something
festive to the room.

PHOTOS
Add a picture to almost
anything and it's instantly
a meaningful, personalized
piece of décor.

white crown
+
bridesmaids' kisses
=
BACHELORETTE
PARTY HAT

party hat
+
stickers
+
lollipop
=
CLOWN HAT

pink party hat
+
white and pink paper
+
*black marker
nose and eyes*
=
BUNNY HAT

paper shark fin
+
wave crown
=
SHARK HAT

stay front & center

An easy, elegant idea is to line up single stems in bud vases as a centerpiece. Pick one type of bloom (shown here, peonies in shades of pink) and arrange stems in light-to-dark order down the table's center. Tie the color of the flowers into the tabletop décor—glasses, linen, and china.

focus on color

For another spin on this idea, pick a hue—say yellow— and line up a row of different blossoms: a tulip next to an aster, then a daffodil.

height check

When arranging flowers
on a dining table, take
a seat to make sure guests
can see across the table.

arrange for flowers

To make the most of your floral décor, keep these
tips in mind at every stage of arranging.

BUY YOUR BUDS

*You can get great flowers almost anywhere—even the grocery
store—if you know what to look for.*

PLAN AHEAD
Buy your flowers a day
or two before your
event so the buds have
time to open up.

THE TEST SQUEEZE
Give buds a little
squeeze before buying.
If they feel sturdy
with a little bounce,
they'll open up and
won't wilt.

SIMPLE IS BETTER
If you won't have much
time to arrange, go
with bundles of all one
flower—tulips are a
great bet.

CLEAN IT UP

Prep your flowers quickly and easily.

CLIP THEM AND SNIP THEM
Snip off any outer bruised petals to
keep flowers looking fresh. Stems
should reach the bottom of the vase,
then extend 4 to 5 inches from
the top. Clip stems at an angle, and
if flowers have harder, woody stems,
split them up the middle a bit, too.

PRACTICE WATER SAFETY:
Don't leave leaves be! An arrangement
looks cleaner when leaves are
clipped off stems, plus foliage makes
water murky and causes the flowers
to spoil faster. Fill, fill, fill the vase
until water is close to the top, then
check it and refill every day.

GET ARRANGING

Create a strong base for blooms and your flowers will be a thing of beauty.

LONG STEMS FIRST
Start by putting
the longest stems in at
an angle, letting
them hit the edge of
the vase.

BUILD THE FRAME
Keep adding stems,
crisscrossing to make
a natural frame for
the rest of your flowers.

FILL THE GAPS
The remaining flowers
can go in vertically and
will stay straight up—
keep going until you've
filled in all the holes.

get together

In a group, tiny vessels can make
a big impact, whether clustered together
or set down the center of the table.

love in blooms

Stacked on a tiered stand,
white flowers reminiscent
of a wedding cake are
perfect for a bridal shower,
engagement party, or
wedding. Or arrange them
in the initials of the
guest of honor.

take it home
—

For a centerpiece that
doubles as favors, let
each guest leave with a
blossom-filled votive.

think outside the vase

Here, blooms are arranged in plain bamboo steamers dressed up
with gold paper trim to match the wooden candy box favors. The roses and sweet
peas in the centerpieces fit the table's pink-and-gold palette.

make a match

Place cards are trimmed with
the same gold paper as
the centerpieces, while the
candy in the boxes reflects
the colors of the flowers.

one and only

Flowers don't have to mean bouquets and intricate arrangements—there are so many easy ways to incorporate them into your décor. A single stem makes a great place card. Just don't set it out too early so that the bloom stays fresh (or use a small, leakproof vial of water to keep from wilting).

Daphne

pro tips from

—

DAVID STARK

DAVID STARK DESIGN AND
PRODUCTION

A fabric cuff spruces up
a plain vessel.

*A New York City event designer since
1995, David amazes me with
his originality, and fresh approach to
entertaining. We've collaborated
on dozens of parties—the photos on
these pages show a few—and
he's the nicest person to work with!
Here's his advice.*

THINK LIKE A GUEST

If you're not sure where to focus your attention or
resources, do a mental walk-through of your space:
When your guests walk into your home, where
will their eyes naturally be drawn? When they turn
the corner into the next room, what's the first
thing they'll see? If you focus on the succession of
"vistas" that your guests will encounter as they
make their way through a party, you land on where
your decorative focus should lie.

DIM THE LIGHTS

Improve your space in minutes by turning the lights
way down, then filling a room with candlelight. I keep bulk packages of tea lights, votives, and
pillar candles in my pantry and can set up
for unexpected parties in a flash. It's a party décor
cliché, but it's true: candles add instant magic.

KEEP SIZE IN MIND

STAY IN SCALE
For a big party, focus on large-scale
elements such as big arrangements, hanging
garlands, or bunches of balloons that
can add impact above the crowd. For a small
party, focus on the details in a way you
just couldn't for a 500-person gathering—
use finely crafted paper flowers or more
refined table linens. The large-scale elements
you would use for a big party are probably
too over-the-top for a small one. I never want
it to look like I tried too hard.

GO BIG—AND SMALL
Consider how your room will look when it's
filled with people. You want design elements
that won't get lost in a standing crowd,
like an arrangement of flowering branches
or a tall candleholder that rises above a
buffet. If guests will sit down, have surprises
at eye level—maybe it's each person's name
written onto a fresh leaf as a place card.

LEAVE ROOM FOR CONVERSATION
Keep centerpieces low or high enough
so they don't create a wall across the table,
blocking guests from one another's view.

Paper "cakes" at Martha's birthday. See page 8.

Paper butterflies fly among poppies.

GET CREATIVE

Exciting is better than expensive. I never want anyone to walk into a party and say, "Oh my! Look how much money they spent!" I want guests to light up with excitement and exclaim, "*Wow! That's cool!*" It's about how much ingenuity you dispense.

STRENGTH IN NUMBERS

Instead of buying a touch of this and a bit of that, pick one element—pumpkins in the fall or potted herbs in the spring—and go all the way. Arrange them on your tabletops, across a mantel, or en masse by the entryway. If you plant flowering plants, herbs, and vegetables in various-sized pots at the beginning of summer, you can use them as décor (and then as dinner!) all season long. Growing your own supplies is planet-friendly and wallet-friendly.

secret weapon
—
Buy a roll of painter's tape and write a giant greeting with it. Stick it on an entry wall as instant décor! Tear it down after the night's a wrap.

why not?

Leave something special on each plate. These sand dollars are decorative elements guests can take them home as favors. They would also work as place cards.

beyond flowers

Blooms aren't the only natural element to call upon for your table décor. Here, sand dollars tied with thin gold ribbons, shells, painted sea urchins, and ocean-inspired centerpieces feel organic and sophisticated.

have it your way

A coastal theme doesn't have to mean a blue palette. If you want to celebrate the ocean, but have your heart set on a whites-and-neutrals color scheme, skip the sea and focus on the shore with sand-colored table linens and painted seashells.

set the table

On occasion—for formal events or when you're feeling fancy—you may want to pull out all the stops and really set the table. Here's how to arrange the elements of a formal place setting.

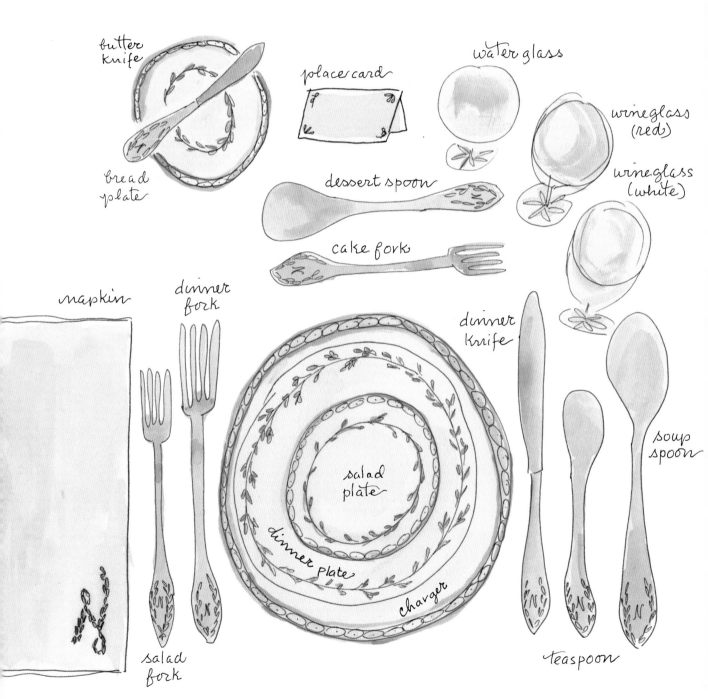

butter knife

bread plate

place card

water glass

wineglass (red)

wineglass (white)

dessert spoon

cake fork

napkin

dinner fork

dinner knife

salad plate

dinner plate

charger

soup spoon

salad fork

teaspoon

ADD SOME AMBIANCE

In the midst of big-picture décor planning, remember
the table is a world of its own, offering many ways
to continue your theme or create a pretty setting. It costs
nothing to fold a napkin in a special way.

white night

Each arrangement has a
different white flower.

float their boats

Float candles in
clear vessels, or a single
large blossom, like
the peony at the far left,
in a silver dish.

tuck them in

Fold napkins ahead
of time and place a single
flower inside just
before the party begins.

hanging out

To hang décor without
making holes in the
walls, use painter's tape or
a suction cup hook.
Or look for curtain rods,
nooks in the molding,
or pre-existing holes that
won't leave a mark.

have the world on a string

Garlands are an easy way to weave your theme and color scheme throughout your space. Run them from corner to corner high above the room, drape them across walls, or string them in doorways. You can make a garland out of anything: flowers, pom-poms, paper, balloons, photos, even candy.

SAY THE
WORD

PEACE OUT

MAKE A
WISH

GET THE
SCOOP

PLAY BALL

blow them away

Balloons always add spirit. Use them as decorations, in games, and as favors—kids love taking home a balloon. (If you're filling these with helium, you can request Hi-Float so they'll last longer.) Here are eight ways to bring them into your party.

1

White balloons arranged against a wall become a rain cloud with blue paper raindrops taped below.

2

Use construction paper to style her hair! Make her wink!

3

Paper ears bring balloons to life. Add pink insides to bunny's.

4

Form a constellation on a black balloon with some star stickers and a metallic paint pen.

5

Wrap balloons in cellophane to turn them into candies.

6

Tape on paper triangles for instant sunbeams.

7

Make animal faces with construction paper, tissue paper, and paint or markers.

8

Attach green balloons side by side into a caterpillar. Decorate the first one with a face. This guy is a great table runner.

siiiiiinging in the rain!

MORE BALLOON IDEAS

Float them on the ceiling.

Use as a centerpiece.

Suspend things from them.

Spell out words or numbers.

Create a backdrop or
frame an entrance.

Bring 7 balloons to school at
pick up for a 7th birthday.

"throw" a party

There are so many ways to toss some confetti into your party. Send it in cello envelopes with invitations, sprinkle some on the table or on serving trays, or put a few handfuls inside a piñata. Here are some ideas for mixing up your own confetti concoctions.

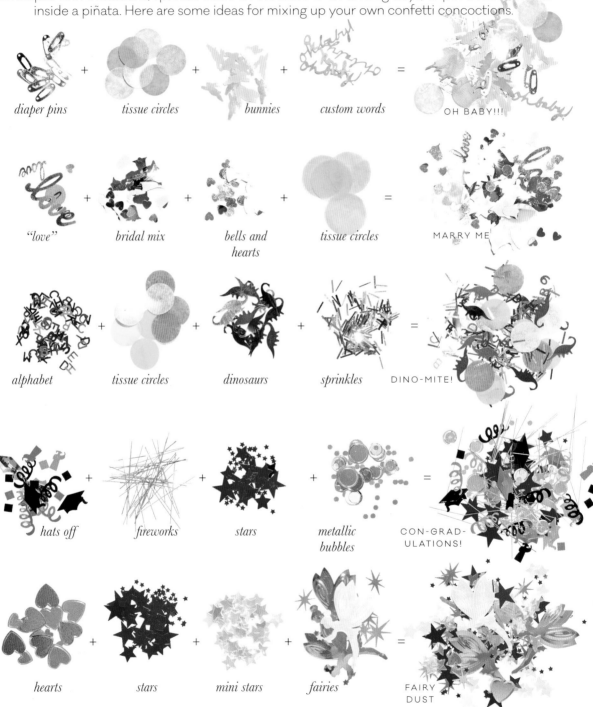

diaper pins + *tissue circles* + *bunnies* + *custom words* = OH BABY!!!

"love" + *bridal mix* + *bells and hearts* + *tissue circles* = MARRY ME

alphabet + *tissue circles* + *dinosaurs* + *sprinkles* = DINO-MITE!

hats off + *fireworks* + *stars* + *metallic bubbles* = CON-GRAD-ULATIONS!

hearts + *stars* + *mini stars* + *fairies* = FAIRY DUST

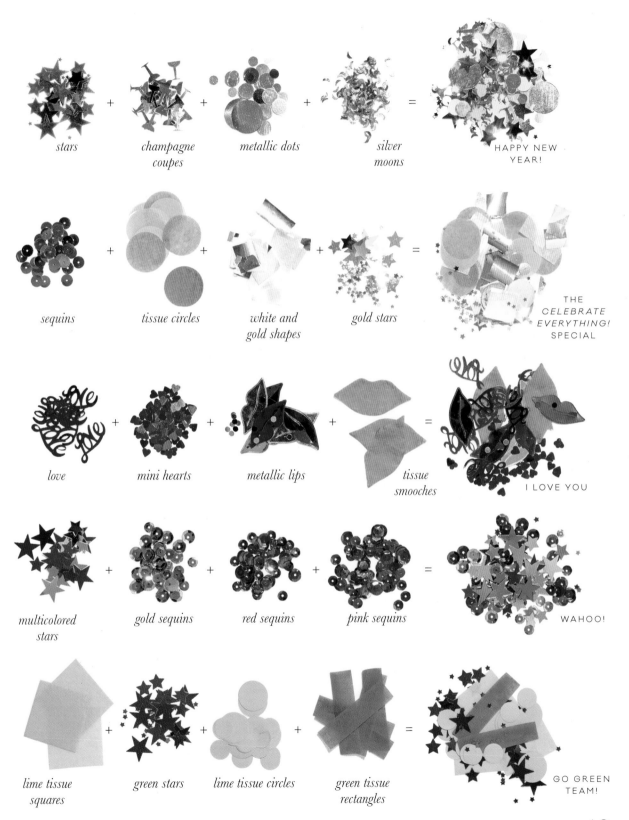

stars + champagne coupes + metallic dots + silver moons = HAPPY NEW YEAR!

sequins + tissue circles + white and gold shapes + gold stars = THE *CELEBRATE EVERYTHING!* SPECIAL

love + mini hearts + metallic lips + tissue smooches = I LOVE YOU

multicolored stars + gold sequins + red sequins + pink sequins = WAHOO!

lime tissue squares + green stars + lime tissue circles + green tissue rectangles = GO GREEN TEAM!

Float light-up beach balls in the pool or scatter them around the backyard.

Sparklers are fun for bigger kids—and for the supervising adults.

A jumbled string of tiny LED lights in a mason jar is a great (and safer) alternative to candles.

Small battery-operated lights let your hedge join the party.

let there be lights

With the flip of a switch or the strike of a match, lighting transforms the mood. It's why a sunny afternoon baby shower feels remarkably different from an elegant candlelit dinner.

take it down a notch

If your party will go from day to night, dim the lights as it gets later. If you don't have dimmers and your space seems too bright, swap out the light bulbs for a lower wattage pre-party.

light the way

If guests need to get from Point A to B (say, your front yard to the party out back), illuminate a path with luminarias, torches, or light-up balloons.

FOOD & DRINK

The menu at a party is about more than feeding
attendees. I like for it to highlight my party's theme,
the season, or the location—and I always include
favorites of the guest of honor. The final touch is clever
presentation, because, with a little dressing up,
even deli sandwiches and pizza can feel special!

D.I.Y.

(darcy it yourself)

Stuck on deciding what
to serve? Here are a few questions
to get you started.

1
who's cooking?

Will you hire a professional, make everything
yourself, or do something in between?
Think about your budget, the number of guests,
and what you have time to do.

I'LL BE IN THE KITCHEN! For a homemade meal, you can cook it all yourself, or . . .	go potluck style—ask guests to each bring a dish, drink, or dessert, or invite friends over for a meal that you prepare together. cook the entrée and serve store-bought sides on your own dishes.
JUST A LITTLE ASSISTANCE, PLEASE! For extra help with set-up, serving, and cleanup . . .	recruit your babysitter/helper. hire a waiter or a bartender— if you have a certain a dress code in mind for servers, make that clear!
I'LL BRING IN THE PROS! For when you are crunched for time, or if cooking isn't your thing . . .	explore the prepared foods section of your specialty market or grocery store, or pick up food from a local restaurant. rent a food truck or hire a local chef or caterer.

2
how are you serving it?

Sit-down or buffet? Choose whatever
style suits your event. Here are
some pros and cons to consider, whether
you're planning a fancy party or
an informal gathering.

SEATED DINNER

The intimate setting encourages
conversation and lets you manage the
seating arrangements and plan
a more limited menu. At a sit-down
dinner, your guest list is restricted to
the number of seats, your menu
has to reflect friends' food restrictions,
and you'll need help serving.

BUFFET

When you set out a spread, you can
serve a wider variety of food, so
individual preferences don't matter as
much, making menu planning easier
if you have a large list. This style also
allows guests to mingle more. But, you'll
still have to provide some seating,
and you will need to monitor food levels
and restock. Plus, it can be tough
keeping dishes the correct temperature.

3
what's for dinner?

Why not serve burgers and
fries at a black-tie party
or break out champagne
when your girlfriends
are over? "Fancy" foods
don't only have to be
for special occasions, and
laid-back favorites
can have a place at formal
events. I personalized
these sliders for my friend's
cocktail party.

start early
—
Begin setting up well before you think you need to in case you discover you're short on napkins or need to run out for ice before getting dressed.

4
what are you drinking?

Your drink menu can be as elaborate as a full bar, or as simple as wine and a few spirits. I like dressing up drinks with on-theme toppers, stirrers, and fun cocktail napkins. Remember to offer a nonalcoholic option like a juice spritzer for those who don't or can't partake.

BUILD-A-BAR

Drinks can personalize a party, but you don't need a full bar. This simple formula offers enough variety for most events:

1 OR 2 KINDS OF WINE   +   1 OR 2 KINDS OF BEER

1 OR 2 SPECIALTY DRINKS
(can be made with or without booze)

+

1 SPECIAL SPIRIT
(vodka, tequila, whiskey, Scotch, etc.)

FORMULA FOR A GOOD TOAST

Don't forget to say cheers!

Thank your guests for coming.

+

Call out any special party helpers.

+

Give a nod to the guest of honor or to the occasion.

=

Keep it short and sweet— under three minutes. (Practice with a timer.) Bonus points if you throw in a good joke!

say cheese!

A cheese plate or table looks beautiful and tastes great—
and there's no cooking involved. Caterer Peter Callahan set up the
spread shown on these pages. Here are his tips plus pairing
advice from the world-famous Murray's Cheese Shop at right.

ADD EXTRAS

Fresh, sweet fruit
complements cheeses.
Go beyond grapes
and strawberries with figs,
dates, or pomegranates
and add nuts, honey-
combs, compotes, and
cured meats.

PICK A RANGE

Offer options made
from a variety of milks
including sheep, goat,
and cow. Not sure which
cheeses to choose?
Ask the cheesemonger
for his or her favorites in
a given price point.

SERVE A SPECTRUM

Along with a range of
milks, look for variety
in texture (hard, soft, semi-
soft) and size.

AIM HIGH

Breadsticks are great for giving dimension to a display. When choosing bread, breadsticks, or crackers make sure the flavor is mild (no garlic or onion) so that it doesn't interfere with the cheese.

MURRAY'S PAIRING TIPS

Try these great tastes that taste great together.

VALENÇAY
(a soft French goat's milk cheese)

sparkling wines	*beer*
champagne, prosecco, cava	farmhouse ale, cider, wheat beer

GREENSWARD
(a creamy cow's milk cheese)

full-bodied whites	*beer*
riesling, viognier, gewürztraminer	porter, stout, farmhouse ale
light-bodied red	
pinot noir	

BERKWELL
(a hard, sheep's milk cheese)

light-bodied red	*beer*
pinot noir	lager
medium-bodied reds	
syrah, rioja, sangiovese	

CHEDDAR
(a firm, cow's milk cheese)

medium-bodied reds	*beer*
syrah, rioja, sangiovese	amber, pale ale
heavier reds	
cabernet sauvignon, merlot	

STILTON
(a blue cow's milk cheese)

sparkling wines	*beer*
sauternes, port, sherry	stout, porter, sweeter cider

Note: When arranging a plate, cheeses should progress from "Mild to Wild" left to right or clockwise starting at noon. Blue is usually placed last as the "wildest" choice.

mix it up!

Do-it-yourself snack mixes can be made in advance, saving you time on the day of the party. If you are making a lot, buy in bulk! Then go ahead and start mixing.

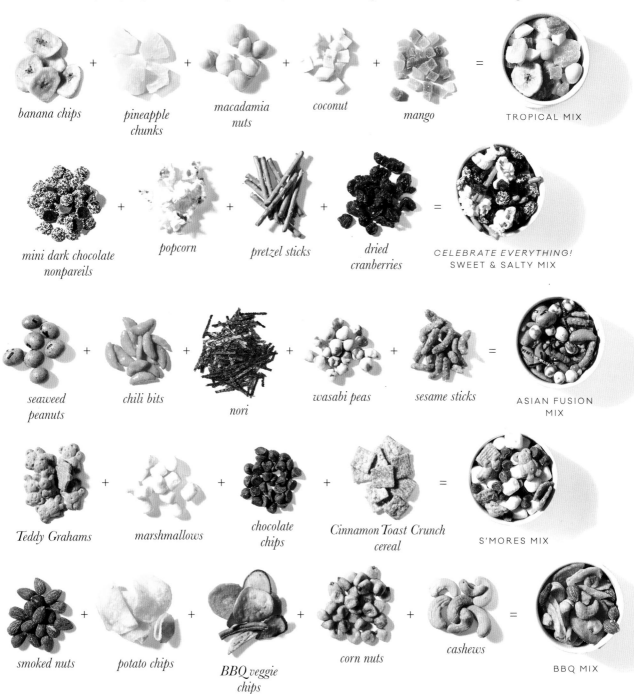

banana chips + pineapple chunks + macadamia nuts + coconut + mango = TROPICAL MIX

mini dark chocolate nonpareils + popcorn + pretzel sticks + dried cranberries = CELEBRATE EVERYTHING! SWEET & SALTY MIX

seaweed peanuts + chili bits + nori + wasabi peas + sesame sticks = ASIAN FUSION MIX

Teddy Grahams + marshmallows + chocolate chips + Cinnamon Toast Crunch cereal = S'MORES MIX

smoked nuts + potato chips + BBQ veggie chips + corn nuts + cashews = BBQ MIX

break it down

If you don't like your snacks all mixed up, another no-cook option is to serve a trio of tastes in individual bowls. Pick unexpected combinations with ingredients that complement each other in flavor and in color and let guests put them together to taste.

PARMESAN, ROASTED RED PEPPERS, ARTICHOKE HEARTS

An explosion of flavor, this popular array is smoky, tangy, and delicious.

RADISHES, BUTTER, SALT

This classic French combo is fresh, sweet, and peppery all at once.

CASTELVETRANO OLIVES, ALMONDS, CARA CARA ORANGES

This trio can be a hit even for those who don't normally like olives, as the Castelvetrano variety is mild and juicy, with a fruity, buttery flavor.

creative crudité

Surprise guests with your presentation of a party favorite, serving veggies and dips in shot glasses for an elegant, fun twist.

5 OTHER FOODS TO SERVE AS
your best shots

1

Chips—or carrots— in dip

2

Mini grilled cheese in tomato soup

3

Shrimp in cocktail sauce

4

Celery or a stick of bacon in a mini Bloody (or Virgin) Mary

5

French toast sticks, syrup at the bottom

CARROT ORANGE LENTIL DIP
MAKES 2½ CUPS

1 tablespoon vegetable oil
1 cup finely diced onion
½ cup finely diced celery
½ cup finely diced carrots
¼ cup minced fresh ginger
½ teaspoon salt
2 garlic cloves, minced
1 plum tomato, finely diced
1 tablespoon curry powder
¼ teaspoon ground cinnamon
1 cup orange lentils
4 cups vegetable stock
½ teaspoon sriracha
1 teaspoon honey
Zest and juice of 1 orange

1. In a large sauté pan over medium heat, heat the oil. Add the onion, celery, carrot, ginger, and salt and sauté for about 5 minutes, or until the vegetables are softened.

2. Add the garlic, tomato, curry powder, and cinnamon and stir to combine. Add the lentils and vegetable stock and stir again.

3. Cover and cook for 20 minutes, or until the lentils are softened. Stir in the sriracha and honey and cook for 10 minutes more, until the mixture has reduced slightly.

4. Remove from the heat and add the orange zest and juice.

5. Process part or all of the lentil mixture in a food processor and pulse to achieve the desired texture. Serve in shot glasses with sliced fennel, sliced jicama, and sugar snap peas. The dip keeps 3 to 4 days refrigerated in an airtight container.

From the kitchen of Peter Callahan

CABBAGE-LEAF-WRAPPED GLASSES

Serve vegetables in containers that match the dip bowls.

Lay a piece of twine horizontally. Arrange two overlapping cabbage leaves on top.

Place a glass on its side on top of the leaves, all the way to the left, then roll it to the right, wrapping it in the leaves as you go.

Knot the twine, trim the ends, and cut the leaves as needed.

CARROT ORANGE LENTIL DIP

HERB DIP

RANCH DIP

let them eat  pie

Pies are the perfect party food for a large group, whether sweet or savory, served whole or as slices. This quiche recipe comes from Haven's Kitchen, a sustainable cooking school and café in Manhattan.

HAVEN'S KITCHEN QUICHE
Makes 1 quiche

CRUST
2 cups all-purpose flour,
  plus more for rolling
1 teaspoon kosher salt
1 cup cold unsalted butter, cubed
¼ cup ice water

CUSTARD FILLING
6 large eggs
2 cups whole milk
2 cups heavy cream
1 tablespoon kosher salt
6 grates of fresh nutmeg

OPTIONAL FILLINGS
1 cup grated Gruyère
¼ cup finely chopped fresh herbs,
  such as chives, parsley, and thyme

1. To make the crust, in a stand mixer using the paddle attachment, combine the flour, salt, and butter. Mix on low speed until the butter is completely incorporated, with no visible butter pieces that will melt and leak while baking. With the mixer on low speed, add the ice water and mix until the dough comes together and pulls away from the sides of the bowl, about 1 to 2 minutes. The dough will be slightly tacky and shiny.

2. Flatten the dough into a disk, wrap it in plastic, and chill for at least 1 hour.

3. Spread a little flour onto a clean surface and roll the chilled dough into a ¼-inch-thick circle that's big enough to go 1 inch over the top of a 9-inch springform pan. Lay the dough over the pan. Carefully press the dough into the edges without tearing it, letting the excess dough drape over the edge. Chill for at least 30 minutes.

4. Preheat the oven to 375°F. Lay a parchment circle or tin foil with at least 4 inches of overlap over the dough and fill with dry beans or pastry weights, pressing them gently over the bottom. Place the pan on a baking sheet.

5. Bake for 30 to 40 minutes, or until the visible part of the crust is light brown. Remove the beans and parchment and bake for 10 minutes more, until the bottom is golden brown. Let cool completely. Lower the heat to 300°F.

6. While the crust is cooling, combine the eggs and 1 cup of the milk in a blender and mix until blended, about 15 seconds. Add the rest of the milk, the cream, salt, and nutmeg and blend for 5 seconds. (If the blender is not large enough, blend the eggs and 1 cup of milk and then whisk the remaining ingredients in a large bowl.)

7. If using the cheese and herbs, spread them over the cooled crust. Pour in the filling and bake for about 1½ hours, or until the custard is richly browned on top and barely set in the center. Let cool in the pan, cover with plastic wrap, and chill overnight.

8. Use a sharp knife to cut the pastry shell flush with the top of the pan. Carefully release the pan hinge and lift the outer ring off the quiche. Cut the quiche into wedges, transfer to plates, and serve chilled or at room temperature.

Note: Quiche must chill overnight.

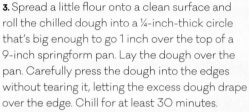

Pick a Pie

Host a potluck pie party:
Ask half the guests to bring savory pies,
and the other half, sweet.
The following are just a few options.

SAVORY

Butternut Squash Tart

Onion and Bacon Tart

Roasted Vegetable Tart

Spinach and Feta Tart

Leek and Goat Cheese Tart

Chicken Pot Pie

Tomato and Herb Tart

Quiche Lorraine

SWEET

Apple Pie

Coconut Cream Pie

Cherry Pie

Blueberry Pie

Grasshopper Pie

Peach Pie

Chocolate Cream Pie

Rhubarb Pie

Banana Cream Pie

Key Lime Pie

Pumpkin Pie

Lemon Meringue Pie

Pecan Pie

why not?
—
Add any favorite flavors to the basic
quiche recipe. This version has piquillo pepper,
chorizo, scallions, and manchego.

burger + hot dogs

THE ALL-AMERICAN CLASSICS

- [ ] buns/rolls
- [ ] variety of cheeses
- [ ] variety of patties
- [ ] french fries
- [ ] ketchup
- [ ] mustard
- [ ] mayo
- [ ] relish
- [ ] onions
- [ ] lettuce
- [ ] bacon
- [ ] pickles
- [ ] fried eggs
- [ ] tomato
- [ ] avocado

Kebab

SERVED ON A STICK

- [ ] beef
- [ ] lamb
- [ ] fish
- [ ] chicken
- [ ] peppers
- [ ] onions
- [ ] tomatoes
- [ ] mushrooms
- [ ] zucchini
- [ ] haloumi cheese
- [ ] beets
- [ ] pineapple
- [ ] garlic cloves
- [ ] eggplant
- [ ] yellow squash

pizza

PICK YOUR TOP TOPPINGS

- [ ] tomato sauce
- [ ] mozzarella
- [ ] tomatoes
- [ ] pepperoni
- [ ] prosciutto
- [ ] arugula
- [ ] mushrooms
- [ ] onion
- [ ] broccoli
- [ ] ricotta
- [ ] sundried tomatoes
- [ ] spinach
- [ ] ham
- [ ] pineapple

taco

TORTILLAS MAKE THINGS TASTY

- [ ] corn shells (hard & soft)
- [ ] ground meat
- [ ] shredded chicken/pork
- [ ] grilled fish
- [ ] lettuce
- [ ] tomatoes
- [ ] guacamole
- [ ] sour cream
- [ ] salsa
- [ ] salsa verde
- [ ] pico de gallo
- [ ] queso fresco
- [ ] shredded cheese
- [ ] black beans
- [ ] refried beans
- [ ] lime wedges
- [ ] radishes
- [ ] cilantro

pancake or waffle

DESSERT AS BREAKFAST

- [ ] berries
- [ ] chocolate chips
- [ ] cinnamon
- [ ] bananas
- [ ] walnuts
- [ ] pecans
- [ ] maple syrup
- [ ] chocolate sauce
- [ ] honey
- [ ] whipped cream
- [ ] crème fraiche
- [ ] butter
- [ ] Greek yogurt
- [ ] powdered sugar

omelet

THE BEST PART OF ANY BRUNCH

- [ ] eggs
- [ ] cheddar cheese
- [ ] mozzarella
- [ ] goat cheese
- [ ] Swiss cheese
- [ ] onions
- [ ] mushrooms
- [ ] tomatoes
- [ ] spinach
- [ ] ham
- [ ] bacon
- [ ] herbs
- [ ] salsa
- [ ] chives
- [ ] broccoli
- [ ] sausage
- [ ] diced potatoes
- [ ] zucchini
- [ ] kale
- [ ] smoked salmon

baked potato

THE ULTIMATE COMFORT FOOD

- [ ] white or sweet potatoes
- [ ] sour cream
- [ ] chives
- [ ] grilled mushrooms
- [ ] cheese
- [ ] crème fraîche
- [ ] bacon
- [ ] smoked trout
- [ ] fried onions
- [ ] creamed spinach

cereal

BREAKFAST OF CHAMPIONS

- [ ] variety of milks
- [ ] cold cereal
- [ ] hot cereal
- [ ] granola
- [ ] strawberries
- [ ] bananas
- [ ] marshmallows
- [ ] blueberries
- [ ] apple slices
- [ ] cinnamon
- [ ] raisins
- [ ] chocolate chips
- [ ] yogurt

grilled cheese

KIDS LOVE THEM—ADULTS, TOO

- [ ] variety of breads
- [ ] variety of cheeses
- [ ] tomato
- [ ] honey
- [ ] jams
- [ ] mustard
- [ ] ham
- [ ] turkey
- [ ] fried eggs
- [ ] apples
- [ ] avocado
- [ ] onion
- [ ] chutneys

pasta

TOSS IN YOUR SPECIAL SAUCE

- [ ] variety of noodles
- [ ] tomato sauce
- [ ] Alfredo sauce
- [ ] Bolognese
- [ ] Pesto
- [ ] broccoli rabe
- [ ] cherry tomatoes
- [ ] peas
- [ ] sausage
- [ ] parmesan cheese
- [ ] olive oil
- [ ] red pepper flakes

smoothie

BREAK OUT THE BLENDER!

- [ ] variety of milks
- [ ] yogurt
- [ ] ice
- [ ] orange juice
- [ ] pineapple juice
- [ ] coconut water
- [ ] bananas
- [ ] frozen berries
- [ ] frozen peaches
- [ ] frozen pineapple
- [ ] watermelon
- [ ] peanut butter

mezze

MEDITERRANEAN DELIGHTS

- [ ] pita
- [ ] falafel
- [ ] tzatziki
- [ ] hummus
- [ ] olives
- [ ] chickpeas
- [ ] eggplant
- [ ] tahini
- [ ] tabouleh
- [ ] roasted nuts
- [ ] labne
- [ ] za'atar
- [ ] man'oushe
- [ ] tarragon
- [ ] baba ghanoush

crepe

START SAVORY, THEN GO SWEET

- [ ] chicken
- [ ] gruyere
- [ ] mozzarella
- [ ] tomatoes
- [ ] ham
- [ ] mushrooms
- [ ] carmelized mushrooms
- [ ] goat cheese
- [ ] roquefort
- [ ] rosemary
- [ ] leeks
- [ ] sugar
- [ ] lemon
- [ ] butter
- [ ] Nutella
- [ ] berries
- [ ] banana slices
- [ ] jam
- [ ] whipped cream
- [ ] honey

say hip, hip, buffet!

Here are some grab-and-go options for buffet or bar-style setups both savory and sweet.

antipasti

PERFETTO FOR A COCKTAIL PARTY

- [ ] salami
- [ ] prosciutto
- [ ] pepperoni
- [ ] provolone
- [ ] mozzarella
- [ ] manchego
- [ ] olives
- [ ] artichoke hearts
- [ ] sliced crusty bread
- [ ] focaccia
- [ ] capers
- [ ] fresh figs
- [ ] bresaola
- [ ] pecorino
- [ ] olive oil
- [ ] basil leaves
- [ ] roasted red peppers
- [ ] pickled vegetables

chili

WARM, HEARTY, A SUPERBOWL HIT

- [ ] vegetarian chili
- [ ] meat chili
- [ ] cornbread
- [ ] sourdough bread
- [ ] sour cream
- [ ] Tabasco
- [ ] onions
- [ ] roasted garlic cloves
- [ ] shredded cheddar
- [ ] shredded jack cheese
- [ ] avocado
- [ ] cumin

bagel

IT'S NOT BRUNCH WITHOUT THEM

- [ ] variety of bagels
- [ ] variety of cream cheeses
- [ ] butter
- [ ] peanut butter
- [ ] bananas
- [ ] avocado
- [ ] tuna salad
- [ ] tomatoes
- [ ] cucumber
- [ ] sprouts
- [ ] capers
- [ ] onion

s'more

ALL THE FUN OF A CAMPFIRE

- [ ] honey graham crackers
- [ ] cinnamon graham crackers
- [ ] chocolate graham crackers
- [ ] marshmallows
- [ ] flavored marshmallows
- [ ] caramels
- [ ] strawberries
- [ ] bananas
- [ ] peanut butter
- [ ] sprinkles

Outrageous Ice cream

STEP 1 PICK AN OUTSIDE.

(SALTY OR SWEET? BOTH ARE NEAT.)

STEP 2 ADD ICE CREAM.

Pretzels

Doughnuts

Palmiers

Sugar Cookies

Pound Cake

Meringues

Sandwich Smörgåsbord

STEP 3 ADD TOPPINGS.

STEP 4 REPEAT STEPS AS NEEDED.

STEP 5 MMMM...

Biscotti

ice cr

macarons

croissants

pro tips from

PETER CALLAHAN

PETER CALLAHAN CATERING

I've been lucky to collaborate with Peter, a New York City—based caterer, on many of my parties since meeting him over 15 years ago—and he whipped up most of the food in this book! His approach is always unique, creative, and fresh. Here, Peter shares his wisdom.

We developed caviar and cracker rings for a shower.

PLANNING A COCKTAIL PARTY
in 5 easy steps

—

1
WHAT TO SERVE
Pick easy, room-temperature food so you can enjoy the party and not have to run back and forth to the kitchen.

2
HOW TO SERVE IT
Consider how you present your food. Upgrade the display with platters of different shapes set at various heights.

3
HOW TO LAY IT OUT
The night before, map out where all your dishes will go. Set up with empty platters and mark what foods will go where with sticky notes.

4
HOW TO STYLE IT
Keep like with like—carrots in one bowl and cherry tomatoes in another. If you have a large platter, avoid mixing more than three colors on one plate.

5
DAY-OF
Fill your bowls and platters as planned— you're ready!

Peter's ultimate

hors d'oeuvres
Mini grilled cheeses are easy to make ahead, freeze, then heat at the party.

entrée
Branzino or strip steak. Marinate either in olive oil and lightly season with maldon salt. Sear in a steel pan.

dessert
Apple tarte tatins.

A bouquet of edible flowers
in a cherry tomato.

"Mark-a-tinis" with melon
Ms for my friend Mark.

SAMPLE MENUS

—

SUMMER
Grilled meats or chilled shellfish
+ assorted salads

FALL
Cinnamon-and-Coriander-Spiced Roasted
Chicken + Fig and Burrata Salad

WINTER
Beef Bourguignon + roasted Jerusalem
artichokes + a light salad

SPRING
Herb-Crusted Rack of Lamb +
grilled asparagus and sautéed morels

ANY TIME, FUSS-FREE MEAL
Pasta salad (can be served at room temp)
+ crusty bread (and feel free to add
store-bought bells and whistles: pesto on the
side, olive oil, and shaved parmesan)

5 TRICKS
OF THE TRADE

—

ADD GARNISH
Snip herbs over roasted carrots right before
serving, or shave watermelon radishes
over vegetables for their crisp color and snap.

USE SMALLER BOWLS
When you lay out snacks (Parmesan shards,
mixed nuts, wasabi peas), use bowls
that are about 6 inches wide. Smaller bowls
look more elegant. For a big group, use
multiples of small bowls.

MAKE SIDES LOOK ABUNDANT
Go for smaller serving pieces for side
dishes, too. They look far more appealing in
bowls or on platters when piled high.

CHOOSE HIGH-IMPACT PLATTERS
For main dishes, oversize platters that are
simple in color make food look amazing.

KEEP DINNER PLATES SIMPLE
If you plate the food before serving, leave
room between items on the plates.
Often, just one accompaniment next to an
entrée looks snazzier than a busy plate.

raise a glass

A party is a great excuse to test out a festive new drink recipe. Serve options with and without alcohol, so everyone can toast. Here are some ideas for big-batch cocktails both spiked and virgin.

SPARKLING CIDER

In a large pitcher, mix 4 cups all-natural apple cider and 1 cup sparkling water. Add ice and strain into tall chilled glasses. Cut a small slit into apple slices and dip each slice lightly in caramel. Garnish the edge of each glass with a slice of caramel apple. Serves 4.

HOT CHOCOLATE

In a medium saucepan over medium-low heat, heat 4 cups half-and-half and ¼ cup sugar until simmering. Remove from heat and add 2 teaspoons pure vanilla extract, 8 ounces dark chocolate (60% or higher), and a pinch of salt. Stir until the chocolate is completely melted, then divide the hot chocolate among four mugs and top with whipped cream and dark chocolate shavings. Serves 4.

Note: For an adult version, add 1 cup Grand Marnier right before serving. Garnish with a vanilla bean and whipped cream and top with a bit of diced candied orange peel.

CALVADOS CIDER WITH SAGE AND BITTERS

In a large pitcher, mix 4 cups all-natural cider, ½ cup Calvados or apple brandy, and 4 dashes bitters with ice. Strain into coupe glasses. Garnish the rim of each glass with a slice of lady apple—or other small apple—and 1 or 2 sage leaves. Serves 4.

To be used as a guide—there
are variables such as time
of day, what alcohol you choose
to serve, and your guest list.
With this equation, everyone will
get the choice they want.

+

=

6 bottles of beer   *2 bottles of wine*   *for every 6 guests
per 1 hour*

STRAWBERRY LEMONADE

Make simple syrup: In a small
saucepan over high heat,
bring ½ cup sugar and ½ cup
water to a simmer and cook
until the sugar is dissolved.
Let cool. In a medium pitcher,
combine the simple syrup,
1 cup fresh lemon juice, and
½ cup water. Stir and add
¾ cup fresh strawberry juice.
Chill before serving. Dip strawberries in sugar and garnish
the rims of the glasses. Serves 4.

FRUIT MOCKTAIL

Mix 4 teaspoons chilled
cherry juice, 2 cups
chilled mango juice, 2 cups
chilled pineapple juice,
and pour in tumbler. Serves 4.

*Note: For a cocktail, this drink is
delicious with ½ cup chilled
vodka mixed in. Use different colors
or numbers of straws
to keep the versions straight.*

PINEAPPLE PEACH CHERRY MARTINI

In a large pitcher, mix ½ cup
vodka, rum, or tequila, 2 cups
pineapple juice, 2 cups fresh
peach juice, and ½ cup
fresh cherry juice (jarred, look
for juice with no added
sugar). Serve over ice. Serves 4.

pomegranate seeds

sugar cubes

mini sugar flowers

mini sugar hearts

pink sugar wedding bells

lemon rinds

be bubbly

Nothing says "Congrats!" or "Here's to You!" like champagne or sparkling wine. Make the occasion even more fun by setting up a bubbly bar with coupes and edible flowers, fruit, candy, or specialty sugars and inviting guests to garnish their own drinks. With all the toppings, it's like a grown-up sundae bar . . . but a little buzzier.

edible roses

brown sugar cubes

sugar roses

diamond candy gems

white sugar wedding bells

flower petals

FUN & GAMES

Activities make a party fun for guests of all ages.
I like to have a few go-tos to fill downtime,
such as sending kids on a scavenger hunt or
giving them a craft project that becomes a
favor to take. Even for adults, activities can add
excitement to a celebration; games like charades
or Would You Rather always break the ice.

D.I.Y.
(darcy it yourself)

Not every party needs a game plan, but it's a good idea to have a few activities up your sleeve to make things even more fun. Here are ways to get your game face on.

little ones, little time
Consider guests's ages. Really little kids don't have the focus to do a craft for half an hour, but teenagers can spend all day on a scavenger hunt.

1
choose an activity
Think about what the guest of honor loves, but also what other attendees will enjoy.

2
break the ice
Guests don't all know one another? Use name tags, and these ideas, to get them chatting.

HELLO, A FUN FACT ABOUT ME IS . . .

Let guests fill in tags with their last book read or favorite movie.

WHO AM I?

Have guests put the name of a celeb on their backs and let everyone figure out who's who.

HOW DO YOU KNOW . . .

Ask every guest to fill in their name and how they know the host or guest of honor, and sign their name, too..

3
make something
A craft keeps guests busy and results in a favor that lasts long after the party is over.

4
have fun with food
More than just what you serve your guests, food can end up being the entertainment, whether you're making your own pizzas or decorating cupcakes.

5
get a game going
Think back to recess and put your own spin on scavenger hunts, board games or just re-name "Duck, Duck, Goose."

strike a pose

Photo booths entertain guests and record your party, and the photos double as a favor. Hire a pro or set up a spot with an instant camera or a portable printer, a backdrop, and props like those shown here. Leave out a book with an example pic and note pasted in so guests can follow suit.

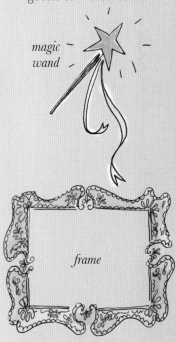

magic wand

frame

animal ears

step and repeat

Create a backdrop by hanging rows of garlands like these tissue paper peace signs.

conversation starters

Get people talking—and the party going—with an ice breaker or two.

SWITCH IT UP

Whether you are celebrating a birthday, graduation, or a new year, turn making wishes and resolutions into a game.

1

Have guests write notes or goals on slips of paper.

2

Collect all the papers in a hat or bowl.

3

Read wishes and vows out loud, and have everyone guess who wrote each one. Or, string all the wishes together in a banner for the guest(s) of honor.

SOMETHING TO TALK ABOUT

Don't let "cheers" fall flat. Left at each place, toast cards with prompts like these inspire sweet stories—or scandalous ones!

My funniest or best memory with ⌣ is _____ .

I love ⌣ because _____ ,

and I always laugh about the time that we _____ .

My favorite thing to do with ⌣ is _____ .

I first met ⌣ when _____ .

This year, ⌣ and I promise to do _____ together.

If you are looking for ⌣ and me, find us _____ because we _____ .

In another world, ⌣ and I would be _____ .

I wish _____ for ⌣ on her birthday.

Something I admire most in ⌣ is _____ .

One of the kindest things I've ever.

seen ⌣ do is _____ .

The first time I knew ⌣ and I were going to be great

friends was when _____ .

The naughtiest thing ⌣ has done is _____ .

My best advice for ⌣ is _____ .

...ream job: ___

Ideal superpower: ___

Celebrity to play me in a movie: ___

My Weirdest habit: ___

Best/worst nickname: ___

Favorite quote: ___

If I were born in a different time, it would be: ___

Favorite TV show: ___

GET TALKING

Help guests get to know each other better with place cards that have a fill-in-the-blank conversation starter on the back. Not having arranged seating? Write the questions on name tags, or read a few out loud and go around the table sharing answers.

My guilty pleasure: ___

I Never leave the house without: ___

My most embarrassing moment: ___

...y worst date: ___

My prediction for the year 3000: ___

Weirdest food I've tried: ___

Best present I've received: ___

My favorite place: ___

I'm most thankful for: ___

put a twist on the classics

Some games are synonymous with kids' parties (though adults can always play, too!). To add your own spin to the fun, update these tried and true games with some simple tweaks.

musical chairs

Try musical balloons instead! Set nonhelium balloons in a circle, one fewer than the amount of players. Everyone spreads out and dances to the music. When it stops, the person who doesn't grab a balloon is out.

hopscotch

Instead of jumping on numbers, challenge guests with instructions on each square. They'll have to clap 3 times, balance on one foot for 10 seconds, or do 4 jumping jacks—all while being timed. Whoever makes it through fastest, wins!

monkey in the middle

Play with a water balloon and see if the "monkey" can catch it without getting soaked! Or, form a circle and have 3 "monkeys" at the same time, trying to intercept 3 balls.

freeze dance

Add an extra action after the music is stopped: "Freeze! Jumping jacks! Freeze again!" or "Freeze! Spin in a circle! Freeze again!" Any players who don't follow instructions (or fall down mid-freeze) are out.

pass the parcel

Wrap a gift in layers of paper for guests to pass around while music plays. Hide small surprises (tattoos, stickers) or instructions ("say the alphabet backward") in random layers for players to unwrap when the music stops. The lucky player who unwraps the last layer gets to keep the grand prize.

pin the tail

Go beyond donkeys! Pin the slippers on the ballerina, the veil on the bride, or the mitt on the baseball player— the possibilities are endless. See page 250 for more ideas.

charades

Tailor the prompts to the celebration: For a Hollywood party, only movies and actors. For a bridal shower, have guests act out wedding and planning-related activities or something significant from the bride's life.

limbo

Play sprinkler or hose limbo on a hot day. Or craft something together (like a paper chain) to use instead of a limbo stick.

hula hoop contest
Who can keep the hoop off the ground? For a bigger challenge, ask guests to hula on one foot or while hopping.

twister
Customize the mat to match your theme. Swap colored circles for different sport balls or pictures of the guest of honor.

ball pit
Instead of filling a space with hundreds of small balls, go bigger with inflatable beach balls of different sizes for guests to play in.

relay races
Ask guests to keep a balloon between their legs the whole way across the course.

summer softball

There are no bases to run, but someone may throw in a towel! Swap out balls for water balloons and see who can smash the most.

———

tug of war

After one side wins, a member of the winning team joins the other side. How small can the winning team get before losing?

tag, you're it

Here are 7 tweaks to the ever-popular game.

tunnel tag

Tagged players freeze in place. Frozen players become unfrozen when another player crawls between their legs. When only one unfrozen player remains, he or she is the new "it."

blob tag

Tagged players hold hands with the original "it" as they chase others together. Every tagged player joins the blob.

shadow tag

Play this version in the late afternoon or early evening, when shadows are long. The "it" player tags people by jumping on their shadows.

reverse tag

In this version, everyone else chases the "it" player. The first person to tag "it" becomes the new "it."

arm and a leg tag

If "it" tags your arm, you can't use that arm. When "it" tags a leg, you can't use that. Players try to escape with unfrozen limbs, and "it" wins when none of the players can move.

tv tag

When "it" approaches a player, he or she yells out the name of a TV character while crouching down—no repeats! If "it" tags you before you sit, you're the new "it." Other categories work, too (movies, foods, animals).

flashlight tag

A mash-up of tag and hide and seek played once the sun goes down. "It" holds the flashlight, and everyone hides. After 50 seconds, players try to sneak to a designated home base before "it" can tag them using the flashlight beam.

LIGHTS OUT!

5 more activities you can do after dark

1
Blow glow-in-the-dark bubbles.

2
Glow-in-the-dark ring toss: Use glow sticks in water bottles as targets, and toss glow-in-the-dark bracelets or necklaces.

3
Glow tic-tac-toe: Tape glow sticks together to make Xs and use bracelets as Os.

4
Hopscotch: Draw your court using glow-in-the-dark chalk or tape.

5
Get crafty (or messy) with glow-in-the-dark clay, slime, or putty.

happy hunting

Scavenger hunts are exciting, creative, fast moving, and cost very little. Get people dashing around in search of odd items—the hilarity that ensues is fun to take part in or to watch. These hunts are endlessly adaptable to any age or occasion: indoor or outdoor, team or individual. Go with a simple checklist, or ask for photo/video proof.

KIDS' SCAVENGER HUNT

☐ Find something that correlates to the birthday child's age

☐ Find something in the guest of honor's favorite color

☐ Find something with the guest of honor's first intial

☐ Sing a song by the guest of honor's favorite band

☐ Find a sports jersey

☐ Have a team member dress up as a superhero

☐ Take a group picture with a neighbor

☐ Find something that is fuzzy

☐ Find something that flies

NATURE SCAVENGER HUNT

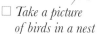

☐ *Take a picture of birds in a nest*

☐ *Bring back fruit from a tree (don't eat it!)*

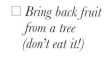

☐ *Take a picture of animal tracks*

☐ *Find a 3-leaf clover (4-leaf for an extra 50 points!)*

☐ *Take a picture of a caterpillar*

☐ *Collect 3 rocks in 3 different colors*

☐ *Collect 3 acorns*

☐ *Draw the most unusual tree you can find*

☐ *Record the sound of a bird chirping*

☐ *Shoot a photo of something that crawls*

☐ *Pick the longest blade of grass*

☐ *Find a stick to use as a cane*

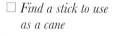

☐ *Pick a leaf that is totally intact*

☐ *Find flowers in every color of the rainbow*

21ST BIRTHDAY SCAVENGER HUNT

- [ ] Get 21 people to wish you "Happy Birthday"

- [ ] Take a picture with 21 different people

- [ ] Find something with the number 21 on it

- [ ] Find a coin dated with your birth year

- [ ] Call the 21st person in your contact list

- [ ] Get someone to buy you a birthday drink

- [ ] Serenade a stranger

- [ ] Start a conga line

- [ ] Find someone who looks like you

- [ ] Collect 5 different coasters

- [ ] Take a photo of your group's reflection in something other than a mirror

- [ ] Do 21 cartwheels or hold a handstand for 21 seconds

ENGAGEMENT PARTY SCAVENGER HUNT

- [ ] Find the numbers of the date the couple got engaged

- [ ] Find the friend who's known the bride the longest

- [ ] Find the friend who's known the groom the longest

- [ ] Ask a relative for a funny story about the bride or groom (or both)

- [ ] Take a picture of a newlywed

- [ ] Take a picture with the couple that's been married the longest

- [ ] Get someone to tell you a secret about the couple

- [ ] Find coins from the year the bride or groom was born

keep in mind

Make your list extra personal: it can revolve around the guest of honor's favorite things, hobby, or a specific location.

BRIDAL/ BACHELORETTE SCAVENGER HUNT

- [ ] Make a veil for the bride and have her wear it during the hunt

- [ ] Get serenaded by a stranger

- [ ] Find another bride-to-be

- [ ] Find a tiara and have someone wear it

- [ ] Find someone with the same first name as the groom

- [ ] Convince a stranger to get down on one knee and propose to someone in the group

- [ ] Collect marriage advice from 5 strangers

- [ ] Spell out "love" with the group's bodies

- [ ] Bring back 5 different items in the bride's favorite color

- [ ] Find two lovebirds

- [ ] Find someone who looks like the groom

- [ ] Find a couple who have been together longer than the bride has been alive

drawing inspiration

Invite guests to get creative as they get to know each other.
A craft can be the main event, or you can set up a few stations with supplies for
crafters to use as people arrive or between activities.

wish boxes

Give guests a wooden box and
supplies to decorate it. Then
have them search for a "lucky" rock,
hold it while they make a wish,
and put it in the box for safe-
keeping. Later they will take home
their magic boxes with the rock
inside. At a birthday or shower, pass
the rock around so friends
and family can make wishes for
the guest of honor.

match point

A roll of green paper turns a
long table into a tennis court—or
a soccer field, football field,
or putting green. Use white tape
to mark lines as needed. Make
nets out of paper, or cut up real
netting. Have guests make
the court, and set out markers
for them to sign it.

place mat picassos

Use pages from coloring books, or
make copies of a sketch to
create place mats and set them
out with markers, crayons,
or colored pencils. Add a maze or
a word search to keep kids
busy while they wait for pizza,
or write a fill-in-the-blank
about the guest of honor that
can be read aloud later.

banner idea

Set out a roll of paper
for everyone to
color in as guests arrive.
The art can hang in
the birthday kid's room
after the party.

play with your foo

Combine snacks with games and a party becomes the setting for edible fun. Just make sure players aren't taking nibbles when they should be making moves!

PROJECT RECIPES

name the flavor

Blindfold guests, give each a bite of something (ice cream, cookie, jelly bean), and ask them to guess the flavor. Better yet, ask them to invent a creative new name for what they taste.

sweet sushi bar

Have guests make candy sushi from Fruit Roll Ups, Rice Krispies Treats, and gummy candy.

(cup)cake boss

Give everyone a cupcake to decorate according to his or her chosen theme (scary, silly, anything goes). Or, work in teams to make a display out of the cupcakes based on your theme. Don't forget to name them, too.

EATING CONTESTS

life saver race

Knot a piece of Life Savers candy in the middle of a long piece of shoestring licorice. Players take their places at each end of the licorice, and race to see who can get to the Life Savers first. Save this one for adults if you're worried about things getting racy!

dough-not touch

Tie doughnuts to strings, then hang them up (on a tree branch or a long stick). The winner is the first person to eat an entire suspended doughnut without using his or her hands. Extra fun (and extra messy) with powdered doughnuts!

and they're off!

Who can eat the fastest using a specific utensil? Have guests try to eat ice cream with chopsticks or spaghetti with a baby spoon.

dig for gummy worms

Fill individual pie pans with whipped cream and gummy worms. The winner is the player who fishes out the most worms without using his or her hands.

EDIBLE EQUIPMENT

egg toss

For an outdoor party, have pairs of guests toss a raw egg between them. The couple that makes it the farthest apart before *splat!* wins.

chewy checkers

Set up a checkerboard with two different kinds of wrapped candies in lieu of playing pieces.

sweet stacks

Have your guests build Jenga-style towers with food like wafer cookies or graham crackers. See how tall the tower can get before it topples!

tic-tac-tasty

Use cookie cutters to make sweets in X and O shapes, or choose
any two treats of different shapes, sizes, or colors. You can play on a grid
made with shoestring licorice or sour straws.

CAKES & SWEETS

If you can't break out dessert for a celebration, when can you? Serving a sweet can turn any gathering into a party—and it doesn't have to be labor-intensive or homemade. Candy and baked goods can also double as décor or party favors, so give your sweet tooth free rein!

D.I.Y.

(darcy it yourself)

A delicious treat served smartly makes a party extra sweet.

GOING BITE SIZE

A bunch of cupcakes or smaller treats can look just as great as one big showstopper of a cake—and you don't have to dismantle your décor to eat them. Plus, you can serve multiple flavors, arrange in any formation, and let guests pick and choose. No plates, no cutting, no silverware!

1
pick a sweet (or a few!)

Whether you gather around a single cake or set up an entire dessert buffet, there's a whole world of goodies to choose from! Pies, cupcakes, cookies, brownies, petits fours, cream puffs, milk shakes, cheesecake . . . the list goes on and on.

2
personalize it

Even the plainest dessert can get dressed up. It's not just about decoration (though there's no end to what you can put on top of a cake!). Think about the flavor, the filling, and the frosting along with what you put on top.

add a toothpick

Attach a cute drawing, a word, a pom-pom, a flower—anything, really— to a simple toothpick, stick it in the top of your chosen dessert, and voilà: instant personalization!

. . . or a cookie

I love using cookies to decorate cakes and cupcakes. Bake a lollipop stick into the cookie and push the stick all the way inside the cupcake to stand the cookie up.

3
display it

Dessert can be décor, too. Cake stands add impressive height to a table, but you can also showcase your sweet on wood boards, marble slabs, embellished trays, or anything else flat and sturdy enough. Don't wait until the end of the party to break out the cake. Display it on a side table or anywhere in view—the cake also makes an impressive centerpiece!

4
top it off

Don't just have a cake at your party; throw a party on your cake!
Crown it with a festive topper, whether it's one simple standout or every
party piece you can find in the house. See the list below for ideas.

play it safe

—

Toppers are great, and
so are candles—but
the two together add up
to a fire hazard. Be
cautious when using both
at the same time!

**MORE
CAKE TOPPERS**

Matchbox cars

Tiara

A Barbie doll

Toy soldiers

Party hat

A mini landmark
(like the Eiffel Tower)

Card on a toothpick

add something extra

Candy. A toy. A flag. Almost anything can be a treat's topper—just remove anything inedible before serving your littlest guests.

candy, blocks

yipes, stripes!

go fish

bon voyage

it's a boy

Surprise!

why not?

—

Use baby chicks to celebrate new arrivals about to hatch.

congratulations!   sugar plum fairy   twins

aloha   class clowns   be mine

make it your own

A cake becomes extra special when personalized for the occasion. Color is one of the easiest ways to customize by using the guest of honor's team colors or favorite hue. Here is my daughter's cake from Pippa's Purple Party (page 22), complete with a mini Pippa swinging from a garland. To make this topper, tie a cutout to a string attached to two skewers.

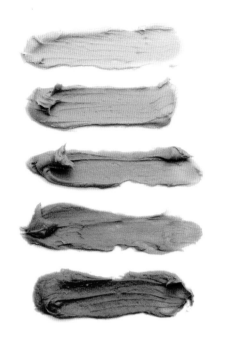

SPANNING THE SPECTRUM

Take your cake up a notch with ombré frosting. Split a batch of icing into five or six bowls. Add a tiny bit of food coloring to one, a little more to the next, and so on. Put the whole gradient on one cake, or frost rows of cupcakes in each shade. For an alternative to frosting, create an ombré cake with sanding sugar, sprinkles, jelly beans, or other candy.

surprise inside

If you're baking a vanilla cake, tint the batter with food coloring for a look that's to *dye* for. A colored inside (pink or blue) is perfect for a baby gender-reveal party, holidays (red, white, and blue for the 4th of July), or just for fun! For an ombré effect, follow the instructions from Spanning the Spectrum on this page, using batter instead of frosting.

crown the queen of cakes

Pink frosting, a tutu, and a paper crown make this cake a royal success.

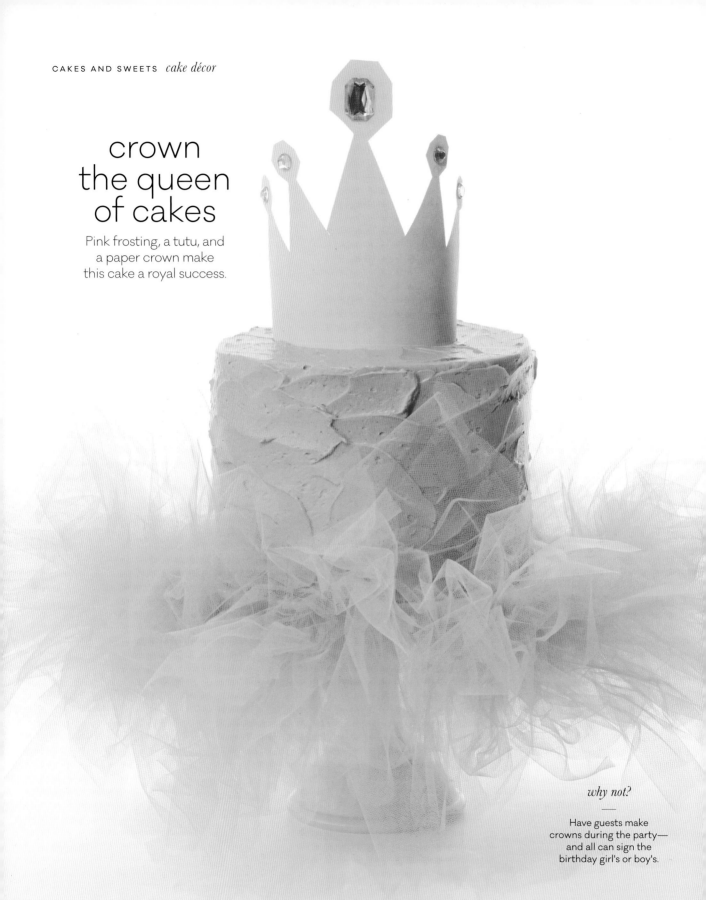

why not?

—

Have guests make crowns during the party— and all can sign the birthday girl's or boy's.

name the winner...

Reward your birthday girl or boy—or gymnast, musician, or graduate— with a prize ribbon cake. Here the frills are made of fondant, but you can get the same effect by using a roll of ribbon or crêpe paper to create a border on a round cake.

4

pin it to win it

What's easier than turning the cake itself into a prize ribbon? Simply use an award ribbon as a cake topper.

make it count

So many celebrations are built around a digit. Whether it's a birthday, anniversary, graduation, reunion, or new year— baby, you've got its number.

5 WAYS
to fill a number mold

—

1
Jell-O

2
Rice Krispies Treats

3
Banana (or zucchini or pumpkin) bread

4
Coffee cake

5
Brownies, blondies, or cookie cakes

DO THE MATH

Have the topper add up to the guest of honor's age: 2 toy cars for a 2-year-old, 3 action figures for a 3-year-old, or 5 lollipops for a 5-year-old. To finish it off, top the frosting with candy dots, and wrap a few strips of the candies around the stand.

GIVE A HIGH FIVE!

Write a number on a plain cake or batch of brownies using pieces of candy, or try berries.

ONE OF A KIND

Cover a number-shaped cake in rows of colored gummies—or pick a single shade and use a mix of candies (red licorice wheels, red jelly beans, red gum drops, and so on).

boo boo

oney

bake

darling

sandwich says
Even ice cream sandwiches
can relay a sweet message.
Write with icing that matches
the color of the chilly filling.

sweetie

spell it out

Send a message with your sweets! Spell out words, or highlight one significant letter using icing, letter-shaped cookies, or candy letters. Get your inspiration from a nickname, word, or initials (maybe those of a newly engaged couple!).

easy as a, b, c

Order or make vanilla-frosted cupcakes topped with fondant letters. One cupcake with chocolate icing adds contrast.

petite sweets

Individual petits fours, each piped with a single letter, can be lined up to make a statement.

the write stuff

Arrange letter cookies frosted in different shades of the same color icing on a basic cake to spell out your message.

hide some treasure

With the first slice, what appears to be a simple cake topped with edible glitter becomes an explosion of confections and color. (Shhhhh! Don't tell the birthday girl or boy!) It's easier than you think to hide candy on the inside—here, baker Seton Rossini shares how.

SURPRISE CAKE

You'll need three layers to make this delightful dessert.

1
stack and frost
2 layers

2
cut out the
middle of
both layers

3
fill with
surprise candy

avoid meltdowns

—

Let the cake layers cool
all the way before adding
candy and frosting.

4
top with frosting
and add remaining
cake layer

5
crumb coat
and frost

why not?

—

Fill with either pink or
blue candies as
a "gender reveal" at a
baby shower.

start your ovens

Roll up your sleeves! Magnolia Bakery, known for making delicious cakes and cupcakes over the past three decades, shared their recipes for chocolate and vanilla cake and buttercream frosting (the vanilla can be tinted any color).

VANILLA CAKE

Makes 2 dozen cupcakes or 1 three-layer, 9" cake

1½ cups self-rising flour
1¼ cups all-purpose flour
1 cup (2 sticks) unsalted butter, softened
2 cups sugar
4 large eggs, at room temperature
1 cup milk
1 teaspoon pure vanilla extract

1. Preheat the oven to 350°F.
2. Lightly flour three 9 × 2-inch round cake pans and line the bottoms with wax paper, or line two 12-cup muffin tins with cupcake liners.
3. In a small bowl, combine the flours. Set aside.
4. In a standing mixer or large bowl, cream the butter on medium speed until smooth. With the mixer running, gradually add the sugar, beating until fluffy, about 3 minutes. Add the eggs one at a time, beating well after each addition.
5. Add the dry ingredients in three parts, alternating with the milk, beating until incorporated, but do not overmix. Mix in the vanilla. Using a rubber spatula, scrape down the sides of the bowl to make sure the ingredients are well blended.
6. Carefully spoon the batter into the cupcake liners, filling them about three-quarters full, or divide the batter among the prepared cake pans.
7. Bake for 20 to 25 minutes, or until a cake tester inserted into the center comes out clean.
8. Cool the cake layers or cupcakes in the pans for 15 minutes, then invert them onto wire racks to cool.
9. Frost as desired with buttercream icing. Be sure the cake is completely cool before icing.

CHOCOLATE BUTTERCREAM ICING

Makes icing for 24 cupcakes or 1 three-layer, 9" cake

12 ounces semisweet chocolate, chopped
2 cups (4 sticks) unsalted butter, softened
3 tablespoons milk
1½ teaspoons pure vanilla extract
3 cups sifted confectioner's sugar

1. Place the chocolate in a double boiler over simmering water on low heat and let it melt, stirring occasionally, for 5 to 10 minutes, or until completely smooth. Set aside to cool for 5 to 15 minutes, or until lukewarm.
2. In a standing mixer or large bowl, with a mixer on medium speed, beat the butter until creamy, about 3 minutes. Add the milk carefully and beat until smooth. Add the melted chocolate and beat well, about 2 minutes. Add the vanilla and beat for 3 minutes.
3. Gradually add the sugar and beat on low speed until the icing is creamy and of the desired consistency.

Note: the chocolate buttercream will get too soft if the room is warm. Place in the fridge for 30 minutes to firm up and then whisk until smooth before using. Use the icing immediately or store it in an airtight container in the refrigerator for up to 3 days.

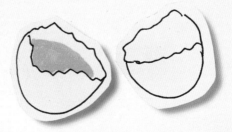

SUPER-RICH CHOCOLATE CAKE

Makes 2 dozen cupcakes or 1 three-layer, 9" cake

2 cups plus 2 tablespoons sugar
1¾ cups all-purpose flour
¾ cup plus 2 tablespoons unsweetened cocoa powder
1½ teaspoons baking powder
1½ teaspoons baking soda
1½ teaspoons salt
2 large eggs
1 cup milk
½ cup vegetable oil
1 tablespoon pure vanilla extract
¾ cup plus 2 tablespoons boiling water

1. Preheat the oven to 350°F. Butter and flour three 9 × 2-inch cake pans or line two 12-cup muffin tins with cupcake liners.
2. In a large bowl, whisk the sugar, flour, cocoa powder, baking powder, baking soda, and salt.
3. In a medium bowl, whisk the eggs, milk, oil, and vanilla.
4. Using a large whisk, combine the egg mixture with the dry mixture. Beat until well combined.
5. Whisk in the boiling water until just combined. The batter will be thin and very watery.
6. Divide the batter between the prepared cake or muffin pans (fill muffin tins three-quarters full; don't overfill! Use an ice cream scoop to make even-size cupcakes) and bake for 22 to 25 minutes, or until a tester inserted into the center comes out clean.
7. Let the cake layers or cupcakes cool in the pans for about 10 minutes, then invert them onto a wire rack to cool.
8. Frost as desired with buttercream icing. Be sure the cake is completely cool before icing.

VANILLA BUTTERCREAM ICING

*Makes icing for 24 cupcakes or
1 three-layer, 9" cake*

1 cup (2 sticks) unsalted butter, softened
1 teaspoon pure vanilla extract
4 cups sifted confectioner's sugar
2 to 3 tablespoons milk
Food coloring, optional

1. In a standing mixer or a large bowl with a hand mixer on medium speed, cream the butter. Mix in the vanilla. Gradually add the sugar, 1 cup at a time, scraping down the bowl often. When the mixture starts to thicken and appears a little dry, add 2 tablespoons of the milk. Beat on medium speed until smooth and creamy, about 2 to 4 minutes. Add more milk as needed for a thinner consistency. If desired, add a few drops of food coloring and mix thoroughly.
2. Use the icing immediately or store it in an airtight container at room temperature for up to 3 days.

let everyone make a wish!

A more sophisticated take on cupcakes, individual cakes—each with their own candle—make everyone feel celebrated. Personalize cakes with guests' names, or let them decorate their own.

just add candles

Who says a cake has to be a cake? Stick a candle into any of these treats, sing "Happy Birthday," and it's an instant party! This trick works for breakfast, lunch, dinner, or any time you want to celebrate! Treats to try: doughnuts, brownies, Rice Krispies squares, candy bars, macarons, waffles, pancakes, bagels, croissants . . .

a cake by any other name

A cake doesn't have to be batter and frosting. Here, ice cream sandwiches do the job when stacked in a pyramid on a cake stand.

keep your cool

—

Ice cream sandwiches melt fast! This tower needs to be assembled, presented, and eaten quickly.

strike a match

Candles instantly upgrade a simple dessert—and there are so many creative options. Plus, their smoke is said to carry wishes away to be granted.

add a cherry on top

spell out a word or silly message

turn a round cake into a carousel

make it a garden cake by adding some gnomes

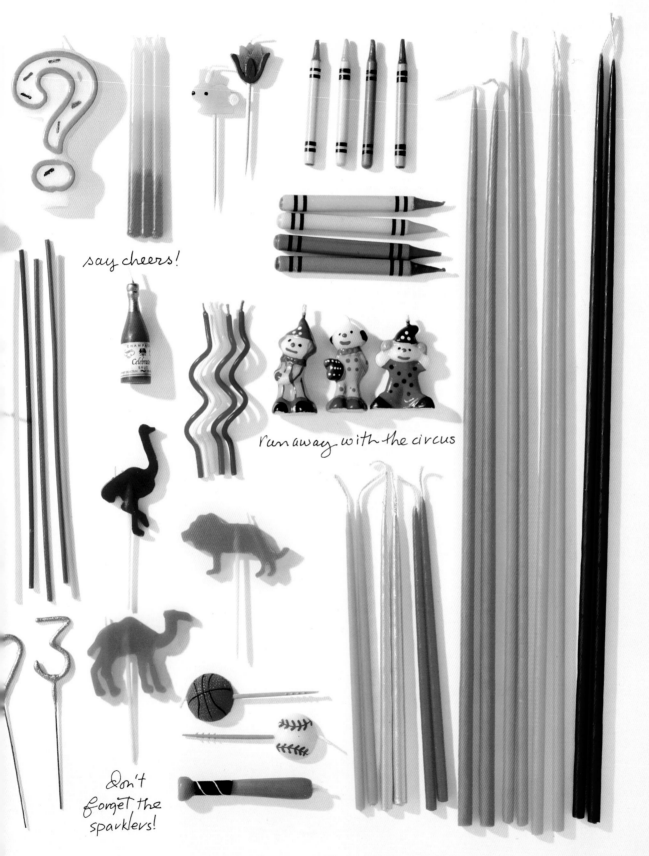

say cheers!

run away with the circus

Don't forget the sparklers!

be a smart cookie

Cookies are easy to make and fun to personalize. Here's a recipe from the home kitchen of Eleni, owner of Eleni's Cookies in New York City.

TRADITIONAL SUGAR COOKIE CUTOUTS

Makes about 20 cookies

1¾ cups all-purpose flour

2 teaspoons baking powder

¼ teaspoon ground nutmeg

½ cup (1 stick) unsalted butter, at room temperature

1 cup confectioner's sugar

2 teaspoons pure vanilla extract

1 egg

1. In a medium bowl, combine the flour, baking powder, and nutmeg and stir well.

2. In a large bowl, beat the butter and sugar with a mixer until light and fluffy. Mix in the vanilla, then the egg, and beat again until fluffy.

3. Gradually add the flour mixture to the wet mixture, beating until just well combined.

4. Wrap the dough in plastic wrap and refrigerate until firm (1 to 2 hours or overnight).

5. Preheat the oven to 325°F and lightly grease baking sheets or line them with parchment paper.

6. Work with about half the dough at a time, keeping the remainder in the refrigerator. On a lightly floured board, or between sheets of parchment paper, roll the dough out to about ⅛-inch thick. Cut with cookie cutters into rounds or other fancy shapes. Carefully transfer them to the prepared baking sheets, leaving at least an inch between each cookie.

7. Bake until cookies are golden brown, about 10 to 12 minutes. Let stand for a few minutes, then transfer to wire racks to cool.

Note: For the best-shaped cookies, especially intricate seasonal cut-outs, it's highly recommended that you freeze the cut-outs before baking them. Place them directly from the freezer onto parchment-paper-lined baking sheet and bake.

ROYAL ICING RECIPE

Makes enough icing for about 20 cookies

At Eleni's New York they refer to this loose icing as "flood" icing. If it's too runny it will spill over your cookie; using "stiff" icing around the edges keeps it in place.

¼ cup meringue powder

4 to 5 tablespoons warm water

3¾ cups (1 pound) sifted confectioner's sugar

TO MAKE FLOOD ICING, in a large bowl, beat the meringue powder and water until soft peaks form. Add the sugar and beat to the desired consistency, about 2 minutes on medium speed. Add more sugar for a firmer icing or a bit of water or egg white for a looser icing.

TO MAKE STIFF ICING, set aside ½ cup of the royal icing in a medium bowl. Slowly add confectioner's sugar and beat to stiffer peaks. Test by dipping a spoon into the icing. Held over the bowl, the icing should not drop from the spoon.

DECORATING COOKIES

For twenty 2½-inch circles, you will need about 1¼ cups of flood icing.

1

Outline cookies first with a stiff icing and allow about 20 minutes for it to set.

2

Flood the surface of the cookies with the looser white icing and set aside for 8 to 12 hours to thoroughly dry and become hard to the touch.

3

Use food-safe markers to decorate! Have fun.

set a sweet table

A display of cakes and goodies can be the heart of
your party décor—add boxes or bags for guests to fill and
the treats double as favors, too.

SWEET SCENE SETTERS

Keep these items in mind as you deck out a display.

COLOR	*monochrome*	pink sweets on a pink cloth for a baby shower
	multicolor	stick to a palette of two or more hues, or use several shades of a color for an ombré look
COMPOSITION	*height*	use serving pieces of varied heights: a cake on a stand, cupcakes on a tiered platter
	depth	place taller items in back and napkins, bags, and cutlery up front
VESSELS	*style*	modern, rustic, global—whatever floats your boat
	size	you'll need an array of serving pieces in small, medium, and large
	shape	go beyond bowls with cloches and platters
FOOD ACCESSORIES	*on-theme toppers*	buy ready-made, or use drawings taped to toothpicks
	wrappers	personalize chocolate bars, cupcakes, and cake stands

spend strategically

Display expensive treats
such as handmade
chocolate truffles in
smaller groups. Fill
any gaps with balloons
or larger items like
cupcakes or pastries.

KEEP THE SETTING SIMPLE

What's behind the buffet? Keep the backdrop as neutral as possible; a busy background
will take away from the display.

size to fit

Bigger treats go in larger
vessels, smaller candies in
smaller dishes (it takes
a lot of jelly beans to fill
a large bowl!).

FAVORS

Favors thank guests for joining in a celebration
and let them take a piece of the party home. A favor
doesn't have to be elaborate, just thoughtful—
something you like or think your guests would enjoy.
Be sure to display takeaways before anyone
leaves, so no one misses out.

D.I.Y.
(darcy it yourself)

Favors are never required, but they're fun to get—and to give, if there's something you want to share with your friends. Here's how to focus on favors.

1
choose an item

The universe of possibilities for party favors is huge. These are a few jumping off points: favors that double as décor (think candy-filled baby bottles at a shower); having guests craft something they can take home (tie-dying blank tote bags); a goodie-to-go, whether it's Rice Krispies Treats or your favorite tea or coffee blend; or a takeaway with a picture or note on it, like a mint tin with a customized label.

2
make it personal

Just a few words—or a guest's name— make a favor more special. Whether you use a paint pen to personalize a water bottle or Frisbee, or attach a tag saying "thanks for coming" to a small flower pot, it will add that extra element to your favor.

3
pick your packaging

Not everything needs to be elaborately wrapped—adding a ribbon, label, or note makes a favor feel unique. Packaging can be as simple as a clear box or as creative as you like. A classic paper bag filled with candy gets a makeover with brightly colored stickers, and a couple of hole punches with a lollipop poked through keep it closed.

4
set it out

Display favors in obvious places so that guests who are busy having fun notice them and pick one up. Either place one on each plate at a seated dinner, or set up a favor table near the door at a cocktail party and sprinkle it with some confetti or tie on balloons.

pip pip hooray!

pip pip hooray!

pip pip hooray!

pip pip hooray!

pun times

Fun wording takes anything up a notch— these Pip Pip Hooray goodie bags were for my daughter Pippa's 5th birthday.

think small

There's a universe of treasures to choose from as a "thanks for coming to my party" token. Here are some classic options. And if you can't choose just one, fill containers with an array of little items or have guests dig into a bucket to pick one fun toy on their way out.

olé olé

ring ring!

Zooooom!

spi

post-its

E ♥ B

iron-on patches

erasers

S.W.A.K

go fish

tattoos

stretch your imagination

A favor becomes more than the sum of its parts if it celebrates the idea of your party. Adding paper-cutout drawings turned candy into balance beams for a gymnastics party.

the kindest cuts
Cut out photos or drawings of guests and attach them to favors, sprinkle throughout décor, or use as cake toppers.

tiny trophies
Everyone's a winner when
a simple favor box is
topped with a toy trophy
filled with candies.

double the fun

Favors can act as decorative focal points if they're hung from the ceiling, pinned to the wall, or set on a table. These balloons are anchored by bags of sweets in a candy-filled bowl used as a centerpiece.

GO UP
AND AWAY!

How to turn even
the plainest favor into décor?
Just tie a balloon onto it.
Add a name tag to personalize
a favor for each guest.

iron on
a shape

draw with
fabric markers

DM
iron on a monogram

stripe it with a
paintbrush

splatter
paint

add a
pom-pom

dip dye
handkerchiefs

name it

Ben

illustrate it

polka dot it
with an eraser top

number it
with a patch

sew on
a few bows

iron on
a love patch

attach a tassel

get crafty

Bring guests in on the favor fun by letting them create or decorate their own takeaway, whether it's a piece of jewelry or a design-it-yourself tote bag, tee, or cap. Just set out the art supplies (add some wine for a grown-up party), and let the crafting, and chatting, begin.

KEEP IN MIND

Wash items first, as some fabrics may shrink.

Use permanent (not washable) markers and paint.

Make sure to leave enough time for things to dry.

Send guests home with any necessary instructions (like rinsing and drying directions for tie-dye).

embroider it

make it two-tone,
use painters tape
for clean lines

decorate it with paint

spray paint it —
cut out a cloud stencil for
sweeter dreams

tie it together

These chic favors are super simple to make.
Guests can add pins, letter beads, or other decorative
touches, and fill with treats.

it's a cinch!

A no-sew project is so
easy. Start with a piece of
round fabric, punch holes
around the perimeter
with a screw punch, and
lace with cord to cinch.

pin-terest

Use beads to create your own phrases, monograms, equations, and abbreviations.

give tasty takeaways

It's easy to package food in a theme-friendly form with personalized labels. Or, turn any baked good into a party animal—or even an alien—by wrapping it in cellophane and using markers, felt, string, glue, and googly eyes to make an adorable assortment of furry (and delicious) friends.

assigned seat treat

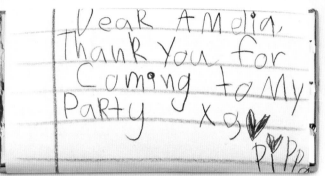

sweet thank you note

SET THE BAR HIGH

A custom label can turn a chocolate bar into something unexpected. To make your own, scan or download anything from a photo to a letter and print—or use colored paper or stickers.

commemorative confection

blank canvas
(set at each place with markers!)

Put a ring on it.

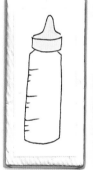

It's a . . . chocolate!

edible escort card

graduation goody

chocolate "popsicles"
(just add the sticks!)

bon bon disguise

keep saying cheers!

Pick a bottle of bubbly or another favorite drink, then dress it up
or personalize it so your guests can raise another toast later.

it's a wrap

Roll a bottle up in light-
weight wrapping paper,
newspaper, or sheets
of decorated tissue paper
and seal with tape,
a sticker, or tie with string.

a fine vintage

Print out a custom label
with the date of the
party or the honoree's
birthday, along with a
photo, and wrap around
the base of the bottle.

perfect pairing

For my friends' wedding
favors, I decorated bottles of
vodka and soda in honor
of Anthony and Rusty's go-to
drink. Citrus candy slices
added a finishing touch.

show me your ID!

For a coming-of-age
birthday, mark half your
bottles of beer with
"2" labels and the other
half with "1" to com-
memorate the big day.

toast with the most

Fringe some tissue paper with scissors and wrap around the top of mini champagne bottles. Add a simple label made with plain black paper and a paint pen and spell out a name, or even "mom" or "pop."

party in a bag

Slip a bottle into a clear cellophane bag along with a party blower and some paper confetti, and you'll have the ingredients for a great celebration.

photo finish

Print a favorite pic on copy paper, then wrap around bottles for a label that's all about the person—or people— you're celebrating.

wrap it up

The simplest toys or treats turn into memorable gifts when
they're boxed, bagged, or decorated in a unique way.
Drum up a style that matches your theme—or dress up
a box fit for a princess (or a superhero).

ALL ABOARD

Almost anything can be packaged in a box—and the
container itself can be transformed into just as
many options. Button wheels, some cardboard, and cotton
balls turn plain white boxes into the train above.

IN ROTATION

Stack two boxes into one supercute favor. These
boxes were custom-printed for my sister's birthday,
where we celebrated her sense of style with
a mix-and-match wardrobe of outfits. You could
also use words or letters; Xs and Os, for example,
would add up to a tower of hugs and kisses.

cupcakes

cookie

pins

chocolate bars

picture this

There's nothing more personal than photos, which makes them perfect for customizing favors and other party details. Put them on lollipops, favor bags, or anything else ... even confetti!

stickers

barley lollipops

deck of playing cards

memory game

tattoo

confetti

coasters

white chocolate lollipops

favor bag

matches

printed chocolates

magnet

4 TIPS FOR *fab photos*

1

Choose a picture with a simple background to avoid visual confusion.

2

Snaps with the subject looking at the camera are the most intimate.

3

If you're showcasing a guest of honor, pick a photo they like. You may find their awkward phase cute, but they likely won't.

4

When in doubt, convert your photos to black and white. They'll instantly look more unified.

NOW, LET THE
CELEBRATIONS BEGIN!

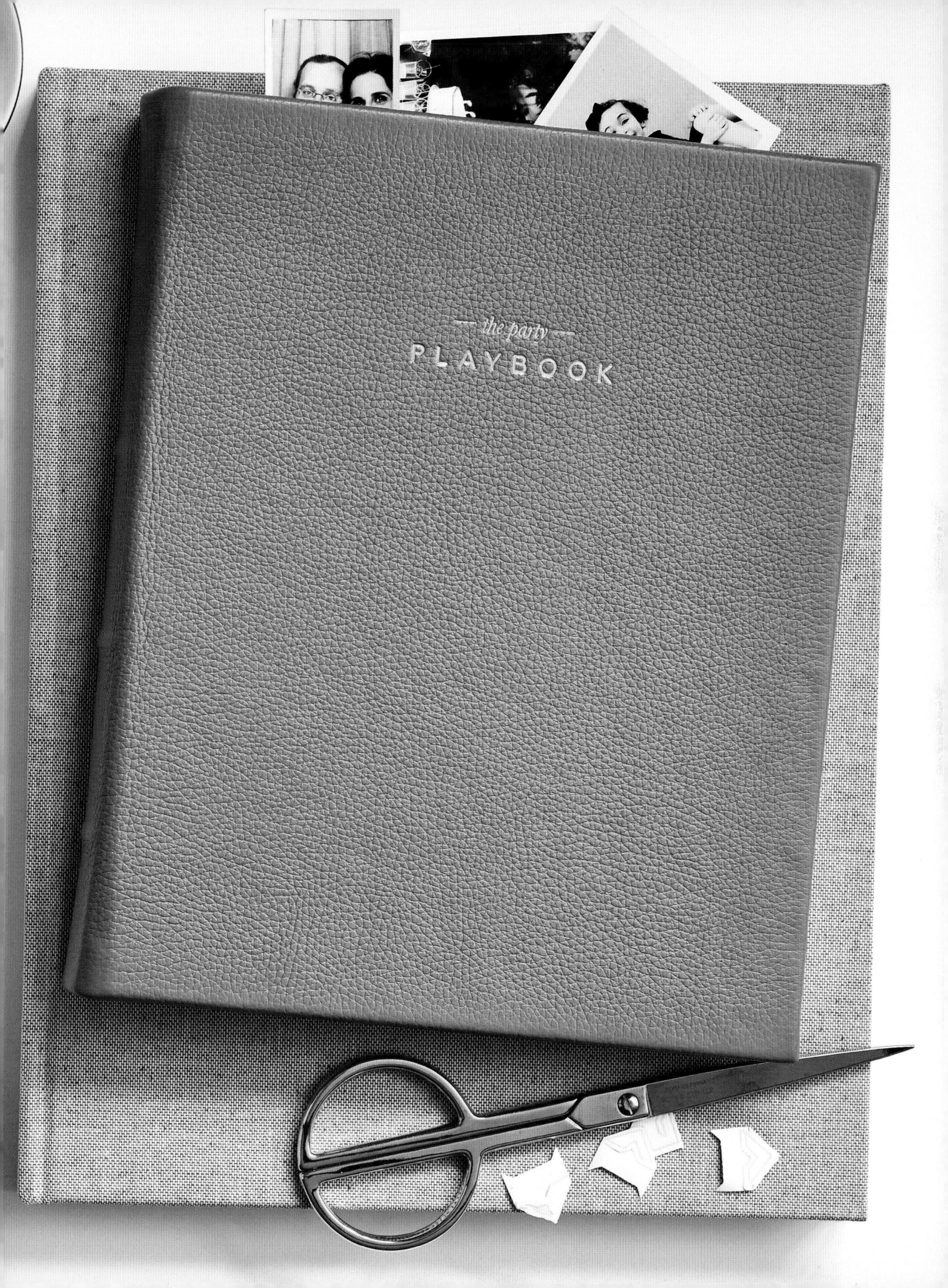
the party
PLAYBOOK

flora and fauna

A variety of white flowers in different vessels played up the nature theme. *Opposite*: Toy deer and sugar mushrooms top a mille-crêpe cake dusted with green tea powder.

Welcome Baby Berry

BABY SHOWER

Baby animals set the scene as we celebrated my friend Kate, a mom-to-be, and her impending arrival. Her love of nature inspired a baby shower that felt like a walk through an enchanted forest, with miniature deer and bunny rabbits at every turn. Flowers and decorative birds' nests rounded out the décor, alongside woodland-inspired bite-size treats that were *almost* too cute to eat.

oh deer!

Choosing one motif to
appear throughout
the food and décor brings
your theme to life.
Here, a fawn was used
in multiple ways.

a little invite

Baby animals on the invitation and
envelope liner set the tone.

group guestbook

Have each guest write well-wishes,
one after the other, along a
strip of paper (quilling paper is
shown in the top photo).
When done, tuck it into a small box;
I used one shaped like a log.

mommy's mobiles

Baby animal cutouts, strung from
embroidery hoops hung overhead,
became a gift for the mom-to-be.

custom soap

Custom-ordered soap printed
with my drawing of a fawn was given
as favors. Each bar came in a
muslin bag decorated with a made-
to-order rubber stamp in gold ink.

toys and treats

Deer figurines were placed
throughout the dessert display.

cute cookies

White frosting spots make
gingerbread deer even sweeter.

the tops
Personalize cupcakes with
on-theme toppers.

MERINGUE
MUSHROOMS

CANELLÉS

CHAMPAGNE
BUBBLE
GUMDROPS

CHOCOLATE
HEDGEHOGS

HAND-CUT
MARSHMALLOWS

MACARONS

CHOCOLATE
CARAMEL EGGS

woodland wonders

An abundant buffet was filled with sweet treats shaped to look like objects you'd see in an enchanted forest.

trees for trays
Birch stumps covered in wood-grain paper served as pedestals on the dessert display.

sweet-nest
Decorative mini nests were filled with coffee-and-cream candy and cocoa-dusted almonds.

Yule log
A *bûche de Noël* topped with buttercream, powdered sugar, and meringue mushrooms, resembled a birch log.

baby bites

Cheese, crackers, and a few appetizers
were presented in keeping with the forest theme.

"birds' nests"

Crème frâiche, smoked
trout, and caviar layered
atop a potato pancake
made a hearty passed app.

nestled eggs

A hardboiled quail egg
topped with black pepper
in a fried-leek nest.

egg-ceptional

Hollowed-out hard-boiled
eggs were halved
and filled with scrambled
egg and garnished with
a truffle slice.

croque mademoiselle

The mini version of a
croque madame: grilled
cheese with bechamel
sauce, Gruyère, and
prosciutto, topped with a
sunny-side up quail egg.

easy peasy

Bunny grilled cheeses are easy to
D.I.Y. with a cookie cutter.

stilton

Herbed chèvre

Parmesan

Crackers

Brie

creative crackers

Serve cheese with crackers you shape with cookie cutters.

MAKES APPROXIMATELY FIFTY 1½-INCH CRACKERS

1 cup all-purpose flour

1 teaspoon kosher salt

3 tablespoons very cold
  butter, cut into small
  pieces

3 tablespoons freshly grated
  Parmesan cheese

¼ cup milk

1. Preheat the oven to 225°F.

2. In a large bowl or standing mixer, combine the flour and salt. Add the butter and mix on medium speed until the mixture resembles coarse meal. Add the cheese and mix until combined. Add the milk and mix until the dough comes together.

3. On a floured surface, roll the dough out to ⅟₁₆-inch thickness. Use woodland animal cookie cutters to cut out your desired shapes. Lay the shapes on a baking sheet with ½-inch of space between them.

4. Bake for 30 minutes. Rotate the pan back to front and bake 30 minutes more, until lightly golden. Let crackers cool on the baking sheet.

From the kitchen of Peter Callahan

natural beauties

The nature theme carried through everything from the food and drink to favors of marshmallow mushrooms.

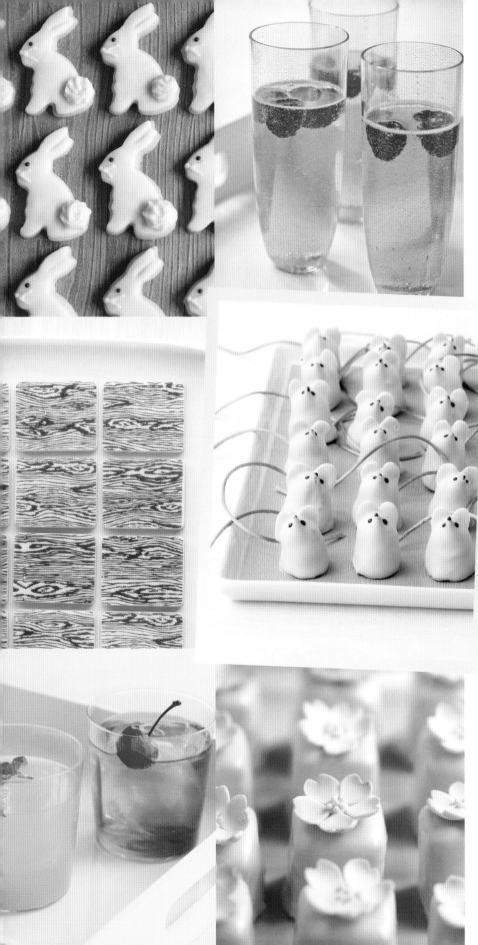

bunny hop

Frosted sugar cookies with piped tails looked ready to jump.

berry bubbly

Champagne was kept cool with frozen raspberries.

"wood" blocks

Chocolate can be silk-screened with any pattern—faux bois fit the forest theme.

18 blind mice

White chocolate versions of our furry friends came complete with ribbon tails.

"mommy" and "daddy" drink

The mom-to be (and other guests) enjoyed nonalcoholic organic peach nectar with a sprig of baby basil. Also offered was a cocktail for the dad—a traditional Manhattan, garnished with a maraschino cherry.

pink petals

Sugar-flower-topped petits fours were an on-theme way to let guests know "it's a girl!"

child's play

Tailor-made for baby showers, these games bring out the kid in everyone.

NURSERY RHYME POP QUIZ

What's mama going to buy if the mockingbird don't sing? What were the occupations of the three men in the tub? And so on. Whoever answers the most correctly wins.

BABY SHOWER BINGO

Make bingo cards with a different baby gift in each square (onesies, bibs, diaper bag, rattle, blanket). Have guests mark off their cards as gifts are opened to see who gets bingo first.

NAME THE CELEBRITY BABY

Give each guest a list of famous offspring. Whoever recognizes the most bold-faced baby names, and can fill in the names of the celeb moms and dads, wins.

DON'T SAY "BABY"

As guests arrive, give each one a sheet of five stickers. Whenever someone says "baby," whomever that person is talking to puts a sticker on the speaker's shirt. The last guest not wearing stickers wins.

NAME THAT STORYBOOK

List memorable lines from favorite kids' books. "In a great green room," "We'll eat you up— we love you so," "Once you are real, you can't be ugly." Whoever guesses the most titles wins. (*Goodnight Moon, Where the Wild Things Are, The Velveteen Rabbit*)

SHOWER CHARADES

Just like the regular version except that guests act out baby-centric activities, whether it's from the point of view of the parent (changing a diaper, swaddling baby, rocking an infant to sleep) or the baby (crying, crawling).

baby mobile

Cut cute shapes (bunnies, boats, butterflies) from felt or paper and use string to tie onto an embroidery hoop. Hang from the ceiling with twine and removable 3M hooks.

SWEET SACHETS

Handmade sachets are easy to sew, and make thoughtful favors. Choose solid or patterned fabric; you can even have fabric custom printed to match your theme.

FILL A SACHET WITH DRIED

lavender   peppermint

rosemary   chamomile

rose petals   lemongrass

sage   cedar chips

PRESS PLAY ▶

The vibe: dreamy, precious, magical

My Baby Just Cares for Me
NINA SIMONE

Northern Sky
NICK DRAKE

Sweet Baby
MACY GREY

Haven't Met You Yet
MICHAEL BUBLÉ

C'est Si Bon (It's So Good)
EARTHA KITT

Banana Splits for My Baby
LOUIS PRIMA

Lucky
KAT EDMONSON

Sweet Pea
AMOS LEE

Baby
SHE & HIM

Baby I Love You
ARETHA FRANKLIN

Crazy Little Thing Called Love
PABLO DAGNINO

Imagine
JACK JOHNSON

made in the shade(s)

Arrange an "ocean" of candy in shades of blue on a serving tray as part of your decor. *Opposite:* This ombré effect is easier than it looks—turn the page!

POOL PARTY

A swim-themed celebration can be held on dry land if color guides the décor and underwater themes get splashed around—I've thrown one in my living room as a cocktail party! If there's a pool available, the entertainment is built in, too. (It took the promise of cake to lure kids out of the water during a birthday party at an indoor pool.) The theme inspires sweet treats for the little ones and savory snacks for grownups. Create an ombré cake with a diving topper and you can have your pool and eat it, too.

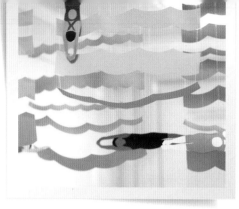

OMBRÉ POOL FROSTING

Divide white icing into four bowls and add blue food coloring in varying amounts.

Frost from the top down, starting with the lightest shade, using darker colors as you go. Make waves by moving a knife up and down.

Cut a strip of blue paper into a wave shape, wrap around the stand, and secure with double-sided tape.

doorway divers

Cut and hang paper garlands of waves and swimmers so guests feel like they're underwater.

life preservers

Doughnut balloons become flotation devices with a little help from some red tape.

a fish out of water

Little touches bring the shore indoors. For events in public pools, beaches, or parks, make paper decorations ahead, then pack them up with grab-and-go snacks for a portable pop-up party.

straw fishies

Cut fish shapes out of paper to make straw toppers.

ice and easy

Snow cones are perfect for a hot day. Personalize them by printing an image on the cone wrapper.

stick 'n' swim

Cut fish out of contact paper: instant stickers!

sea of sweets centerpiece

A fish bowl brimming with candy makes a great focal point.

A DOUGHNUT POOL

*Mini pastries glazed with
aqua icing stay in their own lanes—
until the guests arrive!*

THE WATER
To create a faux pool, place a sheet
of light-blue wrapping paper under a
large, clear tray or sheet of Lucite.

THE LANES
Red and white bakers twine is great
for lanes. Or line up paper dots
punched from color paper as on left.

THE BLUE DOUGHNUTS
You can buy plain mini doughnuts
to frost with your own icing tinted
with food coloring; sprinkle iced
doughnuts with blue sanding sugar; or
just order them already frosted blue.

THE LIFE PRESERVERS
Pipe four stripes of red icing onto
a vanilla-frosted mini doughnut and
voilà—life preservers!

3 WAYS WITH
chocolate medals

As prizes or favors, these
are definitely winners.

—

1

Hand out with blank labels
and markers as a color-
in activity during the party.

2

Fill in labels with guests'
names as place cards.

3

Order custom stickers
with a logo or artwork.

GO FOR THE GOLD!

*Amp up the fun with some of these
wet-and-wild games.*

IN THE POOL

Cannonball contest

Marco Polo
(use the guest of honor's name instead!)

Pool tag

Scavenger hunt using diving toys

Freeze dance

Relay race

Synchronized swimming dance-off

ON THE LAWN

Water balloon toss

Slip 'N' Slide

Sprinklers

Water balloon piñatas

Blow-up toy race

fish food

Simple details really bring the theme of a party to life. A couple of well-placed touches or easy-to-make snacks in fun shapes (hello, cookie cutters!) can turn almost anything into a nautical treat.

here, fishy fishy!

Trim sushi-grade tuna into fish shapes and serve on toast. Crackers with cream cheese and red caviar make tasty life preservers.

sweet suits

Buy or frost and decorate cookies beforehand, or at the party as an activity for guests. A round sugar cookie can be dressed up to look like a porthole or waves.

why not?

Order custom napkins. You can pick a phrase like "Splash Out!" or choose an image.

relay bar

After all that splashing, give your guests an energy boost.

MAKES THIRTY-TWO 1×2-INCH MINI BARS

1½ cups rolled oats
1 cup chopped almonds
1 cup dates
⅓ cup honey
⅓ cup almond or peanut butter
Chopped dried fruits or other nuts, optional
½ cup mini chocolate chips

1. Spread the oats in a single layer on a rimmed baking sheet and toast them in a 350°F oven for 5 to 7 minutes, until lightly browned.
2. Toast the almonds on the same sheet for 8 minutes, until lightly browned. Chop.

3. Roughly puree the dates in a food processor.
4. In a medium bowl, combine the date puree, honey, and almond or peanut butter and stir until smooth. Stir in the almonds and oats and mix well. (Mix in dried fruit or nuts, too, if desired.)
5. Line an 8×8-inch pan with plastic wrap and press the mixture firmly and evenly into the pan. Sprinkle the chocolate chips on top and press gently. Let the mixture cool in the pan. When it is cool to the touch, cut it into bars of the desired size.

From the kitchen of Peter Callahan

AWARD-WINNING CANDY FAVORS

Start with a clear, round box full of blue candy and decorate with paper waves and a "gold" (read: chocolate) medal.

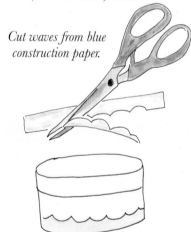

Cut waves from blue construction paper.

Attach paper along bottom edge with doublestick tape, fill with candy.

Top closed box with two strips of gold tape and chocolate coin.

PRESS PLAY

▶

The vibe: sunshine, cabana cool, sublime

Tenderness
GENERAL PUBLIC

Funky Bahia
SERGIO MENDES
FEAT. WILL.I.AM AND
SIEDAH GARRETT

Say Hey (I Love You)
MICHAEL FRANTI
& SPEARHEAD

Boa Sorte (Good Luck)
VANESSA DA MATA
FEAT. BEN HARPER

Gold Silver Diamond
GENERATIONALS

Rivers of Babylon
BONEY M.

Love Generation
BOB SINCLAR

Jamming
BOB MARLEY

Rudy, A Message to You
DANDY LIVINGSTONE

Horchata
VAMPIRE WEEKEND

*Theme from
"The Endless Summer"*
THE SANDALS

SEA-WORTHY SEND-OFF

As favors, give guests a taste of the (sweets!) sea: Fill favor bags with blue candy and gummy fish. Serve pop bottle to-go drinks complete with straws and fishy toppers.

more straw toppers

Any paper cutout can be a straw topper—just punch two holes to thread the straw through the top and bottom! To keep shapes intact, add a small tab at the top and bottom of your design and punch those.

bright ideas

Paper fans in rainbow colors make a great photo backdrop. *Opposite:* A horseshoe-shaped pan plus cake pop clouds add up to an adorable cake.

RAINBOW PARTY

If you can't pick one favorite hue, throw a party that celebrates them all! With a bold palette as your guide, look for colorful favors, food, and activities. At this birthday party, kids were divided into color teams for games. Grown-ups love rainbows, too—set your table in mismatched colored glass and china and serve cocktails in every shade!

rainbow
connections

Decorate with every shade
in the spectrum.

canopy

Start by suspending a
white sheet from the
ceiling to create a canopy,
then add a bright circle
garland and a banner.

message banner

Use a bowl to trace
semicircles on paper,
personalize with letters
(handwritten or stickers),
and staple to the canopy
to spell out your wish.

paper circle garland

Sew colored circles
together, or use a hole
punch on the edge of
each colored circle and
thread string through.
(The garland can also hang
on its own, sans canopy.)

the tabletop

Set your table in rainbow
order with tissue paper
flowers and bowls of
matching candy, napkins,
and colored drinks.

5 WAYS TO GET YOUR
GUESTS TO
dress on-theme

—

1

Invite everyone to
come head-to-toe in
their favorite color.

2

Or, assign each invitee
a color to dress in.

3

Offer accessories like
bracelets or bandanas.

4

Link multicolor
paperclips into jewelry.

5

Set up a rainbow
nail polish or hair chalk
station.

rainbow hopscotch

Draw numbers on colored paper with
a black marker and tape to floor. Or,
use white paper and multicolor digits.

rainbow races

Give regular party games, like relay
races, a rainbow twist by dividing
guests into color teams: red + orange
+ yellow vs. green + blue + purple.

colorful jewelry

Jewelry-making keeps everyone busy,
and gives them on-theme accessories
to wear and take home as favors.
String beads on shoelaces, or have
older kids sew pom-poms together.

large-scale art

Blow up a black-and-white drawing
for everyone to color in together, then
hang it in the birthday kid's room.

design your own

Set out permanent markers to decorate
blank pillowcases, pencil cases,
hats, journals, aprons, T-shirts, or totes.

color them happy

A rainbow theme lends itself to countless crafts
and activities; the list at left is just a jumping-off point!

it's a draw

Print out coloring sheets
for kids to fill in.

taste a rainbow

Brightly hued snacks are one way to play with your theme.

shade-y characters

Chill different flavors of Jell-O one layer at a time, or make single-color cups and arrange in rainbow order.

pink drinks

And every other color, too. Serve multihued beverages, such as Gatorade, in glass bottles.

edible rainbow

Everyone will want a piece of this rainbow! (Try it with veggies, too—tomatoes, carrots, yellow pepper, celery, black olives, purple cabbage.)

sweet skewers

Spear marshmallows tinted with food coloring, or make single-hue kebabs and line them up. As a healthy alternative, try fruit kebabs.

filling fun

Tint white icing in colors of the rainbow and sandwich it between two simple sugar cookies.

rainbow brights

A tube of multicolor jelly beans can double as a place card and a favor. Cut a slit in the top of the tube to slip in a paper cloud name tag.

Anna

Daisy

Jeremy

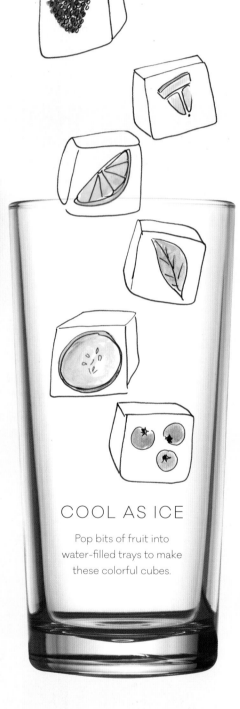

candy necklaces

Make necklaces you can nibble on from peach rings, Fruit Loops, or gummy Life Savers strung onto a piece of licorice. Candy without a ready-made hole, like gumdrops or gummy bears, can be strung using a needle and unflavored, coated dental floss—the candy will slide on more easily than with regular thread.

PRESS PLAY ▶

The vibe: sparkle, shine, soar

Unwritten NATASHA BEDINGFIELD	*Be Okay* OH HONEY	*Brave* SARA BAREILLES
Gold BRITT NICOLE	*Easy Love* SIGALA	*Hey, Soul Sister* TRAIN
Beautiful CARLY RAE JEPSEN FEAT. JUSTIN BIEBER	*Love Myself* HAILEE STEINFELD	*All Night* ICONA POP
Up OLLY MURS FEAT. DEMI LOVATO	*Hold My Hand* JESS GLYNNE	*22* TAYLOR SWIFT

COOL AS ICE

Pop bits of fruit into water-filled trays to make these colorful cubes.

POP-UP INVITATION

1

Paint (or draw) a rainbow in the middle of a piece of 8.5 × 11-inch paper, then make copies.

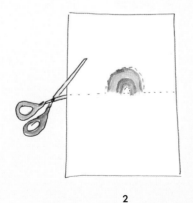

2

Cut as shown around the rainbow.

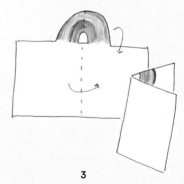

3

Fold the paper in half vertically, then fold the rainbow at its base so it nestles into the paper and pops up as the card opens.

tee time

A gumball and golf tee in a bag of jelly beans makes a favor that's a hole in one.

GOLF PARTY

A golf-themed celebration is right on par for an aspiring golf pro—or a retiree. Tee up for an outdoor party like this one for my friend's son, where a backyard was the perfect stand-in for a putting green. Or, use your imagination (and lots of grass-green accents) for an indoor event. If you're a soccer or baseball fan, many of these ideas easily translate. Play ball!

turn the table into a golf course

Start by rolling out a sheet of artificial grass, fake moss, or a green paper tablecloth as a base, then make putting green place mats out of paper and sand-trap coasters out of sandpaper. Finally, add the elements on the next page.

place settings

Top plates with score pad place cards that double as favors. Bamboo utensils make things even "greener!"

fairway flag

Use a punch to make two holes on the side of a triangle paper flag and poke a straw through.

GOLF BALL PARTY HAT

blue party hat

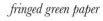

fringed green paper

round label stickers make a great ball above a paint-pen tee

caddie canteens

Label water bottles with a birthday (or hole) number on a paper wrapper.

ball bites

Instead of pressing Rice Krispies Treats into a pan, mold scoops into golf-ball-size spheres.

golf cupcakes

Chocolate cake stands in for soil, green frosting and sanding sugar are grass, and a Sixlet is the ball.

sticker 'staches
Colorful mustache stickers make a fun photo prop for your team. An overhead picture offers a new perspective on the party.

ball + cup games

Decorate paper cups to match your theme, and use them for both drinks and activities.

ball toss

Stack upside-down paper cups in a pyramid, and see who can topple the stack first.

cup toss

Stand face-to-face and a step away from your cup-holding partner. Toss the ball into the cup. For each successful "putt," both take a step backward. See who can get the highest number of holes in one.

three cup monte

Have a guest hide a ball under one cup while the others try to keep tabs on it as the cups are slid around to new positions.

putting practice

No mini golf course needed. Set up paper cups sideways in the grass and secure with tees.

sporty spoon race

Like an egg and spoon race,
but with a golf ball instead!
(A Ping-Pong ball is a lighter
alternative for little kids.)

golf course cake
From the kitchen of Butterfly Bakeshop

1
Start with two rectangular cakes.

2
Spread a layer of buttercream on one, and place the other on top. Refrigerate 15 minutes.

3
Add green food dye to the rest of the buttercream, mixing evenly.

4
Cut a sand trap shape and a putting green shape from parchment or waxed paper to use as templates.

5
Ice the cake and then press the templates gently on top. Pour on green sprinkles, avoiding the two templates.

6
Peel off the templates.

7
Sprinkle crushed graham crackers in the sand trap space and stick a mini flag and candy golf ball on the putting green.

sun tea

MAKES 2 QUARTS

12 tea bags
1 gallon of water
lemon slices, sugar,
or mint to taste

1

Place about 12 tea bags
per gallon of water in
a large container (or 4 tea
bags per quart) in direct
sunlight for 3 to 5 hours.

2

Add lemon slices, sugar,
or mint leaves for extra
flavor. Serve over ice from
a mason jar with a spout.

Arnold Palmer

Serve the famous golfer's
signature drink: equal parts
lemonade and iced tea. For
adults, add a vodka splash.

simple garland
Make an ice cream
cone garland out of brown
paper pennants
and pastel paper scoops.
Opposite: A slice of cake
becomes a cone when
topped with a scoop and
a marzipan cherry.

ICE CREAM PARTY

Everyone loves ice cream—and not just for dessert. I've thrown more than one scoop-centric event, and half the fun of a party like this is figuring out how you're going to serve the sweet stuff: as make-your-own ice cream sandwiches or sundaes, in cakes, or as a feast for the eyes in décor elements. This chapter offers lots of ideas for doing d.) all of the above.

extra large cone

Balloons and a craft paper cone attach to each other with double-sided tape. Adhere them to the wall with painter's tape for a photo backdrop.

scoop dreams

For a chill thrill, pass out balloon "scoops" and cardboard "cones" and start playing games with an ice cream theme.

RELAY RACE

Split guests into teams for an egg-and-spoon-style relay race.

MONKEY IN THE MIDDLE

Use cones to catch and toss the "scoop" over the monkey's head.

UP IN THE AIR

Each guest, or pair of players, gets a cone and scoop. Toss and try to keep the scoop up the longest without dropping it.

CHERRY BALLOON WALL

two red balloons
+
green string
+
a pair of green paper leaves attached at the stem

1
Blow up the balloons,
but not all the way,
so that they stay round.

2
Knot the center of
the string on the stem
of the paper leaves.

3
Fold one leaf down
to cover the knot.

4
Tie the string ends to
a pair of balloons, then
attach to the wall
with painter's tape.

tasteful treats

Sherbet-hued markers let guests color paper cups to fill with treats at the party, and decorate pencil cases to take home.

scooper fun

From party hats to crafty favors, every element of the celebration can get in on the ice cream theme.

cone heads

Fill favor cones of waffle-printed paper with treats or trim in fringed tissue to wear as hats. Or, turn a hat into a favor holder at party's end.

top it off

What's for dessert? An ice cream sandwich bar that lets everyone make their own winning combination. Set out cookies, waffles, and other outsides; ice cream in a few flavors; and ramekins filled with different toppings from mini marshmallows to chocolate chips, gummies, candies, and sprinkles.

Toppings

1. marshmellow
2. sprinkles
3. Sour path kids

Noor's magical

sandwich name

Suprise

PLAY WITH PLACE MATS!

Upgrade the average write-on place mat with these ideas:

Photos of the birthday kid to doodle on (add a mustache!)

Fill-in-the-blank awards

Art to finish (connect the dots)

On-theme word searches

Customized or on-theme crossword puzzles

Personalized Mad Libs

Acrostic puzzle with honoree's name

the big chill

Go ahead and break the ice cream rules. Waffles don't have to be cones, ice cream can be in—not on—the cake, and a single "cone" can line your table. There are so many ways to vary the theme!

cone centerpiece
Line the table center with a wedge-shaped cake slice frosted like a cone, three cupcake "scoops," and a marzipan cherry for a delicious display.

don't stop at waffle cones!
Make your own waffle à la mode. Top with dried coconut and add marzipan cherries to sweeten the deal.

ICE CREAM, ALL GROWN UP

To end the party on a sweet (and caffeinated!) note, serve adults espresso with an amaretto-brioche coffee ice cream sandwich. Other adult combinations include:

*affogato: vanilla
ice cream or gelato
+
a shot of hot espresso
poured on top*

—

*palmier cookies
+
salted caramel
ice cream to dip in*

—

*Limoncello
+
lemon sorbet
served in scooped-out
lemon halves*

*sundae
night lights*
—
Number-shaped sparklers
bring any cake to life.

stack 'em high!
Classic ice cream sandwiches
stacked like logs make for a highly
impressive impromptu cake.
Just make sure you have help to
stack them quickly before they melt!

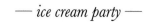

WORKBOOK

larger than life

Supersize an ice cream sandwich with blocks of
ice cream and two sheet cakes. (Use some cake in the
middle as support.) Freeze before serving.

I scream, You scream...

ONE SCOOP TO GO

Cone shaped cellophane bags (or clear disposable pastry bags) are the perfect size to fit a sugar cone. Fill and top with your favorite candy, seal the bag with tape, and top with a pom-pom "cherry."

sweet scenes

Paper wedding bells make just the right backdrop. Tie honeycomb bells together with monofilament or stick them to the wall with painter's tape. Invite the groom to make an appearance at the end of the party—if he brings a bouquet, it's a photo booth prop! *Opposite:* Plain cupcakes were decorated with chocolate gems worthy of engagement rings.

BRIDAL SHOWER

A celebration of love itself, a shower is even more fun if it focuses on the couple. I chose a soft palette of white, gold, and pink for my friend Tiler's party, and filled the room with romantic motifs including wedding bells, lovebirds, hearts, cakes, and more. Pictures of the bride and groom, Robbie, were scattered throughout, sharing their love story.

raspberry-infused champagne
Frozen fruit adds a touch of color while chilling champagne.

photo napkins
Personalize anything from coasters to napkins with a pic. Print each image in black and white for a cohesive look. See page 158 for photo glossary.

"i do's"

Say yes to special touches from petals to hearts that add romance to your menu.

two for tea

Rose petals add a flowery taste to an herbal blend (just make sure they're pesticide-free), and Palmiers are the perfect accompaniment—they're already heart-shaped!

love on ice

A single edible flower was frozen inside each cube in a heart-shaped ice tray. Flowerless hearts or blossoms frozen in regular cubes would work, too.

black-tie affair

Cut toast into a bow-tie shape and top with caviar for an appetizer that's formal and fun.

french bliss

We had *beaucoup* options for our French-themed dessert display. Here are just a few highlights.

MACARON
\ ˌmä-kə-ˈr͞on \

Almond flour meringue cookies fillled with ganache, buttercream or jam.

CHOUX PASTRY
ˌʃuː ˈpeɪstri

Very light pastry made with egg, typically used for eclairs or profiteroles.

RELIGIEUSES
[ruh-lee-zhyæz]

A small choux pastry set atop a larger one, both filled with cream and covered in ganache.

sugar high

At French weddings, dessert is a pyramid of crème puffs bound with caramel called a *croquembouche*. The French bakery Ladurée makes a crème-filled choux tower iced in pink as a twist on the idea.

sweet love

Dessert displays are even more delicious when they're inspired by personal details. Since this couple got engaged in Paris, a display of French pastries was both meaningful and *magnifique!*

gold standard

Gold Dresden trim along the edge of a cake stand mimics "wedding band china," a vintage pattern featuring gold circles that was once a popular gift for newlyweds.

chic shapes

Piped pink frosting turns vanilla cupcakes into different types of flowers.

love letters
Cookie cutters turn home-made marshmallows into hearts and the pair's initials.

ring their bells
Cookies on lollipop sticks make perfect decorations for cupcakes.

marshmallows

With this recipe from One Girl Cookies in Brooklyn, NY, you can bake your own marshmallows and cut them into fun shapes.

MAKES 24 TWO-INCH-SQUARE MARSHMALLOWS

3 envelopes unflavored gelatin
2 cups sugar
¾ cup light corn syrup
½ teaspoon salt
2 teaspoons vanilla extract
1 cup sifted confectioner's sugar

Note: You will need a candy thermometer for this recipe.

1. Coat a 9 × 13-inch baking pan with cooking spray and line the bottom with parchment paper.

2. Pour ½ cup cold water into the bowl of a standing mixer fitted with the whisk attachment. Sprinkle the gelatin over the water and set it aside to absorb the water.

3. In a heavy-bottomed pot over medium heat, combine the sugar, corn syrup, salt, and ½ cup of water. Stir to dissolve the sugar. Bring the mixture to a boil, cover the pot with a tight-fitting lid, and boil for 5 minutes. Uncover and do not stir the syrup any more as it is heating.

4. Taking care not to agitate the pot, attach the candy thermometer and continue to boil the syrup until it reaches 240°F. Do not overheat the syrup. When the syrup reaches 240°F, carefully remove the pot from the heat. Turn the mixer on low speed and carefully pour the hot syrup into the bowl of gelatin. Increase the speed to high and beat for 8 minutes. With the machine on high, add the vanilla. Continue whipping as the mixture becomes light and fluffy. After 5 to 7 minutes, it will be stiff and lukewarm.

Stop the mixer and carefully scrape the mixture into the prepared pan. Using a spatula that has been sprayed with cooking spray, smooth the top of the marshmallow. Let cool for at least 5 hours, uncovered.

5. To cut the marshmallows, sprinkle a generous amount of confectioner's sugar on a cutting board. Turn the marshmallows out of the pan onto the cutting board. Sprinkle the top and sides with more confectioner's sugar. Spray a large chef's knife with cooking spray and carefully cut the marshmallows into cubes. This is very sticky business. Use plenty of confectioner's sugar on your hands and on the marshmallows to help you fight the stickiness. The marshmallows will keep in an airtight container at room temperature for 5 to 6 days.

formal fare
Candy pearls and powdered sugar bow ties dress up brownies.

love bites

Create heartfelt sweets by topping cupcakes with cookies in wedding-inspired shapes like doves, hearts, bells, or even the couple's initials.

life of the party

Celebrate the bride-to-be—and keep guests engaged—with these bridal shower games.

wedding "would you rather?"

At the start of the party, hand each guest a pencil and a printout with a series of this-or-that questions about the bride. Read the questions aloud and have her give the correct answers. The person who knows her best wins. Bonus: Ask the groom to fill a copy in ahead of time and share his responses, too.

Would she rather ...

- ☐ stay in and watch a movie **OR**
- ☐ go to a bar?

- ☐ take endless work-out **OR**
- ☐ cooking classes?

- ☐ vacation in Paris **OR**
- ☐ the Caribbean?

- ☐ drive a U-haul **OR**
- ☐ a golf cart for a year?

- ☐ cook dinner **OR**
- ☐ have someone cook for her?

- ☐ read *Romeo and Juliet* **OR**
- ☐ watch the movie?

- ☐ dine with Beyoncé **OR**
- ☐ Gloria Steinem?

- ☐ skip winter **OR**
- ☐ skip summer?

- ☐ run for president **OR**
- ☐ go to the moon?

- ☐ be overdressed **OR**
- ☐ underdressed?

- ☐ wake up at 5 a.m. **OR**
- ☐ stay up until 5 a.m.?

- ☐ give up heels **OR**
- ☐ sneakers forever?

- ☐ watch a reality TV marathon **OR**
- ☐ train for an *actual* marathon?

- ☐ have a small, intimate birthday party **OR**
- ☐ a big, surprise birthday party?

- ☐ live in a small apartment in the city **OR**
- ☐ a sprawling house 300 miles from town?

- ☐ meet her great-great-great-grandmother **OR**
- ☐ great-great-great-grandchild?

20 questions

When the groom arrives, get him into the action! Give each half of the engaged pair a bride or groom sign and have them sit back-to-back. As questions are read, have them raise their signs to answer, and see how often they agree.

1
Who said "I love you" first?

2
Who is the better gift giver?

3
Who talks more?

4
Who is better at keeping surprises?

5
Who is the better cook?

6
Who is always running late?

7
Who takes the longer shower?

8
Who uses pet names more?

9
Who's the boss?

10
Who is always right?

11
Who hogs the covers?

12
Who is a pickier eater?

13
Who decides most of the plans?

14
Who would be more willing to give up closet space ?

15
Who is more of a morning person?

17
Who likes lingerie more?

18
Who is more romantic?

19
Who is the bigger party animal?

20
Who made the first move?

Wedding wishes...

Wedding wishes...

May you bring each other as much happiness as your friendship has brought me!

xo, Lindsay

make a wish

For a thoughtful upgrade on a traditional guest book, have each attendee leave behind marriage advice, date ideas, memories of the couple, or first impressions of the groom versus how they feel about him now. It'll be much more memorable than a list of names!

MORE BRIDAL SHOWER GAMES

BFF TEST

Compile a list of specific questions about the bride, from her favorite movie to the brand of toothpaste she uses. The person who answers the most correctly wins.

FIANCÉ FACTS

How well does the bride know the groom? Before the shower, give him the same list of questions you used about the bride. When she's done, compare to see what she gets right.

LOOKING BACK

Print photos of the bride and groom at different ages (one each when they were 5, 10, 13, 15, etc.) Have people pair images they think show the couple at the same age.

BRIDAL MAD LIBS

Everyone gets their own, or pass one around for each guest to fill in blanks like "[Bride] is the [superlative] person I know and [Groom] perfect for her because he's [adj.]!"

HE SAID, SHE SAID

Ask the groom questions about the pair's romance ahead of time, then write out a list of his answers along with some made-up responses: have the bride/guests guess what's real.

SHARE THE WISDOM

Have everyone write out their best piece of relationship advice on slips of paper and put them all in a jar, then pull out one at a time and read aloud. Guess who shared what.

"YOU WERE MEANT TO BE"

Give everyone a pencil and a piece of paper, and ask them to write down how they knew the bride and groom were destined to be together. ("I knew they were meant to be when she said, 'He can't spell, but I love him anyway.'") Collect the notes and give them to the bride. She can read them aloud at the party, or save them to look back on later.

TOAST TIME

Everyone recalls when they first could tell that the bride was in love.

EYE ON THE TIMER

Set a timer as the bride unwraps gifts. Each time it pings, whoever gave what she's holding gets a prize.

PIN THE VEIL ON THE BRIDE

Use a drawing or photo of the honoree.

box it

Stack graduated boxes and they'll look like little wedding cakes. You can personalize them with artwork (like I did here), or use plain boxes in your color palette.

stack it

Two-tier white chocolate mini Oreo cookie cakes are topped with a sugar heart.

pop it

Whether it's a lollipop or a cake pop, a wedding-cake shaped sweet on a stick is easy and fun for guests to pick up on the way out.

"slice" it

Slice-shaped boxes are inspired by the tradition of the "groom's cake," a second cake displayed at Southern weddings that is cut and sent home with guests; it's said to make single people dream of their future spouse. Boxes can be filled with cake at the last minute, or pre-packed with candy and confetti.

tie it

Tiny cakes whose name means "small oven" in French, petits fours are ideal for parties because they're bite-sized. Gold trim bows celebrate tying the knot.

take the cake

Don't just stop at dessert! Any way you slice it, "wedding cake" makes gorgeous décor and fun favors, too! Pre-filled with candy before the party starts, these slice-shaped favor boxes double as décor.

"WEDDING CAKE" SANDWICH

This salmon toast appetizer tastes savory but looks so sweet.

open-faced cream cheese and smoked salmon tea sandwiches

+

3 sizes of circular cookie cutters

+

edible flowers on top

=

LOVE NOTES

A garland of folded pennants where guests share wishes at the shower can then decorate the rehearsal dinner, the get-away car, or future anniversary parties.

PRESS PLAY ▶

The vibe: true love, joyous, forever

Question
OLD 97'S

Be My Forever
CHRISTINA PERRI
FEAT. ED SHEERAN

Gotta Have You
THE WEEPIES

I'll Melt with You
NOUVELLE VAGUE

Lucky (Suerte)
JASON MRAZ
FEAT. XIMENA SARIÑANA

I Like the Way This Is Going
THE EELS

Signed, Sealed, Delivered I'm Yours
STEVIE WONDER

Better Together
US THE DUO

If I Ain't Got You
ALICIA KEYS

I Will
THE BEATLES

Let My Love Open the Door
PETE TOWNSHEND

Then Came You
DIONNE WARWICK &
THE SPINNERS

fly the coupe

Jell-O shots *can* be elegant if you swap water for bubbly.
To fill eight standard six-ounce champagne coupes, mix a
packet of Jell-O, ½ cup of hot water, and 2½ cups of
champagne. Chill in plastic coupes and serve with a spoon.

champagne jello shots

the finishing touches
You can garnish coupes with
something extra, like these
sugared organic rose petals.

polar express

Flocked branches add
dimension to this dessert
spread, while cloches
give the look of snow globes.
Opposite: Bear cookies
circle a buttercream cake.

WINTER PARTY

My parents love any excuse for a party. For a December cocktail gathering, they sent out an invitation that read, "come and get toasted with Frosty." I helped them bring winter inside with bite-size food and cocktails inspired by Jack Frost, all set in a silver-and-white palette. Snowflakes and icicles make for a warm welcome when they're used as decorations that re-create a winter wonderland indoors.

have a (snow) ball!

Decorative cookies are easily matched to your theme and can be treats to enjoy at your party or favors for guests to take home. Here, the same polar bear cookies that graced the cake march across a plain white platter.

3 FUN WAYS TO
winterize your party
—

1

Coat the corners
of your windows with
spray-on snow.

2

Line the dessert buffet
with cotton batting and
fake snow.

3

For extra shimmer,
sprinkle open surfaces with
sparkly confetti.

snowy woods
Marshmallows
topped with cotton
candy make a
forest floor for these
paper tree cutouts.

SIMPLE SNOWMAN CUPCAKE TOPPER

*Go beyond just snowflakes!
With a pair of scissors and a few
simple snips, you can transform
plain paper into so many things.*

1

Cut or punch a snowman
from white paper; draw
on buttons and a carrot
nose with markers.

2

Wrap with a scarf
of yarn, sparkly ribbon,
or paper.

3

Attach to a toothpick
with tape.

snow-topped toppers

Decorative dessert toppers add personality to simple sweets.

snowball poms

Buy ready-made or attach a sparkly pom-pom to a toothpick with hot glue.

paper snowflakes

Cut paper or use a decorative punch to make flakes.

top hats

Add an accessory to snowmen cake pops.

tree cookies

A mini cake topped with frosted cookies sits on a bed of cotton candy snow. (If it's not touching food, cotton batting works, too.)

silver bells

Shiny cups and sticker toppers make cupcakes even cooler.

3 SIMPLE STEPS TO
dress up a cupcake

—

1
Top with a sugar
snowflake.

2
Sprinkle the frosting with
white sanding sugar.

3
Swap a plain paper
liner for lacy one.

winter drinks

These seasonal sippers from the kitchen of caterer Peter Callahan are inspired by holiday flavors including cranberry, cinnamon, and ginger.

CRANBERRY CITRUS MOJITO
MAKES 8 SERVINGS

8 cups frozen cranberries

1 cup rum

zest and juice of ½ orange

2 cups simple syrup

Blend the cranberries, zest and juice, and simple syrup until smooth. Strain and add the rum. Serve over ice and garnish with whole cranberries on a skewer and a lime wedge.

GINGER-PEAR-TINI
MAKES 8 SERVINGS

1 cup chopped ginger root

1 cup vodka

1 cup pear juice

1 cup sugar

1 cup water

Puree the ginger, sugar, and one cup water. Strain out the solids to make ginger water. Mix the pear juice, vodka, and 1½ cups of the ginger water. Serve over ice in small juice glasses.

HOT TODDY
MAKES 1 SERVING

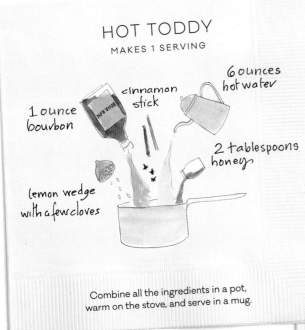

1 ounce bourbon

cinnamon stick

6 ounces hot water

2 tablespoons honey

lemon wedge with a few cloves

Combine all the ingredients in a pot, warm on the stove, and serve in a mug.

LIMONCELLO-TINI
MAKES 8 SERVINGS

1½ cups of your favorite lemonade

1 cup vodka

1 cup limoncello

1 cup sparkling water

Combine the ingredients in a large pitcher and serve over shaved ice in mint julep cups.

icy cool

Keep Limoncello-tinis
chilled on a bed of ice.
Serve in julep cups with
decorative birch straws.

MORE BOOZY
WINTER DRINKS

Eggnog

Moscow Mule

White Russian

Irish coffee

Hot buttered rum

Peppermint Patty

Mulled wine

Spiked hot cocoa

marshmallow man

Cancel that trip to the North Pole.
Your tray of tasty little snowmen can come
right from the grocery store's candy aisle.

1 Rolo candy

1 chocolate coin

SNOWFLAKE COOKIE GARNISH

Use a paring knife to cut slits into cookies just
as they come out of the oven, when they're still
soft. Test one on a glass before cutting them all
to be sure the cut is the right size for the cookies
to rest on the rims of eggnog-filled glasses.

3 big marshmallows

black sprinkles or food-safe markers

PRESS PLAY ▶

The vibe: cool as ice, majestic, cosmopolitan

1 orange sprinkle

silver sprinkles

and a skewer

Let Go
RAC
FEAT. KELE AND MNDR

Ghost
(Lost Kings Remix)
HALSEY

Magic
COLDPLAY

Lose Yourself
to Dance
DAFT PUNK

Sit Still, Look Pretty
DAYA

No Diggity
CHET FAKER

Lose It
OH WONDER

Into the Night
CAROUSEL

Harvest Moon
POOLSIDE

Midnight City
M83

Nocturnal
DISCLOSURE
FEAT. THE WEEKND

Classic
THE KNOCKS
FEAT. POWERS

bed of snow

Use a decorative edger punch to make a string of paper snowflakes. Tape around the edge of a flat piece of styrofoam (make sure snowflakes are taller than the foam). Cover the foam with cotton stuffing or cotton candy and stick marshmallow pops into the styrofoam.

birthday boy balloons!
Paper glasses, hair, and a drawn-on smile lend personality to plain balloons. (Pipe cleaners make snazzy specs, too, or just draw them on!) *Opposite:* Breadsticks tucked inside printed paper bags dress up a place setting.

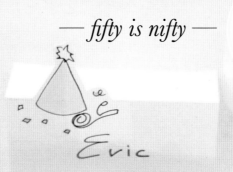

MILESTONE PARTY

Any birthday is something to celebrate—but especially one ending in 0 or 5. It's a chance to honor someone you love, by gathering his or her favorite people (and food, and music)! For my husband Andy's surprise 50th party, everything from centerpieces to games was a reminder of who he is, where he's been, how much we love him, and how glad we are that he was born.

here's to you!

Every element of your party can be a nod to the
guest of honor. This sugar-coated fête was for a birthday boy
with a serious sweet tooth.

décor = dessert

Candy-topped cakes
add color to an all-
white table; wooden
candlestick holders
were painted to match.

place cards
Hand-decorated cards played up the theme of the day.

HAPPY

candy dot strips + painter's tape (for attaching)= wall art!

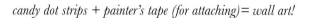

BIRTHDAY

surprise!

bloom service
Single peony stems in small vessels complemented the cakes.

lemon drops

orange gum drops

kaleidoscope cakes

How to dress up a cake for a candy fan?
Gather gummies in all shapes and colors, plan your
design, and get decorating! First, map out a
pattern on a piece of paper cut to the cake's shape
and size. Once you've laid it all out, transfer to
the cake! You can let the dessert's flavor inspire the
taste of your candy decorations.

watermelon slices

lime slices

orange wedges

raspberry gummies

cherry slices

lemon wedges

memorable meals

Serve favorite foods from cherished places. Ask yourself these
questions about the honoree to inspire your menu:
Where has he lived? Traveled? What's his dream vacation?

news flash

Download the front page from the day he
was born, make copies, and roll into
cones to hold fries. (Line with wax paper
cones.) Copied newsprint also works
as place mats, photo backdrops, candy
bar wrappers, and more.

greatest hits

Guests went on
a culinary journey of
Andy's life.

New York nosh

Mini stadium hot dogs
represented Andy's
adulthood in New York.

college try

Bite-size burgers and beers
recalled his undergrad days.

top toast

The birthday boy's drink of
choice was offered in
a self-service Scotch bar.
Inexpensive glass decanters
were dressed up with
personalized labels; we now
use them on our bar at home.

travel tastes

Time spent in Russia and
Italy inspired these tiny
caviar-and-blintz birthday
cakes and spaghetti and
meatballs hors d'oeuvres.

party by number

Sure, age is nothing but a number—but it's a number that can lead to lots of great party themes. Jump-start your imagination with these ideas, whether you're planning for 5 or 50.

50 flavors

Marked with stickers announcing the milestone age, 50 small cups held different toppings. They were set up at a do-it-yourself sundae bar shaped like the number itself.

special delivery

Make a big statement by gathering balloons—as many as the guest of honor's age—and tying them to his or her chair. Not around on the big day? Send the bunch to work as a surprise!

are you
1
are you
2
are you
3

are you...?

OTHER WAYS TO
party by numbers
—

21
types of bottled beer offered at the bar

16
candles on every table

30
Lotto tickets — with an extra one for good luck!

40
different chocolates, delivered on the day

include the kids

Even at a grown-up party, it's nice to get children in on the celebration. Make it fun for all ages with activities for the little ones.

PIN THE FAVORITE THING ON DADDY

Post a life-size image of the guest of honor, then draw or print out some of his or her favorite objects for a witty version of pin-the-tail-on-the-donkey with props such as:

cell phone

sunglasses

tennis racket

hammer

stethoscope

cocktail

remote control

mocktail hour

Dress up sparkling water or ginger ale with a fruit candy wedge so kids can toast. Cover the table with paper and white party hats and set out crayons for budding artists.

why not?
—
Stack layers of candy into an edible centerpiece.

through the years

Photographs are a great way to personalize a party that celebrates a guest of honor. Choose pictures from different eras, and convert them all to black and white to make them uniform. Then try some of these décor and favor ideas.

snap happy

Print customized cookies to look like Polaroids so you can show your honoree's sweet side.

FAVOR BOX TIME LINE

Paste photos of favorite moments onto bags or boxes and arrange them in chronological order as shown opposite. These were filled with birthday-present-shaped bite-size cakes.

wearable memories

Download a party hat template, print out photos, cut, and roll into shape.

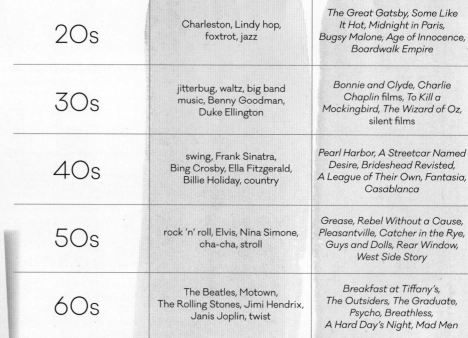

party by decade

Be inspired by a decade you love! Celebrate the one the guest of honor was born in, got married in, or is entering, or embrace them all and have everyone come dressed in the style of a chosen era and bring a dish of the time.

candy by the decade

Package top treats from the era in which the guest of honor grew up.

	MUSIC AND DANCE	BOOKS, FILM, AND TV
20s	Charleston, Lindy hop, foxtrot, jazz	*The Great Gatsby, Some Like It Hot, Midnight in Paris, Bugsy Malone, Age of Innocence, Boardwalk Empire*
30s	jitterbug, waltz, big band music, Benny Goodman, Duke Ellington	*Bonnie and Clyde,* Charlie Chaplin films, *To Kill a Mockingbird, The Wizard of Oz,* silent films
40s	swing, Frank Sinatra, Bing Crosby, Ella Fitzgerald, Billie Holiday, country	*Pearl Harbor, A Streetcar Named Desire, Brideshead Revisted, A League of Their Own, Fantasia, Casablanca*
50s	rock 'n' roll, Elvis, Nina Simone, cha-cha, stroll	*Grease, Rebel Without a Cause, Pleasantville, Catcher in the Rye, Guys and Dolls, Rear Window, West Side Story*
60s	The Beatles, Motown, The Rolling Stones, Jimi Hendrix, Janis Joplin, twist	*Breakfast at Tiffany's, The Outsiders, The Graduate, Psycho, Breathless, A Hard Day's Night, Mad Men*
70s	Blondie, disco, Bob Marley, Led Zeppelin, The Bee Gees, The Jackson 5, Diana Ross, Donna Summer	*Rocky Horror Picture Show, Saturday Night Fever, Star Wars, Annie Hall, Almost Famous*
80s	Madonna, Michael Jackson, Tina Turner, The Police, Bon Jovi, Whitney Houston, Queen, Duran Duran, Bruce Springsteen	*ET, Flashdance, Scooby Doo, Top Gun, Back to the Future, The Breakfast Club, Ghostbusters*
90s	Lauryn Hill, Snoop Dogg, Tupac Shakur, The Notorious B.I.G., Britney Spears, Spice Girls, TLC, Macarena	*Clueless, Friends, Beverly Hills, 90210, Saved by the Bell, Empire Records, The Virgin Suicides, Pulp Fiction, Wayne's World*
OOs	hip hop, pop punk, Destiny's Child, Blink-182, Kelly Clarkson, Foo Fighters, Panic! at the Disco, J. Lo, Usher, Auto-Tune	*Mean Girls, Twilight, The Da Vinci Code, Donnie Darko, High School Musical, Napolean Dynamite, Lost*

CANDY	FASHION	FOOD AND DRINK
Baby Ruth, Bit-O-Honey, Chuckles, Dubble Bubble, Goldenberg's Peanut Chews	Coco Chanel, fringed flapper dresses, drop waist, long gloves, vests, fedoras, pork pie hats	champagne cocktails, Caesar salad, gin cocktails
3 Musketeers, Boston Baked Beans, Candy Buttons, Choward's Violet candy, Life Savers	Katherine Hepburn menswear, Mary Janes, florals, Hollywood glamour, hats	moonshine, Singapore Sling, cheese puffs, Twinkies
M&M's, Almond Joy, licorice ropes, Dots	pin curls, uniforms (army, navy, air force), pumps, high-waisted dresses and skirts, red lipstick, polka dots, pin-up girls, Rosie the Riveter	Hemingway Daiquiri, mai tai, French 75, Cracker Jack
Atomic Fireball, Smarties, Pez, bubble gum cigars	beehives, leather jackets, poodle skirts, neckerchiefs, saddle shoes, cat-eye glasses, cuffed jeans, white T-shirts	glass soda bottles, hot dogs and milk shakes, root beer floats, Jell-O molds, pineapple, pound cake, sloe gin fizz
Lemonhead, Now and Later, wax bottles	Audrey Hepburn, Twiggy, tie-dye, go-go boots, miniskirts, slogan buttons	martinis, Manhattan, whiskey sour, shrimp cocktail
Blow Pop, Big Red, Cherryhead, Chiclets	bell-bottoms, mood rings, platform shoes, Daisy Dukes, maxidresses, floppy hats	piña coladas, fondue, crêpes
AirHeads, Bubble Tape, Nerds, Reese's Pieces	acid-washed jeans, bangle bracelets, crimped hair, side ponytails, Converse, jelly shoes, neon, shoulder pads	Cool Ranch Doritos, Long Island Iced Tea, Tab soda, margaritas
Gobstoppers, Gushers, Ring Pops, Warheads, candy necklaces	grunge, stick-on earrings, flannel, chokers, plaid skirts, fanny packs, overalls, crop tops, baby tees	Cosmopolitan, White Russian, Dunk-a-Roos, pizza bagels, Dippin' Dots
salted caramels and Orbit gum	flare jeans, studded belts, flip phones, trucker hats, peasant tops, cargo pants, velour track suits, Ugg boots, skater style	Appletini, Red Bull & Vodka, cupcakes, smoothies, bacon everything, Starbucks

PRESS PLAY
▶

The vibe: back to the future

Bizarre Love Triangle
NEW ORDER

Electric Feel
MGMT

Just Like Heaven (The Penelopes Remix)
THE CURE

A Little Respect
ERASURE

Wait And See
HOLY GHOST!

Something Good Can Work
TWO DOOR CINEMA CLUB

Train in Vain
THE CLASH

Just Can't Get Enough
DEPECHE MODE

Chase Us Around
VICEROY FEAT. MADI DIAZ

Helena Beat
FOSTER THE PEOPLE

Let's Go
THE CARS

Bruises
CHAIRLIFT

oh, baby

It's often seen as a filler
flower, but baby's breath,
when massed together,
looks so elegant.

ANNIVERSARY PARTY

Love is one of the best reasons to throw a party. No need to wait for silver (25th) or gold (50th) anniversaries; we felt my parents' 45th was a milestone that called for a stylish dinner, with everything glittering in metallic hues. The celebration was packed with reminders of the lovebirds' commitment, from photos of their lives to a menu inspired by the era of their wedding.

Darcy

First Course

WILD MUSHROOM POT PIE

SAUTÉED TRUMPET, GOLDEN OYSTER
AND HEDGEHOG MUSHROOM

Main Course

PHEASANT UNDER GLASS

PLUM GLAZED PHEASANT BREAST,
CREAMED SPINACH, GOLDEN POTATOES
WITH CREME FRAICHE AND CHIVES

Dessert

BAKED ALASKA

... and toasts, toasts, toasts!

two for fun

The menu also served
as a place card,
and a reminder to start
thinking about a toast.

love story

A long marriage is extra special—
send an extra special anniversary party
invitation to match.

book 'em!

I love an invitation that
goes above and beyond to
get guests excited for
the party. This booklet was
a tribute to the details
of my parents' special day.

top tier

Use vintage cake toppers
as décor. It's an especially
nice touch if the couple
saved their own.

put a ring in it

Paper ring cutouts
fell from the invitation
like confetti.

this is your life

Tell the story of their time together in pictures—and find clever ways to incorporate them into your decor.

hanging history

Have photos of the pair through the years around the room, and hanging from monofilament on a festive tassel garland.

memory lane

Display a time line of their life since their wedding. Make an accordion by folding a long strip of paper or by attaching photo mats together.

THE SECRET TO MADGE & MARTIN'S HAPPY MARRIAGE IS...

raise a glass

Your guests will want to toast the couple. Take the pressure off by handing out toast prompt cards to get them started (see suggestions at right).

15 TOAST PROMPTS

These ideas will help your guests say "cheers" with ease.

Their secret to happiness is . . .

My first impression of them was . . .

They make me laugh when . . .

The best lesson they've taught is . . .

The best gift I could give them would be . . .

I'd love to travel with them to . . .

I knew he loved her when . . .

The most fun I've had with them was . . .

They get the most joy from . . .

The best thing about them is . . .

They are happiest when . . .

The wildest thing they've done together was . . .

I love their story about . . .

Before their next anniversary I hope they . . .

worth more than gold
Personalize chocolate
coins with photos, writing, or
artwork. Order custom
stickers or print your pictures
on round stickers or
adhesive paper and punch out.

a menu with meaning

Serve food and drink that pay tribute to the couple's favorite place, their wedding menu, or the era in which they married. I chose a *Mad Men*–style menu in honor of my parents' 1965 wedding.

Endive with smoked trout, horseradish crème frâiche, and dill

Deviled eggs with caviar

cocktail power

Served with personalized coasters and napkins, throwback drinks— a champagne cocktail and a kir royale— transported guests back in time.

Wild mushroom pot pie

celebratory sweets
From sparkling Baked Alaska to edible glitter-covered bonbons to foil-wrapped treats, shiny desserts feel extra festive.

MAKE IT PERSONAL

THE PALETTE
Get inspired by their
wedding colors.

THE FLOWERS
Re-create the wedding
bouquet on the table.

THE DÉCOR
Display sweets with
mementos in cloches.

THE SWEETS
Customize chocolates with
monograms or photos.

tablecloth upgrade
A plain roll of paper gets a D.I.Y. makeover with the help of a circle punch.

child's play

Make the littlest guests feel special with their own table where they can stay busy with bubbles, toy rings, colored pencils, and sweet treats!

kids' meal

The secret to on-theme dishes kids will actually eat: cookie cutters, which shaped the wedding cake grilled cheese as well as the cucumber M (for Madge and Martin), atop the cucumber and cream cheese sandwich. Another "fancy" touch: Shirley Temples in coupes.

big bash

It's not a party without a piñata—and they're not just for kids. Some alternatives to classic candy and toy fillers:

movie tickets

lotto tickets

hair accessories

gift cards

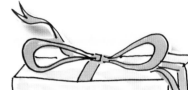

memory-filled cootie catcher

The classic cootie catcher game can be personalized in so many ways. Fold them and add fortunes ahead of time ("Martin will tell you the story of the first time he saw Madge—again!"), or let guests write their own predictions.

Fold diagonally and crease to make fold lines.

Fold up all corners so points meet in the middle . . .

like this!

Fold up the corners so points meet in the middle again . . .

like this!

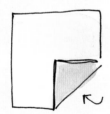

Fold the top back.

Work your fingers into the corners from the fold side.

MILESTONE ANNIVERSARY GIFTS

Mark the occasion with an unexpected twist on the classic present.

1st PAPER
art, tickets (to an event—or a flight!), handwritten letter

5th WOOD
furniture, a tree to plant, a wood-based perfume

10th TIN/ALUMINUM
a keepsake box or decorative tin to hold memories

15th CRYSTAL
predictions from a "crystal ball," a watch, glasses and a nice bottle of wine

20th CHINA
a piece from the couple's wedding pattern, tea or coffee cups and a custom blend

25th SILVER
a silver pen, collar stays, an engraved locket, a moonlit celebration

30th PEARL
an oyster dinner, jewelry, a trip to the South Seas

35th CORAL
scuba-diving lessons, anything coral-colored, a tropical vacation

40th RUBY
a special bottle of red wine (from the year they met)

45th SAPPHIRE
a beach weekend (sapphire blue seas!), a lucky "something blue"

50th GOLD
a watch, their wedding photo in a gold frame, 50 favorite chocolates wrapped in gold foil

60th DIAMONDS
anything sparkly, diamonds themselves are always nice

PRESS PLAY
▶

The vibe:
timeless, eternal, love

Love Is In the Air
JOHN PAUL YOUNG

Ain't Nobody
CHAKA KHAN AND RUFUS

Knock Me a Kiss
LOUIS JORDAN

It's Good to Be in Love
FROU FROU

So in Love
CURTIS MAYFIELD

Let's Stay Together
OBADIAH PARKER

You Are the Best Thing
RAY LaMONTAGNE

Super Duper Love
JOSS STONE

*This Must Be the Place
(Naive Melody)*
TALKING HEADS

Zou Bisou Bisou
JESSICA PARÉ

How Deep Is Your Love
THE BIRD AND THE BEE

*Ain't Nothing Like
the Real Thing*
MARVIN GAYE
AND TAMMI TERRELL

scentimental décor

To add a "floating on cloud nine" vibe
to the room, set fragrant flowers like
gardenias, jasmine, and peonies adrift in
bowls. If you prefer to keep the dining
table scent-free, use tulips and calla lilies
there and aromatic blooms elsewhere.

box it up

Dress up cupcakes in
clear favor boxes
with ribbon and com-
memorative labels.

AFTER THE PARTY

Once you've spent time creating a party, enjoy it! Plans may go astray, but what matters is being with family and friends. Even as you're celebrating, think about the memories you'll want to preserve by keeping an extra invite or taking photos. The fun doesn't have to end when everyone leaves!

D.I.Y.

(darcy it yourself)

When an occasion is really special, you want to relive memories of it. Here are a few tips to help keep the celebration going after candles have been blown out.

1

get snappy

Whether you shoot candids, set up a backdrop for guests to pose in front of, or hire a photographer, it's fun to look back at pictures. No one ever regrets having the photos, but people often say, "Oh, I wish we had a picture—or a video—of so-and-so."

2

save the sweet stuff

Scrapbooks are one of my favorite ways to document important gatherings (I made a 50-pound scrapbook for our wedding!). For an extra special keepsake, I'll make a scrapbox, my personal twist on a shadowbox.

book it

Invitations, pictures, notes from friends, a cocktail napkin, a copy of your toast—paste them all in the pages and you'll keep the memory of your party alive for years to come.

box it

A scrapbox is a great way to keep mementos that don't fit in a book, whether it's the hat from your child's first birthday, or the cake topper or caviar tin lid from your wedding.

3

be grateful

Mail thank-you notes and e-mail pictures to keep the love going long past the party.

IDEAS FOR AN AFTER-THE-PARTY SCRAPBOX

Get creative! When you use a box rather than a book, it opens up all kinds of new possibilities. Consider adding a three-dimensional element or two to a photo, as in these examples:

1

First escort card for you and your significant other as a couple + photo of the two of you taken at the event

2

Invitation to a graduation party + diploma photo of graduate

3

Champagne cork or cage + photo of guests toasting guest of honor and copies of toasts

4

Pressed petals from a bouquet, with a bit of the ribbon + photo of bride holding the bouquet or handkerchief or invitation

pro tips from

—

DONNA
NEWMAN

DONNA NEWMAN PHOTOGRAPHY

*The best photos show the soul of a party—
or a person. Photographer Donna Newman is
known for her unique ability to capture
that spirit. These are her tips for shooting
unforgettable pictures.*

TOP TIPS

WORK WITH THE BEST LIGHTING DESIGNER: MOTHER NATURE!
I love to photograph with natural light in
outdoor settings. I try to avoid placing my
subjects in bright sunlight, and look for a
shady spot with nice backlighting.

KEEP GROUP PORTRAITS INFORMAL
For portraits with multiple people, I let the group
arrange themselves, with the main person in
the middle. People tend to position themselves
around those with whom they feel most
comfortable. Snap it right as they are getting
settled in when they look most relaxed.

DON'T FORCE IT.
Never start directing; just wait for
the right moments. The shots will happen!

HAVE FUN
When you truly enjoy being at the party,
the images reflect that.

BE CANDID
I try to be as discreet as possible, so I can
capture photos of people having fun. That's when
you see someone's inner spirit shine through.

DONNA'S MUST HAVE SHOT LIST

THE GUEST OF HONOR
You'd be surprised how often people come
away from a 40th birthday party
with photos of the food and the friends,
but none of the birthday girl!

YOUR NEAREST AND DEAREST
Make sure you have informed all of your
important people beforehand that
there will be a time allocated for family shots.
This way, no one is left out. You can't go
back in time to capture them and you don't
want to have regrets!

A BIRDS-EYE VIEW
Stand on a chair to shoot some pictures
that show an overhead view, so you get a
sense of the party in its entirety.

THE BIRTHDAY BOY OR GIRL
The classic birthday shot is when the child
is about to blow out the candles.
Try to get all of the kids around the birthday
child and the parents, siblings right
beside him or her.

THE FUN MOMENTS
My number one tip to getting a great picture
at a party is to listen for where the
laughter is in the room. I always gravitate
toward that energy since that is where the
best shots are going to be happening.

thank-you note abc's

Post-party, it's nice to let your guests know you appreciate their company—and their gifts. In a pinch, shoot off an e-mail. But even sitting down and writing a snail-mail note is simple if you boil it down to a few key points. Here's an example to get you started.

1

Say: Hi.
(Dear, Dearest, Hi, Hello, Hey, Ciao, Greetings)

2

Say: It was great to see the person.

3

Say: Something that reflects on the nature of your relationship.

4

Say: Something specific about the gift.

5

Say: The actual words "thank you!"

6

Say: Something that refers to the future, even if it's just "See you soon!"

7

Say: Bye.
(Love, All My Love, Thanks again, xo, Warmly, Sincerely, With a Squeeze)

DARCY MILLER

1 — Dear Wendy,

2 — It was so fun to see you at my party!

3 — Can you believe it's the 26th birthday we've celebrated together? I'll always be so grateful that we were in the same bunk at camp way back when!

4 — Speaking of grateful, I love love love this scarf.

5 — Thank you for the lovely gift (and for having such great taste)! I hope your

6 — first day at the new job is amazing, and would love to hear about it over dinner some time soon.

7 — Big hug and kiss,
XO Darcy

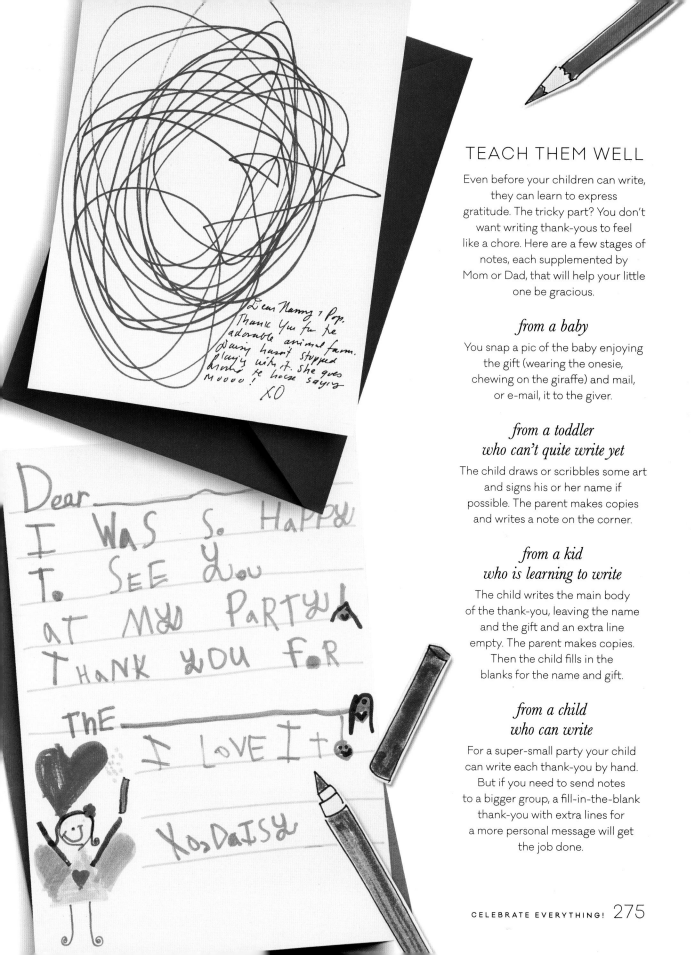

Dear _____
I was so happy to see you at my party. Thank you for the _____ I love it.
XO, Daisy

Dear Nanny & Pop,
Thank you for the adorable animal farm. Daisy hasn't stopped playing with it. She goes around the house saying Moooo!
XO

TEACH THEM WELL

Even before your children can write, they can learn to express gratitude. The tricky part? You don't want writing thank-yous to feel like a chore. Here are a few stages of notes, each supplemented by Mom or Dad, that will help your little one be gracious.

from a baby

You snap a pic of the baby enjoying the gift (wearing the onesie, chewing on the giraffe) and mail, or e-mail, it to the giver.

from a toddler
who can't quite write yet

The child draws or scribbles some art and signs his or her name if possible. The parent makes copies and writes a note on the corner.

from a kid
who is learning to write

The child writes the main body of the thank-you, leaving the name and the gift and an extra line empty. The parent makes copies. Then the child fills in the blanks for the name and gift.

from a child
who can write

For a super-small party your child can write each thank-you by hand. But if you need to send notes to a bigger group, a fill-in-the-blank thank-you with extra lines for a more personal message will get the job done.

DARCY'S FEATURED SOURCES

Want to throw a great celebration? These go-tos have
everything you need to plan a party and so much more too.

BAKED GOODS & BAKING SUPPLIES/ ACCESSORIES

bakedideas.com
bakednyc.com
bakerycrafts.com
bbworldcorp.com
bellacupcakecouture.com
billysbakerynyc.com
butterflybakeshop.com
cakepower.com
cakesnshapes.com
customcookies.com
dragonflycakes.com
elenis.com
etsy.com/shop/iltoccokitchen
etsy.com/shop/manjar
etsy.com/shop/pfconfections
fancyflours.com
frostedpetticoatblog.com
georgetowncupcake.com
Laceycakesnyc.com
laduree.com
ladym.com
madeinheavencakes.com
magnoliabakery.com
nycake.com
nycakepops.com
onegirlcookies.com
paradisesweets.etsy.com
parksidepapers.com
setonrossini.com
shellconyc.com
sprinkles.com
sugarrushny.com
sundaescones.com
twolittleredhens.com

weddingcakes.com
wendykromer.com
whippedbakeshop.com
wilton.com

CANDY, CHOCOLATE, & ICE CREAM

albanesecandy.com
americanchocolatedesigns.com
beau-coup.com
bedazzlemybonbons.com
burdickchocolate.com
candy.com
candystore.com
candywarehouse.com
chambredesucre.com
crossingsfinefoods.com
curiouscandy.com
dylanscandybar.com
economycandy.com
etsy.com/shop/andie
specialtysweets
etsy.com/shop/candiedcakes
etsy.com/shop/pfconfections
etsy.com/shop/pinkcherrymama
etsy.com/shop/sugarartbytami
etsy.com/shop/sweetedibles
etsy.com/shop/sweetiesbykim
foiledagainchocolate.com
frenchconnectionllc.com
groovycandies.com
hammondscandies.com
hersheys.com
jellybelly.com
joycone.com
kimmiecandy.com
kopperschocolate.com

ladyfortunes.com
madelainechocolate.com
maggielouiseconfections.com
mehlenbacherscandies.com
melvillecandy.com
mitchmallows.com
mymms.com
nuts.com
ohnuts.com
purdys.com
prints-on-chocolate.com
sockerbit.com
sugarfina.com
sugarpetals-usa.com
sweetcarolineconfections.com
sweetlifeny.com
sweetworks.net
the5almonds.com
vanleeuwenicecream.com
vintageconfections.com

CRAFT SUPPLIES

americancrafts.com
angelaliguori.com
avery.com
castleintheair.biz
createforless.com
dennisdaniels.com
enasco.com
etsy.com/shop/christmas
keepsakes
Martha Stewart Crafts
melissaanddoug.com
michaels.com
raffit.com
save-on-crafts.com
tuliphomedecor.com

CUSTOMIZING

candywrapperstore.com
cocoagraph.com
evermine.com
justbubbly.com
lucywrubel.com
maptote.com
minted.com
photofetti.com
pinholepress.com
shutterfly.com
spoonflower.com
us.eatsleepdoodle.com

FLOWERS & GARDEN SUPPLIES

davidstarkdesign.com
gourmetsweetbotanicals.com
jamaligarden.com
seaportflowers.com
thegreenvase.com

FOOD & DRINK

havenskitchen.com
murrayscheese.com
petercallahan.com
titosvodka.com

PAPER DÉCOR

beistle.com
birthdaydirect.com
blumchen.com
confettisystem.com
devra-party.com
foryourparty.com
lunabazaar.com
papercupdesign.com
tinseltrading.com
urbanicpaper.com

PACKAGING

clearbags.com
etsy.com/shop/acarrdiancards
etsy.com/shop/imeondesign

papermart.com
smittenonpaper.com
sophiesfavors.com
uline.com

PARTY SUPPLIES

artistryinmotion.com
birthdayexpress.com
brightlablights.com
casparionline.com
creativecandles.com
chicoparty.com
etsy.com
inkscissorspaper.com
kikkerland.com
knotandbow.com
etsy.com/shop/lightandco
merimeri.com
partycity.com
ricebyrice.com
sassafrasstore.com
shop.ohhappyday.com
shopparcel.com
sperrytents.com
sucreshop.com
theconfettibar.com
theflairexchange.com
thimblepress.com
topsmalibu.com

STATIONERY, PENS, & PAPER

appntd.com
calligraphics.info
championstamp.com
chereeberrypaper.com
envelopments.com
graphicimage.com
intlarrivals.com
jampaper.com
lettercdesign.com
moleskine.com
nancyhowell.com
papersource.com
pictureitpostage.com

sharpie.com
sugarpaper.com
zazzle.com

TABLETOP

bambuhome.com
bellocchio.com
biacordonblu.com
buy4asianlife.com
cb2.com
containerstore.com
Craig's Plastics "I love lucite"
fishseddy.com
food52.com
juliska.com
macys.com
mudaustralia.com
sferra.com
surlatable.com
westelm.com

TOYS, CLOTHING, & ACCESSORIES

amazon.com
bando.com
bcmini.com
beachballs.com
dillonimporting.com
espadrillestore.com
favors.com
iwako.com
jcrew.com
jellycat.com
knockoutnovelties.com
oldnavy.com
orientaltrading.com
safariltd.com
shopsweetlulu.com
smilemakers.com
stickeryou.com
tattly.com
toysplash.com
windycitynovelties.com
wineenthusiast.com

sources and credits

photo credits

with thanks

SOURCES AND CREDITS

FRONT AND BACK COVER

Front cover styling by Randi Brookman Harris: www.brookmanharris.com DETAILS Honeycomb: *shop.ohhappyday.com*, Minc from Heidi Swapp Foil Machine (used for artwork): *americancrafts.com* SWEETS AND TREATS Glitter Lollipop: *sweetcarolineconfections.com*, Some Confetti: *thimblepress.com*, Some Candy: *candywarehouse.com*, *nuts.com*, *the5almonds.com*, and *sugarfina.com*

TITLE DOUBLE PAGE SPREAD

Pages 1–2 DÉCOR Ice Cream Bulb Lights: *brightlablights.com* SWEETS AND TREATS Doughnuts: *havenskitchen.com*, Cherries: *wendykromer.com*, Mint Green Cake: *onegirlcookies.com*, Candy Bracelets: *oriental trading.com*, 5 Cake: *cakepower.com*, Blue and Gymnastics Cupcakes: *onegirlcookies.com*, Cupcake Cones: *butterflybakeshop.com*, Mini Hotdogs: *petercallahan.com*, Rose Cupcake: *magnoliabakery.com*, 5O Piñata: *etsy.com*, Cones: *joycone.com*

FOREWORD

Pages 8–9 DÉCOR Paper Magnolias: *thegreenvase.com* DETAILS Gold 'M': *thegreenvase.com*, Personalized Canvas Bag: *maptote.com*, Straws: *foryourparty.com*, Coasters: *evermine.com*, Personalized Bottle Label, Guestbook, and Notepad: *pinholepress.com* SWEETS AND TREATS Baking Cookies: *elenis.com*, Salted Caramel Cake: *bakednyc.com*, Scrabble Petits Fours: *weddingcakes.com*, Food and Drink: *petercallahan.com*

INTRODUCTION

Pages 12–13 DETAILS Confetti: *knotandbow.com* and *photofetti.com* SWEETS AND TREATS Barnyard Cake with Cookies and Color Me! Cookies: *elenis.com*

PARTY HANDBOOK OPENER

Page 14–15 DETAILS Personalized Notebook & Ruler: *appntd.com*, White/Gold Pen: *sugarpaper.com*, Metallic Braided Ribbon: *angelaliguori.com*

GETTING STARTED

Pages 22–23 DETAILS Purple Paper: *papersource.com*, Dresses: *jcrew.com*, Cello Bag: *clearbags.com*, Boa: *windycitynovelties.com*, Bubbles, Pencils, Stadium Horn, Star Confetti, White Journal: *oriental trading.com*, Purple Letter: *smilemakers.com*, Purple Crayons: *enasco.com* SWEETS AND TREATS Giant Marshmallows: *candywarehouse.com*, Long Sugar Sticks, Lollipop, Mint Sticks, and Assorted Candy: *candy.com*, Purple Cupcakes: *onegirlcookies.com*, White and Purple Lollipop: *orientaltrading.com*, Foil-Wrapped Hearts: *dylanscandybar.com*, Sugar Violets and Purple Sprinkles (on donuts): *nycake.com* **Pages 24–25 DETAILS** Stuffed Bunnies: *jellycat.com*, Invitation Paper: *papersource.com*, Martha Stewart Crafts Star and Moon Punch SWEETS AND TREATS Cow Cupcakes, Cat and Star Cookies: *elenis.com*, Cupcakes on Stand: *onegirlcookies.com* **Pages 26–27 DÉCOR** Hanging Tissue Daisies: *beistle.com*, Hanging Paper Daisies: *papersource.com*, Yellow Hanging Fans: *birthdaydirect.com*, Tent: *sperrytents.com* DETAILS Martha Stewart Cake Stand: *macys.com*, Daisy Boxes: *papersource.com*, Daisy Dish: *biacordonblu.com*, Martha Stewart Crafts Daisy Stickers (cupcake toppers) and Paper Cake Stand, Glass Canisters: *containerstore.com* SWEETS AND TREATS Daisy Cookie on Cupcake: *elenis.com*, Daisy Lollipops: *melvillecandy.com*, Round Yellow Lollipops: *hammondscandies.com*, Yellow Cupcakes: *butterflybakeshop.com* **Pages 28–29** Shot on location at The Chord Club: *thechordclub*

.com **DÉCOR** Academy Awards Garland: *foryourparty.com* **DETAILS** Amscan Star Confetti and Ticket Roll: *partycity.com*, Black Cups with White Stars: *inkscissorspaper.com*, Star Peel-n-Place Decals, Black and Gold Boa, Bead Necklace, and Director's Cone: *windycitynovelties.com*, Gold Hair Flower: *bando.com*, Envelope: *envelopments.com*, Toysmith Microphones (we personalized): *amazon.com*, Gold Candy Cups: *nycake .com*, Glass Jars: *containerstore.com*, Award Sticker Seal: *staples.com* **SWEETS AND TREATS** Cake and Cupcakes with Stars: *sugarrushny .com*, Movie Theme Cookies: *customcookies .com*, Star Cake Pops: *nycakepops.com* **Pages 30–31 DÉCOR** Martha Stewart Cupcake Tree: *macys.com*, Wall Decal: *shutterfly.com* **DETAILS** Bone Crayons: *birthdayexpress.com*, Stamps: *championstamp.com*, Stuffed Dogs: *orientaltrading.com* **SWEETS AND TREATS** Dog Cake Pops and Cupcakes: *cakepower.com*, Fire Hydrant Cookies: *elenis.com* **Pages 32–33 DÉCOR** Baking Cups: *wilton.com*, Amscan Snowflake Paper Fans **DETAILS** Ballerina Toppers and Doily on Cake Stand: *nycake .com*, Blossom Baking Cups: *wilton.com*, Lace Cupcake Liners: *fancyflours.com*, Scalloped Cupcake Liners: *bellacupcakecouture.com*, Metallic Presents: *orientaltrading.com* **SWEETS AND TREATS** Cake Pops: *nycakepops .com*, Cake: *twolittleredhens.com*, Edible Sparkle Dust: *nycake.com*, Large Angel Cake and Canelles: *onegirlcookies.com*, sugar walnuts and Snowflake Lollipops: *etsy.com/ shop/andiespecialtysweets*, Sugar Angel Wings: *etsy.com/shop/sugarartbytami*, Sugar Snowflake Toppers: *sugarpetals-usa.com*, Cupcakes: *onegirlcookies.com* **Pages 34–35 DÉTAILS** Stickers (on drink stirrers), Plush and Bouncy Basketballs: *orientaltrading .com*, Amscan Orange and White Popcorn Bag, *partycity.com* Inflatable Basketballs (for limbo): *knockoutnovelties.com*, White and Yellow Pinnies: *amazon.com* **SWEETS AND TREATS** Cake: *cakepower.com*, Foiled chocolates: *madelainechocolate.com*, Cake Pops: *nycakepops.com*, Assorted Candy: *dylanscandybar.com* and *candywarehouse .com* **Pages 36–37** Shot on location at Pins & Needles: *pinsandneedlesnyc.com* **DÉCOR**

Stitch Grid Wall Hanging: *us.eatsleepdoodle .com* **DETAILS** Cheeky Pink Cake Stand: *royalalbert.com*, Measuring Tape Ribbon: *pinsandneedles.com* Custom Fabric: *spoonflower.com*, Felt Shapes: *etsy.com/ shop/christmaskeepsakes*, Personalized Pencils: *orientaltrading.com* **SWEETS AND TREATS** Button Cookies: *etsy.com/ paradisesweets*, Button Lollipops: *etsy .com/shop/candiedcakes*, Cross-Stitched Brownies: *onegirlcookies.com*, Cupcakes: *sprinkles.com*, Spool Cake: *cakepower.com*, Spool Cake Pops: *nycakepops.com*, White Chocolate Buttons and Thimbles: *etsy.com/ shop/sweetiesbykim* **Pages 38–39 DETAILS** D, P, and Heart Shaped Lucite: Craig's Plastics "I Love Lucite", 'D' Stir Sticks: *foryourparty .com*, Invite Design: *chereeberrypaper .com* **SWEETS AND TREATS** Chocolate Bar: *chocolate-editions.com*, Cinnamon Straws: *hammondscandies.com*, Haribo Grapefruit Gummi Slices: *candywarehouse.com*, Jelly Beans and Licorice Wheels: *dylanscandybar .com*, Madelaine Chocolate Hearts, Madelaine Chocolate Malt Balls, Gumballs, Red Sixlets: *candy.com*, Choco Almonds: *kimmiecandy.com*, Taffy Sticks: *mehlenbacherscandies.com*, Red Gummi Bears: *albanesecandy.com* **Page 43** All Playlists by DJ Lucy Wrubel: *lucywrubel.com* **Pages 44–45 DETAILS** Amscan Star Confetti: *partycity.com*, Tissue Circles: *knotandbow .com*, Custom Stamps: *zazzle.com*, Crayons: *orientaltrading.com* **SWEET AND TREATS** Whirly Pop: *dylanscandybar.com* **Pages 46–47 DETAILS** Invitations: *chereeberrypaper.com*, Confetti: *photofetti.com*, *knotandbow.com*, *artistryinmotion.com*, and *confettisystem .com*, Stamp: *pictureitpostage.com*

DÉCOR DETAILS

Pages 50–51 DETAILS Glass Rectangle Vase: *jamaligarden.com*, Gold Paper: *paperpresentation.com*, Enormous Plush Pom-Pom: *orientaltrading.com*, Bunny & Shark Paper: *papersource.com* **Pages 52–53 DETAILS** Bud Vases and Pink Glasses: *cb2.com* **Page 55 DÉCOR** Flowers: *davidstarkdesign.com* **Pages 56–57 DÉCOR** Plates: *bambuhome.com*, Wooden Boxes: *buy4asianlife.com*, Stemmed

photo credits

with thanks

Glasses: *juliska.com* Details Gold Trim (on boxes and cards): blumchen.com, Martha Stewart Crafts Tag **SWEETS AND TREATS** Holland Mints: *sugarfina.com* **Pages 58–59** *davidstarkdesign .com* **Pages 60–61 DÉCOR** Glasses: *juliska.com*, Flatware: *westelm.com*, Napkins: *food52 .com*, Shell: *jamaligarden.com* **Pages 64–65 DÉCOR** Baby's Breath: *thegreenvase.com*, Photo Accordion: *papercupdesign.com*, Wendy Addison Letters (left) and Glitter Doves: *tinseltrading.com*, Gold Leaves Cord: *papermart.com*, Paper for Ice Cream Banner: *papersource.com* **Page 66** Glass Cube: *jamaligarden.com* **Pages 68–69 DETAILS** Baby Pins, Bunnies, Bells and Hearts, School Days Confetti, Dinosaur, Iridescent Stars, Tiny Moons, Red Love and Hearts, Multicolor Metallic Sprinkles, Champagne, Gold and Silver Dots: *chicoparty.com*, Pink Tissue Circles, Red Tissue Lips, Lime Tissue Squares, Green Tissue Rectangles: *artistryinmotion.com*, Candy Shoppe (pink/blue tissue circles), Boardwalk (yellow/pink tissue circles): *theflairexchange .com*, Custom Words: *theconfettibar.com*, Graduation, Silver Dots, Amscan Pink Beveled Hearts, Sassy Kisses, Amscan Colored Stars: *partycity.com*, Fairy Magic: *beistle.com*, Rainbow, Tissue Circles and Metallic Mix: *knotandbow.com*, Green Circles: *photofetti .com*, Gold Flat Sequins: *amazon.com*, Sequins: *orientaltrading.com* **Pages 70–71 DÉCOR** White Firefly Lights (in jar), and White Floralyte 2-LED Submersable Light (in hedges): *save-on-crafts .com*, 16" and 24" White LED Glowing Beach Balls: *beachballs.com*

FOOD AND DRINK

Unless otherwise noted, all food and drink pictured is from Peter Callahan Catering: *petercallahan.com*

Page 75 DETAILS Coupes: *cb2.com* **Pages 76–77 SWEETS AND TREATS** Cheese Tips: *murrayscheese .com* **Pages 78–79**, Banana Chips, Pineapple Chunks, Macadamia Nuts, Coconut, Mango, Mini Dark Chocolate Nonpareils, Seaweed Peanuts, Chili Bits, Wasabi Peas, Sesame Sticks, Marshmallow, Chocolate Chips, BBQ Veggie Chips, Corn Nuts, and Cashews: *nuts.*

com, Skinny Pop **Page 83 SWEETS AND TREATS** Quiche: *havenskitchen.com* **Pages 86–87** Shot on location at and some baked goods provided by: Haven's Kitchen: *havenskitchen.com* **SWEETS AND TREATS** Ice Cream: *vanleeuwenicecream. com*, Macarons: *onegirlcookies.com*, Gummy Ice Cream Cones: *nuts.com* **Pages 88–89** Drink Stirrers: *foryourparty.com*, Glasses: *cb2.com* **Pages 92–93 SWEETS AND TREATS** Begonia Petal Mix: *gourmetsweetbotanicals.com*, Diamond Candy Gems: *candywarehouse.com*, Mini Pink Sugar Hearts, Mini White Flowers, Sugar Cubes (white and brown): *chambredesucre .com*

FUN AND GAMES

Pages 96–97 DETAILS Sports Gear: *amazon.com*, T-shirts, Shorts, Jacket, and Flip Flops: *oldnavy .com*, Peace Sign Garland: *beistle.com* **Page 101 DETAILS** Beach Balls: *beachballs.com*, Shirts: *oldnavy.com*, Iron-on Letters: *michaels.com* **Page 102 DETAILS** T-shirts and Shorts: *oldnavy .com* **Pages 106–107 DETAILS** Wooden Box: *orientaltrading.com*, Table Tennis Set: *amazon .com*, Fish Sunglasses and Pastel Bouncy Balls: *orientaltrading.com* **SWEETS AND TREATS** Neon Cupcake Sprinkles: *nycake.com*

CAKES AND SWEETS

Pages 112–113 DETAILS Gold Present: *oriental trading.com*, Photo: *photofetti.com*, Bow: *urbanicpaper.com*, Honecomb: *etsy.com/ shop/lightandco*, Giraffe: *safariltd.com* **SWEETS AND TREATS** Cake: *bakednyc.com*, Bird and Star Cookie: *bakedideas.com*, Ribbon Candy: *ohnuts.com*, Glitter Lollipop: *sweetcarolineconfections.com*, Champagne Bubbles: *sugarfina.com*, Mini Meringue: *etsy .com/shop/iltoccokitchen* **Pages 114–115 DETAILS** Champagne, Flag, and Tinsel Pick: *bakerycrafts .com*, Ballerina: *nycake.com*, Chenille Chick: *partycity.com*, Zebra Topper: *safariltd .com*, Lego Style Candy: *ohnuts.com*, Party Partners Clown Toppers and Party Partners Fruit Toppers: *parksidepapers.com*, Barley Heart Lollipop: *sweetcarolineconfections .com*, Stork: *bbworldcorp.com*, Goldfish Topper: *dillonimporting.com* **SWEETS AND TREATS** Cupcakes: *bakednyc.com* **Pages 116–117**

DETAILS Martha Stewart Domed Cake Stand and Cloche: *macys.com*, Beeswax Candles: *knotandbow.com* Sweets and Treats Purple Cake: *onegirlcookies.com*, Kubli Violettes: *the5almonds.com*, Other Purple Candies: *dylanscandybar.com* Pages 118–119 DETAILS Crown Paper: *papersource.com*, Amscan Gold Star Confetti: *partycity.com* SWEETS AND TREATS Pink Cake: *bakednyc.com*, Ribbon Cake: *cakepower.com* Pages 120–122 DETAILS Cake Stand: *fishseddy.com* SWEETS AND TREATS "5" Cake (gummies not included): *cakepower.com*, Blue Cupcakes: *billysbakerynyc.com*, Pink Candies: *dylanscandybar.com* Pages 122–123 Nickname Cookies: *elenis.com*, Birthday Cake (cookies not included): *onegirlcookies.com*, "D-A-D" Cupcakes (cookies not included): *georgetowncupcake.com*, "I Love You" Cupcakes: *sprinkles.com*, Letter Cookies: *bakedideas.com*, Petit Fours: *shellconyc.com* Pages 124–125 DETAILS Amscan Gold Mini Taper Candles: *partycity.com* SWEETS AND TREATS Edible Glitter: *nycake.com*, "Fruity Loops" Pastel Candy Balls and Champagne Bubbles: *sugarfina.com*, Surprise Cake: *setonrossini.com* Page 127 DETAILS Cake Stand: *mudaustralia.com* SWEETS AND TREATS Cake and Cupcakes: *magnoliabakery.com* Pages 128–129 DETAILS Candles: *creativecandles.com* SWEETS AND TREATS Mini Cakes: *onegirlcookies.com* Page 131 DETAILS Amscan Birthday Candles: *partycity.com*, Cake Stand: *surlatable.com* Pages 132–133 DETAILS Party Partners Pink "3", Party Partners Peace Sign, and Party Partners Circus Animal: *parksidepapers.com*, Heart, Bunny, and Tulip: *sassafrasstore.com*, "1", Amscan Baseball, Basketball, and Amscan Skinny Coil: *partycity.com* Construction, Baseball Bat, Crayon, Champagne, and Ducky: *wilton.com*, Caspari Birthday: *casparionline.com*, Carousel Horse, Gnome, and Clown Candles: *ricebyrice.com*, Tall & Tapered (6" and 15"): *creativecandles.com*, Heart and "3" Sparklers: *topsmalibu.com*, Amscan Coil Spirals, Amscan Happy Birthday Letters, Amscan Cherries, Unique Neon Candles, Bakery Crafts Glitter "8", Bakery Crafts Question Mark, Bakery Crafts

Pink Ombré, Bakery Crafts Sparkler Sticks, Bakery Crafts Swirl Candles Page 135 SWEETS AND TREATS Color Me Cookies: *elenis.com*

FAVORS

Pages 140–141 DETAILS Frisbees and Mini Brown Bags: *amazon.com*, Heart Stickers: *knotandbow.com*, Ice Cream Cone Shooters: *orientaltrading.com*, Retro Sunglasses: *windycitynovelties.com* Page 142–143 DETAILS Cloud Post-its and Mini Bell Alarm Clock: *kikkerland.com*, Dessert Erasers: *iwako.com*, "Girl Talk" Bobbi Pins: *bando.com* Glasses & Nose Disguise: *favors.com*, Hand Fan: *paperpresentation.com*, Ice Cream Cone Shooters, Jacks, Maraca, Whistle, Yo-yo Personalized Pencils, Mushroom Spinner, *orientaltrading.com*, Mini Magnifying Glass, Mini Playing Cards Mini Trophy: *partycity.com*, Mini Notebook: *moleskine.com*, Mini Pencil Pouches and Tubes: *bcmini.com*, Rainbow Tatttoos: *tattly.com*, Toysmith Mini Paint Set: *amazon.com*, Very Best Supply Co. Neon Pencils, MT Masking Tape: *masking-tape.jp/en/* Pages 144–145 DETAILS Trophies: *partycity.com*, Tape: *orientaltrading.com*, Star Stickers: *amazon.com* SWEETS AND TREATS Hard Candy Sticks: *partycity.com*, Hershey Bars: *hersheys.com*, Sixlets: *partycity.com* Pages 146–147 DÉCOR Balloons: *partycity.com* DETAILS Gold & Glitter Twine: *knotandbow.com*, Bakery Boxes: *smittenonpaper.com* SWEETS AND TREATS Gold Stars: *madelainechocolate.com*, Foil Wrapped Balls and Wrapped Mints: *economycandy.com* Pages 148–149 DETAILS Canvas Pencil Case, Mini Drawstring Bags, Parasol, Pot Holders, Small Canvas Tote, White Backpack, and Wood Sailboat: *orientaltrading.com*, Espadrilles: *espadrillestore.com*, Pillow Cover: *tuliphomedecor.com* Pages 150–151 DETAILS Wood Color Beads: *melissaanddoug.com*, White Beads: *orientaltrading.com* Pages 152–153 DETAILS Cello Bags: *nycake.com*, Letterman Alphabet Stickers: *michaels.com*, Tuck Top Box: *uline.com* SWEETS AND TREATS Giant Blue Jawbreaker Lollipop: *ohnuts.com*, Pastel Foil Wrapped Chocolates: *the5almonds.com* Pages 154–155 DETAILS Toasting Bottle

photo credits

with thanks

Wraps: *chereeberrypaper.com* **SWEET AND TREATS** Candy Fruit Slices: *ohnuts.com*, Vodka: *titosvodka.com* **Pages 156–157 DETAILS** Gray Token Boxes and Personalized Boxes: *smittenonpaper.com* **Pages 158–159 DETAILS** Barley Lollipops: *vintageconfections.com*, Chocolate Bars: *candywrapperstore.com*, Coasters and Pins: *evermine.com*, Cocoa Squares: *cocoagraph.com*, Confetti: *photofetti.com*, Favor Bag, Magnet, and Matches: *foryourparty.com*, Memory Game: *pinholepress.com*, Playing Cards: *shutterfly.com*, Stickers and Tattoos: *stickeryou.com* **SWEETS AND TREATS** Cookies: *elenis.com*, Cupcakes: *laceycakesnyc.com*, White Chocolate Lollipop: *beau-coup.com*

PARTY PLAYBOOK OPENER

Pages 160–161 DETAILS Napkin: *foryourparty.com*, Album: *graphicimage.com*, Scissors: *angelaliguori.com,* Matchbook: *mrsstrong.com*

BABY SHOWER

All food and drink: *petercallahan.com*

Pages 162–163 DÉCOR Flowers: *seaportflowers.com* **DETAILS** Calligraphy: *calligraphics.info*, Deer Figurines: *safariltd.com*, Woodland Cake Décor: *etsy.com/shop/andiespecialtysweets* **SWEETS AND TREATS** Green Tea Mille Crepes Cake: *ladym.com* **Pages 164–165 DETAILS** Animal Figurines (except for on cupcakes): *safariltd.com*, Deer on Cupcake: *shopsweetlulu.com,* Birch Log and Tray: *bellocchio.com*, Quilling Paper: *amazon.com*, Invitation: *chereeberrypaper.com*, Custom Soap: *just bubbly.com*, Muslin Bag: *papersource.com* **SWEETS AND TREATS** Canelles and Cupcakes: *onegirlcookies.com*, Gingerbread Deer: *etsy.com/shop/pfconfections* **Pages 166–167 DETAILS** Birch Rounds: *michaels.com*, Crepe Paper Candy Cups: *shopsweetlulu.com*, Small Nests: *beau-coup.com*, Gold Trimmed Oval Platter: *calvinklein.com* **SWEETS AND TREATS** *Bûche de Noël*, Canelles, Cupcakes, Macarons, Sandwich Cookies, and Marshmallow Squares: *onegirlcookies.com*, Sugar Ladybugs and Chocolate Deer: *etsy.com/shop/andiespecialtysweets*, Chocolate Caramel Eggs: *candywarehouse.com*, Chocolate

Hedgehogs:*purdys.com*, Cocoa Dusted Almonds and Coffee and Cream Almonds: *nuts.com*, Jelly Beans: *jellybelly.com*, Meringue Acorns and Mushrooms: *frenchconnectionllc.com*, Champagne Bubbles: *sugarfina.com* **Pages 168–169 DETAILS** Personalized Napkin: *foryourparty.com* **Pages 170–171 DETAILS** Box for Marshmallows: *uline.com* **SWEETS AND TREATS** Candy Mushrooms: *sockerbit.com*, Bunny Cookies: *etsy.com/shop/pfconfections*, Faux Bois Chocolates: *americanchocolatedesigns.com*, Chocolate Mice: *burdickchocolate.com*, Petit Four: *shellconyc.com*, Sugar Flowers: *wendykromer.com* **Pages 172–173 DETAILS** Custom Fabric: *spoonflower.com*, Sachet Favors Sewn By: *pinsandneedlesnyc.com*

POOL PARTY

All food: *petercallahan.com*

Shot on Location at Asphalt Green: *asphaltgreen.org* **Pages 174–175 DETAILS** Paper for Waves: *papersource.com* **SWEETS AND TREATS** Pearlescent Powder Blue Gum Balls, Tiny Candy Hearts, Caribbean Blue Foiled Milk Chocolate Balls, Jelly Belly Jelly Beans, Wildberry Chewy Sourballs: *candywarehouse.com*, Powder Blue Sixlets: *nuts.com*, M&M's: *mymms.com*, Ombre Wave Cake: *onegirlcookies.com* **Pages 176–177 DETAILS** Footed Fish Bowls: *amazon.com*, Sip Sticks Straws: *parksidepapers.com* **SWEETS AND TREATS** Sour Gum Drops (top): *ohnuts.com*, For other blue candy See **Page 174**, Orange Swedish Fish: *candywarehouse.com* **Page 178–179 DETAILS** Lucite tray: Craig's Plastic's "I Love Lucite" **SWEETS AND TREATS** Donuts: *shellconyc.com* **Pages 180–181 DETAILS** Personalized Napkins: *foryourparty.com*, Dolphin Pool Rider: *toysplash.com*, Nike Junior Swim Cap: *allamericanswim.com* **SWEETS AND TREATS** Chocolate Medals: *foiledagainchocolate.com*, Swimsuit Cookies: *elenis.com*, Wave Cookies: *shellconyc.com* **Pages 182–183 DETAILS** Clear Round Plastic Container: *papermart.com*, Gold Tape: *orientaltrading.com* **SWEETS AND TREATS** Blue Candy: repeated from opener, Caribbean Blue Maltballs: *candywarehouse.com*, Chocolate Coins: *foiledagainchocolate.com*

RAINBOW PARTY

Shot on Location at E.A.T.: *elizabar.com* **Pages 184–185 DÉCOR** Tissue Fans: *birthdaydirect .com* and *lunabazaar.com* **SWEETS AND TREATS** Rainbow Cake: *cakepower.com* **Pages 186–187 DETAILS** Napkins: *foryourparty.com*, Paper for Garlands: *papersource.com* **SWEETS AND TREATS** Jelly Beans: *jellybelly.com*, M&M's: *mymms.com* **Pages 188–189 DETAILS** Colored Pens and Art Supplies: *intlarrivals.com*, Star Beads and White DIY Bag: *orientaltrading.com*, Vintage Travelers European Mini Rainbow Suitcases: *amazon.com*, Sharpies: *sharpie .com*, Multicolor Paper Clips: *jampaper.com* **Pages 190–191 DETAILS** Glass Bottles: *surlatable .com*, Clear Tube: *uline.com* **SWEETS AND TREATS** Fruit Tray from E.A.T.: *elizabar.com*, Gold Chocolate Coins: *candywarehouse .com*, Jelly Beans: *jellybelly.com*, Marshmallow Kebabs: *bakednyc.com*, Rainbow Cookies: *onegirlcookies.com* **Pages 192–193 DETAILS** Rainbow Confetti: *knotandbow.com* **SWEETS AND TREATS** Gummy Rings: *albanesecandy .com*

GOLF PARTY

Pages 194–195 DETAILS "8" Adhesive Vinyl Number: *amazon.com*, Candy Stripe Candles: bakerycrafts.com, Cello Bag: *nycake.com*, Flag Straw: *foryourparty.com*, Green Cups and Napkins: *partycity.com*, Mini Metal Bucket: *amazon.com*, Trophies: *partycity.com* **SWEETS AND TREATS** Cake Pops: *nycakepops .com*, Golf Cake: *butterflybakeshop.com*, Green Jelly Beans and Oversize Gumball: *dylanscandybar.com*, White Chocolate Golf Ball (half & whole): *ladyfortunes.com* **Pages 196–197 DÉCOR** Artificial Grass Turf: *jamaligarden .com* **DETAILS** Amscan Green Party Hats, *Bambu* Flatware: *bambuhome.com*, Trophies: *partycity.com*, Flag Straws: *foryourparty .com*, "Golf Ball" Avery Label: *staples.com*, "Golf Tee" MT Washi Tape: *amazon.com*, Martha Stewart Crafts Fringe Scissors, White "Par-Tee" Picks: *orientaltrading.com* **SWEETS AND TREATS** Cupcakes: *butterflybakeshop .com*, Foil-Wrapped Chocolate Golf Balls: *madelainechocolate.com* **Pages 198–199 DETAILS** Little Joker Stick-On Mustaches and Plastic

Golf Clubs: *amazon.com* **Pages 202–203 DETAILS** Platter: *cb2.com*, Striped Straws: *for yourparty.com*

ICE CREAM PARTY

Shot on location at Haven's Kitchen: *havenskitchen.com* **Pages 204–205 DETAILS** Marble Round: *surlatable.com*, Tissue Paper Ice Cream Cones: *devra-party.com* **SWEETS AND TREATS** Cherry on Black Wire: *madeinheavencakes.com*, Ice Cream: *vanleeuwenicecream.com* **Pages 206–207 DETAILS** Tall Craft Cones: *createforless .com* **Pages 208–209 DETAILS** Canvas Pencil Case, Ice Cream Pints, Sweet Treats Erasers: *orientaltrading.com*, Colored Chocolate Coins: *partycity.com*, Bubbles, Pen, Popsicle Lip Gloss: *amazon.com*, Shaped Erasers: *iwako.com* **SWEETS AND TREATS** Candy Bracelet, Gumballs, and Sixlets: *partycity .com*, Gummy Sour Cherries: *nuts.com* **Pages 212–213 DETAILS** "9" Golden Sparkler Wand: *topsmalibu.com* **SWEETS AND TREATS** Belgian Waffle and Brioche: *havenskitchen.com*, Cherry on Black Wire: *madeinheavencakes .com*, Cherries on Green Wire: *wendykromer .com*, Cupcakes: *magnoliabakery.com*, Ice Cream: *vanleeuwenicecream.com*, Waffle Cake Slice: *madeinheavencakes.com* **Pages 214–215 DETAILS** Wilton Gold Spiral Candles, Pastry Bag: *amazon.com*, White Candles: *creativecandles.com*, White Metallic Confetti: *knotandbow.com* **SWEETS AND TREATS** Giant Ice Cream Sandwich Cake: *sundaescones.com*, Raspberry Gum Drops: *ohnuts.com*, Waffle Cones: *joycone.com*, Yellow Pufflettes: *candywarehouse.com*

BRIDAL SHOWER

All Food and Drink: *petercallahan.com*

Pages 216–217 DÉCOR "French Vanilla" Honeycomb Wedding Bells: *devra-party .com* **SWEETS AND TREATS** Chocolate Jewels: *frostedpetticoatblog.com*, Cupcakes: *bakednyc.com* **Pages 218–219 DETAILS** Photo Cocktail Napkins: *foryourparty.com* **Pages 220–221 DÉCOR** Flowers: *davidstarkdesign .com* **DETAILS** Cake Stand Trimming:

photo credits

with thanks

castleintheair.biz and *blumchen.com*, Crystallized Rose: *gourmetsweetbotanicals .com*, Custom Wedding Cake Favor Boxes: *smittenonpaper.com*, Gold Cupcake Liners: *bellacupcakecouture.com*, Mini Glass Bell Jar with White Fluted Base: *beau-coup.com* **SWEETS AND TREATS** Croquembouche Macarons, Religieuse: *laduree.com*, Flower Cupcakes: *magnoliabakery.com*, Frosted Canelles with Coconut Flakes: *onegirlcookies.com*, White Chocolate Hearts: *maggielouiseconfections .com* **Pages 222–223 DETAILS** White Cupcake Liners: *bellacupcakecouture.com* **SWEETS AND TREATS** Brownies: *petercallahan.com*, Cupcakes, Dove and Heart Cookies, Shaped Marshmallows: *onegirlcookies.com*, Personalized Wedding Bell Cookies: *bakedideas.com* **Pages 224–225 DETAILS** Bride and Groom Fans, Wedding Wishes Cards: *chereeberrypaper.com*, Pencil: *letterdesign.com* **Pages 225–226 DETAILS** Custom Wedding Cake Favor Boxes: *smittenonpaper .com*, Cake Slice-Shaped Favor Boxes with Flowers and Ribbons: *etsy.com/shop/ imeondesign*, Scalloped-Top Cake Favor Box (flower not included): *etsy.com/shop/ acarrdiancards* **SWEETS AND TREATS** Mini 2-Tier Oreo "Cake": *beau-coup.com*, Tiny Candy Hearts: *candywarehouse.com*, Mini Wedding Cake Cake Pops: *nycakepops.com*, Petit Fours: *dragonflycakes.com* **Pages 228–229 DÉCOR** Wedding Wishes Guestbook Garland *chereeberrypaper.com* **DETAILS** Crystallized Rose Petals: *gourmetsweetbotanicals.com*

WINTER PARTY

All Food and Drink: *petercallahan.com*

Pages 230–231 DÉCOR Flocked Branches: *davidstarkdesign.com* **DETAILS** Paper Around Cake Stand: *papersource.com* **SWEETS AND TREATS** Chocolate Snowmen: *burdickchocolate .com*, Fransk Nogat *sockerbit.com*, Gingerbread House: *elenis.com*, Meringues: *onegirlcookies .com*, Cake Balls Tower: *nycakepops.com*, Cake: *twolittleredhens.com*, Edible Glitter Cotton Candy: *curiouscandy.com*, Polar Bear Cookies: *whippedbakeshop.com*, Sugar Snowflakes: *etsy.com/shop/sweetedibles* **Pages 232–233**

DETAILS Martha Stewart Crafts Doily Lace Cupcake Wrapper **SWEETS AND TREATS** Cupcake: *onegirlcookies.com*, Edible Glitter Cotton Candy: *curiouscandy.com*, Fluffy Stuff Snow Balls Cotton Candy: *candywarehouse .com*, Marshmallow Cubes: *mitchmallows.com* **Pages 234–235 DETAILS** *Martha Stewart Crafts* Snowflake Punch, *Martha Stewart Crafts* Snowflake Stickers, Mini Silver Cupcake Cups: *nycake.com* **SWEETS AND TREATS** Canelles, Cupcakes, Macaron: *onegirlcookies.com*, Snowman Cake Pops: *nycakepops.com*, Sugar Snowflakes: *etsy.com/shop/pinkcherry mama* and *etsy.com/shop/sweetedibles*, Christmas Tree Cookies: *elenis.com*, Mini Cake: *twolittleredhens.com* **Pages 236–237 DETAILS** Napkins: *foryourparty.com* Birch Straws: *kikkerland.com* **Pages 238–239 DETAILS** *Martha Stewart Crafts* Snowflake Punch

MILESTONE PARTY

Food by and shot on location at Callahan Catering: *petercallahan.com* **Pages 240–241 DETAILS** Personalized Breadsticks Bag: *smittenonpaper.com*, White Blossom Baking Cups: *wilton.com*, Paper for Balloon Decoration: *papersource.com* **SWEETS AND TREATS** Champagne Bubble Candy: *candystore .com* **Pages 242–243 DÉCOR** Flowers and Candle Sticks: *davidstarkdesign.com* **SWEETS AND TREATS** Candy Buttons: *candystore.com* and *dylanscandybar.com* **Pages 244–245 SWEETS AND TREATS** Gumdrops, Haribo and Assorted Fruit Slices, Sunkist Fruit Gems: *candystore .com*, Raspberry Gummies: *sockerbit.com* **Pages 246–247 DETAILS** Decanters: *wineenthusiast .com* **Pages 248–249 DETAILS** Plain Ice Cream Cups: *inkscissorspaper.com*, Polka Dot Spoon: *sucreshop.com*, Adhesive Numbers: *amazon .com* **SWEETS AND TREATS** Assorted "50" Candy: *candystore.com*, *sockerbit.com*, and *candywarehouse.com* **Pages 251 DETAILS** Polka Dot Napkins: *merimeri.com* **Pages 252–253 DETAILS** Petit Fours Favor Boxes: *sophiesfavors .com* **SWEETS AND TREATS** Petit Fours: *onegirlcookies.com*, Polaroid Cookies: *etsy.com/ shop/manjar* **Page 254 DETAILS** "1960's" Tag: *chereeberrypaper.com*

ANNIVERSARY PARTY

All food and Drink: *petercallahan.com* **Pages 256–257 DÉCOR** All Flowers: *thegreenvase.com* **DETAILS** Candles: *creativecandles.com* **Pages 258–259 DETAILS** Calligraphy: *nancyhowell.com*, Invitation and Menu Card: *chereeberrypaper.com*, Vintage Bride & Groom Toppers: *fancyflours.com*, Napkin: *sferra.com* **Pages 260–261 DÉCOR** Photo Garland: *minted.com* **DETAILS** Accordion: *papercupdesign.com*, Toast Cards: *chereeberrypaper.com*, Avery Label Paper: *avery.com* **SWEETS AND TREATS** Chocolate Coins: *groovycandies.com* **Pages 262–263 DETAILS** Custom Coasters, Napkins, and matches: *foryourparty.com* **Pages 264–265 DETAILS** Gold Candy Cups: *nycake.com*, St. Gallen Shimmering Metallic Sheer Ribbon: *raffit.com* **SWEETS AND TREATS** White Round Pearl "Milkies": *sweetlifeny.com*, Gold-Wrapped Paris Caramels: *crossingsfinefoods.com*, Almond Jewels: *kopperschocolate.com*, Heart-Shaped Marshmallow and Meringues: *onegirlcookies.com*, "M" Lollipops and Chocolates with Photos: *prints-on-chocolate.com*, Silver Chocolate Stars: *madelainechocolate.com*, Metallic Bonbons: *bedazzlemybonbons.com* **Pages 266–267 DETAILS** Cupcake Wraps: *bellacupcakecouture.com*, BC Mini Pencils: *bcmini.com*, Illustrated Confetti: *photofetti.com*, Piñata: confettisystem.com, Wedding Cake Bubbles: *beistle.com*, Cupcake Wraps: *bellacupcakecouture.com* **Pages 268–269 DÉCOR** Wendy Addison Glitter Letters, *tinseltrading.com* **DETAILS** Clear Tuck Top Boxes: *papermart.com* **SWEETS AND TREATS** Cupcakes: *onegirlcookies.com*

AFTER THE PARTY

Pages 272–273 DETAILS Shadow Boxes: *dennisdaniels.com* **SWEETS AND TREATS** Barbie Cake: *cakesnshapes.com*

photo credits

with thanks

PHOTO CREDITS

featured sources

sources and credits

photo credits

WITH THANKS

Much like the planning of any great party, creating this book has been a celebration of the talent of so many friends and colleagues.

TO MY AMAZING TEAM Jesse Kase, my long-term creative collaborator, Lindsay Lanier, whose tireless effort always backed me up, Caroline Hulsey, who brilliantly wore every hat imaginable from designer to air traffic controller, Mary Weng, whose attention to detail is unparalleled, and Susie Flax, who understood what this book was from the very beginning.

TO MY TALENTED ART DIRECTORS & DESIGNERS I am forever grateful to Vanessa Holden for her creative genius, motivation, and friendship, and to my design idol, Stephen Doyle, for mentoring me and helping me realize my vision. To David Bowman and Rosemary Turk at Doyle Partners; Melanie Wiesenthal and Yael Eisele at Deerfield; Christy Sheppard, and Lauren O'Neill: your incredible art direction and design helped make this book a reality.

TO MY EDITORIAL WORDSMITHS Rory Evans, Kim Fusaro, Eleni Gage, Michelle Stacey—your keen editorial eyes saved me from rambling on too long about cupcakes and confetti!

TO MY DARCY'S DREAM PARTY EXPERTS TEAM Cheree Berry, David Stark, Peter Callahan, Donna Newman, and Lucy Wrubel for adding brilliance and creativity to our profession.

TO MY CULINARY EXPERTS EXTRAORDINAIRE Thank you to Eleni's Cookies, Haven's Kitchen, Magnolia Bakery, One Girl Cookie and Murray's Cheese for sharing your recipes and tips.

TO MY SUPPORTIVE COLLEAGUES AND FRIENDS Matthew Axe, Doug Bernheim, Katie Berry, Randi Brookman-Harris, Paulie Dibner, Dani Evans, Monica Faillace, Erin Furey, the Fuhrman Family, Katie Hatch, Cassidy Iwersen, the Myers Family, Rachel Stout and so many others. Your input was invaluable in pulling this book together.

TO MY BOOK-SMART "BOOK PEOPLE" Carla Glasser, my incredible agent, and my wonderful editor, Cassie Jones, at HarperCollins, for her tremendous support, and granting me more deadline extensions than there are jelly beans in this book!

TO MY PARTY PARTNERS IN CRIME
Thank you to all of the industry talents credited in this book, with whom I've collaborated over the years—bakers, crafters, chefs, designers, artisans and amazing resources—who make party planning inspiring and fun.

TO MY MENTOR Thanks to Martha Stewart, for her kind words in the beginning of this book and for paving the way, both in the industry and for myself, for serious celebrating.

FINALLY, BECAUSE MY CELEBRATIONS ALWAYS BEGIN AT HOME . . .

TO MY PARENTS Who taught my sister and me how important it is to celebrate each other. Daddy for always supporting me and Mommy, who has always been on call with her calligraphy pens since my childhood to now, in the pages of this book.

TO MY SISTER Jenny, a partner-in-celebration, even over oceans. And to her entire family, whom I love and who are always ready to party.

TO JEAN AND BUD and the entire Nussbaum clan for always being there and your love and help.

TO MY DAUGHTERS, Daisy, Ella, and Pippa, with whom I share my markers, and count down to birthdays a year in advance, who make life magical and give me a reason to celebrate every day.

AND TO ANDY . . . for his patience, support, and love through this process, and in every aspect of our lives. With you, I want to celebrate everything!

with thanks

Dear Reader,

I'm so glad you came to my parties. I hope you left full of ideas for your own fêtes. Thanks for reading and remember no matter what goes wrong at a party, being with loved ones makes everything right. So, whatever you do, be sure to D I T - Do it together! Life is short.

Celebrate Everything!!!

XO,
Darcy

Introduction
to Microcomputing

Introduction
to Microcomputing

Sydney B. Newell

HARPER & ROW, PUBLISHERS, New York
Cambridge, Philadelphia, San Francisco,
London, Mexico City, São Paulo, Sydney

1817

Sponsoring Editor: John Willig
Project Editor: David Nickol
Designer: Helen Iranyi
Production Manager: Marion Palen
Compositor: Science Typographers, Inc.

Art Studio: J&R Art Services, Inc.

Introduction to Microcomputing

ISBN 0-06-044802-4

Contents

Preface

Living in the age of the "LSI Revolution" is exciting. Changes are taking place so rapidly that no one can really comprehend what progress we will have made ten years from now or, for that matter, next year. Microprocessors have become a very real part of our lives, and yet the word *microprocessor* represents something vague and mysterious to many people.

This book introduces microprocessors and microcomputers, assuming absolutely no prior knowledge of computers, electronics, or engineering. It can be used as (1) a textbook for a first- or second-year college course; (2) a supplement to more advanced courses; (3) a self-teaching manual for readers wishing to learn about microprocessors on their own; and (4) a quick reference for those already familiar with the field.

Rather than dealing in abstract generalities, I've chosen to use a specific microprocessor—the 6800—to provide readers with a concrete, working example. Having mastered the initial concepts of any specific microprocessor, one can easily make the transition to other microprocessors. Successful completion of this book will enable one to program the 6800 in both machine and assembly language and to appreciate hardware considerations sufficiently to use more advanced texts dealing with interfacing.

To facilitate the learning process, I've used a number of pedagogical aids: Learning objectives at the beginning of each chapter tell the readers what to expect in that chapter. New words are emphasized by setting them in **boldface** type where they are first defined, making it easy to find words again if necessary. Many in-chapter worked examples reinforce each topic. Review questions at the end of every chapter, with answers to be found directly within the chapter, help readers to test their knowledge and understanding. Two equivalent sets of end-of-chapter exercises—set A, with all answers at the back of the book, and set B, with answers in a separate Instructor's Manual—allow readers to work on their own with instant feedback, while giving an instructor the option of assigning homework where the answers are not available. Suggestions for programming applications are given in lists of programming ideas following some of the later chapters. Finally, all the words defined in the book are listed in the Glossary for quick reference.

"Number-crunching" isn't very interesting to most people, so for motivation I've introduced I/O concepts early in the book, with the PIA discussed in Chapter 5. Even without any knowledge of interfacing, readers can gain an appreciation of some of the many applications of microprocessors and how to program them for such applications. The latter rather than arithmetic is the theme throughout the book, although arithmetic receives some attention in Chapter 7.

The 6800 Instruction Set, simplified to suit the needs of this book, is presented in Appendix A. Appendix B is the M6800 Cross Assembler Reference Manual; Appendix C gives answers to the set A exercises. And since 16-bit microprocessors are becoming very important, some information on the 68000—Motorola's 16-bit microprocessor—is included in Appendix D.

Many people have contributed to the final product. The students at the University of Maine at Orono, where I first taught the course, provided valuable feedback, using the material in its initial incarnation. This feedback continued through a course introduced at the University by Professor Waldo Libbey, who used this text in its second incarnation. I am grateful to Professor Libbey and his students for inputs obtainable only from the classroom. Dr. Ronald Rohrer acted as electrical engineering consultant, providing essential critiques of accuracy, clarity, relevance, and readability. Detailed advice that contributed to the structure and direction of the work came from Steven Conley, Virginia Technological Institute; Robert D. Guyton, Mississippi State University; Donald F. Hanson, University of Mississippi; Gerald R. Kane, Southern Methodist University; Waldo Libbey, University of Maine at Orono; Donald Pederson, University of California at Berkeley; Ronald Rohrer, University of Colorado at Colorado Springs; Martha Sloan, Michigan Technological University; K. Vairavain, University of Wisconsin at Milwaukee; Mac Van Valkenburg, University of Illinois; and Claude Wiatrowski, University of Colorado at Colorado Springs. In addition, Teresa Byers, a student at the University of Colorado at Colorado Springs, capably performed the gargantuan task of detailed error-checking. To all of them I extend my thanks.

I am grateful to the staff of Motorola, Inc. In particular, Don Aldrich, Ben LeDonne, and Ron Bishop were very helpful in contributing technical information and answers to specific questions. Marshall Rothen kindly supplied documentary materials, photographs, and permissions. Thanks also go to the Heath Company, and Phil Cole, who provided materials, photographs, and permissions regarding the microprocessor trainer.

The staff of Harper & Row has my appreciation for completing this project. Engineering Editor Charlie Dresser, who was responsible for initiating this text, provided helpful reviews and suggestions. Later, Fred Henry, Executive Editor, contributed excellent guidance, support and enthusiasm. Finally, David Nickol, the project editor, saw the manuscript through to the final text product. I am also indebted to those staff members who are responsible for the editing, design, production, and other functions necessary in book publication.

Although the preface may mark the end for an author, it is the beginning for a reader. I hope that users of *Introduction to Microcomputing* will find it enjoyable as well as educational, and that they may catch the excitement that pervades the world of microprocessors.

S. B. NEWELL

Introduction
to Microcomputing

1 Introduction to Computers, Microprocessors, and Microcomputers

LEARNING OBJECTIVES

After completing this chapter, you should be able to:

1. Give a definition, explanation, or example for each of these: *computer, program control, computer program, execute, memory, fetch, address, transfer of control, decode, input, output, processor, central processor unit, microprocessor, integrated circuit, chip, pin, dual in-line package, LSI, VLSI, microprocessor system, microcomputer, hardware, software, architecture, block diagram, bus, RAM, read, write, read/write memory, volatile, nonvolatile, garbage, ROM, monitor, PROM, EPROM, EAROM, input/output, memory-mapped I/O, pin-out, high voltage, low voltage, data bus, bidirectional, address bus, unidirectional, control bus.*
2. List the characteristics of a computer.
3. Describe the organization of a computer program.
4. Explain in a general way how a computer executes a program.
5. Explain the difference between a microprocessor and a microcomputer.
6. Describe the duties of the microprocessor, I/O, memory, and buses in a microprocessor system.
7. Sketch a block diagram of a microprocessor system and its buses.

Right now we're living in a period that some people call the "Microprocessor Revolution," because microprocessors have revolutionized many aspects of our lives. Because of their small size, microprocessors let us computerize watches, calculators, appliances, TV sets, electronic games, and many other devices. Cash registers that

1

scan an item's code, record the item and its price, keep a running total, and provide a detailed printout are microprocessor based. Microprocessors are used to control automobile emissions—in some cars even monitor and display the status of the gas tank, temperature, and oil pressure—and to allow relatively sophisticated mileage and time calculations. Many industries use microprocessors to monitor and control their assembly lines and also to help them comply with EPA (Environmental Protection Agency) standards for emissions and pollution control. Newspapers use microprocessors for composition. Microprocessors are used in telephones and traffic controllers. Each day more and more specialized uses of microprocessors are being developed.

We're conscious of the presence of microprocessors in almost every aspect of our lives. But what *is* a microprocessor? And what is a microcomputer?

Before we can begin learning about microprocessors and microcomputers, first, we need to know a bit about computers in general.

1.1 COMPUTERS AND COMPUTER PROGRAMS

To many people the word *computer* brings to mind a science fictionlike setting: in a room filled with a large amount of complex equipment, spools of tape spin, various lights on panels flash mysteriously, cathode-ray tubes display messages in cryptic languages, dials are turned, switches are flipped, meter needles move. Perhaps there is an intermittent "beep" added to the hum and spin of the moving tapes.

A computer *can* be as large and as complex as that. Or it can be as small and as simple as the "brains" of a digital watch or hand-held calculator. Even in the case of the large and complex computer system, though, only a small amount of the equipment is the computer itself. Most of the rest is taken up with storage of information and methods of communicating with the computer (cathode-ray tube screens, printers, keypunches, and teletypewriters).

What is a computer?

A **computer** is a machine that processes data. As far as a computer is concerned, this data has to be numerical. If we, the users, have some nonnumerical data that we want a computer to process (such as text material), it is necessary that the nonnumerical data be translated into numbers before the computer gets it.

To perform even the simplest task, a computer needs to be told exactly how to do it. A computer operates under **program control**, meaning that the computer's actions are controlled by a series of instructions that make up a **computer program**. When a computer **executes** a program, it carries out the instructions the program contains. A computer executes a program much as we humans follow a set of written instructions.

Building a typewriter table

Suppose you've bought a typewriter table that needs to be assembled. Assume that it comes with assembly directions, as shown in Figure 1.1.1. You've followed written instructions like this so many times that you do it without even thinking about the steps involved. In order to see how a computer executes a program, let's think about some of the characteristics of the typewriter table instructions of Figure 1.1.1.

First, just *having* the instructions doesn't get the table built. To build the table, you have to read, interpret, and follow the directions, using the materials supplied by the manufacturer.

Second, the instructions are in the form of English words, which have meaning to those of us who read English.

Third, the words that make up the instructions are stored in a physical location (the paper and ink). If anyone wanted to change the instructions, they'd have to do it physically by changing the words on the paper.

Fourth, reading the instructions doesn't destroy them; you can read them as many times as you like and they'll stay the same.

Fifth, the instructions are numbered in sequence. You expect to follow this sequence unless one of the instructions says otherwise. For instance, step 5 says to skip step 6 if you don't want rolling casters on the table. In that case, you go from step 5 to step 7.

You carry out the instructions like this:

Read an instruction. (When you read an instruction, you "copy" the information from the paper into your brain.)

Interpret the instruction. (For instance, the words in the instruction "Remove table top from box" would have a certain meaning to you. You'd interpret this instruction as meaning that you should go to the box, put your hands into it, and lift out the table top.)

Carry out the instruction. (Do what it says.)

Read the next instruction.

Interpret the instruction.

Carry out the instruction.

—and so on

FIGURE 1.1.1   Instructions for Assembling Typewriter Table

1. Remove table top (part 1) from box.
2. Remove folding extension (part 2) from box.
3. Attach folding extension to table top with two nuts and bolts from envelope A.
4. Remove legs (parts 3 to 6) from box.
5. If casters are not to be used, skip step 6 and go on to step 7.
6. Remove casters from small box B. Insert metal end of each caster into hole at bottom of each leg and push until it clicks.
7. Attach legs to each corner of table top using two nuts and bolts from envelope A.
8. Table is ready for use.

When you've read, interpreted, and carried out all the instructions, you have a typewriter table ready to use.

A computer program

Figure 1.1.2 shows a pictorial representation of a computer program. The program is like the typewriter table instructions in some ways and unlike them in others.

First, as with the typewriter table instructions, just *having* the program doesn't get the job done. To perform the task specified by the program, the computer must read the program's instructions and interpret and execute them.

Second, unlike the typewriter table instructions, the instructions in the program are in the form of numbers, which have meaning to the computer.

Third, like the typewriter table instructions, a computer program is stored in a set of physical locations. But instead of on paper, the numbers that make up the computer program are stored in the computer's **memory**, which we define as a set of physical locations that can contain numbers. If we wanted to change the program, we'd have to change physically that part of memory where the program was stored.

Fourth, as with reading the typewriter table instructions, reading the instructions in a computer program doesn't destroy them. The reading of an instruction by a computer is called a **fetch**.

FIGURE 1.1.2   Organization of a Computer Program

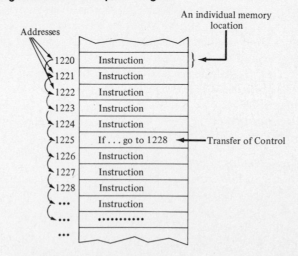

Program is stored in **memory**.
Each memory location is identified by a unique **address**.
Computer proceeds through addresses in sequence unless a **transfer of control** is encountered.

Fifth, like the typewriter table instructions, instructions in a computer program are arranged in sequence. Instead of a sequence number, a number called an **address** is used to identify a single memory location. Unlike the typewriter table directions, a computer program doesn't have to begin its sequence with 1. In Figure 1.1.2 the computer program starts at address 1220. A computer program can start at any address, but the computer must be told what that address is. Then, the computer begins at the starting address of the program and follows the addresses in sequence, unless one of the instructions tells it otherwise. An instruction that tells the computer to go to an address that is out of sequence is called a **transfer of control** instruction, which is illustrated in Figure 1.1.2.

A computer executes a program like this:

FETCH (*read*) *an instruction*. (When the computer fetches an instruction, it "copies" the instruction from memory into its "brain.")

DECODE (*interpret*) *the instruction*. (Each number that represents an instruction in the program has a certain meaning to the computer in terms of what action it should take. When the computer decodes the instruction, it finds out what the instruction means.)

EXECUTE (*carry out*) *the instruction*.

FETCH the next instruction.

DECODE the next instruction.

EXECUTE the next instruction.

—and so on

Features of a computer

Generally, computers have these characteristics:

1. an **input** medium (a way of putting numbers in)
2. a **memory**, where numbers are stored
3. a **control** section, where instructions are decoded
4. a **calculating** section, where the data is processed
5. a **decision** capability, where alternate courses of action can be taken based on data
6. an **output** medium (a way of getting results from the computer)

Computers are especially good at tasks that include performing mathematical operations; performing routine tasks over and over again without any mistakes; counting out exact quantities; responding in the same way to the same stimulus, which might bore or fatigue a human being; carrying out any set of instructions *exactly*.

A computer can perform the function of a watch if we program it to do so. Such a program might contain instructions for counting out a minute's worth of time and changing a visual display each minute. We can't carry around a roomful of computers on our wrist, though, so using a large computer to run a digital watch isn't practical. Instead, digital watches (and hand-held calculators, electric appliances, microwave ovens, and so on) are controlled by the microprocessors they contain.

1.2   WHAT IS A MICROPROCESSOR?

Before discussing microprocessors, let's define the word *processor*. The **processor**, also called the **Central Processor Unit (CPU)**, is that part of a computer, that fetches, decodes, and executes programmed instructions; it contains the control, calculating, and decision-making sections of a computer. In a large, room-sized computer, the processor might be rather large.

A **microprocessor (MPU)** is a single small device that performs the functions of a CPU. The MPU contains the calculating, decoding, and decision-making parts of a computer, but they are all on a single tiny piece of silicon (hence the *micro* part of *microprocessor*). A piece of silicon that has several electronic parts on it is called an **Integrated Circuit (IC)**, or, colloquially, a **chip**. There are many different kinds of ICs. A microprocessor is a special kind of IC that is programmable.

What does a microprocessor look like?

Figure 1.2.1 shows a typical microprocessor as we would buy it ready to use from the manufacturer. The device in the figure is about 2 inches long and 0.5 inch wide, but the actual microprocessor chip is much smaller and occupies a small area underneath the white square. Most of the size of the microprocessor comes from its packaging.

In the figure, we see two sets of leglike protrusions, called **pins**. These pins plug into a socket and connect the device to the rest of a system. This type of packaging is called a **Dual In-line Package (DIP)**. The device in the figure has 40 pins, but other integrated circuit DIPs may have different (even) numbers of pins.

Microprocessors in their DIPs all look pretty much alike from the outside; the one in Figure 1.2.1 could be a picture of any one of many. However, the microprocessor in Figure 1.2.1 is actually one called the 6800. The 6800, which we'll be

FIGURE 1.2.1   A Typical Microprocessor in a Dual In-Line Package

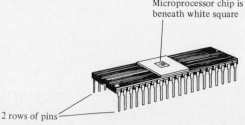

Microprocessor chip is
beneath white square

2 rows of pins

discussing in this book, was originally made by Motorola but is now being manufactured by several other companies.

Other microprocessors

There are many other microprocessor types besides the 6800. Although they all resemble one another from the outside, they have different operating characteristics.

Some microprocessors are designed to be used for a single, specific purpose, such as running a digital watch. Such microprocessors may contain some memory right on the same chip to store programs for their own use. A microprocessor for a digital watch might contain the program it uses to run the watch. At the time of this writing, microprocessors that contain larger and larger amounts of memory are being manufactured.

Microprocessors were made possible because of a technology called **Large-Scale Integration (LSI)**, which means the ability to get more and more electronic parts onto smaller and smaller chips. Large-scale integration is now giving way to **Very Large-Scale Integration (VLSI)**. Right now a piece of silicon about half a centimeter square could contain over 100,000 electronic parts. Every one to two years, the number of parts that can be put onto an IC has doubled, and there's no indication when this trend will stop. As time passes, it becomes possible to put more and more devices onto smaller and smaller spaces for less and less money. With capabilities increasing and prices dropping as time progresses, it is difficult to predict how far reaching the implications of the availability of the microprocessor might be.

Next, we'll see how microprocessors are combined with other devices to make a system.

1.3   MICROPROCESSOR SYSTEMS AND MICROCOMPUTERS

Microprocessors are powerful computing devices, but they're not much good by themselves. Just as a human brain needs hands, feet, eyes, ears, a nose, and a mouth to be able to direct physical actions, a microprocessor needs to be connected to other devices. A **microprocessor system** is a microprocessor plus all the devices it requires to do a certain job. A microcomputer is one type of microprocessor system.

What is a microcomputer?

A **microcomputer** has all the parts of a computer described in Section 1.1. For its calculating and decision-making sections it uses a microprocessor. So a microcomputer is a microprocessor plus input, memory, and output. Figure 1.3.1 shows two simple microcomputers with their microprocessors (MPUs). We see that there are many ICs on each board besides the microprocessor. Some of these ICs are

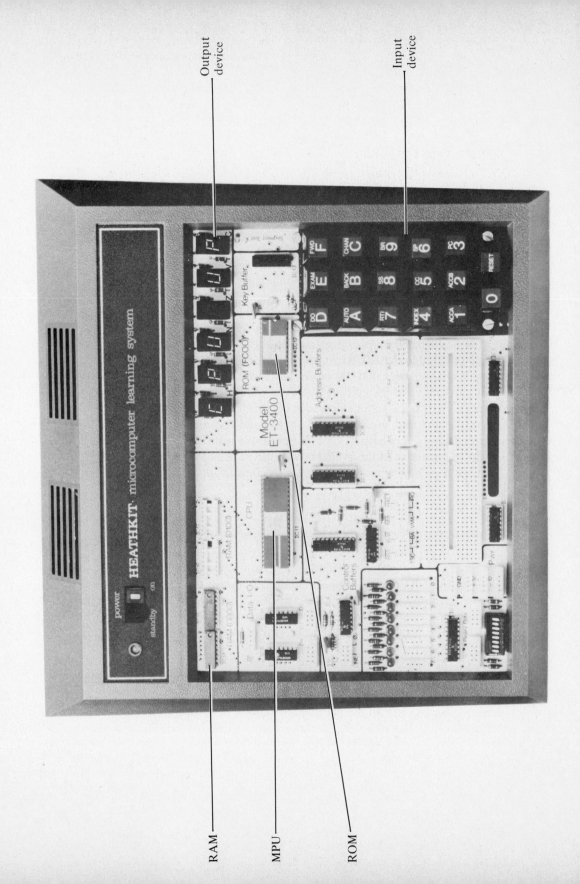

Output device

Input device

RAM

MPU

ROM

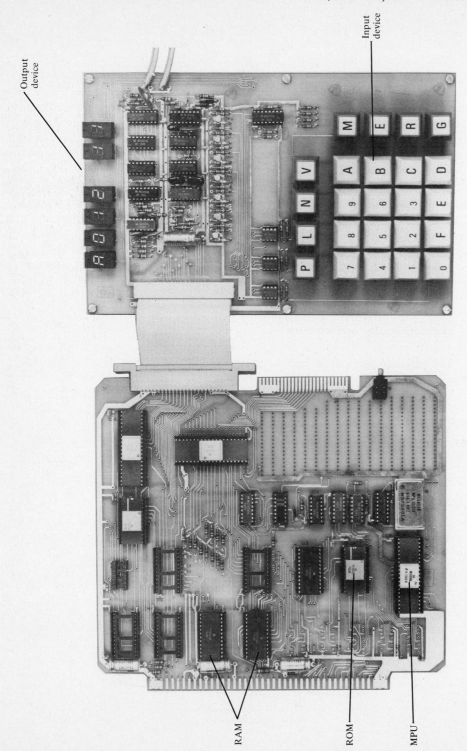

FIGURE 1.3.1 Two Sample Microcomputers.

memory; others are electronic parts for connecting the microprocessor to its memory, input, and output. These will be discussed in the next section.

Microcomputers take up far less space and cost far less than full-scale computers. The average person can now afford a home computer for business and pleasure. Educational institutions can provide one computer work station for each small group of students instead of one large computer to serve all students. Word processors—microcomputers that let the user input text and edit, store, and print it—are now affordable. Such word processors are useful to authors (this book was written using a word processor based on a microcomputer) and also to firms that deal with large quantities of printed material such as form letters.

In the near future each home may well have microcomputer systems that perform functions such as keeping financial records, writing letters, filing recipes with nutritional information, and computing income tax. With more hardware, home computers can also control external devices such as burglar and fire alarms, garage doors, home heating and cooling systems, and house and garden plant care devices. Even now, owning a home computer can be a very enjoyable, educational, and—at times—obsessing experience.

Microcomputer architecture

The physical parts of a microcomputer are its **hardware**; its programs are **software**. By microcomputer **architecture** we mean a description of its hardware parts, how they are connected, and how they communicate with each other.

FIGURE 1.3.2 Block Diagram of Microprocessor System

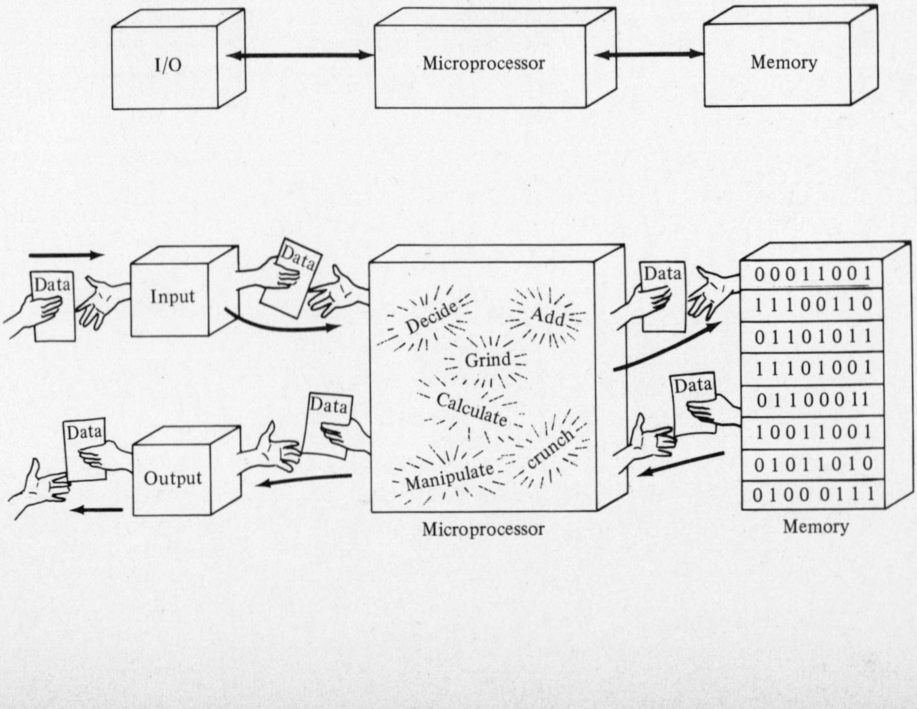

Anyone studying microprocessor will sooner or later encounter one or more block diagrams. A **block diagram** is a graphic description of individual parts of a system and how they interact. Figure 1.3.2 is a block diagram showing a general microprocessor system.

In the figure, we've defined four basic parts of a microcomputer, although microprocessor systems may have more than four parts. Three include the microprocessor, memory, and input/output, all of which we've already mentioned. The fourth part, not mentioned yet, is the microcomputer's system of buses. A **bus** is a set of wires that is used to transmit information among two or more devices. The other three parts of the microcomputer need the buses to exchange information.

First, we'll summarize the duties of each of the parts that are symbolized by the blocks of Figure 1.3.2. Then, we'll talk about each part in more detail.

Duties of the microprocessor

- to execute programs that are stored in memory
  - a. to do all the data manipulations (e.g., arithmetic)
  - b. to make all the decisions based on data
- to provide timing and control for the memory and I/O sections

Duties of the I/O section

I/O means **input/output** and is the link between the microprocessor and the outside world. Its duties are:

- to allow the microprocessor to read input data under program control
- to output data from the microprocessor under program control

Duties of the memory

- to store programs and data
- to provide data to the microprocessor upon request
- to accept new data from the microprocessor for storage

Duties of the bus system

- the bus system transmits information among the other three parts of the microcomputer

In each section, we'll refer to the two microcomputers shown in Figure 1.3.1: the Motorola D2 and the Heathkit Microprocessor Trainer. Even though these two microcomputers have the same microprocessor—the 6800—they don't look alike and are not exactly the same. That is, there is a great variety of components besides microprocessors to choose from, and different choices are made by different people who design microcomputers. In the same way, two people might buy identical amplifiers but end up with very different stereo systems because of differences in speakers, turntables, and so on.

Next, we'll talk about each microcomputer part in slightly more detail.

1.4   MEMORY AND I/O

There are many different kinds of memories, which can be classified in many different ways. Here, we'll define a few terms used to describe memories.

RAM

RAM stands for **Random Access Memory**. Random access means that we can access (get to) any individual location directly, without having to go through any other locations first. Getting a book from the stacks of a library is a familiar example of random access. After locating its reference number in the card file, we can go right to the book and pull it off the shelf (assuming that someone hasn't checked it out already) without having to start with the lowest-numbered book and look at every one until we get to the one we want.

Usually, RAM has both read and write capability, meaning that both we and the microprocessor can read from and write into the memory. **Read** means to copy a number nondestructively from one location to another. Reading is nondestructive because whatever was in the location read from is still there afterward. And **write** means to store a number destructively in a location. Writing is destructive because whatever was in the location before writing into it is destroyed when the new value is written in. *Read/write* means that we (or the microprocessor) can change as well as examine values in memory whenever we want. For writing user programs, and for doing calculations with different numbers, we need to be able to change values in memory. The name **read/write memory** is used to describe memories that have both read and write capability.

The RAM chips on the two sample microcomputers are shown in Figure 1.3.1.

Many types of RAM are **volatile**, meaning that the memory keeps the data stored in it only as long as power is supplied. If we turn off the microcomputer, or if the power fails, the data stored in volatile memory is lost. Some newer kinds of RAM are **nonvolatile**, meaning that the memory keeps its data intact even when the power is shut off.

The RAM chips used by both example microcomputers are volatile. When we turn off the microcomputer, all the values stored in RAM are destroyed. When we turn the microcomputer on, random values will be stored in all the memory locations. We call these random values **garbage** because they have no meaning to us.

RAM is "working" memory—a space we can use as a scratch pad, or to store a program we want to run at the moment. But for programs that are essential to running the microcomputer itself, we'd like a way of storing them that is more permanent.

ROM

ROM stands for **Read Only Memory** and means that we or the microprocessor can read values from it but can't write values into it. If we try to write to ROM, it won't accept the new data. ROM, like RAM, is usually randomly accessible.

Storing a program on ROM prevents the program from accidentally being erased or changed. All types of ROM are nonvolatile. When the microcomputer is turned off, the contents of ROM locations stay the same. When the microcomputer is turned on, the ROM locations contain the same values that they did before it was turned off.

The ROM chips for the two microcomputers are shown in Figure 1.3.1. We need ROM to store operational programs, called *monitors*. A **monitor** is a program that lets the user communicate with the microprocessor, using the keyboard and display. The monitor translates the physical actions of pressing the keys into numerical data for the microprocessor. The monitor also lets us run our programs and examine and change contents of RAM locations. The monitor programs of the two microcomputers were written by different persons and so are quite different from each other. Both, however, accomplish the same purpose of establishing communication between the user and the microprocessor.

ROM chips are usually custom made by manufacturers. But there are some read-only memories, called **Programmable Read-Only Memories** (PROMs) that can be programmed by the user. Such a PROM chip starts out containing a number of fusible links. The desired program is stored in the PROM, and then a high current is applied. The program is permanently stored by blowing appropriate links and retaining others.

Other read-only memory chips, called **Erasable Programmable Read Only Memories (EPROMs),** can be erased by applying ultraviolet light. Then they can be reprogrammed. EPROMs are programmed with an electrical stimulus rather than with fusible links as PROMs are. Still others, called **Electrically Alterable Read Only Memories (EAROMs)**, can be both programmed and erased with electrical stimuli.

Input/Output (I/O)

We've learned that input is the information given the microcomputer, and the information it gives is output. Here, we've lumped these together into **Input/Output (I/O)**. We're discussing I/O in the same section as memory because the 6800 handles I/O in the same way it does memory. **Memory-mapped I/O** means that input and output devices are assigned specific addresses in memory to be read from (input) or written to (output). In later chapters we'll be looking at some chips that help the 6800 handle memory-mapped I/O.

Both example microcomputers have keypads for input. The keys we punch are translated into numbers for internal use by the microprocessor system.

For output both microcomputers have digital displays, but they're slightly different from each other. The Heathkit's digits are spaced equidistant from one another. The Motorola D2's 6 digits are arranged in groups of 4 and 2, separated by a larger space. But both displays can give us output that we can read.

As with input, there has to be a translator to change the computer's numerical results into visual output on the display. In Figure 1.3.1 both displays are showing a "prompt" (a message from the microprocessor that it is waiting for instructions). The prompts for these two microcomputers are different because their translator programs were written by different people. But the end result is the same: Even though microprocessors work in numbers, they can provide information in other forms.

1.5 BUSES

The MPU uses its buses to communicate with the other parts of the system. To get an idea of the type of information to be transmitted, let's look at a few of the 6800's pins.

Pins of the 6800

Figure 1.5.1 shows a diagram, called a **pin-out**, of the 6800. The 6800 has 8 data pins (D0–D7), which are used to output data from or input data to the microprocessor. These pins can be either outputs or inputs to the microprocessor, because the microprocessor can either receive or transmit data.

The 6800 also has 16 address pins (A0–A15), which are used to select a particular location in memory. The address pins are outputs only from the microprocessor, because only the microprocessor determines the location to be addressed.

Also shown in the figure are 4 pins used for control; 1 pin for power (+5V) and 2 for ground (GND, 0 volts) give the chip the power it needs to operate. These 3 pins are inputs to the MPU. The fourth control pin shown is the READ/WRITE (R/W) pin, which determines whether the MPU is reading from or writing to memory. When the R/W pin has a **high voltage**—around 5 volts—the MPU is reading from memory. And when the R/W pin has a **low voltage**—around 0 volts—the MPU is writing to memory. The R/W pin is an output from the MPU, because only the MPU determines whether it is reading or writing.

We'll be discussing some of the other pins later on, but for now these will be enough to let us describe the bus system. We distinguish three kinds of buses according to the kind of information they're transmitting.

FIGURE 1.5.1 Pin-Out of the 6800

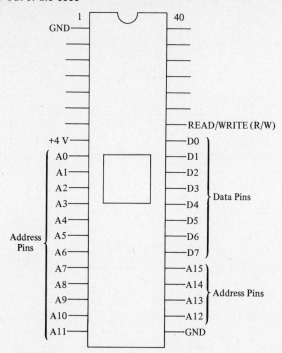

The data bus

The **data bus** transmits data into and out of the MPU. By *data* here, we mean any values stored in memory or to be written into memory. There are 8 data pins on the 6800, and the data bus has 8 lines, one for each pin. We say that the data bus is **bidirectional** (*bi* means "two"), because the data can flow in either direction, from MPU to memory or from memory to MPU.

Here's where the READ/WRITE pin of the MPU comes in. When this pin contains a high voltage, the MPU is reading (data is input to the MPU from the data bus). When the READ/WRITE pin contains a low voltage, the MPU is writing (placing data onto the data bus).

The address bus

The **address bus** lets the MPU select an individual location in memory, to or from which data is to be transferred. The 6800 has 16 address pins, and there are 16 lines on the address bus. The address bus is **unidirectional** (*uni* means "one") because information goes one way only: from the MPU to the memory.

FIGURE 1.5.2 Block Diagram of a Microcomputer System, Showing Buses

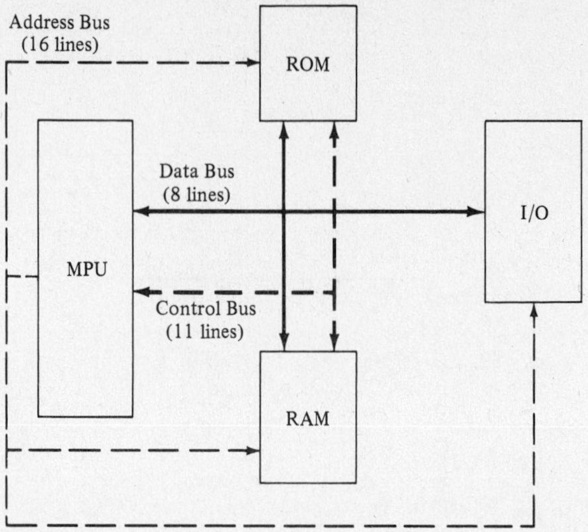

The control bus

The **control bus** contains control lines from other pins of the MPU, such as the READ/WRITE. A control bus has as many lines as it needs. The 6800 has 11 control lines. The control bus is unidirectional: That is, each line of the control bus goes only one way. Some lines (such as the READ/WRITE line) go only out of the MPU. Others, which we'll discuss later, go only into the MPU.

Figure 1.5.2 shows a block diagram of a microcomputer system with its buses.

In this chapter we've had a slight introduction to microcomputers. To use microcomputers, we need to be able to program them to do what we want. We've said that instructions in microcomputer programs must be in numbers and not in words. In the next two chapters we'll learn some of the number codes we need in order to communicate with microcomputers.

REVIEW QUESTIONS

1. What does microprocessor revolution mean? Explain and give examples.
2. What is a **computer**? Does a computer have to occupy a large space?
3. What is **program** control? What is a **computer program**?
4. What do we mean when we say that a computer **executes** a program?
5. Describe the similarities and differences between a human being following a set of written instructions and a computer executing a program.
6. What do we mean by computer **memory**? What is a **fetch**?
7. How do we identify each location in memory?

8. Does a computer program have to begin its sequence with 1? What is a **transfer of control** instruction? Explain.
9. Explain what the word **decode** means in terms of a computer program.
10. List five characteristics of a computer.
11. Name some tasks that computers are especially good at.
12. What is a **processor**? What is another name for it?
13. What is a **microprocessor**? Why is it ''micro''?
14. What is an **IC**? What is another name for it?
15. What is a **DIP**? What are **pins**?
16. What is **LSI**? How did it make microprocessors possible?
17. What is a **microprocessor system**? What is a **microcomputer**? What is the difference between a microcomputer and a microprocessor?
18. What do we mean by **hardware** and **software**? What is **microcomputer architecture**?
19. What is a **block diagram**? Draw a block diagram of a microprocessor system. What is a **bus**?
20. What are the duties of the microprocessor, I/O, memory, and buses?
21. Are microcomputers that use the same microprocessor necessarily exactly alike? Explain.
22. What is **RAM**? What does random access mean?
23. Explain what we mean by **read** and **write** with reference to memory. Which is destructive and which nondestructive? What is **read/write memory**?
24. What do we mean by **volatile** and **nonvolatile** memory? Is the RAM in each of the sample microcomputers volatile or nonvolatile?
25. What happens to values stored in RAM when we turn off the power? What is stored in the RAM locations when we turn on the power?
26. What is **read-only memory**? What is another term for it? Is it volatile or nonvolatile?
27. What is a **monitor**? Why should a monitor be stored in ROM?
28. What is a **PROM**? an **EPROM**? an **EAROM**? How are these like ROM, and how are they different?
29. What is I/O? **Memory-mapped I/O**? What I/O devices do the two example microcomputers use?
30. What does the MPU use its buses for? What is a **pin-out**?
31. How many data pins and how many address pins does the 6800 have? Are these inputs or outputs to the MPU?
32. What is the function of the READ/WRITE pin? What is meant by a **high** and a **low voltage**? What is happening when the READ/WRITE pin has a high or a low voltage?
33. List the three buses. How many lines does each have on the 6800? Which are **bidirectional** and which, **unidirectional**?

2 Number Codes

LEARNING OBJECTIVES

After completing this chapter, you should be able to:

1. Give a definition, explanation, or example for each of these: *base ten, base, radix, digit, base two, base sixteen, positional notation, least significant digit, most significant digit, binary, binary representation, flip-flop, bit, toggle, byte, nibble, data word, address word, kilobyte, megabyte, Binary Coded Decimal (BCD), hexadecimal, hexadecimal representation, hexadecimal digit, unsigned binary number, signed binary number, sign bit.*
2. Describe the three base number systems in this chapter in terms of number of digits and characters used for their digits.
3. Use positional notation to describe numbers in decimal, binary, and hexadecimal.
4. Use powers of two to determine how many unique values may be represented by a given number of bits.
5. Count in binary and in hexadecimal.
6. Convert among binary, BCD, decimal, and hexadecimal representation in any combination.
7. Recognize a signed binary or hexadecimal number as positive or negative.

In Chapter 1 we learned that computers work exclusively in numbers, but we avoided saying what kind of numbers. In this chapter we'll be considering some important number codes used in computing.

2.1 NUMBER SYSTEMS

The number system we're used to, the decimal system, is a **base ten** number system. A **base** (or **radix**) is a number used as reference for constructing a number system.

Digits

A **digit** is a nonnegative integer that is smaller than the base. In the base ten system we have ten digits, expressed by the characters 0–9. It's been said, half-jokingly, that humans developed the base ten system because we have ten fingers. We can count from 0–9 on our fingers if each finger represents a digit in base ten.

Now that we're dealing with computers, we'll need to know two other number systems: base two and base sixteen. In the **base two** system we have two digits, expressed by the characters 0 and 1. In the **base sixteen** system we have sixteen digits. To represent sixteen digits, we need sixteen characters. The decimal system gives us only ten: 0–9. Thus for the other six we borrow the first six alphabetic characters: A–F.

Figure 2.1.1 summarizes these three number systems, their digits, and the characters used to symbolize those digits. We see that the base itself can't be expressed with a single digit. So although we're used to the representation "10" meaning "ten," this is only true if we're working in the base ten number system. In base two "10" means "two," and in base sixteen, "10" means "sixteen." In cases where there might be confusion as to the base, we identify a number's base by using a subscript, such as: 10_2 (for base two), 10_{10} (for base ten), and 10_{16} (for base sixteen). We can omit the base subscripts when the base is obvious. For instance, the

FIGURE 2.1.1 Three Number Systems and the Characters Used to Represent Their Digits

Base Two Two Digits	Base Ten Ten Digits	Base Sixteen Sixteen Digits
0	0	0
1	1	1
	2	2
	3	3
	4	4
	5	5
	6	6
	7	7
	8	8
	9	9
		A
		B
		C
		D
		E
		F
10 is two	10 is ten	10 is sixteen

number F3E0 is obviously a number in base sixteen. And a number such as 237, without a subscript, is assumed to be in the familiar base ten number system.

Positional notation

In grammar schools, students are taught that the rightmost place of a multi-digit number is the "1's place," the place just to its left is the "10's place," the next, the "100's place," and so on. Thus the number

444_{10}

contains three 4s, but each has a different value because of its position. The "rightmost" 4, in the 1's place, is worth four 1s (4). The middle 4, in the 10's place, is worth four 10s (40). And the "leftmost" 4, in the 100's place, is worth four 100s (400). Adding these up (400 plus 40 plus 4) gives us 444.

Another way to express the number 444_{10} is to use powers of ten. Thus the rightmost place is the 10^0's place, the place just to its left is the 10^1's place, the next place to the left is the 10^2's place, and so on. When we express a number in **positional notation**, we write it as a sum of individual digits, multiplied by exponentials, which represent the digits' positional values. Thus the number 444_{10} is written in positional notation, in base ten, like this:

$$(4 \times 10^0) + (4 \times 10^1) + (4 \times 10^2)$$

Figure 2.1.2 summarizes positional notation in the decimal system. In any system we call the rightmost digit the **Least Significant Digit (LSD)** because its value has the least significance of any in the number. The leftmost digit then represents the **Most Significant Digit (MSD).** The number 444 has only 3 digits, but we can use as many digits as we need to express a number of any value.

FIGURE 2.1.2   Positional Notation in the Decimal System

Thousands Place	Hundreds Place	Tens Place	Ones Place
1000	100	10	1
10^3	10^2	10^1	10^0

Most Significant Digit $\longrightarrow$ **4** **4** **4** $\longleftarrow$ Least Significant Digit

$(4 \times 100) + (4 \times 10) + (4 \times 1) = 444$

$(4 \times 10^2) + (4 \times 10^1) + (4 \times 10^0) = 444$

2.2 BINARY REPRESENTATION

Binary means having two states. Many things can have two states. A switch may be on or off. A door may be open or closed. The answer may be yes or no. We may win or lose, pass or fail, sink or swim. **Binary representation** is the name given to the base two number system.

Why binary?

Computers keep track of numbers by means of a great many electronic switches called **flip-flops**. Each flip-flop is binary, because it can be in one of two possible states—the high and low voltages (5 and 0 volts, respectively), of which we spoke in Chapter 1. We could also call these two states "on" and "off." The wires on the microcomputer's buses, too, carry binary values: a high or a low voltage.

Computers naturally use the base two number system because it is also binary. We use the word **bit** to mean BInary digiT. Each bit can have one of two possible states, designated 1 or 0. A bit value is represented by a single flip-flop, which is either on (1) or off (0). To change a bit value, the computer **toggles** (reverses the state of) the flip-flop. Similarly, the wires in the data, address, and control buses carry bit values with a high voltage representing 1 and a low voltage representing 0.

Counting in binary

When we count in any number system, we start with the lowest single digit and count until we run out of digits. Then we go to two digits, and so on. In binary

FIGURE 2.2.1 Counting from Zero to Sixteen in Binary

Binary		Decimal Equivalent
0	This far, binary and	0
1	decimal are the same.	1
10		2
11		3
100		4
101		5
110		6
111		7
1000		8
1001		9
1010		10
1011		11
1100		12
1101		13
1110		14
1111		15
10000		16

representation we count like this: 0, 1—and we've already run out of bits, so we go to two places: 10, 11. Now we have to go to three: 100, 101, 110, 111, and so on. Figure 2.2.1 illustrates counting from zero to sixteen in binary.

We recall from Chapter 1 that the 6800 has 8 data pins and 8 lines on the data bus. This corresponds to a set of 8 bits, a convenient number called a **byte.** Half a byte, or 4 bits, is called a **nibble**. Since the 6800 has 8 data pins, we say that its **data word** is 8 bits, or 1 byte. We can count a lot further using 8 bits than we could with the 4 bits of Figure 2.2.1. If we were to write out all the binary values possible with an 8-bit data word, we'd get the list in Table 2.2.1. With 256 different numbers, we can express 256 values using an 8-bit (1-byte) data word.

In Table 2.2.1 we've grouped the bits in fours (nibbles). This we'll do often throughout the book just to make the numbers easier to read. Also, we see in the table that the more significant bits are filled in with 0s: for example, 0000 0011 instead of just 11 to represent "three." Each bit in a computer word is represented by a switch and must contain some binary value, either 0 or 1. As in the decimal system, putting 0s in front of a number doesn't change its value.

The 6800's **address word** is 16 bits, or 2 bytes. How many values can we express with a 16-bit word? In order not to have to count all the values possible with 16 bits, let's establish the pattern of values for numbers of bits.

Powers of two

Looking back at Figure 2.2.1, we see that with just 1 bit we can express two values: 0 and 1. With 2 bits we have four possibilities: 00, 01, 10, and 11. For 3 bits we have 8 possibilities; for 4 bits, 16; and for 8 bits, 256 (Table 2.2.1). The pattern to the number of possible values that can be represented by a certain number of bits has to do with powers of two. If we have n bits, we'll have 2^n possible values. Some powers of two are listed in Table 2.2.2. After awhile some of these values may become familiar, but there is no need to memorize them.

Now we see that a 16-bit word can represent 65,536 values. Because the 6800 has a 16-bit address word, it can specify 65,536 different addresses. Some of the newer microprocessors have 16-bit data words and 20 to 24-bit address words and can address from 1,048,576 to 16,777,216 different locations.

Writing numbers such as 1,048,576 and 16,777,216 becomes cumbersome and error prone. Instead of writing the numbers out each time, we often use the letter K, meaning *Kilo-* for multiples of 1024 (2^{10}). Thus 1024 is 1K; $2^1 \times 1024$ (2048) is 2K; $2^2 \times 1024$ (4096) is 4K; and so on. When we get to 2^{20} (1,048,576), we use the letter M, meaning *Mega-*, which is 1K squared: $1024^2 = 1,048,576$. Thus 2^{21} (2,097,152) is 2M; 2^{22} (4,194,304) is 4M; and so on.

K and M are quantities and not units. We usually use them to describe the number of bits or bytes that can be stored. For instance, a memory size of 64 kilobits (Kbits) means that 65,536 bit values can be stored. But for a microprocessor with a 1-byte data word, such as the 6800, it's more useful to describe the number of bytes

TABLE 2.2.1 One-Byte Binary Values

Binary	Decimal	Binary	Decimal
0000 0000	0	0011 0111	55
0000 0001	1	0011 1000	56
0000 0010	2	0011 1001	57
0000 0011	3	0011 1010	58
0000 0100	4	0011 1011	59
0000 0101	5	0011 1100	60
0000 0110	6	0011 1101	61
0000 0111	7	0011 1110	62
0000 1000	8	0011 1111	63
0000 1001	9	0100 0000	64
0000 1010	10	0100 0001	65
0000 1011	11	0100 0010	66
0000 1100	12	0100 0011	67
0000 1101	13	0100 0100	68
0000 1110	14	0100 0101	69
0000 1111	15	0100 0110	70
0001 0000	16	0100 0111	71
0001 0001	17	0100 1000	72
0001 0010	18	0100 1001	73
0001 0011	19	0100 1010	74
0001 0100	20	0100 1011	75
0001 0101	21	0100 1100	76
0001 0110	22	0100 1101	77
0001 0111	23	0100 1110	78
0001 1000	24	0100 1111	79
0001 1001	25	0101 0000	80
0001 1010	26	0101 0001	81
0001 1011	27	0101 0010	82
0001 1100	28	0101 0011	83
0001 1101	29	0101 0100	84
0001 1110	30	0101 0101	85
0001 1111	31	0101 0110	86
0010 0000	32	0101 0111	87
0010 0001	33	0101 1000	88
0010 0010	34	0101 1001	89
0010 0011	35	0101 1010	90
0010 0100	36	0101 1011	91
0010 0101	37	0101 1100	92
0010 0110	38	0101 1101	93
0010 0111	39	0101 1110	94
0010 1000	40	0101 1111	95
0010 1001	41	0110 0000	96
0010 1010	42	0110 0001	97
0010 1011	43	0110 0010	98
0010 1100	44	0110 0011	99
0010 1101	45	0110 0100	100
0010 1110	46	0110 0101	101
0010 1111	47	0110 0110	102
0011 0000	48	0110 0111	103
0011 0001	49	0110 1000	104
0011 0010	50	0110 1001	105
0011 0011	51	0110 1010	106
0011 0100	52	0110 1011	107
0011 0101	53	0110 1100	108
0011 0110	54	0110 1101	109

TABLE 2.2.1 (*Continued*)

Binary	Decimal	Binary	Decimal
0110 1110	110	1010 0110	166
0110 1111	111	1010 0111	167
0111 0000	112	1010 1000	168
0111 0001	113	1010 1001	169
0111 0010	114	1010 1010	170
0111 0011	115	1010 1011	171
0111 0100	116	1010 1100	172
0111 0101	117	1010 1101	173
0111 0110	118	1010 1110	174
0111 0111	119	1010 1111	175
0111 1000	120	1011 0000	176
0111 1001	121	1011 0001	177
0111 1010	122	1011 0010	178
0111 1011	123	1011 0011	179
0111 1100	124	1011 0100	180
0111 1101	125	1011 0101	181
0111 1110	126	1011 0110	182
0111 1111	127	1011 0111	183
1000 0000	128	1011 1000	184
1000 0001	129	1011 1001	185
1000 0010	130	1011 1010	186
1000 0011	131	1011 1011	187
1000 0100	132	1011 1100	188
1000 0101	133	1011 1101	189
1000 0110	134	1011 1110	190
1000 0111	135	1011 1111	191
1000 1000	136	1100 0000	192
1000 1001	137	1100 0001	193
1000 1010	138	1100 0010	194
1000 1011	139	1100 0011	195
1000 1100	140	1100 0100	196
1000 1101	141	1100 0101	197
1000 1110	142	1100 0110	198
1000 1111	143	1100 0111	199
1001 0000	144	1100 1000	200
1001 0001	145	1100 1001	201
1001 0010	146	1100 1010	202
1001 0011	147	1100 1011	203
1001 0100	148	1100 1100	204
1001 0101	149	1100 1101	205
1001 0110	150	1100 1110	206
1001 0111	151	1100 1111	207
1001 1000	152	1101 0000	208
1001 1001	153	1101 0001	209
1001 1010	154	1101 0010	210
1001 1011	155	1101 0011	211
1001 1100	156	1101 0100	212
1001 1101	157	1101 0101	213
1001 1110	158	1101 0110	214
1001 1111	159	1101 0111	215
1010 0000	160	1101 1000	216
1010 0001	161	1101 1001	217
1010 0010	162	1101 1010	218
1010 0011	163	1101 1011	219
1010 0100	164	1101 1100	220
1010 0101	165	1101 1101	221

TABLE 2.2.1 (*Continued*)

Binary	Decimal	Binary	Decimal
1101 1110	222	1110 1111	239
1101 1111	223	1111 0000	240
1110 0000	224	1111 0001	241
1110 0001	225	1111 0010	242
1110 0010	226	1111 0011	243
1110 0011	227	1111 0100	244
1110 0100	228	1111 0101	245
1110 0101	229	1111 0110	246
1110 0110	230	1111 0111	247
1110 0111	231	1111 1000	248
1110 1000	232	1111 1001	249
1110 1001	233	1111 1010	250
1110 1010	234	1111 1011	251
1110 1011	235	1111 1100	252
1110 1100	236	1111 1101	253
1110 1101	237	1111 1110	254
1110 1110	238	1111 1111	255

that can be stored. So the terms **kilobyte (Kbyte),** meaning 1024 bytes of data, and **megabyte (Mbyte),** meaning 1,048,576 bytes, are commonly used. Because each memory location can contain 1 byte, we say that the 6800's 16-bit address word can address 64 Kbytes of memory. The prefix *Giga* (2^{30}) hasn't been extensively used to describe computer memories, but it probably will be in the future.

Figure 2.2.2 shows the address and data word structure of the 6800. Each bit is identified with a bit number: 0–15 for the address word and 0–7 for the data word. We'll see next how these bit numbers came about.

Positional notation

As in the decimal system, each bit in binary representation is given a value using positional notation. Instead of using powers of ten, we now use powers of two.

TABLE 2.2.2 Powers of Two

$2^0 = 1$	$2^{14} = 16{,}384 \ (16\,K)$
$2^1 = 2$	$2^{15} = 32{,}768 \ (32\,K)$
$2^2 = 4$	$2^{16} = 65{,}536 \ (64\,K)$
$2^3 = 8$	$2^{17} = 131{,}072 \ (128\,K)$
$2^4 = 16$	$2^{18} = 262{,}144 \ (256\,K)$
$2^5 = 32$	$2^{19} = 524{,}288 \ (512\,K)$
$2^6 = 64$	$2^{20} = 1{,}048{,}576 \ (1\,M)$
$2^7 = 128$	$2^{21} = 2{,}097{,}152 \ (2\,M)$
$2^8 = 256$	$2^{22} = 4{,}194{,}304 \ (4\,M)$
$2^9 = 512$	$2^{23} = 8{,}388{,}608 \ (8\,M)$
$2^{10} = 1{,}024 \ (1\,K)$	$2^{24} = 16{,}777{,}216 \ (16\,M)$
$2^{11} = 2{,}048 \ (2\,K)$	
$2^{12} = 4{,}096 \ (4\,K)$	
$2^{13} = 8{,}192 \ (8\,K)$	

FIGURE 2.2.2   Word Structure of 6800

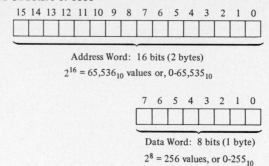

Address Word: 16 bits (2 bytes)

$2^{16} = 65,536_{10}$ values or, $0\text{-}65,535_{10}$

Data Word: 8 bits (1 byte)

$2^8 = 256$ values, or $0\text{-}255_{10}$

Thus the least significant bit is the 2^0 place, the next the 2^1 place, the next the 2^2 place, and so on.

We write the 8-bit binary number 1110 1011 in positional notation like this:

$$(1\times2^7)+(1\times2^6)+(1\times2^5)+(0\times2^4)+(1\times2^3)$$
$$+(0\times2^2)+(1\times2^1)+(1\times2^0)$$

Figure 2.2.3 shows positional notation for the 8-bit binary number 1110 1011. Three ways of describing each bit are shown. In addition to the powers of two notation, we use bit 0, bit 1, bit 2, and so forth to identify the bits. (Note that these numbers correspond to the powers of two). Finally, we can evaluate the powers of two in decimal: the 1's place, the 2's place, the 4's place, the 8's place, and so on.

FIGURE 2.2.3   Positional Notation in Binary

One Hundred Twenty-eights Place	Sixty-Fours Place	Thirty-Twos Place	Sixteens Place	Eights Place	Fours Place	Twos Place	Ones Place	
2^7	2^6	2^5	2^4	2^3	2^2	2^1	2^0	Power of 2
7	6	5	4	3	2	1	0	Bit #
128	64	32	16	8	4	2	1	Evaluated power of 2
I	I	I	O	I	O	I	I	

|← 4 bits = 1 nibble →|← 4 bits = 1 nibble →|

|← 8 bits = 1 byte →|

1110 1011 expressed in positional notation:

$(1 \times 2^7) + (1 \times 2^6) + (1 \times 2^5) + (0 \times 2^4) + (1 \times 2^3) + (0 \times 2^2) + (1 \times 2^1) + (1 \times 2^0)$

FIGURE 2.2.4 Using Positional Notation in Binary–Decimal Conversion

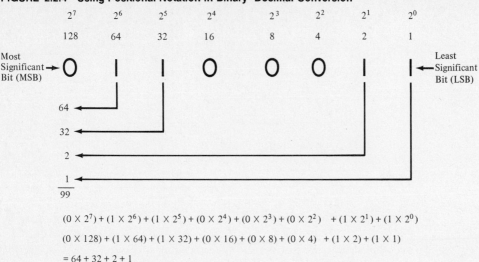

$$(0 \times 2^7) + (1 \times 2^6) + (1 \times 2^5) + (0 \times 2^4) + (0 \times 2^3) + (0 \times 2^2) \ + (1 \times 2^1) + (1 \times 2^0)$$

$$(0 \times 128) + (1 \times 64) + (1 \times 32) + (0 \times 16) + (0 \times 8) + (0 \times 4) \ + (1 \times 2) + (1 \times 1)$$

$$= 64 + 32 + 2 + 1$$

$$= 99$$

Binary-decimal conversion

We don't have to use Table 2.2.1 to convert between binary and decimal. There are several different methods for converting from binary to decimal. We'll discuss only one of them.

Positional notation will be helpful in this conversion. Figure 2.2.4 shows the 8-bit (1-byte) binary number 0110 0011 expressed, using positional notation, both with powers of two and with the powers of two evaluated. Our number has a 0 in the 128's place, a 1 in the 64's place, a 1 in the 32's place, a 0 in the 16's place, a 0 in the 8's place, a 0 in the 4's place, a 1 in the 2's place, and a 1 in the 1's place. We could also say that the number contains one 64, one 32, one 2, and one 1. Adding $64 + 32 + 2 + 1$ gives us 99 in decimal.

EXAMPLE 2.2.1

Convert the binary number 1011 0101 to decimal.

Solution

First, write the evaluated powers of two over the digits:

128	64	32	16	8	4	2	1
1	0	1	1	0	1	0	1

Next, wherever there is a 1, write down the power of two that corresponds to that digit. Then add them.

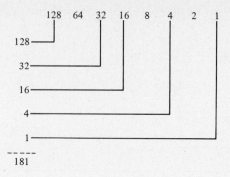

Answer: 181

Decimal-binary conversions

To accomplish this, we just reverse the preceding process. To convert decimal 157 to binary, first, we label the place for each binary digit:

128   64   32   16   8   4   2   1

Next, we look at the number. Because 157 is greater than 128, there is one 128 in 157. We write a 1 in the 128's place and subtract 128 from 157.

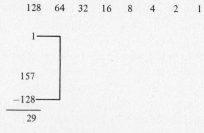

The number 29 contains no 64s and no 32s, so we write a 0 in each of those places. There is a 16 in 29, so we write a 1 in the 16's place and subtract 16 from 29.

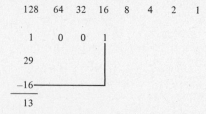

This number contains an 8, a 4, no 2s, and a 1, so we write a 1 in each of the 8's, 4's, and 1's places, and our binary equivalent is finished.

128   64   32   16   8   4   2   1
 1   0   0   1   1   1   0   1

EXAMPLE 2.2.2

Convert the decimal number 79 to binary.

Solution

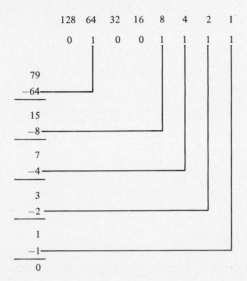

Answer: 0100 1111

2.3   BINARY CODED DECIMAL (BCD) REPRESENTATION

This system effects a compromise between the decimal system, which human beings find more comfortable, and the binary system, which computers need to do their work. In **Binary Coded Decimal (BCD)** we define a set of 4 bits (a nibble) as equivalent to 1 decimal digit. That is, we use a nibble of binary to represent each decimal digit from 0–9. A nibble can represent sixteen numbers—0 through 15 in decimal—but BCD uses only ten of the fifteen bit patterns. Table 2.3.1 illustrates BCD and its relationship to the binary and decimal systems.

For the decimal numbers 0–9, binary and BCD representations are the same. Just as we must use 2 digits to represent numbers above 9 in decimal, we must use 2 nibbles to represent the same number in BCD. Thus these representations aren't valid in BCD:

1010
1011
1100
1101
1110
1111

TABLE 2.3.1   Relationship Among Binary, Decimal, and BCD

Binary Representation	Decimal Representation		BCD Representation
0000	0		0000
0001	1		0001
0010	2		0010
0011	3		0011
0100	4		0100
0101	5		0101
0110	6		0110
0111	7		0111
1000	8		1000
1001[a]	9[a]		1001[a]
1010	10	Decimal must	0001 0000
1011	11	use 2 digits	0001 0001
1100	12	here; so, too	0001 0010
1101	13	must BCD	0001 0011
1110	14		0001 0100
1111	15		0001 0101

[a]Up to this point, binary and BCD representation are the same.

Decimal-BCD conversions

To represent a decimal number in BCD, we merely express each decimal digit as an independent nibble of binary representation.

EXAMPLE 2.3.1

Convert the decimal number 4095 to BCD.

Solution

Take each decimal digit separately and convert it to a nibble of binary. Thus 4 becomes 0100, 0 is 0000, 9 is 1001, and 5 is 0101.

Answer: 0100 0000 1001 0101

That conversion was much easier than it would have been to convert 4095 in decimal into binary. The number 4095_{10} expressed in binary is

1111   1111   1111

We express this number using 12 bits in binary representation, but we had to use 16 bits to express the same number in BCD. BCD is wasteful of digits. The larger the word size is, the more bits are wasted using BCD. But depending on the particular application, the greater convenience of BCD often makes up for its inefficiency.

For instance, we humans operate in base ten most of the time. For some devices that do decimal calculations we might not care that they waste some bit patterns, because base ten is what we want to use. When we enter a decimal number onto the keypad of a calculator, a program inside the calculator might translate the decimal number into BCD. Some microprocessors can add, subtract, multiply, and divide in BCD with only a little more effort than in their natural language, binary. The microprocessor's program lets it translate the answer from BCD to decimal to display it.

BCD-decimal conversions

Converting from BCD to decimal is just as easy.

EXAMPLE 2.3.2

Convert the BCD number 0110 1001 1000 to decimal.

Solution

We evaluate each nibble as a decimal digit. Thus 0110 is 6, 1001 is 9, and 1000 is 8.

Answer: 698

One word of caution: BCD representation looks just like binary, so we must be very careful and specify which number system we're using. For instance, the number in Example 2.3.2, if interpreted as a binary number, would be equivalent to decimal 1688.

BCD-binary conversions

To convert BCD to binary and vice versa, we find it easiest to change either number to decimal representation first.

EXAMPLE 2.3.3

Convert the BCD number 1001 0111 into binary representation.

Solution

First, change to decimal: 97. Next, change to binary in the usual way.

Answer: 0110 0001 (quite different from the BCD representation)

EXAMPLE 2.3.4

Convert the binary number 0111 1001 into BCD.

Solution

First, change to decimal: 121. Next, change decimal to BCD in the usual way.

Answer: 0001 0010 0001

Next, we'll look at a number system that is more convenient than binary but which doesn't waste all the digits that BCD does.

2.4 HEXADECIMAL REPRESENTATION

Hexadecimal is the name for the base sixteen number system. In **hexadecimal representation** we define a set of 4 binary digits (a nibble) as equivalent to 1 hexadecimal digit. A **hexadecimal digit** is a digit in base sixteen. In Figure 2.1.1, we listed the characters (0–F), that represent the hexadecimal digits. Table 2.4.1 shows decimal, hexadecimal, and binary equivalents.

Binary-hexadecimal and hexadecimal-binary conversions

These are easy. All we do is evaluate each nibble or each digit with its equivalent from Table 2.4.1.

EXAMPLE 2.4.1

Convert the binary number 1011 0111 to hexadecimal.

Solution

Find each bit pattern on Table 2.4.1 and use its hexadecimal equivalent. Thus 1011 is B and 0111 is 7.

Answer: B7

EXAMPLE 2.4.2

Convert the hexadecimal number 9F to binary.

Solution

9 is 1001 and F is 1111.

Answer: 1001 1111

Most often, we use hexadecimal representation in place of binary for programming microcomputers such as the Motorola D2 Evaluation Kit of Figure 1.3.1.

TABLE 2.4.1 Hexadecimal, Decimal, and Binary Equivalents

Decimal	Hexadecimal	Binary
0	0	0000
1	1	0001
2	2	0010
3	3	0011
4	4	0100
5	5	0101
6	6	0110
7	7	0111
8	8	1000
9	9	1001
10	A	1010
11	B	1011
12	C	1100
13	D	1101
14	E	1110
15	F	1111

Looking back at that figure, we see that the microcomputer has a hexadecimal keypad. As the calculator does between decimal and BCD, the microcomputer has a program that translates binary into hexadecimal when it outputs to the display. We can input numbers in hexadecimal with the keypad, because the microcomputer interprets each key as a pattern of bits. The ability to work in hexadecimal instead of binary makes life a lot easier for users.

Hexadecimal-decimal conversions

To accomplish these, we use positional notation as we did with binary-decimal conversions. The largest word that the 6800 uses is its 16-bit address word,

FIGURE 2.4.1 Positional Notation in Base Sixteen

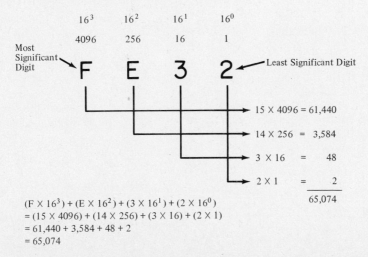

$$(F \times 16^3) + (E \times 16^2) + (3 \times 16^1) + (2 \times 16^0)$$
$$= (15 \times 4096) + (14 \times 256) + (3 \times 16) + (2 \times 1)$$
$$= 61,440 + 3,584 + 48 + 2$$
$$= 65,074$$

equivalent to 4 hexadecimal digits. Thus 4 hexadecimal digits are all we'll ever have to worry about, fortunately. Powers of sixteen get large very fast.

Figure 2.4.1 shows a hexadecimal-decimal conversion using positional notation. In converting the hexadecimal number FE32 to decimal, we have an F (15 in decimal) in the 4096's place, so we multiply 15×4096. We have an E (14 in decimal) in the 256's place, so we multiply 14×256. Then, we multiply 3×16 and finally, 2×1. Using a calculator makes these conversions easier.

EXAMPLE 2.4.3

Convert the hexadecimal number 100F to decimal.

Solution

First, write the evaluated powers of sixteen over the digits:

```
4096   256   16   1
  1     0     0   F
```

Next, multiply each digit by its evaluated power of sixteen:

$$1 \times 4096 = 4096$$
$$0 \times 256 = 0$$
$$0 \times 16 = 0$$
$$15 \times 1 = 15$$

Next, add them: 4111

Answer: 4111 in decimal

To convert from decimal to hexadecimal, we reverse the preceding process.

EXAMPLE 2.4.4

Convert the decimal number 10,495 to hexadecimal.

Solution

First, write down the evaluated powers of sixteen:

```
4096   256   16   1
```

Next, there are two 4096s in 10,495. So we write a 2 in the 4096's place and subtract $2 \times 4096 = 8192$ from 10,495:

```
4096        256     16     1
  2
10,495
−8,192
────────
 2,303
```

Next, there are eight 256s in 2,303. Thus we write an 8 in the 256's place and subtract $8 \times 256 = 2048$ from 2303.

$$
\begin{array}{cc}
2 & 8 \\
10{,}495 & \\
-8{,}192 & \\
\hline
2{,}303 & \\
-2{,}048 & \\
\hline
255 &
\end{array}
$$

Next, there are fifteen 16s in 255. So we write an F in the 16's place and subtract $15 \times 16 = 240$ from 255.

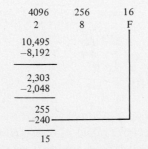

$$
\begin{array}{cccc}
4096 & 256 & 16 & \\
2 & 8 & F & 1 \\
10{,}495 & & & \\
-8{,}192 & & & \\
\hline
2{,}303 & & & \\
-2{,}048 & & & \\
\hline
255 & & & \\
-240 & & & \\
\hline
15 & & &
\end{array}
$$

Finally, there are fifteen 1s in 15. Thus we write an F in the least significant digit.

Answer: 28FF

Hexadecimal-BCD conversions

These are best done by first converting either number to decimal.

EXAMPLE 2.4.5

Convert the hexadecimal number D1 to BCD notation.

Solution

First, convert D1 to decimal:

$$
\begin{array}{r}
13 \times 16 = 208 \\
+ \ 1 \times \ 1 = \ \underline{1} \\
209
\end{array}
$$

Next, convert 209 to BCD in the usual way.

Answer: 0010 0000 1001

EXAMPLE 2.4.6

Convert the BCD number 1001 0110 to hexadecimal.

Solution

First, convert 1001 0110 to decimal: 96. Next, convert 96 to hexadecimal: There are no 4096s and no 256s in this number, so it will have only 2 hexadecimal digits:

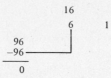

Answer: 60 in hexadecimal

2.5 SIGNED BINARY NUMBERS

Earlier in this chapter we said that a byte of data with values 0000 0000 through 1111 1111 could correspond to decimal values of 0 through 255. This is true if we're talking about **unsigned binary numbers,** meaning that we can't specify a number as positive or negative. Now, we're going to introduce a code that uses those same

FIGURE 2.5.1   Making a One-Byte Binary Odometer

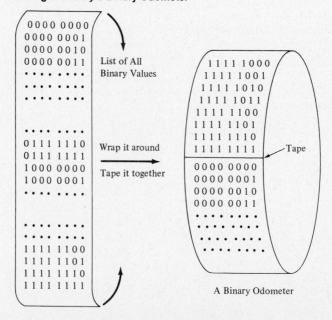

binary values (0000 0000 to 1111 1111) to represent signed numbers from decimal −128 to +127. By **signed binary numbers** we mean numbers that can be specified as either positive or negative.

Imagine all the possible values of 1-byte binary numbers (Table 2.2.1) typed out on a piece of adding machine tape in increasing numerical order. Now, imagine that we tape the two ends together to form a "binary odometer" as shown in Figure 2.5.1.

First, we see that if we turn the odometer back from zero (0000 0000) we get 1111 1111 (FF in hexadecimal). So 1111 1111 can be the same as −1 (decimal), 1111 1110 (FE) can be the same as decimal −2, and so on.

Next, let's turn over our taped odometer so that it resembles Figure 2.5.2. With a pair of scissors we cut between the numbers 0111 1111 (7F) and 1000 0000 (80), and spread the tape out flat again so that 1000 0000 is at the top and 0111 1111 is at the bottom. If we counted forward from zero, we'd find that 0111 1111 equals +127 (decimal). And if we counted backward from zero, we'd find that 1000 0000 equals −128 (decimal). By taping and cutting the list in this way, we've rearranged the same set of binary values without changing the total number that are on the list.

Table 2.5.1 shows the list of signed binary numbers, with their decimal and hexadecimal equivalents, which we just created. In our code of signed binary numbers we define the most significant bit (in this case, bit 7) as the **sign bit.** All negative numbers have a 1 in the sign bit; all positive numbers have a 0 in the sign bit. (By this token, 0 is considered to be a positive number.)

We see in Table 2.5.1 that the smallest negative 8-bit binary number equals decimal −128 and that the largest positive 8-bit binary number equals decimal +127. There isn't any binary equivalent to decimal +128 for an 8-bit binary number. No matter how many bits we use, it's always true that *the smallest negative*

FIGURE 2.5.2   Making a Restructured List of Binary Values

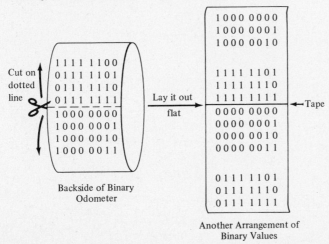

Backside of Binary Odometer

Another Arrangement of Binary Values

TABLE 2.5.1 List of One-Byte Signed Binary Numbers

Binary	Decimal	Hexadecimal	Binary	Decimal	Hexadecimal
1000 0000	−128	80	1011 0111	−73	B7
1000 0001	−127	81	1011 1000	−72	B8
1000 0010	−126	82	1011 1001	−71	B9
1000 0011	−125	83	1011 1010	−70	BA
1000 0100	−124	84	1011 1011	−69	BB
1000 0101	−123	85	1011 1100	−68	BC
1000 0110	−122	86	1011 1101	−67	BD
1000 0111	−121	87	1011 1110	−66	BE
1000 1000	−120	88	1011 1111	−65	BF
1000 1001	−119	89	1100 0000	−64	C0
1000 1010	−118	8A	1100 0001	−63	C1
1000 1011	−117	8B	1100 0010	−62	C2
1000 1100	−116	8C	1100 0011	−61	C3
1000 1101	−115	8D	1100 0100	−60	C4
1000 1110	−114	8E	1100 0101	−59	C5
1000 1111	−113	8F	1100 0110	−58	C6
1001 0000	−112	90	1100 0111	−57	C7
1001 0001	−111	91	1100 1000	−56	C8
1001 0010	−110	92	1100 1001	−55	C9
1001 0011	−109	93	1100 1010	−54	CA
1001 0100	−108	94	1100 1011	−53	CB
1001 0101	−107	95	1100 1100	−52	CC
1001 0110	−106	96	1100 1101	−51	CD
1001 0111	−105	97	1100 1110	−50	CE
1001 1000	−104	98	1100 1111	−49	CF
1001 1001	−103	99	1101 0000	−48	D0
1001 1010	−102	9A	1101 0001	−47	D1
1001 1011	−101	9B	1101 0010	−46	D2
1001 1100	−100	9C	1101 0011	−45	D3
1001 1101	−99	9D	1101 0100	−44	D4
1001 1110	−98	9E	1101 0101	−43	D5
1001 1111	−97	9F	1101 0110	−42	D6
1010 0000	−96	A0	1101 0111	−41	D7
1010 0001	−95	A1	1101 1000	−40	D8
1010 0010	−94	A2	1101 1001	−39	D9
1010 0011	−93	A3	1101 1010	−38	DA
1010 0100	−92	A4	1101 1011	−37	DB
1010 0101	−91	A5	1101 1100	−36	DC
1010 0110	−90	A6	1101 1101	−35	DD
1010 0111	−89	A7	1101 1110	−34	DE
1010 1000	−88	A8	1101 1111	−33	DF
1010 1001	−87	A9	1110 0000	−32	E0
1010 1010	−86	AA	1110 0001	−31	E1
1010 1011	−85	AB	1110 0010	−30	E2
1010 1100	−84	AC	1110 0011	−29	E3
1010 1101	−83	AD	1110 0100	−28	E4
1010 1110	−82	AE	1110 0101	−27	E5
1010 1111	−81	AF	1110 0110	−26	E6
1011 0000	−80	B0	1110 0111	−25	E7
1011 0001	−79	B1	1110 1000	−24	E8
1011 0010	−78	B2	1110 1001	−23	E9
1011 0011	−77	B3	1110 1010	−22	EA
1011 0100	−76	B4	1110 1011	−21	EB
1011 0101	−75	B5	1110 1100	−20	EC
1011 0110	−74	B6	1110 1101	−19	ED

TABLE 2.5.1 (*Continued*)

Binary	Decimal	Hexadecimal	Binary	Decimal	Hexadecimal
1110 1110	−18	EE	0010 0101	+37	25
1110 1111	−17	EF	0010 0110	+38	26
1111 0000	−16	F0	0010 0111	+39	27
1111 0001	−15	F1	0010 1000	+40	28
1111 0010	−14	F2	0010 1001	+41	29
1111 0011	−13	F3	0010 1010	+42	2A
1111 0100	−12	F4	0010 1011	+43	2B
1111 0101	−11	F5	0010 1100	+44	2C
1111 0110	−10	F6	0010 1101	+45	2D
1111 0111	−9	F7	0010 1110	+46	2E
1111 1000	−8	F8	0010 1111	+47	2F
1111 1001	−7	F9	0011 0000	+48	30
1111 1010	−6	FA	0011 0001	+49	31
1111 1011	−5	FB	0011 0010	+50	32
1111 1100	−4	FC	0011 0011	+51	33
1111 1101	−3	FD	0011 0100	+52	34
1111 1110	−2	FE	0011 0101	+53	35
1111 1111	−1	FF	0011 0110	+54	36
0000 0000	0	00	0011 0111	+55	37
0000 0001	+1	01	0011 1000	+56	38
0000 0010	+2	02	0011 1001	+57	39
0000 0011	+3	03	0011 1010	+58	3A
0000 0100	+4	04	0011 1011	+59	3B
0000 0101	+5	05	0011 1100	+60	3C
0000 0110	+6	06	0011 1101	+61	3D
0000 0111	+7	07	0011 1110	+62	3E
0000 1000	+8	08	0011 1111	+63	3F
0000 1001	+9	09	0100 0000	+64	40
0000 1010	+10	0A	0100 0001	+65	41
0000 1011	+11	0B	0100 0010	+66	42
0000 1100	+12	0C	0100 0011	+67	43
0000 1101	+13	0D	0100 0100	+68	44
0000 1110	+14	0E	0100 0101	+69	45
0000 1111	+15	0F	0100 0110	+70	46
0001 0000	+16	10	0100 0111	+71	47
0001 0001	+17	11	0100 1000	+72	48
0001 0010	+18	12	0100 1001	+73	49
0001 0011	+19	13	0100 1010	+74	4A
0001 0100	+20	14	0100 1011	+75	4B
0001 0101	+21	15	0100 1100	+76	4C
0001 0110	+22	16	0100 1101	+77	4D
0001 0111	+23	17	0100 1110	+78	4E
0001 1000	+24	18	0100 1111	+79	4F
0001 1001	+25	19	0101 0000	+80	50
0001 1010	+26	1A	0101 0001	+81	51
0001 1011	+27	1B	0101 0010	+82	52
0001 1100	+28	1C	0101 0011	+83	53
0001 1101	+29	1D	0101 0100	+84	54
0001 1110	+30	1E	0101 0101	+85	55
0001 1111	+31	1F	0101 0110	+86	56
0010 0000	+32	20	0101 0111	+87	57
0010 0001	+33	21	0101 1000	+88	58
0010 0010	+34	22	0101 1001	+89	59
0010 0011	+35	23	0101 1010	+90	5A
0010 0100	+36	24	0101 1011	+91	5B

TABLE 2.5.1 (*Continued*)

Binary	Decimal	Hexadecimal	Binary	Decimal	Hexadecimal
0101 1100	+92	5C	0110 1110	+110	6E
0101 1101	+93	5D	0110 1111	+111	6F
0101 1110	+94	5E	0111 0000	+112	70
0101 1111	+95	5F	0111 0001	+113	71
0110 0000	+96	60	0111 0010	+114	72
0110 0001	+97	61	0111 0011	+115	73
0110 0010	+98	62	0111 0100	+116	74
0110 0011	+99	63	0111 0101	+117	75
0110 0100	+100	64	0111 0110	+118	76
0110 0101	+101	65	0111 0111	+119	77
0110 0110	+102	66	0111 1000	+120	78
0110 0111	+103	67	0111 1001	+121	79
0110 1000	+104	68	0111 1010	+122	7A
0110 1001	+105	69	0111 1011	+123	7B
0110 1010	+106	6A	0111 1100	+124	7C
0110 1011	+107	6B	0111 1101	+125	7D
0110 1100	+108	6C	0111 1110	+126	7E
0110 1101	+109	6D	0111 1111	+127	7F

number has no positive counterpart. This isn't too surprising when we realize that 0, considered a positive number, is taking up one of the positive bit patterns, leaving one fewer for the rest of the positive numbers.

EXAMPLE 2.5.1

Without consulting Table 2.5.1, identify the numbers 0110 1100 and A7 as positive or negative signed numbers.

Solution

We look at the sign bit (bit 7, in this case). 0110 1100 has a 0 in the sign bit, so it's positive. The binary equivalent of A7 (1010 0111) has a 1 in the sign bit, thus it's negative.

Answer: 0110 1100, positive; A7, negative

We can formulate a rule for hexadecimal numbers so that they don't have to be converted into binary each time we want to known their sign. From the last example we found out that an A in the most significant hexadecimal digit meant a negative number, because an A has a 1 in the most significant bit of its binary equivalent. Thus all the other hexadecimal digits whose binary equivalents have a 1 in the most significant bit will cause a hexadecimal number to be negative. These digits are 8 through F. We can say, then, that *any hexadecimal number having 8 through F for its most significant digit (MSD) represents a negative value in signed binary notation.* Thus the number C2 is negative; 2C is positive.

For now, to find the decimal equivalent of a negative binary number, we must consult Table 2.5.1. We'll be working more with signed binary numbers in Chapter 8, where we'll see a more systematic way of converting a negative binary (or hexadecimal) number to its decimal equivalent.

There are other number codes besides those discussed in this chapter. One that's sometimes used is the octal system, which is base eight. Octal won't be discussed in this book, because it isn't especially convenient to use with the 6800.

In the next chapter we'll see that other kinds of data besides numbers can have binary codes.

REVIEW QUESTIONS

1. What do we mean by the **base ten** number system? What is a **base**, and what is another name for it? What is a **digit**?
2. What three number systems will we be using? List their bases and digits.
3. Does 10 always mean ten? Explain.
4. What is **positional notation**? Give an example in base ten.
5. Give examples of the **least** and **most significant digits** in a decimal number.
6. What does **binary** mean? What is **binary representation**? What is a **bit**?
7. What is a **flip-flop**? Why do computers use the **base two** number system? What does **toggle** mean?
8. Count from zero to sixteen in binary.
9. How many bits are in a **byte**? A **nibble**?
10. What is a computer's **data word**? **Address word**? How long are the 6800's data and address words?
11. How do we know how many values can be represented by a given set of bits? How many locations can be addressed with a 16-bit address word?
12. What does the abbreviation K mean? What does ''64K'' mean? What is a kilobyte? A megabyte?
13. Express 8 bits of a binary number in positional notation, describing each bit as a power of two, as a bit number, and as the power of two evaluated in decimal.
18. Explain how to convert from binary to decimal and from decimal to binary.
19. What is **binary coded decimal** (BCD) representation? How is it similar to binary? How is it different?
20. What binary values aren't valid in BCD? Why?
21. How many BCD nibbles would be needed to express the decimal number 10?
22. Explain how to convert from decimal to BCD and vice versa.
23. Explain why BCD is wasteful of digits, and why it is nevertheless used.
24. Why must we be careful to specify whether a certain number is in BCD or in binary?
25. Explain how to convert from BCD to binary and vice versa.
26. What is the **hexadecimal** number system? What is **hexadecimal representation**?
27. How can we program microcomputers in hexadecimal when the microcomputer needs the information in binary?
28. What is the maximum number of hexadecimal digits that we'll need here? Explain.
29. Use positional notation to describe a 4-digit hexadecimal number.
30. Explain how to convert from hexadecimal to binary and vice versa.

31. Explain how to convert from hexadecimal to decimal and vice versa.
32. Explain how to convert from hexadecimal to BCD and vice versa.
33. What do we mean by **unsigned** and **signed** binary numbers? How many signed binary numbers can be represented in 1 byte? What are their decimal equivalents?
34. Can we express decimal +128 using 1 byte of signed binary numbers? Explain.
35. How can we identify a signed binary or hexadecimal number as positive or negative?

EXERCISES

Set A (answers at back of book)

1. What is the value of 10 in the base eight number system?
2. Write these decimal numbers in base ten positional notation:
   a. 25   b. 99,999   c. 4
3. The 68000 microprocessor, related to the 6800, has a 16-bit data word and a 24-bit address word. (a) How many decimal values can be represented by its data word? (b) How many bytes can be addressed, if each address represents a byte?
4. Write the binary number 1001 1111 in positional notation.
5. Give the range, in decimal, of each binary number having the following number of bits: (Example: a 2-bit number has a range of 0–3)
   a. 3 bits   b. 4 bits   c. 6 bits   d. 10 bits
   e. 8 bits
6. How many bits would be needed to represent these decimal numbers?
   a. 16K   b. 144   c. 5000
7. Write 8-bit binary numbers that have these characteristics:
   a. a 1 in bits 7, 3, and 2, and the rest 0s
   b. a 1 in the 8's place and the rest 0s
   c. a 1 in the 32's place, the 4's place, and the 1's place
   d. a 1 in all bits except bit 5
   e. a 1 in all bits that represent odd-numbered powers of two
8. Convert these numbers from binary to decimal representation:
   a. 0000 0111   b. 0010 1010   c. 1100 1100
   d. 0001 1000   e. 1111 1111
9. Convert these numbers from decimal to binary representation:
   a.   8   b. 33   c. 19   d. 222   e. 69
10. Which bit should be examined to tell whether a number in binary representation is odd or even?
11. Convert these decimal numbers to BCD:
    a. 496   b. 78   c. 5280
12. Convert these BCD numbers to decimal:
    a. 0001 0101   b. 1000 0111 0110   c. 0100 1001
13. Assume that the numbers in Exercise 12 are binary, and convert them to decimal. Compare your answers with those of Exercise 12.
14. Which of these numbers could not be interpreted as BCD numbers? Explain.
    a. 0100 0011   b. 1010 0011
    c. 0111 1110   d. 0110 1001

15. Convert these BCD numbers to binary:
    a. 0110 1000   b. 0111 0111
16. Convert these binary numbers to BCD:
    a. 1101 0001   b. 1111 1101
17. Convert these binary numbers to hexadecimal:
    a. 0010 1100   b. 1111 1010 1101 1110
    c. 1101 0000
18. Convert these hexadecimal numbers to binary:
    a. 1A   b. 40BD   c. 0F
19. Convert these hexadecimal numbers to decimal:
    a. F3   b. 2A47   c. 0A
20. Convert these decimal numbers to hexadecimal:
    a. 255   b. 83   c. 632
21. Convert the values in Exercise 19 to BCD.
22. Convert the binary number 1011 0111 to:
    a. decimal   b. BCD   c. hexadecimal
23. Convert the decimal number 456 to:
    a. binary   b. BCD   c. hexadecimal
24. Convert the hexadecimal number EA to:
    a. binary   b. decimal   c. BCD
25. Convert the BCD number 0110 0111 to:
    a. decimal   b. binary   c. hexadecimal
26. What is the smallest negative 16-bit binary number? What are its decimal and hexadecimal equivalents?
27. Without consulting Table 2.5.1, identify the numbers 9C and 1100 1111 as positive or negative.
28. Consult Table 2.5.1 and express the decimal number −123 in binary and hexadecimal.

EXERCISES

Set B (answers not given)

1. How do we write "twelve" in base twelve?
2. Write these decimal numbers in positional notation:
   a. 439   b. 88   c. 4,976
3. The 8086 microprocessor can represent 65,536 data values and can address 1 Mbyte of locations. (a) How many lines are in its data bus? (b) How many lines are in its address bus?
4. Write the binary number 1111 0110 in positional notation.
5. Give the range, in decimal, of each binary representation having the following number of bits: (Example: a 2-bit number has a range of 0–3)
   a. 5 bits   b. 7 bits   c. 9 bits
   d. 11 bits   e. 16 bits
6. How many bits would be needed to represent these decimal numbers?
   a. 512   b. 32K   c. 822
7. Write 8-bit binary numbers that have these characteristics:
   a. a 1 in bits 0, 4, and 5 and the rest 0s

   b. a 0 in all odd-numbered bits

   c. a 1 in the most and least significant bits and the rest 0s

   d. a 0 in the 64's place, the 16's place, and the 1's place and the rest 1s

   e. a 0 in all bits except bit 7

8. Convert these numbers from binary to decimal representation:

   a. 1111 0000   **b.** 1001 1001   **c.** 0100 1100

   d. 0101 1111   **e.** 0011 1110

9. Convert these numbers from decimal to binary representation:

   a. 167   **b.** 44   **c.** 22

   d. 102   **e.** 244

10. What is the limit of decimal values that can be expressed in the 6800's data word?

11. Convert these decimal numbers to BCD:

   a. 807   **b.** 12   **c.** 1345

12. Convert these BCD numbers to decimal:

   a. 1001 1000   **b.** 0111 1000 0001

   c. 0110 0000

13. Assume that the numbers in Exercise 12 are binary, and convert them to decimal.

14. Which of these numbers could not be interpreted as BCD numbers? Explain.

   a. 1110 0000   **b.** 1000 0000 1000

   c. 1111 0000   **d.** 0011 1100

15. Convert these BCD numbers to binary:

   a. 1001 0110   **b.** 0001 0111 0100

16. Convert these binary numbers to BCD:

   a. 1011 0011   **b.** 1000 0111

17. Convert these binary numbers to hexadecimal:

   a. 1101 1110 1010 1111   **b.** 1100 0011   **c.** 0011 0011

18. Convert these hexadecimal numbers to binary:

   a. 7C   **b.** ACED   **c.** B9

19. Convert these hexadecimal numbers to decimal:

   a. 2B   **b.** 9D07   **c.** DF

20. Convert these decimal numbers to hexadecimal:

   a. 63   **b.** 977   **c.** 34

21. Convert the values in Exercise 19 to BCD.

22. Convert the binary number 1001 1001 to:

   a. decimal   **b.** BCD   **c.** hexadecimal

23. Convert the decimal number 1097 to:

   a. binary   **b.** BCD   **c.** hexadecimal

24. Convert the hexadecimal number AD to:

   a. binary   **b.** decimal   **c.** BCD

25. Convert the BCD number 0111 1000 to:

   a. decimal   **b.** binary   **c.** hexadecimal

26. What is the largest positive 16-bit binary number? What are its decimal and hexadecimal equivalents?

27. Without consulting Table 2.5.1, identify the numbers 7F and 1000 0000 as positive or negative.

28. Consult Table 2.5.1 and express the signed binary number 1111 0000 in decimal and in hexadecimal.

3 Nonnumerical Computer Codes

LEARNING OBJECTIVES

After having completed this chapter, you should be able to:

1. Give a definition, explanation, or example for each of these: *character code, ASCII code, control character, even parity, odd parity, parity bit, serial, interface circuitry, don't care, control word, register, accumulator, working register, OP code, operation code, instruction code, instruction set, load, store, operation, operand, instruction, high-order byte, low-order byte, program address, data address.*
2. Use the *ASCII* chart to convert between binary numbers and characters, with and without parity.
3. Explain how a bit may be used as a single electrical switch or a byte may be used as a group of switches.
4. Provide or interpret a control word for a given hardware control scheme.
5. Explain what information is contained in an OP code.
6. Explain why we need two program words to store an address.
7. Interpret a binary number in any of six ways.
8. Explain how a microcomputer interprets a binary number.
9. Given a program with each instruction marked, tell the function of the number in each program address.

In Chapter 1 we've hinted at the tremendous versatility of microprocessors. In Chapter 2 we emphasized the number codes that let us communicate with them. Although microprocessors work strictly in binary representation and treat all data as numerical, they actually perform many functions that aren't numerical. If we want a microprocessor to perform nonnumerical functions, we, the users, must translate our nonnumerical functions into numbers.

For example, to use a microcomputer as a text editor, we need a code that translates the characters on our typewriter keyboard into binary numbers. We need another code if we want a microcomputer to do household control of heating, security, and so on. Even the program that tells the microcomputer what to do has code numbers for the individual instructions.

In this chapter we'll look at three nonnumerical computer codes.

3.1 CHARACTER CODES

What if we had a typewriter that had only numerals and no letters? Could we still use it to communicate with other humans in English? We could make up a code such as $A = 1$, $B = 2$, and so on. As long as the person we were communicating with knew the code too, we'd have no trouble. In the same way, we can have a **character code** for binary numbers.

The ASCII

How many bits do we need? Let's take a look at what we might want to represent. First, we'll require 26 upper case letters and 26 lower case letters. Then, we might want about 25 miscellaneous characters (the common punctuation marks, and $, #, %, &, and so on.) And we need 10 numerals (0–9). That's a total roughly of 90 characters to represent. Looking back at the powers of two table (Table 2.2.2), we see that 6 bits gives us 64 values (not enough). Seven bits gives us 128 values (more than enough).

Many character codes have been developed. We'll look at only one: the ASCII. **ASCII** stands for **American Standard Code for Information Interchange**, which is a

TABLE 3.1.1   ASCII Chart

Most Significant Digit		0	1	2	3	4	5	6	7
	0	NUL	DLE	SP	0	@	P		p
	1	SOH	DC1	!	1	A	Q	a	q
	2	STX	DC2	''	2	B	R	b	r
	3	ETX	DC3	#	3	C	S	c	s
	4	EOT	DC4	$	4	D	T	d	t
	5	ENQ	NAK	%	5	E	U	e	u
	6	ACK	SYN	&	6	F	V	f	v
Least Significant	7	BEL	ETB	'	7	G	W	g	w
Digit	8	BS	CAN	(	8	H	X	h	x
	9	HT	EM	)	9	I	Y	i	y
	A	LF	SUB	*	:	J	Z	j	z
	B	VT	ESC	+	;	K	[	k	{
	C	FF	FS	'	<	L	/	l	/
	D	CR	GS	—	=	M	]	m	}
	E	SO	RS	.	>	N	↑	n	≈
	F	SI	US	/	?	O	→	o	DEL

7-bit character code. Table 3.1.1 shows ASCII in hexadecimal representation. A 2-digit hexadecimal value means 8 bits, and ASCII is a 7-bit code. To fill out the remaining bit in the byte, we set the most significant bit to zero.

To use the chart to find the binary equivalent of a character, we first locate the character on the chart. Then we read up its column to find the most significant hexadecimal digit. Reading horizontally to the left across a row gives the least significant digit. Then we can translate this 2-digit hexadecimal number into binary.

EXAMPLE 3.1.1

Find the ASCII equivalents in hexadecimal and in binary for a capital S.

Solution

First, locate capital S on the chart. Read up its column to find the most significant digit (5, in this case). Next, read across the row to the left to find the least significant digit (3, in this case). Put the 2 digits together (53) and translate into binary.

Answer: 53 in hexadecimal; 0101 0011 in binary

To find the character associated with a binary or hexadecimal number, we do the opposite. We use the most significant hexadecimal digit to locate the character's column and the least significant digit to locate its row. Where these intersect, we'll find the character. Figure 3.1.1 shows some ASCII messages and their English translations.

EXAMPLE 3.1.2

What character is represented by the binary number 0010 1011?

Solution

First, convert the number to hexadecimal: 2B. Next, find the column with 2 above it. Then, find the row with B opposite it. Find the character at the intersection. (+, in this case.)

Answer: A plus sign (+)

FIGURE 3.1.1   Some ASCII Messages and Their English Translations

0100 1000	48		0100 1001	49	
0100 0101	45		0010 0111	27	
0100 1100	4C	HELP!	0100 1101	4D	
0101 0000	50		0010 0000	20	I'M OK.
0010 0001	21		0100 1111	4F	
			0100 1011	4B	
			0010 1110	2E	

Now that we know how to use the ASCII chart, we can notice a few things. First, because the ASCII uses only 7 bits, the most significant nibble of the binary number has values only between 0000 to 0111. Because the chart assumes a 0 in bit 7, the most significant hexadecimal digit on the chart is never above 7.

Next, we see that the type of character can be identified by its most significant hexadecimal digit. Working our way across the chart from left to right, we come to columns 0 and 1. These columns are **control characters**, which perform functions but don't result in anything that is typed. Some obvious ones are CR, which causes a carriage return, and BEL, which causes a bell sound.

Column 2 contains special characters that are neither letters nor numbers. Column 3 contains the decimal numerals 0–9, plus some special characters left over from column 2. We see that the least significant hexadecimal digit of the numerals is the same as its decimal value. Thus 30 is the ASCII equivalent of 0, 31 and 32 are 1 and 2, and so on.

Columns 4 and 5 contain upper case (capital) letters, with a few special characters added to fill out the columns. The numerical values of the least significant digits of the letters increase with their positions in the alphabet. Thus A is 41, B is 42, C is 43, and so on. This ordering lets us use a computer to alphabetize words (for instance, B is greater than A) or search a list of words for a certain word. These techniques and others are used in computerized text editing.

Finally, columns 6 and 7 contain lower case letters with more special characters to fill the spaces. The lower case letters have the same least significant digit as the corresponding capital letters, and the most significant digit is 2 greater than that of the corresponding capital letter. Thus A is 41 and a is 61, B is 42 and b is 62, and so on.

Parity

Sometimes the idle bit (bit 7) is used to adjust the parity of ASCII characters. A computer word has **even parity** if it has an even number of 1 bits; it has **odd parity** if it has an odd number of 1 bits. Thus the number 0110 1111 (6F) has six 1 bits and therefore even parity; the number 0001 1010 has three 1 bits and therefore, odd parity.

If we choose, we can declare even or odd parity for a system that uses ASCII characters. If we choose even parity, then the **parity bit** (bit 7) is used to make an extra 1 bit if it is needed. Thus with even parity the ASCII 001 0101 would become 1001 0101 (95 in hexadecimal). In odd parity the ASCII 110 1111 would become 1110 1111 (EF). Notice that when we establish parity, the high-order hexadecimal digit can be greater than 7. But the extra 1 in bit 7 doesn't change the character. ASCII characters 0110 1111 (6F) and 1110 1111 (EF) are both o; the former has even and the latter has odd parity.

Parity is useful as an error check. Many computers have typewriter keyboards, teletypewriters, or video terminals attached to them. The terminals have translators for codes such as ASCII so that the information given to them can be converted to the binary representation that the microcomputer needs. ASCII characters are often transmitted through wires in **serial** form (1 bit after another). Errors in transmission can occur, and an error of a single bit can cause a wrong character to be interpreted. If parity has been established, the receiver looks for each character to have that parity. If one doesn't, then an error has been made and the receiver can ask that the message be repeated. This method catches all errors of a single bit per byte, but not 2-bit errors. Sometimes a ninth bit may be added to memory words to provide parity for 8-bit data bytes.

3.2 INDIVIDUAL BIT ASSIGNMENTS

So far, we've talked about groups of bits (bytes or nibbles) as units in various codes. One BCD or hexadecimal digit is 1 nibble of binary representation; 1 ASCII character is essentially 1 byte of binary representation. But a bit is a single entity, and it's perfectly valid to use a single bit to represent almost anything we want. Bits in a microcomputer are usually arranged in bytes, so we have our choice of using from 1 to 8 bits in a single byte for individual purposes. First, let's see how a single bit could be used.

A bit as an electrical switch

In Chapter 1 we said that a computer represents a bit value in a single switch, or flip-flop. By the same token, we can use the value of a computer's bit to turn an external switch off or on.

In the discussions that follow, and throughout the rest of the book, we'll be talking about controlling external devices with a microcomputer. This involves connecting parts of the data and address buses to the devices through appropriate electrical interface circuitry. By **interface circuitry**, we mean an assembly of electrical circuit elements that provide the necessary connection between a microcomputer and an external device. The circuitry itself could be different for each particular device, and we'll represent it with a box labeled "interface circuitry" rather than attempting to define it. The purpose of our discussions is to show how to program the microcomputer to control these devices. The design of the interface circuitry itself is another topic and is beyond the scope of this book. For now, we should realize that we probably can't connect one of a microcomputer's flip-flops directly to an electrical device without the possibility of serious damage to the computer, the device, or both.

Figure 3.2.1 shows a data byte at an arbitrary memory location whose address is 00F0. Data line 0 is connected through its interface circuitry to an electric light switch. We can turn the light on by storing a 1 in bit 0 of location 00F0, and turn the light off by storing a 0 in bit 0.

FIGURE 3.2.1   A Single Bit May Be Used to Control a Device

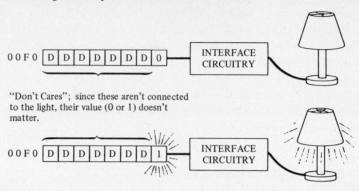

"Don't Cares"; since these aren't connected
to the light, their value (0 or 1) doesn't
matter.

In the figure the d's in bits 1–7 are called **don't cares** because we don't care what's in them. So far, bit 0 is the only bit at address 00F0 whose data line is connected to anything external, thus its contents are the only contents that matter. We could make the don't cares all 0s so that light off would be 00 in hexadecimal and light on would be 01 in hexadecimal. If the don't cares were all 1s, then light off would be FE and light on would be FF. Any even number stored at this address would mean light off, and any odd number would mean light on.

When we use a computer to turn a light off and on, we're using the computer for output—it is controlling some device in the outside world. We can wire a memory location for input too. To input a 1, we want to cause a high voltage (around 5 volts) to appear on a wire connected to the bit. And to input a 0, we want a low voltage (around 0 volts) on the wire. If we connected a 5-volt source to data line 0 through a switch, then the computer would receive a 0 in bit 0 if the switch were off and a 1 if the switch were on. If that switch were the only device we had wired at that address, then bits 1–7 would be don't cares, too. Figure 3.2.2 shows a bit wired for input from a switch.

FIGURE 3.2.2   A Switch Connected to a 5-Volt Source Can Input a Binary Value of 0 or 1

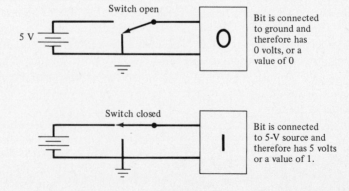

Multiple bits

In order to be able to control many lights with a microcomputer, we could wire each light to 1 data line of a separate location. Or we could wire each light to 1 data line of the same location. If 8 lights were wired each to 1 data line at the same location, then FF would turn on all the lights and 00 would turn them all off. To turn on some, but not all, of the lights, we would just store a 1 in each appropriate bit. For instance, 80 would turn on only the light wired to data line 7.

The uses of individual bits in a byte don't even have to be related to each other. We could wire all 8 data lines, for example, to high power electronic switches to control all the devices shown in Figure 3.2.3. The nighttime situation of all appliances off, window shades down, and bathroom thermostat turned down to 55 degrees would be represented by all zeros, or 00 in hexadecimal. Storing F2 at this location (00F0) would turn on the bedroom light, start the coffee, turn the bathroom thermostat up to 68, turn the TV on to the morning news, and raise the window shades. If your microcomputer were programmed to store F2 in location 00F0 a half-hour before you wanted to get up, you could wake up and watch the news, then get up to a warm bathroom and a pot of coffee. The word (F2, in this case) stored in a location used for control is called the **control word**.

FIGURE 3.2.3 Example: Control of Individual Devices

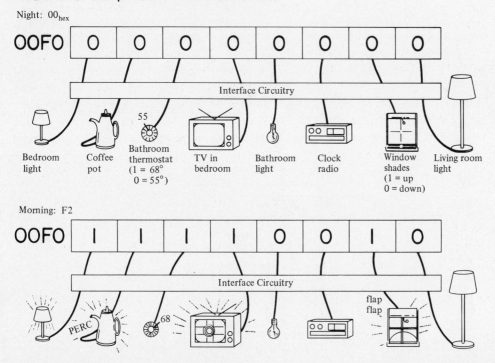

We could use 8 data lines for input, too, as well as for the output we've described. In later chapters we'll see some specific examples of input. Now, it's important just to understand that we, the users, can let a bit, several bits, a nibble, or a byte stand for anything we choose, even though the computer interprets a byte as an 8-bit binary number.

3.3 OPERATION CODES (OP CODES)

We've said that everything—even instructions—must be given to the microprocessor in binary representation. This means another code, in which a given 1-byte binary number stands for a given operation.

Suppose you have wired the devices in Figure 3.2.3 through appropriate interface circuitry to data lines at location 00F0. You want to program your home computer to activate these devices at 6:30 in the morning. A microprocessor can keep track of time, so at 6:30 it could activate these devices by placing the control word F2 in location 00F0. (You could do this yourself using the microcomputer's monitor. But the whole point is to activate the devices while you're still asleep.) You need a program to get the microprocessor to store F2 in location 00F0. What would such a program be like?

A program stored in memory

Figure 3.3.1 shows a hexadecimal program, which would be stored in memory as a sequence of binary numbers. Executing this program would cause the microprocessor to store F2 in location 00F0.

In the 6800, and in some other microprocessors, there isn't any way of moving a number directly from one memory location to another. Many such microprocessors use one of their internal registers as temporary storage in between. A

FIGURE 3.3.1   A Program That Causes the Microprocessor to Place the Value F2 in Location 00F0

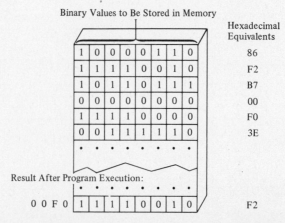

register is a physical location that can contain a binary number. Under this definition, memory locations are also registers. But normally, when we use the word *register*, we mean registers that are internal to the MPU.

The 6800 has internal registers that can be accessed by the user. Two of these are 8-bit registers called Accumulator A (ACCA) and Accumulator B (ACCB). An **accumulator** is a working register. A **working register** does more than just store a number. For example, an accumulator is often used to accumulate results (hence the origin of the name). In the 6800, memory-to-memory data transfers are usually done by using one of the accumulators (A or B) as a "go-between." That is, the data is first copied from a memory location into an accumulator and then copied from the accumulator to another memory location.

The program of Figure 3.3.1 doesn't mean much to a human being who's reading it, just as the English directions for building a typewriter table wouldn't mean anything to a microprocessor. But the microprocessor does understand the program. To the microprocessor the program means this sequence of steps:

1. Copy a number (in this case, F2) from location 0101 into accumulator A.
2. Copy the number in accumulator A (in this case, F2) into location 00F0.
3. Wait.

Now, we'll look at this program rather closely and see what these hexadecimal numbers mean.

Hexadecimal OP codes

To **load** means to copy a number from a memory location into a register. The hexadecimal number 86 means *Load accumulator A with a value that follows in the next memory location*. This number (86) is a code for a particular operation and is called an **OP code**, an **operation code**, or an **instruction code**. Each microprocessor has a set of operations that it can perform. This set of operations, with corresponding OP codes, make up the microprocessor's **instruction set**. There are 197 OP codes in the 6800's instruction set, listed in Appendix A.

To **store** means to copy a number from a register into a memory location. The hexadecimal number B7 means "Store the contents of accumulator A in a memory

TABLE 3.3.1   Some 6800 OP Codes

Hexadecimal OP Code	Meaning
86	"Load a value into accumulator A. Read the next word to get the value to be loaded."
B7	"Store the contents of accumulator A in a memory location. Read the next two words to get the address of the location."
3E	"Wait."
B6	"Load accumulator A with the contents of a memory location. Read the next two words to get the address of the location."
BB	"Add the contents of a memory location to the contents of accumulator A, and put the results into accumulator A. Read the next two words to get the address of the location.

location whose address follows in the next location." The number 3E means "wait." These, and a few other hexadecimal OP codes, are shown in Table 3.3.1.

Numbers in a microcomputer program

In Chapter 1 we saw a set of instructions for building a typewriter table. In it, each instruction is a complete sentence, which has the subject "you," understood. Each sentence has a verb, which tells what to do ("Remove...") and what to do it *to* ("...table top..."). It also tells *where* to find things ("...from box..."). So we have a sentence with a subject, a verb, a direct object, and an indirect object.

In the program instructions of Figure 3.3.1, each instruction is also a complete sentence, which has the subject "you" understood ("you," in this case, is the microprocessor). Each instruction has a verb, which tells the MPU what to do. The instruction's verb is called the **operation**, and the code that we use to describe the operation is the OP code. Like an English instruction, each microcomputer instruction may have a direct object and/or an indirect object. The name for the object, direct *or* indirect, is the **operand**. An operand may be data itself (a "direct" object) or an address that tells where the data is (an "indirect" object). A microcomputer **instruction** consists of an operation plus zero to two operands.

A microcomputer instruction, like an English instruction, may consist of varying numbers of words. For the 6800, a word is 1-byte long and an instruction may consist of 1, 2, or 3 bytes. The first instruction in Figure 3.3.1 consists of 2 bytes: 86 and F2. This instruction translates into English as:

Load accumulator A with the value F2.

Here, we have two operands: accumulator A (an indirect object) and F2 (a direct object). The OP code itself, 86, contains this information:

1. This is a "load" instruction.
2. Accumulator A is the operand to be loaded.
3. The instruction contains one word in addition to the OP code. This word is the other operand (the value to be loaded), and it's a direct object.

When one of the operands is an accumulator, this information is part of the OP code, as well as the information as to *which* accumulator (A or B). For nearly every instruction that uses accumulator A there is an equivalent instruction for accumulator B. The OP code, C6, for accumulator B corresponds to 86 for accumulator A.

The next instruction has three words: B7, 00, and F0. This instruction translates into English as:

Store the value in accumulator A in memory location 00F0.

Here, we have two operands, accumulator A and location 00F0 (both indirect objects). The OP code, B7, contains this information:

1. This is a "store" instruction.

2. Accumulator A is the operand to be stored from.

3. The instruction has two words in addition to the OP code. The next two words contain an address, which is the second operand (an indirect object).

In this instruction B7 is the OP code and 00 and F0 make up the operand. We see that two words are needed for a single operand if that operand is a memory location. Addresses of memory locations are 2 bytes long, and our data word is only 1 byte long. We can't store 2 bytes' worth of information in a space that's only 1 byte long. So we store it in pieces. The leftmost 2 hexadecimal digits (00, in this case) we call the **high-order byte** of the address and the next 2 (F0, in this case), the **low-order byte** of the address. The 6800 expects to find the high-order byte of the address in the second word of the instruction (immediately after the OP code) and the low-order byte in the third and final word of the instruction. Figure 3.3.2 illustrates the way in which an address is stored in a program.

The last instruction, 3E, means "wait" and has no operand. In English, too, the instruction, wait, has no object.

Figure 3.3.3 illustrates the function of each program word in this stored program. In Chapter 1 we said that a microcomputer program occupies consecutive

FIGURE 3.3.2   A 2-Byte Address Must Be Stored in Two 1-Byte Memory Locations

The Address of the Memory
Location (2 bytes long)

A Memory Location
(contains 1 byte)

0 0 F 0

A 2-byte address is too large to store in one 1-byte memory location.

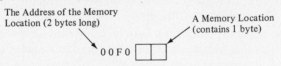

0 1 0 1   0 0   F 0

So we break the address into two parts—

and store it in two consecutive memory locations.

0 1 0 1   0 0

0 1 0 2   F 0

FIGURE 3.3.3   Function of Each Value in a Stored Program

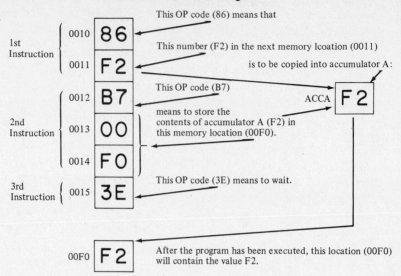

locations in memory. In Figure 3.3.3 we've chosen to begin our program at location 0010 and to occupy consecutive locations to 0015. In this case 00F0 is a location apart from the program. Now, we can make a distinction between a **program address**, whose location contains a word that's part of a program instruction, and a **data address**, whose location contains the value (the data) to be operated on by the program.

The instructions for building a typewriter table are located on paper. To build the table using the instructions we must use real quantities (the parts). The parts aren't on the paper with the instructions; the parts are somewhere else (in the box). In the same way, the microcomputer's instructions for executing a program are in a set of memory locations. To execute the program using the instructions, the microprocessor has to use real quantities (the data). Usually, the data isn't located in the set of memory locations with the instructions; the data is somewhere else (in different memory locations). Program addresses should be sequential, but data addresses don't have to be. The only requirement for a data address is that it mustn't interfere with the execution of the program.

3.4   INTERPRETATION OF BINARY DATA

We've seen some numerical and some nonnumerical codes. Using these codes, we could interpret a binary (or hexadecimal) number in any of these ways:

1. as a pure binary number, with a decimal or hexadecimal equivalent
2. as an ASCII character

3. as individual bits used for external control
4. as an OP code
5. as an operand (address or data)
6. as a BCD number

For example, let's take the binary number 1011 1011. All these meanings are valid for this number:

1. the binary number itself (equivalent to decimal 187, or hexadecimal BB)
2. ASCII for a semicolon (;), with even parity
3. for the setup of Figure 3.2.3: bedroom light on, bathroom thermostat to 68, TV on, bathroom light on, window shades up, living room light on
4. an OP code (see Table 3.3.1) meaning to get a number from a memory location, add it to the contents of accumulator A, where the result is accumulated.
5. half an address (recall that addresses are 2 bytes long)

Note that we couldn't interpret BB as a BCD number, because the bit patterns in both digits are invalid in BCD.

EXAMPLE 3.4.1

Give as many interpretations as possible for the binary number 1000 0110.

Solution

We go through the preceding list and use as many values as possible. First, we find numerical equivalents: 134 in decimal, 86 in hexadecimal. Next, looking at the ASCII chart (Figure 3.1.1), we see that 86 can only be an ASCII character if the parity bit is set. Without the parity bit, it's 06. This corresponds to the control character ACK (acknowledge). So 86 can be interpreted as the control character ACK, with odd parity. For the setup of Figure 3.2.3, the bedroom light and clock radio would be on and the window shades up. Looking at Table 3.3.1, we find 86 at the top of the OP code list, meaning to load a value into accumulator A. The number 86 could be either the high- or low-order byte of an address. As a BCD number: 86 in decimal

Answer: Decimal 134; hexadecimal 86; ASCII ACK (odd parity); bedroom light and clock radio on, window shades up; OP code for "Load accumulator A with a value"; half of an address; BCD 86

With all these possibilities, how does a microprocessor decide which of these meanings a given binary number might have? First, for some possibilities, the decision is already made in hardware or software. If a number code (like hexadecimal or BCD) is used, then a method of translating is usually provided. Terminals with typewriter keyboards have translators, called encoders and decoders, to handle

ASCII. If a word is to be used to control external devices, this decision is made when the bits at that address are wired, through appropriate circuitry, to the devices.Thus all that's left for the computer to decide is whether a binary number in a program means an OP code, part of an address, or a value. As it turns out, even this isn't much of a decision. We'll see why by looking again at a familiar English example.

Just as the binary number 86 could be interpreted as an OP code or an operand (address or data), we have many words in English that can be used as either verbs or nouns. Take the word *program*, for example:

Verb. I will *program* the microcomputer.
Noun. This is a microcomputer *program*.

If someone asked us, out of context, whether the word *program* were a verb or a noun, we wouldn't be able to answer. In the same way, the function of a binary number in a program is determined by its context. The microcomputer doesn't look at a binary number singly to determine its function. It looks at the whole instruction, and each binary number is interpreted according to its context. Here are the rules of

FIGURE 3.4.1 Program to Add Two Numbers and Store the Answer

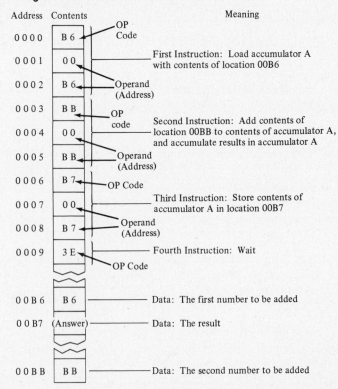

grammar for 6800 microprocessor instructions:

1. A program must begin with an instruction.
2. The first word in an instruction is an OP code. The OP code tells whether the instruction is 1, 2, or 3 words long.
3. In a three-word instruction, the word following the OP code is the high-order byte of an address. The next word is the low-order byte of the address.
4. In a two-word instruction, the word following the OP code may be either pure numerical data or the low-order byte of an address (more about this later).

Figure 3.4.1 is a program to add 2 numbers and store the result in a memory location. The function of each number, determined by its context, is shown in the figure. The data locations and their contents are also shown. The contents of data locations are always interpreted by the microprocessor as pure binary data. The user may attach other significance to numbers in data locations (such as the control word for the household devices), even though the microprocessor treats them as numbers.

To show how binary data is interpreted, we've used the same numerical values on purpose to mean different things. We used the number B6 in three ways: to represent an OP code (in program address 0000); to represent the low-order byte of an address (in program address 0002); and to represent pure numerical data corresponding to decimal 182 (in data location 00B6). The fact that this number has three different meanings according to its context in the program isn't a bit confusing to the microprocessor, and it shouldn't be to us either. Similarly, the number BB is used in three different ways, and the number B7, in two different ways.

EXAMPLE 3.4.2

The following is a program of an unspecified nature. Interpret each number as an OP code, part of an address, or pure numeric data.

PROGRAM ADDRESS   CONTENTS

1A00	7F	⎫
1A01	01	⎬ First instruction
1A02	9A	⎭
1A03	B6	⎫
1A04	01	⎬ Second instruction
1A05	9B	⎭
1A06	B7	⎫
1A07	01	⎬ Third instruction
1A08	9A	⎭
1A09	3E	Fourth instruction

DATA ADDRESS

| 019A | 9A |
| 019B | 9B |

Solution

The instructions are marked off for us, so we know how many bytes each contains. We know that the first number, 7F, is an OP code, even though it isn't on Table 3.3.1. A program must begin with an instruction, and an instruction must begin with an OP code. Therefore the first word in a program must be an OP code. This is a three-word instruction, thus 01 is the high-order byte of an address and 9A, the low-order byte. This brings us to the beginning of the next instruction, so B6 must be an OP code (we do find this in Table 3.3.1). This is another 3-word instruction, so the operand is an address: 01 is its high-order byte and 9B its low-order byte. For the next instruction, B7 is the OP code, and 01 and 9A make up its operand, which is an address. The last instruction is only one word long, and that word is an OP code, 3E.

Answer: 7F, OP code; 01, high-order byte of address; 9A, low-order byte of address; B6, OP code; 01, high-order byte of address; 9B, low-order byte of address; B7, OP code; 01, high-order byte of address; 9A, low-order byte of address; 3E, OP code

Note that in this example the 2 data locations, 019A and 019B, contain the values 9A and 9B. These values would be treated as data by the microprocessor, because they are contained in data locations. The values were made the same numerically as the low-order byte of the corresponding data address itself, for the purpose of illustration. When the values 9A and 9B appear in the context of the instructions given here, the microcomputer interprets them as low-order bytes of addresses.

In the next chapter we'll be taking a closer look at instructions and their components.

REVIEW QUESTIONS

1. Why do we need nonnumerical computer codes? Give some examples.
2. What do we mean by a **character code**? What character code will we use?
3. Why does ASCII use only 7 bits?
4. Explain how to use the ASCII chart to find the binary equivalent of a character or the character equivalent of a binary number.
5. Why is 7 the greatest value of the most significant hexadecimal digit on the ASCII chart?
6. What are **control characters**? Give a few examples.
7. Explain how the columns of the ASCII chart roughly classify the types of characters.
8. What is **even** and **odd parity**? a **parity bit**? What is parity used for?
9. Explain how the parity bit may affect the most significant hexadecimal digit of a 1-byte ASCII character.
10. How is a letter's position in the alphabet related to its ASCII representation?
11. What is meant by transmitting binary data in **serial** form?

12. Explain how a bit can represent an electrical switch.
13. What is **interface circuitry**? Why do we need it?
14. What are **don't cares**? Give an example. What values may a don't care have?
15. Explain how we could use a byte as a set of electrical switches. What is a **control word**?
16. Explain how we arrived at the control word of F2 for Figure 3.2.3.
17. What is a **register**? an **accumulator**? How many accumulators does the 6800 have? What is a **working register**?
18. Using the 6800, how do we cause a number to be copied from one memory location to another?
19. What sequence of steps is represented by the program of Figure 3.3.1?
20. What does **load** mean?
21. What is an **OP code**? What are some other names for it?
22. What is an **instruction set**? How many instructions are in the 6800's instruction set?
23. What does **store** mean?
24. What is a microcomputer **instruction**? How is it like an English instruction?
25. What is an **operation**? an **operand**? Compare these to parts of a sentence.
26. What information is contained in the OP code 86?
27. Explain the OP codes B7, 3E, B6, and BB.
28. What tells the microprocessor which accumulator to use?
29. How many words do we need to specify an address? Explain.
30. What do we mean by **high-order byte** and **low-order byte**?
31. What is the difference between a **data address** and a **program address**?
32. May we have an instruction with no operand? Give an example.
33. Name six ways that a binary number may be interpreted.
34. Explain how the microprocessor decides how to interpret a binary number.
35. What are the rules of grammar for microcomputer instructions?
36. Explain how the number B6 is used and interpreted in three different ways in Figure 3.4.1.

EXERCISES

SET A (answers at back of book)

1. For which of the ASCII characters A–Z does the code have the largest numerical value? the smallest?
2. Write these characters in increasing numerical order according to their ASCII representations: R, 5, $, C, J, 9, 2
3. How are upper case and lower case letters similar? How are they different?
4. Decode this ASCII message:

    54, 45, 53, 54, 49, 4E, 47, 3A, 20, 31, 2C, 32, 2C, 33, 2C, 34

5. Translate this message into ASCII: What's up, doc?
6. Adjust the numbers in Exercise 5 for (a) even parity and (b) for odd parity.
7. With reference to Figure 3.2.1, which of these values stored in location 00F0 would turn on the light?
    a. 34 b. 49 c. F0 d. 0F e. CA f. 27

8. Imagine that we have wired an electric light to bit 7 of an address and a buzzer to bit 5 of the same address.
   a. Which of the bits are don't cares?
   b. Give 2 numbers (in hexadecimal) that would turn on the light and the buzzer.
   c. Give 2 numbers (in hexadecimal) that would turn on the light but not the buzzer.

9. For the setup of Figure 3.2.3, we wish to program the computer so that the house looks "lived in" while we are away for a time. Write the hexadecimal word that would be stored in 00F0 for each of these situations:
   a. (6:00 A.M.) Turn on bedroom light, TV, pull up shades.
   b. (6:30 A.M.) Turn on bathroom light, turn off TV and bedroom light.
   c. (7:30 A.M.) Turn everything off, but leave window shades up.
   d. (7:00 P.M.) turn on living room light, pull down shades.
   e. (10:00 P.M.) Turn on bedroom light and TV, turn off living room light.
   f. (11:30 P.M.) Turn off TV, turn on bathroom light.
   g. (12:00 A.M.) Turn everything off.

10. With reference to Figure 3.2.3, tell what each of these control words does:
    a. E3 b. 0F c. 99

11. Give as many alternate interpretations as possible for each of these:
    a. The binary number 1011 0110 b. The ASCII for s

12. The following is a program of an unspecified nature. Interpret each number as an OP code, part of an address, or pure numeric data.

ADDRESS	CONTENTS	
0000	B6	
0001	B6	First instruction
0002	00	
0003	B0	
0004	B0	Second instruction
0005	00	
0006	B7	
0007	B7	Third instruction
0008	00	
0009	3E	Fourth instruction

DATA ADDRESSES

B000	1A	
B600	3F	
B700	25	

EXERCISES

SET B (answers not given)

1. Which hexadecimal digit should be checked so as to tell whether an ASCII character is a letter or a numeral? What value does this digit have for each?

2. Write these characters in increasing numerical order according to their ASCII representations: u, CR, 4, T, %, ?

3. Here is an ASCII message, using odd parity. Translate into English:

   CE, EF, 20, D0, 61, F2, 6B, E9, 6E, 67, AE

4. Translate this message into ASCII (no parity)

   Who's There?

5. Adjust the numbers in Exercise 3 for even parity.
6. Adjust the numbers in Exercise 4 for odd parity.
7. With reference to Figure 3.2.1, which of these values stored in location 00F0 would turn off the light?
   a. A3 b. 76 c. F0 d. 0F e. 49 f. CB
8. Imagine that we have wired bits 0, 1, and 2 of an address to a red, yellow, and green traffic light, respectively.
   a. Which bits are don't cares?
   b. Give 2 numbers that would turn on the red and yellow lights.
   c. Give 2 numbers that would turn on only the green light.
9. For the setup of Figure 3.2.3, give hexadecimal words to accomplish these:
   a. coffee pot on, window shades up, bathroom thermostat to 68
   b. living room light on, clock radio on, window shades down, bathroom thermostat to 55
   c. bathroom light on, clock radio on, window shades up, living room light on, bathroom thermostat to 55
10. With reference to Figure 3.2.3, tell what each of these control words does:
    a. A0 b. 05 c. BB
11. Give as many alternate interpretations as possible for each of these (ignore OP code interpretation if not listed in Table 3.3.1):
    a. the binary number 0101 1110
    b. the OP code for Wait
12. The following is a program of an unspecified nature. Interpret each number as an OP code, part of an address, or pure numeric data.

ADDRESS	CONTENTS	
0000	F6	First instruction
0001	01	
0002	A0	
0003	FB	Second instruction
0004	01	
0005	A1	
0006	F7	Third instruction
0007	01	
0008	A2	
0009	3E	Fourth instruction

DATA ADDRESSES

01A0	07
01A1	05
01A2	0C

LEARNING OBJECTIVES

After completing this chapter, you should be able to:

1. Give a definition, explanation, or example for each of these: *Arithmetic and Logic Unit (ALU), microprogram, micro instructions, control unit, program counter, increment, status or Condition Code register (CC), set, cleared, negative status bit, zero status bit, carry status bit, Memory Data Register (MDR), Memory Address Register (MAR), Instruction Register (IR) internal bus, mnemonic, register transfer notation, source, destination, general register transfer notation, specific register transfer notation, addressing mode, extended addressing mode, machine code, direct addressing mode, page zero addressing, immediate operand, immediate addressing mode, inherent addressing mode, machine language, assembly language, label, assembling, hand-assembling, hand-coding, assembler, listing, source program, source code, object program, object code, variable data.*

2. Convert among hexadecimal status register contents and contents of individual status bits.

3. Describe the fetching and executing of an instruction in terms of the registers and memory of the MPU.

4. Write and interpret statements in general and specific register transfer notation.

5. Determine how any instruction affects the carry, zero, and negative status bits by reading the microprocessor's instruction information sheet.

6. Use the table of addressing modes on an instruction information sheet to select an appropriate OP code for a specific purpose.

7. Read and interpret a typical instruction information sheet.

8. Write a simple program in assembly language and hand code it.

In Chapter 3 we saw two simple programs using just 5 of the 197 OP codes in the 6800's instruction set. To write microcomputer programs, we need to understand how to use these and others of the 6800's OP codes.

In this chapter we'll take a detailed look at the instruction information sheets of Appendix A, and see how to use the information on the sheets. And we'll show how to write a simple program.

Many of the 6800's OP codes cause data to be transferred from one part of the MPU to another. So that we can understand how to use the OP codes, first, we need to know something about what's inside the MPU.

4.1   INTERNAL ARCHITECTURE OF THE 6800

Figure 4.1.1 shows a simplified block diagram of the 6800 MPU. Let's look at each component separately.

The ALU

The **Arithmetic and Logic Unit (ALU)** is that part of a CPU that performs arithmetic and logical operations and executes data transfers. (We know what arithmetic operations are; we'll be finding out about logical operations a little later.) The actual execution of an instruction takes place in the ALU. The ALU selects the proper operation called for by the instruction when it receives an appropriate signal from the control unit. Each instruction requires a series of hardware operations to execute it. The set of operations for each instruction is called a **microprogram** and is often stored in a small ROM on the MPU. When the ALU receives a control signal for, say, ADD, it executes the **micro instructions** in the microprogram stored for the operation ADD. Each of the 6800's instructions initiates the execution of its own microprogram.

FIGURE 4.1.1   Simplified Block Diagram of a Microprocessor Unit

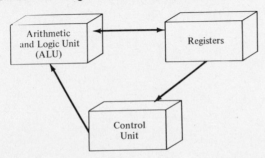

The control unit

The **control unit** directs the fetching and executing of instructions, which it does by providing timing and control signals that tell the ALU and other circuits what to do and when to do it. The control unit causes each instruction to be fetched by sending a control signal. Then it decodes the instruction and sends another control signal to the ALU that tells the ALU what operation to perform.

The registers

We've already seen two of the 6800's registers: accumulators A and B. The 6800 has four more internal registers that are programmable by the user. Figure 4.1.2 shows a diagram of the 6800's user-programmable registers.

The **Program Counter (PC)** is a 2-byte register that holds the address of the next location whose contents are to be fetched. (The program counter is 2 bytes because the 6800 has a 2-byte address word.) In Chapter 1 we said that the MPU expects to fetch the contents of memory addresses in sequence unless it encounters a transfer of control instruction. The program counter is responsible for keeping track of this sequence. As soon as the contents of a memory location are fetched, the program counter contents are **incremented** (increased by 1). Then the program counter contents "point" to the next program location.

Before the MPU can execute a program, the program counter must contain the starting address of the program. When we execute a user program, we give the monitor the starting address. Then the monitor loads the program counter for us.

FIGURE 4.1.2   User-Programmable Registers of the 6800

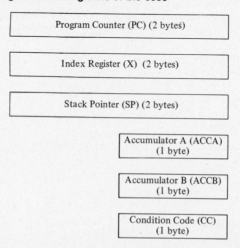

Program Counter (PC) (2 bytes)

Index Register (X) (2 bytes)

Stack Pointer (SP) (2 bytes)

Accumulator A (ACCA)
(1 byte)

Accumulator B (ACCB)
(1 byte)

Condition Code (CC)
(1 byte)

FIGURE 4.1.3 The Condition Code (Status) Register

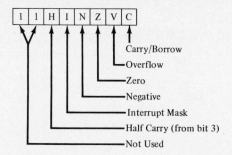

Two other user-programmable registers that have to do with addressing are the **indeX Register (XR)**, and the **Stack Pointer (SP)**, both 2 bytes. We'll reserve a discussion of these until later, but meanwhile we can examine their contents with the help of the monitor in both the Heathkit trainer and the Motorola D2.

The **status register**, or **Condition Code register (CC)**, is a 1-byte register whose individual bits contain information about the results of the last operation. Though the 6800's status register is 8 bits, all those bits aren't used.

Figure 4.1.3 shows a diagram of the 6800's status register. Each bit may be **set** (to 1) or **cleared** (to 0) by an operation.

We'll discuss only 3 of the status bits now and save the others for later. The **Negative status bit**, N, is set if bit 7 of the result is set after an ALU operation, otherwise the N bit is cleared. If we're not working with signed numbers, or using the contents of bit 7 for anything else, we can usually ignore this bit. The **Zero status bit**, Z, is set if the result of an ALU operation is 0; otherwise Z is cleared.

Finally, the **Carry status bit, C,** is set if the result of an ALU operation (like adding) is a number greater than 8 bits—that is, too big to be contained in an 8-bit register or memory location. We can compare this with an automobile odometer that has 5 digits. As we go from 99,999 to 100,000, we see only 00000 on the odometer because we have generated a number too big for the register on the odometer. If an odometer had a carry bit, we'd examine its contents and find that it contained a 1—a decided help when purchasing a used car! Unfortunately, a mechanical odometer doesn't have a carry bit, but the 6800 does.

We'll discuss the other status bits later when we need to use them.

To find out whether a given status bit is set or cleared, we could first examine the contents of the status register, write those contents in binary representation, and then locate the desired bit or bits from Figure 4.1.3.

EXAMPLE 4.1.1

The contents of the status register are CA. Determine whether each status bit is set or clear.

Solution

First, write the contents in binary:

1 1 0 0   1 0 1 0

Next, line up the binary contents with the individual bit locations given in Figure 4.1.3:

1 1 0 0 1 0 1 0
1 1 H I N Z V C

We note that the 2 most significant bits aren't used and are always set. Beyond those, we read off the contents of each bit.

Answer: H, Clear; I, Clear; N, Set; Z, Clear; V, Set; C, Clear

By using the preceding method in reverse, we can figure out the contents of the status register from the contents of its individual bits.

EXAMPLE 4.1.2

The C and Z bits are set; the rest of the status register bits are clear. Determine the contents (in hexadecimal) of the status register.

Solution

Write down the bit order of Figure 4.1.2:

1 1 H I N Z V C

As before, the two most significant bits automatically contain 1s. Beyond that, place a 1 in the Carry (C) and Zero (Z) bits, and a 0 in every other bit:

1 1 H I N Z V C
1 1 0 0 0 1 0 1

Finally, we convert this binary number to hexadecimal.

Answer: C5

(Notice that the first hexadecimal digit of the status register contents will never be a number lower than C, because the 2 most significant bits are always set.)

In addition to these six user-programmable registers, the 6800 microprocessor has some internal registers that are not accessible to the user.

The **Memory Data Register (MDR)** is a 1-byte register that the MPU uses to store data temporarily. When the MPU reads the contents of a memory location, those contents are read into the MDR via the data bus. And when the MPU writes new data into a memory location, the new data is written into that location from the MDR via the data bus.

The **Memory Address Register (MAR)** is a 2-byte register that temporarily holds an address that has been fetched from memory. That is, it holds a data address until it is time to fetch the data. We said in Chapter 3 that a 2-byte address that is part of a program occupies two program locations. This address is written into the MAR from the program locations 1 byte at a time, as directed by signals from the control unit. When the MAR has the complete address, that address goes out on the address bus as directed by another control signal.

The **Instruction Register (IR)** is a 1-byte register that holds the OP code temporarily until it can be interpreted. When the OP code is fetched from memory, it is written into the instruction register via the data bus. Then the control unit decodes the OP code.

Function of the 6800's registers

Figure 4.1.4 is a detailed block diagram showing the relationship among some of the parts of the MPU and memory. The MAR and the PC can each access the address bus, on the appropriate signal from the control unit. The MDR can receive data from the data bus when the R/W line is high and transmit data to the data bus when the R/W line is low. The lines between the parts of the MPU represent the

FIGURE 4.1.4   Relationship Among Parts of MPU and Memory

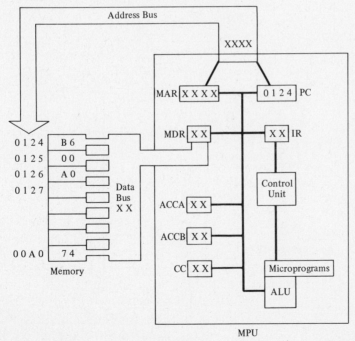

MPU's **internal bus,** a set of conductors over which signals are exchanged among these parts.

The figure shows a 3-byte instruction loaded in memory. Before the instruction is fetched, the registers of the MPU contain the values shown. The program counter contains the value 0124, loaded by the user via the system's monitor. The X's in the other registers and buses indicate that they contain garbage insofar as this particular instruction is concerned.

Figure 4.1.5 shows the fetching of the first word of the instruction. We've numbered the registers or buses in sequence, where changes take place. At (1) the contents of the program counter are transferred onto the address bus, which points to the memory location having address 0124. At (2) the program counter contents are incremented (increased by 1). At (3) the contents of location 0124 (B6) are placed on the data bus (4) and then into the MDR (5). Because the word B6 is the first word of an instruction, it next goes to the instruction register (6) and then to the control unit (7) for decoding. The control unit decodes B6 and finds that it is the OP code for an instruction to load accumulator A with a value. To get the value, the microprocessor must first fetch the 2-byte address in the next two program locations.

Figure 4.1.6 shows the fetching of the second byte of the instruction. At (1) the PC contents (0125) are loaded onto the address bus. The program counter contents are incremented (2). At (3) the address bus points to address 0125; at (4) the

FIGURE 4.1.5   First Byte of Instruction Is Fetched

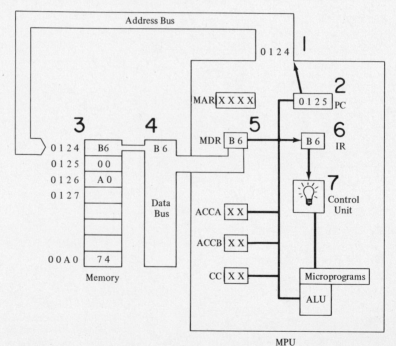

FIGURE 4.1.6   Second Byte of Instruction Is Fetched

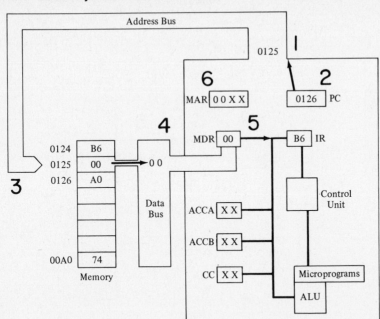

contents of location 0125 (00) are placed on the data bus and then at (5) into the MDR. When the control unit decoded the OP code B6, it determined that the destination of this value, 00, would be the high-order byte of the MAR. So at (6) the contents of the MDR (00) are placed in the high-order byte of the MAR.

Notice that the IR still contains the value B6 and that ACCA, ACCB, and CC still contain garbage.

In Figure 4.1.7 the third byte of the instruction is fetched. At (1) the PC contents (0126) are loaded onto the address bus and at (2) the PC contents are incremented. At (3) the address bus points to address 0126 and at (4) the contents of location 0126 (A0) are placed on the data bus. At (5) the data bus writes its contents (A0) into the MDR. When the control unit decoded the instruction B6, it predetermined that the destination of A0 would be the low-order byte of the MAR. Thus at (6) the value A0 is written into the low-order byte of the MAR. Notice that the contents of the IR, ACCA, ACCB, and CC still haven't changed.

Figure 4.1.8 shows the execution of the instruction. This time, the MAR, and not the PC, puts its contents onto the address bus (1). The address bus points to location 00A0 (2), and its contents (74) are placed on the data bus (3). At (4) the contents of the data bus (74) are written into the MDR. Because this was a "Load accumulator A" instruction, at (5) the value 74 is loaded into ACCA, and also some of the bits in the status (CC) register have been changed. We'll see in the next section why these status bits have received these values.

FIGURE 4.1.7 Third Byte of Instruction Is Fetched

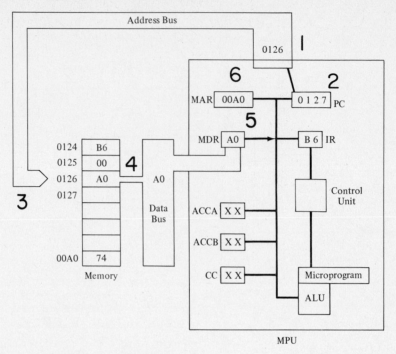

FIGURE 4.1.8 Execution of the Instruction

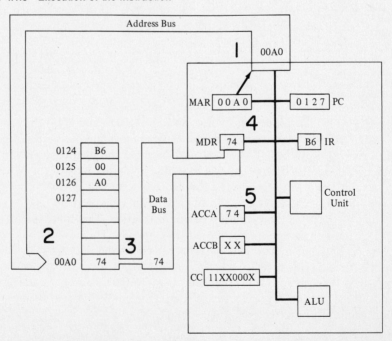

We should note that each event described for all of the fetch and execution operations happens under the direction of an appropriate signal from the control unit. Also, we see from Figure 4.1.8 that the PC contents weren't incremented during the execution of the instruction. Now that this instruction is executed, the PC still points to the next location in memory (0127). And at the completion of this instruction the contents of the registers remain until they are changed by a subsequent instruction.

4.2 THE INSTRUCTION INFORMATION SHEET

The 6800's instruction set, summarized in Appendix A, p. XXX, is the set of vocabulary words that we'll use to write programs. In addition to this summary, each instruction has a full page devoted to it, giving all the detailed information we need to know about that instruction. Here we find the meaning of that particular vocabulary word, as well as all the rules of grammar for using it correctly. These individual instruction information sheets start on p. XXX of Appendix A. We'll take some time to go through one of these sheets in detail and to explain how to get meaningful information from it.

Mnemonics

Figure 4.2.1 is the instruction information sheet for one of the most commonly used instructions of the 6800 instruction set. In the upper right-hand corner we find the letters LDA. This set of three letters is the instruction's symbol, or mnemonic, which is what we use in writing programs. The dictionary defines the word *mnemonic* as a device to help in remembering something. In microcomputer programming we'll define **mnemonic** as a group of letters (usually 3, sometimes 4) that symbolize an instruction. Webster's definition of the word still applies, though, because the letters that are chosen as a mnemonic for a particular operation usually suggest what that operation is.

In the upper left-hand corner of Figure 4.2.1 we find the instruction's definition; in this case, "Load Accumulator." We see that the mnemonic, LDA, does in fact suggest LoaD Accumulator.

Register transfer notation

Directly underneath the definition, Load Accumulator, on Figure 4.2.1, is a line that says:

Operation: $(ACCX) \leftarrow (M)$

This line describes the instruction in a kind of shorthand, which we call **register**

FIGURE 4.2.1 A Sample Instruction Information Sheet

Instruction definition

Mnemonic

**Register transfer
Statement**

Load Accumulator

LDA

Operation: $(ACCX) \leftarrow (M)$

Description: The contents of a memory location are placed in (loaded into) the accumulator.

Condition Codes:
H: Not affected.
I: Not affected.
N: Set if the number loaded is negative; cleared otherwise.
Z: Set if the number loaded is zero; cleared otherwise.
V: Cleared.
C: Not affected.

Addressing Modes, Execution Time, and Machine Code (hexadecimal).
(Dual Operand)

Addressing Modes	Execution Time (No. of cycles)	Number of Bytes of Machine Code	Machine Code HEX.
A IMM	2	2	86
A DIR	3	2	96
A EXT	4	3	B6
A IND	5	2	A6
B IMM	2	2	C6
B DIR	3	2	D6
B EXT	4	3	F6
B IND	5	2	E6

transfer notation. Much of what a microprocessor does is to transfer data from one register or memory location to another register or memory location. In register transfer notation we tell what happens to the contents of a registor and/or a memory location by using these devices:

( ) means that the contents of the parentheses is a location and not a value.
← means "is transferred to," "is placed in," or, simply, "gets."
X means either accumulator A or B; we substitute the one we want.
M means a memory location.

We call the place where the data comes from the **source** and the place where the data goes to the **destination**. In a statement written in register transfer notation, the destination is on the left, then an arrow pointing to it, then the source(s) on the right. Thus in the preceding statement, M is the source and ACCX, the destination.

Directly below the register transfer statement on Figure 4.2.1 is a line that says "Description: The contents of a memory location are placed in the accumulator." This line is an English translation of the register transfer notation statement. This translation was obtained by reading the statement from right to left. Normally, when the source is enclosed in parentheses we read it as "the contents of ...," because it means the contents of the address and not its numerical value. Thus on the right (M) translates to "The contents of memory location M"; the arrow means "are placed in", and ACCX means "accumulator X."

In **general register transfer notation** we use the general terms X and M. All the instruction sheets use general register transfer notation. To describe an instruction for a specific use in a program that we may be writing, we use **specific register transfer notation**. In it, we replace the general terms X and M with specific symbols. For instance, the notation

$$(ACCA) \leftarrow (00A0)$$

is a specific example of $(ACCX) \leftarrow (M)$ and can be translated as "The contents of memory location 00A0 are placed in accumulator A."

EXAMPLE 4.2.1

Translate into English:

$$(ACCA) \leftarrow (ACCA) + (00B2)$$

Solution

ACCA means accumulator A. Because it appears on the left, it's the destination and gets the data. On the right of the arrow, ACCA and 00B2 are the sources and will provide the data. The plus sign means what it usually means: to add. And the parentheses mean "the contents of."

Answer: Right to left: "The contents of memory location 00B2 are added to the contents of accumulator A and the result placed in accumulator A."

The statement of Example 4.2.1 is the specific register transfer notation for the instruction having mnemonic ADD, on p. XXX of Appendix A. Looking at this instruction sheet, we see that the general register transfer notation is

$$(ACCX) \leftarrow (ACCX) + (M)$$

and translates to "the contents of a memory location are added to the contents of the accumulator, and the results placed in the accumulator." Note that for this instruction the same accumulator—A or B—is used throughout.

Just as we can translate register transfer notation into English, we can translate some English into register transfer notation.

EXAMPLE 4.2.2

Write the following English description in specific register transfer notation: "The contents of accumulator A are placed in memory location 00C2."

Solution

From the sentence, the words "are placed in… " tell us that memory location 00C2 is the destination. Accumulator A is the source. So we put (00C2) on the left side, then the arrow, and then (ACCA) on the right. We put parentheses around ACCA and 00C2 because they're both locations and not values.

Answer: $(00C2) \leftarrow (ACCA)$

This instruction, called "Store Accumulator," has the mnemonic STA and is found on p. 464 of Appendix A. It, like the LDA instruction, is one of the more commonly used of the 6800 instruction set. As its description states, it stores (places) the contents of either accumulator in a memory location.

Condition codes

The instruction information sheet tells how each instruction affects the status register (condition code) bits. Every instruction doesn't affect every status register bit. In fact, there are some instructions that don't affect any status register bits. We can look at Figure 4.2.1 to see how the LDA instruction affects the status bits.

The list under "Condition Codes" tells us that H, I, and C are not affected by the LDA instruction. Also, it tells us that V is cleared regardless of the result of the LDA instruction. The only bits that depend on the result are N and Z. N will be set if the number loaded into the accumulator has a 1 in bit 7. And Z will be set if the number loaded is 0. Now we see why the contents of CC (Figure 4.1.8) were 11XX000X after loading 74 into ACCA. N is clear because 74 isn't negative; Z is clear because 74 isn't 0; and V is clear because LDA automatically clears it. The bits containing X weren't affected by the LDA instruction and contain whatever values they had before.

EXAMPLE 4.2.3

Tell how each of the status bits are affected by the STA operation.

Solution

We find the instruction information sheet for STA on p. 464, Appendix A. Looking at the condition codes list gives us the answer.

Answer: H, I, and C are not affected; V is cleared always; N is set if the number stored is negative; Z is set if the number stored is 0.

When a status bit isn't affected by an operation, it retains the same contents after the operation that it had beforehand.

EXAMPLE 4.2.4

The status register contains E3 before performing an operation (STA A) on a negative number. What will be the contents of the status register after this operation?

Solution

First, write the initial contents in binary and line them up with the bit letters:

```
1   1   1   0   0   0   1   1
1   1   H   I   N   Z   V   C
```

Next, look at the STA A instruction sheet to see what bits are affected. Bring down the values of any bits that aren't affected. We see that H, I, and C aren't affected, so we bring them down along with the first two:

```
1   1   1   0   0   0   1   1
1   1   H   I   N   Z   V   C
1   1   1   0               1
```

Next, determine how the remainder of the bits will be affected. First, N will be set because the number being stored is negative. Z will be cleared because the number being stored isn't 0. And V will be cleared because it always is for this operation. We bring these values down:

```
1  1  1  0  0  0  1  1
1  1  H  I  N  Z  V  C
1  1  1  0  1  0  0  1
```

Finally, we write this number in hexadecimal.

Answer: E9

The table at the bottom of the instruction information sheet deals mostly with addressing modes. This is a rather large topic and deserves its own section.

4.3 ADDRESSING MODES

Recall that an instruction consists of an operation and one or more operands. By selecting a particular **addressing mode**, we specify exactly how the operand identifies the data.

Looking back at Figure 4.2.1, we find a table at the bottom. For convenience, we've repeated this table here in Figure 4.3.1. In this exhibit there is a column called "Addressing Modes" on the left. We have 8 choices of addressing modes for this instruction. The letters A and B let us choose between accumulators A and B. The next 3 letters specify the addressing mode: IMM stands for immediate addressing, DIR for direct, EXT for extended, and IND for indexed. We'll explain the first 3 now and save indexed addressing for later.

Extended addressing

The addressing mode that we've used mostly so far is the **extended addressing mode**. In it, the data to be processed is in a memory location identified by a 2-byte address (the operand). The program of Figure 3.4.1 used this addressing mode for the LDA, ADD, and STA instructions.

Let's read across from the entry A EXT in the column under Addressing Modes in Figure 4.3.1. (A EXT specifies accumulator A and the extended addressing mode.) The first column we come to, called "Execution Time," we'll be discussing a little later and won't go into right now. The next column is called "Number of Bytes of Machine Code." The binary or hexadecimal numbers used to convey instructions are called **machine code**, because this is the code the machine (i.e., the microcomputer) must have in order to execute the instructions. This column contains a 3 for the entry A EXT, which means that three program addresses are needed to contain the instruction using this addressing mode. Recall from Chapter 3 that we need one address for the OP code, one for the high-order byte of the address, and one for the low-order byte of the address.

FIGURE 4.3.1   Table of Addressing Modes for LDA Instruction

LDA

For ACCA: LDA A
For ACCB: LDA B

IMM = Immediate
DIR = Direct
EXT = Extended

Addressing Modes, Execution Time, and Machine Code (hexadecimal)
(Dual Operand)

	Addressing Modes	Execution Time (No. of cycles)	Number of Bytes of Machine code	Machine Code
				HEX.
For ACCA	A IMM	2	2	86
	A DIR	3	2	96
	A EXT	4	3	B6
	A IND	5	2	A6
For ACCB	B IMM	2	2	C6
	B DIR	3	2	D6
	B EXT	4	3	F6
	B IND	5	2	E6

Going across to the last column, we find the OP code in hexadecimal. In this case its value is B6, the same number that was used in the program of Figure 3.4.1. If we look on the instruction information sheets for ADD and STA (p. 405 and 464, Appendix A) in the extended addressing mode, we find the OP codes BB and B7, respectively. These OP codes were also used in the program of Figure 3.4.1.

Direct addressing

This mode is similar to extended addressing. In the **direct addressing mode** the data to be processed is in a memory location identified by a 1-byte address (the operand). In order to qualify for the direct addressing mode, the memory location addressed must have 00 as its high-order address byte. Sometimes the high-order byte of a 2-byte address is called the "page number" (00 through FF). For this reason, direct addressing is also called **page zero addressing**.

Let's look at the entry "A DIR" on Figure 4.3.1. Reading across, we find that this addressing mode uses only two program addresses: one for the OP code and one for the low-order byte of the address, the high-order address byte being understood

FIGURE 4.3.2   Using the Direct Addressing Mode Where Possible Saves Program Words

Program to Add Two Numbers and Store the Answer

Extended			Direct	
Address	Contents		Address	Contents
0000	B6 ⎫	*First Instruction:* Load ACCA	⎧ 0000	96
0001	00 ⎬	with contents of location 00B6	⎩ 0001	B6
0002	B6 ⎭			
0003	BB ⎫	*Second Instruction:* Add contents	⎧ 0002	9B
0004	00 ⎬	of location 00BB to contents of	⎩ 0003	BB
0005	BB ⎭	ACCA, and accumulate results		
		in ACCA.		
0006	B7 ⎫	*Third Instruction:* Store contents	⎧ 0004	97
0007	00 ⎬	of ACCA in location 00B7.	⎩ 0005	B7
0008	B7 ⎭			
0009	3E	Wait.	0006	3E

from the OP code to be 00. Looking in the next column, we see that the OP code for this instruction, using the direct addressing mode, is 96.

To use fewer program addresses and thus end up with a simpler program, we'd like to use direct addressing whenever possible. The program of Figure 3.4.1, which uses extended addressing, contains operands that all qualify for the direct addressing mode. This program, rewritten using direct addressing (Figure 4.3.2), is 3 bytes shorter than the same program using extended addressing. However, we may not always be able to use direct addressing exclusively, for two reasons: (1) the high-order byte of the operand may not be 00 and (2) the rules of a particular instruction, as stated on its information sheet, may not allow the direct addressing mode as an option.

Immediate addressing

In the **immediate addressing mode**, the data to be processed is the operand that follows immediately after the OP code. In Figure 4.3.1 we find A IMM at the top of the addressing modes column. Reading across, we see that this instruction takes 2 bytes: one for the OP code and one for the immediate operand. The immediate addressing mode will always require two program addresses. Looking across to the next column, we find that the OP code for this is 86.

The program of Figure 3.3.3, repeated for convenience in Figure 4.3.3, uses the immediate addressing mode in the first instruction:

86
F2

Here, the number that follows the OP code (in this case, F2) is the **immediate operand** and is the value that is to be placed in accumulator A.

FIGURE 4.3.3   The Immediate Addressing Mode Used in a Program

Program to Store F2 in Location 00F0

Address	Contents	
0010	86 ⎫	*First Instruction*: Load ACCA with
0011	F2 ⎭	Immediate Operand (F2). (Immediate Mode)
0012	B7 ⎫	*Second Instruction*: Store Contents
0013	00 ⎬	of ACCA in Location 00F0. (Extended Mode)
0014	F0 ⎭	
0015	3E	*Third Instruction*: Wait.

We write the description using specific register transfer notation in this way:

(ACCA) ← F2

and the English translation of this is "The hexadecimal value F2 is placed in accumulator A" or "Accumulator A gets the hexadecimal value F2." The lack of parentheses around F2 means that the *value* F2, and not the *contents* of location 00F2, is placed into accumulator A.

In contrast to the first instruction, the second instruction in Figure 4.3.3 uses the extended addressing mode. Notice that we could save a byte of program address here by using the direct addressing mode instead, because we have a page zero operand (00F0), and the STA instruction does give us the option of the direct addressing mode.

Figure 4.3.4 summarizes the three addressing modes that we've just discussed. Each instruction accomplishes the same thing (places a value of FF in accumulator A), but each does it in a different way. In both the extended and direct addressing

FIGURE 4.3.4   Three Addressing Modes

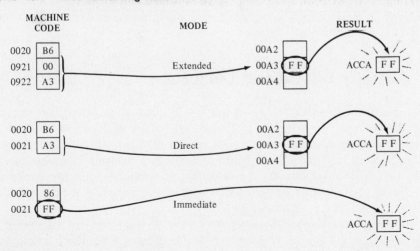

FIGURE 4.3.5   Table of Addressing Modes for the WAI Instruction

Addressing Modes, Execution Time, and Machine Code (hexadecimal)

Addressing Modes	Execution Time (No. of cycles)	Number of Bytes of Machine code	Machine Code
			HEX.
Inherent	9	1	3E

modes the operand is an address (00A3) whose contents (FF) are loaded into accumulator A. In the immediate addressing mode the operand (FF) is the value to be loaded into accumulator A.

In addition to the general addressing modes given on Figure 4.3.1, we can discuss one more at this time.

Inherent addressing

Some instructions don't have any operand or have as an operand one of the MPU's internal registers. In that case no operand needs to be specified. In the **inherent addressing mode** the data to be processed is either found in an internal register or is nonexistent. An example is the WAI (wait) instruction, whose table of addressing modes from its instruction information sheet is shown in Figure 4.3.5. We find that WAI has only one addressing mode available: INH, or inherent. And it takes only 1 byte of machine code: the OP code (3E), because no operand needs to be specified. In fact, here, there is no data; the microprocessor must simply *wait*.

There are two more addressing modes: indexed and relative. We'll be talking about each of these later. Now, we have enough addressing modes to write a simple program in a programming language.

4.4   ASSEMBLY, OR SYMBOLIC, LANGUAGE

We've seen that mnemonics make identifying an instruction easier than numerical OP codes, because we associate meaning with groups of letters more than with groups of numbers. Now, we'll see how to use mnemonics to write programs that are simpler to write and read than programs written in **machine language**, meaning binary or hexadecimal numbers. In **assembly**, or **symbolic, language**, symbols are used instead of numbers to represent OP codes and operands. In the case of the OP code the symbol used is its mnemonic.

To illustrate assembly language, let's look at the format of an instruction, shown in Figure 4.4.1. Here we see the instruction both in assembly language and

FIGURE 4.4.1   Format of an Instruction

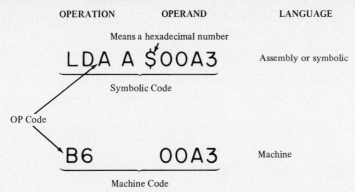

machine language. To the microprocessor this instruction means "Place the contents of memory location 00A3 in accumulator A."

In assembly language the machine language OP code B6 has been replaced with the symbol LDA A. This is an assembly language OP code, where we use letters instead of numbers to identify the instruction. The dollar sign ($) means that the number that follows it is hexadecimal and not decimal or binary. A prefix of % means that the number is binary. And no prefix means decimal. We'll sometimes use these prefixes in text material where ambiguity might result otherwise.

Figure 4.4.2 shows a program to add 2 numbers and store the result, written in both machine and assembly language. Here, each statement means either the direct or the extended addressing mode, with preference given to the direct if possible.

The program of Figure 4.3.3 uses the immediate addressing mode in the first instruction. To denote the immediate mode in assembly language, we use the pounds

FIGURE 4.4.2   A Program to Add Two Numbers in Assembly and Machine Language

MACHINE LANGUAGE   ASSEMBLY LANGUAGE

B6
00 } LDA A $00F0   Place the contents of location 00F0 in accumulator A.
F0

BB
00 } ADD A $00F1   Add the contents of location 00F1 to the contents of accumulator A, and place the sum in accumulator A.
F1

B7
00 } STA A $00F2   Place the contents of accumulator A in location 00F2.
F2

3E   WAI   Wait for further instructions.

sign (#) as a prefix. Thus the program of Figure 4.3.3 is written in assembly language like this:

```
LDA A   #$F2   LOAD ACCA WITH IMMEDIATE OPERAND $F2
STA A   $00F0  STORE (ACCA) IN LOCATION $00F0
WAI
```

Although the machine language program is what the microprocessor must have in order to execute the program, the assembly language program is a lot easier to read and write.

Next, we'll see how to write a program in assembly language.

A simple program

Suppose we want to write a program to solve the following problem.

The Problem: Through appropriate interface circuitry, we have wired a set of 8 lights, one to each data line at address $CC00. We want to write a program that will display a binary number with the 8 lights. The binary number should be the equivalent of whatever 2-digit hexadecimal number is in memory location $0000. Start the program at address $0010.

Figure 4.4.3 illustrates the problem. For each light that is to be on, we store a 1 in the corresponding bit of address $CC00. And for each light that is to be off, we store a 0 in that bit.

The problem says that, for instance, if the hexadecimal number 6A were in memory location $0000, our lights should represent a binary 0110 1010 with the light pattern shown in Figure 4.4.3.

FIGURE 4.4.3   A Programming Problem

Problem: Display a binary number on a set of eight lights.
          The number displayed should be the same as the
          contents of memory location $0000. The eight lines a
          are appropriately wired to data lines at location $CC00.

For example, if location $0000 has these contents:

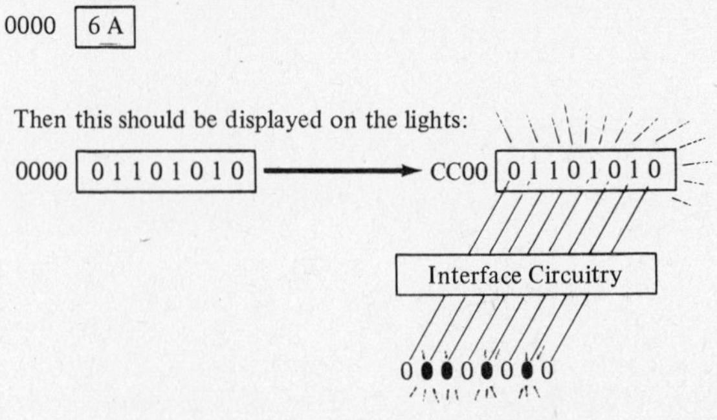

```
0000  │ 6 A │
```

Then this should be displayed on the lights:

To do this, transfer the contents of location $0000
through an accumulator to location $CC00.

Writing the program

We want to move the value that's in location $0000 into location $CC00. Or, translated into register transfer notation,

($CC00)←($0000)

As we know, there isn't any one instruction in the 6800 instruction set that does this. But we can use one of the accumulators as a go-between, by transferring the contents of location $0000 to an accumulator and then to location $CC00. Or

(ACCB)←($0000)

($CC00)←(ACCB)

(Here, we've used ACCB just for variety.)

The two instructions that will do these transfers are LDA B and STA B. We write the program on a worksheet:

ADDRESS	CODE	LABEL	MNEMONIC	OPERAND	COMMENT
		START	LDA B	$0000	PUT CONTENTS OF 0000 INTO ACCB
			STA B	$CC00	PUT CONTENTS OF ACCB INTO CC00
			WAI		WAIT FOR FURTHER INSTRUCTIONS

Here, a **label** is a group of up to 6 characters (the first of which must be a letter), used to identify a location in a program. We'll be defining a broader meaning of the word *label* later. For now, we've put a label, START, at the beginning of the program, although we didn't have to. But as our programs get more interesting, it'll be handy to know where the program actually starts. We leave the address and OP code columns blank while we're writing the assembly language program.

Assembling the program

Translating an assembly language program into a machine language program is called **assembling** the program. If we, the users, do it ourselves, we call it **hand assembling** or **hand coding**. There are also programs, called **assemblers**, that do the assembling for us. More about that later. Right now, we're going to hand assemble our assembly language program.

First, the problem said to start our program at address $0010. So we write 0010 in the address column opposite LDA B:

ADDRESS	CODE	LABEL	MNEMONIC	OPERAND	COMMENT
0010		START	LDA B	$0000	PUT ($0000) INTO ACCB

Next, we look on the instruction sheet for the first instruction, LDA B, to find out its OP code and how many bytes it takes. We see that LDA B gives a choice among four addressing modes. To load the contents of a memory location requires either the direct or the extended mode. Our first address, $0000, qualifies for the direct mode because its first 2 digits are 0s. The OP code for LDA B in the direct mode is D6. So we write D6 under CODE on the same line with 0010.

ADDRESS	CODE	LABEL	MNEMONIC	OPERAND	COMMENT
0010	D6	START	LDA B	$0000	PUT ($0000) INTO ACCB

Our instruction requires 2 bytes: one for the OP code and one for the low-order byte of the memory location. So we enter a 00 in the box next to D6:

ADDRESS	CODE	LABEL	MNEMONIC	OPERAND	COMMENT
0010	D6 00	START	LDA B	$0000	PUT ($0000) INTO ACCB

This is a 2-byte instruction; therefore memory locations $0010 and $0011 must be used to store it. We only listed the $0010 and not the $0011. But we understand that if there are two 1-byte values under CODE, two addresses are needed.

Next, we write 0012 in the ADDRESS column because that'll be the address where the next instruction starts.

ADDRESS	CODE	LABEL	MNEMONIC	OPERAND	COMMENT
0010	D6 00	START	LDA B	$0000	PUT ($0000) INTO ACCB
0012					

We look at the information sheet for the STA B instruction. For addressing modes we have only one choice: the extended mode; because the first 2 digits of CC00 are not 0s. We find that the OP code for STA B in the extended mode is F7. So we write F7 in the first box under CODE.

ADDRESS	CODE	LABEL	MNEMONIC	OPERAND	COMMENT
0012	F7		STA B	$CC00	PUT (ACCB) INTO CC00

This instruction is 3 bytes long. In the second box we write CC, the high-order byte of the address, and in the third box, 00, the low-order byte.

ADDRESS	CODE	LABEL	MNEMONIC	OPERAND	COMMENT
0012	F7 CC 00		STA B	$CC00	PUT (ACCB) INTO CC00

Since this instruction took 3 bytes (one for OP code, two for address), our next program address will be $0015, and we write it in. We find the OP code for WAI to be 3E. That's a 1-byte instruction, so we're done.

ADDRESS	CODE	LABEL	MNEMONIC	OPERAND	COMMENT
0015	3E		WAI		WAIT FOR INSTRUCTIONS

TABLE 4.4.1   A Program Listing

Address		Code			Label	Mnemonic	Operand	Comment
0010		D6	00		START	LDA B	$0000	Put (0000) into ACCB
0012		F7	CC	00		STA B	$CC00	Now store it in location of set of lights (display bit pattern on set of lights)
0015		3E				WAI		Wait

When we have finished writing down all the addresses and codes for the program, we have produced its listing. A **listing** is a document that shows a side-by-side comparison of the assembly language program and the machine language program that results from it. The assembly language program is also called the **source program** (because it's the source from which the machine language program is derived), and the specific symbols in it are called the **source code**. The machine language program is called the **object program** (because it's the object of what we do when we assemble) and the hexadecimal or binary numbers contained in it are called **object code**.

Table 4.4.1 shows the completed listing of the program we just assembled.

Loading and executing the program

Before the microprocessor can execute the program, we must store the object code in the microcomputer's memory. The starting address of the program is $0010, so we load the microcomputer's memory locations $0010 through $0015 with the object code, using the microcomputer's monitor. First, we look at the first instruction, which starts at address $0010 and is 2 bytes long. Thus we should load location $0010 with the first byte of code (D6). Although it isn't written down anywhere, the next location is $0011 and should contain the second byte of code (00). We load location $0010 with D6 and location $0011 with 00.

The next instruction starts at address $0012 and is 3 bytes long: locations $0012, $0013, and $0014. We load location $0012 with F7, $0013 with CC, and $0014 with 00.

The last instruction starts at address $0015 and is only 1 byte long. So we load location $0015 with 3E.

When the program is loaded into memory, we're still not quite ready to run it. Usually, the whole point of a program is that we want to process some data. Thus we have to **input** the data, which means that we store it in memory too. In this case our data are whatever 2-digit hexadecimal number corresponds to the binary number we want the lights to display. This is called **variable data**, because the number we input may vary from one time to the next.

Let's arbitrarily choose the number 3C as our data. We load it into memory location $0000, because that's where our program expects to find it. When we run the program according to the procedure specified by the microcomputer, we should find that the 8 lights look like this:

0 0 1 1 1 1 0 0

If we hadn't loaded location $0000 with a number we wanted, the lights would still display some value, corresponding to whatever garbage was in location $0000.

We used a simple programming example to illustrate the use of assembly language. Now that we know how to write in assembly language and how to produce a listing, we'll be ready to write more interesting programs in later chapters.

REVIEW QUESTIONS

1. What is the **ALU**? What is a **microprogram**, and what are **micro instructions**?
2. Name the six user-programmable registers of the 6800.
3. What is the **program counter**? What does **increment** mean?
4. What is the **status register**? What is another name for it? How can we tell whether each bit is **set** or **cleared** by looking at the hexadecimal contents of the status register?
5. Why is the first digit of the status register always hexadecimal C or greater?
6. What are the **negative, zero,** and **carry** bits of the status register? What are their functions?
7. What are the names and functions of the **MDR**, the **MAR**, and the **IR**?
8. What is the MPU's **internal bus**? Describe what happens during an instruction fetch and execute, using Figures 4.1.4–4.1.8.
9. What is a **mnemonic**? Give an example of a mnemonic, and explain how it conforms to Webster's definition of "mnemonic."
10. What is **register transfer notation**? Give an example.
11. What do parentheses mean in register transfer notation? What does an arrow mean?
12. What do we mean by **source** and **destination**? On which side of the arrow in a register transfer notation statement is each found?
13. What is the difference between **general** and **specific** register transfer notation?
14. Explain how to translate a register transfer notation statement into English, and vice versa.
15. Does every instruction affect each status bit? Explain.
16. How do we know how each instruction affects the status register bits?
17. What happens to a status bit that isn't affected by an operation?
18. Explain what we mean by **addressing modes**.
19. What is the **extended addressing mode**? How many program addresses does it take?
20. What is **machine code**?
21. How do we find the numerical OP code for a particular instruction and addressing mode?
22. What is the **direct addressing mode**? How is it like the extended addressing mode? How is it different? What is the requirement for an operand to use the direct addressing mode?
23. What is another name for **direct addressing**?
24. What is the **immediate addressing mode**? What is an **immediate operand**? How do we symbolize this mode in assembly language?

25. How many program addresses do the direct and immediate addressing modes use?
26. What is the **inherent addressing mode**? Why does it require no operands?
27. What is **machine language**? What does it consist of?
28. What is **assembly**, or **symbolic, language**? How is it different from machine language? How is it similar?
29. What do a dollar sign ($) and a percent sign (%) mean in assembly language? What if a number has no prefix?
30. How do we specify the immediate addressing mode in assembly language?
31. Explain the steps necessary to write an assembly language program. What is a **label**?
32. What is **assembling**? Explain how to **hand assemble** a program.
33. When hand assembling a program, how do we decide whether to use the direct or the extended addressing mode?
34. What is a **listing**? Is every program address written down in a listing? Explain.
35. What is meant by the terms **source program, source code, object program, object code**?
36. Explain how to read a listing and decide what contents to load into what memory locations.
37. What do we mean by **input**? What is **variable data**? Give an example.
38. In the sample program in the text, what would be the result if we didn't input data?

EXERCISES

Set A (answers at back of book)

1. For the following status register contents, determine whether each status bit is set or clear:
   a. D7   b. C0   c. EF
2. Determine the contents (in hexadecimal) of the status register for each of these conditions:
   b. all clear except N
   a. H, Z, and V set; the rest clear
   c. all set except Z
3. Give definitions and general register transfer notation for these mnemonics (consult Appendix A):
   a. ABA   b. DEC   c. SUB   d. TAB
4. Give English translations of the general register transfer statements in Exercise 3. Indicate the source(s) and destination for each.
5. Translate into English:
   a. (ACCB)←(ACCB)−($0054)
   b. (ACCB)←($2054)
   c. (ACCB)←(ACCB)−01
   d. (ACCA)←(ACCA)+($0015)
6. Identify the mnemonic for each operation in Exercise 5.
7. Write these English descriptions in specific register transfer notation:
   a. "The contents of accumulator A are placed in accumulator B."
   b. "Memory location 00A3 gets the contents of accumulator A."

c. "The contents of accumulator A are added to the contents of accumulator B, and the sum is placed in accumulator A."

d. "The number 1 is subtracted from the contents of memory location 0053, and the result is placed in memory location 0053."

8. Identify the mnemonic for each operation in Exercise 7.

9. Tell how the C, Z, and N status bits are affected by each instruction in Exercise 3. (Consult Appendix A.)

10. The status register contains C3 before performing a LDA A operation where the number loaded is 0. What will be the contents of the status register after this operation?

11. What addressing mode is indicated by each of these statements? (More than one may be correct; in that case, give all.)

a. (ACCB)←$F0

b. ($00A3)←(ACCA)

c. (ACCA)←($1200)

d. (ACCB)←(ACCA)

12. Write an assembly language statement for each part of Exercise 11, and give the machine code for each (consult Appendix A).

13. State which addressing mode(s) are indicated by each of these:

a. ADD A #$45   b. LDA B $1298   c. DEC A

14. Refer to Figure 3.2.3, and modify the assembly language program of Table 4.4.1 so as to turn on the bedroom light, the coffee pot, and the TV. What is the value of the input data, and where should it be input?

15. Hand assemble the program of Exercise 14. Start the program at location $0200.

For Exercises 16 to 18 create a listing for each program. Use the direct instead of the extended mode wherever possible.

16.

```
START   LDA A   $0034   GET CONTENTS OF LOCATION $0034
        SUB A   $0152   SUBTRACT CONTENTS OF $0152, RESULT IN ACCA
        STA A   $0035   PUT ANSWER IN LOCATION $0035
        WAI             WAIT
```

Start the program at location $0000.

17.

```
START   LDA A   #$32    PUT $32 IN ACCA
        LDA B   #$10    PUT $10 IN ACCB
        ABA             ADD THE TWO VALUES, PLACE RESULT IN ACCA
        STA A   $0073   NOW PUT RESULT IN LOCATION $0073
        WAI             WAIT
```

Start the program at location $0100.

18.

```
START   LDA A   #$FF    PUT $FF INTO ACCA
        DEC A           SUBTRACT ONE FROM (ACCA)
        TAB             PUT RESULT IN ACCB
        STA B   $0230   NOW PUT RESULT IN LOCATION $0230
        WAI             WAIT
```

Start the program at location $0020.

EXERCISES

Set B (Answers not given)

1. For the following status register contents, determine whether each status bit is set or clear.
   a. F0 b. C9 c. DE
2. Determine the contents (in hexadecimal) of the status register for each of these conditions.
   a. I and Z set; the rest clear
   b. Z, V, and C clear; the rest set
   c. All set except V
3. Give definitions and general register transfer notation for these mnemonics (consult Appendix A).
   a. SBA b. INC c. CLR d. TBA
4. Give English translations of the general register transfer statements in Exercise 3. Indicate the source(s) and destination for each.
5. Translate into English:
   a. ($00A3)←($00A3)+01
   b. (ACCB)←$00
   c. ($0500)←(ACCA)
   d. (ACCB)←(ACCB)+($0245)
6. Identify the mnemonic for each operation in Exercise 5.
7. Write these English descriptions in specific register transfer notation:
   a. "The contents of accumulator B are subtracted from the contents of accumulator A, and the result is placed in accumulator A."
   b. "The contents of accumulator B are placed in accumulator A."
   c. "One is added to the contents of accumulator A, and the results are placed in accumulator A."
   d. "Zero is placed in location $00F0."
8. Identify the mnemonic for each operation in Exercise 7.
9. Tell how the C, Z, and N status bits are affected by each instruction in Exercise 3. (Consult Appendix A.)
10. The status register contains E9 before performing a STA A operation where the number stored is positive. What will be the contents of the status register after this operation?
11. What addressing mode is indicated by each of these statements? (More than one may be correct; in that case, give both.)
    a. (ACCB)←(ACCB)+($F3C1)
    b. (ACCA)←(ACCA)+02
    c. ($0096)←($0096)+01
    d. (ACCA)←(ACCA)−(ACCB)
12. Write an assembly language statement for each part of Exercise 11, and give the machine code for each. (Consult Appendix A.)
13. State which addressing mode(s) is(are) indicated by each of these:
    a. INC B b. LDA A #$37 c. CLR $0567
14. Refer to Figure 3.2.3, and modify the assembly language program of Table 4.4.1 so as to raise the shade and turn on the bathroom light. What is the value of the input data, and where should it be input?

15. Hand assemble the program of Exercise 14. Start the program at location $1000.

For Exercises 16–18 create a listing for each program. Use the direct instead of the extended mode wherever possible.

16.

```
START   LDA B   #$32    PUT $32 INTO ACCB
        LDA A   #$10    PUT $10 INTO ACCA
        SBA             SUBTRACT (ACCB) FROM (ACCA), PUT RESULT IN ACCA
        STA A   $0343   PUT RESULT IN $0343
        WAI             WAIT.
```

Start the program at location $0080.

17.

```
SWAP    STA A   $0000   SAVE (ACCA) IN LOCATION $0000
        TBA             PUT (ACCB) IN (ACCA)
        LDA B   $0000   NOW GET ORIGINAL ACCA CONTENTS BACK
        WAI             WAIT
```

Start the program at location $0120.

18.

```
START   CLR A           PUT ZEROS IN ACCA
        INC A           NOW PUT 01 IN ACCA
        CLR B           PUT ZEROS IN ACCB
        SBA             SUBTRACT (ACCB) FROM (ACCA)
        STA A   $0067   PUT RESULT IN $0067
        WAI             WAIT
```

Start the program at location $0A26.

5 Introducing the PIA

LEARNING OBJECTIVES

After completing this chapter, you should be able to:

1. Give a definition, explanation or example for these words: *I/O port, peripheral interface adapter (PIA), peripheral, peripheral data pins, peripheral data register, data direction register, control register, Light-Emitting Diode (LED), configure, seven-segment display.*
2. Describe the PIA's pins shown in Figure 5.1.2.
3. List the internal registers of the PIA and state their functions.
4. Describe, using Figures 5.2.1 and 5.2.2, how input and output data is exchanged between the MPU and peripherals via the PIA's data register.
5. Explain how to configure the PIA's data registers for input and output.
6. Given specific addresses for a user and system PIA, state what values should be loaded into what addresses to configure the PIA for input and for output and to input data from and output data to the data registers.
7. Write program segments to configure the PIA in a specific way.
8. Derive a hexadecimal code for the seven-segment display.
9. Given a hardware setup, write programs to configure the PIA and handle the input and output.

In Chapter 3 we talked about wiring a set of lights as though it were a memory location (memory-mapped I/O). In that case we were using a memory location as an **Input/Output (I/O) port,** which means the place where data comes into and goes out of the microprocessor.

In this chapter we're going to introduce a special chip that handles I/O. This is the **Peripheral Interface Adapter (PIA).** The PIA interfaces with a peripheral under direction from the CPU. A **peripheral** is a unit of processing equipment external to the CPU, such as a keypad, display, or printer. A microcomputer could receive input from a hexadecimal keypad or send output to a display, light, loudspeaker, or printer by interfacing the CPU with a PIA. Figure 5.1.1 shows a diagram of this

FIGURE 5.1.1 The CPU Controls External Devices Through the PIA

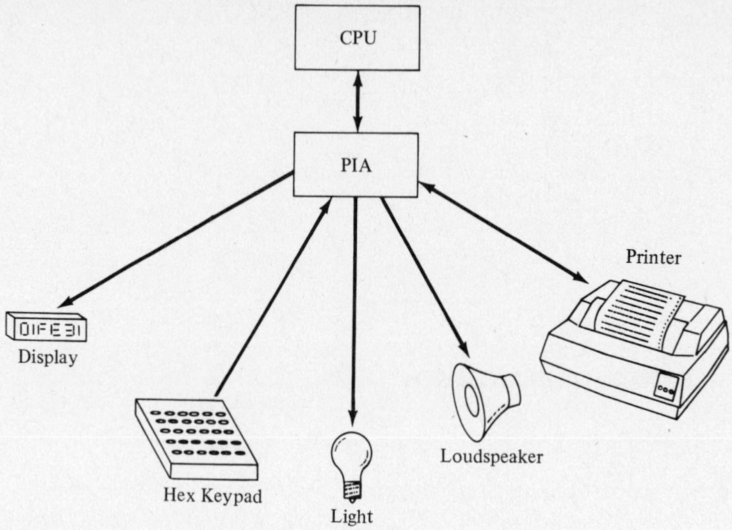

communication. To see how this interface works, first, we have to know a little about the PIA itself.

5.1 ARCHITECTURE OF THE PIA

In Chapter 1 we discussed a few pins of the 6800: the data, address, power, ground, and READ/WRITE (R/W) pins. Now we'll look at similar pins of the PIA.

Pin-out of the PIA

Figure 5.1.2 shows a pin-out of the PIA. Like the 6800, the PIA has 40 pins, which connect to the various buses. First, we'll discuss 4 pins on the control bus that are inputs to the PIA. Like the 6800, the PIA has pins that supply its power: +5V and GND. The R/W pin is connected to the MPU's R/W pin and is high when the MPU is reading from the PIA and low when the MPU is writing to the PIA. Like the 6800, the PIA has some internal registers, which we'll discuss later. A low voltage on the PIA's RESET pin clears all of its registers. (When a register or memory location is cleared, each bit is cleared to zero.)

Right now we'll focus our attention on the data pins. The PIA acts as "go-between" for the 6800 and one or more peripherals, so it has two kinds of data pins: one kind for exchanging data with the microprocessor, and another for exchanging data with peripherals.

FIGURE 5.1.2   The PIA

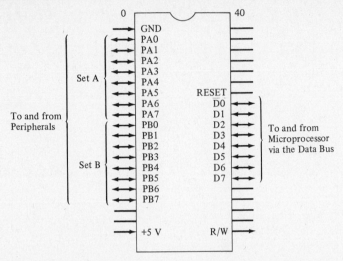

The PIA has 8 data pins (D0 through D7) for exchanging data with the microprocessor. These are connected to the 6800's bidirectional data bus.

In addition, the PIA has 16 **peripheral data pins** (PA0 through PA7 and PB0 through PB7) for sending or receiving data to or from peripheral devices. The peripheral data pins are organized into two sets of 8, called set A and set B, corresponding to sides A and B of the PIA.

Each peripheral data line can be either an input or an output of the PIA, but not both at once. We program each peripheral data line individually to be an input or an output, depending on what we need. These lines can be all inputs, all outputs, or any combination. To see how to program the peripheral data lines, first, we need to take a look inside the PIA.

Registers of the PIA

Figure 5.1.3 shows a diagram of the PIA, its data lines, and its registers. Besides 8 peripheral data lines, each of the A and B sides has three registers. Although there are subtle differences between the two sides, we won't discuss those differences in this book. For most of the discussions that follow it will be simpler to talk about just one side, and we'll arbitrarily choose side A. For our purposes we assume that whatever we say about side A goes for side B, too.

On side A, **peripheral data register A**, sometimes called **Data Register A (DRA)**, is an 8-bit register in the PIA that holds the current data to be input to or output from the A side of the PIA.

FIGURE 5.1.3   Registers and Data Lines of the PIA

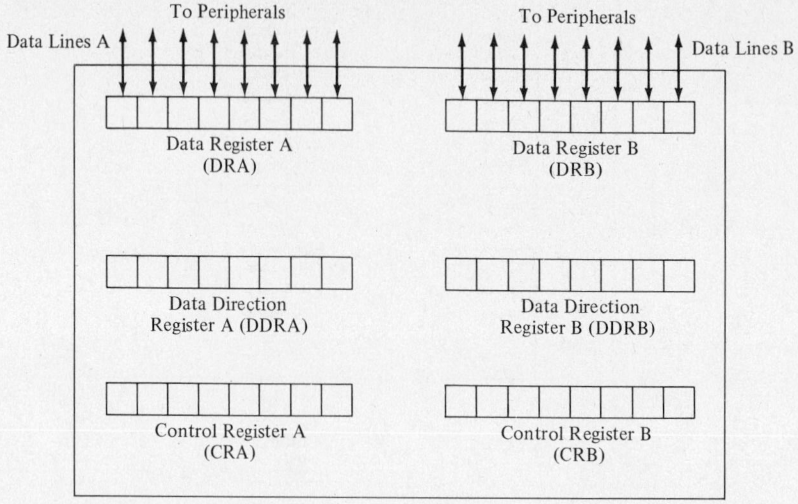

To determine whether each bit in DRA is used for input or output, we use **Data Direction Register A (DDRA).** If a bit in DDRA is a 1, then the corresponding bit in DRA will be an output; if 0, an input.

Control Register A (CRA) lets the user set up side A for a variety of functions. In this chapter we'll be concerned with only one of the bits in the control register. Next, we'll look at the data lines and registers in some detail.

5.2   INPUT, OUTPUT, AND THE PIA

In this section we'll see how to use the PIA's data lines and registers to input and output data.

Peripheral data lines and Data Register A

In Chapter 3 (Figure 3.2.2) we showed how a switch could be wired to input a 1 or a 0 onto a line of the MPU's data bus. Because the PIA is handling I/O for the MPU, we can wire one of the PIA's peripheral data lines to a switch in the same way. Figure 5.2.1 is a block diagram showing the communication between side A's peripheral data lines and a set of 8 switches to be used for input. The MPU can read the data input on the switches after the data has first passed through the PIA. Here, "switch up" causes a 1 to be input, and "switch down" causes a 0 to be input. Thus all of the switches up would allow the MPU to read %11111111 ($FF), and all switches down would allow the MPU to read %00000000 ($00). Figure 5.2.1 illustrates a typical case. At (1) the user inputs a value (in this case, $C2) on the switches. At (2) the data, $C2, goes to data register A via side A's peripheral data

FIGURE 5.2.1   Side A of the PIA Using Eight Switches as Inputs

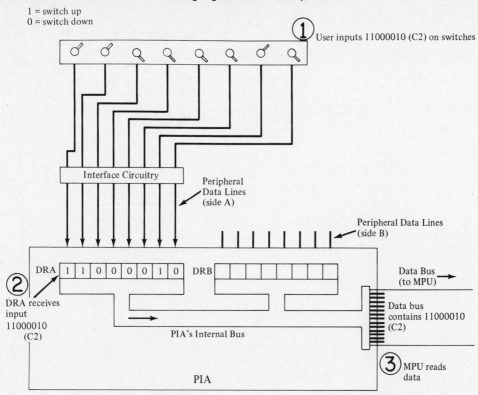

1 = switch up
0 = switch down

① User inputs 11000010 (C2) on switches

Interface Circuitry

Peripheral
Data Lines
(side A)

Peripheral Data Lines
(side B)

DRA | 1 | 1 | 0 | 0 | 0 | 0 | 1 | 0 | DRB

Data Bus
(to MPU)

②

DRA receives
input
11000010
(C2)

PIA's Internal Bus

Data bus
contains 11000010
(C2)

③ MPU reads
data

PIA

lines. At (3) the data gets onto the data bus via the PIA's internal bus. Then the MPU can read the data. In this case side A is set up for all 8 lines to be inputs. Once we have wired side A for all inputs, it would naturally stay that way until we rewired it.

Alternatively, we could wire side A so that all 8 lines were outputs. For an output device, we'll use a **Light-Emitting Diode (LED)**, a small device that produces a red light when turned on. LEDs are very commonly used in microcomputer displays. An LED can be wired so that a 1 means "light on" and a 0 means "light off." Or it can be wired in the opposite way: 1 = "light off" and 0 = "light on."

Figure 5.2.2 shows side A of the PIA wired through interface circuitry so that all 8 peripheral data lines are outputs to 8 LEDs. In this case the MPU can write data into the LEDs by first passing the data through the PIA. Here, a 1 output by the MPU to the PIA causes an output of light on, and a 0 causes light off. So if the MPU writes %11111111 ($FF), all the lights will be turned on. And if the MPU writes %00000000 ($00), all the lights will be turned off. Figure 5.2.2 illustrates a particular example. At (1) the MPU places the data ($A7, in this case) onto the data bus. At (2) the data is placed into DRA via the PIA's internal bus. At (3) the data is

FIGURE 5.2.2   Side A of PIA Using Eight LEDs as Outputs

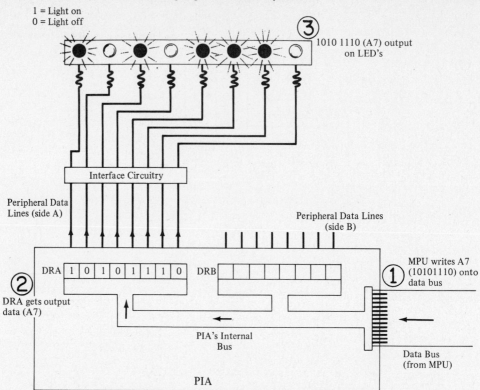

1 = Light on
0 = Light off

③ 1010 1110 (A7) output on LED's

Interface Circuitry

Peripheral Data Lines (side A)

Peripheral Data Lines (side B)

DRA | 1 | 0 | 1 | 0 | 1 | 1 | 1 | 0 | DRB

① MPU writes A7 (10101110) onto data bus

② DRA gets output data (A7)

PIA's Internal Bus

Data Bus (from MPU)

PIA

output onto the LEDs through the PIA's side A peripheral data lines, and the binary number 1010 1110 ($A7) appears as the pattern on the lights.

We've shown examples of side A of the PIA being used for all input and all output. But we can use each line individually for either input or output. We could wire 4 peripheral data lines to switches and 4 to LEDs or 7 to switches and 1 to an LED or 3 to switches and 4 to LEDs, and so on.

But how do we establish which peripheral data lines are inputs and which are outputs?

Configuring the PIA

When we set the peripheral data lines of the PIA to be inputs or outputs, we say that we **configure** them. To configure side A of the PIA, we use Data Direction Register A (DDRA) and Control Register A (CRA).

The contents of DDRA determine whether a peripheral data line is an input or an output: a 0 means input, and a 1 means output. To set the A side for all inputs, as was done in Figure 5.2.1, DDRA had to be loaded with all 1s, or $FF in hexadecimal. Loading different words into the data direction register will cause all possible combinations of inputs and outputs. For instance, loading C7 (binary 1100 0111) into DDRA will put 1s into bits 0, 1, 2, 6, and 7, so data lines DA0, 1, 2, 6, and 7 will be outputs. And bits 3, 4, and 5 contain 0s, so lines DA3, 4, and 5 will be inputs.

EXAMPLE 5.2.1

Lines DA0–3 are wired to switches and DA4–7 to LEDs. What hexadecimal value must be written into DDRA to configure side A for this situation?

Solution

First, we recognize that a switch is an input device, so lines DA0–3 are to be inputs. And an LED is an output device, so lines DA4–7 are to be outputs.

Next, write the word in binary. Put a 1 in each bit that is to be an output and a 0 in each bit that is to be an input.

1 1 1 1 0 0 0 0

Finally, translate the binary number to hexadecimal.

Answer: $F0

Now that we see what values to write into DDRA, we need to find out *how* to write values into DDRA. To access DDRA, we use Control Register A (CRA). CRA lets us access either DRA or DDRA. We can't access both at once.

Like the other registers in the PIA, the control register contains 8 bits. But for now, bit 2 is the only one we'll discuss. The contents of bit 2 determine whether we're accessing the data direction register (DDRA) or the data register (DRA). A 0 in bit 2 of CRA means the data direction register, and a 1 in bit 2 of CRA means the data register.

EXAMPLE 5.2.2

What hexadecimal value should CRA be loaded with (a) to access DDRA; (b) to access DRA?

Solution

Bit 2 of CRA is the only one of concern here now; we don't as yet know the function of the other CRA bits. We'll clear them to 0s because that will do less harm than setting them to 1s.

(a) To access DDRA, bit 2 of CRA must contain 0. Clearing all other bits to 0 gives us (binary) %00000000 or (hexadecimal) $00.

(b) To access DRA, bit 2 of CRA must contain 1. Setting bit 2 and clearing all the others gives us %00000100, or $04.

Answer: (a) $00; (b) $04

Let's summarize what we must do to configure side A for inputs and outputs and to input or output data.

1. Load CRA with $00 so as to access DDRA.
2. Load DDRA with an appropriate value depending on what inputs and outputs are desired.
3. Load CRA with $04 so as to access DRA.
4. If outputting, write output data into DRA. If inputting, read data from DRA.

But how do we write into and read from the PIA's registers?

5.3 ADDRESSING THE PIA

Each register of the PIA has an address, and is accessed like a memory location. To load a register in the PIA, we write a number to the register's address. And to examine the contents of a PIA register, we read the contents of that register's address.

There are six registers altogether; three on each side. But a PIA requires only four addresses: two for each side. The control register has its own address. The data register and the data direction register share a single address. The actual numerical values of these addresses depend on the individual system.

The Motorola D2 Evaluation Kit is an example of a microcomputer that uses two PIAs: one to run the system's keyboard and display (the System PIA), and one for the user to configure (the User PIA). Each PIA has four addresses, corresponding to CRA, CRB, DRA/DDRA, and DRB/DDRB. DRA and DDRA share the same address. DRB and DDRB share another address. Table 5.3.1 gives the values used by the Motorola D2 Evaluation Kit.

TABLE 5.3.1 Motorola D2 Address Assignments for PIA Registers

Register	User PIA	System PIA
CRA	8005	8021
CRB	8007	8023
DRA/DDRA	8004	8020
DRB/DDRB	8006	8022

Note: Selection of DR or DDR is made by the contents of bit 2 of the CR:
(bit 2)=0: Address is valid for DDR
(bit 2)=1: Address is valid for DR

FIGURE 5.3.1 Addressing Control Register A

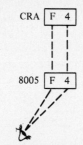

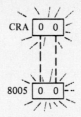

To read CRA, we examine location $8005. We see that location $8005 contains $F4, so CRA contains $F4. Bit 2 is set.

To write into CRA, we write into location $8005. Here, we clear CRA by clearing location $8005. Now bit 2 of CRA is clear.

Addressing the control register

We saw in the previous section that we load bit 2 of CRA with a 0 or a 1 to determine whether we're accessing DRA or DDRA. Now, we see why: DRA and DDRA both use the same address, so we must have some way of distinguishing between them.

For the moment, we'll concentrate just on the user PIA. Figure 5.3.1 illustrates accessing the control register. Examining location $8005 shows the contents of CRA, which we can change just by loading a different number into that location.

EXAMPLE 5.3.1

What location should be loaded with what value to be able to access DDRA of the user PIA?

Solution

To access the data direction register, first, we need to load CRA with $00. The address of CRA is $8005. Accessing DDRA means loading bit 2 of location $8005 with 0. We found in Example 5.2.2 that loading CRA with $00 does the job.

Answer: Load location $8005 with $00 (clear location $8005).

Some of the other bits in the control registers can be changed in the course of program execution. Thus we may find that locations $8005 and $8007 have had some of their contents altered since we loaded them with 00. Typically, bit 2 will not be changed in this fashion.

Now CRA is set so that we can get at DDRA through location $8004.

Addressing the data direction register

From Table 5.3.1 we see that the Motorola D2 Evaluation Kit uses address $8004 for DRA and DDRA of the user PIA. Once we've cleared CRA, we've assigned address $8004 to DDRA. So the contents of location $8004 (the address of DDRA) determines which of the data lines will function as input and which will function as output.

EXAMPLE 5.3.2

These locations were found to have these contents:

    8004   15
    8005   00

Which lines are configured for input and which for output?

Solution

Because location $8005 contains $00 (bit 2 of CRA is clear), we're looking at DDRA.

Write the contents of location $8004 (DDRA) in binary, then evaluate each bit individually. All bits that contain a 1 are outputs; all those that contain a 0 are inputs.

    0 0 0 1 0 1 0 1

Answer: PA1, PA3, and PA5–7 are inputs; PA0, PA2, and PA4 are outputs.

EXAMPLE 5.3.3

We want to configure PA0, PA2, and PA7 as inputs and the rest of the A lines as outputs. What locations should be loaded with what values to configure the system PIA in this way?

Solution

First, we consult Table 5.3.1 to find the addresses of DRA/DDRA and CRA for the system PIA. We find that $8021 is CRA's address, and DRA/DDRA share address $8020.

Next, load CRA with $00 to address DDRA. To do this, load location $8021 with $00. The address for DDRA for the system PIA is $8020. To determine what to load location $8020 with, write the word in binary:

    0 1 1 1 1 0 1 0

Finally, translate the word to hexadecimal.

Answer: Load location $8021 with $00, and location $8020 with $7A.

To address the B side, we look on Table 5.3.1 to get the addresses of the B registers, and proceed as in Examples 5.3.1 and 5.3.2.

Now that we've configured the data lines for input and output, we can use them to pass the actual data.

Addressing the data register

As we've said, the data registers have to share addresses with the data direction registers. So far, by setting bit 2 of CRA to 0, we've established that location $8004 would access DDRA. But now, we are finished with DDRA and need to access DRA. Thus, we go back to CRA and set bit 2 to 1. Then location $8004 will address DRA.

EXAMPLE 5.3.4

Assume that we have wired DA0–3 to 4 switches and DA4–7 to 4 LEDs and that we have just configured the data lines for input and output. What locations must be loaded with what values to load DRA with $6E?

Solution

First, we must set bit 2 of CRA to 1 so as to access DRA. We determined in Example 5.2.2 that the hexadecimal value $04 should be loaded into CRA to set bit 2. CRA is at location $8005, so we load location $8005 with $04. Next, we load location $8004 (DRA) with the data.

Answer: First, load location $8005 with $04. Next, load location $8004 with $6E. (Notice that the order makes a difference. If we loaded location $8004 with $6E first, we'd be loading DDRA and not DRA. To access DRA, first, we must load CRA's bit 2 with 1.)

In the previous example we stored $6E in DRA. Note that only the 6 part would be output, because bits DA0–3 were configured as inputs. Any hexadecimal digit could replace E with the same results output. Similarly, if we were to read DRA, only the contents of bits DA0–3 would be valid input data.

We should make a distinction here between hardware and software. When we decide which lines to use for input and which for output, that's a software decision. When we actually wire the lines to input or output devices, that's a hardware decision. Once we've made the hardware decision, the software decision has to go along with it. If we had, say, wired the A side to be all inputs, we'd have to program it to be all inputs from then on. We could program it to be all outputs, but it wouldn't work, because the lines wouldn't be attached to output devices.

Even though wiring the peripheral data lines commits us to a specific input/output configuration, we must still configure the PIA each time we use it. Recall that a low voltage on the PIA's RESET pin clears all its registers. Usually, the PIA's RESET pin is attached to the MPU's RESET pin, which may in turn be attached to a RESET button or switch on the microcomputer's console. Both the Motorola D2 and Heathkit trainer have such switches. Pushing the RESET button clears both DDRA and DDRB and therefore configures both sides for input.

It's not by accident that RESET automatically configures all peripheral data lines as inputs. When the microcomputer is turned on, a signal output by mistake to a peripheral might do some damage to the peripheral if it weren't prepared to receive the signal. Configuring all the lines as inputs will prevent a mistake like this from happening. Because of this automatic clearing of the PIA's registers, we must reconfigure the PIA each time we use it.

Figure 5.3.2 summarizes the sequencing necessary to configure side A. We can think of location $8004 as a "window" on *either* DRA or DDRA, depending on the contents of CRA's bit 2. Clearing location $8005 clears CRA's bit 2 and converts location $8004 into a window for DDRA. After we configure DRA for all inputs by storing all 0s in location $8004, we go back to location $8005 (CRA) and set bit 2 to 1 by storing $04. Now location $8004 is a window for DRA and not DDRA, and we can read the contents of DRA (in this case, 2E).

FIGURE 5.3.2   Configuring Side A for All Inputs and Reading DRA

First, clear location $8005.
This clears bit 2 of CRA
and lets location $8004
access DDRA.

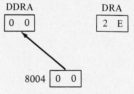

Next, clear location $8004.
This stores all 0s in DDRA
and configures DRA for
all inputs.

Next, store $04 in location
$8005. This sets bit 2 of
CRA and lets location $8004
access DRA.

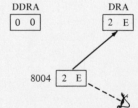

Now, reading location $8004 lets
us read whatever input data is in
DRA. Here, the value $2E is
being input.

FIGURE 5.3.3   Configuring Side A for All Outputs and Writing into DRA

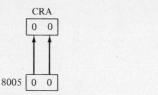

First, clear location $8005.
This clears bit 2 of CRA
and lets location $8004
access DDRA.

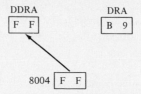

Next, store $FF in location $8004.
This stores all 1s in DDRA and
configures DRA for all outputs.

Next, store $04 in location
$8005. This sets bit 2 of
CRA and lets location $8004
access DRA.

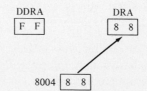

Now, writing any data into location
$8004 writes the data into DRA and
outputs the data. Here, the value
$88 is being output.

Figure 5.3.3 summarizes configuring side A for all outputs and writing into DRA. First, clearing bit 2 of CRA lets $8004 be a window for DDRA. Storing FF in location $8004 configures side A for all outputs. Then storing a 1 in bit 2 of CRA ($04 in location $8005) changes location $8004 into a window for DRA. Now writing a value (in this case, $88) into location $8004 outputs the value. Note that the previous contents of DRA ($B9) are destroyed.

Next, we'll see how to write some programs dealing with input and output.

5.4   PROGRAMMING THE PIA

Now that we know how to address the registers of the PIA, we can begin writing programs that configure and use the PIA.

Reading and writing in the PIA

To cause the CPU to read the contents of a location, we use LDA A or LDA B. To cause it to write into a location, we use STA A or STA B. Because the registers of the PIA are all represented by addresses, writing a program to read and write in them is easy.

EXAMPLE 5.4.1

Write a program segment to configure the A side of the user PIA for all inputs and the B side for all outputs.

Solution

So far, we've just been working with side A. But side B is configured in the same way, using its unique addresses. To configure side A for input, first, we must load CRA (in this case, location $8005) with $00 (that is, clear CRA). One way to load location $8005 with $00 would be to load accumulator A with $00 and then store it in location $8005, like this:

```
CONFIG   LDA A   #$00    GET READY TO CLEAR CRA
         STA A   $8005   LOAD CRA WITH ALL ZEROS
```

However, a shorter way to clear CRA is with the CLR (clear) instruction. Turning to its instruction information sheet, we see that CLR clears either an accumulator or a memory location. So we can clear CRA with just one instruction:

```
CONFIG    CLR  $8005   CLEAR CRA BIT 2 TO ADDRESS DDRA
```

Next, to set DDRA for all inputs, we load location $8004 with all 0s, which we can do by clearing as before.

```
          CLR    $8004      SET DDRA FOR ALL INPUTS BY LOADING ALL ZEROS
```

These two instructions configure side A for all inputs. Now for side B. First, we clear CRB (location $8007):

```
          CLR    $8007      CLEAR CRB BIT 2 TO ADDRESS DDRB
```

Next, to set DDRB for all outputs, we load location $8006 with all 1s ($FF). We can use ACCA for this.

```
          LDA A   #$FF    PUT ALL ONES IN ACCA TO STORE IN DDRB
          STA A   $8006   CONFIGURE DDRB FOR ALL OUTPUTS
```

Answer: Here's our finished assembly language program segment:

```
CONFIG   CLR     $8005   CLEAR CRA BIT 2 TO ADDRESS DDRA
         CLR     $8004   SET DDRA FOR ALL INPUTS
         CLR     $8007   CLEAR BIT 2 OF CRB
         LDA A   #$FF    PUT ALL ONES IN ACCA
         STA A   $8006   CONFIGURE DDRB FOR ALL OUTPUTS
```

Now that we've set up the A and B sides for input and for output, we're ready to actually do something.

The seven-segment display

Figure 5.4.1 shows a diagram of a **seven-segment display**, used in hand-held calculators, digital watches and clocks, and as output for many microcomputers, including the Motorola D2 Evaluation Kit and the Heathkit Microprocessor Trainer.

Each segment of the display is a bar-shaped LED. We cause the desired digit to be displayed by making the appropriate segments light up. All segments lit make an 8; segments 0, 3, 4, 5 make a C, and so on. In a microcomputer display we need numerals 0–F. The hexadecimal digits B and D show up as lowercase letters, and in Figure 5.4.1 we see why. If we tried to make a capital B, it would look just like an 8. And if we tried to make a capital D, it would look just like a 0.

The Motorola D2 Evaluation Kit uses a PIA to light its display. There are 6 digits on the D2's display, but we'll take a simple example using only one.

We want to light a seven-segment display using a PIA. We've already config-ured side B for all outputs, so we'll use this side. We'll attach each of the data lines on the B side to one segment of the display, as follows: PB0 to segment 0, PB1 to segment 1, and so on.

Next, let's assume a system in which a 0 in a bit in DRB causes the corresponding segment to be on, and a 1 causes it to be off. Then, to display digit 0, segments 0, 1, 2, 3, 4, and 5 have to be lit. This means putting a 0 in each of the corresponding data lines. We want segment 6 to be off, so that means putting a 1 in PB6. There are 8 data lines and only 7 segments, so we have 1 bit left over, which

FIGURE 5.4.1   The Seven-Segment Display

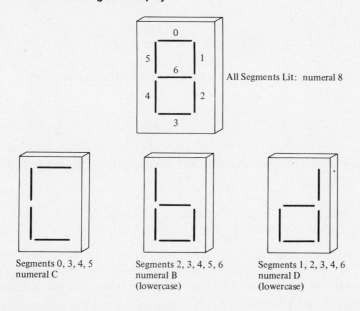

All Segments Lit: numeral 8

Segments 0, 3, 4, 5
numeral C

Segments 2, 3, 4, 5, 6
numeral B
(lowercase)

Segments 1, 2, 3, 4, 6
numeral D
(lowercase)

we'll always load with a 0. (Some seven-segment displays have a decimal point, and in this case bit 7 can be used for that.)

To display a 0 on the seven-segment display, we'd load DRB with the binary number 0100 0000, or 40 in hexadecimal. We could figure out a code for each digit in much the same way.

EXAMPLE 5.4.2

Referring to Figure 5.4.1 and the previous discussion, derive the code for displaying a 1 on the seven-segment display.

Solution

First, write out the DRB bit positions:

```
7   6   5   4   3   2   1   0
```

Next, figure out which segments need to be lit. For a 1 we want to light segments 1 and 2, which means that these bits get 0s. Bit 7 does, too, because it's not being used. We put 0s in these bits:

```
7   6   5   4   3   2   1   0
0                   0   0
```

Obviously, the remaining bits get 1s:

```
7   6   5   4   3   2   1   0
0   1   1   1   1   0   0   1
```

Finally, we translate the binary number to hexadecimal.

Answer: $79

Figure 5.4.2 shows a code for each hexadecimal digit. Now that we have this code, we can write a program that displays a hexadecimal digit when its corresponding digit code is input.

EXAMPLE 5.4.3

With side A configured for input and wired to a set of 8 switches and side B configured for output and wired to a seven-segment display as in Figure 5.4.2, write a program to display a hexadecimal digit based on the code input on the switches. Assume the user PIA addresses given in Table 5.3.1.

FIGURE 5.4.2   Derivation of Seven-Segment Code

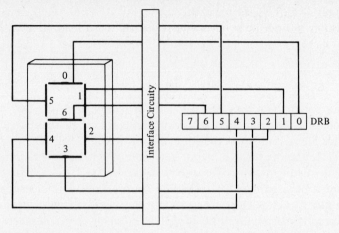

Hexadecimal Digit	Segments	Bianry Code	Hex Code
0	0, 1, 2, 3, 4, 5	0 1 0 0 0 0 0 0	40
1	1, 2	0 1 1 1 1 0 0 1	79
2	0, 1, 2, 4, 6	0 0 1 0 0 1 0 0	24
3	0, 1, 2, 3, 6	0 0 1 1 0 0 0 0	30
4	1, 2, 5, 6	0 0 0 1 1 0 0 1	19
5	0, 2, 3, 5, 6	0 0 0 1 0 0 1 0	12
6	0, 2, 3, 4, 5, 6	0 0 0 0 0 0 1 0	02
7	0, 1, 2	0 1 1 1 1 0 0 0	78
8	0, 1, 2, 3, 4, 5, 6	0 0 0 0 0 0 0 0	00
9	0, 1, 2, 5, 6	0 0 0 1 1 0 0 0	18
A	0, 1, 2, 4, 5, 6	0 0 0 0 1 0 0 0	08
B	2, 3, 4, 5, 6	0 0 0 0 0 0 1 1	03
C	0, 3, 4, 5	0 1 0 0 0 1 1 0	46
D	1, 2, 3, 4, 6	0 0 1 0 0 0 0 1	21
E	0, 3, 4, 5, 6	0 0 0 0 0 1 1 0	06
F	0, 4, 5, 6	0 0 0 0 1 1 1 0	0E

Solution

The program segment of Example 5.4.1 will work for configuring the PIA, so we assume that the segment we're writing has to do only with the actual input and output data.

First, we load the control registers' bit 2 with 1 to get at DRA and DRB:

```
DATREG  LDA A   #$04   LOAD ACCA WITH 04
        STA A   $8005  SET CRA BIT 2 TO ADDRESS DRA
        STA A   $8007  AND SET CRB BIT 2 TO ADDRESS DRB
```

Next, we read DRA:

```
GETDIG  LDA A   $8004  READ CODE INPUT ON SWITCHES
```

Next, we transfer the code to DRB:

```
        STA A   $8006  PUT CODE IN DRB TO LIGHT DISPLAY
```

Answer: Our program segment is

```
DATREG  LDA A   #$04    LOAD ACCA WITH 04
        STA A   $8005   SET CRA BIT 2 TO ADDRESS DRA
        STA A   $8007   AND SET CRB BIT 2 TO ADDRESS DRB
GETDIG  LDA A   $8004   READ CODE INPUT ON SWITCHES
        STA A   $8006   PUT CODE IN DRB TO LIGHT DISPLAY
```

We can put the two program segments in Examples 5.4.1 and 5.4.3 together. Then we'll have a program that configures side A for all inputs, side B for all outputs, reads DRA, and stores the contents of DRA in DRB. Whatever gets stored in DRB will determine what numeral gets output on the seven-segment display. Figure 5.4.3 is a listing of this composite program.

Writing a program can be simplified by breaking it into smaller segments, which are easier to write. Then, when we put the small segments together, we have finished a larger program. Writing programs in small pieces has another specific advantage where input/output is concerned.

We've said that once a PIA is wired for input and output, it has to be programmed that way thereafter. So that we don't have to keep writing the same program segment over and over again to configure the PIA, we write it just once, make sure it's correct, and then just have it handy to attach to the beginning of all the other programs we might write for this configuration of the PIA. We'll have occasion to do this in later chapters.

We can notice a few things about this program. First, we weren't able to use the direct mode, because none of the PIA addresses were on page zero. Second, we've put labels in the program: CONFIG (for *configure*), DATREG (for *data register*), and GETDIG (for *get digit*). A label should mean something to the

FIGURE 5.4.3   Listing of Composite Program from Examples 5.4.1 and 5.4.3

```
                        ;THIS PROGRAM CONFIGURES SIDE A OF
                        ;THE USER PIA FOR ALL INPUTS AND
                        ;SIDE B FOR ALL OUTPUTS. SIDE A
                        ;IS ATTACHED TO A SET OF EIGHT SWITCHES
                        ;SIDE B TO A 7-SEGMENT DISPLAY.
                        ;THIS PROGRAM CAUSES A NUMERAL TO BE
                        ;OUTPUT ON THE 7-SEGMENT DISPLAY
                        ;IN RESPONSE TO A HEXADECIMAL CODE
                        ;INPUT ON THE SWITCHES.
0000 7F 80 05   CONFIG  CLR     $8005   CLEAR CRA BIT 2
0003 7F 80 04           CLR     $8004   SET DDRA ALL INPUTS
0006 7F 80 07           CLR     $8007   CLEAR CRB BIT 2
0009 B6 FF              LDA A   #$FF    PUT ALL ONES INTO ACCA
000B B7 80 06           STA A   $8006   CONFIGURE DDRB ALL OUTPUTS
000E 86 04      DATREG  LDA A   #$04    LOAD ACCA WITH 04
0010 B7 80 05           STA A   $8005   SET CRA BIT 2 TO 1, ADDRESS DRA
0013 B7 80 07           STA A   $8007   SET CRB BIT 2, ADDRESS DRB
0016 B6 80 04   GETDIG  LDA A   $8004   READ CODE INPUT ON SWITCHES
0019 B7 80 06           STA A   $8006   PUT CODE IN DRB, LIGHT DISPLAY
001C 3E                 WAI
```

programmer and others reading the program. For now, it may not be obvious where to put labels—and in this program it really doesn't matter, because they aren't used for anything except to provide a few reference points in the program. Later, as we become more sophisticated, we'll learn where to put labels.

Third, the first few lines tell what the program does. Each line has a semicolon (;) in front of it, a convention we'll use to mean that a comment follows. For the sake of people reading the program it's always a good idea to put such an explanation at the front of every program.

We've now had some experience at writing simple programs. Most programs we'll eventually want to write won't be this simple. Next, we'll be looking at some aids to program writing that will help us when we get to more interesting problems.

REVIEW QUESTIONS

1. What is an **I/O port**? What is a **peripheral interface adapter (PIA)**? What is a **peripheral**?
2. What do the PIA's R/W and RESET pins do?
3. Why does the PIA have two kinds of data pins? Name each kind, the number of pins in each, and tell what each is for.
4. Is there a rule for how many data lines may be input and how many may be output? Explain.
5. Name the three types of registers in the PIA and state their functions.
6. Explain how we can use a set of 8 switches to input data to the MPU through the PIA. (Refer to Figure 5.2.1.)
7. What is an **LED**? Are LEDs always wired so that a 1 means light on and a 0 means light off?
8. Explain how we can use a set of 8 LEDs to receive output data from the MPU through the PIA. (Refer to Figure 5.2.2.)
9. How do we set the A side for all inputs or all outputs?
10. Which bit of CRA determines whether DRA or DDRA is being accessed? Explain.
11. What does it mean to **configure** the data lines of the PIA?
12. How do we access the registers of the PIA?
13. What do we mean by **user** and **system** PIA?
14. How do we read from and write into CRA? What value should be loaded into CRA to access DDRA?
15. How do we read from and write into DDRA? How do we know what value to write into DDRA?
16. Explain how we can tell from the contents of DDRA which lines are configured for input and which for output.
17. Since the data register and data direction register share the same address, how do we know which one we're addressing?
18. Why must we load bit 2 of the control register before loading data into the data register?
19. Why must we reconfigure the PIA each time we use it, even though it might be wired in the same way as it was the last time we used it?

20. Does storing an 8-bit word in DRA mean that 8 bits will always be output? When might all 8 bits not be output?
21. What instructions do we use to allow the CPU to read from and write into the PIA?
22. What are two program instructions we can use to load a register with 00?
23. What is a **seven-segment** display? How does it work?
24. Explain how the digit code of Figure 5.4.2 was derived.
25. Explain how to write a program to read input on switches and display a numeral on a seven-segment display.
26. Can we use the direct addressing mode when dealing with PIA addresses? Explain.
27. What does a semicolon in front of a line of assembly language program mean?

EXERCISES

Set A (answers at back of book)

1. What would be the contents of DRA for the following switch settings, left to right? (Refer to Figure 5.2.1.)
   a. up up down down up down up up
   b. down up down up down down up down
2. Refer to Figure 5.2.2. Assume a system set up so that a 1 = light on and a 0 = light off. What would be the contents of DRA for the following (left to right):
   a. on off off on on on on off
   b. off off off on on on on on
3. Bits 0, 1, and 2 are to be used as inputs and the rest outputs on the A side. Give the contents of DDRA that would accomplish this.
4. The contents of DDRA is $F2. Which data lines are inputs, and which are outputs?
5. We read the contents of CRA as follows:
   a. $A5   b. $26   c. $47   d. $B3
   For each, state whether DRA or DDRA is being addressed.
6. We wish to accomplish the following:
   a. Address DRA
   b. Address DDRB
   State the contents of CRA and CRB needed for each.
7. What locations should be loaded with what values to be able to access DDRA and DRB of the system PIA?
8. For these locations and their contents determine which lines of the system PIA are configured for input and which for output:

   $8021   00
   $8023   00
   $8020   C9
   $8022   30

9. What locations should be loaded with what values to configure the system PIA in this way:

   Side A: lines 0–3 inputs, the rest outputs
   Side B: lines 1, 3, 5, and 7 inputs, the rest outputs

10. Assume that we have configured the system PIA for input and output. What locations should be loaded with what values to place $77 in DRA and $90 in DRB?

11. For Exercise 10 assume that DDRA contains $00 and DDRB contains $FF. Will both values stored in Exercise 10 be output? Explain.

12. Referring to Figure 5.4.2, assume a system where a 1 in DRB causes a segment to be on and that the unused bit is still loaded with 0. Derive the hexadecimal code for numerals 0 through 3.

13. Refer to Figure 5.4.2, and assume a system where a 0 in DRB causes a segment to be on. Derive hexadecimal codes for these letters:
a. J b. P c. L d. U

EXERCISES

Set B (answers not given)

1. Assume a system set up so that a 1=switch up and a 0=switch down. What would be the contents of DRA for the following switch settings? (Left to right; refer to Figure 5.2.1.)
a. up up down up down down up up
b. down up up down down down up down

2. Refer to Figure 5.2.2, and state the contents of DRB for the following (left to right):
a. on on on off off on off on
b. off on on off on on on off

3. Bits 0, 5, and 6 are to be used as outputs and the rest inputs on the B side. Give the contents of DDRB that would accomplish this.

4. The contents of DDRA is $A7. Which data lines are inputs, and which are outputs?

5. We read the contents of CRB as follows:
a. $FA b. $34 c. $0E d. $B1
For each, state whether DRB or DDRB is being addressed.

6. We wish to accomplish the following:
a. Address DDRA
b. Address DRB
State the contents of CRA and CRB needed for each.

7. What location should be loaded with what values to be able to access DRA and DDRB of the user PIA?

8. For these locations and their contents, determine which lines of the user PIA are configured for input and which for output:

$8005 $00 $8004 $39
$8007 $00 $8006 $E1

9. What locations should be loaded with what values to configure the user PIA in this way:

   Side A: Lines 1 and 4 outputs, the rest inputs
   Side B: Line 7 input, the rest outputs

10. Assume that we have configured the user PIA for input and output. What locations should be loaded with what values to place $AA in DRA and $4C in DRB?

11. For Exercise 10 assume that DDRA contains $27 and DDRB contains $95. What values in what bits will be output?
12. Referring to Figure 5.4.2, assume a system where a 1 in DRB causes a segment to be on and that the unused bit is still loaded with 0. Derive the hexadecimal code for numerals A through D.
13. Refer to Figure 5.4.2, and assume a system where a 0 in DRB causes a segment to be on. Derive hexadecimal codes for these letters:
    a. lower case r
    b. lower case y
    c. lower case g
    d. lower case h

PROGRAMMING IDEAS

1. Write a program segment to configure the B side of the system PIA for all inputs and the A side for all outputs.
2. Write a program that controls a set of 8 lights with 8 switches so that a switch or switches on turns on the corresponding light or lights. Assume switches are on the A side and lights on the B side. Light on=0; switch on=0.
3. Same as 2, but for light on=1, switch on=1.
4. Modify the program of Figure 5.4.3 to use the system PIA and for side A=seven-segment display and side B=switches.

6 Aids to Program Writing

LEARNING OBJECTIVES

After completing this chapter, you should be able to:

1. Give a definition, explanation, or example for each of these: *algorithm, flowchart, element, terminal box, task box, decision box, conditional branch, connection box, utility program, software aid, editor, resident assembler, cross assembler, assembler directive, field, sequence field, line number, label field, operation field, operand field, comment field.*
2. Write an algorithm and a general flowchart for a simple problem.
3. Write detailed flowcharts for simple problems.
4. Explain and carry out the steps necessary for program development.
5. Explain and use correctly the assembler directives NAM, END, EQU, and ORG.
6. Explain and use correctly the assembly language statement format.
7. Write an assembly language program from a flowchart.
8. If an assembler is available, use it to obtain a listing.
9. Explain the use of labels and use them correctly.
10. Know and use correctly the conventions for using numbers in assembly language statements.
11. Explain the most common sources of error messages.

So far, we've written simple programs using a few basic programming tools. But we'd like to be able to tackle more interesting problems and their microcomputer solutions. Fortunately, programming aids have been developed that will let us program much more comfortably, systematically, and successfully than would be possible without them. In this chapter we'll learn how to make use of some of these programming aids.

6.1 ALGORITHMS AND FLOWCHARTS

Almost anyone could make ice cubes or a piece of toast without benefit of a recipe, but most of us would need one if we wanted to make a cake. In the same way, we've written some programs without formalizing the method we used for writing them. Now, though, we're ready to start writing programs that will require the equivalent of a "recipe."

Most computer programs are developed by first writing an algorithm. An **algorithm** is a series of logical steps to be followed sequentially in order to solve a problem or perform a task. A recipe is an algorithm, as is a set of instructions for building a kit. Developing a microcomputer program is a job that lends itself well to the application of an algorithm. Figure 6.1.1 gives an algorithm for developing a microcomputer program. Although we're introducing this algorithm now to serve as an example, we'll also be using it as a guide for developing programs throughout the book.

A **flowchart** is a graphical representation of an algorithm. Instead of numbered steps, a flowchart contains boxes, called **elements**, which represent the steps. Figure 6.1.2 shows some basic flowchart elements.

The **terminal box** shows where the flowchart starts or stops. The **task box** contains an operation, or something to do. This operation can be very specific (like "clear accumulator A") or very general (like "sort a list"). A general task statement would usually be broken down into several specific tasks at a later time.

The **decision box** has one input and two outputs. In the decision box, we ask a question that can be answered "Yes" or "No," depending on whether or not a certain condition is true. If yes, one exit path is taken; if no, the other is taken. A point in a flowchart that contains a decision box is called a **conditional branch**,

FIGURE 6.1.1 Algorithm for Program Development

1. Define the problem.
2. Describe the problem in terms of what is to be put in, what is to be gotten out, and what processing is to be done.
3. Write a general algorithm and/or flowchart in English to solve the problem.
4. Write successively more detailed flowcharts until each box can be translated into a single assembly language instruction.
5. Write an assembly language program from the flowchart.
6. Assemble the program.
7. Load the program into the microcomputer's memory.
8. Verify that the program has been loaded correctly.
9. Execute the program. If it works, go to 11.
10. If it doesn't work, go back to 3, 4, 5, 6, 7, or 8, depending on where the error(s) is (are). Find the error(s) and correct it (them).
11. Done.

FIGURE 6.1.2 Flowchart Elements

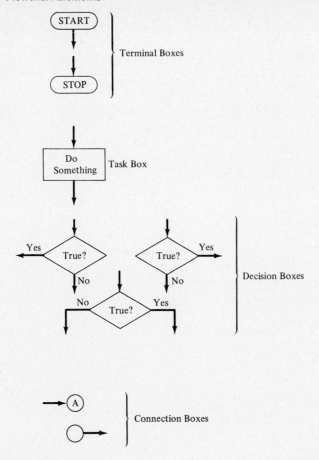

because the flowchart branches in one of two directions, depending on a certain condition.

The **connection box** lets us connect one segment of a flowchart to another segment. Putting a letter inside the connection box tells us where the connection is. Connection boxes are useful if we run out of room on a page and have to continue a flowchart to another page. Or we may want to take a segment of a flowchart out to look at it more closely, to expand or use it in another flowchart. Without any letter inside it, a connection box tells us that we're dealing with a segment and not with a complete flowchart.

We can illustrate how these elements are used by translating the algorithm developed earlier into a flowchart, shown in Figure 6.1.3.

FIGURE 6.1.3 Flowchart Showing Program Development

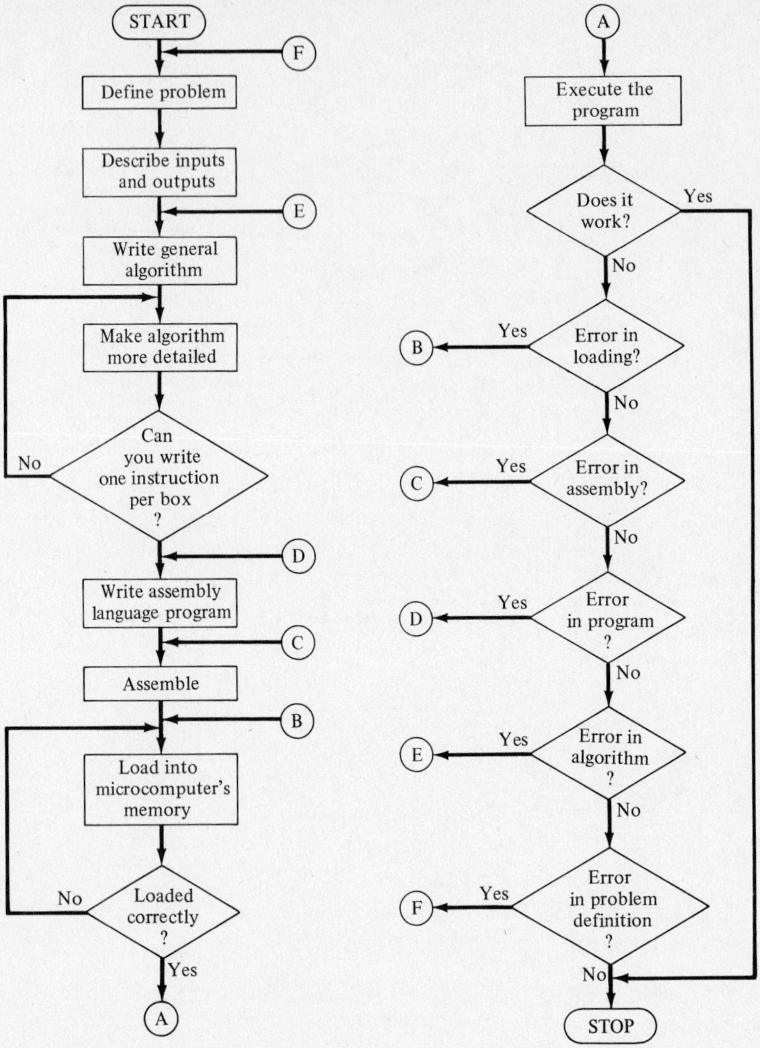

6.2 PROGRAM DEVELOPMENT

To illustrate how to use the algorithm of Figure 6.1.1, or the flowchart of Figure 6.1.3, we'll use a program with which we're already familiar: the program that appears in Chapter 5, Figure 5.4.3. Refer to Figure 6.1.1 as we carry out each step of the algorithm.

1. Define the problem:
A seven-segment display is wired to the B side of a PIA in such a way that a

0 turns a segment on and a 1 turns a segment off, as in Figure 5.4.2. A set of 8 switches is wired to the A side in such a way that a switch on is a 0 and a switch off is a 1. The PIA's addresses are $8005 and $8007 for CRA and CRB, and $8004 and $8006 for DRA/DDRA and DRB/DDRB. Write a program that will light the segments of the seven-segment display according to a binary seven-segment code that is input on the switches.

2. State the desired inputs and outputs:
   Inputs: A 7-bit code on the switches.
   Outputs: The desired lighted segments on the seven-segment display.
3. Write a simple algorithm in English:
   a. Read the data from the switches.
   b. Output the same data to the seven-segment display.
4. Write successively more detailed flowcharts until each box can be translated into an assembly language instruction.

Here, as will usually be the case, our simple English algorithm is a far cry from this goal. To achieve it, we break down each step into smaller steps. We ask "What is necessary for the microprocessor to be able to read the data from the switches and output data to the seven-segment display?" First, the PIA has to be configured for input and output. Next, we must get the PIA ready to be read from and written into.

FIGURE 6.2.1 A General Flowchart

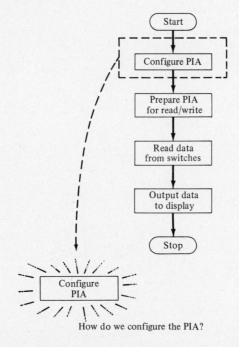

How do we configure the PIA?

Finally, we read from side A and write into side B. So we can write this more detailed algorithm:

1. Configure the PIA.
2. Prepare the PIA for reading and writing.
3. Read the data from side A.
4. Write the same data into side B.

At this point we can start writing flowcharts. Figure 6.2.1 shows a general flowchart that corresponds to the algorithm we just wrote. To develop this flowchart, we expand each box into several smaller boxes. Taking the first box, we ask "How

FIGURE 6.2.2 Flowchart Development

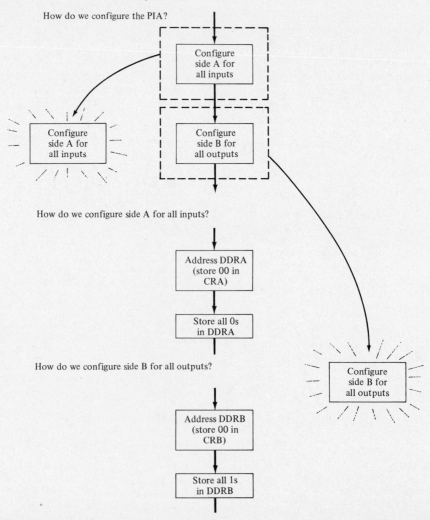

do we configure the PIA?" The answer is:

1. Configure side A of the PIA for all inputs.
2. Configure side B of the PIA for all outputs.

Figure 6.2.2 shows the box configure PIA expanded to these two boxes. But this still isn't detailed enough, so next we ask "How do we configure side A for all inputs?" The answer is:

a. Address DDRA (store 00 in CRA).
b. Store all zeros in DDRA.

Now, at last we're at the point where we can write an instruction for each of these. Thus we go to the next box, and ask "How do we configure side B for all outputs?" The answer is:

a. Address DDRB (store 00 in CRB).
b. Store all ones (FF) in DDRB.

FIGURE 6.2.3 Final Details Added to First Element of Flowchart

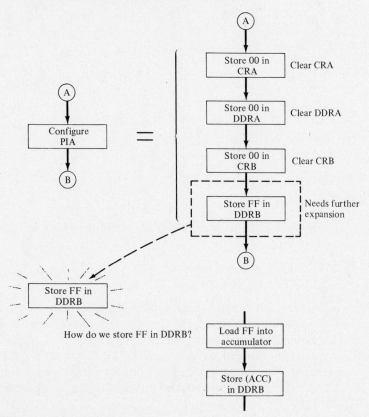

FIGURE 6.2.4 Two Ways to Represent Flowchart Details

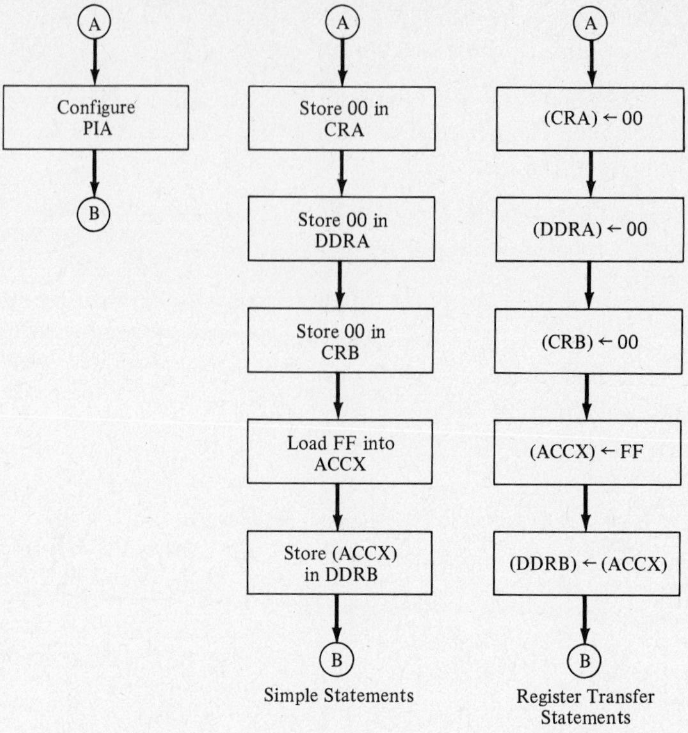

Simple Statements

Register Transfer Statements

We can store 00 in DDRA in one instruction, but it takes two to store FF in DDRB. We could show this by using register transfer notation:

$(ACCX) \leftarrow FF$

$(DDRB) \leftarrow (ACCX)$

So the last box in Figure 6.2.3, entitled "Store FF in DDRB" needs to be expanded further:

1. Load $FF into an accumulator.
2. Store (ACCX) in (DDRB).

Figure 6.2.4 shows the detailed expansion of the general box "Configure PIA," expressed in two ways. We can put simple, descriptive statements in the task boxes, or we can use register transfer notation. Each way has its advantages. Descriptive statements have more meaning to someone reading the flowchart for the first time (or even to the person who wrote it). Register transfer notation gives a more exact picture of what is taking place and makes it easier to translate to an assembly

FIGURE 6.2.5 Expansion of Remaining Task Boxes

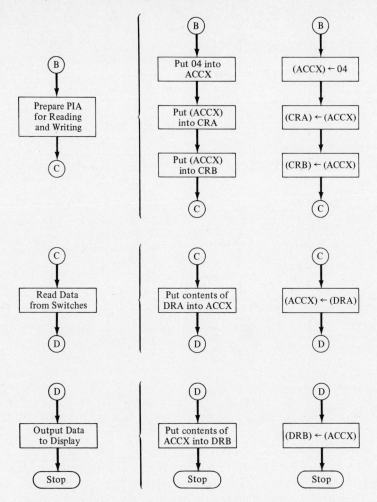

language instruction later on. It's a matter of individual preference. Some people like to use a combination of the two. Each individual should write flowcharts in whatever kind of notation is most comfortable and clear.

To expand the remaining three task boxes in Figure 6.2.1, we'd go through the same process as for the first. The result is shown in Figure 6.2.5. The last two task boxes from the general flowchart each translate into only 1 detailed box.

Figure 6.2.6 shows the completed, detailed flowchart. Here, we've written simple statements in one flowchart in still another way, just to show that there are as many ways of expression as there are programmers.

FIGURE 6.2.6 Finished Detailed Flowchart Showing Alternate Statements

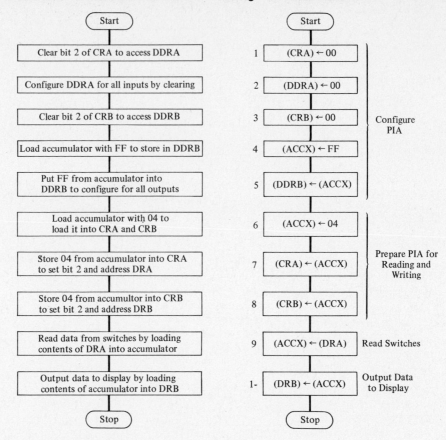

Looking back at the flowchart on Figure 6.1.3, we see that we've done the tasks in the first three task boxes, and can now answer "yes" to "Can you write one instruction per box?" So this brings us down to the next task: "Write assembly language program."

Before we do this, we need an introduction to another programming aid.

6.3 THE ASSEMBLER

To make program writing easier for the user, a number of programs have been developed, called **utility programs** or **software aids**. Among the utility programs generally available are:

Monitors. As we saw before, these let us examine and change contents of memory and registers and execute and debug user programs.

Editors. These programs let us correct or modify what we've written. Usually, only microcomputers that were equipped with a CRT terminal or typewriter would have editors.

Assemblers. These programs translate assembly language statements into machine language. Again, usually only microcomputers that have CRT terminals or printers have assemblers, but there are a few exceptions.

We could have a microcomputer that had its own assembler in ROM or on disk. Then, we'd write an assembly language program, call on the assembler to assemble it, and then run the program on the same microcomputer. When the assembler resides on the same microcomputer on which the program will be run, we call this assembler a **resident assembler**.

Large computers can run assemblers for microcomputers or other computers. An assembler that assembles a program to be run on another computer is called a **cross assembler**. To use a cross assembler, we write a program in assembly language, let the cross assembler provide us with a listing, then take the listing to our microcomputer, load the object program, and run it. Because neither the Motorola D2 Evaluation Kit nor the Heathkit Microprocessor Trainer have resident assemblers, we must use cross assemblers (or hand assembly) to get an object program to run on these microcomputers.

To use an assembler, we have to obey its rules of grammar. Each assembler has its own rules, and most differ from one another. We'll look at some of the rules for our particular cross assembler next.

Minimum requirements for use of the assembler

We already wrote an assembly language program, shown in Figure 5.4.3. We wrote this program to be hand assembled. We're almost ready to give this program to an assembler, but not quite. An assembler can't think and reason the way we can, so we have to give it more explicit instructions. Here are a few basic requirements for this particular cross assembler:

1. We must give our program a name of 6 letters or fewer. For our own convenience, we'd usually make up a name that suggests what the program does: for instance, DISPLY for our program to light a seven-segment display. The first statement in an assembly language program has to tell the name of the program, like this:

NAM DISPLY

The symbol NAM is one of several assembler directives. Assembler directives are to the assembler what mnemonics are to the microprocessor. An **assembler directive** is an instruction to the assembler. Unlike mnemonics, assembler directives don't get translated into machine code. They are used only to tell the assembler what to do.

The statement NAM DISPLY tells the assembler, "This is the beginning of a source program whose name is DISPLY."

2. We must tell the assembler where the end of the source program is. This we do with the assembler directive END. The last statement of an assembly language program must be

END

This statement tells the assembler "This is the end of the source program." The assembler assembles everything between the NAM and END statements, and stops assembling when it comes to END.

3. We must conform to a very strict statement format, which we'll discuss next.

Format of an assembly language statement

We've already seen that assembly language statements have a label, operation, operand, and comment column. These columns are called **fields**. When we're writing programs for use with an assembler, there is usually one additional field: the **sequence field**. The sequence field contains a **line number**, used for identifying or locating a line. Most assemblers allow line numbers from 0 to 1000. Usually, it's convenient to number lines in increments of ten (100, 110, 120, and so on) because this leaves room for us to insert lines during later revisions of the program. Some assemblers require the user to type in the line numbers. Other assemblers provide the line numbers automatically.

Figure 6.3.1 shows an assembly language statement that contains entries in all possible fields. On the left is the sequence field. Next is the **label field**, which may contain any of these:

1. A label
2. A comment, preceded by a comment symbol in the first space of the label field. For the cross assembler we're using, this symbol is a semicolon (;). The Motorola M68SAM cross assembler (Appendix B) uses an asterisk (*) as a comment symbol. Following the comment symbol is the comment,

FIGURE 6.3.1 **Format of an Assembly Language Statement**

Sequence	Label	Operation	Operand	Comment
170	GETDIG	LDA A	$8004	READ CODE INPUT ON SWITCHES

FIGURE 6.3.2   Alternative Contents of Label Field

Sequence	Semicolon at start of label field indicates a comment			
	Label	Operation	Operand	Comment
100	;THIS IS JUST A COMMENT, AND CAN OCCUPY THE WHOLE LINE			
110	;OR MORE. Each line of comment begins with a comment symbol.			
150		LDA A	# $05	THIS LINE HAS NO LABEL.
	Nothing in label field			

which then occupies the entire line. A comment may occupy more than one line, but each line of comment must begin with a comment symbol.

3. Nothing (the label field is blank)

We've already seen (1) in Figure 6.3.1. The other two possibilities are shown in Figure 6.3.2.

After the label field comes the **operation field**, which contains either a mnemonic or an assembler directive. For mnemonics where accumulator A or accumulator B must be specified, some assemblers expect a space between: for instance, LDA A. Others require them to be strung together: LDAA. Every instruction in an assembly language program must have something in the operation field.

Next comes the **operand field**. Sometimes the operand field can be empty, if the instruction is one that doesn't take an operand. (For example, the WAI instruction.) The assembler, when it interprets the operation, also gets the information on whether or not to expect an operand.

Last is the **comment field**. This can be empty, too, but a few words explaining the instruction makes the program more understandable.

Now we have enough information to write a simple assembly language program.

6.4   WRITING AN ASSEMBLY LANGUAGE PROGRAM

Let's refer to Figure 6.1.3 and see where we are in the development of our program. We're on the task box labeled "Write assembly language program." To do that, we'll refer to the flowchart we made (Figure 6.2.6).

EXAMPLE 6.4.1

Write an assembly language program from the flowchart of Figure 6.2.6.

Solution

We obey the rules for assembly language programming, and translate each box into an assembly language statement, using a worksheet as in Chapter 4. If the source program is to be given to an assembler, we can leave out the address and OP code columns, because these will be provided in the listing.

The first statement must contain the NAM assembler directive, so we translate the START box like this:

SEQ.	LABEL	OP'N	OPERAND	COMMENT
100		NAM	DISPLY	

Here, we arbitrarily chose 100 for our starting line number. We could choose any other number. Note that NAM is an assembler directive and so must appear in the operation field. We arbitrarily chose DISPLY for the name of our program, but any other would work as long as it obeyed the rules for labels (to be explained in Section 6.5).

It's a good idea to have a few lines of comment next, telling what the program is about.

```
110 ;THIS PROGRAM CONFIGURES SIDE A OF THE USER PIA FOR ALL
120 ;INPUTS AND SIDE B FOR ALL OUTPUTS. SIDE A IS ATTACHED
130 ;TO A SET OF EIGHT SWITCHES AND SIDE B TO A 7-SEGMENT
140 ;DISPLAY. THIS PROGRAM CAUSES A CHARACTER TO BE OUTPUT
150 ;ON THE 7-SEGMENT DISPLAY IN RESPONSE TO A BINARY CODE
160 ;INPUT ON THE SWITCHES.
```

Notice that we must put a semicolon at the start of *each* line of comment.

Next, we look at Box 1 in Figure 6.2.6. We can use the CLR mnemonic to put 0s into a location (in this case, $8005, the location of CRA).

SEQ.	LABEL	OP'N	OPERAND	COMMENT
170	CONFIG	CLR	$8005	CLEAR CRA BIT 2 TO ADDRESS DDRA

We've chosen the label CONFIG to remind us that this program segment is supposed to configure the PIA for input and output. The label doesn't have to be there but is useful for providing clarity.

The CLR mnemonic can be used for boxes 2 and 3:

SEQ.	LABEL	OP'N	OPERAND	COMMENT
180		CLR	$8004	CLEAR DDRA FOR SIDE A ALL INPUTS
190		CLR	$8007	CLEAR CRB BIT 2 TO ADDRESS DDRB

Boxes 4 and 5: To load an accumulator (A or B) with $FF, we use the immediate mode. Then we store $FF in location $8006, the address of DDRB.

SEQ.	LABEL	OP'N	OPERAND	COMMENT
200		LDA B	#$FF	PUT ALL ONES INTO ACCB TO STORE IN DDRB
210		STA B	$8006	SET SIDE B ALL OUTPUTS

Boxes 6, 7, and 8: We can identify this program segment with the label INOUT for input/output.

SEQ.	LABEL	OP'N	OPERAND	COMMENT
220	INOUT	LDA A	#$04	GET READY TO SET BIT 2
230		STA A	$8005	SET BIT 2 OF CRA TO ADDRESS DRA
240		STA A	$8007	SET BIT 2 OF CRB TO ADDRESS DRB

FIGURE 6.4.1 Finished Source Program for Example 6.4.1

Seq.	Label	Op'n	Operand	Comment
100		NAM	DISPLY	
110		;THIS PROGRAM CONFIGURES SIDE A OF THE USER PIA FOR ALL		
120		;INPUTS AND SIDE B FOR ALL OUTPUTS. SIDE A IS ATTACHED TO		
130		;A SET OF EIGHT SWITCHES AND SIDE B TO A 7-SEGMENT DISPLAY.		
140		;THIS PROGRAM CAUSES A NUMERAL TO BE OUTPUT ON THE 7-SEGMENT		
150		;DISPLAY IN RESPONSE TO A		
160		;HEXADECIMAL CODE INPUT ON THE SWITCHES.		
170	CONFIG	CLR	$8005	CLEAR CRA BIT 2 TO ADDRESS DDRA
180		CLR	$8004	CLEAR DDRA FOR SIDE A ALL INPUTS
190		CLR	$8007	CLEAR CRB BIT 2 TO ADDRESS DDRB
200		LDA B	#$FF	PUT ALL ONES INTO ACCB TO STORE IN DDRB
210		STA B	$8006	SET SIDE B ALL OUTPUTS
220	INOUT	LDA A	#$04	GET READY TO SET BIT 2
230		STA A	$8005	SET BIT 2 OF CRA TO ADDRESS DRA
240		STA A	$8007	SET BIT 2 OF CRB TO ADDRESS DRB
250	GETDIG	LDA A	$8004	READ INPUT DATA FROM DRA
260		STA A	$8006	OUTPUT IT TO DRB
270		WAI		WAIT
280		END		

Boxes 9 and 10: We can identify the input statement with the label GETDIG, for Get Digit.

SEQ.	LABEL	OP'N	OPERAND	COMMENT
250	GETDIG	LDA A	$8004	READ INPUT DATA FROM DRA
260		STA A	$8006	OUTPUT IT TO DRB

Finally, the STOP box must have two statements: one for the microprocessor and one for the assembler.

SEQ.	LABEL	OP'N	OPERAND	COMMENT
270		WAI		WAIT
280		END		

Notice that line 270 has entries only in the operation and comment fields and line 280, only in the operation field.

Answer: Figure 6.4.1 shows the completed source program.

The next box in Figure 6.1.3 says "Assemble." To do this, submit your source program to an assembler as directed by your instructor according to the requirements of the particular assembler you may be using. The assembler produces a listing. A listing generated by the particular assembler we are discussing is shown in Figure 6.4.2. This assembler does not accept our line numbers, so we had to get rid of those before giving the source program to the assembler.

FIGURE 6.4.2 Assembly Listing of Figure 6.4.1

```
DISPLY
M6800 ASSEMBLER LISTING VERSION 1.6      14OCT 80 20:27   PAGE   2
FIG 641   DAT      14 OCT 80 20:23

                                 5 ;THIS PROGRAM CONFIGURES SIDE A OF THE USER PIA FOR ALL
                                 6 ;INPUTS AND SIDE B FOR ALL OUTPUTS. SIDE A IS ATTACHED TO
                                 7 ;A SET OF EIGHT SWITCHES AND SIDE B TO A 7-SEGMENT DISPLAY.
                                 8 ;THIS PROGRAM CAUSES A NUMERAL TO BE OUTPUT ON THE 7-SEGMENT
                                 9 ;DISPLAY IN RESPONSE TO A
                                10 ;HEXADECIMAL CODE INPUT ON THE SWITCHES.
0000 7F 80 05                   11 CONFIG  CLR    $8005   CLEAR CRA BIT 2 TO ADDRESS DDRA
0003 7F 80 04                   12         CLR    $8004   CLEAR DDRA FOR SIDE A ALL INPUTS
0006 7F 80 07                   13         CLR    $8007   CLEAR CRB BIT 2 TO ADDRESS DDRB
0009 C6 FF                      14         LDA B  #$FF    PUT ALL ONES INTO ACCB TO STORE IN DDRB
000B F7 80 06                   15         STA B  $8006   SET SIDE B ALL OUTPUTS
000E 86 04                      16 INOUT   LDA A  #$04    GET READY TO SET BIT 2
0010 B7 80 05                   17         STA A  $8005   SET BIT 2 OF CRA TO ADDRESS DRA
0013 B7 80 07                   18         STA A  $8007   SET BIT 2 OF CRB TO ADDRESS DRB
0016 B6 80 04                   19 GETDIG  LDA A  $8004   READ INPUT DATA FROM DRA
0019 B7 80 06                   20         STA A  $8006   OUTPUT IT TO DRB
001C 3E                         21         WAI            WAIT
001D                            22         END


NO STATEMENTS FLAGGED


CROSS-REFERENCE TABL

CONFIG         0000              11
GETDIG         0016              19
INOUT          000E              16
OK
```

Assemblers differ from one another, even those using the same language. The listing of Figure 6.4.2 may not look exactly like one produced by another assembler. Still, we can notice a few things about the listing. (1) The assembler assigned it $0000 as a starting address, without being told where the program is to start in memory. (2) The assembler has used the extended mode exclusively. (Like us, the assembler would choose the direct mode if that were possible.) (3) The assembler has generated line numbers, for it and us to use as reference. (4) The message "NO STATE-MENTS FLAGGED" means that there were no errors. (This is always a heartening message to read.) (5) Note the cross-reference table. The assembler has listed each label, its corresponding address, and the line number where it appears.

Now that we have the listing, the next step is to load the machine code into the microcomputer's memory, verify the loading, then execute the program. If the program worked, we'd be done. If it didn't, we'd debug it by following the rest of the flowchart. Although the assembler gave our program a clean bill of health by saying NO STATEMENTS FLAGGED, it means only that we didn't break any of the assembler's rules. We could still have made errors in logic at any other point in the program.

6.5   MORE ABOUT THE ASSEMBLER

We learned enough about the assembler in the last section to be able to write a simple assembly language program that the assembler would accept. There is much more to know about the assembler. In this section we'll touch on a few more points and leave the rest until we need it.

Labels

Let's expand the definition of a label introduced in Chapter 4. Each assembler has rules for what can be a label and what can't. To be used with our particular cross assembler, a valid label must:

1. consist of 1 to 6 characters
2. contain only characters A–Z and 0–9
3. have a letter for the first character
4. not be A, B, or X

Thus DOG, NUM1, and G are valid labels; ELEPHANT, 1NUM, HI-HO, and X are not. If we disobey the rules for labeling, the assembler will give us an error message.

Labels are used in assembly language programs in three ways:

1. to identify a program (example: DISPLY)
2. to identify a program statement (example: CONFIG)
3. to identify a memory location (We haven't used labels for this yet, but it makes programming a lot easier.)

For instance, instead of having to remember the addresses of CRA, CRB, DDRA, DDRB, and so on, it would be much easier if we could just call them by their names. Then, instead of writing

```
140  CONFIG  CLR  $8005   CLEAR CRA BIT 2 TO ADDRESS DDRA
```

We'd write

```
140  CONFIG  CLR  CRA   CLEAR CRA BIT 2 TO ADDRESS DDRA
```

Here, CRA is the operand. Of course, CRA means location $8005. Somewhere we have to tell the assembler this, for which we use another assembler directive.

More assembler directives

The directive EQU is used for equating a label with a hexadecimal number. For example, to tell the assembler that CRA equals location $8005, we write this statement:

```
080  CRA  EQU  $8005
```

Notice that CRA is a label and appears in the label field. This statement won't get translated into machine code, because EQU is an assembler directive and not a mnemonic. The assembler "remembers" the numerical value of each label defined with the EQU directive by storing the label and its value in a symbol table in the microcomputer's RAM.

Equate statements normally are placed before the program statements. We'd write these equate statements for our addresses:

```
161   CRA    EQU   $8005
162   CRB    EQU   $8007
163   DDRA   EQU   $8004
164   DDRB   EQU   $8006
165   DRA    EQU   DDRA
166   DRB    EQU   DDRB
```

DRA EQU DDRA means that DRA has the same value as DDRA. This form defines the new label (DRA) in terms of an already defined label (DDRA). If we tried to do it the other way around

```
165   DDRA   EQU   DRA
```

the assembler would give us an error message, because we hadn't defined DRA yet. Similarly, DRB EQU DDRB means that DRB and DDRB have the same value.

Another assembler directive that's useful is ORG (origin). When we hand assemble a program, we decide on the memory location where we want our program to start. The assembler has to decide that too. If we don't tell it anything, it assigns $0000 as the starting address. We see in Figure 6.4.2 that $0000 is the starting address.

To start a program at any other location than $0000—say, $0020—we use this statement:

```
167   ORG   $0020
```

The assembler will assign the first piece of machine code in the program to the address following the ORG statement (here, $0020) and others in sequence from there.

Appendix B has a table of assembler directives. We'll be using more of them as our programs get more interesting. We should note that the directives NAM, END, and ORG must not be preceded by a label.

Numbers in statements

We already know that the dollar sign ($) is used to denote hexadecimal notation and that the percent sign (%) means binary. Some other facts about numbers are:

1. Leading zeros on numbers may be left off. Thus we may write LDA A #$4 instead of LDA A #$04 and %10 instead of %00000010.

2. If there is no numeric prefix before a number, the assembler interprets the number as decimal, and converts the number to hexadecimal on the listing. Thus the number 10 is interpreted by the assembler as decimal ten and appears on the listing as hexadecimal 0A.

Errors

Appendix B contains a list of error messages used by the assembler. At first, these messages won't mean much. Some of the most common errors are:

1. typing errors
2. label field errors. That is, erroneously placing a mnemonic or assembler directive in the label field or beginning a label in the operation field. Thus both these statements would produce error messages:

```
100  LDA A  DRA    GET INPUT FROM DRA
250         INPUT  LDA A DRA GET INPUT FROM DRA
```

FIGURE 6.5.1   A Source Program for Use with an Assembler

Seq.	Label	Op'n	Operand	Comment
010		NAM	DISPLY	
020		;THIS PROGRAM CONFIGURES SIDE A OF THE USER PIA FOR ALL		
030		;INPUTS AND SIDE B FOR ALL OUTPUTS. SIDE A IS ATTACHED		
040		;TO A SET OF EIGHT SWITCHES AND SIDE B TO A 7-SEGMENT DISPLAY.		
050		;THIS PROGRAM CAUSES A CHARACTER TO BE OUTPUT ON THE DISPLAY		
060		;IN RESPONSE TO A HEXADECIMAL CODE INPUT ON THE SWITCHES.		
070		ORG	$20	
080	PIACRA	EQU	$8005	
090	PIACRB	EQU	$8007	
100	DDRA	EQU	$8004	
110	DDRB	EQU	$8006	
120	DRA	EQU	DDRA	
130	DRB	EQU	DDRB	
140	CONFIG	CLR	PIACRA	CLEAR CRA BIT 2 TO ADDRESS DDRA
150		CLR	DDRA	SET A SIDE ALL INPUTS
160		CLR	PIACRB	CLEAR CRB BIT 2 TO ADDRESS DDRB
170		LDA B	#$FF	PUT ALL ONES INTO ACCB TO STORE IN DDRB
180		STA B	DDRB	SET B SIDE ALL OUTPUTS
190	INOUT	LDA A	#$4	GET READY TO SET BIT 2
200		STA A	PIACRA	SET BIT 2 OF CRA TO ADDRESS DRA
210		STA A	PIACRB	SET BIT 2 OF CRB TO ADDRESS DRB
220	GETDIG	LDA A	DRA	READ INPUT DATA FROM DRA
230		STA A	DRB	OUTPUT IT TO DRB
240		WAI		WAIT FOR INSTRUCTIONS
250		END		

FIGURE 6.5.2 Assembly Listing of Figure 6.5.1 Program DISPLY

```
DISPLY
M6800 ASSEMBLER LISTING VERSION 1.6      16 OCT 80 19:18      PAGE   2
FIG651   DAT     14 OCT 80 22:58
                             3 ;THIS PROGRAM CONFIGURES SIDE A OF THE USER PIA FOR ALL
                             4 ;INPUTS AND SIDE B FOR ALL OUTPUTS. SIDE A IS ATTACHED
                             5 ;TO A SET OF EIGHT SWITCHES AND SIDE B TO A 7-SEGMENT DISPLAY.
                             6 ;THIS PROGRAM CAUSES A CHARACTER TO BE OUTPUT ON THE 7-SEGMENT
                             7 ;IN RESPONSE TO A HEXADECIMAL CODE INPUT ON THE SWITCHES.
0000                         8          ORG    $20
8005                         9 PIACRA   EQU    $8005
8007                        10 PIACRB   EQU    $8007
8004                        11 DDRA     EQU    $8004
8006                        12 DDRB     EQU    $8006
8004                        13 DRA      EQU    DDRA
8006                        14 DRB      EQU    DDRB
0020 7F 80 05               15 CONFIG   CLR    PIACRA   CLEAR CRA BIT 2 TO ADDRESS DDRA
0023 7F 80 04               16          CLR    DDRA     SET A SIDE ALL INPUTS
0026 7F 80 07               17          CLR    PIACRB   CLEAR CRB BIT 2 TO ADDRESS DDRB
0029 C6 FF                  18          LDA B  #$FF     PUT ALL ONES INTO ACCB TO STORE IN DDRB
002B F7 80 06               19          STA B  DDRB     SET B SIDE ALL OUTPUTS
002E 86 04                  20 INOUT    LDA A  #$4      GET READY TO SET BIT 2
0030 B7 80 05               21          STA A  PIACRA   SET BIT 2 OF CRA TO ADDRESS DRA
0033 B7 80 07               22          STA A  PIACRB   SET BIT 2 OF CRB TO ADDRESS DRB
0036 B6 80 04               23 GETDIG   LDA A  DRA      READ INPUT DATA FROM DRA
0039 B7 80 06               24          STA A  DRB      OUTPUT IT TO DRB
003C 3E                     25          WAI             WAIT FOR INSTRUCTIONS
003D                        26          END
NO STATEMENTS FLAGGED
CROSS-REFERENCE TABLE
CONFIG        0020           15
DDRA          8004           11           13  16
DDRB          8006           12           14  19
DRA           8004           13           23
DRB           8006           14           24
GETDIG        0036           23
INOUT         002E           20
PIACRA        8005            9           15  21
PIACRB        8007           10           17  22
```

3. violation of labeling rules

4. typing an O ("oh") instead of a 0 ("zero") or vice versa

5. improper use of mnemonics (misspelling, trying to use an unavailable addressing mode, and so on)

6. leaving out the $ from a number that cannot be interpreted as a decimal number (that is, any number that contains the hexadecimal numerals A–F)

7. attempting to use a mnemonic or an assembler directive as a label

Typing or spelling errors in the comment field will not generate any error messages, because the assembler ignores characters in this field.

An alternate program

Figure 6.5.1 is a source program, written using some of the conveniences discussed in this section. Figure 6.5.2 is the corresponding listing generated by the assembler. Notice that the cross-reference table is much more extensive than that of Figure 6.4.2, because we have more labels. Also, some of the labels have more than one entry. The assembler has listed each line where each label appears.

Appendix B contains the Motorola M68SAM Cross Assembler Reference Manual. Everything we've discussed in this chapter, and some things we haven't, can be found in this appendix.

REVIEW QUESTIONS

1. What is an **algorithm**? A **flowchart**? Why do we need them?
2. Name and describe four flowchart **elements**.
3. Explain the relationship of the algorithm of Figure 6.1.1 to the flowchart of Figure 6.1.3.
4. Explain how to make a more detailed flowchart from a general one.
5. At what point is a flowchart detailed enough?
6. Explain how the register transfer statements of Figure 6.2.6 relate to the English statements on the same figure.
7. Name three utility programs and their functions.
8. What is the difference between a **resident assembler** and a **cross assembler**?
9. What modifications must be made to the program of Figure 5.4.3 before it can be assembled by our particular assembler?
10. What is an **assembler directive**? What do the assembler directives NAM and END mean?
11. What are the five fields in an assembly language statement? Must we have an entry in each field? Explain.
12. What may be contained in the **label field**?
13. Into what field should we put an assembler directive?
14. How do we designate an entire line as a comment?
15. Explain how to write an assembly language program from a flowchart.
16. How do we translate the START and STOP boxes of a flowchart into assembly language statements?
17. How does the assembler know whether to use the direct or the extended addressing mode?
18. What rules must we obey with regard to labels? What are three ways that labels are used in assembly language programs?
19. When we use a label to mean a memory location, how do we tell the assembler the address of the memory location?
20. How do we tell the assembler at what memory location to start the program? What will happen if we don't tell it at all?
21. Must we supply leading zeros on numbers in assembly language statements? How do we distinguish among decimal, binary, and hexadecimal numbers?
22. What are four common causes of assembler error messages?

EXERCISES

Set A (answers at back of book)

1. Write assembly language programs from these detailed flowcharts:

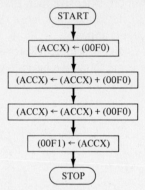

a. This program multiplies a number by 3 by adding it to itself twice. Start the program at location $0000. Name the program TIMES3.

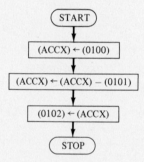

b. This program subtracts one number from another. Start the program at location $0200. Name the program SBTRCT.

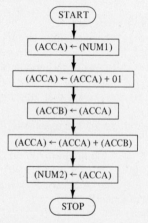

c. This program evaluates the equation NUM2 = 2(NUM1 + 1). Use the labels NUM1 and NUM2 in the program, and assign them to memory locations $0000 and $0001. Start the program at $0010. The name of the program is EQUATN.

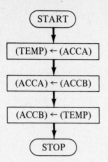

```
        ( START )
            │
            ▼
  ┌──────────────────┐
  │ (TEMP) ← (ACCA)  │
  └──────────────────┘
            │
            ▼
  ┌──────────────────┐
  │ (ACCA) ← (ACCB)  │
  └──────────────────┘
            │
            ▼
  ┌──────────────────┐
  │ (ACCB) ← (TEMP)  │
  └──────────────────┘
            │
            ▼
        ( STOP )
```

d. This program swaps the contents of accumulators A and B. Use the label TEMP in the program, and assign it to location $0040. Start the program at location $0010. The name of the program is SWAP.

2. Fill in the blanks in this assembly language program.

SEQ.	LABEL	OP'N	OPERAND	COMMENT
100		_____	EIGHT	
110	;THIS PROGRAM DISPLAYS THE DIGIT 8 ON A 7-SEGMENT DISPLAY,			
120	;WHICH IS WIRED TO SIDE A OF THE USER PIA.			
130	CRA	EQU	_____	
140	DRA	EQU	_____	
150	DDRA	EQU	_____	
160		CLR	_____	CLEAR CRA BIT 2 TO ADDRESS DDRA
170		LDA A	#$_____	READY TO SET SIDE A ALL OUTPUTS
180		_____	DDRA	SET SIDE A ALL OUTPUTS
190		_____	#$04	GET READY TO ADDRESS DRA
200		STA A	_____	SIDE A READY TO OUTPUT DATA
210	GET8	LDA A	#$_____	GET 7-SEGMENT CODE FOR 8
220		STA A	_____	PUT IT INTO DRA
230		WAI		WAIT
240				

3. Modify the program of (2) so that any digit may be displayed. Use the label DIGIT to store the appropriate seven-segment code, and place DIGIT equal to $0300. Have the program start at address $0010. There is a margin of ten between line numbers, so added lines may be inserted without renumbering the rest of the program. Give line numbers for added lines; Where a line is being replaced, use its original line number.

4. These statements would generate error messages. Tell what is wrong with each.

a.	210	LDA	#$FF	READY TO SET ALL OUTPUTS
b.	100	START	NAM	PROGRM
c.	010		HERE STA A	PLACE
d.	020		LDB	#$02	PUT 2 INTO ACCB
e.	000		CLR	$8OO5	CLEAR CRA
f.	150	2TIMES	LDA A	MULT	GET THE MULTIPLICAND
g.	220		INC	00FF	INCREMENT LOCATION 00FF
h.	130			$THIS IS A COMMENT

5. Correct each of the statements in Exercise 4.

EXERCISES

Set B (answers not given)

1. Write assembly language programs for these detailed flowcharts. Consult Appendix A for mnemonics.

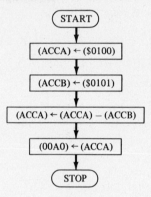

a. This program subtracts one number from another. Start the program at location $0040. Name the program MINUS.

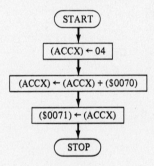

b. This program adds 4 to a number. Start the program at location $00A0. Name the program ADFOUR.

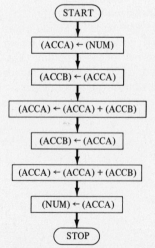

c. This program multiplies a number, NUM, by 4 by adding it to itself three times. Use the label NUM, and assign it to memory location $00B0. Start the program at $0040. Name the program TIMES4.

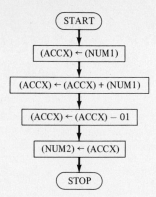

START

(ACCX) ← (NUM1)

(ACCX) ← (ACCX) + (NUM1)

(ACCX) ← (ACCX) − 01

(NUM2) ← (ACCX)

STOP

d. This program evaluates the equation NUM2 = 2NUM1 − 1. Use the labels NUM1 and NUM2 in the program, and assign them to memory locations $0110 and $0111. Start the program at location 0A00. Name the program VALUE.

2. Fill in the blanks in this assembly language program.

SEQ.	LABEL	OP'N.	OPERAND	COMMENT
010		NAM	THERMS	
020	;THIS PROGRAM TURNS ON A FURNACE WHEN THE TEMPERATURE DROPS			
030	;BELOW 60 DEGREES FAHRENHEIT. BIT 0 OF SIDE B OF THE USER PIA			
040	;IS WIRED TO A TEMPERATURE SENSOR, WHERE 1 INDICATES A TEMPER-			
050	;ATURE BELOW 60. BIT 1 OF SIDE B IS WIRED TO THE FURNACE, WHERE			
060	;"1" TURNS IT ON. THE CONTENTS OF BIT 0 ARE TRANSFERRED TO BIT			
070	;1 BY MULTIPLYING THE CONTENTS OF DRB BY TWO (THAT IS, ADDING			
075	;IT TO ITSELF)			
080	CRB	_____	$8007	
090	DRB	_____	_____	SET DRB EQUAL TO ADDRESS $8006
100	DDRB	_____	_____	SET DDRB EQUAL TO ADDRESS $8006 ALSO
110		_____	CRB	CLEAR CRB BIT 2 TO ADDRESS DDRB
120		_____	#$02	READY TO SET BIT 0 IN, BIT 1 OUT
130	STA A	_____		CONFIGURE PIA AS ABOVE
140		_____	_____	GET READY TO ADDRESS DRB
150		_____	CRB	SIDE B READY FOR INPUT AND OUTPUT
160	BRR	LDA A	_____	GET CONTENTS OF DRB
170		_____		TRANSFER TO ACCUMULATOR
180		_____		PUT CONTENTS OF BIT 0 INTO BIT 1
190		_____		WAIT
200		_____		

3. Modify the program of (2) so that bit 1 of side B is wired to the temperature sensor and bit 2 is wired to the furnace. Start the program at address $0100. There is a margin of ten between line numbers, so added lines may be inserted without renumbering the rest of the program. Give line numbers for added lines; where a line is being replaced, use its original line number.

4. These statements would generate error messages. Tell what is wrong with each.

A.	100	DONE	END		
B.	130		NAM	PATRICK	
C.	170	JOE	EQU	$0030	
D.	300		STO A	PLACE	(ACCA) IN LOC PLACE
E.	220	THIS IS A COMMENT TELLING HOW THE PROGRAM WORKS			
F.	050	ORG	$0200		START PROG. AT LOC $0200

G. 190		STA A	$0030	STORE (ACCA) IN LOC $0030
H. 200		STA A	#$0020	STORE (ACCA) IN LOC $0020

5. Correct each of the statements in Exercise 4.

PROGRAMMING IDEAS

For each of these, write an algorithm, general and detailed flowcharts, and an assembly language program. Assemble the program (on an assembler, if available; otherwise by hand), load the program into a microcomputer, run, and debug.

1. Convert an ASCII numeral to its binary equivalent. That is,

INPUT   OUTPUT

30   00
31   01
32   02
AND SO ON

Assume no parity. (Hint: We must convert the most significant digit, which is always 3, to 0.)
2. Evaluate the expression $Y = 2X + B$.
3. Modify the program of Exercise 1 so that an ASCII numeral input on side A of the user PIA via a set of switches is output on side B as its binary equivalent via a set of 8 lights.

7 Arithmetic Operations

LEARNING OBJECTIVES

After having completed this chapter, you should be able to:

1. Give a definition, explanation or example for each of these: *carry, truth table, full adder, base complement, tens complement, twos complement, nines complement, ones complement, fifteens complement, overflow, overflow status bit, double-precision arithmetic, half-carry status bit.*
2. Perform multidigit addition in binary and in hexadecimal representation.
3. Form base complements in binary and in hexadecimal, and verify that the numbers are complementary.
4. Perform subtraction in binary and in hexadecimal by base complementation and addition.
5. Express a signed number as its decimal equivalent, and convert a negative binary or hexadecimal number to its positive counterpart.
6. Add signed binary or hexadecimal numbers, convert the answer to decimal, and determine the contents of the carry and overflow bits as a result of the addition.
7. For each new instruction in the chapter, read the instruction information sheet to obtain information about the instruction, such as the operation of the instruction and how it affects certain status bits.
8. Perform BCD addition and explain the use of the DAA instruction.
9. Use any of the new instructions in this chapter in a simple program.

So far, we've learned a bit about input and output devices, the PIA, and how to use an assembler. Before we go much further, we need to know some of the operations that take place in the Arithmetic and Logic Unit (ALU).

As stated in Chapter 4, the ALU makes all the decisions for the microprocessor, and performs arithmetic and logical operations as well. In this chapter we'll look at the arithmetic operations only.

7.1 ADDITION

We've all done addition in the decimal system for as long as we can remember. As we discuss addition in binary and in hexadecimal, it will be helpful to use the familiar decimal system as a model. If we analyze the steps that we go through in decimal addition, the analogous steps in the other systems will seem quite logical.

Single-digit addition

If we add 2 or more single-digit numbers in any system, we get an answer that has 1 digit if the sum is less than the base (e.g., $4+4+1=9$ in base ten). And we get an answer that has 2 digits if the sum is equal to or greater than the base (e.g., $5+4+1=10$).

For this discussion we're going to confine our answer (sum) to a single digit. Then, the sum of 2 single digits will always be a 1-digit sum and a carry. We define a **carry** as a digit that has a nonzero value when the sum of 2 or more digits equals or exceeds the base of the number system. So, even though we've said since grammar school "five plus five equals ten," we're going to rethink now and say instead "five plus five equals zero with a carry of one." Figure 7.1.1 illustrates single-digit addition in base ten.

To do addition, we need to know all of the single-digit sums for each number system. In the decimal system this is easy because we've known all the combinations since grammar school: $0+0=0$, $0+1=1$, $1+1=2$, and so on. If we were to tabulate all the possible combinations for adding 2 decimal digits, we'd get 10^2, or 100, combinations. For adding 3 decimal digits ($1+1+2=4$, and so on) there are 10^3, or 1000, combinations.

FIGURE 7.1.1   Single-Digit Addition in Decimal

6	SIX PLUS THREE EQUALS NINE, WITH
+3	A CARRY OF ZERO
(0) 9	

9	NINE PLUS SEVEN EQUALS SIX, WITH
+7	A CARRY OF ONE
(1) 6	

3	THREE PLUS TWO PLUS ONE EQUALS SIX,
2	WITH A CARRY OF ZERO
+1	
(0) 6	

9	NINE PLUS SIX PLUS EIGHT EQUALS
6	THREE, WITH A CARRY OF TWO
+8	
(2) 3	

FIGURE 7.1.2   Rules for Addition of 2 and 3 Single Binary Digits

0	0	1	1
+0	+1	+0	+1
(0) 0	(0) 1	(0) 1	(1) 0

0	0	0	1
0	0	1	0
+0	+1	+0	+0
(0) 0	(0) 1	(0) 1	(0) 1

0	1	1	1
1	0	1	1
+1	+1	+0	+1
(1) 0	(1) 0	(1) 0	(1) 1

Note: Parentheses around number to left indicates a carry.

Binary is even easier. With only 2 possible digits, we have far fewer combinations. For adding 2 digits there are 2^2, or 4, combinations: $0+0=0$, $0+1=1$, $1+0=1$, and $1+1=0$ with a carry of 1. For adding 3 binary digits, there are 2^3, or 8, combinations. Figure 7.1.2 gives all possible combinations of 2 and 3 single binary digits. These rules of addition are summarized in Figure 7.1.3 in two truth tables. A **truth table** gives the outputs for all possible inputs to a system. In Figure 7.1.3 the inputs are A, B, and C, and the outputs are S and carry.

Because hexadecimal has 16 integers, there are 16^2, or 256, possible combinations of 2 digits. Also, there are 16^3, or 4096, combinations of 3 hexadecimal digits. Because there are so many values, we won't tabulate the truth tables for decimal or for hexadecimal single-digit addition. A few examples of single-digit addition of 2

FIGURE 7.1.3   Truth Tables for Binary Addition of Two and of Three Bits

Two Bits: Inputs A and B, Outputs S and Carry

A	B	S	Carry
0	0	0	0
0	1	1	0
1	0	1	0
1	1	0	1

Three Bits: Inputs A, B, and C; Outputs S and Carry

A	B	C	S	Carry
0	0	0	0	0
0	0	1	1	0
0	1	0	1	0
0	1	1	0	1
1	0	0	1	0
1	0	1	0	1
1	1	0	0	1
1	1	1	1	1

FIGURE 7.1.4   Single-Digit Addition in Hexadecimal

A	A plus 5 equals F, with a
+5	carry of zero.
(0) F	
B	B plus C equals 7, with a
+C	carry of one.
(1) 7	
9	9 plus 8 plus 2 equals 3,
8	with a carry of one.
+2	
(1) 3	
D	D plus E plus 1 equals C,
E	with a carry of one.
+1	
(1) C	

and 3 hexadecimal digits are shown in Figure 7.1.4. We'll show how to compute such sums in the next example.

EXAMPLE 7.1.1

Express each of these base sixteen operations as a single-digit sum and a carry:
a. F+A; b. C+2+1; c. B+A+C

Solution

We convert the digits to decimal, add them, and convert the sum back to hexadecimal.

a. F (fifteen) plus A (ten) equals twenty-five (sixteen plus nine, or 19 in hexadecimal). Sum: 9. Carry: 1

b. C (twelve) plus two plus one equals fifteen (F in hexadecimal). Sum: F. Carry: 0

c. B (eleven) plus A (ten) plus C (twelve) equals thirty-three (two sixteens plus one, or 21 in hexadecimal). Sum: 1. Carry: 2

Answer: a. 9, with a carry of 1; b. F, with a carry of 0; c. 1, with a carry of 2

Multidigit addition

In decimal addition we often add multidigit rather than single-digit numbers. When we do, the carry out of a digit becomes the carry in for the next, more significant digit. In binary addition we'll want to add numbers that are at least 8 bits (1 byte) wide, because that's the size of our data word. As in decimal addition, the carry out of each digit becomes the carry in to the next.

Figure 7.1.5 shows multidigit addition in decimal, binary, and hexadecimal representation. For each we can think of the "carry in" to the least significant digit as being 0.

FIGURE 7.1.5 Multidigit Addition in Decimal, Binary, and Hexadecimal Systems

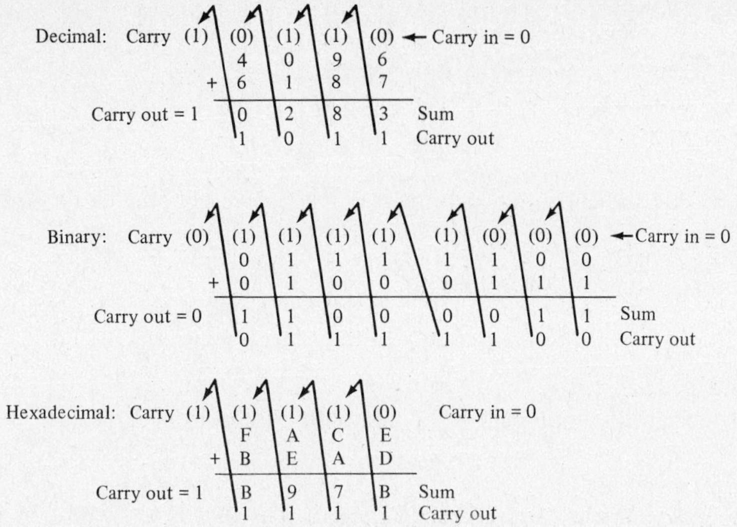

EXAMPLE 7.1.2

Add the binary numbers 0100 1110 and 1001 1111. Assume that the carry in to the least significant bit is 0. Report the carry out also.

Solution

We use the rules for single-bit binary addition and, starting on the right, add each column plus the carry. Starting with the least significant (2^0's) place, we have an initial carry in of 0, plus 0 plus 1 equals 1 with a carry out of 0:

```
                                          INITIAL
CARRY IN                        0         CARRY IN = 0
              0 1 0 0   1 1 1 0
            + 1 0 0 1   1 1 1 1
            ─────────────────────
                                1         SUM
                                0         CARRY OUT
```

For the next more significant place (2^1's place), we bring up the carry out from the 2^0's place and add it to the other 2 digits. Then, 0 plus 1 plus 1 is 0 with a carry of 1:

```
CARRY IN
                                    0 0
                0 1 0 0       1 1 1 0
              + 1 0 0 1       1 1 1 1
              ───────────────────────
                      0         0 1     SUM
                                1 0     CARRY OUT
```

Adding the rest of the digits in this way gives this result:

CARRY IN	0 0 0 1 1	1 1 0 0	
	0 1 0 0	1 1 1 0	
	+1 0 0 1	1 1 1 1	
	1 1 1 0	1 1 0 1	SUM
	0 0 0 1	1 1 1 0	CARRY OUT

Notice that the carry out of bit 7 is 0. This represents the carry for the 8-bit addition.

Answer: 1110 1101, with a carry of 0.

EXAMPLE 7.1.3

Add the 2 hexadecimal numbers A3F7 and 60BC. Report the carry out.

Solution

As before, we assume a carry in of 0. Then, 0 plus 7 plus C (twelve) is nineteen (sixteen plus three) or three with a carry of 1:

CARRY IN	0	
	A 3 F 7	
	+6 0 B C	
	3	SUM
	1	CARRY OUT

Next, one plus F is sixteen, plus B (eleven) is twenty-seven (sixteen plus eleven) or B with a carry of 1. The complete addition, with carries, looks like this:

CARRY IN	0	1	1	0	
	A	3	F	7	
	6	0	B	C	
	0	4	B	3	SUM
	1	0	1	1	CARRY OUT

Here, the carry out of the MSD is 1, so the carry out of the addition is 1.

Answer: 04B3, with a carry out of 1

One way that an ALU can add 8-bit numbers is by using a set of eight full adders. A **full adder** is a device that adds 3 single-digit inputs and produces 2 outputs (sum and carry). The carry out of each adder is connected to the carry in of the adder on its left. Starting at bit 0, the carry in can be set to 0 or 1 by using an appropriate instruction (more about this later). The carry out from bit 7 goes into the carry bit of the status register, which we discussed in Chapter 4 (p. 67). If the

FIGURE 7.1.6 A Set of Eight Full Adders

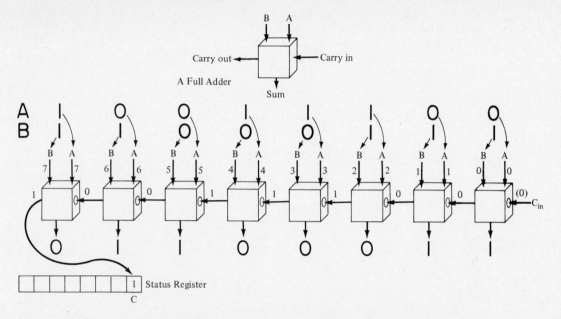

carry out is 0, the carry bit will be cleared. If the carry out is 1, the carry bit will be set.

Figure 7.1.6 shows a set of eight full adders connected as described. The sum shown underneath would set the carry bit, indicating that the answer was too large for the data word to contain.

7.2 SUBTRACTION

For most of us, subtraction is more troublesome than addition. First, there's the fact that subtraction isn't commutative, as addition is. That is, it matters whether we subtract B from A or A from B. Then there's all that borrowing, which seems to be harder than the carrying we have to do in addition.

Subtraction is harder for microcomputers, too. In fact, the ALU can't subtract at all. But there is an instruction Subtract (SUB), which does find the difference between 2 numbers. The ALU performs subtraction by adding. Next, we'll see how we and the ALU can actually subtract by adding.

Subtraction by addition

We can subtract a number from another in any base system by adding the minuend (the number to be subtracted from) to the base complement of the subtrahend (the number to be subtracted). When two numbers add up to 0 with a carry of 1 (which we ignore), we define the two numbers as **base complements** of one another. In the decimal system, such numbers are **tens complements**.

EXAMPLE 7.2.1

Verify that 126 is or is not the tens complement of 874.

Solution

We add the numbers:
$$\begin{array}{r} 874 \\ +126 \\ \hline \end{array}$$
(1)000, with a carry of 1.

Answer: 126 is the tens complement of 874, because their sum is 0 with a carry of 1.

EXAMPLE 7.2.2

Subtract 874 from 923 (a) by normal subtraction and (b) by adding the tens complement of the subtrahend to the minuend.

Solution

(a)

$$\begin{array}{r} 923 \\ -874 \\ \hline 49 \end{array}$$

(b) 874 is the subtrahend. We know from the previous example that 126 is the tens complement of 874, so we add 126 to 923:

$$\begin{array}{r} 923 \\ +126 \\ \hline (1)\ 49 \end{array}$$

In part (b), we get the same answer as in part (a), except for the carry, which we ignore.

Answer: (a) 49; (b) 49 (with a carry of 1)

In Chapter 3 we introduced a system of signed binary numbers and gave all the values for 8-bit positive and negative numbers in Table 2.5.1. In this table the positive and negative counterparts are **twos complements** of each other.

EXAMPLE 7.2.3

Refer to Table 2.5.1. Verify that the binary equivalents of decimal $+35$ and -35 are twos complements of each other.

Solution

Looking at the table, we find these binary equivalents:

$+35$: 0010 0011
-35: 1101 1101

If these numbers are indeed base complementary, their sum will be 0 with a carry of 1. So we add them:

```
    0010  0011
  + 1101  1101
 ---------------
 (1) 0000  0000
```

Answer: The numbers are twos complements, because their sum is 0 with a carry of 1.

We can use the values of twos complement binary numbers from Table 2.5.1 to subtract in binary by adding.

EXAMPLE 7.2.4

Perform the following subtraction (a) in decimal by normal subtraction; (b) by converting the decimal numbers to their appropriate binary equivalents (Table 2.5.1) and adding. Verify that the answer is correct by converting it to decimal and comparing it with the answer in (a).

```
   28
 - 43
```

Solution

(a)
```
   28
 - 43
 -----
 - 15
```

(b) We find the binary equivalents on Table 2.5.1 and add them:

```
  28: 0001 1100
 -43: 1101 0101
 ---------------
      1111 0001
```

To convert to decimal, we consult the table again. We find that 1111 0001 is equivalent to -15 in decimal, so our answer is correct.

Answer: (a) -15; (b) 1111 0001, or -15 in decimal

We see that subtracting by adding the base complement of the subtrahend works. Next, we'll find out how to convert any number to its base complement without having to consult Table 2.5.1 or a similar table.

Base complementation

To find the complement of a number in any system, we follow these rules:

1. On a digit-by-digit basis, subtract each digit from a number one less than the base. (This subtraction is simple because it doesn't involve carrying.)
2. Add 1 to the least significant digit of the overall result.

EXAMPLE 7.2.5

Find the tens complement of 6709.

Solution

We apply the preceding rules. First, subtract each digit one at a time from 9, which is one less than the base (ten) in this case.

$$
\begin{array}{r}
9\ 9\ 9\ 9 \\
-6\ 7\ 0\ 9 \\
\hline
3\ 2\ 9\ 0
\end{array}
$$

This number, 3290, is the **nines complement** of 6709, expressed in base ten. Next, we add 1 to this nines complement:

$$
\begin{array}{r}
3\ 2\ 9\ 0 \\
+\qquad 1 \\
\hline
3\ 2\ 9\ 1
\end{array}
$$

To verify that 3291 is the tens complement of 6709, we add them:

$$
\begin{array}{r}
3\ 2\ 9\ 1 \\
6\ 7\ 0\ 9 \\
\hline
(1)\ 0\ 0\ 0\ 0 \quad \text{(verified)}
\end{array}
$$

Answer: 3291

EXAMPLE 7.2.6

Find the twos complement of 1011 0101.

Solution

"1" is one less than the base (two) so we subtract the number from all 1s:

```
   1 1 1 1   1 1 1 1
 − 1 0 1 1   0 1 0 1
 ─────────────────────
   0 1 0 0   1 0 1 0
```

This number, 0100 1010, is the **ones complement** of 1011 0101, expressed in base two. We add 1 to the ones complement to form the twos complement:

```
          0 1 0 0   1 0 1 0
                       + 1
        ──────────────────────
          0 1 0 0   1 0 1 1   The twos complement
verify:   1 0 1 1   0 1 0 1
        ──────────────────────
      (1) 0 0 0 0   0 0 0 0   (verified)
```

For additional verification we refer to Table 2.5.1 and find that 1011 0101 is decimal −75, and 0100 1011 is decimal +75. So the 2 binary numbers are twos complements.

Answer: 0100 1011

EXAMPLE 7.2.7

Find the sixteens complement of $A3DF.

Solution

1. F is one less than the base (sixteen) so we subtract the number from all F's:

```
              F F F F
            − A 3 D F
            ──────────
              5 C 2 0          The fifteens complement,
                              expressed in base sixteen
2. Add 1:            + 1
            ──────────
              5 C 2 1          The sixteens complement
Verify:       A 3 D F
            + 5 C 2 1
            ──────────
          (1) 0 0 0 0          (verified)
```

Answer: $5C21

We can make three useful statements about complementation:

1. An equivalent, simpler way to form the ones complement of a binary number is to invert each bit (change each 0 to a 1 and each 1 to a 0).

2. The sixteens complement in hexadecimal is equivalent to the twos complement in binary.

3. Complementation is circular. That is, when we take the complement of a complement, we get the original number back.

EXAMPLE 7.2.8

To verify the three previous statements (a) find the ones complement of binary 0101 1110 in two ways and show that they are the same; (b) convert the result of (a) to twos complement and show that this twos complement is equivalent to the sixteens complement of hexadecimal 5E (the hexadecimal equivalent of binary 0101 1110) (c) find the complements of the results of (b) and show that the original numbers are obtained.

Solution

(a)   By subtracting from 1111 1111:

$$
\begin{array}{r}
1111\ 1111 \\
-0101\ 1110 \\
\hline
1010\ 0001 \quad \text{The ones complement}
\end{array}
$$

By inverting each bit: (0101 1110) inverted is 1010 0001. (The same as above.)

(b)
$$
\begin{array}{rr}
1111\ 1111 & FF \\
-0101\ 1110 & -5E \\
\hline
1010\ 0001 & A1 \\
+1 & +1 \\
\hline
1010\ 0010 & A2
\end{array}
$$

A2 is indeed the hexadecimal equivalent of binary 1010 0010.

(c)
$$
\begin{array}{rr}
1111\ 1111 & FF \\
-1010\ 0010 & -A2 \\
\hline
0101\ 1101 & 5D \\
+1 & +1 \\
\hline
0101\ 1110 & 5E
\end{array}
$$

Answer: (a) 1010 0001 both ways; (b) 1010 0010, $A2; these are equivalent. (c) 0101 1110, $5E; these are the original numbers.

Subtraction by complementation and addition

Now that we know how to subtract by addition and how to find base complements, we can combine the two techniques. Also, we've shown that the sixteens and twos complements are equivalent, so we'll find it much more convenient to work in base sixteen, because working in binary is subject to more error.

EXAMPLE 7.2.9

Subtract by sixteens complementation and addition:

$$\begin{array}{r} \$A3 \\ -\$9D \\ \hline \end{array}$$

Solution

First, we find the sixteens complement of the subtrahend (9D):

$$\begin{array}{r} FF \\ -9D \\ \hline 62 \\ +\ 1 \\ \hline 63 \end{array} \quad \text{(the sixteens complement of 9D)}$$

Next, we add 63 to the minuend:

$$\begin{array}{r} A3 \\ +63 \\ \hline (1)\ \ 06 \end{array} \quad \text{(we ignore the carry)}$$

Answer: $6

EXAMPLE 7.2.10

Subtract by sixteens complementation and addition:

$$\begin{array}{r} \$08 \\ -\$10 \\ \hline \end{array}$$

Solution

We'll do this problem more concisely:

$$\begin{array}{r} \$08 \\ -\$10 \\ \hline \end{array} \qquad \begin{array}{r} \$08 \\ +\$F0 \\ \hline \$F8 \end{array} \quad \begin{array}{l} \text{(the sixteens complement of \$10)} \\ \ \\ \text{(the answer)} \end{array}$$

Notice that this time we got a negative answer (recall that hexadecimal numbers 8–F in the most significant digit indicate a negative number in signed notation). This is reasonable, because the subtrahend ($10) is larger numerically than the minuend ($08).

Answer: $F8

When we subtract by complementation and addition, we're working with signed numbers. Next, we'll go into more detail about signed number arithmetic.

7.3 WORKING WITH SIGNED NUMBERS

In Chapter 2 we saw that the range of absolute values of binary numbers in signed notation is only half what it was in unsigned notation. That is, we have assigned half the binary values to negative numbers and half to positive numbers. In this section we'll see how to deal with signed numbers and avoid errors.

For some of our later discussions we'll find it useful to be able to convert a signed hexadecimal (or binary) number to its signed decimal equivalent without always having to look at Table 2.5.1.

Decimal equivalents of signed numbers

To express a signed binary or hexadecimal number as its decimal equivalent, we follow these steps:

1. Identify the number as positive or negative (this we did in Chapter 2).
2. If the number is negative, convert it to its twos or sixteens complement. Otherwise proceed directly to step 3.
3. Convert the result of step 1 or 2 to its decimal equivalent.
4. Affix a plus or minus sign, whichever is appropriate, to the result of step 3.

EXAMPLE 7.3.1

Express the signed numbers $7B and $B7 as their decimal equivalents.

Solution

We apply the preceding rules first to $7B:

1. $7B is positive.
2. Proceed to step 3.
3. $(7 \times 16) + (11 \times 1) = 123$ in decimal
4. $+123$ in decimal

Now we apply the rules to $B7:

1. $B7 is negative.
2. $$\begin{array}{r} F\ F \\ -B\ 7 \\ \hline 4\ 8 \\ +\ 1 \\ \hline 4\ 9 \end{array}$$

3. $(4 \times 16) + (9 \times 1) = 73$ in decimal.

4. -73 in decimal

Answer: $+123, -73$ (decimal)

Addition of signed numbers

Addition of signed numbers is just like addition of unsigned numbers, except that we ignore the carry. We determine the sign of the answer in the usual way.

EXAMPLE 7.3.2

Add the signed hexadecimal numbers $3F and $02. Give the answer in decimal notation.

Solution

First, add the numbers:
$$\begin{array}{r} 3F \\ +02 \\ \hline 41 \end{array}$$

Next, determine the sign of the answer. The most significant hexadecimal digit is 4, so the answer is positive.

Next, convert the number to decimal and affix a positive sign.

Answer: $+65$ in decimal

EXAMPLE 7.3.3

Add the signed hexadecimal numbers $FE and $FD.

Solution

$$\begin{array}{r} FE \\ +FD \\ \hline (1)\ FB \end{array}$$ (we ignore the carry)

The result is negative, because of the F in the most significant hexadecimal digit. So we apply the rules for conversion of negative numbers.

Sixteens Complement:
$$\begin{array}{r} FF \\ -FB \\ \hline 04 + 1 = 5 \end{array}$$

Decimal equivalent: 5

Answer: -5 in decimal

Addition of signed binary numbers works fine as long as we don't exceed the range of our signed numbers. Recall that in adding unsigned numbers we get an apparent wrong answer if we try to exceed our 8-bit range (255 in decimal). In the same way, if we add 2 negative numbers that would give an answer less than -128 (the smallest negative number we can have with 1 byte), we'll exceed the range and get an apparent wrong answer. If we add 2 positive numbers that would give an answer greater than $+127$ (the largest positive number we can have with 1 byte), we'll get an apparent wrong answer, too.

EXAMPLE 7.3.4

Add the signed numbers $9F and $A3. Give the answer in decimal notation.

Solution

$$\begin{array}{r} 9F \\ +A3 \\ \hline (1)\ 42 \end{array}$$

Because of the 4 in the most significant hexadecimal digit, the answer is positive. But both 9F and A3 are negative. We know that adding two negative numbers can't give a positive result. Something is wrong. We can compute the apparent value:

$$(4 \times 16) + (2 \times 1) = 66$$

Answer: Appears to be $+66$ in decimal but cannot be correct.

Let's work the problem in decimal and try to see what happened.

EXAMPLE 7.3.5

Convert the signed numbers $9F and $A3 to their decimal equivalents, add them in decimal, and report the answer both in decimal and in hexadecimal notation.

Solution

We apply the rules for converting these numbers to their decimal equivalents:

1. Both numbers are negative.
2. Take sixteens complement:

$$\begin{array}{r} F\ F \\ -9\ F \\ \hline 6\ 0 \\ +\ 1 \\ \hline 6\ 1 \end{array} \qquad \begin{array}{r} F\ F \\ -A\ 3 \\ \hline 5\ C \\ +\ 1 \\ \hline 5\ D \end{array}$$

3. Convert to decimal: $(6 \times 16) + (1 \times 1) = 97$

$(5 \times 16) + (D \times 1) = 93$

4. Affix minus signs: -97, -93

Having converted the numbers to their decimal equivalents, we'll add them:

$$
\begin{array}{r}
-97 \\
-93 \\
\hline
-190
\end{array}
$$

Now to convert this answer to hexadecimal. Recall that -128 is the smallest decimal number we can express in signed notation using only 1 byte (2 hexadecimal digits). So the decimal number -190 is out of range for a 2-digit hexadecimal number.

Answer: -190 in decimal, no 2-digit hexadecimal equivalent (out of range for 1-byte signed numbers)

In Example 7.3.4, we got an apparent answer of $+66$ in decimal by adding the numbers in hexadecimal and converting the answer to decimal. But in Example 7.3.5, we got a different answer of -190 by converting the numbers to decimal and adding them. We know that the answer $+66$ is wrong because it's positive.

We got an apparently incorrect answer because we tried to add 2 numbers whose sum, -190, was outside our range of signed numbers. The number $+66$ came about when we "wrapped around" the zero point and entered the region of positive numbers. (Adding -256 to $+66$ gives us -190, showing that we were effectively trying to enter another set of 256 numbers.)

Overflow

Whenever we exceed our range of signed numbers, we say that **overflow** has occurred. The addition in Example 7.3.4 would cause an overflow. Overflow is to signed arithmetic what carry is to unsigned arithmetic: It means that our answer appears wrong because we've tried to exceed our allowed range of binary values.

Determining whether or not overflow will occur for the addition of 2 signed numbers is easy. All we have to do is to look at the signs of the 2 numbers and the sum, and apply these rules:

1. When the signs of the 2 numbers to be added are opposite, overflow can't occur.

2. When the signs of the 2 numbers to be added are equal, overflow may or may not occur, depending on the sign of the answer.

3. When the sign of the answer is opposite the signs of the operands, overflow has occurred.

EXAMPLE 7.3.6

Will overflow occur when the signed numbers $8F and $3D are added?

Solution

We look at the preceding rules. According to Rule 1, overflow is impossible because $8F and $3D have opposite signs. We need go no further to answer the question.

Answer: No. $8F and $3D have opposite signs.

EXAMPLE 7.3.7

Will overflow occur when the signed numbers $46 and $62 are added?

Solution

According to Rule 2, overflow is possible because both numbers have the same sign ($+$). To find out whether overflow does occur, we must carry out the addition.

$$
\begin{array}{r}
46 \\
+62 \\
\hline
A8
\end{array}
$$

The sign of the answer (negative) is opposite the signs of the operands (positive), so overflow does occur.

Answer: Yes. The sign of the answer is opposite those of the operands.

The microprocessor has a way of telling us whether an overflow has occurred: in the **overflow status bit** (V). We mentioned this bit briefly in Chapter 4 but didn't explain it. Now we can say that the overflow status bit (bit 2 of the status register) will be set when an arithmetic operation results in an overflow and clear when no overflow results.

How does the microprocessor know whether we are working in signed or unsigned numbers? The answer is that *it doesn't*. It gives us all possible information by setting or clearing the carry and overflow bits each time. It's up to us to pick the one we want and to pay attention to it. In unsigned number arithmetic, we'd look to see whether the carry bit were set to catch a possible incorrect answer. In signed number arithmetic, we'd look at the overflow bit for the same information. Either way, the microprocessor provides information in both bits.

EXAMPLE 7.3.8

State whether the carry and/or overflow bits would be set or clear after these signed number additions: a. $D3+$F7; b. $80+$80.

Solution

First, we see that overflow is possible in both cases because the signs of the operands are alike. So we carry out the additions:

(a)   D3   (b)   80
               F7   80
        ──────────   ──────────
        (1) CA   (1) 00

In (a) the carry bit would be set because there is a carry of 1. The overflow bit would be clear because the sign of the answer is the same as the sign of the operands. In (b) the carry bit would also be set. The overflow bit would be set because the sign of the answer is opposite the sign of the operands (recall that 0 is considered to be a positive number.)

Answer: a. Carry set, overflow clear; b. Carry and overflow both set.

───

Next, we'll look at some of the arithmetic instructions in the 6800 instruction set.

7.4 SOME ARITHMETIC INSTRUCTIONS

Now that we know something about binary arithmetic, we can look at some of the instructions that can be used to program the microprocessor to do arithmetic.

Table 7.4.1 shows some of the 6800's arithmetic instructions. A few of them—ADD, ABA, SUB, SBA—we've already seen in Chapter 4. The instruction COM is new to us and means to form the ones complement or to invert each bit of a binary number. All the instructions in Table 7.4.1 affect the status bits N (negative), Z (zero), and C (carry). And all but COM affect the V (overflow) bit. To find out how each instruction affects each of these 4 status bits, and to find out anything else about an instruction, we consult the individual instruction sheets referenced in Table 7.4.1.

TABLE 7.4.1   Some of the 6800's Arithmetic Instructions

Mnemonic	Instruction Definition	Location
ADD	Add	p. 405
ADC	Add with carry	p. 404
ABA	Add ACCB to ACCA	p. 403
NEG	Negate	p. 449
SBA	Subtract ACCB from ACCA	p. 459
SBC	Subtract with carry	p. 460
SUB	Subtract	p. 467
DAA	Decimal adjust	p. 434
COM	Complement (ones)	p. 432

Double-precision addition

The second instruction in Table 7.4.1, ADC (ADd with Carry), is unfamiliar. We'll look at some of its properties and see what it can be used for.

EXAMPLE 7.4.1

Suppose the numbers $A3 and $DC are to be added using ADC. If the carry status bit were set prior to the addition, what would be (a) the result and (b) the contents of the status bits N, Z, V, and C?

Solution

First, we consult page 404 of Appendix A to get the instruction information for ADC. We find that this instruction causes the two operands, plus the contents of the carry bit, to be added together. In our case the carry bit contains a 1. So the result will be

$$
\begin{array}{r}
A\ 3 \\
D\ C \\
+\ 1 \\
\hline
(1)\ 8\ \ 0
\end{array}
$$

The N status bit will be set because bit 7 of the result is set.

The Z status bit will be clear because the answer is not 0.

The V status bit will be clear, because there is no overflow (the sign of the result is the same as that of the operands).

The C status bit will be set, because there is a carry of 1.

Answer: a. $80; b. (N)=1, (Z)=0, (V)=0, (C)=1

Now, we see how the ADC instruction works. But why would we want such an instruction?

What if we wanted to add two 2-byte numbers, such as $6CFE and $10BA? We can't do that in a single data word, because our data word is only 1 byte wide. And yet a microprocessor that didn't let us add numbers whose sums were greater than 255 (decimal) wouldn't be much use to us. The ADC instruction lets us add as many digits as we want, by making sure that the carry out from each byte gets carried in to the next most significant byte.

To add $6CFE and $10BA, we first input these numbers in 2 halves each and store each byte in a separate memory location. Next, we add the 2 least significant bytes, FE and BA, using the ADD instruction:

$$
\begin{array}{r}
FE \\
BA \\
\hline
(1)\ B\ 8
\end{array}
$$

Then, we add the most significant bytes using the ADC instruction. Because there was a carry of 1 from the previous addition, the carry status bit will contain a 1. The ADC instruction will accomplish this:

```
 6C
 10
+ 1
───
 7D
```

We store each result in a separate memory location and read them and put them together after executing the program. Our result in this case would be $7DB8.

Arithmetic involving 2-byte numbers is called **double-precision arithmetic.** For 3-byte numbers it would be **triple-precision**, and so on.

Figure 7.4.1 illustrates the use of the ADC instruction.

Most of the other instructions in Table 7.4.1 are familiar, except for NEG, SBC, and DAA. NEG is an instruction that forms the twos complement of the operand. To find out how to use it, we could consult the instruction information sheet in appendix A. The Subtract with Carry (SBC) instruction is analogous to the Add with Carry (ADC) instruction, except with SBC the carry behaves like a borrow. If there were a borrow from a less significant byte during a subtraction, this borrow would be subtracted from the next more significant byte.

FIGURE 7.4.1   Illustration of Double-Precision Addition.

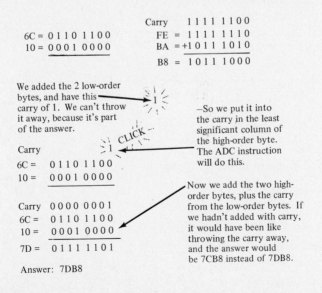

```
6CFE = 0110 1100 1111 1110      We can't add these numbers all at
+ 10BA = 0001 0000 1011 1010    once, because we only have room
                                for 1 byte of data. We must add the
                                high-and low-order bytes separately.
```

```
                          Carry   1111 1100
     6C = 0110 1100         FE =  1111 1110
     10 = 0001 0000         BA = +1011 1010
     ───────────            B8 =  1011 1000
```

We added the 2 low-order
bytes, and have this
carry of 1. We can't throw   1
it away, because it's part   CLICK
of the answer.   —So we put it into
                                                      the carry in the least
Carry   1   significant column of
                                                      the high-order byte.
6C =   0110 1100   The ADC instruction
10 =   0001 0000   will do this.

Carry   0000 0001   Now we add the two high-
6C =   0110 1100   order bytes, plus the carry
10 =   0001 0000   from the low-order bytes. If
──────────────   we hadn't added with carry,
7D =   0111 1101   it would have been like
                                         throwing the carry away,
Answer: 7DB8   and the answer would
                                         be 7CB8 instead of 7DB8.

Decimal adjust

The DAA instruction is new to us at this point. It's used when the micro-processor is doing BCD addition. Consider a hand-held calculator, a cash register, a game, or other device that may deal exclusively with base ten numbers. The microprocessor can represent decimal numbers internally as BCD numbers.

In BCD addition we follow some of the rules of binary addition and some of the rules of decimal addition. We add the bits together as in binary addition, but we carry out of a BCD digit (a nibble) when we reach a number larger than 9 (1001 in BCD). Consider this addition in decimal and in binary:

$$
\begin{array}{rl}
34 & 0011\ 0100 \\
+27 & 0010\ 0111 \\
\hline
61 & 0101\ 1011 \quad (\$5B)
\end{array}
$$

The binary answer, 0101 1011, is different from the BCD number 0110 0001 equivalent to decimal 61. To convert the binary answer to BCD, we add \$06 to it:

$$
\begin{array}{ll}
0\ 1\ 0\ 1\ \ 1\ 0\ 1\ 1 & (5B) \\
+0\ 0\ 0\ 0\ \ 0\ 1\ 1\ 0 & (06) \\
\hline
0\ 1\ 1\ 0\ \ 0\ 0\ 0\ 1 & (61)
\end{array}
$$

The BCD addition had an extra step: We had to add \$06 (0000 0110) to the first answer to adjust it to BCD. Recall that there are 6 binary bit patterns—1010 through 1111—that aren't allowed in BCD. Our first answer, \$5B, contained one of those bit patterns, so we added 6 to it to let us skip over those 6 forbidden patterns. This is the algorithm for adjusting the result of a binary addition to BCD:

1. If the hexadecimal sum in a single digit is less than ten, leave it.
2. If the sum is ten or greater, add 6 to it.
3. Add the resulting carry to the next more significant pair of digits to be added.

EXAMPLE 7.4.2

Perform BCD addition: 38+29.

Solution

Write in BCD and add in binary, 1 digit at a time:

$$
\begin{array}{ll}
0\ 0\ 1\ 1 & 1\ 0\ 0\ 0 \\
0\ 0\ 1\ 0 & 1\ 0\ 0\ 1 \\
\hline
& 0\ 0\ 0\ 1 \quad (1),\ \text{with a carry of 1}
\end{array}
$$

Here, it might seem at first as if this digit were correct. After all, 0001 is a valid bit pattern in BCD. But there was a carry out of the least significant BCD digit, thus that sum was ten or greater (actually, greater than fifteen) and we apply Rule 2:

```
    0 1 1 0  0 0 0 1
 +           0 1 1 0
    _____
             0 1 1 1    (7, the correct digit)
```

Next, we add the most significant nibble, not forgetting the carry out from the least significant nibble:

```
         1
   0 0 1 1
   0 0 1 0
   _____
   0 1 1 0    (6, a correct digit)
```

Notice that there was no carry from this nibble, so nothing needs to be added.

Answer: 0110 0111 (67)

Fortunately, we as users don't have to worry about adjusting for BCD addition when we're writing programs for the 6800. The Decimal Adjust instruction, DAA, does it all for us. To use DAA, we place that instruction directly after an addition, as shown in this program segment:

```
ADD A  $B0    ADD CONTENTS OF B0 TO ACCA
DAA           DECIMAL ADJUST
```

The DAA instruction uses the preceding algorithm for BCD addition, and if necessary, adds 6 to either digit. The operand must be contained in accumulator A only (this is one of several cases where ACCA and ACCB are not exactly alike). The DAA instruction doesn't function as a binary-to-BCD converter. It will work only if it's used after an addition (not after a subtraction), because it needs the input from one of the status bits that's affected by an addition.

As yet, we haven't mentioned the **half-carry status bit**, H, which is set when there is a carry from the least significant nibble during an addition. The DAA instruction uses the contents of the H bit to determine whether there was a carry from the LSB, as we had in Example 7.4.1. Unless we wanted to write a program to simulate the decimal adjust, we as users won't have much use for the H status bit.

We've had a brief introduction to arithmetic operations. By consulting the individual instruction information sheets, we should be able to write programs using the arithmetic instructions given in this chapter.

REVIEW QUESTIONS

1. Explain what is meant by sum and carry when speaking of adding single-digit numbers.
2. What is a **truth table**? Write a truth table for the addition of 3 single-digit binary inputs to give a sum and a carry.
3. Explain how to add single hexadecimal digits to get a sum and a carry.

4. Explain how to add multidigit numbers in binary and hexadecimal.
5. What is a **full adder**? Where in the microprocessor is it located, and what does it do?
6. How does the output of the ALU affect the carry status bit? Explain.
7. Does the ALU perform subtraction by subtracting? Explain.
8. What are **base complements**? How can we tell whether or not 2 numbers are base complements of one another?
9. How do we find the base complement of a number?
10. How do we form the **nines complement**, the **ones complement**, and the **fifteens complement**?
11. Explain how to subtract by complementation and addition.
12. How do we convert a negative number to its positive counterpart? How do we express a signed number as its decimal equivalent?
13. Explain how we may get a wrong answer when adding 2 signed numbers.
14. What is **overflow**? How do we know whether overflow has occurred?
15. What is the **overflow status bit**? How is it set or cleared?
16. How does the microprocessor know whether we are working in signed or in unsigned numbers? Explain.
17. Explain how to perform signed addition and determine the contents of the overflow and carry bits.
18. How do we find out how an instruction affects the status bits?
19. Explain what the ADC instruction does.
20. What is **double-precision addition**? Explain how we use the ADC instruction in double-precision addition.
21. Explain how to perform BCD addition. How do we correct a number that contains an invalid BCD digit?
22. What instruction is used for correcting a BCD sum? What is the **half-carry status bit**, and what is it used for?

EXERCISES

Set A (answers at back of book)

1. Add these binary numbers, and report the carry out:
   a. 0110 1111+1100 0110
   b. 1110 0011+0001 1011
   c. 0110 0011+0101 1110
   d. 1100 1011+1011 0011
2. Add these hexadecimal numbers, and report the carry out:
   a. $C7+$3F   b. $FACE+$F00D   c. $4A+$79   d. $BAAA+$78C3
3. In each of Exercises 1 and 2, state which operations give answers that are too large for the number of digits available.
4. Find the twos complement of each of these, and verify that the numbers are complementary:
   a. 1111 1111   b. 0111 1000   c. 1010 0011   d. 1000 0000
5. Find the sixteens complement of each of these, and verify that the numbers are complementary:
   a. $34   b. $ACED   c. $7D   d. $000F
6. Using the hexadecimal number CE, verify that the sixteens complement in hexadecimal is equivalent to the twos complement in binary.

7. Subtract by sixteens complementation and addition:
   a. $4C-$1B   **b.** $D8-$A1   **c.** $ACDC-$1212   **d.** $F1F0-$A127

8. Form the ones complements by inverting each bit:
   a. 0011 1001   **b.** 1000 1011   **c.** $84   **d.** $79

9. Express these signed numbers as their decimal equivalents:
   a. 1101 0110   **b.** 0011 1001   **c.** $40   **d.** $EE

10. Add these signed numbers, and give the answers in decimal notation, as well as in binary or hexadecimal:
    a. 1101 1000 + 0101 1001
    b. $6A + $88
    c. 1001 0010 + 1010 0100
    d. $EEFF + $CAFE

11. State, for Exercise 10, those instances in which overflow would result, indicating an apparently wrong answer.

12. Add these signed numbers, and state the contents of C and V:
    a. $97+$12   **b.** $85+$AF   **c.** $40+$40   **d.** $35+$B2

13. Suppose the 2 numbers $E3 and $1C are to be added using the instruction ADD. Give (a) the result and (b) the contents of the status bits N, Z, V, and C.

14. Repeat Exercise 13 using the instruction ADC and assuming that (C)=1.

15. Suppose (ACCA)=$45 and (ACCB)=$97. Give the result and the contents of the status bits N, Z, V, and C that would occur after executing each of these instructions independently. (Consult the individual instruction information sheets in Appendix A.)
    a. NEG A   **b.** ABA   **c.** NEG B

16. Perform BCD addition:
    a. 0010 1000+0100 0111
    b. 0110 0011+0101 0100
    c. 0111 1000+1000 0111
    d. 1001 0010+0011 0010

17. Suppose that (ACCA)=$19. Give the contents of ACCA after executing this program segment:

    ```
    ADD A   #$27
    DAA
    ```

EXERCISES

Set B (answers not given)

1. Add these binary numbers, and report the carry out:
   a. 1110 0110 + 0101 1010   **b.** 0111 1101 + 0011 1100
   c. 0110 1101 + 1111 0000   **d.** 1001 1100 + 1110 0110

2. Add these hexadecimal numbers, and report the carry out:
   a. $49+$AE   **b.** $BEEF+$A1DE   **c.** $7F+$B9   **d.** $9865+$ABCD

3. In each of Exercises 1 and 2, state which operations give answers that are too large for the number of digits available.

4. Find the twos complement of each of these, and verify that the numbers are complementary:
   a. 1110 0111   **b.** 0001 1111   **c.** 0111 1111   **d.** 1011 0001

5. Find the sixteens complement of each of these, and verify that the numbers are

complementary:

a. $FE b. $DEED c. $63 d. $0100

6. Using the hexadecimal number $A3, verify that complementation is circular.
7. Subtract by sixteens complementation and addition:

a. $23−$EA b. $97−$A3 c. $BABA−$6543 d. $F0AA−$F1FE

8. Form the ones complements by inverting each bit:

a. 1000 0111 b. 0110 1001 c. $72 d. $B3

9. Express these signed numbers as their decimal equivalents:

a. $3A b. 1011 0001

c. $98 d. 0100 1010

10. Add these signed numbers, and give the answers in decimal notation, as well as in binary or hexadecimal.

a. 1100 0010 + 1110 0110 b. $F3 + $47

c. 0100 0111 + 0111 0011 d. $BEAD + $FEED

11. State, for Exercise 10, those instances in which overflow would result, indicating an apparently wrong answer.
12. Add these signed numbers, and state the contents of C and V:

a. $80+$80 b. $F2+$CD c. $30+$3F d. $54+$97

13. Suppose the 2 numbers $97 and $69 (hexadecimal) are to be added using ADD. Give (a) the result and (b) the contents of the status bits N, Z, V, and C.
14. Repeat Exercise 13 using the instruction ADC and assuming that (C)=1.
15. Suppose (ACCA)=$A1 and (ACCB)=$C8. Give the result and the contents of the status bits N, Z, V, and C that would occur after executing each of these instructions independently (consult the individual instruction information sheets in appendix A):

a. ABA b. NEG B c. NEG A

16. Perform BCD addition:

a. 1001 1000 + 0011 0111 b. 0101 1000 + 1000 0100

c. 0110 1000 + 0100 0100 d. 0010 0110 + 1001 0111

17. Suppose that (ACCB)=$93. Give the contents of ACCB after executing this program segment:

```
ADD B   #$32
DAA
```

PROGRAMMING IDEAS

1. Write a program for double-precision addition.
2. Write a program for double-precision subtraction.
3. Write a program to add two 1-byte numbers and take the twos complement of the result.
4. Write a program to subtract one 1-byte number from another and take the twos complement of the result.
5. Write a program to add 2 BCD numbers and give the result in BCD.
6. Write a program to convert a hexadecimal number to BCD.
7. Write a program to subtract 1 BCD number from another and give the result in BCD.
8. Write a program for triple-precision addition.
9. Write a program for triple-precision subtraction.

8 Decisions

LEARNING OBJECTIVES

After completing this chapter, you should be able to:

1. Give a definition, explanation, or example for each of these: *relative addressing mode, relative address, sign extension, unconditional transfer of control, absolute address, conditional transfer of control, IF-THEN-ELSE unit, loop, DO-WHILE unit.*
2. Explain what is meant by a "signed displacement" and give the range of relative addressing.
3. Explain how to calculate the new program counter contents, given the old contents and a relative address.
4. Explain the difference between a "jump" and a "branch" instruction.
5. Explain the relationship between the contents of the status bits and the conditional branching instructions.
6. State three things necessary to use a conditional branch effectively.
7. Explain the difference between a two-dimensional and a one-dimensional flowchart, and why we use a one-dimensional flowchart to write a program.
8. Choose an appropriate branch instruction for a given situation, and write the flowchart.
9. Construct a one-dimensional flowchart from a two-dimensional one.
10. Explain how a loop may be terminated.
11. Hand assemble programs using the two-pass method given.
12. Write flowcharts and programs that contain IF-THEN-ELSE units and loops terminated by input data.

One of the more useful things a computer can do is to make decisions based on inputs. For instance, we might want a computer to monitor a set of security switches and sound an alarm if any of them were closed. The flowchart for a program to accomplish this would contain at least one decision box, because the microprocessor would have to decide whether or not any switches were closed.

In Chapter 6 we learned to write programs from flowcharts by substituting one instruction for each flowchart element. So far, none of these flowcharts have contained decision boxes. To write more interesting and useful programs, we need to know what instructions to substitute for decision boxes. In this chapter we'll learn about some of these instructions, and write programs that contain one or more decisions.

The instructions that take the place of decision boxes are transfer of control instructions.

8.1 TRANSFER OF CONTROL INSTRUCTIONS

In Chapter 1 we said that instructions are executed sequentially unless the microprocessor comes to a transfer of control instruction. A transfer of control instruction causes the program counter to point to a location other than the next sequential one. The 6800's transfer of control instructions are listed in Table 8.1.1. Most of these instructions begin with B, or Branch. To see how these work, we need to look at a new addressing mode.

Relative addressing

The **relative addressing mode** requires 2 bytes per instruction: an OP code, followed by a 1-byte number. This number, called a **relative address**, is a signed

TABLE 8.1.1 6800 Transfer of Control Instructions

Mnemonic	Definition
Unconditional	
BRA	BRANCH ALWAYS
BSR	BRANCH TO SUBROUTINE
JMP	JUMP
JSR	JUMP TO SUBROUTINE
Conditional	
BCC	BRANCH IF CARRY CLEAR
BCS	BRANCH IF CARRY SET
BNE	BRANCH IF NOT EQUAL
BEQ	BRANCH IF EQUAL
BPL	BRANCH IF PLUS
BMI	BRANCH IF MINUS
BVC	BRANCH IF OVERFLOW CLEAR
BVS	BRANCH IF OVERFLOW SET
BGE	Branch IF GREATER THAN OR EQUAL TO ZERO
BGT	Branch IF GREATER THAN ZERO
BHI	Branch IF HIGHER
BLE	Branch IF LESS THAN OR EQUAL TO ZERO
BLS	Branch IF LOWER OR SAME
BLT	Branch IF LESS THAN ZERO

displacement that is added to the current program counter contents. The result of the addition is placed back in the program counter to effect the transfer of control.

When we say "signed displacement," we mean that the branch can be forward in the program (that is, toward higher memory) or backward in the program (toward lower memory), depending on whether the relative address is positive or negative. Relative addresses $00 through $7F will cause a forward branch and relative addresses $80 through $FF will cause a backward branch. We know that the range of signed 1-byte numbers is -128 to $+127$ (decimal), which means that we can branch only as far as 128 locations backward or 127 locations forward. Thus the relative addressing mode has a limited range of -128 to $+127$ locations.

Relative addresses are 1 byte long, but addresses of memory locations are 2 bytes long. To add a signed 1-byte number to a 2-byte number, we first perform a **sign extension** by filling out the 8 more significant bits with all 0s ($00 in hexadecimal) if the number is positive and with all 1s ($FF in hexadecimal) if the number is negative.

Figure 8.1.1 illustrates forward and backward branching. In the top illustration the contents of location $0017 is $20, the OP code for BRA. The relative address, $05, is contained in location $0018. After the microprocessor has fetched the 2-byte instruction, the program counter is pointing to the next address, $0019. To execute the instruction, the microprocessor sign extends the positive relative address, $05, to

FIGURE 8.1.1 The Relative Addressing Mode May Cause a Forward or a Backward Branch in the Program

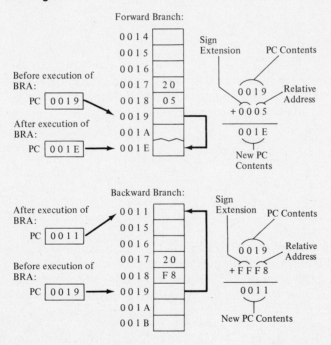

$0005. Adding this number to the current program counter contents ($0019) yields $001E, the new program counter contents. After execution of this branch instruction, the program counter will point to location $001E.

In the bottom illustration of Figure 8.1.1 the program counter is also pointing to location $0019 after fetching the instruction. To execute the instruction, the microprocessor sign extends the negative relative address, $F8, to $FFF8. Then the microprocessor adds $FFF8 to $0019 to get $0011 (as usual, we and the microprocessor ignore any carry that results from adding signed numbers). Then the program counter points to location $0011.

EXAMPLE 8.1.1

Determine the program counter contents before and after execution of a BRA instruction for each of these conditions: (a) The OP code, $20, is contained in location $FF02 and the relative address, $12, is contained in location $FF03; (b) the OP code, $20, is contained in location $F2E3 and the relative address, $FE, is contained in location $F2E4.

Solution

(a) The program counter contents before execution is $FF04, the address of the location immediately following the instruction. To get the program counter contents after execution, we sign extend the positive relative address, $12, to $0012 and add it to the program counter contents, $FF04:

$$
\begin{array}{cccc}
 \text{F} & \text{F} & 0 & 4 \\
+0 & 0 & 1 & 2 \\
\hline
 \text{F} & \text{F} & 1 & 6 \\
\end{array}
$$

(b) The program counter contents before execution is $F2E5. To get the program counter contents after execution, we sign extend the negative relative address, $FE, to $FFFE, and add it to the program counter contents:

$$
\begin{array}{cccc}
 \text{F} & 2 & \text{E} & 5 \\
 \text{F} & \text{F} & \text{F} & \text{E} \\
\hline
 \text{F} & 2 & \text{E} & 3 \\
\end{array}
$$

Answer: (a) $FF04, $FF16; (b) $F2E5, $F2E3

We see in part (b) of Example 8.1.1 that a negative displacement of -2 locations ($FE in hexadecimal) puts the program counter back to the location of the branch instruction itself ($F2E3). Recall that the program counter always points to the *next* instruction. When the microprocessor is executing the contents of location $F2E3, the PC is pointing to $F2E5. So a negative displacement of 2 is needed to get the PC back to $F2E3.

The transfer of control instructions in Table 8.1.1 are classified as unconditional or conditional. We'll look at these classifications next.

Unconditional transfer of control

In this classification, transfer of control takes place no matter what, with no decision involved. We already used BRA, Branch Always, to illustrate relative addressing. Of these four instructions, two begin with B or Branch, and the other two with J or Jump. If we look at the instruction information sheet for either JMP or JSR, we find that only two addressing modes are available: the familiar extended addressing mode and the indexed addressing mode, which we won't discuss until Chapter 9. Either way, 3 bytes of machine code are required. In the extended addressing mode the operand is a 2-byte address, which is loaded into the program counter to effect the transfer of control. This operand is called an **absolute address** to distinguish it from the relative address of a branch instruction. That is, transfer of control goes absolutely to that address. Thus a jump instruction has an unlimited range and can cause a transfer of control to anywhere in memory.

Later we'll discuss the instructions BSR and JSR. Figure 8.1.2 illustrates the difference between the BRA and JMP instructions.

Here's an example of the use of BRA and JMP in two assembly language program segments:

```
100 . . . .          
110    BRA  HERE      110    JMP  HERE
120 . . .             120 . . .
130 HERE . . . .      130 HERE . . . .
```

FIGURE 8.1.2 Comparison of JMP and BRA Instructions

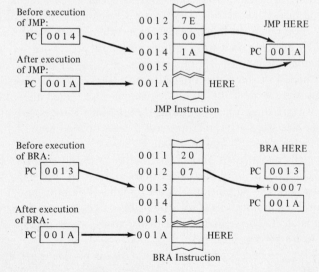

JMP Instruction

BRA Instruction

Both instructions accomplish the same thing: They transfer control to the location identified by the label HERE. We recall from Chapter 7 that a label may be used to identify a program statement. When the assembler assembles the source code, it automatically assigns the address of the instruction of (in this case) line 130 to the label HERE. For branch instructions the assembler calculates the relative address, too. BRA and JMP appear to be the same when we write them in assembly language, but their machine codes and addressing modes are different.

How would we decide whether to use JMP or BRA in a given situation? First, if the location where control is to be transferred is outside the range of -128 to $+127$ bytes, we'd have no choice but to use JMP. However, if the location were inside this range, we'd probably pick BRA. As a branch instruction, BRA takes one less program word than JMP.

To find out more about each individual transfer of control instruction, we consult the individual instruction information sheets in Appendix A. One thing we'd notice is that none of the transfer of control instructions affect the status register bits. But most of these instructions depend on conditions of one or more of the status bits, as we'll see in the next subsection.

Conditional transfer of control

In this classification a transfer of control takes place only if a specific condition is satisfied. All these are branch, rather than jump, instructions and therefore use the relative addressing mode.

When we humans make a decision based on a condition being true or false, we test that condition, then make the decision. We're so used to doing this that we don't usually think of it in such a formal way. Suppose, for instance, that you planned to attend a Fourth of July picnic, which was to be canceled in case of rain. On the day of the picnic you make the decision whether to go or not by first testing whether or not it's raining. You could do this by looking outside or by sticking your hand out, or maybe even by listening, if it were raining very hard.

Just as human beings use various sources of data for making decisions, the microprocessor uses 4 of the status bits: Negative (N), Zero (Z), Overflow (V), and Carry (C). Now we see why the status register is also called the condition code register: It keeps track of various conditions that the microprocessor will need to test in order to make decisions. The microprocessor tests one or more of the status bits each time it executes a conditional branch.

The first eight conditional branch instructions are the simplest, because they depend on the contents of only one of the four status bits. For each of these four status bits there are two conditional branching instructions: one that causes a transfer of control if the status bit is set and another that causes a transfer of control if the status bit is clear. The remaining six instructions, which depend on more than one status bit, won't be discussed here.

Before asking the microprocessor to test a status bit, we must first set up the condition of that bit by using an instruction that affects the bit. To see how this works, let's look at this program segment:

```
140     ADD A   $B0   ADD CONTENTS OF $00B0 TO ACCA
150     BVS     ERR   IF V BIT SET, BRANCH TO ERR
160 . . . .
170 . . . .
180 ERR . . .
```

We know that ADD A affects all four status bits, so this instruction will set up the condition in the overflow bit (V), the bit we want to test. In line 150 the branch instruction BVS ERR will cause the microprocessor to test the overflow bit. If V is set, control will be transferred to the location of the label ERR. If the condition is not met (that is, if the overflow bit is clear), no transfer of control will take place and the instruction at line 160 will be the next instruction fetched.

Three things are necessary to use a conditional branch effectively:

1. We must set up the condition we want to test by using an appropriate instruction just before the conditional branch. To find out how each instruction affects the status bits, we consult the instruction information sheets in Appendix A.
2. We test the condition by using an appropriate branch instruction *immediately* after setting up the condition. (Here, the BVC instruction came right after the ADD instruction. If we had put another instruction in between, it might have changed the condition of the bit we wanted to test.)
3. We must tell the microprocessor where the control is to be transferred if the condition is met. (Here, we used a label ERR.)

In addition to following these rules, we must also select a conditional branch instruction for our particular situation. In the next section we'll find out how to do this.

8.2   USING TRANSFER OF CONTROL INSTRUCTIONS

We've seen that for each status bit there's a conditional branch instruction that causes transfer of control if the status bit is set, and one that causes transfer of control if the status bit is clear. How do we decide which to use for a given situation? If we wanted to make a decision based on the contents of the carry bit, for instance, how would we know whether to use BCC or BCS?

For each situation one conditional branch will usually be preferable to the other and will result in a simpler program. We'll see how to make the right choice.

Flowcharting for conditional branch instructions

Let's compare the structure of a flowchart with the structure of a program stored in memory. Flowcharts that contain no decision boxes are one-dimensional; that is, the flow is linear. This corresponds to the one-dimensional nature of a stored

FIGURE 8.2.1 A One-Dimensional Flowchart Contains No Tasks Within Its Branches

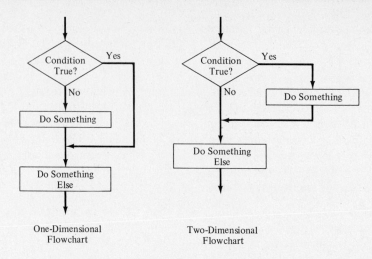

One-Dimensional
Flowchart

Two-Dimensional
Flowchart

program, where the sequence of addresses is linear. However, a flowchart that contains decision boxes can be two-dimensional. We can't write a one-dimensional program from a two-dimensional flowchart, so in this section we'll emphasize writing one-dimensional flowcharts. A one-dimensional flowchart contains no tasks within its branches; the branches return directly to the body of the flowchart. A two-dimensional flowchart contains one or more tasks within its branches. Figure 8.2.1 illustrates the difference between a one- and a two-dimensional flowchart.

A flowchart segment that contains a decision box and its alternative task boxes as in Figure 8.2.1 is called an **IF-THEN-ELSE unit**. That is, *if* the condition is true, *then* do something; otherwise (*else*) do something else. Although one of the

FIGURE 8.2.2 Decision Box Equivalents for Some Conditional Branching Instructions

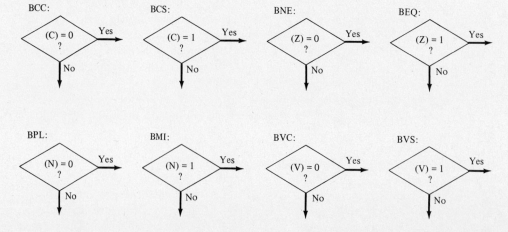

units in the figure is one-dimensional and the other two-dimensional, both are IF-THEN-ELSE units.

Next, let's look at the structure of a conditional branch instruction. Each instruction causes a branch *if* its condition is met; this corresponds to a yes on a decision box (there *is* a branch). If the condition is not met, the program proceeds in sequence; this corresponds to a no on a decision box (there is *no* branch). Figure 8.2.2 shows decision boxes equivalent to the first eight conditional branching instructions of Table 8.1.1.

We want to use the decision boxes so that the flowchart stays one-dimensional (linear); that way, we can translate the flowchart to a program. To keep the flowchart linear, we'd like to have the no path continue in the program and the yes path skip the next task or tasks in the program. With this restriction, the choice of the better branching instruction is easy.

EXAMPLE 8.2.1

We want to program the microprocessor to act like a burglar alarm. We have wired DA7 of the PIA to a sensor on a door, so that if the door is opened a 1 is present in that bit; otherwise a 0 is in that bit. We have wired DA0 to an alarm. Storing a 1 in that bit causes the alarm to turn on. We can test whether DA7 is set by loading it into an accumulator and then using either BMI or BPL to make the decision as to whether or not the door has been opened. The program should cause the micro-processor to check the door and, if it's closed, to stop. If the door is opened, the microprocessor should sound the alarm and then stop. Which is the better choice, BPL or BMI?

Solution

Looking at Figure 8.2.2, we see that BMI causes a branch if N is set, and BPL causes

FIGURE 8.2.3 Two Alternative IF-THEN-ELSE Units for Example 8.2.1

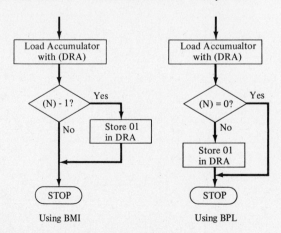

Using BMI   Using BPL

a branch if N is clear. N will be set if the door is opened ((DA7)=1) and clear if the door is closed ((DA7)=0).

Step 1: Write two separate flowchart segments, using each of the two possible branch instructions, which are shown in Figure 8.2.3.

Step 2: Choose the branching instruction that results in a one-dimensional flowchart segment. We choose BPL.

Answer: BPL

With a little experience, we'll be able to pick the better branch instruction without actually writing out the flowcharts. But at first, writing them out will make the choice clear.

FIGURE 8.2.4   Detailed Flowchart for Program of Example 8.2.1

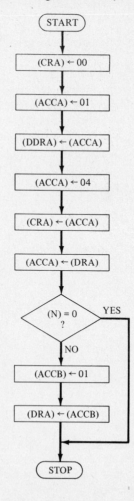

FIGURE 8.2.5   Program for Example 8.2.1

Seq	Label	Op'n	Operand	Comment
100		NAM	BURGLR	
110	;THIS PROGRAM SOUNDS AN ALARM WIRED TO DA0 WHEN A DOOR IS OPENED.			
120	;A SENSOR ON THE DOOR IS WIRED TO DA7.			
130	CRA	EQU	$8005	DEFINE CONTROL REG
140	DRA	EQU	$8004	DEFINE DATA REG
150	DDRA	EQU	DRA	DEFINE DATA DIRECTION REG
160	START	CLR	CRA	SET BIT 2 OF CRA TO 0
170		LDA A	#$01	SET BIT 0 OF DRA OUT, REST IN
180		STA A	DDRA	CONFIGURE SIDE A FOR I/O
190		LDA A	#$04	READY TO SET CRA BIT 2 TO 1
200		STA A	CRA	ADDRESS DRA; READY FOR I/O
210		LDA A	DRA	GET CONTENTS OF DRA
220		BPL	SHUT	IF BIT 7=0, DOOR SHUT
230		LDA B	#$01	OTHERWISE READY TO TURN ON ALARM
240		STA B	DRA	TURN IT ON
250	SHUT	WAI		STOP.
260		END		

Figure 8.2.4 shows a complete, detailed flowchart to do the job described in Example 8.2.1. In this problem we set up the condition to test N by loading the contents of DRA into accumulator A. Figure 8.2.5 shows the corresponding assembly language program.

Notice that although this program will work and do what it's supposed to, it will only do it once and then stop. To be an effective burglar alarm, the microprocessor should keep checking and checking the door. As the program is written now, the only way to do that is for us to keep reexecuting the program, and if we're going to do that, we might as well just watch the door instead. Later we'll see how to make such programs more useful.

Because the 6800's instruction set contains two opposite branch instructions for each status bit, we should always be able to pick one branch instruction that gives us a one-dimensional flowchart. There are other microprocessors, however, that don't have two opposite branch instructions for each status bit. For these, we might have to construct a one-dimensional flowchart out of a two-dimensional one.

Constructing a one-dimensional flowchart from a two-dimensional one

We chose BPL as the better choice to do the job of Example 8.2.1. But what if we were using a microprocessor that had only the equivalent of a BMI, and no BPL? Then, we'd have to make do with BMI and would be stuck with a two-dimensional flowchart. Figure 8.2.6 shows the decision part of Figure 8.2.4 rewritten, using BMI instead of BPL. To make this flowchart one-dimensional, we must move the task boxes in the yes path down so that they are in the line of flow.

FIGURE 8.2.6   IF-THEN-ELSE Unit Rewritten Using BMI Instead of BPL

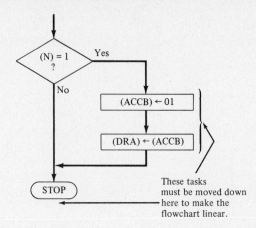

Figure 8.2.7 shows the construction of a one-dimensional flowchart. To return the yes branch to the main flow, we need to do more than just draw an arrow. We need to use an unconditional transfer of control, either BRA or JMP. The finished flowchart has one more task box in it because of this transfer of control instruction.

The program corresponding to this flowchart is shown in Figure 8.2.8. This program will work just as well as that of Figure 8.2.5, but it is slightly longer and a

FIGURE 8.2.7   Construction of One-Dimensional Unit Using Unconditional Transfer of Control

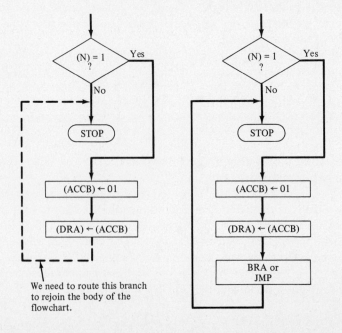

FIGURE 8.2.8 Program from Figure 8.2.7

Seq	Label	Op'n	Operand	Comment
100		NAM	BURGLR	
110	;THIS PROGRAM SOUNDS AN ALARM WIRED TO DA0 WHEN A DOOR IS OPENED.			
120	;A SENSOR ON THE DOOR IS WIRED TO DA7.			
130	CRA	EQU	$8005	DEFINE CONTROL REG
140	DRA	EQU	$8004	DEFINE DATA REG
150	DDRA	EQU	DRA	DEFINE DATA DIRECTION REG
160	START	CLR	CRA	SET BIT 2 OF CRA TO 0
170		LDA A	#$01	SET BIT 0 OF DRA OUT, REST IN
180		STA A	DDRA	CONFIGURE SIDE A FOR I/O
190		LDA A	#$04	READY TO SET CRA BIT 2 TO 1
200		STA A	CRA	ADDRESS DRA; READY FOR I/O
210		LDA A	DRA	GET CONTENTS OF DRA
220		BMI	OPEN	IF BIT 7=1, DOOR OPEN
230	DONE	WAI		STOP.
240	OPEN	LDA B	#$01	READY TO TURN ON ALARM
250		STA B	DRA	TURN IT ON
260		BRA	DONE	AND STOP.
270		END		

bit awkward. Having the end of the program somewhere at the middle is confusing and makes following the program difficult. We see why the program of Figure 8.2.5 is preferable.

Next, we'll see how to use decision boxes to perform a task more than once.

8.3 INTRODUCTION TO LOOPS

In the last section we saw how to use decision boxes to construct an IF-THEN-ELSE unit. We also saw that our burglar alarm program would be much more useful if we could cause the microprocessor to monitor the door constantly instead of checking it just once. To do this, we need to know something about loops.

A **loop** causes certain operations to be performed over and over until some end condition is reached. Another name for loop is **DO-WHILE unit**. That is, the microprocessor is to *do* the operations *while* some nonterminal condition exists. Figure 8.3.1 shows a general loop, or do-while, structure.

Going through the set of operations once is called "going through the loop." We speak of the "first pass through the loop," "second pass through the loop," and so on until the end condition is reached. Then the microprocessor exits the loop. There are several ways we can define the end condition: (1) We could give the microprocessor a certain number of times to go through the loop; for instance, to process a list of 20 words. (2) We could let the appearance of a predetermined piece of data—say, an ASCII period—define the end condition. (3) We could let the end condition be determined by some outside event, as the "door open" input on our burglar alarm. In the latter two cases the loop would be passed through an indefinite number of times.

FIGURE 8.3.1   Generalized DO-WHILE Unit, or Loop, Structure

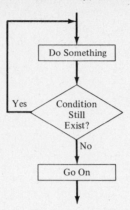

Figure 8.3.2 shows the IF-THEN-ELSE unit of Figure 8.2.4 converted to a DO-WHILE unit. Here, we want the microprocessor to *do* the task (check the door by loading the contents of DRA into accumulator A) *while* the nonterminal condition exists (door shut, or (N)=0). If at any time (N) is no longer 0, the condition no longer exists and the microprocessor will exit the loop and sound the alarm. The program segment that corresponds to this unit is also shown in Figure 8.3.2.

FIGURE 8.3.2   Conversion of IF-THEN-ELSE to DO-WHILE Unit

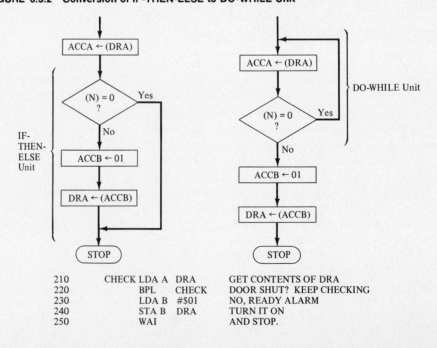

210	CHECK	LDA A	DRA	GET CONTENTS OF DRA
220		BPL	CHECK	DOOR SHUT? KEEP CHECKING
230		LDA B	#$01	NO, READY ALARM
240		STA B	DRA	TURN IT ON
250		WAI		AND STOP.

This brief introduction to loops will pave the way for the more detailed treatment that follows in Chapter 9.

8.4   MORE ABOUT HAND ASSEMBLING

In Chapter 4 we had an introduction to hand assembly. We learned how to code instructions using the direct, extended, and inherent modes. Now that we've learned about the relative addressing mode, we need to know a little more about hand assembly.

Let's look at Figure 8.4.1, which is an assembler's listing of the complete program corresponding to the source program of Figure 8.2.4. We noted earlier that the assembler makes a cross-reference table at the bottom. To make this table, the assembler constructs a symbol table, in RAM, which contains each label and its value.

Usually, an assembler makes 2 passes through a source program. During the first pass, the assembler creates the symbol table. As it comes to a symbol and its value, it records these in memory. It gets the values of CRA, DRA, and DDRA as they are defined by the equate statements. It equates START with $0000, because there is no ORG statement and START is the first statement that contains executable code (that is, an OP code). Also, during the first pass the assembler puts in the OP codes and the values of any labels that have been defined. When it comes to line 220, BPL SHUT, it leaves a blank, because the label SHUT hasn't been defined yet. At the end of the first pass the symbol table should be complete.

During the second pass the assembler substitutes any remaining label values and calculates the relative address values for any transfer of control instructions.

We're going to take about the same approach to hand assembling as the assembler does and follow this procedure:

1. Make 2 passes through the source code. During the first pass, keep track of labels by keeping a symbol table as an assembler does. As you come to each label, write down its value in the symbol table.
2. During the first pass, leave blank spaces for any operands that are represented by labels that haven't yet been defined. Also, leave blank the relative addresses.
3. When you complete the first pass, go back and compute the relative addresses using this formula: Relative address = destination address − address of branching instruction + $FFFE (this value, equivalent to −$0002, compensates for the fact that the program counter is already pointing to the next instruction, two locations after the branch instruction).
4. Make the second pass through. Fill in the missing operands and relative addresses.

Now, we'll use these rules as we hand assemble a sample program.

FIGURE 8.4.1   Assembly Listing of Program of Figure 8.2.5

```
BURGLR
M6800 ASSEMBLER LISTING VERSION 1.6      14 OCT 80 23:14    PAGE   2
FIG825   DAT     14 OCT 80 22:32

                      3  ;THIS PROGRAM SOUNDS AN ALARM WIRED TO DA0 WHEN A DOOR IS OPENED.
                      4  ;A SENSOR ON THE DOOR IS WIRED TO DA7.
8005                  5  CRA    EQU   $8005      DEFINE CONTROL REG
8004                  6  DRA    EQU   $8004      DEFINE DATA REG
8004                  7  DDRA   EQU   DRA        DEFINE DATA DIRECTION REG
0000 7F 80 05         8  START  CLR   CRA        SET BIT 2 OF CRA TO 0
0003 86 01            9         LDA A #$01       SET BIT 0 OF DRA OUT, REST IN
0005 B7 80 04        10         STA A DDRA       CONFIGURE SIDE A FOR I/O
0008 86 04           11         LDA A #$04       READY TO SET CRA BIT 2 TO 1
000A B7 80 05        12         STA A CRA        ADDRESS DRA; READY FOR I/O
000D B6 80 04        13         LDA A DRA        GET CONTENTS OF DRA
0010 2A 05           14         BPL   SHUT       IF BIT 7 = 0, DOOR SHUT
0012 C6 01           15         LDA B #$01       OTHERWISE READY TO TURN ON ALARM
0014 F7 80 04        16         STA B DRA        TURN IT ON
0017 3E              17  SHUT   WAI              STOP.
0018                 18         END

NO STATEMENTS FLAGGED

CROSS-REFERENCE TABLE

DRA      8005     5     8    12
DDRA     8004     7    10
DRA      8004     6     7    13   16
SHUT     0017    17    14
START    0000     8
```

EXAMPLE 8.4.1

Hand assemble the program of Figure 8.4.2.

Solution

We follow the preceding rules. After copying the comments, we come to the first symbols: NUM and SIGN. We put them and their values in a symbol table:

SYMBOL TABLE

NUM	00B0
SIGN	00B1

Next, we assemble each line of source code, leaving blanks for operands represented by symbols not yet defined. We also leave the relative address for BPL blank. So far, the executable code of our assembly language program looks like this after the first pass:

ADDRESS	CODE	LABEL	MNEMONIC	OPERAND	COMMENT
0000	7F 00 B1	START	CLR	SIGN	PUT ZEROS IN SIGN
0003	96 B0		LDA A	NUM	GET NUM, TEST NEG BIT
0005	2A —		BPL	POS	IF POS, LEAVE ALONE
0007	70 00 B0		NEG	NUM	ELSE FORM 25 COMP
000A	C6 FF		LDA B	#$FF	READY TO STORE NEG MSGE
000C	D7 B1		STA B	SIGN	PUT FF INTO SIGN
000E	3E	POS	WAI		AND STOP

We see that the label START comes at address 0000, and POS at address 000E. So we add these to our symbol table.

FIGURE 8.4.2 **Sample Program for Hand Assembly**

Addr.	Code	Seq.	Label	Op'n	Operand	Comment
		100		NAM	NEGATE	
		110	;THIS PROGRAM IDENTIFIES A NUMBER INPUT			
		115	;IN ADDRESS $00B0 AS			
		120	;POSITIVE OR NEGATIVE. IF NEGATIVE,			
		125	;THE NUMBER IS CHANGED			
		130	;TO POSITIVE AND FF IS STORED IN LOCATION 00B1.			
		135	;IF POSITIVE, THE NUMBER IS LEFT INTACT			
		140	;AND $00 IS LEFT IN LOCATION $00B1.			
		150	NUM	EQU	$00B0	
		160	SIGN	EQU	$00B1	SAVE NUM AND SIGN
		170	START	CLR	SIGN	PUT ZEROS IN SIGN
		180		LDA A	NUM	GET NUM, TEST NEG BIT
		190		BPL	POS	IF POS, THEN LEAVE ALONE
		200		NEG	NUM	ELSE FORM 2S COMP
		210		LDA B	#$FF	READY TO STORE NEG MSGE
		220		STA B	SIGN	PUT $FF INTO $00B0
		230	POS	WAI		AND STOP
		240		END		

Symbol Table

NUM	00B0
SIGN	00B1
START	0000
POS	000E

Now, we're finished with the first pass. Next, we calculate the relative address for the branching instruction:

$$000E - 0005 - 02 = 0007 \ (07)$$

Next, we make the second pass through, filling in all the blanks with the values in the symbol table and the relative address we just calculated. The address and code portion of our finished program will look like this:

Address	Code
0000	7F 00 B1
0003	96 B0
0005	2A 07
0007	70 00 B0
000A	C6 FF
000C	D7 B1
000E	3E

Answer: The complete listing is identical with that of Figure 8.4.3.

FIGURE 8.4.3 Hand Assembled Sample Program

Addr.	Code	Seq.	Label	Op'n	Operand	Comment
		100		NAM	NEGATE	
		110	;THIS PROGRAM IDENTIFIES A NUMBER INPUT			
		115	;IN ADDRESS $00B0 AS			
		120	;POSITIVE OR NEGATIVE. IF NEGATIVE,			
		125	;THE NUMBER IS CHANGED			
		130	;TO POSITIVE AND FF IS STORED IN LOCATION $00B1.			
		135	;IF POSITIVE, THE NUMBER IS LEFT INTACT			
		140	;AND $00 IS LEFT IN LOCATION $00B1.			
		150	NUM	EQU	$00B0	
		160	SIGN	EQU	$00B1	SAVE NUM AND SIGN
0000	7F 00 B1	170	START	CLR	SIGN	PUT ZEROS IN SIGN
0003	96 B0	180		LDA A	NUM	GET NUM, TEST NEG BIT
0005	2A 07	190		BPL	POS	IF POS, THEN LEAVE ALONE
0007	70 00 B0	200		NEG	NUM	ELSE FORM 25 COMP
000A	C6 FF.	210		LDA B	#$FF	READY TO STORE NEG MSGE
000C	D7 B1	220		STA B	SIGN	PUT $FF INTO $00B0
000E	3E	230	POS	WAI		AND STOP
		240		END		

Symbol Table

NUM	00B0
SIGN	00B1
START	0000
POS	000E

In this chapter we've introduced an important aspect of programming: the implementation of transfer of control instructions in IF-THEN-ELSE and DO-WHILE units. In the next chapter we'll look at DO-WHILE units in more detail.

REVIEW QUESTIONS

1. What kind of instructions take the place of a decision box?
2. What is the **relative addressing mode**? What is a **relative address**?
3. What does signed displacement mean? Explain.
4. What is the range of branch and jump instructions? Explain.
5. What is a **sign extension**? How do we use sign extension to calculate new program counter contents?
6. What is **unconditional transfer of control**? What are the instructions for unconditional transfer of control? What is an **absolute address**?
7. What addressing mode is used by jump instructions? Explain the difference between JMP and BRA.
8. How do transfer of control instructions affect the status bits? How are they dependent on contents of the status bits?
9. What three things are necessary to use a conditional transfer of control instruction effectively?
10. Explain what we mean by one-dimensional and two-dimensional flowcharts. Why must we have a one-dimensional flowchart to write a program?
11. Sketch decision boxes that illustrate the first eight conditional branch instructions.
12. Explain how to use decision boxes to keep flowcharts one dimensional.
13. How do we choose the best branch instruction for a given situation?
14. What is an **IF-THEN-ELSE unit**? Why is it called that?
15. Explain how to construct a one-dimensional flowchart from a two-dimensional one. Why might we need to do that?
16. What is a **loop**? What is another name for it?
17. How do we cause the microprocessor to exit a loop?
18. Explain how to write a flowchart and program containing a loop that is terminated by input data.
19. Describe briefly how an assembler assembles a program. What is a symbol table?
20. Explain how to hand assemble a program using the method given in this chapter. How do we calculate a relative address?

EXERCISES

Set A (answers at back of book)

1. Refer to Figure 8.1.1, and calculate the new PC contents if location $0018 contains (a) $00; (b) $F2; (c) $10
2. Determine the PC contents before and after execution of a BRA instruction for each of these conditions:
   a. The OP code, $20, is contained in location $0103 and the relative address, $F1, is contained in location $0104.

b. The OP code is contained in location $00F7 and the relative address, $08, is contained in location $00F8.

3. Refer to Figure 8.1.2. For the JMP instruction, what would be the contents of locations $0012 and $0013 if the new PC contents are to be $0005?

4. We wish to transfer control from address $0011 to $3000. Could either unconditional branch instruction be used? Explain.

5. Which of these instructions would set up the condition for BPL or BMI: (a) LDA B; (b) TBA; (c) SBA; (d) JMP; (e) BVC

6. Which of these instructions would set up the condition for BCC or BCS: (a) LDA A; (b) ABA; (c) ADC; (d) BEQ; (e) CLC; (f) TAB (g) SBC

7. We want to program the microprocessor to add 2 numbers and, if the answer is less than 256, add a third number. Select the correct branch instruction, and state how the condition will be set up.

8. We have wired side A of the PIA to 8 individual security switches. If any one of these switches is closed, its bit will contain a 1. We want the microprocessor to sound an alarm by storing a 1 in bit 0 of side B of the PIA if any of the switches are closed. Select the correct branch instruction and state how the condition will be set up.

9. Refer to Exercise 7 and construct a one-dimensional flowchart using the opposite branch instruction.

10. Refer to Exercise 8, and construct a one-dimensional flowchart using the opposite branch instruction.

11. We wish to set up the program of Exercise 8 so that the microprocessor constantly monitors the security switches. Sketch the DO-WHILE unit that would accomplish this.

EXERCISES

Set B (answers not given)

1. Refer to Figure 8.1.1, and calculate the new PC contents if location $0018 contains: (a) $FD; (b) $02; (c) $22

2. Determine the PC contents before and after execution of a BRA instruction for each of these conditions:

   a. The OP code, $20, is contained in location $0011 and the relative address, $0B, is contained in location $0012.

   b. The OP code is in location $00A3 and the relative address, $F5, is in location $00A4.

3. Refer to the JMP instruction of Figure 8.1.2. If location $0012 contained $01 and location $0013 contained $00, what would the new PC contents be?

4. We wish to transfer control unconditionally from location $0010 to location $0000. Could either BRA or JMP be used? Explain.

5. Which of these instructions could be used to set up the condition for BVC or BVS: (a) LDA A; (b) ADC; (c) BCC; (d) CLR; (e) DEC; (f) STA A

6. Which of these instructions could be used to set up the condition for BEQ or BNE: (a) INC; (b) LDA B; (c) SEV; (d) NOP; (e) JMP; (f) CLR

7. We want to program the microprocessor to add 2 numbers and, if there is no overflow, to store the answer in location LOC, otherwise stop. Select the correct branch instruction, and state how the condition would be set up.

8. A priceless Javanese vase in a museum is protected with an electric eye. As long as the beam is unbroken, a 1 is input into DA0 of the PIA. If the beam is broken (meaning possibly that someone is trying to steal the vase), then a 0 is input into DA0. The other bits of side A are permanently wired to 0. We want the microprocessor to sound an alarm if someone is trying to steal the vase. Choose the correct branch instruction and state how the condition would be set up.

9. Refer to Exercise 7, and construct a one-dimensional flowchart using the opposite branch instruction.

10. Refer to Exercise 8, and construct a one-dimensional flowchart using the opposite branch instruction.

11. We wish to set up the program of Exercise 8 so that the microprocessor constantly monitors the vase. Sketch the DO-WHILE unit that would accomplish this.

PROGRAMMING IDEAS

Write flowcharts and programs for these. If necessary, hand assemble the programs.

1. DA7 is wired to a temperature sensor. When the temperature is 65 or above, DA7 contains a 1. When the temperature drops below 65, DA7 contains a 0. DA0 is wired to a switch that turns the furnace on when a 1 is stored in that bit. We want to monitor the temperature constantly, and to turn the furnace on when it drops below 65.

2. Modify program 1 so that it also turns the furnace back off when the temperature reaches 66 or above.

3. Add 2 numbers and store the answer in location $00FE. If there is a carry of 1, store $FF in location $00FF, otherwise leave $00 in location $00FF.

4. Subtract 1 number from another and store the answer in location $00AA. If the result is negative, turn on a light wired to DB0. If the result is 0, turn on a light wired to DB1.

9 Loops

LEARNING OBJECTIVES

After completing this chapter, you should be able to:

1. Give a definition, explanation, or example for each of these: *iterative, sensing loop, counting loop, loop counter, timing loop, cycle time, clock, positive transition, negative transition, clock cycle, clock frequency, routine, delay routine, nested loops.*
2. Name, describe, and implement the five basic elements of a loop.
3. Use these new instructions correctly in a program: CMP, CBA, ASL, LSR, LDX, DEX, INX, NOP.
4. Explain the instructions in (3) in terms of their results and how they affect the status register.
5. Explain, modify, and write similar programs to the examples given in the chapter.
6. Explain the difference between incrementing and decrementing a loop counter.
7. Given the time for each instruction, calculate the elapsed time in a loop.
8. Use the index register as a loop counter.
9. Calculate the elapsed time in a loop for a specific cycle time, using the clock cycle information on the instruction information sheets.
10. Create a delay routine that produces a specific time delay.
11. Use nested loops to create longer time delays in programs.
12. Write programs similar to those given in the chapter.

In the last chapter we briefly described loops and noted that without them it's pretty hard to use a microprocessor to advantage. In this chapter we'll look more closely at loops and learn some new instructions that will be useful in their implementation.

9.1 PARTS OF A LOOP

We can divide a loop into five basic elements:

1. *Initialization*. Here, we establish starting values of registers, and so on.
2. *Processing*. Here, we do the actual work.
3. *Loop Control*. Here, we set up the condition that will be tested in order for the microprocessor to decide whether or not to exit the loop.
4. *Decision*. Here, we test a condition and decide to exit or to stay in the loop.
5. *Termination*. Here, we end the operation.

Figure 9.1.1 shows a flowchart of this scheme. Parts 2, 3, and 4 make up the **iterative portion of the loop** (to *iterate* means "to repeat"). In a properly working program that contains a loop, the iterative portion is executed many times. In contrast, the initialization (part 1) and the termination (part 5) are normally executed only once.

In our burglar alarm program of Chapter 8 the instruction LDA DRA was the loop control section, because this instruction set up the condition to be tested by the BPL branch instruction. In this case the loop's terminal condition was caused by an external event. The microprocessor continued through the loop until it found (sensed) the terminal condition. We call this kind of loop a **sensing loop**.

FIGURE 9.1.1 Basic Parts of a Loop

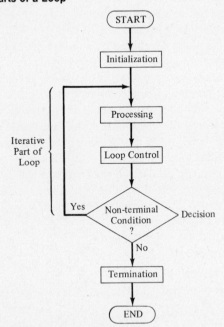

9.2 SENSING LOOPS

In our simple burglar alarm problem we were dealing with just one bit (DA7) and an easy one to detect at that. Let's look at a more interesting problem.

We want to make a combination lock. The combination, known only to the user, is a 1-byte binary number to be input by means of 8 switches wired to side A of the PIA. When the right combination is entered, the microprocessor stores a 1 in DB0, which causes the safe to be unlocked. For the microprocessor to know whether or not we've input the right combination, it has to compare our input value with the predetermined combination. To do that, it needs another instruction.

The Compare Instruction

If we look up CMP in Appendix A, we find that this instruction compares the contents of an accumulator with the contents of a memory location by subtracting the contents of memory from the contents of the accumulator.

When we compare (ACCA) with (M), there are three possibilities:

1. (ACCA) is greater than (M).
2. (ACCA) is equal to (M).
3. (ACCA) is less than (M).

In our particular case we're only interested in (2), because either the number we input is equal to the predetermined combination or it isn't. Beyond that, we don't care whether one is larger or smaller than the other. Later, we may use these other potential results of the CMP instruction.

Although the numbers are compared by subtraction, the result of the subtraction isn't stored anywhere, and the 2 values stay the same as they were before the comparison. The only effect is on the 4 status bits N, Z, V, and C, and for now we'll focus on Z. When the 2 numbers being compared are equal, their difference is zero and Z is set. When the 2 numbers are not equal, Z is cleared.

We see on the sheet that the immediate addressing mode is available for CMP, so we can compare the contents of an accumulator with an immediate operand instead of with the contents of a memory location if that suits our purpose.

The CMP instruction can be used in the loop control section of a loop, to set up the condition that is to be tested (in this case, the Z status bit). Normally, the CMP is followed by a branch instruction (in this case, BNE or BEQ), which tests the condition of the bit that has been set up.

EXAMPLE 9.2.1

State whether or not the branch would be taken for these program segments:

```
(a)  CMP B   #$4F      ((ACCB)=$4F)
     BNE     NOPE
```

(b) CMP A   COMB   ((ACCA)=$46, (COMB)=$92)
     BEQ   BUMP

Solution

(a) The two values are the same, so $(Z)=1$. The branch would not be taken. (b) The two values are not the same, so $(Z)=0$. The branch would not be taken.

Answer: (a) No; (b) No

Related to the CMP instruction is CBA, which compares the contents of the two accumulators by subtracting (ACCB) from (ACCA). As in the CMP instruction, the result of the subtraction isn't stored anywhere, the two values stay the same, and the status bits are affected in the same way as they are with the CMP instruction.

EXAMPLE 9.2.2

For this program segment

```
LDA A   COMB
LDA B   #$3E
CBA
BNE     FORK
```

Would the branch be taken (a) if (COMB)=$3E; (b) if (COMB)=$80?

Solution

(a) The contents of the two accumulators are equal, and $(Z)=1$. The branch would not be taken. (b) The contents of the two accumulators are not equal, and $(Z)=0$. The branch would be taken.

Answer: (a) No; (b) Yes.

A Combination Lock

Figure 9.2.1 shows a general flowchart that will work as a combination lock. In the program the microprocessor keeps getting the 2 numbers and comparing them as long as they are different. If they are the same, the microprocessor opens the safe. The owner can change the combination at any time by storing a different value in the memory location assigned to the combination.

From now on, let's assume that we know how to configure the PIA for such applications. So that we can focus on current programming aspects, we'll just write "configure PIA" and understand that this statement will have to be expanded into its true series of instructions in the program. Figure 9.2.2 shows a detailed flowchart for our combination lock program.

FIGURE 9.2.1   General Flowchart for
                Combination Lock

FIGURE 9.2.2   Detailed Flowchart for
                Combination Lock

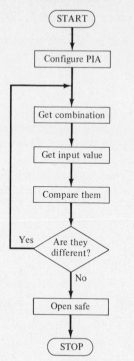

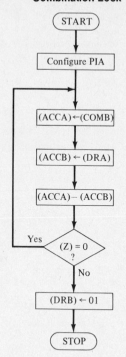

Figures 9.2.3 and 9.2.4 show the completed program as source code and listing. As with most programs, this isn't the only program that would work, but it is one possibility.

Some Shift Instructions

In the burglar alarm problem of Chapter 8 we were able to detect a single security switch attached to bit 7 by focusing on the N status bit. And if 8 switches are attached to DRA, we can tell if any of them are closed by using the Z status bit. But suppose we had a series of switches wired to DRA and each switch required a different action. For instance, one security switch might detect a door being opened, indicating a possible burglary. Then we'd want to sound an alarm and dial the police. Another switch might mean a fire; then we'd want to turn on the sprinkler and dial the fire department. Still another might indicate a power failure; then we'd want to activate the emergency power backup system and dial the building manager, and so on.

FIGURE 9.2.3   Combination Lock Program

```
100              NAM      COMBIN
110     ;THIS PROGRAM COMPARES A NUMBER INPUT ON A SET OF 8 SWITCHES
120     ;WIRED TO SIDE A OF THE PIA WITH A PREDETERMINED COMBINATION.
130     ;IF THE NUMBERS ARE THE SAME, A LOCK IS UNLOCKED BY STORING
140     ;01 IN DRB.
150     CRA      EQU      $8005
160     DRA      EQU      $8004
170     DDRA     EQU      DRA
180     CRB      EQU      $8007
190     DRB      EQU      $8006
200     DDRB     EQU      DRB
210     COMB     EQU      $B0
220     CONF     CLR      CRA      ADDRESS DDRA
230              CLR      DDRA     SET ALL SIDE A INPUTS
240              CLR      CRB      ADDRESS DDRB
250              LDA A    #$1      READY TO SET DB0 OUTPUT
260              STA A    DDRB     BIT 0 READY TO UNLOCK SAFE
270              LDA A    #$4      READY TO SET CR BIT 2
280              STA A    CRA      SIDE A READY TO RECEIVE INPUTS
290              STA A    CRB      SIDE B READY TO OUTPUT
300     START    LDA A    COMB     GET PREDETERMINED COMBINATION
310              LDA B    DRA      GET INPUT VALUE
320              CBA               COMPARE THEM
330              BNE      START    IF NOT EQUAL, KEEP LOOKING
340              LDA A    #$01     IF EQUAL, READY TO OPEN SAFE
250              STA A    DRB      OPEN IT
360              WAI               AND STOP.
370              END
```

We need a way of examining 1 bit at a time and identifying which switch might be closed. One such way is with shift instructions, which shift the data word to the right or to the left, one bit at a time.

There are several shift instructions, but right now we'll just look at two: ASL (Arithmetic Shift Left) and LSR (Logical Shift Right). Without worrying about the words *arithmetic* and *logical*, we can see what these instructions do.

Turning to the instruction information sheet for ASL, we see that it shifts all bits of the operand one place left. A 0 is shifted into bit 0 of the operand and the contents of bit 7 are shifted out of the operand and into the carry status bit. The previous contents of the carry bit are shifted out and lost.

Looking at LSR, we find an analogous situation for shifting to the right. The instruction shifts all bits of the operand one place right. A 0 is shifted into bit 7 of the operand and the contents of bit 0 are shifted out of the operand and into the carry status bit. As with ASL, the previous contents of the carry bit are shifted out and lost.

ASL and LSR are illustrated in Figure 9.2.5.

Both instructions give us the option of shifting in an accumulator (inherent mode) or in a memory location (extended mode).

FIGURE 9.2.4 Assembly Listing of Combination Lock Program

COMBIN
M6800 ASSEMBLER LISTING VERSION 1.6   14 OCT 80 23:14   PAGE   2
FIG923   DAT   14 OCT 80 22:34

```
                  3 ;THIS PROGRAM COMPARES A NUMBER INPUT ON A SET OF 8 SWITCHES
                  4 ;WIRED TO SIDE A OF THE PIA WITH A PREDETERMINED COMBINATION.
                  5 ;IF THE NUMBERS ARE THE SAME, A LOCK IS UNLOCKED BY STORING
                  6 ;01 IN DRB.
8005              7 CRA      EQU      $8005
8004              8 DRA      EQU      $8004
8004              9 DDRA     EQU      DRA
8007             10 CRB      EQU      $8007
8006             11 DRB      EQU      $8006
8006             12 DDRB     EQU      DRB
0000             13 COMB     EQU      $B0
0000 7F 80 05    14 CONF     CLR      CRA        ADDRESS DDRA
0003 7F 80 04    15          CLR      DDRA       SET ALL SIDE A INPUTS
0006 7F 80 07    16          CLR      CRB        ADDRESS DDRB
0009 86 01       17          LDA A    #$1        READY TO SET DB0 OUTPUT
000B B7 80 06    18          STA A    DDRB       BIT 0 READY TO UNLOCK SAFE
000E 86 04       19          LDA A    #$4        READY TO SET CR BIT 2
0010 B7 80 05    20          STA A    CRA        SIDE A READY TO RECEIVE INPUTS
0013 B7 80 07    21          STA A    CRB        SIDE B READY TO OUTPUT
0016 96 B0       22 START    LDA A    COMB       GET PREDETERMINED COMBINATION
0018 F6 80 04    23          LDA B    DRA        GET INPUT VALUE
001B 11          24          CBA                 COMPARE THEM
001C 26 F8       25          BNE      START      IF NOT EQUAL, KEEP LOOKING
001E 86 01       26          LDA A    #$01       IF EQUAL, READY TO OPEN SAFE
0020 B7 80 06    27          STA A    DRB        OPEN IT
0023 3E          28          WAI                 AND STOP.
0024             29          END
```

NO STATEMENTS FLAGGED

CROSS-REFERENCE TABLE

COMB	00B0	13	22	
CONF	0000	14		
CRA	8005	7	14	20
CRB	8007	10	16	21
DDRA	8004	9	15	
DDRB	8006	12	18	
DRA	8004	8	9	23
DRB	8006	11	12	27
START	0016	22	25	

EXAMPLE 9.2.3

For this program segment

```
ASL A
BCC    BACK
```

state whether or not the branch would be taken and what the new contents of ACCA would be if the initial contents of ACCA were (a) $72; (b) $8A.

FIGURE 9.2.5   Illustration of ASL and LSR

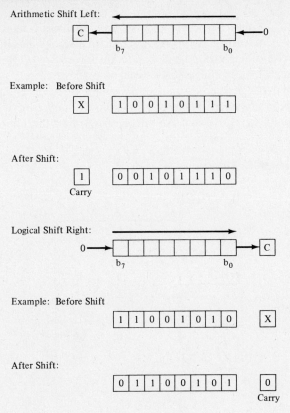

Arithmetic Shift Left:

Example: Before Shift

After Shift:

Logical Shift Right:

Example: Before Shift

After Shift:

Solution

(a) Write the number $72 in binary: 0111 0010. Next, shift it one place left, with bit 7 going into C:

```
0   1110 0100
C
```

Now the carry bit contains a 0, so the branch will be taken. The new contents of ACCA are $E4. (b) $8A in binary is 1000 1010. Shift one place left:

```
1   0001 0100
C
```

Now the carry bit contains a 1 so the branch will not be taken. The new contents of ACCA are $14.

Answer: (a) Yes, $E4; (b) No, $14

Surveillance Program

Now we can write a flowchart and program to handle multiple inputs. We assume that DA0 is wired to a door sensor; DA1, to a smoke alarm; and DA2, to a power monitor. The other lines on the A side are forced to 0. Lines DA0 through DA2 will be 0 unless one of the security switches is activated.

We assume that elsewhere in memory we have three programs stored, called "routines," which tell the microprocessor exactly how to take care of each emergency situation. Our problem is to direct the microprocessor to the appropriate routine,

FIGURE 9.2.6   Flowchart for Surveillance Program

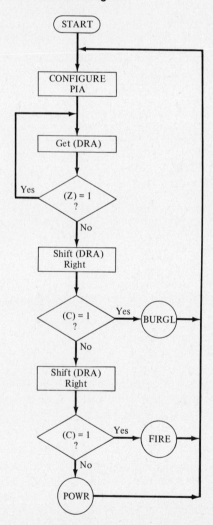

FIGURE 9.2.7 Surveillance Program

```
100              NAM    SRVLNC
110     ;THIS PROGRAM MONITORS THREE SECURITY SWITCHES AND BRANCHES
120     ;TO AN APPROPRIATE ROUTINE IF ONE IS FOUND CLOSED
130     CRA      EQU    $8005
140     DRA      EQU    $8004
150     DDRA     EQU    DRA
160     BURG     EQU    $E073
170     FIRE     EQU    $E09A
180     POWR     EQU    $E033
185              ORG    $E000
190     CONF     CLR    CRA       ADDRESS DDRA
200              CLR    DDRA      SET SIDE A ALL INPUTS
210              LDA A  #$4       READY TO STORE 1 IN BIT 2
220              STA A  CRA       READY TO RECEIVE INPUTS
230     CHECK    LDA A  DRA       GET INPUT FROM DRA
240              BEQ    CHECK     IF ZERO, KEEP CHECKING
250              LSR A            OTHERWISE SEE WHICH SWITCH IS ON
260              BCS    BURG      IF THIS ONE, BRANCH TO BURG
270              LSR A            OTHERWISE CHECK NEXT BIT
280              BCS    FIRE      IF THIS ONE, BRANCH TO FIRE
290              BRA    POWR      MUST BE A POWER FAILURE
300              END
```

depending on what the emergency is. The routine BURG starts at $E073; the routine FIRE starts at $E09A; and the routine POWR starts at $E033. We assume that the routines contain instructions for returning to the beginning of the surveillance program. The program is to start at location $E000.

Figure 9.2.6 is a flowchart for the surveillance program. The loop at the top repeatedly checks DRA for a nonzero value. As long as (DRA) stays zero, everything is fine and no switches have been activated. As soon as (DRA) becomes nonzero, the microprocessor checks to see which switch has been activated, by shifting each bit one at a time into the carry. Notice that we need to shift only twice, even though there are 3 bits to check. If there is a nonzero value in DRA, then one of the switches must be closed. If it isn't one of the first two, then it must be the third.

This flowchart is detailed enough so that we can write a program directly from it. The program and its listing is shown in Figures 9.2.7 and 9.2.8.

9.3 COUNTING LOOPS

In a **counting loop** we go through the loop a definite number of times. We define a **loop counter** as a device used to keep track of the number of times through a loop. The loop counter can be a register (such as ACCA or ACCB) or a memory location; the only requirement is that we must be able to load, increment, and decrement the loop counter.

FIGURE 9.2.8   Assembly Listing of Surveillance Program

```
SRVLNC
M6800 ASSEMBLER LISTING VERSION 1.6      14 OCT 80 23:05   PAGE    2
FIG926   DAT    14 OCT 80 23:03

                    3 ;THIS PROGRAM MONITORS THREE SECURITY SWITCHES AND BRANCHES
                    4 ;TO AN APPROPRIATE ROUTINE IF ONE IS FOUND CLOSED
8005                5 CRA      EQU     $8005
8004                6 DRA      EQU     $8004
8004                7 DDRA     EQU     DRA
E073                8 BURG     EQU     $E073
E09A                9 FIRE     EQU     $E09A
E033               10 POWR     EQU     $E033
0000               11          ORG     $E000
E000 7F 80 05      12 CONF     CLR     CRA       ADDRESS DDRA
E003 7F 80 04      13          CLR     DDRA      SET SIDE A ALL INPUTS
E006 86 04         14          LDA A   #$4       READY TO STORE 1 IN BIT 2
E008 B7 80 05      15          STA A   CRA       READY TO RECEIVE INPUTS
E00B B6 80 04      16 CHECK    LDA A   DRA       GET INPUT FROM DRA
E00E 27 FB         17          BEQ     CHECK     IF ZERO, KEEP CHECKING
E010 44            18          LSR A             OTHERWISE SEE WHICH SWITCH IS ON
E011 25 60         19          BCS     BURG      IF THIS ONE, BRANCH TO BURG
E013 44            20          LSR A             OTHERWISE CHECK NEXT BIT
E014 25 84         21          BCS     FIRE      IF THIS ONE, BRANCH TO FIRE
E016 20 1B         22          BRA     POWR      MUST BE A POWER FAILURE
E018               23          END

NO STATEMENTS FLAGGED

CROSS-REFERENCE TABLE

BURG          E073        8        19
CHECK         E00B       16        17
CONF          E000       12
CRA           8005        5        12        15
DDRA          8004        7        13
DRA           8004        6         7        16
FIRE          E09A        9        21
POWR          E033       10        22
```

Incrementing or Decrementing the Loop Counter

Say we want to go through a loop 6 times. We have our choice of counting up or down. If we start at 0 and count up, we want the microprocessor to execute the loop for counter values of 0 through 5 (0 through 5 is 6 iterations). The microprocessor should exit the loop *after* the loop counter hits the value 6, but *before* executing the loop for the seventh time.

If we start at 6 and count down, the microprocessor should execute the loop for counter values of 6 through 1 (6 iterations). The microprocessor should exit the loop *after* the loop counter hits 0, but *before* executing the loop for the seventh time.

In general, decrementing (counting down) is more efficient than incrementing (counting up), because the microprocessor has an automatic way of detecting 0 (the Z status bit). For the microprocessor to detect any nonzero number (in this case, 6), we must give it a Compare instruction. Figure 9.3.1 contrasts incrementing and

FIGURE 9.3.1 Flowcharts for Incrementing or Decrementing Loop Counter

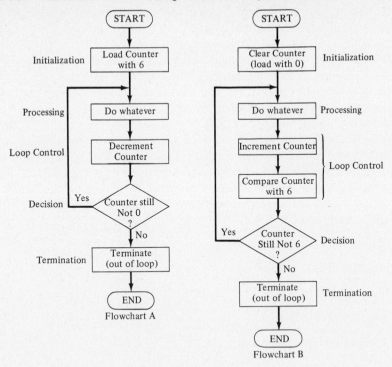

Flowchart A

Flowchart B

decrementing a loop counter. In flowchart A the loop control section has only one task: to decrement the loop counter. As soon as the loop counter contains 0, the Z status bit is set and the microprocessor exits the loop before performing the seventh iteration.

In flowchart B the loop control section has two tasks: to increment the loop counter and to compare it with its maximum value (6, in this case). When the loop counter contains 6, the microprocessor exits the loop before performing the seventh iteration. Because of the need to compare the loop counter contents with a maximum value, flowchart B has one more task box than flowchart A ("Compare Counter with 6"). This means that one more instruction (CMP) is needed in the program for flowchart B than in the program for flowchart A. In general, we try to decrement rather than increment a loop counter, because decrementing a loop counter usually results in a simpler program.

Timing Loops

Counting can be a way of "stalling for time." Recall that children playing hide-and-seek use this method. The person who is "it" counts to, say, 100, giving the others enough time to get well hidden. The amount of time that elapses depends on two factors: the speed at which "it" can count, and how far "it" counts.

Suppose we wanted a neon advertising sign to blink on and off at 1 sec intervals. We could do it this way: Turn the sign on, then stall for 1 sec. Turn the sign off, then stall for 1 sec. Keep doing this in a continuous loop. We could write a program segment for a loop that could count to 1 sec.

Stalling for time by going through a loop many times is very similar to the hide and seek "it" stalling for time by counting. The amount of time that elapses when we use a counting loop depends on: (1) how long it takes to go through the loop once and (2) how many times we go through the loop. A loop whose purpose is to provide a time delay is a **timing loop**.

We can calculate how long it takes to make a certain number of passes through a loop much more accurately than we can calculate how long it takes for a child to count to 100. In a given microcomputer each instruction in each addressing mode takes a *precise*, known amount of time to execute. By adding up the time for each instruction in a loop, we can calculate the elapsed time in a loop. Some of the time units we'll be using are:

Microsecond (μsec): 10^{-6} sec

Millisecond (msec): 10^{-3} sec

1 msec $= 1000\ (10^3)\ \mu$sec

1 sec $= 1000\ (10^3)$ msec

1 sec $= 1,000,000\ (10^6)\ \mu$sec

EXAMPLE 9.3.1

This timing loop is to be run on the Heathkit Microprocessor Trainer:

```
        LDA     #VAL
COUNT   DEC A
        BNE     COUNT
```

Each instruction takes this long to execute on the trainer:

LDA A: 4 μsec

DEC A: 4 μsec

BNE: 8 μsec

Calculate the time elapsed for: (a) one pass through the loop; (b) VAL $=$ \$50; (c) maximum possible number of passes.

Solution

(a) To get the time for 1 pass, we add the times for the instructions in the loop:

LDA A: 4 μsec

DEC A: 4 μsec

BNE: 8 μsec

Total: 16 μsec

(b) For VAL = $50, that's 80 (decimal) passes through the loop. However, only the instructions DEC A and BNE (the iterative part of the loop) will be executed 80 times. LDA #VAL (the initialization part of the loop) will be executed only once. So first, we calculate the time for the iterative part of the loop:

DEC A: 4 μsec

   BNE: 8 μsec

 Total: 12 μsec

Next, we calculate the time for 80 passes through the iterative part of the loop:

80 passes × 12 μsec/pass = 960 μsec

Finally, we add on the amount of time for one execution of the loop initialization (LDA A #VAL):

   960 μsec   (iterative part of loop)

+   4 μsec   (initialization part of loop)
——————————

   964 μsec   (0.964 msec)

(c) Accumulator A is a 1-byte register, so it can count from 0 to 255 (decimal), for a maximum of 256 passes through the iterative part of the loop:

Iteration: 256 passes × 12 μsec/pass =   3072 μsec

Initialization (LDA A):   +   4 μsec
                             ——————————

Total: 3076 μsec (3.076 msec)

Answer: (a) 16 μsec; (b) 0.964 msec; (c) 3.076 msec

_____

We notice two facts from Example 9.3.1. First, for the maximum number of passes we count from 0 to 0, and it doesn't matter whether we count up or down. Either direction gives us 256 passes through the iterative part of the loop, and sets the Z bit when 0 is reached. The instruction INC and DEC take the same amount of execution time, so in this case (maximum number of passes) incrementing or decrementing the loop counter is equally efficient.

Second, the execution time for the initialization part of the loop becomes less and less significant the more passes we make through the iterative part. For 1 pass, LDA A contributed about 25 percent of the total execution time; for 80 passes, 0.4 percent; and for 256 passes, only 0.1 percent. In applications that don't demand a high degree of accuracy (as in the blinking sign), the initialization can be neglected in calculating the total execution time.

In Example 9.3.1 the execution times were supplied, but we can find these values for ourselves. Looking at each instruction's information sheet, we find a heading: "Execution Time (No. of Cycles)." To translate the execution time from "cycles" to μsec, we need a conversion factor, called the **cycle time**, that gives microseconds per cycle. For the Heathkit Microprocessor Trainer the cycle time is

2.000 μsec/cycle. We multiply the number of cycles by 2.000 μsec/cycle to get an instruction's execution time in μsec on the Heathkit trainer.

EXAMPLE 9.3.2

Refer to appropriate instruction information sheets, and verify the execution times in microseconds for the instructions in the timing loop of Example 9.3.1. Assume that the instructions are to be executed on the Heathkit Microprocessor Trainer, whose cycle time is 2.000 μsec/cycle.

Solution

On the information sheet for each instruction, we select the appropriate addressing mode and read the number of cycles under the column Execution Time.

Looking at the information sheet for LDA, we find a variety of execution times, depending on the addressing mode used. The statement LDA A #VAL indicates the immediate addressing mode, so we locate LDA A (IMM) in the table and find that it takes 2 cycles. Multiplying 2 cycles by the Heathkit trainer's conversion factor (2.000 μsec/cycle) gives us the cycle time in μsec:

LDA   A (IMM):   2 cycles $\times$ 2.000 μsec/cycle = 4.000 μsec

(the same value as that given in Example 9.3.1.)

Next, we find the execution times for DEC A (2 cycles) and for BNE (4 cycles) on their information sheets. We multiply these values by the conversion factor:

DEC A: 2 cycles $\times$ 2.000 μsec/cycle = 4.000 μsec

BNE: 4 cycles $\times$ 2.000 μsec/cycle = 8.000 μsec

Answer: LDA A (IMM), 4.000 μsec; DEC A, 4.000 μsec; BNE, 8.000 μsec (These values are the same as those given in Example 9.3.1.)

We won't get a delay of 1 sec by using the loop of Example 9.3.1. That loop produces a delay of only about 3 msec. To increase the amount of delay time, we have several options: (1) to use more loops, one inside another, (2) to put more instructions within the loop to take up more time, or (3) to use a larger register for a loop counter so that the maximum number of iterations is greater. We'll choose the latter option for now and save the others for later.

The Index Register as Loop Counter

The index register (XR) is a very powerful register that we mentioned briefly in Chapter 4. In Chapter 10 we'll learn to use it for what it does best. Now we'll find it handy as a larger sized loop counter. We recall that the index register is 2 bytes long. Therefore it can count to decimal 65,535, much further than an accumulator's 255.

The index register has instructions similar to those for the accumulators: LDX, Load Index Register; INX, Increment Index Register; and DEX, Decrement Index Register. With these instructions, we can use the index register as a loop counter.

EXAMPLE 9.3.3

For this timing loop

```
        LDX     #VAL
COUNT   DEX
        BNE     COUNT
```

calculate the maximum delay time that can be produced on the Heathkit Microprocessor Trainer.

Solution

We find the total number of cycles and multiply it by the Heathkit's cycle time, 2.000 μsec/cycle.

First, find the number of cycles for the iterative part of the loop (DEX and BNE). Looking on the information sheets, we find these values:

DEX: 4 cycles

BNE: 4 cycles

Total: 8 cycles/pass

Next, multiply by 65,536 passes for the maximum delay:

8 cycles/pass $\times$ 65,536 passes $=$ 524,288 cycles

Next, look up the execution time for the initialization part of the loop (LDX), and add it onto the total for the iterative part:

Iterative portion of loop: 524,288 cycles

Initialization portion: $+$ 3 cycles (LDX (IMM))

Total: 524,291 cycles

Finally, multiply the number of cycles by 2.000 μsec/cycle:

524,291 cycles $\times$ 2.000 μsec/cycle $=$ 1,048,582 μsec (1.048582 sec)

Answer: 1.048582 sec (or about 1.05 sec)

Here, where we're making many more passes through the loop, we see that the initialization portion contributes even less to the total execution time (in this case, about 0.0006 percent).

Microcomputer Timing

Where does the Heathkit trainer's cycle time of 2.000 μsec/cycle come from? To find out, we'll briefly discuss the microcomputer's **clock**, a device that produces a series of regular pulses that synchronize the operations within the microcomputer. The pulses come about from changes in voltage. A change from a low to a high voltage is called a **positive transition**, and a change from a high to a low voltage is called a **negative transition**. These transitions are usually shown pictorially as a series of square waves, seen in Figure 9.3.2. When the clock goes from one positive transition to another or from one negative transition to another, it has completed 1 **clock cycle**. The time between positive (or negative) transitions is the cycle time. A microcomputer's cycle time depends on its **clock frequency**, which is the reciprocal of cycle time.

To do calculations involving frequencies, we'll need to use some of these units:

1 Hertz (Hz) $= 1 \text{ sec}^{-1} = 1$ cycle/sec

1 kiloHertz (kHz) $= 1 \times 10^3 \text{ sec}^{-1} = 1 \times 10^3$ cycles/sec

1 megaHertz (mHz) $= 1 \times 10^6 \text{ sec}^{-1} = 1 \times 10^6$ cycles/sec

---

EXAMPLE 9.3.4

Calculate the cycle time for (a) the Motorola D2 Evaluation Kit, whose clock frequency is 614.4 kHz; (b) the Heathkit Microprocessor Trainer, whose clock frequency is 500.0 kHz.

Solution

To calculate cycle times, we take reciprocals of the clock frequencies.

(a) 614.4 kHz $= 614.4 \times 10^3$ cycles/sec $= 6.144 \times 10^5$ cycles/sec

Cycle time $= 1 \text{ sec}/(6.144 \times 10^5 \text{ cycles})$

$= 0.1627 \times 10^{-5}$ sec/cycle, or 1.627 μsec/cycle

FIGURE 9.3.2   A Microcomputer's Clock Generates a Series of Regular Pulses

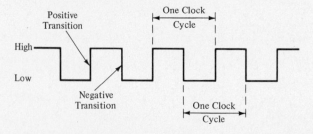

Time to complete one clock cycle = Cycle Time

Cycle Time $= \dfrac{1}{\text{Clock Frequency}}$

(b) 500.0 kHz $= 500.0 \times 10^3$ Hz $= 5.000 \times 10^5$ cycles/sec

Cycle time $= 1$ sec/$(5.000 \times 10^5$ cycles$)$

$\qquad = 0.2000 \times 10^{-5}$ sec/cycle $= 2.000$ μsec/cycle

(The same value that was given in Example 9.3.2.)

Answer: (a) 1.627 μsec/cycle; (b) 2.000 μsec/cycle

The cycle time depends on the clock used by a particular microcomputer. The clock produces the square wave clock signal to a high degree of accuracy (similar circuitry is used in digital watches). Some microprocessors have a clock right on the MPU chip itself, but the 6800 doesn't; it needs inputs from an external clock. On the board of the Evaluation Kit is a small rectangular component labeled MC6871B, which is the microcomputer's clock. The Heathkit Microprocessor Trainer has a MC6875 clock generator, not visible on the outside of the board.

EXAMPLE 9.3.5

Calculate the execution time for the loop of Example 9.3.3 if it is to be executed on the Motorola D2 Evaluation Kit.

Solution

We've already done most of the calculations. We know from Example 9.3.3 that the loop takes 524,291 cycles. We multiply this by the cycle time for the Evaluation Kit:

524,291 cycles $\times$ 1.627 μsec/cycle

$\qquad = 853,021$ μsec, or 0.853 sec

Answer: 0.853 sec (Less time than the Heathkit trainer, because the Heathkit's cycle time is longer.)

Next, we'll see how to write a program segment for a timing loop that produces nearly the exact time delay we want.

9.4 PROGRAMS THAT CONTAIN TIMING LOOPS

We've seen that a microcomputer instruction is executed in a matter of microseconds—a relatively short time compared with human reflex time. If we turned a light on and off by alternately storing a 1 and a 0 in a bit that controlled the light, we wouldn't even see it blinking because our eyes can't detect such a fast change. So to adjust microcomputer programs to allow for human response time, we often have to slow the processes down with timing loops.

A program segment that performs a specialized task and can be part of a larger program is called a **routine**. In this section we'll see how to use timing loops to construct **delay routines** that can be used in any program where we want a specific time delay.

Blinking Sign Program

Assume that we have wired a switch to DA0 that controls a soft drink advertising sign, "Drink Whoopee Cola." A 0 in DA0 turns the sign off, and a 1 turns it on. We want to leave the sign on for 1 sec and turn it off for 1 sec, over and over without stopping. Figure 9.4.1 is a general flowchart that describes a possible solution to this problem.

We should notice a few factors about this flowchart. First, it doesn't matter whether the sign is off or on initially, so we don't have to bother storing anything in DA0 initially. We will toggle the switch later anyway.

Next, we see that there is no end point to the program. We assume that the sign is just to blink on and off forever unless someone shuts off the power. Note that we must reinitialize the counter each time we begin a new counting loop.

FIGURE 9.4.1 General Flowchart for Blinking Sign Program

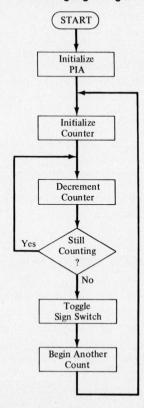

To write a detailed flowchart and finally a program, we need first to figure out our timing loop. The actual loop we use depends on the clock frequency of the microcomputer used to control the sign.

EXAMPLE 9.4.1

Write a detailed flowchart and program to blink a sign as previously described, using the Heathkit Microprocessor Trainer to control the sign. The sign should be on for 1 sec (plus or minus 0.10 sec) and off for the same amount of time.

Solution

In Example 9.3.3 this loop

```
        LDX   #VAL
COUNT   DEX
        BNE   COUNT
```

was found to take about 1.05 sec for the maximum count ($0000 to $0000 in the index register). Because 1.05 sec is well within the specifications (0.90 to 1.10 sec), we can use that loop.

Next, we look at the general flowchart (Figure 9.4.1). We know how to initialize the PIA by now. For "Initialize Counter," we load XR with $0000. The next two boxes are DEX and BNE. But how do we toggle the sign switch?

One way to toggle the sign switch would be just to increment or decrement DRA each time, which would alternately place a 1 and a 0 in bit 0.

An instruction that specifically reverses each bit value is the instruction Complement (COM), which we encountered briefly in Chapter 7. Looking at its information sheet, we find that either the inherent or the extended mode is available. We can use COM DRA to toggle the sign switch. Of course COM will toggle all 8 bits in the data word, and not just the one we want (bit DA0). This does no harm as long as the other bits aren't connected to anything.

Answer: Figure 9.4.2 shows a detailed flowchart, and Figures 9.4.3 and 9.4.4, a program.

Notice that after the first pass through the loop, the index register contents will always be $0000 at the start of each new pass, because $0000 will have triggered the microprocessor's exiting the loop. This means that we could save one program instruction by omitting the initialization entirely. Then, when the sign program is first turned on, the index register will contain some random value (probably not 0). The sign will be on or off (depending on the random contents of DA0) for less than 1 sec the first time, but who cares? After the first pass all times will be 1 sec. For such applications, where exact timing isn't critical, we can save programming time and space by making approximations.

Note, in Figure 9.4.3, that even though the program itself doesn't have an end, the source code does. We still have to tell the assembler where to stop assembling.

FIGURE 9.4.2 Detailed Flowchart for Blinking Sign Program Using Heathkit Microprocessor Trainer

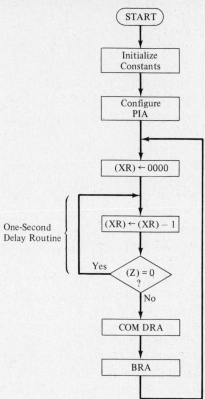

FIGURE 9.4.3 Blinking Sign Program for Execution on Heathkit Microprocessor Trainer

```
100                    NAM      BLINK
110       ;THIS PROGRAM CAUSES A NEON SIGN TO BLINK OFF AND ON AT
120       ;ONE-SECOND INTERVALS. THE SWITCH IS WIRED TO DA0.
130       CRA          EQU      $8005
140       DRA          EQU      $8004
150       DDRA         EQU      DRA
170       CONF         CLR      CRA      ADDRESS DDRA
180                    LDA A    #$1      READY TO CONFIGURE DA0 OUT
190                    STA A    DDRA     DA0 IS OUTPUT
200                    LDA A    #$4      READY TO ADDRESS DRA
210                    STA A    CRA      NOW DRA READY FOR OUTPUT
220       START        LDX      $0       INITIALIZE COUNTER IN XR
230       COUNT        DEX               DECREMENT COUNTER
250                    BNE      COUNT    STILL COUNTING?
260                    COM      DRA      NO, TOGGLE SIGN SWITCH
270                    BRA      START    AND START ANOTHER COUNT
280                    END
```

FIGURE 9.4.4 Assembly Listing for BLINK program

BLINK
M6800 ASSEMBLER LISTING VERSION 1.6   06 NOV 80 21:15 PAGE   2
FIG943   DAT   06 NOV 80 21:06

	3 ;THIS PROGRAM CAUSES A NEON SIGN TO BLINK OFF AND ON AT			
	4 ;ONE-SECOND INTERVALS. THE SWITCH IS WIRED TO DA0.			
8005	5 CRA	EQU	$8005	
8004	6 DRA	EQU	$8004	
8004	7 DDRA	EQU	DRA	
0000 7F 80 05	8 CONF	CLR	CRA	ADDRESS DDRA
0003 86 01	9	LDA A	#$1	READY TO CONFIGURE DA0 OUT
0005 B7 80 04	10	STA A	DDRA	DA0 IS OUTPUT
0008 86 04	11	LDA A	#$4	READY TO ADDRESS DRA
000A B7 80 05	12	STA A	CRA	NOW DRA READY FOR OUTPUT
000D CE 00 00	13 START	LDX	#0	INITIALIZE COUNTER IN XR
0010 09	14 COUNT	DEX		DECREMENT COUNTER
0011 26 FD	15	BNE	COUNT	STILL COUNTING?
0013 73 80 04	16	COM	DRA	NO, TOGGLE SIGN SWITCH
0016 20 F5	17	BRA	START	AND START ANOTHER COUNT
0018	18	END		

NO STATEMENTS FLAGGED

CROSS-REFERENCE TABLE

CONF	0000	8		
COUNT	0010	14	15	
CRA	8005	5	8	12
DDRA	8004	7	10	
DRA	8004	6	7	16
START	000D			

In arranging the 1-second delay , we assumed the delay caused by the routine would be the sole contribution to the delay time. For this application this assumption is close enough. But a look at Figure 9.4.2 shows that, for each toggling of the sign switch, the instructions COM DRA and BRA are each executed once. These instructions contribute a small amount to the total execution time.

EXAMPLE 9.4.2

Calculate the on or off time caused by the program of Figure 9.4.3.

Solution

We find the total cycles for one toggling of the sign switch. Then we multiply by 2.000 μsec/cycle for the Heathkit Microprocessor Trainer.

Iterative Portion: 65,536 passes $\times$ 8 cycles/pass = 524,288 cycles
Initialization (LDX):   3 cycles
COM (EXT.):   6 cycles
BRA: 4 cycles
Total: 524,301 cycles

$$524{,}301 \text{ cycles} \times 2.000 \ \mu\text{sec/cycle} = 1{,}048{,}602 \ \mu\text{sec}, \text{ or about } 1.049 \text{ sec}$$

Answer: 1.048602 sec (still about 1.05 sec)

We see that the extra 10 cycles makes a small difference, which is unimportant in our application but which might not be if the timing were more critical.

In Example 9.4.1 we were lucky in that our timing loop happened to take the right amount of time for our application. In other examples we probably won't be so fortunate.

To adjust a loop for a time less than its maximum value, we initialize the counter with a value we can calculate like this:

No. of passes = (desired delay time)/(cycle time)(cycles per pass)

Counter value = no. of passes (decimal) converted to hexadecimal

To adjust a loop for a time more than its maximum value, we can insert instructions in the loop to take up more time. Any instruction can be used, but we should be careful to choose one that won't do any harm. The instruction "No Operation" (NOP) is sometimes used in timing loops to provide more delay. NOP does just what its name says: It performs no operation (and therefore can do no harm). As with any instruction, however, the program counter contents are incremented.

To find out how many cycles/loop we need, we use this formula:

Cycles/loop = (desired delay time)/(cycle time)(max # of loops)

EXAMPLE 9.4.3

Design a flowchart and program for the same problem as Example 9.4.1, but using the Motorola D2 Evaluation Kit.

Solution

Looking at Example 9.3.5, we find that the timing loop we've been using takes only 0.853 sec on the D2: too short a time.

First, let's calculate the number of cycles per loop we need. The desired time is 1 sec ($10^6 \ \mu\text{sec}$), so

$$\text{Cycles/loop} = (10^6 \ \mu\text{sec})/(1.627 \ \mu\text{sec/cycle})(65{,}536 \text{ loops})$$

$$= 9.378 \text{ cycles/loop}$$

We can't have a fractional number of clock cycles, so we'll round 9.378 to 10. (Note that we should always round upward, because we can adjust the loop downward with the initial value.) The loop we now have is 8 clock cycles. If we add another 2 clock cycles we'll have our 10.

Looking at the instruction information sheet for NOP, we find, happily enough, that it takes 2 cycles. So we could write a loop like this:

```
          LDX    #VAL
   TICK   NOP
          DEX
          BNE    TICK
```

This loop would take (10 cycles)(1.627 μsec/cycle)$=16.27$ μsec to execute. Then, to get the number of passes through the loop for our 1-sec delay, we use this formula:

No. of passes $=$ Desired time (in μsec)$/(\mu$sec/pass)

No. of passes $=10^6$ μsec$/(16.27$ μsec/pass)$=61{,}462.8$ passes

which we round up to 61463.

FIGURE 9.4.5 Detailed Flowchart for Blinking Sign Program Using Motorola D2

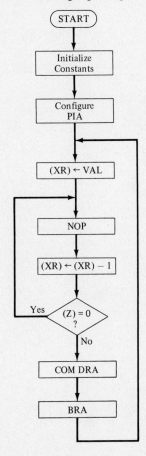

FIGURE 9.4.6   Blinking Sign Program for Execution on Motorola D2 Evaluation Kit

```
100                 NAM     BLINK
110     ;THIS PROGRAM CAUSES A NEON SIGN TO BLINK OFF AND ON AT
120     ;ONE-SECOND INTERVALS. THE SWITCH IS WIRED TO DA0.
130     CRA         EQU     $8005
140     DRA         EQU     $8004
150     DDRA        EQU     DRA
160     VAL         EQU     $F017
170     CONF        CLR     CRA       ADDRESS DDRA
180                 LDA A   #$1       READY TO CONFIGURE DA0 OUT
190                 STA A   DDRA      DA0 IS OUTPUT
200                 LDA A   #$4       READY TO ADDRESS DRA
210                 STA A   CRA       NOW DRA READY FOR OUTPUT
220     START       LDX     #VAL      INITIALIZE COUNTER IN XR
230     COUNT       NOP               STALL FOR TIME
240                 DEX               DECREMENT COUNTER
250                 BNE     COUNT     STILL COUNTING?
260                 COM     DRA       NO, TOGGLE SIGN SWITCH
270                 BRA     START     AND START ANOTHER COUNT
280                 END
```

FIGURE 9.4.7   Assembly Listing of BLINK Program for Motorola D2

```
BLINK
M6800 ASSEMBLER LISTING VERSION 1.6      10 NOV 80 21:06   PAGE      2
FIG945    DAT   10 NOV 80 21:03

                   4 ;THIS PROGRAM CAUSES A NEON SIGN TO BLINK OFF AND ON AT
                   5 ;ONE-SECOND INTERVALS. THE SWITCH IS WIRED TO DA0.
                   6 ;EXECUTION IS ON MOTOROLA D2
8005               7 CRA       EQU     $8005
8004               8 DRA       EQU     $8004
8004               9 DDRA      EQU     DRA
F017              10 VAL       EQU     $F017
0000 7F 80 05     11 CONF      CLR     CRA       ADDRESS DDRA
0003 86 01        12           LDA A   #$1       READY TO CONFIGURE DA0 OUT
0005 B7 80 04     13           STA A   DDRA      DA0 IS OUTPUT
0008 86 04        14           LDA A   #$4       READY TO ADDRESS DRA
000A B7 80 05     15           STA A   CRA       NOW DRA READY FOR OUTPUT
000D CE F0 17     16 START     LDX     #VAL      INITIALIZE COUNTER IN XR
0010 02           17 COUNT     NOP               STALL FOR TIME
0011 09           18           DEX               DECREMENT COUNTER
0012 26 FC        19           BNE     COUNT     STILL COUNTING?
0014 73 80 04     20           COM     DRA       NO, TOGGLE SIGN SWITCH
0017 20 F4        21           BRA     START     AND START ANOTHER COUNT
0019              22           END
```

NO STATEMENTS FLAGGED

CROSS-REFERENCE TABLE

CONF	0000	11		
COUNT	0010	17	19	
CRA	8005	7	11	15
DDRA	8004	9	13	
DRA	8004	8	9	20
START	000D	16	21	
VAL	F017	10	16	

Next, convert to hexadecimal:

61,463 (decimal) = $F017 (hexadecimal).

Finally, calculate the delay time for this loop:

Iterative portion: 61,463 passes × 10 cycles/pass = 614,630 cycles

Initialization portion (LDX):	3 cycles
COM(EXT.):	6 cycles
BRA:	4 cycles
Total:	614,643 cycles

Execution time = 614,643 cycles × 1.627 μsec/cycle

= 1.000024 sec (close enough!!)

Answer: Figure 9.4.5 shows the detailed flowchart, and Figures 9.4.6 and 9.4.7 the finished assembly language program.

Notice that LDX, COM, and BRA accounted for a tiny 0.0021 percent of the delay time. We could have neglected them in our calculations for this application.

In Figure 9.4.5 we put in the box "Initialize Constants" to remind us that we must establish values for our labels. In Figure 9.4.6 note that establishing the value of VAL at the beginning gives the owner of the sign the option of changing the off and on time without having to disrupt the program itself.

We've learned some new instructions in this chapter, which are summarized in Table 9.4.1.

TABLE 9.4.1   Summary of New Instructions in Chapter 9

Mnemonic	Name	Function
CMP	COMPARE	Compares the contents of ACCX with the contents of M, and sets or clears status bits depending on results. Both operands remain unchanged.
CBA	COMPARE ACCUMULATORS	Compares contents of ACCA and ACCB, and sets or clears status bits depending on results. Both operands remain unchanged.
ASL	ARITHMETIC SHIFT LEFT	Shifts operand left one bit. (Bit 7) goes into C, 0 goes into Bit 0.
LSR	LOGICAL SHIFT RIGHT	Shifts operand right one bit. (Bit 0) goes into C, 0 goes into Bit 7.
LDX	LOAD INDEX REGISTER	Loads XR with a value.
DEX	DECREMENT INDEX REGISTER	Decrements the contents of XR.
INX	INCREMENT INDEX REGISTER	Increments the contents of XR.
NOP	NO OPERATION	Does nothing but increment PC.

Nested Timing Loops

We've seen how to use a timing loop to create a 1-sec delay routine. To produce delays longer than 1 sec, we just execute the 1-sec delay routine more than once. For example, to delay for 15 sec, we execute the 1-sec delay routine 15 times; to delay for 1 min, 60 times; for a half-hour, 1800 times; and so on.

We can control the number of times we go through the 1-sec delay by using another counting loop outside the delay routine. Thus we create a system of **nested loops**, which means loops within loops. We can nest one loop inside another for a nest two levels deep. For a nest that's three levels deep, we'd place a loop within a loop within a loop, and so on.

Figure 9.4.8 shows a general flowchart for a two-level system of nested loops. The outer loop counter controls the number of times the inner delay routine is executed. Each pass through the outer loop reinitializes the inner loop counter. If we

FIGURE 9.4.8   Two-Level System of Nested Loops

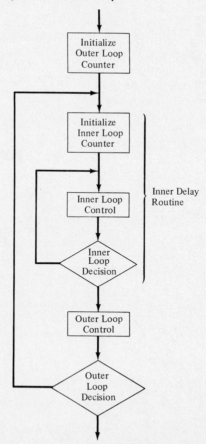

were counting from 0 to 0 on the inner loop counter, this reinitialization would be done automatically. But for any other number, we need to reinitialize the inner loop counter each time.

Figure 9.4.9 shows a two-level system of nested loops to be executed on the Heathkit Microprocessor Trainer. In it we used the 1-sec delay routine (from Figure 9.4.3) for the inner loop. The outer loop now controls how many times we execute the 1-sec delay routine. That is, loading the outer loop counter (accumulator A, in this case) with $09 would cause a delay of about 9 sec. We say *about* 9 sec because (1) the delay routine produces a delay of 1.05, and not 1.00, sec. This discrepancy of 0.05 sec will accumulate each time the routine is executed (9 times through the routine causes a discrepancy of 0.45 sec) and (2) as we saw earlier, some extra time has been added to the delay routine because of the additional instructions (in this case, DEC A and BNE) needed for the outer loop. For each pass through the outer loop, DEC A is executed once (2 cycles), and BNE once (4 cycles). This extra 6 cycles contributes a small amount to the total execution time.

FIGURE 9.4.9   Outer Loop Instructions Contribute to Total Time in a Nested Loop System

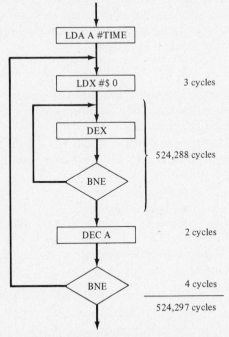

1 pass × 524,297 cycles/pass × 2.000 μsec/cycle = 1.048594 sec (1.05 sec)

9 passes × 524,297 cycles/pass × 2.000 μsec/cycle = 9.437346 sec (9.44 sec)

256 passes × 524,297 cycles/pass × 2.000 μsec/cycle = 268.44 sec (268.4 sec)

(HEATHKIT MICROPROCESSOR TRAINER)

The calculations on Figure 9.4.9 show the accumulation of these discrepancies. For one pass through the loop we still get a delay of about 1.05 sec (the 6 additional cycles is small compared with the 524,291 cycles we already have for the inner routine). For 9 passes through the loop we get an extra 0.44 sec. And with the maximum number of times through the loop—256—we get an extra 14 sec beyond the 256 we wanted. In our blinking sign application we probably wouldn't notice even an extra 14 sec. But in high-precision timing—as in the programming of a digital clock, for instance—this could be a problem. Most of the discrepancy came from the fact that our 1-sec delay routine was really 1.05 sec. For some applications we'd need to time 1 sec more accurately.

EXAMPLE 9.4.4

Refer to Figure 9.4.9. Calculate the contents of the inner and outer loop counters needed for a delay routine of 1.0000 ± 0.0001 min when executed on the Heathkit trainer.

Solution

We adjust the inner loop to 1 sec as accurately as possible, taking into account the two extra instructions DEC A and BNE. Then we load the outer loop counter with $3C (decimal 60) for 60 sec. To adjust the inner loop, first, we calculate the total number of cycles needed for a 1-sec delay:

$$10^6 \ \mu\text{sec}/(2 \ \mu\text{sec}/\text{cycle}) = 500,000 \text{ cycles}$$

This 500,000 cycles is the total needed to go through the outer loop once. In it, we execute LDX once; the inner loop, some number of times we've yet to determine; and DEC A and BNE, once apiece.

Second, calculate the number of cycles left for the inner loop after we have allowed for the instructions that are executed only once (LDX, DEC A, and BNE):

500,000	cycles	
−3	cycles	(LDX IMM.)
−2	cycles	(DEC A)
−4	cycles	(BNE)

499,991 cycles left for inner loop

Third, calculate the number of passes through the inner loop:

No. passes $= (499,991 \text{ cycles})/(8 \text{ cycles}/\text{pass}) = 62,498.9$ passes

which we round to 62,499.

Fourth, calculate the hexadecimal value to be loaded into the inner loop counter:

62,499 (decimal) equals $F423

Fifth, calculate the hexadecimal value to be loaded into the outer loop counter:

60 (decimal) equals $3C

Finally, calculate the elapsed time to make sure that it is within the allowed tolerance:

Inner routine:

62,499 passes $\times$ 8 cycles/pass = 499,992 cycles

LDX (IMM):	3 cycles
DEC A:	2 cycles
BNE:	4 cycles
Total:	500,001 cycles

Elapsed time = 500,001 cycles/pass $\times$ 2 μsec/cycle $\times$ 60 passes

= 60,000,120 μsec = 60.000120 sec

Time in minutes = 60.000120 sec/(60 sec/min) = 1.000002 min.

(well within the accuracy specified)

Answer: Inner loop counter, $F423; inner loop counter, $3C

FIGURE 9.4.10   Timing Routine for Example 9.4.4 (Heathkit Microprocessor Trainer)

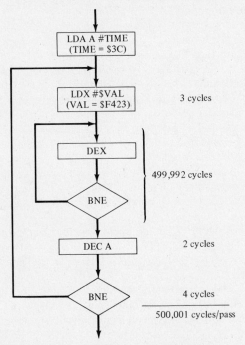

1 pass $\times$ 500,001 cycles/pass $\times$ 2.000 μsec/cycle = 1.000002 sec

60 passes $\times$ 500,001 cycles/pass $\times$ 2.000 μsec/cycle = 60.000120 sec

(1.000002 min.)

Figure 9.4.10 repeats the flowchart of Figure 9.4.7, with new values.

We can notice a few facts about this example. First, the value 1.000002 min, accurate as it seems, still would not make an absolutely perfect digital clock. Such a clock would gain a minute in about 33 days—an annoyance, however, with which many of us could live. Second, the maximum delay we can get with the two-level nested loop system of Figure 9.4.10 is 256 sec, or 4 min and 16 sec. If we wanted an hour's delay time, we could construct a third level loop to go through the 1-min delay routine 60 times.

We've had an introduction to loops with an emphasis on timing. In the next chapter we'll see how to use loops to process lists and tables of data.

REVIEW QUESTIONS

1. Sketch a flowchart showing the five basic loop elements. Name and describe each element.
2. What do we mean by a **sensing loop**? Give an example.
3. How does CMP differ from SUB? How is it similar? What is the function of CMP in a loop?
4. Explain the ASL and LSR instructions. How does each affect the carry status bit?
5. Explain how LSR is used in the surveillance program.
6. What is a **counting loop**? A **loop counter**?
7. Describe the loop control sections of a loop for incrementing and decrementing the loop counter. Which method is generally preferable?
8. What is a **timing loop**? Why might we want one?
9. Explain how to calculate the elapsed time in a loop if we know the time for each individual instruction.
10. If we count from 0 to 0 in a register, does it matter whether we increment or decrement? Explain.
11. How can we increase the elapsed time in a timing loop?
12. How high can the index register count? Name and describe three instructions connected with the index register.
13. Explain how to use the Execution Time found on the instruction information sheets to calculate the elapsed time in a timing loop.
14. What is a microcomputer's **clock**? What do we mean by **positive** and **negative** transition?
15. What is a **clock cycle**? What are **cycle time** and **clock frequency**, and how are they related?
16. What is the cycle time for the Heathkit trainer? Is this time the same for all microcomputers? Explain.
17. Explain how COM is used in the blinking sign program. Could COM be used if other bits of DRA were being used for output?
18. Explain how we can adjust a timing loop so that it is as long or as short as we want it to be.
19. What do we mean by **nested loops**? How can we use these to make longer time delays? Sketch a flowchart for a two-level system of nested loops.

20. Explain how to calculate the amount of time elapsed in a two-level system of nested loops.
21. Explain how to create a delay routine that is very close to the desired time delay.

EXERCISES

Set A (answers at back of book)

1. State whether or not the branch would be taken for these program segments:

   (a) CMP A LUMP   (ACCA)=$0A, (LUMP)=$09
       BNE   LOC
   (b) CMP B #$10   (ACCB)=$10
       BEQ   FUZZ
   (c) LDA A #$7
       INC A
       CBA
       BNE   GNAW   (ACCB)=$8

2. Modify the combination lock program to use CMP instead of CBA. Give only that program segment that would be different.
3. For each of these program segments, state whether or not the branch would be taken, and state the new contents of the appropriate register or memory location:

   (a) LDA A #$A3
       ASL A
       BCS   LOOK   (ACCA)=?
   (b) LDA A #$40
       STA A NUM1
       LSR   NUM1
       BCC   HERE   (ACCA)=? (NUM1)=?
   (c) LDA B #$40
       ASL B
       ASL B
       BCS   GONE   (ACCB)=?

4. Modify the surveillance program to use ASL instead of LSR. Give only that program segment that is different.
5. Modify the surveillance program for the case that DA0 through DA2 are cleared for "switch closed" and the rest of the lines are forced to 1. (For all switches open DRA will contain FF.) Give only that program segment that is different.
6. Refer to Example 9.3.1. What is the elapsed time if:
   (a) (VAL)=$80   (b) (VAL)=0
7. Refer to the appropriate instruction information sheets, and calculate the execution times, in μsec, for these instructions: (a) LDA A (ext.); (b) DEC (EXT.); (c) LSR A. Assume the instructions are to be executed on the Heathkit Microprocessor Trainer.
8. Refer to Example 9.3.3. What is the elapsed time if VAL=$0A00 and we are running the loop on a microcomputer that has a conversion factor of 1.627 μsec/cycle?
9. Calculate the cycle time for a clock frequency of 1 MHz.
10. Modify the blinking sign program (Figure 9.4.3) so that the elapsed time is 0.5 sec. Give only the program segment that is different.

11. Calculate the elapsed time in this loop, to be executed on the Heathkit Microprocessor Trainer:

```
        CLR   CNTR
STALL   INC   CNTR
        BNE   STALL
```

12. Refer to Example 9.4.3. Calculate the value of VAL for a delay of 0.800 ± 0.001 sec.
13. Refer to Figure 9.4.9, and calculate the elapsed time if TIME=$7F and XR is loaded with $A3D7.
14. Refer to Figure 9.4.9. Using the loop of Example 9.4.3 for an inner loop, calculate the contents of the inner and outer loop counters needed to produce a delay of 4.0000 ± 0.0001 min when executed on the Motorola D2 Evaluation Kit.
15. Incorporate the 4-min delay routine of Exercise 14 into a three-level nested loop system that produces a delay of 1 hr. Use ACCB for the third-level loop counter and write the program segment for this. You may neglect execution times of instructions added as part of the third-level loop.

EXERCISES

Set B (answers not given)

1. State whether or not the branch would be taken for these program segments:

    (a)
    ```
    LDA B   #$FE
    CMP B   MOSS    (MOSS)=$FE
    BNE     WHIZ
    ```
    (b)
    ```
    LDA A   #$05
    DEC A
    CMP A   #$03
    BNE     WOOP
    ```
    (c)
    ```
    LDA A   HASH
    DEC A           (HASH)=$0A
    LDA B   #$0B
    CBA
    BEQ     JADE
    ```

2. Modify the combination lock program so that CMP A (immediate) is used instead of CBA. Give only that program segment that is different.
3. For each of these program segments, state whether or not the branch would be taken, and state the new contents of the appropriate register or memory location:

    (a)
    ```
    LDA A   #$FF
    LSR A
    LSR A
    BCC     GOON    (ACCA)=?
    ```
    (b)
    ```
    LDA B   #$36
    DEC B
    ASL B
    BCS     REAP    (ACCB)=?
    ```
    (c)
    ```
    LDA A   #$1B
    TAB
    ASL B
    STA B   KEEN
    BCS     GOGO
    ASL     KEEN    (ACCB)=? (KEEN)=?
    ```

4. Modify the surveillance program so that CMP, instead of LSR, is used to test each switch.
5. Modify the surveillance program for the case where the burglar sensor is wired to DA7, the smoke alarm to DA6, and the power sensor to DA5.
6. Refer to Example 9.3.1, and calculate the elapsed time of this loop (assume execution on the Heathkit Microprocessor Trainer, where CLR (EXT) and INC (EXT) each take 12 μsec and BNE takes 8 μsec):

```
        CLR   BILL
COUNT   INC   BILL
        BNE   COUNT   (INC A TAKES THE SAME TIME AS DEC A)
```

7. Refer to the appropriate instruction information sheets, and calculate the execution times, in μsec, for these instructions: (a) ADD (dir.); (b) NEG (EXT); (c) STA A (DIR). Assume execution on the Motorola D2.
8. Refer to Example 9.3.3. What is the elapsed time if VAL = $0500 and we replace DEX with INX for a microcomputer having a cycle time of 1.50 μsec?
9. Calculate the clock frequency for a cycle time of 12.5 μsec/cycle.
10. Modify the blinking sign program (Figure 9.4.6) so that the elapsed time is 0.80 sec. Give only the program segment that is different.
11. Calculate the elapsed time in this loop, to be executed on the Motorola D2 Evaluation Kit:

```
        LDA A   #$64
        STA A   CTR   (EXTENDED ADDRESSING MODE)
WAIT    NOP
        DEC     CTR
        BNE     WAIT
```

12. Refer to Example 9.4.1. Calculate the value of VAL for a delay of 0.500 ± .001 sec.
13. Refer to Figure 9.4.7, and calculate the elapsed time if TIME = $3C and XR is loaded with $1234.
14. Refer to Figure 9.4.9. Using the loop of Example 9.4.2 for an inner loop, calculate the contents of the inner and outer loop counters needed to produce a delay of 4.0000 ± 0.0001 min on the Heathkit Microprocessor Trainer.
15. Incorporate the 4-min delay routine of Exercise 14 into a three-level nested loop system that produces a delay of 20 min. Use ACCB for the third-level loop counter and write the program segment. You may neglect execution times for instructions added for the third-level loop.

PROGRAMMING IDEAS

1. We wish to make a more sophisticated combination lock program, so that 3 consecutive different correct numbers must be input in order for the safe to be opened. The program should search for the first correct number in a continuous loop. When the first correct number is input, the microprocessor should wait for 2 sec, then look for the second number. If this number is correct, it should wait for 2 more seconds, then look for the third number. If this is correct, the safe should be opened. If any number is incorrect, the program should ring a bell (wired to DB7) and branch to the beginning of the program.
2. Write a program to square a number (e.g., N^2) by adding N to itself N times.

3. A traffic light has the red light wired to DB0; the yellow, wired to DB1; and the green, wired to DB2. Write a program that turns the red light on for 2 min, the yellow on for 10 sec, and the green light on for 4 min. The program should run continuously.

4. Modify program (4) so that after midnight (as indicated by a 1 input on DA7) the green light is on continuously unless a car approaches the cross street (indicated by a 1 input on DA6). In that event the red-yellow-green cycle of Exercise 4 should run once and then revert to continuous green.

5. Write a railroad crossing monitor program. If a train is coming from either direction (indicated by sensors wired to DA0 and DA1), flash the light (DB1) and sound the bell (DB2). Next, check to see whether any pedestrians or cars are in the crossing (DA2). If there are, wait until they are out, then lower the gate. When the train is gone (sensor off) inactivate the gate.

10 Tables and Lists

LEARNING OBJECTIVES

After completing this chapter, you should be able to:

1. Supply a definition, explanation, or example for each of these: *indexed addressing mode, offset, index register, table, look-up table.*
2. Explain and use in programs the five instructions listed in Table 10.1.1 and the branching instructions of Table 10.4.1.
3. Load the index register using the immediate, direct, or extended addressing modes.
4. Write, use, and interpret programs involving look-up tables.
5. Write, use, and interpret programs with indexed addressing.
6. Explain and use in programs the assembler directives RMB and FCB.
7. Write, use, and interpret programs that step through lists.
8. Modify programs to accommodate varying offsets or direction of stepping through a list.
9. Explain and use three ways of detecting the end of a list.
10. Use the index register for a counter and for indexed addressing in the same program without causing an error.
11. Write, use, and interpret searching and sorting programs of the type explained in this chapter.

Tables and lists are two important ways to organize data. Microprocessors are especially well suited to keep track of and access tables and lists. For example, lighting a seven-segment display can be conveniently done by first storing the seven-segment codes in a table. Then the microprocessor can access each code when it's needed.

We can think of a list as a one-dimensional table. There are many ways to manipulate a list: We can sort it, move it to another location, search it for specific items, rearrange it, perform an operation on each member of it. In text-editing, for example, we might want to locate a word or group of letters (a list of ASCII characters) to delete it, replace it, or change it in some way. We might want to move a paragraph (a block of ASCII characters) from one location to another. In this chapter we'll discuss problems involving some list manipulations.

First, let's take a simple example. Suppose we want to create a list containing all zeros starting with location $00A0 and ending with location $00FF. We could do this by clearing all the locations between and including these addresses.

EXAMPLE 10.1.1

Write a program to clear locations $00A0 through $00FF.

Solution

Here's one way to do it:

```
100   NAM   CLEAR
110    ;THIS PROGRAM CLEARS LOCATIONS $00A0 THROUGH $00FF
120   CLR   $00A0   CLEAR THE FIRST LOCATION
130   CLR   $00A1   CLEAR THE NEXT ONE
140   CLR   $00A2   CLEAR THE NEXT
150   CLR   $00A3   AND THE NEXT
160   CLR   $00A4   AND THE NEXT
170   CLR   $00A5   NEXT
180   CLR   $00A6   GOOD THING COMPUTERS DON'T GET BORED
190   CLR   $00A7   STILL, IT DOES SEEM WASTEFUL OF MEMORY
200   CLR   $00A8   TO CLEAR THESE ONE AT A TIME LIKE THIS
210   CLR   $00A9   HELP! HOW MANY MORE TO GO?
---   CLR   " " "

---
1060  CLR   $00FF   DONE! AND IT ONLY TOOK 95 COMMANDS…
```

Answer: See preceding program.

Obviously, this isn't what computing is all about. What we'd like to do is to make a loop with just one CLR instruction and have it step through the list clearing each location sequentially. To do this efficiently, we need to know of another useful tool that's standard with the 6800 and available on other microprocessors.

10.1 INDEXED ADDRESSING

The Indexed Addressing Mode

In the 6800's **indexed addressing mode** the address of the operand is computed by adding an 8-bit unsigned number, called an **offset**, to the contents of the index register. In Chapter 9 we used the index register as a 16-bit loop counter. Now we'll use the index register to do what it was designed for: to step through tables and lists.

The 6800's **Index Register (XR)** is a 2-byte register whose contents are used to compute an indexed address.

The indexed addressing mode is best illustrated by example. Figure 10.1.1 shows an assembly language instruction using indexed addressing. In the instruction, LDA A $10,X, the X part tells the assembler that this is the indexed addressing mode. To execute the instruction, the microprocessor adds the offset ($10, in this case) to the contents of the index register ($01AC, in this case) and the sum ($01BC) is the address of the data ($A3), which is loaded into accumulator A.

Indexed addressing works almost like relative addressing, but not quite. Like relative addressing, indexed addressing computes an address by adding a 16-bit number to an 8-bit number. In relative addressing the 8-bit number is signed. A sign extension must be performed on the relative address before adding it, and the displacement can be either backward (toward lower memory) or forward (toward higher memory). However, indexed addressing uses an 8-bit *unsigned* offset. With an unsigned offset, no sign extension is performed before adding, so the displacement is only forward (toward higher memory). A 1-byte displacement therefore gives us a range of 255 bytes beyond the address given by the contents of the index register.

Other examples of the indexed addressing mode are (assume (XR)=$01AC):

```
STA A   $10,X   STORE (ACCA) IN LOCATION $01BC
CMP A   $10,X   COMPARE (ACCA) WITH ($01BC)
ADD A   $10,X   ADD (ACCA) TO ($01BC), RESULT IN (ACCA)
```

In these examples we were stuck with whatever the index register contained ($01AC). But we can affect those contents by using appropriate instructions.

FIGURE 10.1.1   In Indexed Addressing, the Address of the Operand is Computed by Adding the Contents of the Index Register to an Offset

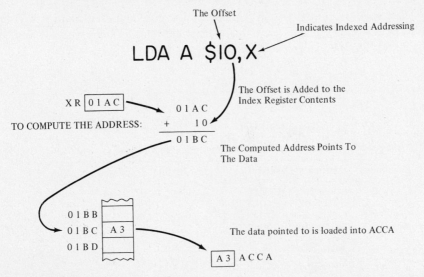

Instructions That Affect the Index Register

Table 10.1.1 lists some instructions that deal with the index register. In Chapter 9 we used three of them: LDX, INX, and DEX. The instruction STX is similar to STA; the contents of the index register is stored in two consecutive memory locations (remember that the index register is 2 bytes wide). The instruction CPX compares the contents of the index register with a 2-byte value and sets or clears the N, Z, and V status bits according to the result. Of the 3 status bits, only Z is meaningful at this point. If (XR) is equal to the compared value, Z is set; otherwise Z is cleared.

EXAMPLE 10.1.2

State (a) into what location the contents of accumulator A would be stored and (b) whether or not the branch would be taken, for this program segment:

```
       LDX    #$10
KNOT   STA A  $A0,X
       DEX
       CPX    #$5
       BNE    KNOT
```

Solution

The first statement loads the index register with $0010. The second statement we recognize as the indexed addressing mode because of the 'X' part. So to find the address of the operand, we add the offset ($A0) to the contents of the index register ($0010) and get $00B0, the address into which the contents of accumulator A will be stored.

The next statement, DEX, decrements the contents of the index register to $000F. Next, CPX compares the index register contents ($000F) with the immediate value $0005. The two values aren't equal, so the branch will be taken.

Answer: (a) $00B0; (b) Yes

TABLE 10.1.1   Instructions That Affect the Index Register

Mnemonic	Instruction definition	Addressing modes available				
LDX	LOAD INDEX REGISTER	IMM,	DIR,	EXT,	IND	
STX	STORE INDEX REGISTER	—	DIR,	EXT,	IND	
CPX	COMPARE INDEX REGISTER	IMM,	DIR,	EXT,	IND	
DEX	DECREMENT INDEX REGISTER	—	—	—	—	INH
INX	INCREMENT INDEX REGISTER	—	—	—	—	INH

Using Indexed Addressing

To see whether a given instruction has indexed addressing available, we look at the individual instruction information sheet. Usually, any instruction that has the extended mode also has the indexed mode.

EXAMPLE 10.1.3

Write a program segment that loads the index register with $0010 and then adds the contents of location $00B2 to accumulator A, using indexed addressing.

Solution

The first statement is easy: LDX #$10. Next, we look at the instruction information sheet for ADD to make sure that the indexed addressing mode is available: It is. Our next statement will then have this form:

ADD A —— ,X

where the blank is some offset that we have to determine. We get the offset this way:

$$\text{offset} = [\text{desired address} - (XR)], \text{ truncated to 2 LSDs}$$

$$= \$00B2 - \$0010 = \$00A2, \text{ which we truncate to } \$A2.$$

Answer

```
LDX    #$10
ADD A  $A2,X
```

We may use the CMP instruction in the indexed addressing mode. The instruction CMP A,X is easily confused with CPX because both are compare instructions and have to do with the index register. CMP A,X compares an indexed memory value with the contents of accumulator A, whereas CPX compares the contents of the index register with a 2-byte value. The next example illustrates the difference between CMP (indexed), and CPX.

EXAMPLE 10.1.4

For each of these program segments, state what values are being compared and whether or not the branch will be taken.

```
(a) LDX    #$1234   (b) LDX   #$1234
    LDA A  #$FF         INX
    STA A  $1235        CPX   #$1235
    LDA B  #$FF         BNE   MOON
    CMP B  $1,X
    BEQ    STAR
```

Solution

(a) First, we look at the CMP B instruction. The contents of ACCB ($FF, in this case) are being compared with the contents of an indexed memory location. We get the location by adding the offset, $0001, to the contents of the index register, $1234: location $1235. The contents of $1235 are $FF. We compare (ACCB)=$FF to ($1235)=$FF and find that they're the same. So the branch will be taken. (b) This one is easier. We compare the contents of the index register ($1235, after the INX) with the immediate value $1235, and find that they're the same. So the branch won't be taken.

Answer: (a) (ACCB)=$FF is being compared with ($1235)=$FF. Because the two values are equal, the BEQ (Branch on Equal) branch will be taken. (b) (XR)=$1235 is being compared with $1235. Again, the two values are equal, but because the instruction BNE (Branch if Not Equal) is used here, the branch will not be taken.

FIGURE 10.1.2 Example 10.1.4(a) Illustrated

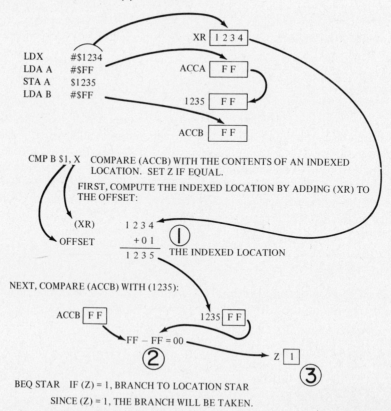

FIGURE 10.1.3   Example 10.1.4(b) Illustrated

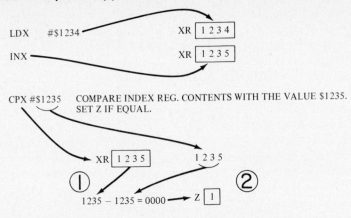

CPX #$1235   COMPARE INDEX REG. CONTENTS WITH THE VALUE $1235.
                SET Z IF EQUAL.

BNE   MOON   BRANCH TO LOCATION MOON IF (Z) = 0.

SINCE (Z) ≠ 0, BRANCH WILL NOT BE TAKEN.

Figure 10.1.2 illustrates (a) of Example 10.1.4. The first four instructions load XR, ACCA, location 1235, and ACCB with contents, as shown on the right. The CMP B instruction causes this sequence of events: at (1), the indexed address is computed by adding the XR contents ($1234) to the offset ($01), getting $1235. At (2) the contents of $1235 ($FF) are compared with the contents of ACCB ($FF). The two values are equal; that is, subtracting one from the other results in zero. At (3) the Z status bit is set as a result of the comparison.

The condition has been set up for the next instruction, BEQ STAR. The condition is true: The two compared values are equal ((Z) = 1). So the branch will be taken.

Figure 10.1.3 illustrates (b) of Example 10.1.4. The first two instructions give the index register the contents $1235. The CPX instruction causes this sequence of events: At (1) the contents of XR ($1235) are compared with the immediate value $1235. At (2) the Z status bit is set because the two values are equal.

For the BNE MOON instruction the condition is false: That is, the compared values are *not* unequal. So the branch will not be taken.

10.2   TABLES

A **table** is a systematic arrangement of data in rows and columns for ready reference. In a **look-up table** two equivalent sets of values are stored side by side so that any one of them can be retrieved at will. An ASCII chart is a familiar example of a look-up table. To look up the ASCII for a character on the chart, we locate the character itself, then retrieve its hexadecimal equivalent from its row and column. To look up the character for an ASCII, we do the reverse.

There are many uses of tables in computing. For example, when an assembler creates a symbol table, it stores the ASCII values of the characters contained in each symbol opposite the numerical value equated with that symbol. Then the next time the assembler encounters the symbol, it retrieves the symbol's numerical value.

A computer can do multiplication in a variety of ways. One is to calculate mathematically the answer directly from the data. Another way is to store a table of all the possible values of multiplying numbers together and look up the answer for a given set. A look-up table is often an alternative to the computer doing a mathematical operation each time. Sometimes it's better to do the computation; sometimes a look-up table is better, depending on factors such as the length of the calculation, the size of the table, the relative frequency of accessing the table, and the like. The programmer should choose the method that is best for a particular situation.

Table of Squares

Table 10.2.1 is a table of squares of decimal numbers 0 through 15. The squares, in hexadecimal, are stored in locations $0096 through $00A5.

We cause the microprocessor to retrieve a value in a look-up table by using indexed addressing. The sum of the offset and the contents of the index register form a "pointer." The address that is pointed to contains the value to be retrieved.

TABLE 10.2.1   Partial Look-up Table of Squares

Address	No. Being Squared (DEC.)	Square (HEX.)	
0096	0	00	(Zero)
0097	1	01	(Decimal 1)
0098	2	04	(Decimal 4)
0099	3	09	(Decimal 9)
009A	4	10	(Decimal 16)
009B	5	19	(Decimal 25)
009C	6	24	(Decimal 36)
009D	7	31	(Decimal 49)
009E	8	40	(Decimal 64)
009F	9	51	(Decimal 81)
00A0	10	64	(Decimal 100)
00A1	11	79	(Decimal 121)
00A2	12	90	(Decimal 144)
00A3	13	A9	(Decimal 169)
00A4	14	C4	(Decimal 196)
00A5	15	E1	(Decimal 225)

XR 0096   LDA A $5, X

+ 05

009B   "Pointer"

1 9   ACCA

EXAMPLE 10.2.1

For this program segment, refer to Table 10.2.1.

```
LDX    #$96
LDA A  $5,X
STA A  SQUR
```

(a) What value is stored in SQUR? (b) What number has been squared? (c) Modify the program segment so that the number to be squared is contained in XR.

Solution

(a) To find the address being pointed to, we add the offset ($5) to the contents of the index register ($0096) and get $009B. The contents of $009B are $19, so this value is stored in SQUR. (b) $19 (decimal 25) is the square of decimal 5. (c) If XR contains $0005, then we must have an offset of $0096 if we are to point to location $009B.

Answer: (a) $19 (decimal 25); (b) decimal 5; (c)
```
LDX    #$5
LDA A  $96,X
STA A  SQUR
```

An illustration at the bottom of Table 10.2.1 shows the computing of the address. The resulting pointer points to $009B, and its contents, $19, are retrieved and loaded into accumulator A.

Digit Table

In Chapter 5 we derived a table of seven-segment code for displaying the 16 hexadecimal digits (Figure 5.4.2). A microprocessor system could have this information permanently stored as a table in ROM so that it could display the correct digit as needed. Before we can consider this problem, we should look more closely at the LDX instruction.

Up to now, we've found it convenient to load the index register using the immediate addressing mode. But sometimes we'll have to use the extended mode. Because the index register is 2 bytes long and memory locations are only 1 byte long, we must load the index register with the contents of two memory locations.

EXAMPLE 10.2.2

For this program segment:

```
XRH  EQU    $B0
XRL  EQU    $B1
     LDA A  #$D0
     STA A  XRH
     LDA A  #$06
     STA A  XRL
     LDX    XRH
```

What is the contents of the index register after executing this program segment?

Solution

Looking at the instruction information sheet for LDX, we see that the high-order byte of the index register is loaded from the memory location specified in the program. The low-order byte is loaded from the next memory location (M + 1).

The statement LDX XRH means to load the high-order byte of XR with the contents of the address XRH (equated with $00B0) and the low-order byte of XR with the contents $00B0 + 1 (in this case, XRL). From the rest of the program these contents are:

XRH = $00B0 CONTENTS: $D0
XRL = $00B1 CONTENTS: $06

Answer: (XR) = $D006

Figure 10.2.1 compares the immediate, direct, and extended addressing modes of the LDX instruction. The immediate mode is so easy to use with an assembly language statement that we haven't had to consider that it, too, must load XR with

FIGURE 10.2.1 Loading the Index Register Using Three Addressing Modes

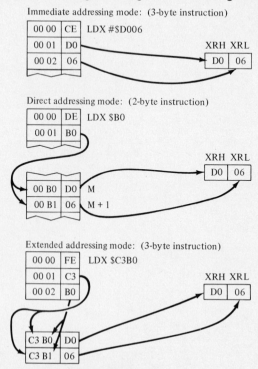

the contents of two memory locations. As usual, the assembler chooses between the direct and extended modes.

EXAMPLE 10.2.3

A digit table of seven-segment codes is stored in ROM starting at location $E097, shown in Table 10.2.2. Assume side A of the PIA is wired to a set of 8 switches (0 = off, 1 = on) and side B is wired to a seven-segment display. A 0 means "segment on" and a 1 means "segment off." Bit 7 of side B is permanently forced to 0.

Write a program that takes a 4-bit binary number input on the switches, converts it to a seven-segment code for the corresponding hex digit, and displays the digit on the seven-segment display. For example, if we input the binary number 1101 (hexadecimal D) on the switches, the corresponding code, $21, should be retrieved from the table and stored in DRB. Storing $21 in DRB causes a "d" to appear on the display.

Solution

In this problem we have to take a different approach because the table is stored at high memory. The high-order byte of the address is $E0. We can't put the input number into XR and use the rest of the address as an offset, because only a 1-byte offset is allowed. One way to get around this is to store $E0 permanently in the high-order byte of XR, to let the input value be placed into the low-order byte of XR each time, and to make up the difference with the offset ($97).

We'll use an arrangement similiar to that in Example 10.2.3. The flowchart is shown in Figure 10.2.2.

Answer: The program is shown in Figure 10.2.3.

TABLE 10.2.2   Table of Seven-Segment Code

Hex digit	Address	Code
0	E097	40
1	E098	79
2	E099	24
3	E09A	30
4	E09B	19
5	E09C	12
6	E09D	02
7	E09E	78
8	E09F	00
9	E0A0	18
A	E0A1	08
B	E0A2	03
C	E0A3	46
D	E0A4	21
E	E0A5	06
F	E0A6	0E

FIGURE 10.2.2 Flowchart for Digit Display Program

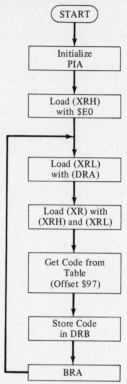

In this program we loaded XR using the extended mode. The assembler directive RMB, Reserve Memory Byte, used in lines 195 and 196, is new to us. RMB directs the assembler to save some number of bytes (in this case, 1) for each label. We don't care what the actual addresses of XRH and XRL are because the assembler will keep track of them.

In lines 290 and 300 we place the value $E0 into XRH; this is a fixed value. In lines 310 and 320 we place the variable value input into DRA into XRL. Line 330 points to the corresponding value and puts the appropriate seven-segment code into accumulator A.

Displaying a Square

Now that we've explored the loading of the index register, we can look at another example of loading the low-order byte of the index register with a variable.

FIGURE 10.2.3 HEXDIG: Displaying a Hexadecimal Digit

```
100              NAM      HEXDIG
110    ;THIS PROGRAM CONVERTS A 4-BIT NUMBER INPUT ON A SET OF
120    ;SWITCHES TO ITS HEX DIGIT CODE VIA A LOOK-UP TABLE AND DISPLAYS
130    ;THE DIGIT ON A 7-SEGMENT DISPLAY
140    CRA       EQU      $8005
150    DRA       EQU      $8004
160    DDRA      EQU      DRA
170    CRB       EQU      $8007
180    DRB       EQU      $8006
190    DDRB      EQU      DRB
195    XRH       RMB      1          SAVE 1 LOCATION FOR XRH
196    XRL       RMB      1          SAVE 1 LOCATION FOR XRL
200    INIT      CLR      CRA        ADDRESS DDRA
210              CLR      DDRA       SET ALL SIDE A INPUTS
220              LDA B    #$04       READY TO ADDRESS DRA
230              STA B    CRA        READY TO RECEIVE INPUTS
240              CLR      CRB        ADDRESS DDRB
250              LDA A    #$FF       READY TO SET SIDE B ALL OUTPUTS
260              STA A    DDRB       SIDE B ALL OUT
270              STA B    CRB        READY TO OUTPUT
290              LDA A    #$E0       READY TO LOAD XRH WITH E0
300              STA A    XRH        XRH IS PERMANENTLY E0
310    GETDIG    LDA A    DRA        GET HEX VALUE INPUT ON SWITCHES
320              STA A    XRL        PUT IT INTO XL
325              LDX      XRH        POINT TO SWITCH VALUE ON TABLE
330              LDA A    $97,X      CONVERT TO 7-SEG CODE VIA TABLE
340              STA A    DRB        DISPLAY THE DIGIT
340              BRA      GETDIG     GET ANOTHER INPUT
360              END
```

EXAMPLE 10.2.4

We have wired lines DA0 through DA3 to a set of 4 switches (1=on) and DA4 through DA7, permanently to 0. DRB is wired to a set of 8 LEDs. Write a program that takes a binary bit pattern input on the 4 switches (1 hex digit), squares its decimal equivalent, and displays the result in binary on the 8 LEDs.

Solution

Here, the number that we want to square is variable. The 6800's indexed addressing mode doesn't allow a variable offset. However, the index register contents can be variable. Recall, though, that the index register contents are 2 bytes long. Our high-order byte (XRH) will always be 00, so we store 00 in a temporary location XRH. Our variable (the number we want to square) can be put into the next consecutive address, XRL, which we'll reserve. Then we'll retrieve the square using an offset of $96 (the beginning of the table of squares, minus one).

Answer: Figure 10.2.4 shows a flowchart, and Figure 10.2.5, the program.

FIGURE 10.2.4 Retrieving and Displaying a Square from a Look-up Table

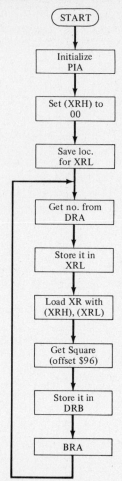

In this program we've proceeded slightly differently from what was done in the digit display program. First, in line 195 we used another assembler directive: FCB, Form Constant Byte. The FCB directive tells the assembler that the 1-byte number that follows (in this case, $00) is to be stored in an address corresponding to the label (in this case, XRH). RMB and FCB are similar. RMB reserves a byte or bytes for variable data. FCB reserves a byte or bytes for constant data.

Second, in the HEXDIG program we made use of a table that was already stored in ROM. In the square program, however, we need to set up the table ourselves. Lines 340 and 350 set up the table, called SQTBL, at origin $0096 as specified by ORG $96. Again, we find the FCB directive useful, this time to store a table of constants instead of a single value. Notice that there is a comma, but no

FIGURE 10.2.5   Program SQUARE

```
100           NAM    SQUARE
110     ;THIS PROGRAM CONVERTS A 4-BIT NUMBER INPUT ON A SET OF
120     ;SWITCHES TO ITS SQUARE VIA A LOOK UP TABLE AND DISPLAYS
130     ;THE SQUARE ON A SET OF 8 LED'S
140     CRA   EQU    $8005
150     DRA   EQU    $8004
160     DDRA  EQU    DRA
170     CRB   EQU    $8007
180     DRB   EQU    $8006
190     DDRB  EQU    DRB
195     XRH   FCB    $00       SET XRH AT $00
197     XRL   RMB    1         AND SAVE A BYTE FOR XRL
200     INIT  CLR    CRA       ADDRESS DDRA
210           CLR    DDRA      SET ALL SIDE A INPUTS
220           LDA B  #$04      READY TO ADDRESS DRA
230           STA B  CRA       READY TO RECEIVE INPUTS
240           CLR    CRB       ADDRESS DDRB
250           LDA A  #$FF      READY TO SET SIDE B ALL OUTPUTS
260           STA A  DDRB      SIDE B ALL OUT
270           STA B  CRB       READY TO OUTPUT
280     START LDA A  DRA       GET NO. TO BE SQUARED
282           STA A  XRL       PUT IT IN XRL FOR POINTER
285           LDX    XRH       LOAD XR WITH 2-BYTE VALUE TO SQUARE
290           LDA A  $96,X     GET SQUARE, PUT IN ACCA
300           STA A  DRB       OUTPUT IT TO LED'S
310           BRA    START     DO IT AGAIN
320           ORG    $96       START SQUARE TABLE AT $0096
330     SQTBL FCB    $00,$01,$04,$09,$10,$19,$24,$31
340           FCB    $40,$51,$64,$79,$90,$A9,$C4,$E1
350           END
```

space, after each constant. When we have more constant values than will fit on a line, we use another line, without repeating the label. The FCB directive handles a series of data words by placing each value in a consecutive location after the origin (in this case, $0096.)

In this section we've seen how to use the index register to retrieve a single value from a table. In the next, we'll see how to step through a list of values so that we address each value one after another.

10.3   STEPPING THROUGH A LIST

In computing, we'd like to be able to step through a list and do something to each member of the list. In text processing we might want to step through a string (list) of ASCII characters and compare each character with one we wanted to locate, or check the parity of each one. Or add a constant value to each member of a list. The way we approach any of these problems is the same regardless of the actual process carried out on the members of the list.

FIGURE 10.3.1   General Flowchart for Program to Step Through and Process a List

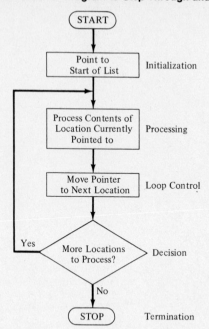

Figure 10.3.1 is a general flowchart for simple list processing. We'll refer to this flowchart as we look at a few specific examples.

Clearing a Set of Locations

Let's go back to the problem of Example 10.1.1 and solve it using the plan of Figure 10.3.1. We want to clear locations $00A0 through $00FF, inclusive. Figure 10.3.2 shows a flowchart that will do this using indexed addressing.

In Figure 10.3.2 we point to the start of the list by loading the index register with $00A0, the first address listed. The next process we want is to clear the location. In this loop control section we move the pointer by incrementing the index register. Then we set up the condition for the decision by comparing the index register contents with an address that's one *higher* than the last address on the list (in this case, $0100). Note that if we compared the index register contents with the last address on the list, the microprocessor would exit the loop before clearing the last location.

Figure 10.3.3 illustrates how the "pointer" moves through the list for the first 2 passes. First, the pointer is initialized by the LDX instruction. The instruction CLR $0,X then points to location $00A0 and clears it. Incrementing the index register moves the pointer down one location so that during the next pass $00A1 is the location pointed to and cleared, and so on.

FIGURE 10.3.2 Flowchart to Clear a Set of Locations

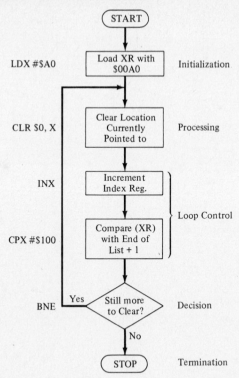

In Figure 10.3.2 we set it up so that the "start" of the list was the lowest address and moved the pointer down the list by using INX. To know when to stop, we compared the index register contents with the highest address plus one.

Another way is to start the list at the highest address ($00FF, in this case) and to move the pointer down the list by using DEX. To know when to stop, we'd compare the index register contents with the lowest address minus one. Figure 10.3.4 compares the two ways of stepping through a list, and Figure 10.3.5 shows programs for both.

When using indexed addressing, we always have an option as to what specific values to use for the offset and the index register contents. In order to point to address $00A0, we loaded the index register with $00A0 and used an offset of $00. But we could just as well load the index register with $0000 and use an offset of $A0. Or we could load the index register with $0010 and use an offset of $90—any 2 numbers that add up to $00A0 will work. Often one set is preferable to another.

EXAMPLE 10.3.1

Modify program A of Figure 10.3.5 so that XR is loaded with $0000 initially.

FIGURE 10.3.3 Incrementing the Index Register Moves the Pointer Down the List

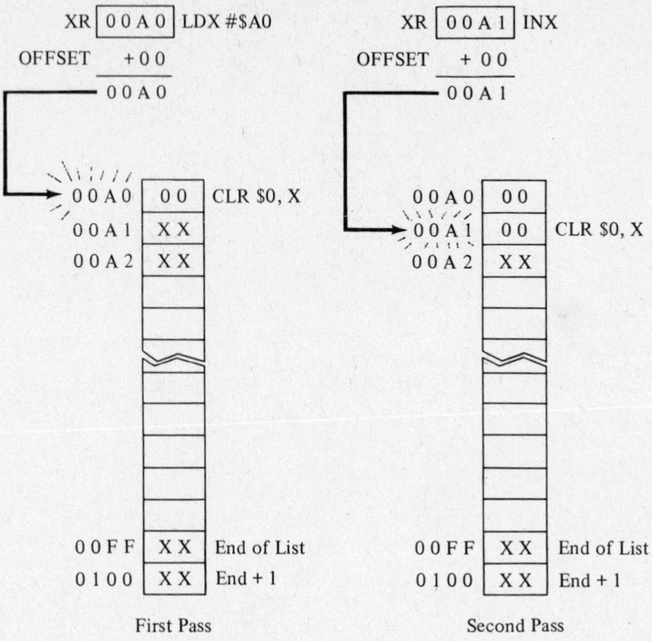

XR 00A0 LDX #$A0
OFFSET +00
00A0
00A0 00 CLR $0, X
00A1 XX
00A2 XX
00FF XX End of List
0100 XX End + 1
First Pass
XR 00A1 INX
OFFSET +00
00A1
00A0 00
00A1 00 CLR $0, X
00A2 XX
00FF XX End of List
0100 XX End + 1
Second Pass

FIGURE 10.3.4 A List May Be Stepped Through in Either Direction

START
009F XX
00A0 00
00A1 00
00A2 00
00FE 00
00FF 00
0100 XX
STOP
STOP
009F XX
00A0 00
00A1 00
00A2 00
00 FE 00
00FF 00
START
0100 XX

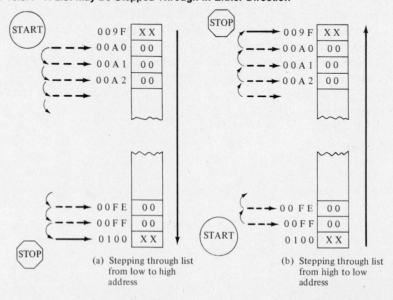

(a) Stepping through list from low to high address

(b) Stepping through list from high to low address

FIGURE 10.3.5   Program to Clear a Set of Locations

```
PROGRAM A
100                 NAM    CLRUP
110     ;THIS PROGRAM CLEARS LOCATIONS $00A0 THROUGH $00FF
115     ;FROM LOWER TO HIGHER MEMORY
120     START    LDX    #$A0      LOAD XR W/START OF LIST
130     ZAP      CLR    $0,X      CLEAR CURRENT LOC OF POINTER
140              INX              MOVE POINTER TO NEXT (HIGHER) LOCATION
150              CPX    #$100     MORE LOCATIONS TO CLEAR?
160              BNE    ZAP       YES, KEEP ZAPPING
170              WAI              NO, STOP
180              END

PROGRAM B
100                 NAM    CLRDN
110     ;THIS PROGRAM CLEARS LOCATIONS $00A0 THROUGH $00FF
115     ;FROM HIGHER TO LOWER MEMORY
120     START    LDX    #$FF      LOAD XR W/START OF LIST
130     ZAP      CLR    $0,X      CLEAR CURRENT LOC OF POINTER
140              DEX              MOVE POINTER TO NEXT (LOWER) LOCATION
150              CPX    #$9F      MORE LOCATIONS TO CLEAR?
160              BNE    ZAP       YES, KEEP ZAPPING
170              WAI              NO, STOP
180              END
```

Solution

If XR is loaded with $0000 initially, we need an offset of $A0. So Lines 120 and 130 would be replaced by:

```
120   START  LDX   #$0    POINT TO $0000
130   ZAP    CLR   $A0,X  CLEAR CURRENT LOCATION OF POINTER
```

Next, in line 150 we need to compare (XR) with a different value. When we're finished with the list, the address pointed to will be $0100. With an offset of $A0, this means that XR will contain $0060 ($0100 minus $A0 is $0060).

```
150   CPX   #$60   MORE LOCATIONS TO CLEAR?
```

Answer: Shown in Figure 10.3.6, Program A.

We see from the previous example that the number of locations to be cleared is $60. Sometimes we can gain program efficiency by loading the index register with the number of locations to be processed. Then we use the index register as a loop counter as well as a pointer.

EXAMPLE 10.3.2

Modify program B (Figure 10.3.5) by loading the index register with $0060.

FIGURE 10.3.6 Programs for Examples 10.3.1 and 10.3.2

```
PROGRAM A
100                NAM   CLERA
110    ;THIS PROGRAM CLEARS LOCATIONS 00A0 THROUGH 00FF
115    ;FROM LOWER TO HIGHER ADDRESS
120    START       LDX   #$0      POINT TO 0000
130    ZAP         CLR   $A0,X    CLEAR CURRENT LOCATION
140                INX            MOVE POINTER TO HIGHER ADDRESS
150                CPX   #$60     MORE LOCATIONS TO CLEAR?
160                BNE   ZAP      YES, KEEP ZAPPING
170                WAI            NO, STOP
180                END

PROGRAM B
100                NAM   CLERB
110    ;THIS PROGRAM CLEARS LOCATIONS 00A0 THROUGH 00FF
115    ;FROM HIGHER TO LOWER ADDRESS
120    START       LDX   #$60     LOAD XR WITH LENGTH
130    ZAP         CLR   $9F,X    CLEAR CURRENT LOCATION
140                DEX            MOVE POINTER TO LOWER ADDRESS
150                BNE   ZAP      MORE TO CLEAR? KEEP ZAPPING
160                WAI            NO, STOP
170                END
```

Solution

To step through the list from high to low address, we want to start with address $00FF. This means an offset of $00FF − $0060 = $9F.

```
120  START  LDX  #$60  LOAD INDEX REG WITH LENGTH
130  ZAP    CLR  $9F,X  CLEAR CURRENT LOCATION
```

When we are through with the list, we'll be pointing at location $009F, meaning that the index register will have been decremented to zero. Looking at the instruction information sheet for DEX, we see that the Z status bit is set when XR is decremented to zero. So our condition will be set without having to use CPX. For this program we don't need line 150 at all.

Answer: Shown in Figure 10.3.6, Program B.

Moving a List

There are many reasons for wanting to move a list from one portion of memory to another. One common reason is in text editing, when we want to switch paragraphs—lists of ASCII characters—around. This job is easily done by using indexed addressing.

Moving a list is similar to clearing one. However, the processing part of the flowchart to move a list now contains two operations: (1) getting a number from the old list and (2) storing it in the new list location. As with clearing a list, we have the same options of stepping up or down, and the values for the offset and the index register contents are flexible as before. Now we can look at another option: how to signal the microprocessor that it has reached the end of the list. In the previous section our example was for a list of definite length and definite starting and ending address. In this case we detected our end condition by comparing the value of the index register to the end address plus one or by counting down.

Many computer applications require moving blocks of data of indefinite length. Word processors constantly move blocks of text of indefinite length, and files that get moved from one storage medium to another almost never have constant length. To signal the end of such a list, we can use a predetermined end marker. We'll write a program that moves a block of ASCII characters starting at location

FIGURE 10.3.7 List Terminated with a Marker

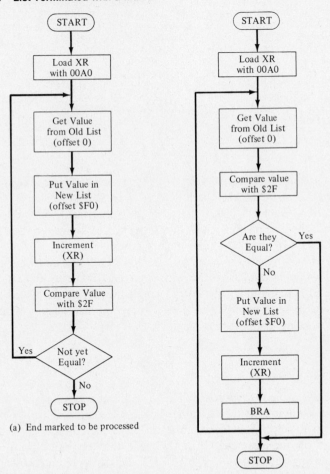

(a) End marked to be processed

(b) End marker not to be processed

FIGURE 10.3.8 **Programs for Figure 10.3.7**

```
PROGRAM A
100              NAM      MOVEA
110    ;THIS PROGRAM MOVES A LIST OF NUMBERS OF INDEFINITE LENGTH FROM
120    ;A BLOCK STARTING WITH 0A00 TO A BLOCK STARTING WITH 0AF0. THE
130    ;LIST IS TERMINATED BY AN ASCII SLASH, WHICH IS MOVED TOO.
140    START     LDX      $A00          XR GETS START OF LIST
150    MOVIT     LDA A    0,X           GET A VALUE
160              STA A    $F0,X         STORE IT IN NEW LOCATION
170              INX                    ADVANCE POINTER TO NEXT ADDRESS
180              CMP A    #$2F          COMPARE VALUE WITH ASCII SLASH
190              BNE      MOVIT         NOT EQUAL? MOVE ANOTHER VALUE
200              WAI                    EQUAL? STOP.
210              END

PROGRAM B
100              NAM      MOVEB
110    ;THIS PROGRAM MOVES A LIST OF NUMBERS OF INDEFINITE LENGTH FROM
120    ;A BLOCK STARTING WITH 0A00 TO A BLOCK STARTING WITH 0AF0. THE
130    ;LIST IS TERMINATED BY AN ASCII SLASH, WHICH IS NOT TO BE MOVED.
140    START     LDX      #$A00         XR GETS START OF LIST
150    MOVIT     LDA A    0,X           GET A VALUE
160              CMP A    #$2F          IS IT A SLASH?
170              BEQ      OUT           YES, DONE
180              STA A    $F0,X         NO, STORE IT IN NEW LIST
190              INX                    ADVANCE POINTER TO NEXT VALUE
200              BRA      MOVIT         BRANCH TO TOP OF LOOP
210    OUT       WAI                    STOP.
220              END
```

$0A00 to a location starting at $0AF0. An ASCII slash (/), whose equivalent is $2F, will mark the end of the block. The list is less than $F0 words long.

Figure 10.3.7 shows two flowcharts for this program. The problem didn't say whether or not the end marker itself (the slash) was to be moved. The figure shows both possibilities. Figure 10.3.8 shows the programs.

Note that moving a list starting with the lowest address and working upward in memory only works in this case if the list is less than $F0 items long. If, for example, the list were $FF items long, the last 15 entries would be destroyed as they were replaced by the first 15. In that case we'd move the list starting with the highest address and working toward lower memory.

One-Digit Message

We'll use the Motorola D2 Evaluation Kit to spell out a message on a seven-segment display. First, we'll store a table of digit codes in memory. Then we'll instruct the microprocessor to step through the table and place each digit code one at a time in DRB. To spell out the message "HELLO," we'll store the digit code for the message in a table, starting with location $00C0. Each digit is to be on for 0.5 sec, and the display is to be blank for 0.5 sec between each letter. The message should be

TABLE 10.3.1   Seven-Segment Code Table for Message

Letter	Address	Seven-segment code
H	00C0	09
BLANK	00C1	7F
E	00C2	06
BLANK	00C3	7F
L	00C4	47
BLANK	00C5	7F
L	00C6	47
BLANK	00C7	7F
0	00C8	40
BLANK	00C9	7F

repeated continuously. We assume the same PIA configuration as in Example 10.2.3. The program should start at location $0000.

In Chapter 6 we learned how to make a seven-segment code for some letters. Table 10.3.1 shows our seven-segment code table for the message HELLO. Because we want each letter to have a blank after it, we put the code for a blank—7F—in every other location. From Chapter 9 we know how to make time delays. In this chapter we learned to step through a list and process each member one by one. Figure 10.3.9 shows a general flowchart. Because we want the message to be displayed continuously, the program won't have any end. When we have finished the message, we reset the pointer to the start of the table and step through it again.

Before we can write a detailed flowchart and finally a program, we should consider what to use for the delay loop. In Chapter 9 we wrote a 1-sec delay routine for the Motorola D2. We can use the same routine, making half as many passes through it. The 1-sec routine made 61,463 passes. Half of 61,463 is 30,731.5 (which we round to 30,732), or $780C.

There is a potential problem in using this delay routine, because it uses the index register for a counter. The program itself uses the index register to point to entries in the table. After the microprocessor has executed the delay routine once, the index register will contain $0000 and therefore won't be pointing to the table. One way to avoid this problem, of course, is to use a delay routine that doesn't use the index register for a counter. However, we can use the index register as both a counter and a pointer if we save its contents before the timing loop and restore them after the timing loop. We can do this by storing the index register contents in a memory location using STX and restoring them using LDX.

Figure 10.3.10 shows a detailed flowchart. We use boxes for "Configure PIA" and for "Delay 0.5 sec," because it is assumed we know how to write those program segments.

Figure 10.3.11 is the program for the 1-digit message. Let's go over parts of the detailed flowchart and see how they are implemented in the program.

In the box, *Set Origin of DGTBL*, we start the table at $00C0 with line 193, ORG $C0. This way, the assembler knows to start at $00C0. To *put values in DGTBL*, we use the assembler directive FCB (line 195), Form Constant Bytes. The

FIGURE 10.3.9 Flowchart for One-Digit Message

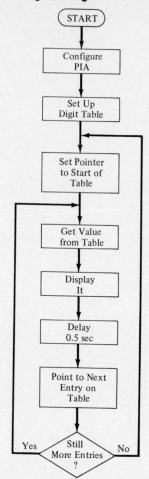

assembler starts with whatever location it is currently addressing (in this case, $00C0) and loads that location and subsequent ones with the values following the FCB directive. So $09 is loaded into $00C0; $7F, into $00C1; and so on. When the table is finished, the assembler will be at location $00CA. We put a comma, but no space, between the constant values.

To *define other labels*, we remember that it is necessary to establish a value for VAL. Also, in order to save the index register, we reserve 2 bytes for that in line 196. The assembler will save locations $00CA and $00CB for TEMPXR.

To start the program at $0000, we need another ORG statement because the assembler is currently addressing location $00CC. (Note that we may have more

FIGURE 10.3.10   Detailed Flowchart for One-Digit Message

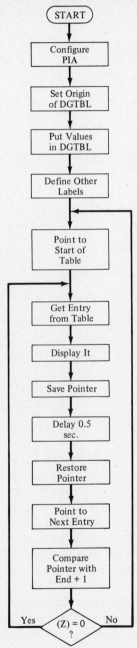

FIGURE 10.3.11 Program MSSGE

```
100              NAM    MSSGE
110     ;THIS PROGRAM SPELLS OUT A MESSAGE IN A 7-SEGMENT DISPLAY
120     ;WITH EACH LETTER ON FOR 0.5 SEC AND A BLANK OF 0.5 SEC
130     ;BETWEEN LETTERS. DISPLAY IS WIRED TO DRB. D2 EVAL KIT.
170     CRB      EQU    $8007
180     DRB      EQU    $8006
190     DDRB     EQU    DRB
192     VAL      EQU    $780C      COUNTER VALUE FOR 0.5 SEC DELAY
193              ORG    $C0        START DIGIT TABLE AT 00C0
195     DGTBL    FCB    $09,$7F, $06,$7F,$47,$7F,$47,$7F,$40,$7F
196     TEMPXR   RMB    2          SAVE 2 BYTES FOR TEMP STORAGE OF (XR)
199              ORG    $0         START PROGRAM AT LOCATION 0000
200     INIT     CLR    CRB        ADDRESS DDRB
250              LDA A  #$FF       READY TO SET SIDE B ALL OUTPUTS
260              STA A  DDRB       SIDE B ALL OUT
270              STA A  CRB        READY TO OUTPUT
290     START    LDX    #DGTBL     POINT TO START OF DIGIT TABLE
300     GETLTR   LDA A  0,X        GET CODE VALUE FROM TABLE
310              STA A  DRB        OUTPUT IT INTO DRB TO DISPLAY LETTER
320              STX    TEMPXR     SAVE POINTER DURING DELAY
330     DELAY    LDX    #VAL       INITIALIZE DELAY COUNTER
340     COUNT    NOP               STALL FOR TIME
350              DEX               DECREMENT COUNTER
360              BNE    COUNT      STILL COUNTING?
370              LDX    TEMPXR     NO, RESTORE POINTER
380              INX               AND POINT TO NEXT ENTRY IN TABLE
390              CPX    #$CA       COMPARE WITH LAST ENTRY +1
400              BNE    GETLTR     NOT DONE? GET NEXT ENTRY
410              BRA    START      NO, RESET AND PLAY AGAIN
420              END
```

than one ORG statement in a program.) Line 199, ORG $0, will cause the assembler now to start assembling at $0000.

To *point to start of table*, we use line 290, LDX #DGTBL. The index register will then be loaded with the value of DGTBL (not its contents), in this case, $00C0. To *get entry from table*, we load the accumulator using an offset of 0; to *display it* we store that value in DRB. To *save pointer*, line 320 stores the index register contents in the two locations saved at TEMPXR. The delay loop is familiar to us; to *restore pointer*, Line 370 loads the index register from its temporary storage location. To *point to next entry* we of course use INX; and to see whether we're done with the table, we use line 390 and compare the current index register contents with the last table address plus one.

We can notice a few factors about this program. First, there are some other options: We could have stored the message backward in the table and stepped through it by decrementing the index register. Instead of saving and restoring the pointer, we might have used a set of nested timing loops that used an accumulator instead of an index register as a loop counter. We could have stored 0 in the index register and used $C0 as an offset, and so on.

FIGURE 10.3.12   MSSGE ASSEMBLY LISTING

```
MSSGE
M6800 ASSEMBLER LISTING VERSION 1.6      19 NOV 80 20:57   PAGE      2
MSSGE   DAT      19 NOV 80 20:55

                        3 ;THIS PROGRAM SPELLS OUT A MESSAGE IN A 7-SEGMENT DISPLAY
                        4 ;WITH EACH LETTER ON FOR 0.5 SEC AND A BLANK OF 0.5 SEC
                        5 ;BETWEEN LETTERS, DISPLAY IS WIRED TO DRB. D2 EVAL KIT.
8007                    6 CRB    EQU   $8007
8006                    7 DRB    EQU   $8006
8006                    8 DDRB   EQU   DRB
780C                   9 VAL    EQU   $780C      COUNTER VALUE FOR 0.5 SEC DELAY
0000                   10       ORG   $C0        START DIGIT TABLE AT 00C0
00C0 09 7F 06 7F       11 DGTBL  FCB   $09,$7F,$06,$7F,$47,$7F,$47,$7F,$40,$7F
00C4 47 7F 47 7F       11
00C8 40 EF             11
00CA 00 00             12 TEMPXR RMB   2          SAVE 2 BYTES FOR TEMP STORAGE OF (XR)
00CC                   13       ORG   $0         START PROGRAM AT LOCATION 0000
0000 7F 80 07          14 INIT   CLR   CRB        ADDRESS DDRB
0003 86 FF             15       LDA A #$FF        READY TO SET SIDE B ALL OUTPUTS
0005 B7 80 06          16       STA A DDRB        SIDE B ALL OUT
0008 B7 80 07          17       STA A CRB         READY TO OUTPUT
000B CE 00 C0          18 START  LDX   #DGTBL     POINT TO START OF DIGIT TABLE
000E A6 00             19 GETLTR LDA A 0,X        GET CODE VALUE FROM TABLE
0010 B7 80 06          20       STA A DRB         OUTPUT IT INTO DRB TO DISPLAY LETTER
0013 DF CA             21       STX   TEMPXR     SAVE POINTER DURING DELAY
0015 CE 78 0C          22 DELAY  LDX   #VAL       INITIALIZE DELAY COUNTER
0018 02                23 COUNT  NOP              STALL FOR TIME
0019 09                24       DEX              DECREMENT COUNTER
001A 26 FC             25       BNE   COUNT      STILL COUNTING?
001C DE CA             26       LDX   TEMPXR     NO, RESTORE POINTER
001E 08                27       INX              AND POINT TO NEXT ENTRY IN TABLE
001F 8C 00 CA          28       CPX   #$CA       COMPARE WITH LAST ENTRY +1
0022 26 EA             29       BNE   GETLTR     NOT DONE? GET NEXT ENTRY
0024 20 E5             30       BRA   START      NO, RESET AND PLAY AGAIN
0026                   31       END

NO STATEMENTS FLAGGED

CROSS-REFERENCE TABLE

COUNT      0018      23    25
CRB        8007       6    14     17
DDRB       8006       8    16
DELAY      0015      22
DGTBL      00C0      11    18
DRB        8006       7     8     20
GETLTR     000E      19    29
INIT       0000      14
START      000B      18    30
TEMPXR     00CA      12    21     26
VAL        780C       9    22
```

In this program we've made use of two routines that we've already written: the configuration of the PIA and the delay loop. Utilizing routines previously written makes for greater programming efficiency. We'll find it convenient to ask, when writing a new routine, whether it was made as general as possible so that we can apply it to something else later.

Next, we'll look at an important pair of list manipulations.

10.4 SEARCHING AND SORTING

We often want to search a list for a specific value or to sort a list according to some condition (alphabetical or numerical order, and so on). Searching and sorting are important aspects of computing, about which whole books have been written. In this section we attempt only a brief introduction rather than an exhaustive discussion of searching and sorting.

Program to Search for Smallest Value

To illustrate searching, we'll take a specific example. In a given list, starting with location $A000 and ending with location $A010, we want to find the smallest *unsigned* value and place it at the top of the list (that is, at the lowest address). The value that used to be at the top should then occupy some other position in the list.

Figure 10.4.1 shows some sample values with the desired results, and also a general flowchart to solve the problem. We define a value, called *RUNT*, as the smallest current value on the list, and another value, called *NEWNUM*, as a previously unseen value that we want to compare with RUNT. The plan will be to point to the top of the list and get the first value. Whatever that value is, it's the smallest we've seen so far, so we call it RUNT. Then we step down the list, get the next value NEWNUM, and compare RUNT with NEWNUM. If NEWNUM is smaller than RUNT, we swap it with the contents of RUNT. (Note that if RUNT=NEWNUM, there's no point in swapping them.) We step down the list and look at each NEWNUM. When we get to the bottom of the list, RUNT should contain the smallest value. Then we point to the start of the list again and store RUNT in the first location. Note that the value formerly at the top of the list will have been stored back in the list during a swap.

To write a detailed flowchart and a program, we should consider two factors. First, in comparing RUNT with NEWNUM, we'll of course use the CMP instruction. So far, we've only used CMP to determine whether or not 2 numbers were equal, by using BNE or BEQ immediately after CMP. Now we need to use CMP to determine whether one number is less than or equal to another. Looking in the instruction information sheets, we find six instructions that deal with inequalities. These are summarized in Table 10.4.1, with some examples and explanations.

We've defined our system of numbers as *unsigned*, so $FF is the largest number we can have and $00, the smallest. In *signed* numbers $7F is the largest

FiGURE 10.4.1 General Flowchart to Search List for Smallest Value

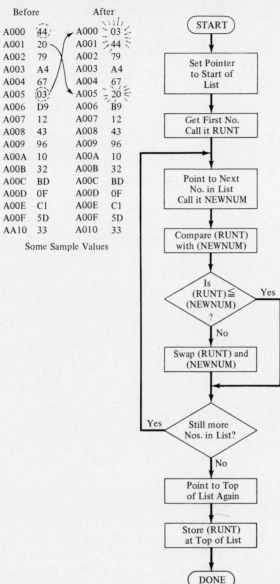

Before		After	
A000	44	A000	03
A001	20	A001	44
A002	79	A002	79
A003	A4	A003	A4
A004	67	A004	67
A005	03	A005	20
A006	D9	A006	B9
A007	12	A007	12
A008	43	A008	43
A009	96	A009	96
A00A	10	A00A	10
A00B	32	A00B	32
A00C	BD	A00C	BD
A00D	0F	A00D	0F
A00E	C1	A00E	C1
A00F	5D	A00F	5D
AA10	33	A010	33

Some Sample Values

number we can have and $80, the smallest. The various branching instructions let us choose whether we're comparing signed or unsigned numbers. Looking through the branching instructions, we find two that say they're for unsigned numbers: BHI, Branch if Higher; and BLS, Branch if Lower or Same.

Let's use ACCA to contain the current value of RUNT. An indexed memory location will be NEWNUM. Then, we'll be comparing the contents of ACCA with

TABLE 10.4.1 Some "Inequality" Branch Instructions

Mnemonic	Instruction	Result
BGE	BRANCH IF GREATER THAN OR EQUAL TO ZERO	BRANCH IS TAKEN IF (ACCX)$\geqq$ (M), SIGNED NUMBERS
BGT	BRANCH IF GREATER THAN ZERO	BRANCH IS TAKEN IF (ACCX)$>$ (M), SIGNED NUMBERS
BHI	BRANCH IF HIGHER	BRANCH IS TAKEN IF (ACCX)$>$ (M), UNSIGNED NUMBERS
BLE	BRANCH IF LESS THAN OR EQUAL TO ZERO	BRANCH IS TAKEN IF (ACCX)$\leqq$ (M), SIGNED NUMBERS
BLS	BRANCH IF LOWER OR SAME	BRANCH IS TAKEN IF (ACCX)$\leqq$ (M), UNSIGNED NUMBERS
BLT	BRANCH IF LESS THAN ZERO	BRANCH IS TAKEN IF (ACCX)$<$ (M), SIGNED NUMBERS

Some Examples
For the instruction CMP A MEM
where (ACCA) = \$FF and (MEM) = \$01,

Instruction	Branch Taken?	Comment
BGE	NO	\$FF IS NEGATIVE; THEREFORE NOT GREATER THAN OR EQUAL TO \$01.
BGT	NO	\$FF IS NEGATIVE; THEREFORE NOT GREATER THAN \$01.
BHI	YES	\$FF IS A LARGER UNSIGNED NUMBER THAN \$01.
BLE	YES	\$FF IS NEGATIVE; THEREFORE LESS THAN \$01.
BLS	NO	\$FF IS NOT A LOWER (OR SAME) UN-SIGNED NUMBER THAN \$01.
BLT	YES	\$FF IS NEGATIVE; THEREFORE LESS THAN \$01.

the contents of a memory location. Looking at the flowchart, we see that we *want* to branch if RUNT (ACCA) is less than or equal to NEWNUM (memory). Table 10.4.1 says that BLS performs exactly that function, so BLS is our choice. The example confirms it: if (ACCA) contains \$FF and (MEM) contains \$01, the branch will *not* be taken, and the swap on our flowchart will take place. This is what we want if (ACCA) is to contain the current *smallest* value.

Note that we could easily change our SEARCH routine to locate the smallest *signed* number just by using the signed equivalent of BLS. Looking at Table 10.4.1, we see that this equivalent is BLE, Branch if Less Than or Equal to Zero.

Our second consideration is with the box "Swap RUNT and NEWNUM." Suppose you have a stack of plates in your right hand and a tray of martinis in your left. To swap these between your two hands without destroying either, you'd first put one of them down temporarily. Here's a possible swap: First, put the stack of plates on a table. Next, transfer the tray of martinis to your right hand. Finally, retrieve the stack of plates from the table with your left hand.

Similarly, we swap contents of two locations (or registers) by first putting one into a temporary location. We could do it this way: First, put RUNT into ACCB

FIGURE 10.4.2 Flowchart for SEARCH Program

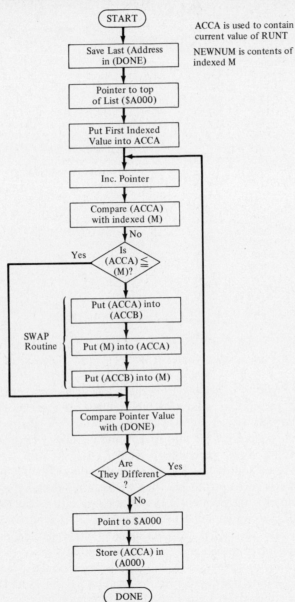

ACCA is used to contain
current value of RUNT

NEWNUM is contents of
indexed M

FIGURE 10.4.3   Program SEARCH

100	NAM	SEARCH	
110	;THIS PROGRAM SEARCHES A LIST IN LOCATIONS		
120	;$A000 THROUGH $A010 FOR THE SMALLEST UN-		
130	;SIGNED VALUE, AND PLACES THAT VALUE AT THE		
140	;TOP OF THE LIST ($A000).		
150	DONE	FCB	$A0,$10	SAVE END ADDRESS
155	XRH	FCB	$A0	
158	XRL	FCB	$00	
160		LDX	XRH	POINT TO TOP OF LIST
170		LDA A	0,X	GET RUNT
180	LOOK	INX		POINT TO NEWNUM
190		CMP A	0,X	COMPARE IT WITH RUNT
200		BLS	NOSWP	UNLESS RUNT>NEWNUM, DON'T SWAP
210		TAB		TO SWAP, PUT RUNT INTO ACCB
220		LDA A	0,X	PUT NEWNUM INTO ACCA
230		STA B	0,X	PUT FORMER RUNT BACK IN LIST
240	NOSWP	CPX	DONE	STILL MORE NEWNUMS?
250		BNE	LOOK	YES, KEEP LOOKING
260		LDX	XRH	NO, POINT TO TOP OF LIST
270		STA A	0,X	PUT RUNT AT TOP
280		WAI		AND STOP
290		END		

temporarily. Next, transfer NEWNUM to RUNT's location. Finally, retrieve the value from ACCB (the former value of RUNT) and place it in NEWNUM's location.

Figure 10.4.2 shows a detailed flowchart for the search program. We use ACCA to contain the current value of RUNT. First, we save the end address in location DONE, so that we can use it to know when to stop. Next, we point to the top of the list. Then we put RUNT into ACCA and increment the pointer so that it points to NEWNUM. Next, we compare RUNT (ACCA) with NEWNUM (the contents of the indexed address). If RUNT is smaller than NEWNUM, we skip the swap routine; otherwise we swap them. Then we see whether this was the last value on the list by comparing the pointer (XR) with the last address (DONE). If not, we go back, increment the pointer, and get the next value of NEWNUM. When we have compared the last value on the list, (ACCA) should contain the smallest value on the list. We point to the top of the list and store RUNT in that location ($A000).

Figure 10.4.3 shows a program for this search. We used the assembler directive FCB to store the 2-byte address $A010 in location DONE and DONE+1. As before, we store the high-order byte of the index register contents in XRH and the low-order byte in XRL. We chose the branch instruction BLS instead of BHI in order to *skip* the swap if it's true that (ACCA) (RUNT, in this case) *is* lower or the same as the contents of M (NEWNUM, in this case).

We can use this searching routine to sort a list.

FIGURE 10.4.4 SEARCH Assembly Listing

```
SEARCH
M6800 ASSEMBLER LISTING VERSION 1.6      18 NOV 80 20:22   PAGE     2
SERCH   DAT     18 NOV 80 20:20

               3 ;THIS PROGRAM SEARCHES A LIST IN LOCATIONS
               4 ;$A000 THROUGH $A010 FOR THE SMALLEST UN-
               5 ;SIGNED VALUE, AND PLACES THAT VALUE AT THE
               6 ;TOP OF THE LIST ($A000).
0000 A0 10     7 DONE    FCB     $A0,$10     SAVE END ADDRESS
0002 A0        8 XRH     FCB     $A0
0003 00        9 XRL     FCB     $00
0004 DE 02    10         LDX     XRH         POINT TO TOP OF LIST
0006 A6 00    11         LDA A   0,X         GET RUNT
0008 08       12 LOOK    INX                 POINT TO NEWNUM
0009 A1 00    13         CMP A   0,X         COMPARE IT WITH RUNT
000B 23 05    14         BLS     NOSWP       UNLESS RUNT>NEWNUM, DON'T SWAP
000D 16       15         TAB                 TO SWAP, PUT RUNT INTO ACCB
000E A6 00    16         LDA A   0,X         PUT NEWNUM INTO ACCA
0010 E7 00    17         STA B   0,X         PUT FORMER RUNT BACK IN LIST
0012 9C 00    18 NOSWP   CPX     DONE        STILL MORE NEWNUMS?
0014 26 F2    19         BNE     LOOK        YES, KEEP LOOKING
0016 DE 02    20         LDX     XRH         NO, POINT TO TOP OF LIST
0018 A7 00    21         STA A   0,X         PUT RUNT AT TOP
001A 3E       22         WAI                 AND STOP
001B          23         END

NO STATEMENTS FLAGGED

CROSS-REFERENCE TABLE

DONE            0000      7      18
LOOK            0008     12      19
NOSWP           0012     18      14
XRH             0002      8
XRL             0003      9
```

Program to Sort in Numerical Order

In this example we want to sort a list so that the smallest unsigned number is at the top of the list (lowest memory) and the largest unsigned number is at the bottom (highest memory). The numbers should be arranged in increasing (unsigned) numerical order.

Figure 10.4.5 shows an example with the desired results and an illustration of the general plan. Executing the SEARCH routine once puts the smallest value at the top of the list. Once we've gotten the smallest value, we can forget about it and find the smallest value of those remaining. We want to execute SEARCH $(N-1)$ times, where N is the number of items on the list. Note that when we have arranged all but the last value, the last value must necessarily be the largest by default.

When we execute SEARCH once, we point to each value of NEWNUM to compare it with RUNT. We'll call this pointer the "Inner Pointer." We'll now need

FIGURE 10.4.5 SORT Program Uses SEARCH Routine to Find Smallest Value in Remaining Members of List

Before		After		
A000	44	A000	03	
A001	20	A001	0F	
A002	79	A002	10	
A003	A4	A003	12	
A004	67	A004	20	
A005	03	A005	32	
A006	D9	A006	33	
A007	12	A007	43	
A008	43	A008	44	Desired Results of SORT program
A009	96	A009	5D	
A00A	10	A00A	67	
A00B	32	A00B	79	
A00C	BD	A00C	96	
A00D	0F	A00D	A4	
A00E	C1	A00E	BD	
A00F	5D	A00F	C1	
A010	33	A010	D9	

One pass through
SEARCH puts smallest
value at top:

A000	03
A001	20
- - -	
- - -	
- - -	
A010	33

Outer pointer
defines new "top"
of list:

A000	03
A001	20 ◄— Outer Pointer
A002	79
- - -	
- - -	
- - -	
A010	33

Now we find smallest of these remaining values

Second pass through
SEARCH puts next
smallest value
in 2nd position:

A000	03
A001	0F
A002	79
- - -	
- - -	
- - -	
A010	33

Outer pointer moves
down to new "top" of
list:

A000	03
A001	0F
A002	79 ◄—Outer Pointer
- - -	
- - -	
- - -	
A010	33

Now choose smallest of these values

to define an "Outer Pointer" that defines the new "top" of the list; that is, the beginning of the values that still have to be searched for the smallest value.

Before the first pass through the search routine, both inner and outer pointers point to $A000. During the first execution of SEARCH the inner pointer has moved from $A000 through $A010 and back to $A000. Now we have the smallest number in location $A000, so we don't want to search location $A000 any more. We move the outer pointer to location $A001 so that we can now use SEARCH to find the smallest value contained in locations $A001 through $A010.

FIGURE 10.4.6 General Flowchart for SORT Program

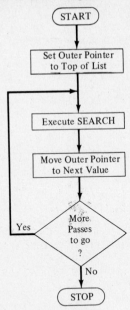

FIGURE 10.4.7 Detailed Flowchart for SORT Routine

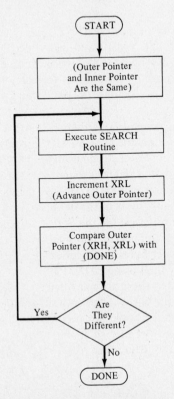

FIGURE 10.4.8 SORT Program

```
100            NAM    SORT
110 ;THIS PROGRAM SORTS A LIST IN LOCATIONS
120 ;$A000 THROUGH $A010 IN INCREASING NUMERICAL
130 ;ORDER.
140 DONE      FCB    $A0,$10  SAVE END ADDRESS
150 XRH       FCB    $A0      SET OUTER AND INNER POINTERS
160 XRL       FCB    $00      TO TOP OF LIST
170 SEARCH    LDX    XRH      SET INNER POINTER AT CURRENT TOP
180           LDA A  0,X      GET RUNT
190 LOOK      INX             POINT TO NEWNUM
200           CMP A  0,X      COMPARE IT WITH RUNT
210           BLS    NOSWP    UNLESS RUNT>NEWNUM, DON'T SWAP
220           TAB             TO SWAP, PUT RUNT INTO ACCB
230           LDA A  0,X      PUT OLD NEWNUM INTO ACCA
240           STA B  0,X      PUT OLD RUNT BACK IN LIST
250 NOSWP     CPX    DONE     STILL MORE NEWNUMS?
260           BNE    LOOK     YES, KEEP LOOKING
270           LDX    XRH      NO, POINT TO TOP OF LIST
280           STA A  0,X      PUT RUNT AT TOP
290           INC    XRL      ADVANCE OUTER POINTER
300           CPX    DONE     MORE SEARCHES TO DO?
310           BNE    SEARCH   YES, DO ANOTHER SEARCH
320           WAI             NO, STOP
330           END
```

During the second execution of SEARCH, the inner pointer now starts with location $A001, moves through $A010 and gets back to $A001, where the next smallest value (in this case, $0F) gets stored. Now we don't want to search location $A001 any more, and the outer pointer moves to location $A002, and so on. Note that the outer pointer value also defines the first value of the inner pointer at the beginning of each pass.

Figure 10.4.6 shows a general, and Figure 10.4.7 a detailed, flowchart to do this job. Note that we haven't detailed the SEARCH routine, because it has already been done. We use the location XRL to determine the outer pointer (XRH stays at $A0). Incrementing XRL lets the index register be loaded with the next address at the beginning of each execution of SEARCH. The detailed flowchart is almost the same as the general one, because most of the details have been done in SEARCH.

Figure 10.4.8 shows a program for the SORT routine. We see that only a few instructions more are needed to construct this program from the SEARCH routine. Storing the high- and low-order bytes of the index register in separate, defined labels usually gives more flexibility than using LDX (IMM).

Again, we emphasize that there are many ways of sorting a list. The way we've chosen isn't the most efficient, but it is the easiest to understand.

As we progress through the book, our programs will get longer. But they're not necessarily more complicated, because so far we've been putting together routines that have already been written. Rewriting previously written routines is boring and

FIGURE 10.4.9 SORT Assembly Listing

SORT
M6800 ASSEMBLER LISTING VERSION 1.6   19 NOV 80 20:04   PAGE   2
SORT   DAT   19 NOV 80 20:02

```
                    3 ;THIS PROGRAM SORTS A LIST IN LOCATIONS
                    4 ;$A000 THROUGH $A010 IN INCREASING NUMERICAL
                    5 ;ORDER.
0000 A0 10          6 END      FCB    $A0,$10    SAVE END ADDRESS
0002 A0             7 XRH      FCB    $A0        SET OUTER AND INNER POINTERS
0003 00             8 XRL      FCB    $00        TO TOP OF LIST
0004 DE 02          9 SEARCH   LDX    XRH        SET INNER POINTER AT CURRENT TOP
0006 A6 00         10          LDA A  0,X        GET RUNT
0008 08            11 LOOK     INX               POINT TO NEWNUM
0009 A1 00         12          CMP A  0,X        COMPARE IT WITH RUNT
000B 23 05         13          BLS    NOSWP      UNLESS RUNT>NEWNUM, DON'T SWAP
000D 16            14          TAB               TO SWAP, PUT RUNT INTO ACCB
000E A6 00         15          LDA A  0,X        PUT OLD NEWNUM INTO ACCA
0010 E7 00         16          STA B  0,X        PUT OLD RUNT BACK IN LIST
0012 9C 00         17 NOSWP    CPX    DONE       STILL MORE NEWNUMS?
0014 26 F2         18          BNE    LOOK       YES, KEEP LOOKING
0016 DE 02         19          LDX    XRH        NO, POINT TO TOP OF LIST
0018 A7 00         20          STA A  0,X        PUT RUNT AT TOP
001A 7C 00 03      21          INC    XRL        ADVANCE OUTER POINTER
001D 9C 00         22          CPX    DONE       MORE SEARCHES TO DO?
001F 26 E3         23          BNE    SEARCH     YES, DO ANOTHER SEARCH
0021 3E            24          WAI               NO, STOP
0022              25          END
```

NO STATEMENTS FLAGGED

CROSS-REFERENCE TABLE

DONE	0000	6	17	22
LOOK	0008	11		
NOSWP	0012	17	13	
SEARCH	0004	9	18	23
XRH	0002	7		
XRL	0003	8	21	

subject to error. What we'd like is to write a routine to do a certain job only once, be sure that it works, and then just insert it by name if it's needed in a bigger program.

This is what we'll learn in the next chapter.

REVIEW QUESTIONS

1. What is the **indexed addressing mode**? What is an **offset**? Give an example.
2. How are relative and indexed addressing similar? How are they different?
3. What is the range of indexed addressing?
4. Explain how the instructions STX and CPX work.
5. What is a **table**? Give an example of a **look-up table**.

6. How do we form a pointer in a look-up table? Explain how to use indexed addressing to retrieve a value from a table.

7. Explain how to determine the offset and index register contents for a desired indexed address.

8. Explain how to load the index register using the direct or extended modes. Why might we need to establish individual labels for the high- and the low-order byte of the index register contents?

9. What does the assembler directive RMB do? Give an example of its use in a program.

10. Sketch a general flowchart for a program to step through and process a list.

11. Explain the differences between stepping through a list from high to low memory and from low to high memory. How do we know when we reach the end of the list?

12. What options do we have with regard to what values to use for the offset and the index register contents?

13. Illustrate how we may use the index register as a loop counter as well as a pointer. What is the advantage of this?

14. Explain how to detect the end of a list of variable length by the use of a marker. How will the program be different according to whether or not we want the marker itself to be processed?

15. Can we use the index register for indexed addressing and for a counter in a timing loop in the same program without causing an error? How?

16. Explain how to use ORG to set the origin of a table at a specific location.

17. What does the FCB assembler directive do? Give an example.

18. Explain how the SEARCH program of Figure 10.4.3 works. How do we swap the contents of two registers or memory locations?

19. What branching instructions treat the 2 numbers compared in CMP as unsigned numbers? How do we know which instruction to use?

20. Explain how to use the SEARCH program to sort a list of numbers in increasing numerical order. How do we advance the outer pointer?

EXERCISES

Set A (answers at back of book)

1. State (a) from what location accumulator A would be loaded and (b) whether or not the branch would be taken, for this program segment:

```
LDX     #$F
LDA A   $11,X
INX
BNE     LAST
```

2. Write a program segment that loads the index register with $00A0 and then stores the contents of accumulator B in location $00B3, using indexed addressing.

3. Write a program segment that loads the index register with some value and then adds the contents of accumulator A to the contents of location $0040, using indexed addressing with an offset of $10.

4. Refer to Table 10.2.1, and state what value is retrieved from the table by each of these program segments:

   (a) LDX   #$9C   (b) LDX   #$0   (c) LDX $90   (d) LDX   #$A0
        LDA A 0,X   LDA A $A0,X   LDA A $10,X   LDA A $1,X

5. Using the addresses and contents of Table 10.2.1, state whether or not the branch would be taken in each of these program segments:

   (a) LDX   #$90   (b) LDX #$96   (c) LDX   #$0
        LDA A #$10   DEX   INX
        CPA $9,X   CPX #$10   LDA A #$64
        BEQ   SNAP   BNE POP   CPA $A0,X
                                        BEQ   BANG

6. Write program segments for each: (a) Retrieve the square of 4, using an offset of $96; (b) retrieve the square of 6, with the index register loaded with $96; (c) retrieve the square of 3, using an offset of 3; (d) retrieve the square of 9, with the index register loaded with 0.

7. State the contents of the index register after executing each of these program segments:

   (a) INDH EQU $33   (b) LDA A #$3   (c) CLR $15   (d) LDX $9D
        INDL EQU $34   STA A $A0   LDA B #$65
        LDA A #$FF   LDA A #$A7   STA B $16
        STA A INDH   STA A $A1   LDX $15
        LDA A #$4   LDX $A0
        STA A INDL
        LDX   INDH

   (Assume addresses and contents of Table 10.2.1)

8. Give the new line or lines for these modifications of the HEXDIG program (Figure 10.2.3): (a) The digit table is to begin at address $B097. (b) The digit table is to begin at address $E0AB. (c) The digit table is to begin at address $C042.

9. Give the new line or lines for programs A and B of Figure 10.3.5 if the list to be cleared is in locations $1001 to $1021.

10. Give the new line or lines for program B of Figure 10.3.5 if the list is in locations $00E0 to $00F0 and the index register is to be loaded with the number of locations to be processed (refer to Example 10.3.2).

11. Give the new line or lines for programs A and B of Figure 10.3.9 if the list is to be moved from $00C0 to $00A0 and the end marker is an ASCII carriage return (CR).

12. For each of these program segments, give the starting address of DGTBL, the addresses of TEMPXR, and the starting address of the program:

    (a)   ORG 0
        DGTBL   FCB $0B, $EF,$06,$EF,$63,$EF,$63
        TEMPXR   RMB 2
                 ORG $20
        INIT   CLR CRA   START PROGRAM

    (b)   ORG $1000
        TEMPXR   RMB 2
        DGTBL   FCB $0B, $EF,$06,$EF
                 ORG $10
        INIT   CLR CRA   START PROGRAM

13. Modify the MSSAGE program so that the message HELLO ends with an exclamation point, which is also to be displayed. Give only the lines that are to be inserted or to replace others.

14. Modify the MSSAGE program so that it is stepped through by decrementing the index register. Give only the lines that are to be inserted or to replace others.

15. What would be the result of replacing BLS in the SEARCH program (Figure 10.4.3) by (a) BLT; (b) BGT?

16. Modify the SEARCH program (Figure 10.4.3) so that it searches (a) for the largest unsigned value; (b) from higher to lower memory and places RUNT at the bottom of the list; (c) a list of variable length whose end is marked by an ASCII carriage return (CR), followed by a line feed (lf).

17. Modify the SORT program so that it sorts from bottom to top.

18. Would the SORT program be effective as it stands for sorting a list of ASCII characters into alphabetical order if the characters had (a) no parity; (b) odd parity; (c) even parity? If the answer to any of these is "no," state briefly what modifications must be made to the program.

EXERCISES

Set B (answers not given)

1. State (a) into what address accumulator A would be stored and (b) whether or not the branch would be taken, for this program segment:

```
LDX     #$AF
LDA A   $5,X
DEX
CPX     #$AE
BNE     FUDGE
```

2. Write a program segment that loads the index register with some value and then loads the contents of location $01AE into accumulator A with an offset of $A0, using indexed addressing.

3. Write a program segment that loads the index register with $1234 and then stores the contents of accumulator A in location 1300, using indexed addressing.

4. Refer to Table 10.2.1, and state what value is retrieved from the table by each of these program segments:

```
(a)  LDX    #$10   (b)  LDX    #$97   (c)  LDX  #$0      (d)  LDX    #$96
     LDA A  $93,X       LDA A  $0,X        LDA A  $A5,X       LDA A  $1,X
```

5. Using the addresses and contents of Table 10.2.1, state whether or not the branch would be taken in each of these program segments:

```
(a)  LDX  #$0    (b)  LDX    #$98   (c)  LDX    #$B
     INX              INX               LDA A  #$7A
     CPX  #$64        LDA A  #$9        DEC A
     BNE  WOOF        CMP A  $0,X       CMP A  $96,X
                      BNE    MEOW       BEQ    CHIRP
```

6. Refer to Table 10.2.1, and write program segments for each of these: (a) retrieve the square of 5_{10} with an offset of 0; (b) retrieve the square of 13_{10} with the index register contents 0; (c) retrieve the square of 10_{10} with an offset of $0A; (d) retrieve the square of 1 with an offset of $0A.

7. State the contents of the index register after execution of each of these program segments:

(a) Assume addresses and   (b) Assume addresses and
     contents of Table 10.2.2:   contents of Table 10.2.2:

     LDX $E0A5   LOCH EQU $E097
                               LDX   LOCH

(c)   LDA A   #$04   (d) VAL   EQU $8076
       STA A $A0   LDX   #VAL
       LDA A   #$97
       STA A $9F
       LDX $9F

8. Give the new line or lines for the HEXDIG program if the digit table is to begin at: (a) 4797; (b) E033; (c) 0115.

9. Give the new line or lines for programs A and B of Figure 10.3.5 if the list to be cleared is in locations $0100 to $0200 inclusive.

10. Give the new line or lines for program B of Figure 10.3.5 if the list is in locations $00DF to $0100 and the index register is to be loaded with the number of locations to be processed (refer to Example 10.3.2).

11. Modify program A of Figure 10.3.9 to move a block of definite length $10 locations long and starting in location $0260 to a set of addresses starting with location $0200. Give only the line or lines that are new.

12. For each of these program segments, give the starting address of DGTBL, the addresses of TEMPXR, and the starting address of the program:

(a)
```
              ORG  0
    TEMPXR    RMB  2
    DGTBL     FCB  $0B,$EF,$06,$EF,$63,$EF,$63,$EF,$40
    INIT      CLR  CRA      START PROGRAM
```

(b)
```
              ORG  0
    DGTBL     FCB  $0B,$EF,$06,$EF,$63,$EF
              ORG  $A0
    TEMPXR    RMB  2
    INIT      CLR  CRA      START PROGRAM
```

13. Give the new line or lines for the MSSAGE program if it is to detect the end of the message by using the numeral "0" as a marker.

14. Give the new line or lines for the MSSAGE program if it is to allow for a message of variable length, to be supplied by the user in a location called LENGTH.

15. What would be the result of replacing BLS in the SEARCH program by (a) BGT; (b) BHI?

16. Modify the SEARCH program (Figure 10.4.3) so that it searches (a) for the largest signed value; (b) a list occupying locations C310 through C400.

17. Modify the SORT program so that it sorts from bottom to top.

PROGRAMMING IDEAS

1. Write a program to evaluate $y = 5x^2$ using a look-up table of squares.

2. Create a hexadecimal-to-BCD look-up table for BCD values 10 to 20. Put the table in your assembly language program at location $00B0. Start the program at $0000. Assume side A of the PIA is wired to a set of 8 switches (0 = off, 1 = on) and side B, to 8 LEDs (0 = off, 1 = on). The program should input a 2-digit hexadecimal number from $0 to $14 on the switches and display its BCD equivalent on the 8 LEDs. (Note that for digits 0 to 9 no conversion is necessary and the number can be displayed directly.) If the number input on the switches is too large for the conversion table, display $FF on the LEDs.

3. Calculate the sum of a series of 1-byte numbers for a list (a) having a fixed length of 8 values; (b) having variable length, stored by user in location LENGTH; (c) having variable length where $00 is the end marker.

4. Find the largest number in a list that starts at location $0020 and ends at location $0030. Store the largest number in location $0031.

5. Move a list from $00B0–$00D0–$00A0–$00C0. Note that the two lists overlap; write the program so that no values are destroyed.

6. Search a list of values for an ASCII period, and report its address in locations labeled PRD1 and PRD2. The list occupies locations $00C0 to $00D0.

7. Count the number of negative values in a list, starting at $00C0 and having variable length input into location LENGTH. Store the number of negative values in location NEGVAL.

8. Assume the PIA is set up as in Example 10.2.3 and Table 10.2.2 is stored in ROM. Cause the display to count in sequence repeatedly until an F is input on the switches, at which time the program should blank the display and stop. Place a 0.5-sec delay between numbers.

9. Each side of the PIA is wired to a seven-segment display, side A to the leftmost and side B to the rightmost. Write a program that will cause the message HELLO to flow across the 2 digits, ticker-tape fashion, with a 0.5-sec delay between changes. That is, the digits should look like this:

```
FIRST POSITION:      H  E
        SECOND:      E  L
         THIRD:      L  L
        FOURTH:      L  O
         FIFTH:      O  (BLANK)
         SIXTH:  (BLANK)  H
AND SO ON.
```

10. Transpose two lists of ASCII characters. One list starts at location $00C0 and the other starts at location $00D0. They both contain ten characters.

11. Alphabetize a list of words of varying length. An ASCII carriage return marks the end of each word. The words are stored in memory, beginning at location $C000 and ending with location $C0FF.

11 Subroutines

LEARNING OBJECTIVES

After completing this chapter, you should be able to:

1. Supply a definition, explanation, or example for each of these: *subroutine, stack, LIFO, pulling from the stack, pushing onto the stack, stack pointer, calling instruction, call, calling program, return instruction, return, nested subroutines, parameters, passing parameters.*
2. Explain and use correctly in programs the stack instructions of Table 11.1.1.
3. Use the instructions BSR, JSR, and RTS correctly in subroutines, and explain their effect on the stack and stack pointer.
4. Create a subroutine from a routine, saving register contents.
5. Use PSH and PUL within a subroutine without causing error.
6. Explain or discuss errors resulting from improper loading or failure to load the stack pointer.
7. Explain how to pass parameters between a main program and a subroutine, and implement parameter passing.

In Chapter 10 we recognized that there are routines that can be used over and over again. Once our system PIA is wired in a certain way, we'll configure it identically each time we use it. After writing a program segment that causes a 1-sec delay, we'd like to use it whenever a delay of 1 sec is needed.

For instance, we have a 1-sec delay routine for the Motorola D2, which we could call DELAY:

```
DELAY   LDX   #$F017   LOAD COUNTER WITH 1-SEC VALUE
COUNT   NOP            STALL FOR TIME
        DEX            DECREMENT COUNTER
        BNE   COUNT    STILL COUNTING?
```

Then, as part of a larger program—for instance, the blinking sign program—we could just branch to the routine DELAY.

```
STA A   CRA     NOW DRA READY FOR OUTPUT
BRA     DELAY   GO TO 1-SEC DELAY ROUTINE
COM     DRA     TOGGLE SIGN SWITCH
```

There's just one problem with this. Once the delay routine is finished, where will the microprocessor go next to get an instruction? We'd like it to come back to the main program at the instruction COM DRA. One way to do this would be to give our return point a label and cause the routine to branch there:

```
DELAY   LDX   #$F017   LOAD COUNTER WITH 1-SEC VALUE
COUNT   NOP            STALL FOR TIME
        DEX            DECREMENT COUNTER
        BNE   COUNT    STILL COUNTING?
        BRA   RET      NO, RETURN TO MAIN PROGRAM
```

Then the main program would look like this:

```
        STA A  CRA     NOW DRA READY FOR OUTPUT
        BRA    DELAY   GO TO 1-SEC DELAY ROUTING
RET     COM    DRA     TOGGLE SIGN SWITCH
```

This would work, but now our routine is specific for this particular return point, RET. Instead, we'd like the routine to be so general that it can be used anywhere in the main program. A routine that causes the microprocessor to return to the main program automatically at the correct point is called a **subroutine**.

When reading a book, you might stop temporarily to do something else. To resume reading where you left off, you'd probably use a bookmark. If none were available, you could write down, or save, the page number where you stopped reading. When you finish what you're doing and return to the book, you could resume reading at the right place by getting the saved page number, looking at it, turning to the right page, and reading from there.

Similarly, a microprocessor might stop executing a main program temporarily to execute a subroutine. A microprocessor doesn't have a "bookmark" available to help it resume execution at the right place. However, a microprocessor does have a mechanism for "writing down" (saving) the program counter contents at the point where it temporarily stops executing a main program to execute a subroutine. When the microprocessor finishes the subroutine, it can resume the main program at the right place by retrieving the saved program counter contents and executing from there.

One way for a human being to save information is to write it on paper. Microprocessors save information by storing (writing) it in registers or memory. To save program counter contents during the execution of a subroutine, most microprocessors use a special organization of memory. We'll learn about that next.

11.1 THE STACK AND STACK POINTER

When the 6800 stops executing a main program temporarily to execute a subroutine, it automatically saves the current program counter contents in the microprocessor's **stack**, a set of contiguous memory locations used in Last-In-First-Out (LIFO) fashion. We can illustrate **LIFO** with a stack of trays in a cafeteria. When we pull a tray off the stack, it's always the one on top of the stack—and the last one that was put back by someone else. When we put a tray on the stack, we put it on top, and it'll be the first one pulled off by someone else. Like taking the top cafeteria tray, taking the top value from a microprocessor's stack is called **pulling from the stack**. Placing a value on top of the microprocessor's stack is **pushing onto the stack** (if a stack of trays were supported by a spring under the counter, we might have to push the top tray down to bring the stack down to a reasonable height).

Some microprocessors have a stack of definite length within the CPU itself, but the 6800's stack is located in memory. In the former case there is no problem knowing where the stack begins or ends. But the 6800's stack can be anywhere in memory and can have any length. In that case we need to be able to know where the stack begins in a particular instance. The **stack pointer**, which we've mentioned briefly in Chapter 3 without defining, is a 16-bit register in the CPU whose contents determine the location where data is to be pushed onto the stack. The length of the stack depends on how many values have been pushed onto it.

Some Stack Manipulating Instructions

Table 11.1.1 lists some instructions connected with the stack and stack pointer. We, the users, can set the stack anywhere we like by loading the stack pointer with a 2-byte value. To do this, we use the instruction Load Stack Pointer, LDS. The instructions LDS, STS (Store Stack Pointer), INS (Increment Stack Pointer) and DES (Decrement Stack Pointer) work just like the corresponding index register instructions LDX, STX, INX, and DEX.

TABLE 11.1.1   Some Instructions That Affect the Stack and Stack Pointer

Mnemonic	Instruction	Operation
LDS	LOAD STACK POINTER	PLACES 2-BYTE VALUE IN SP
STS	STORE STACK POINTER	STORES (SP) IN 2 MEMORY LOCS
INS	INCREMENT STACK POINTER	ADDS ONE TO (SP)
DES	DECREMENT STACK POINTER	SUBTRACTS ONE FROM (SP)
PSH A PSH B	PUSH DATA ONTO STACK	1. PLACES (ACCA) OR (ACCB) INTO MEM LOC POINTED TO BY (SP) 2. DECREMENTS (SP)
PUL A PUL B	PULL DATA FROM STACK	1. INCREMENTS (SP) 2. PLACES CONTENTS OF MEM LOC POINTED TO BY (SP), INTO ACCA OR ACCB.

EXAMPLE 11.1.1

For this program segment:

```
SAVIT   EQU   $0500
SPH     FCB   $00
SPL     FCB   $FF
        LDS   SPH
        INS
        STS   SAVIT
        DES
        DES
```

state (a) the stack pointer contents and (b) the contents of locations $0500 and $0501 after the program segment is executed.

Solution

(a) Looking at the LDS instruction, we see that the high-order byte of the stack pointer is loaded with the contents of a memory location, M (in this case, SPH). And the low-order byte of the stack pointer is loaded with the contents of the next memory location, M + 1 (in this case, SPL). So the first instruction LDS SPH loads the stack pointer with $00FF. The instruction INS increments the stack pointer contents to $0100. Two DES instructions decrement the stack pointer contents twice to $00FE. (b) Location SAVIT is defined as $0500. Looking at the STS instruction, we see that the high-order byte of the stack pointer contents is stored in the operand M (in this case, SAVIT, $0500). The low-order byte of the stack pointer contents is stored in location M + 1 (in this case, $0501). At the time the STS instruction is executed, the stack pointer contains $0100. So location $0500 gets the value $01 and location $0501, $00.

Answer: (a) (SP) = $00FE; (b) ($0500) = $01; ($0501) = $00

The instructions LDS, STS, INS, and DES affect only the stack pointer contents. But the next two instructions on Table 11.1.1, PSH and PUL, affect both the stack pointer contents and the stack itself.

Pushing onto the Stack

Turning to the instruction information sheet for PSH, Push Data onto Stack, we see first that only the accumulator addressing modes are available; we may push only the contents of accumulator A or B onto the stack. Next, we see a new kind of register transfer notation:

(ACCX) ↓

Here, the arrow pointing down means "is pushed onto the stack." So the register transfer statement reads "The contents of an accumulator is pushed onto the stack."

To push onto the stack means, precisely, to place the accumulator contents into a memory location whose address is the current stack pointer contents.

There is a second register transfer statement:

$$(SP) \leftarrow (SP) - 0001$$

This type of statement is familiar to us and means "The stack pointer contents are decremented by one."

The instruction PSH therefore causes the microprocessor to do two things: (1) to push the contents of the accumulator onto the stack and (2) to decrement the contents of the stack pointer.

EXAMPLE 11.1.2

Consider this program segment:

```
LDS     #$FF
LDA A   #$AA
LDA B   #$BB
PSH A
PSH B
```

After the microprocessor has executed this, (a) What locations will contain what new values? (b) What will be the contents of the stack pointer? and (c) What values will be contained in ACCA and ACCB?

Solution

The first instruction loads the stack pointer with $00FF. Next, we load accumulator A with $AA and accumulator B with $BB. We saw from the instruction information sheet for PSH that its activities are to push the contents of an accumulator onto the stack and to decrement the stack pointer contents. So PSH A pushes the value in ACCA ($AA) onto the stack at location $00FF and decrements the stack pointer contents to $00FE. Next, PSH B pushes the value in ACCB ($BB) onto the stack at location $00FE and decrements the stack pointer contents to $00FD.

Answer: (a) ($00FE) = $BB; ($00FF) = $AA; (b) (SP) = $00FD; (c) (ACCA) = $AA; (ACCB) = $BB

Figure 11.1.1 illustrates what happens in this program segment. First, the instruction LDS #$FF uses the immediate mode to load the stack pointer with $00FF. The stack pointer points to the location where data will be pushed next. Right now, that location ($00FF) contains garbage.

At (1), the next instruction, PSH A pushes the contents of accumulator A (in this case, $AA) onto the stack where the stack pointer is pointing (in this case, $00FF). At (2), after pushing (ACCA) onto the stack, PSH A decrements the stack pointer contents (in this case, to $00FE). So at the end of this PSH A instruction,

FIGURE 11.1.1 Pushing onto Stack with PSH

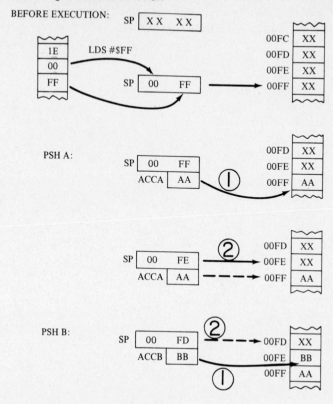

location $00FF contains $AA and the stack pointer contains $00FE. $00FE is now the next location where data will be pushed.

The next instruction, PSH B (1), pushes the contents of accumulator B (in this case, $BB) onto the stack at $00FE. At (2) it decrements the stack pointer contents to $00FD. Thus at the end of this program segment, ($00FF)=$AA, ($00FE)=BB, and (SP)=$00FD.

Pushing onto the stack is destructive to the stack. When a new value is pushed onto the stack, whatever was contained in that memory location is destroyed. For this reason it's very important to place the stack somewhere in memory where it won't interfere with the program instructions. To get the stack as far as possible from program addresses, we usually load the stack pointer with the highest available RAM address. Normally, the first instruction in a program where the stack is to be used loads the stack pointer with the highest available RAM address. The value $00FF is the highest available RAM address for the Motorola D2.

We retrieve values pushed onto the stack, in LIFO fashion, by pulling them from the stack.

Pulling from the Stack

On the instruction information sheet for PUL, Pull Data from Stack, we see that, like PSH, only the accumulator addressing modes are available. Next, we see two register transfer statements:

$$SP \leftarrow (SP) + 0001$$
$$(ACCX) \uparrow$$

These statements mean that, first, the stack pointer contents are incremented. Next, the arrow pointing up means "is pulled from the stack." So the second register transfer statement reads "A value is pulled from the stack and placed in the accumulator." To pull from the stack means, precisely, to copy the contents of a memory location whose address is the current stack pointer contents. Note that the PUL instruction increments the stack pointer contents *before* pulling, because the stack pointer always points one location lower than the location of the next value to be pulled.

The instruction PUL therefore causes the microprocessor to do two things: (1) to increment the contents of the stack pointer and (2) to pull from the stack and place the contents in an accumulator.

EXAMPLE 11.1.3

Assume the values of (SP) and memory locations as they were left by Example 11.1.2. Then assume that this program segment is executed:

```
PUL   A
PUL   B
```

After execution of this segment, state (a) the contents of ACCA and ACCB; (b) the contents of the stack pointer; and (c) the contents of locations $00FD, $00FE, and $00FF.

Solution

From the instruction information sheet for PUL we saw that the first operation is to increment the stack pointer contents. Those contents, at the end of Example 11.1.2, were $00FD. So after incrementing, the stack pointer contains $00FE. The next operation for PUL A is to place the contents of the location pointed to by the stack pointer ($00FE) into accumulator A. The contents of $00FE are $BB. Thus after PUL A, the stack pointer contains $00FE and ACCA contains $BB. Location $00FE still contains $BB.

For the PUL B instruction, first, the stack pointer contents ($00FE) are incremented to $00FF. Next, the contents of $00FF ($AA) are placed in accumulator B. So after PUL B the stack pointer contains $00FF and ACCB contains $AA. Location $00FF still contains $AA.

Answer: (a) (ACCA)=$BB; (ACCB)=$AA. (b) (SP)=$00FF. (c) ($00FD)= garbage; ($00FE)=$BB; ($00FF)=$AA

Figure 11.1.2 illustrates pulling from the stack using this program segment. After Example 11.1.2 the stack pointer contained $00FD, ACCA contained $AA, and ACCB contained $BB. The stack pointer points to location $00FD, whose contents are garbage. Location $00FE contains $BB and location $00FF contains $AA.

Next is the PUL A instruction. At (1) the stack pointer contents are incremented to $00FE. Now the stack pointer is pointing to $00FE, whose contents are $BB. At (2) the value pointed to by the stack pointer ($BB) is placed in accumulator A, destroying the value $AA, which was in there before.

The PUL B instruction is shown a little more briefly than PUL A. At (1) the stack pointer is incremented to $FF and now points to the value $AA. At (2) the value $AA is loaded into ACCB, destroying its previous contents ($BB).

Summary: Pushing onto and Pulling from the Stack

We can notice several factors from Examples 11.1.2 and 11.1.3. First, let's put those two program segments together:

```
LDS    #$FF
LDA A  #$AA
LDA B  #$BB
PSH A
PSH B
PUL A
PUL B
```

Now we have a routine that swaps the contents of accumulators A and B. The initial contents (ACCA)=$AA and (ACCB)=$BB were loaded into the accumulators for the purpose of illustration. After executing the preceding sequence, (ACCA)=$BB and (ACCB)=$AA. Regardless of the initial contents of ACCA and ACCB, the sequence

```
PSH A
PSH B
PUL A
PUL B
```

will always swap their contents. Because of the LIFO way of accessing the stack, the *last* value pushed onto the stack ($BB) is the *first* one pulled. So if we pull first into ACCA and second into ACCB, we'll have reversed their original contents.

Second, notice that *equal numbers of pushes and pulls return the stack pointer contents to their original value*. Here, we had two pushes and two pulls. At the end (SP)=$00FF as it was in the beginning.

Third, notice that the instructions PSH and PUL aren't symmetrical when it comes to the order in which they access the stack and change the stack pointer

FIGURE 11.1.2 Pulling from Stack with PUL

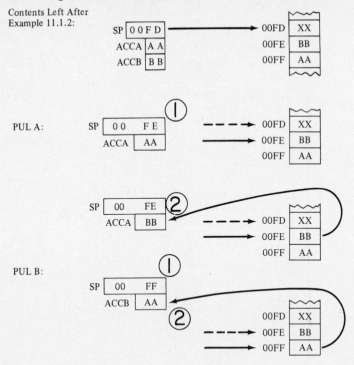

contents. That is, PSH accesses the stack and *then* decrements (SP). However, PUL *first* increments (SP) and then accesses the stack. This could be confusing unless we remember that *before a PSH instruction, the stack pointer points to the location where data will be pushed* and that *before a PUL instruction, the stack pointer points to the next (lower) location from which data will be pulled*. That way, pushing onto the stack will destroy nothing we want. Once we've pushed onto the stack, the stack pointer points to the next available location. If we want to retrieve a value from the stack, we must first increment the stack pointer so that it points to the value we want.

Finally, notice that pushing is destructive to the stack. Like putting trays onto a stack, we place new values into a microcomputer's stack by pushing onto it. However, pulling is nondestructive to the stack. Unlike pulling trays off a stack, pulling a value from the microcomputer's stack doesn't remove it from the stack. If we examine stack locations before and after pulling, we find their contents to be the same.

The stack is useful in programming whenever we want to temporarily "stash" the contents of an accumulator and then retrieve them. The 6800 has only two accumulators. When we're writing large programs, there may be times when two

FIGURE 11.1.3 A Three-Level Nested Timing Loop with only ACCA as Counter, Using Stack

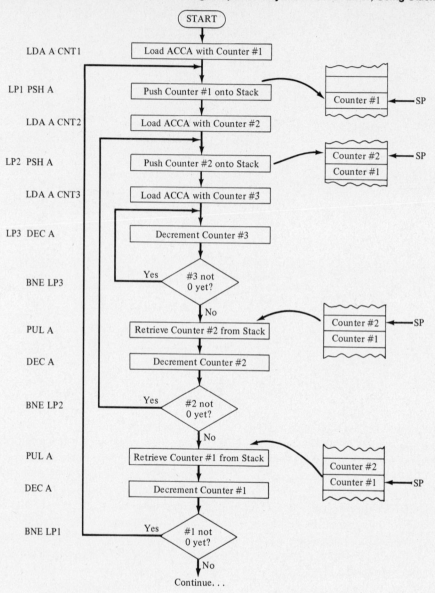

accumulators just aren't enough. In that case we can "borrow" one by pushing its contents onto the stack, using the accumulator, then pulling the old contents back from the stack.

Figure 11.1.3 is a flowchart for a three-level nested timing loop that uses only one accumulator for all three counters. We accomplish this by pushing each of the two outer counter values onto the stack before loading ACCA with the inner counter value. Note that we don't need to push counter #3 because it will be decremented to zero in loop 3. When loop 3 has finished executing, counter #2 is pulled from the stack, decremented once and tested, and then (if it isn't zero yet) its new value is pushed onto the stack again so that accumulator A can be reloaded with counter 3.

When counter 2 does reach zero, the stack pointer is pointing to counter 1 and is retrieved from the stack, decremented, tested, and if not zero, pushed onto the stack so that accumulator A can be initialized for another pass through loop 2. We can construct as many levels of loops as we like, as long as each counter value is pulled before decrementing and pushed on entering the next level of inner loop.

Next, we'll see how the microprocessor uses the stack to implement subroutines.

11.2 SUBROUTINES AND THE STACK

We said that when the microprocessor finishes executing the subroutine, it must be directed back to the main program. To keep track of where it stopped executing the main program to execute a subroutine, it pushes the program counter contents onto the stack. This frees the program counter for subroutine use. After the microprocessor finishes executing the subroutine, it pulls the old program counter contents from the stack, places them in the program counter, and resumes executing the main program.

To understand the sequences involved in getting back and forth between a program and a subroutine, we'll next look at the 6800's subroutine instructions.

Subroutine Instructions

These three instructions are listed in Table 11.2.1. Two of them, BSR and JSR, were introduced briefly but without explanation in Chapter 8. Now we'll learn how to use them and their companion, RTS, to implement subroutines.

TABLE 11.2.1   Subroutine Instructions

Mnemonic	Instruction Name	Addressing Modes
BSR	BRANCH TO SUBROUTINE	RELATIVE
JSR	JUMP TO SUBROUTINE	INDEXED, EXTENDED
RTS	RETURN FROM SUBROUTINE	INHERENT

FIGURE 11.2.1 Transfer of Control in a Subroutine Call

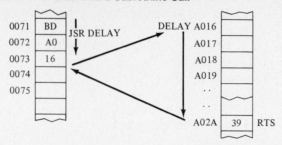

The two instructions BSR and JSR are **calling instructions**. When we **call** a subroutine, we transfer control from the main program, the **calling program**, to the subroutine. Both these instructions automatically cause the microprocessor to save the current program counter contents before executing the transfer of control. The difference between these instructions is that JSR uses the extended addressing mode and therefore has unlimited range, whereas BSR uses the relative mode and has a limited range of -128 to $+127$ addresses. We'd usually use BSR unless the subroutine were outside this limited range.

The instruction RTS is a **return instruction**. When we *return* from a subroutine, we transfer control from the subroutine back to the calling program. Note that RTS uses the inherent mode and therefore has no operand. A subroutine always ends with RTS.

Figure 11.2.1 illustrates pictorially a transfer of control during a subroutine call and return. At location $0071 the microprocessor encounters the JSR instruction (OP code $BD) and, when it fetches the entire instruction ((PC)=$0074), it saves the program counter contents and then transfers control to DELAY by loading the program counter with $A016. The subroutine is executed until the microprocessor encounters RTS ($39) in location $A02A. Then control is transferred back to the calling program at the point where it left off ($0074) by restoring the saved $0074 to the program counter.

The JSR and BSR Instructions

Turning to the JSR information sheet, we see first that there are two addressing modes available: extended and indexed. Next, we see that JSR is a very busy instruction, with five register transfer statements that describe its operation. The new notation we saw in the PSH instruction—the arrow pointing down—is used here again in some of the statements.

Translating all of the register transfer statements, we have:

1. $\downarrow$(PCL)   The contents of the low-order byte of the program counter are pushed onto the stack.

2. (SP)$\leftarrow$(SP)-0001 The stack pointer contents are decremented.

3. ↓(PCH)   The contents of the high-order byte of the program counter are pushed onto the stack.

4. (SP)←(SP)−0001 The stack pointer contents are decremented.

5. (PC)←operand   The operand of JSR is loaded into the PC.

The operations described by these register transfer statements take place exactly in the preceding order. To illustrate this sequence of events, let's take this program segment:

```
ORG   #$0
LDS   #$FF
JSR   $A037
```

Figure 11.2.2 diagrams the functions of the JSR instruction as they are listed by the register transfer statements above. First, we see that the program starts at location $0000 and that the original stack pointer contents are $00FF, shown at START on

FIGURE 11.2.2 JSR Register Transfer Statements Illustrated

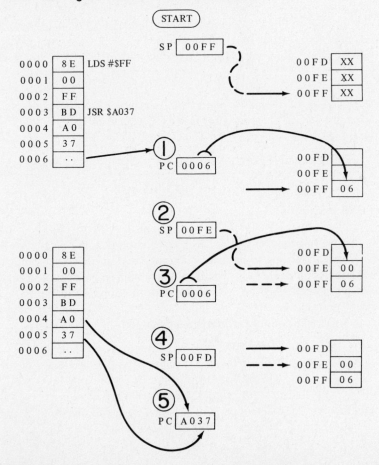

the figure. At (1) the program counter contents are $0006. The contents of PCL, $06, are pushed onto the stack at the location the stack pointer is pointing to ($00FF). At (2) the contents of the stack pointer are decremented to $00FE. At (3) the contents of PCH, $00, are pushed onto the stack at the location the stack pointer is pointing to ($00FE). At (4) the contents of the stack pointer are decremented to $00FD. At (5) the address of the subroutine, $A037, is loaded into the program counter. After the JSR is executed, the stack pointer contents are $00FD, because they were decremented twice.

All this happens automatically with the JSR (and BSR) instruction. We, the users, don't have to keep track of or do anything about it, but we should know what the microprocessor is doing so that we can use the stack ourselves.

EXAMPLE 11.2.1

For this program segment:

```
LDS  #$3FF
BSR  PONY
```

assume the subroutine PONY is located at $0047 and the LDS instruction starts at $0021. After execution of the BSR instruction, state (a) the stack pointer contents; (b) the contents of locations $03FE and $03FF; and (c) the new PC contents.

Solution

(a) Before execution of the BSR instruction, the stack pointer contains $03FF. Decrementing this twice gives us $03FD. (b) Location $03FE contains $00 and $03FF contains $26. (c) Since PONY = $0047, then (PC) = $0047.

Answer: (a) $03FD; (b) ($03FE) = $00, ($03FF) = $26; (c) (PC) = $0047

The RTS Instruction

Now that we've been through the JSR instruction in some detail, the RTS will be somewhat easier. Turning to its instruction information sheet, we see that it uses the inherent addressing mode only. The RTS instruction has only four instead of five register transfer statements. And we see the same notation as in the PUL instruction: an arrow pointing up.

We can write translations for all the statements:

1. $(SP) \leftarrow (SP) + 0001$ The stack pointer contents are incremented.
2. $\uparrow(PCH)$ The top value is pulled from the stack and placed in the high-order byte of the PC.
3. $(SP) \leftarrow (SP) + 0001$ The stack pointer contents are incremented.
4. $\uparrow(PCL)$ The top value is pulled from the stack and placed in the low-order byte of the PC.

FIGURE 11.2.3 RTS Register Transfer Statements Illustrated

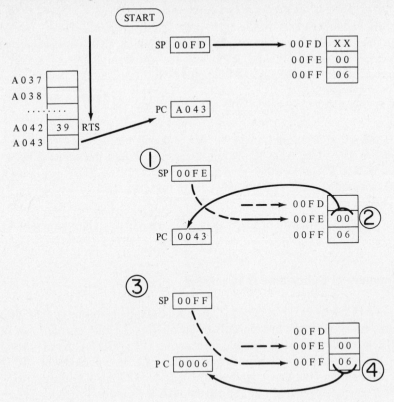

Figure 11.2.3 diagrams the functions of the RTS instruction. In this figure we assume the same conditions as those in Figure 11.2.2: that is, the stack pointer contains $00FD and locations $00FE and $00FF contain $00 and $06, respectively. The microprocessor executes the subroutine until it encounters the RTS instruction (OP code $39) in location $A042. At that time (PC)=$A043. At START the stack pointer is pointing at $00FD, which contains some value but not one that we're interested in. At (1) the stack pointer contents are incremented to $00FE. At (2) the value $00 is pulled from the stack and placed in PCH. At (3) the stack pointer contents are incremented to $00FF. And at (4) the value $06 is pulled from the stack and placed in PCL. We have reversed the process of pushing almost exactly, but not quite. The stack pointer contents are now the same as they were before the subroutine call, and (PC) has the value it had before the subroutine call. But the contents of $00FE and $00FF don't have their original values restored, because of the destructive nature of the push operation.

EXAMPLE 11.2.2

Assume the conditions left by the BSR instruction in Exercise 11.2.2 are present when the microprocessor encounters the RTS instruction. Give (a) the stack pointer contents after execution of the RTS; (b) the program counter contents after execution of the RTS; and (c) the contents of locations $03FE and $03FF after execution of the RTS.

Solution

(a) The stack pointer contents were $03FD and will be incremented twice by the RTS: $03FF. (b) PCH is contained in $03FE and has the value $00; PCL is contained in $03FF and has the value $26. Therefore (PC)=$0026. (c) Pulling PCH and PCL from the stack does not remove them from the stack, so ($03FE)=$00 and ($03FF)=$26.

Answer: (a) (SP)=$03FF; (b) (PC)=$0026; (c) ($03FE)=$00, ($03FF)=$26

Summary of Subroutine Instructions

Figure 11.2.4 gives a bird's-eye view of what happens during a subroutine call and return. At START, the microprocessor encounters the JSR instruction (OP code $BD). When it has fetched the whole instruction, (PC)=$0074. At (1) the old PC contents are saved by pushing onto the stack, PCL and then PCH. At (2) the program counter gets the new contents ($A016). At (3) control is transferred to the subroutine, which is executed until at (4) the RTS instruction is encountered. Then, at (5), the old PC contents are pulled from the stack, PCH first, and loaded into the program counter. Finally, at (6), control is returned to the calling program.

Like pushing with PSH, pushing onto the stack by a subroutine instruction is destructive to the stack. And like pulling with PUL, getting back the PC contents doesn't remove them from the stack. We see in Figure 11.2.4 that the old PC contents, $00 and $74, are still there after the RET has been executed.

Any program that uses subroutines should always load the stack pointer. As seen with the PSH and PUL instructions, keeping the stack as far as possible from the rest of the program prevents the program from being destroyed when a subroutine call pushes onto the stack. Like other registers and like RAM locations, the stack pointer will have a random value in it when the microprocessor is powered up. So during a subroutine call the microprocessor will be pushing the program counter contents wherever the stack pointer happens to be pointing. If it's pointing to a ROM location, the push won't work. Later when the RTS instruction is executed, wrong values from the ROM location will be loaded into the PC. If the stack pointer is pointing to a location that's part of a program's instructions, the program will be ruined.

FIGURE 11.2.4 Transfer of Control to and from Subroutine

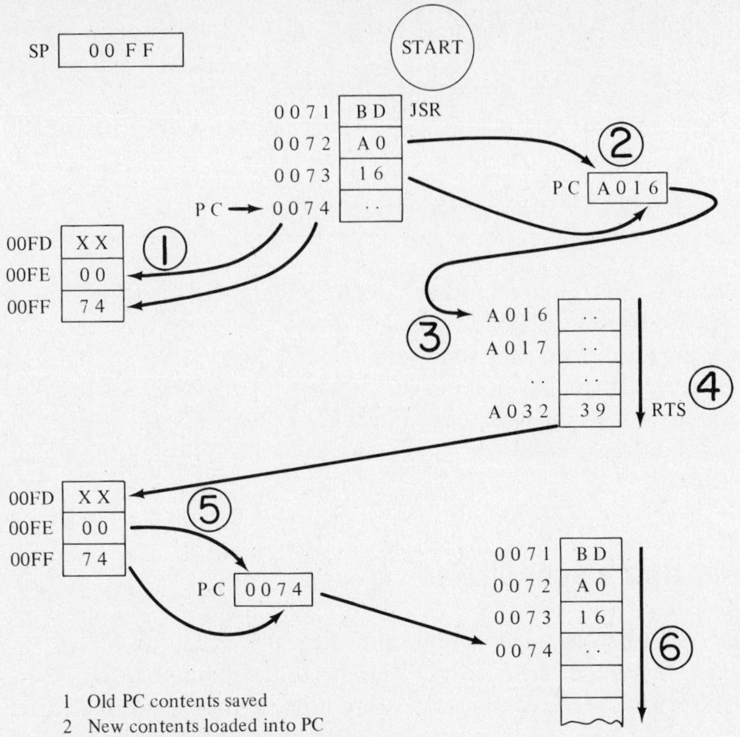

1 Old PC contents saved
2 New contents loaded into PC
3 Control transferred to subroutine
4 RTS causes µp to access stack
5 Old PC contents restored
6 Control transferred to calling program

EXAMPLE 11.2.3

For this program segment:

```
ORG   $100
BSR   CONFIG
```

no LDS statement has been given. Suppose the stack pointer were loaded with the random value $009D which by chance just happens to be in the middle of our table of squares of Table 10.2.1. (a) After execution of BSR, would any values in the table be changed? If so, give the locations and their new contents. (b) When the subroutine CONFIG has finished execution with the RTS instruction, will control be transferred back to the correct location in the calling program? If not, give the new program counter contents.

Solution

(a) Looking at the table of squares, we find that $009D contains the value $31. When (PCL) is pushed into this location, $31 will be removed and replaced by $02. And $009C will contain $01 (PCH) instead of $24. (b) The correct values would be pulled by the RTS instruction, so control will be transferred back to the correct location.

Answer: (a) ($009C)=$01, ($009D)=$02. (b) Yes.

We see that our table of squares would be tampered with in this case. If our program needed to use the table, we might get some strange answers.

Some monitors load the stack pointer and keep track of it for themselves and for the user. Others have one value they use for themselves—usually in system RAM—and leave it to the user to load his or her own value in user RAM. If you're not sure which of these applies to your system, it's always safe to just load the stack pointer yourself.

11.3 CREATING A SUBROUTINE

A routine doesn't become a subroutine automatically. When we make a routine into a subroutine, we have to satisfy two obligations to the main program. First, when the microprocessor finishes executing the subroutine, it must be directed back to the main program. Second, the subroutine mustn't cause the microprocessor to destroy any data that might be needed by the main program.

To satisfy the first obligation, we use the 6800's subroutine instructions.

Using Subroutine Instructions

To make a subroutine out of a routine, we must give it a label at its beginning and an RTS at its end. The calling program must contain either JSR or BSR at the point in the program where the subroutine is to be called.

EXAMPLE 11.3.1

Use JSR and RTS to modify the blinking sign program (Figure 9.4.5) so that the 1-sec delay is a subroutine. Give only those portions of the program that are different. Call the subroutine DELAY and cause it to delay for a fixed time of 1 sec.

Solution

A subroutine must begin with an identifying label and end with RTS. To cause a fixed delay of 1 sec, we substitute some immediate value (the value for 1 sec) for the variable VAL. Then, our subroutine is

```
DELAY  LDX  #VAL    LOAD COUNTER WITH 1-SEC VALUE
COUNT  NOP          STALL FOR TIME
       DEX          DECREMENT COUNTER
       BNE  COUNT   STILL COUNTING?
       RTS          NO, RETURN TO CALLING PROGRAM
```

Now, we must insert JSR DELAY in the main program after Line 210. We remove the subroutine to its own program space, so the main program segment looks like this:

```
210  STA A  CRA    NOW DRA READY FOR OUTPUT
220  JSR    DELAY  GO WAIT 1 SEC
230  COM    DRA    TOGGLE SIGN SWITCH
```

Now, let's figure out with what value to load the counter. If we were satisfied to delay for approximately 1 sec, we could just load VAL with #F017, the previous value for 1 sec. But for more precise measurements, we should note that the timing has been changed slightly by making the routine into a subroutine. From the time the microprocessor "leaves" the main program to delay, it must execute JSR DELAY (9 cycles) and RTS (5 cycles) in addition to the instructions in the delay routine. These subroutine instructions contribute to the time of the delay.

Total no. of cycles needed: $10^6 \, \mu sec/1.627 \, \mu sec/cycle = 614{,}629$ cycles

Instructions executed once:

JSR	9 cycles
LDX (IMM)	3 cycles
RTS	5 cycles
COM	6 cycles
BRA	4 cycles
	27 cycles

Cycles left for loop = $614{,}629 - 27 = 614{,}602$ cycles

$614{,}602$ cycles/10 cycles/loop = $61{,}460.2$ loops, rounded to 61,460 loops

Convert to hexadecimal: $F014 (Value for VAL)

(Note that we don't have to identify the return point (line 230) with any label. The JSR instruction causes the microprocessor to keep track of the return point.)

Answer: See preceding solution.

The subroutine may be at higher or at lower memory than the calling program. Often subroutines are placed at the end of an assembly language program, but they can also be at the beginning. In this example we could have used BSR instead of JSR as long as the subroutine were located within the range of -128 to $+127$ addresses.

Figure 11.3.1 shows a flowchart for the blinking sign program modified to use two subroutines: CONFIG and DELAY. This flowchart is simpler than that of Figure 9.4.5 because we assume that the subroutines have been documented elsewhere. In this figure we've introduced the subroutine task box with its characteristic shape.

FIGURE 11.3.1 Blinking Sign Flowchart Using Subroutines

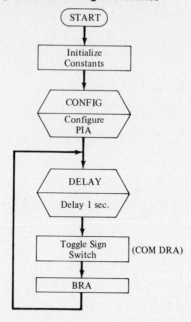

FIGURE 11.3.2 Blinking Sign Program Using Subroutines

```
100                NAM     BLKSUB
110     ;THIS PROGRAM CAUSES A NEON SIGN TO BLINK OFF AND ON AT
120     ;ONE-SECOND INTERVALS USING THE MOTOROLA D2.
124     ;THE SWITCH IS WIRED TO DA0. SUBROUTINES ARE USED.
130     CRA        EQU     $8005
140     DRA        EQU     $8004
150     DDRA       EQU     DRA
155                LDS     #$FF      INITIALIZE STACK POINTER
160     START      BSR     CONFIG    GO CONFIGURE PIA
170     CONT       JSR     DELAY     DELAY 1 SEC
180                COM     DRA       TOGGLE SIGN SWITCH
190                BRA     CONT      CONTINUE BLINKING
195     ;;;;;;;;;;;;;;;;;;
200     ;THIS SUBROUTINE CONFIGURES THE PIA FOR DA0 OUT
210     CONFIG     CLR     CRA       ADDRESS DDRA
220                LDA A   #$1       READY TO CONFIGURE DA0 OUT
230                STA A   DDRA      DA0 IS OUTPUT
240                LDA A   #$4       READY TO ADDRESS DRA
250                STA A   CRA       NOW DRA READY FOR OUTPUT
260                RTS               RETURN TO CALLING PROGRAM
265     ;;;;;;;;;;;;;;;;;;
270     ;THIS SUBROUTINE CAUSES A 1-SEC DELAY
280     DELAY      LDX     #$F014    LOAD COUNTER WITH 1-SEC VALUE
290     COUNT      NOP               STALL FOR TIME
300                DEX               DECREMENT COUNTER
310                BNE     COUNT     STILL COUNTING?
320                RTS               NO, RETURN TO CALLING PROGRAM
330                END
```

We write the name of the subroutine at the top of the box and what it does underneath. Note that the subroutine CONFIG is used only once in the program, but DELAY is used over and over.

Figure 11.3.2 shows the program for the flowchart of Figure 11.3.1. We see that the main program occupies only lines 160 through 190. The subroutines will use the same labels as those defined by the main program in lines 130 through 150. Line 155 loads the stack pointer, as we know is necessary when using the stack with or without subroutines. In line 160 control is transferred to the subroutine CONFIG (line 210). RTS, in line 260, transfers control back to the main program at line 170.

FIGURE 11.3.3 BLKSUB Assembly Listing

```
BLKSUB
M6800 ASSEMBLER LISTING VERSION 1.6     26 NOV 80 20:10   PAGE     2
BLKSUB   DAT    26 NOV 80 20:09

                    3 ;THIS PROGRAM CAUSES A NEON SIGN TO BLINK OFF AND ON AT
                    4 ;ONE-SECOND INTERVALS USING THE MOTOROLA D2.
                    5 ;THE SWITCH IS WIRED TO DA0. SUBROUTINES ARE USED.
8005                6 CRA      EQU     $8005
8004                7 DRA      EQU     $8004
8004                8 DDRA     EQU     DRA
0000 8E 00 FF       9        LDS     #$FF        INITIALIZE STACK POINTER
0003 8D 08         10 START   BSR     CONFIG      GO CONFIGURE PIA
0005 BD 00 1B      11 CONT    JSR     DELAY       DELAY 1 SEC
0008 73 80 04      12        COM     DRA         TOGGLE SIGN SWITCH
000B 20 F8         13        BRA     CONT        CONTINUE BLINKING
                   14 ;;;;;;;;;;;;;;;;;;;
                   15 ;THIS SUBROUTINE CONFIGURES THE PIA FOR DA0 OUT
000D 7F 80 05      16 CONFIG  CLR     CRA         ADDRESS DDRA
0010 86 01         17        LDA A   #$1         READY TO CONFIGURE DA0 OUT
0012 B7 80 04      18        STA A   DDRA        DA0 IS OUTPUT
0015 86 04         19        LDA A   #$4         READY TO ADDRESS DRA
0017 B7 80 05      20        STA A   CRA         NOW DRA READY FOR OUTPUT
001A 39            21        RTS                 RETURN TO CALLING PROGRAM
                   22 ;;;;;;;;;;;;;;;;;
                   23 ;THIS SUBROUTINE CAUSES A 1-SEC DELAY
001B CE F0 14      24 DELAY   LDX     #$F014      LOAD COUNTER WITH 1-SEC VALUE
001E 02            25 COUNT   NOP                 STALL FOR TIME
001F 09            26        DEX                 DECREMENT COUNTER
0020 26 FC         27        BNE     COUNT       STILL COUNTING?
0022 39            28        RTS                 NO, RETURN TO CALLING PROGRAM
0023              29        END

NO STATEMENTS FLAGGED

CROSS-REFERENCE TABLE

CONFIG      000D      16      10
CONT        0005      11      13
COUNT       001E      25      27
CRA         8005       6      16      20
DDRA        8004       8      18
DELAY       001B      24      11
DRA         8004       7       8      12
START       0003      10
```

Then a JSR transfers control to the subroutine DELAY (line 270) and RTS (line 320) transfers control back to the main program at line 180.

We put in a line of comment before each subroutine for the purpose of documentation. In that way, someone reading the program will know where each subroutine begins and what it does. Here, we put the subroutines after the main program, but it wasn't necessary. We could have put them at the beginning. Also, the subroutines don't have to be listed in the order in which they are called. Note that the assembler directive END appears at the very end of all the code and not at the end of the main program.

Figure 11.3.3 gives the assembly listing for BLKSUB.

Saving Register Contents

A subroutine has a second obligation to a main program: it mustn't destroy any data being used by the main program.

Why should this be a problem? Suppose, for instance, the main program used accumulator A as a loop counter. Somewhere in the loop it used a subroutine, which also used accumulator A, but for another purpose. As soon as the subroutine was executed, the main program's counter value would be replaced by the subroutine's value. Then the main program couldn't execute its loop the correct number of times. Thus the subroutine could destroy the main program's data.

A subroutine almost always uses one or more registers, as does the main program. The main program and the subroutines must share the 6800's registers, because the 6800 doesn't have enough registers for each program and subroutine to have its own.

In Chapter 10 we encountered a similar problem in the program MSSAGE (Figure 10.3.11) where the index register was used as a loop counter in the delay loop. To save the index register contents needed to access the digit table, we stored those contents in a temporary location (TEMPXR) and restored them after the delay loop had been executed. To be of universal value, a subroutine should do this for all the registers it uses.

We don't usually know exactly where or how many times a subroutine will be called in a main program. A properly written subroutine should be usable anywhere in any program regardless of what registers the main program uses. Therefore a subroutine should assume the main program will already be using any registers that the subroutine needs. To keep from destroying the main program's data, the subroutine with its first instruction(s) should save the contents of all registers it uses. Then its last instruction(s) before the RTS should be to restore those register contents.

To make a subroutine out of the delay routine of Figure 10.3.11, we'd write it like this:

```
DELAY   STX   TEMPXR   SAVE XR CONTENTS
        LDX   #$780C   LOAD COUNTER WITH 0.5-SEC VALUE
```

```
COUNT  NOP            STALL FOR TIME
       DEX            DECREMENT COUNTER
       BNE    COUNT   STILL COUNTING?
       LDX    TEMPXR  NO, RESTORE XR CONTENTS
       RTS            AND RETURN TO CALLING PROGRAM
```

(Here, we've neglected the extra time added to the delay by the JSR and RTS instructions.) In this case we know that the label TEMPXR has already been defined and 2 bytes saved for it in the calling program. When we write a calling program, we can establish temporary storage for registers in case they are needed. The program can always be pared down later.

EXAMPLE 11.3.2

Modify the message program (Figure 10.3.11) so that the PIA is configured by a subroutine called CONFIG. CONFIG should save and restore all registers it uses. Show appropriate lines of the calling program that would be inserted or changed, and show appropriate statements in the calling program that define temporary locations for saving registers.

Solution

Looking at the program, we see that the routine to configure the PIA uses accumulator A, so that's the register we need to save in the first line of the subroutine. We restore it again just before RTS.

Saving the contents of the accumulators is easier than saving other registers' contents. We can save (ACCA) and (ACCB) by pushing them onto the stack. Then we can pull them just before the RTS. (Unfortunately, there are no instructions that push the contents of the index register or stack pointer onto the stack.)

```
CONFIG  PSH A           SAVE USER ACCA CONTENTS
        CLR    CRB      ADDRESS DDRB
        LDA A  #$FF     READY TO SET SIDE B ALL OUTPUTS
        STA A  DDRB     SIDE B ALL OUT
        LDA A  #$04     READY TO ADDRESS DRB
        STA A  CRB      READY TO OUTPUT DATA
        PUL A           RESTORE USER ACCA CONTENTS
        RTS             RETURN TO CALLING PROGRAM
```

The calling program would contain these lines:

```
220  ORG  $0       START PROGRAM AT LOCATION 0000
230  BSR  CONFIG   GO CONFIGURE PIA
```

Answer: See preceding solution.

Figure 11.3.4 shows a flowchart and Figure 11.3.5, a program, for the message program adapted to use subroutines and with the subroutines saving the contents of all registers they use. Also, statements are included to reserve space for temporary storage of the index register. Any labels or constant values the subroutine uses have to be defined by the main program. Here, the table DGTBL was set up for the subroutine by the main program. The DELAY subroutine didn't need any data.

FIGURE 11.3.4 MSSAGE Program, with Subroutines

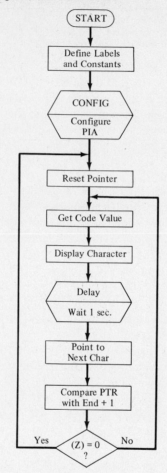

Pushing and pulling within a subroutine won't interfere with the subroutine use of the stack, as long as we observe these rules:

1. For every PSH, there must be a PUL.
2. Each PUL must have been preceded by a PSH.

Thus these are all right:

...PSH PSH PSH... PUL PUL PUL
...PSH PUL PSH PUL...

But not these:

...PUL PUL PUL... PSH PSH PSH
...PUL PSH PUL PSH...

FIGURE 11.3.5   Displaying a One-Digit Message, with Subroutines

```
100                 NAM     MSGSUB
110     ;THIS PROGRAM SPELLS OUT A MESSAGE IN A 7-SEGMENT DISPLAY
120     ;WITH EACH LETTER ON FOR 0.5 SEC AND A BLANK OF 0.5 SEC
130     ;BETWEEN LETTERS. DISPLAY IS WIRED TO DRB.
140     CRB     EQU     $8007
150     DRB     EQU     $8006
160     DDRB    EQU     DRB
170             ORG     $C0             START DIGIT TABLE AT 00C0
180     DGTBL   FCB     $09,$7F,$06,$7F,$47,$7F,$47,$7F,$40,$7F
210     TEMPXR  RMB     2               SAVE 2 BYTES FOR TEMP XR STORAGE
220             ORG     $0              START PROGRAM AT LOCATION 0000
225             LDS     #$FF            INITIALIZE STACK
230             BSR     CONFIG          GO CONFIGURE PIA
240     RESET   LDX     #DGTBL          POINT TO START OF DIGIT TABLE
250     GETCHR  LDA A   0,X             GET CODE VALUE FROM TABLE
260             STA A   DRB             OUTPUT IT TO DRB TO DISPLAY CHARACTER
270             BSR     DELAY           HOLD IT 0.5 SEC
280             INX                     POINT TO NEXT CHARACTER
290             CPX     #$CA            COMPARE WITH LAST ADDRESS+1
300             BNE     GETCHR          STILL MORE CHARACTERS?
310             BRA     RESET           NO, RESET AND PLAY AGAIN
320     ;THIS SUBROUTINE CONFIGURES THE PIA FOR SIDE B ALL OUTPUTS
330     CONFIG  PSH A                   SAVE USER ACCA CONTENTS
340             CLR     CRB             ADDRESS DDRB
350             LDA A   #$FF            READY TO SET SIDE B ALL OUTPUTS
360             STA A   DDRB            SIDE B ALL OUT
370             LDA A   #$04            READY TO ADDRESS DRB
380             STA A   CRB             READY TO OUTPUT DATA
390             PUL A                   RESTORE USER'S ACCA VALUE
400             RTS                     RETURN TO CALLING PROGRAM
410     ;THIS SUBROUTINE CAUSES A DELAY OF 0.5 SEC
420     DELAY   STX     TEMPXR          SAVE USER'S XR CONTENTS
430             LDX     #$780C          LOAD COUNTER WITH VALUE FOR 0.5 SEC
440     COUNT   NOP                     STALL FOR TIME
450             DEX                     DECREMENT COUNTER
460             BNE     COUNT           STILL COUNTING?
470             LDX     TEMPXR          NO, RESTORE USER'S XR CONTENTS
480             RTS                     AND RETURN TO CALLING PROGRAM
490             END
```

From this we see that it's all right to have a subroutine within a subroutine, because each subroutine pushes twice before executing and pulls twice after executing. **Nested subroutines** contain subroutines within subroutines. We can have as many levels of nested subroutines as we like.

EXAMPLE 11.3.3

Verify that the instructions PSH A and PUL A within the subroutine CONFIG will cause no error in the subroutine's return to the main program. That is, trace the contents of the PC, the stack pointer, and the stack locations from the BSR to the RTS.

FIGURE 11.3.6 MSGSUB Assembly Listing

MSGSUB
M6800 ASSEMBLER LISTING VERSION 1.6   26 NOV 80 20:05   PAGE   2
MSGSUB   DAT   26 NOV 80 20:04

```
                      3 ;THIS PROGRAM SPELLS OUT A MESSAGE IN A 7-SEGMENT DISPLAY
                      4 ;WITH EACH LETTER ON FOR 0.5 SEC AND A BLANK OF 0.5 SEC
                      5 ;BETWEEN LETTERS. DISPLAY IS WIRED TO DRB.
8007                  6 CRB     EQU   $8007
8006                  7 DRB     EQU   $8006
8006                  8 DDRB    EQU   DRB
0000                  9         ORG   $C0          START DIGIT TABLE AT 00C0
00C0 09 7F 06 7F 10 DGTBL   FCB   $09,$7F,$06,$7F,$47,$7F,$47,$7F,$40,$7F
00C4 47 7F 47 7F 10
00C8 40 7F           10
00CA 00 00           11 TEMPXR  RMB   2            SAVE 2 BYTES FOR TEMP XR STORAGE
00CC                 12         ORG   $0           START PROGRAM AT LOCATION 0000
0000 8E 00 FF        13         LDS   #$FF         INITIALIZE STACK
0003 8D 12           14         BSR   CONFIG       GO CONFIGURE PIA
0005 CE 00 C0        15 RESET   LDX   #DGTBL       POINT TO START OF DIGIT TABLE
0008 A6 00           16 GETCHR  LDA A 0,X          GET CODE VALUE FROM TABLE
000A B7 80 06        17         STA A DRB          OUTPUT IT TO DRB TO DISPLAY CHARACTER
000D 8D 18           18         BSR   DELAY        HOLD IT 0.5 SEC
000F 08              19         INX                POINT TO NEXT CHARACTER
0010 8C 00 CA        20         CPX   #$CA         COMPARE WITH LAST ADDRESS+1
0013 26 F3           21         BNE   GETCHR       STILL MORE CHARACTERS?
0015 20 EE           22         BRA   RESET        NO, RESET AND PLAY AGAIN
                     23 ;THIS SUBROUTINE CONFIGURES THE PIA FOR SIDE B ALL OUTPUTS
0017 36              24 CONFIG  PSH A              SAVE USER ACCA CONTENTS
0018 7F 80 07        25         CLR   CRB          ADDRESS DDRB
001B 86 FF           26         LDA A #$FF         READY TO SET SIDE B ALL OUTPUTS
001D B7 80 06        27         STA A DDRB         SIDE B ALL OUT
0020 86 04           28         LDA A #$04         READY TO ADDRESS DRB
0022 B7 80 07        29         STA A CRB          READY TO OUTPUT DATA
0025 32              30         PUL A              RESTORE USER'S ACCA VALUE
0026 39              31         RTS                RETURN TO CALLING PROGRAM
                     32 ;THIS SUBROUTINE CAUSES A DELAY OF 0.5 SEC
0027 DF CA           33 DELAY   STX   TEMPXR       SAVE USER'S XR CONTENTS
0029 CE 78 0C        34         LDX   #$780C       LOAD COUNTER WITH VALUE FOR 0.5 SEC
002C 02              35 COUNT   NOP                STALL FOR TIME
002D 09              36         DEX                DECREMENT COUNTER
002E 26 FC           37         BNE   COUNT        STILL COUNTING?
0030 DE CA           38         LDX   TEMPXR       NO, RESTORE USER'S XR CONTENTS
0032 39              39         RTS                AND RETURN TO CALLING PROGRAM
0033                 40         END
```

NO STATEMENTS FLAGGED

CROSS-REFERENCE TABLE

CONFIG	0017	24	14	
COUNT	002C	35	37	
CRB	8007	6	25	29
DDRB	8006	8	27	
DELAY	0027	33	18	
DGTBL	00C0	10	15	
DRB	8006	7	8	17
GETCHR	0008	16	21	
RESET	0005	15	22	
TEMPXR	00CA	11	33	38

Solution

Figure 11.3.7 illustrates this example. First, calculate the value of the PC before the BSR is executed. The program starts at $0000. LDS #$FF takes $0000, $0001, and $0002. BSR takes $0003 and $0004, so after fetching BSR but before executing it, the PC should contain $0005, the address of LDX #DGTBL.

During the execution of BSR the following things occur: at (1) PCL is pushed onto the stack at location $00FF and (SP) is decremented. At (2) PCH is pushed onto the stack at location $00FE and (SP) is decremented. At (3) the address of CONFIG (whatever it is) is loaded into PC for the transfer of control. At the end of the BSR instruction, (SP)=$00FD.

Next, at (4) the PSH A pushes (ACCA) onto the stack at $00FD and decrements (SP) to $00FC. At (5) PUL A increments (SP) to $00FD and pulls its contents ($AA).

FIGURE 11.3.7 A Subroutine May Contain PSH Instructions Followed by Equal Numbers of PUL Instructions

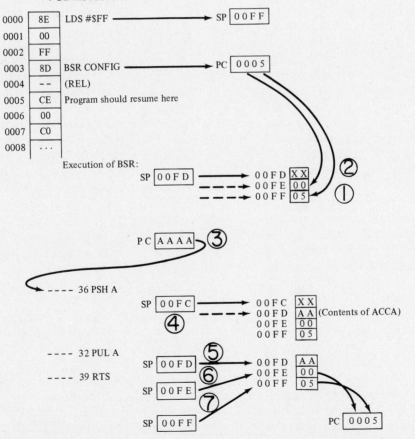

At (6) the RTS increments (SP) and pulls PCH ($00). At (7) (SP) is incremented and PCL is pulled ($05). The result is that the program counter does indeed contain $0005, the address of the next instruction in the main program.

Answer: See preceding solution.

From the diagram of Figure 11.3.6, we see why no errors were caused by the PSH and PUL instructions. The PUL put the SP back where it was before the PSH, almost as if nothing had happened.

11.4   PASSING PARAMETERS

Sometimes a subroutine doesn't need to have any data supplied to it. For instance, the 1-sec DELAY routine had its own data. But usually, we want a subroutine to operate on variable data that is supplied by the main program. In that case we need a mechanism of giving data, called **parameters**, to the subroutine and getting the results (more parameters) back afterward. Giving data to and getting data from subroutines is called **passing parameters**.

Suppose you've given some friends permission to use your ski cabin for a weekend. To get in, they need the key, and you won't see them before they plan to use it. You mutually agree on a location where you will secret the key, which they will retrieve. You also agree that they will return the key afterward by placing it in your mailbox, where you can retrieve it later.

In the same way, a main program and a subroutine mutually "agree" (or rather, the programmer causes them to agree) on a location or locations where the main program will store the data and the subroutine will retrieve it. Also, a location or locations are defined where the subroutine will store the results and the main program will retrieve them. The locations can be the same or they can be different.

One way of passing parameters is through an accumulator. For example, Figure 11.4.1 shows a modification of the square program used as a subroutine. The number to be squared is left in accumulator A by the main program. The subroutine takes the number, finds its square, and leaves the square in accumulator A before returning to the main program.

Another way of passing parameters is through memory locations. The program of Figure 11.4.1 uses this method, too. The memory locations XRH and XRL are defined by the main program and used by the subroutine to locate the square on the table. The MSGSUB program (Figure 11.3.5) also uses memory locations to pass parameters. The main program defines locations CRB, DRB, DDRB, and TEMPA, which are used by the subroutine CONFIG.

If we have a lot of parameters to pass—for example, a list of numbers to be searched—it's not convenient to pass the numbers themselves. Instead, we usually pass a pointer that tells where the numbers are. Figure 11.4.2 shows the search program modified into a subroutine. The main program establishes a place for the

FIGURE 11.4.1 Parameters Passed Through an Accumulator

```
MAIN PROGRAM
———
———
XRH        FCB         00              SET XRH AT 00
XRL        RMB         1               SAVE BYTE FOR XRL
———
———
SQTBL      FCB         ———(ETC)
———
———
           LDA A       #VBL            PUT VARIABLE INTO ACCA
           JSR         SQRSUB          GO GET SQUARE
———
———
;;;;;;;;;;;;;;;;;;;;;;;;;;;;;;;;;;;;;;;;;;
; SUBROUTINE SQRSUB TAKES A VALUE IN ACCUMULATOR A
; LOCATES ITS SQUARE ON THE SQTBL AND RETURNS THE
; RESULT IN ACCUMULATOR A
SQRSUB     STA A       XRL             PUT NO. TO BE SQUD IN XRL
           LDX         XRH             POINT TO ITS SQUARE
           LDA A       $96,X           PUT SQUARE INTO ACCA
           RTS                         AND RETURN.
;;;;;;;;;;;;;;;;;;;;;;;;;;;;;;;;;;;;;;;;;;
```

FIGURE 11.4.2 Passing a Set of Parameters via a Pointer

```
———
LIST       RMB         50              SAVE BYTES FOR LIST
LENGTH     RMB         1               SAVE BYTE FOR LENGTH
———
           LDX         #LIST           POINT TO START OF LIST
           LDA B       LENGTH          GET LENGTH
           DEC B                       SUBTRACT ONE FROM LENGTH
           BSR         SMLSUB          GO GET SMALLEST VALUE
———
———
;THIS SUBROUTINE SEARCHES A LIST FOR THE SMALLEST
;UNSIGNED VALUE. THE STARTING ADDRESS OF THE LIST
;IS IN THE INDEX REGISTER. THE LENGTH OF THE LIST
MINUS ONE
IS IN ACCB. THE SUBROUTINE RETURNS THE SMALLEST
VALUE IN ACCA.
SMLSUB     LDA A       0,X             GET RUNT
LOOK       INX                         POINT TO NEWNUM
           CMP A       0,X             COMPARE IT WITH RUNT
           BLS         NOSWP           UNLESS RUNT>NEWNUM, NO SWAP
           LDA A       0,X             REPLACE RUNT WITH NEWNUM
NOSWP      DEC B                       DECREMENT LIST LENGTH
           BNE         LOOK            STILL MORE LIST?
           RTS                         NO, RETURN RUNT IN ACCA
———
```

list and its length. Before calling the subroutine, it puts the starting address of the list into the index register and the length of the list into accumulator B. Note that we've varied the method of swapping in this subroutine, and also the method of telling when we've reached the end of the list. Because we're not asked to put RUNT at the top of the list, no values in the list will be destroyed if we just load ACCA with the current smallest value and don't save the contents of ACCA.

Instead of comparing the index register value with the end address, we use accumulator B as a counter to tell when we've reached the end of the list. We subtract one from the list length because we increment the index register once *before* decrementing ACCB. If we didn't subtract one from the list length, we'd leave out the last item on the list.

In the next chapter we'll see another important way that the microprocessor uses the stack.

REVIEW QUESTIONS

1. What is a **subroutine**?
2. What is a microprocessor's **stack**? What is **LIFO**? Give an example.
3. What is meant by pushing onto and pulling from the stack?
4. What is the **stack pointer**? How does it control the stack? How do we load, increment, decrement, and store the stack pointer?
5. Explain the register transfer statements of the PSH instruction. What does an arrow pointing down mean?
6. What does PSH do? List its operations in order. Is PSH destructive to the stack?
7. Does it matter where in memory we place the stack? Explain.
8. Explain the register transfer statements of the PUL instruction. What does an arrow pointing up mean?
9. What does PUL do? List its operations in order. Is PUL destructive to the stack?
10. Explain how to use the stack to swap the contents of accumulators A and B.
11. Do PSH and PUL access the stack and change the stack pointer contents in the same order? Explain.
12. Explain why the stack pointer is incremented before pulling but decremented after pushing.
13. Does pulling from the stack remove values from the stack? Explain.
14. Explain what is meant by a subroutine **call** and a calling program. What are the two calling instructions? Explain how they work and the difference between them.
15. Explain what is meant by **return**. What is the **return instruction**, and how does it work?
16. Explain the register transfer statements for the JSR and BSR instructions.
17. After executing the BSR or JSR instruction, by how many locations and in which direction have the stack pointer contents changed?
18. Explain the register transfer statements for the RTS instruction.
19. Answer the question in (17) for the RTS instruction.
20. Does the RTS instruction exactly reverse everything that happened during the BSR or JRS instruction? Explain.

21. Why is it important to load the stack pointer? Explain what might happen if the stack pointer were loaded with a random value.
22. Must a subroutine be at higher or lower memory than the calling program? Explain.
23. Why should a subroutine save the registers it uses? How can it do this?
24. What rules must we observe when using PSH and PUL within a subroutine? Explain.
25. What are **parameters**? What is meant by **passing parameters**?
26. Give some examples of passing parameters.

EXERCISES

Set A (answers at back of book)

1. Consider this program segment:

```
STKH     EQU   $A0D0
TMPSTK   EQU   $AA00
         LDS   STKH
         DES
         STS   TMPSTK
```

After execution of the preceding segment, it was found that (SP) = $01F1. What were the contents of locations $A0D0, $A0D1, $AA00, and $AA01?

2. Consider this program segment:

```
LDS     #$EE
CLR A
LDA B   #$FF
PSH A
PSH A
PSH B
```

After the microprocessor has executed this, (a) What locations will contain what new values? (b) What will be the contents of the stack pointer? (c) What will be the contents of ACCA and ACCB?

3. Given the following addresses and their contents:

```
00EC   EC
00ED   ED
00EE   EE
00EF   EF
00F0   F0
00F1   F1
00F2   F2
```

consider this program segment:

```
LDS     #$EF
PUL A
PUL B
STA A   $F2
PUL A
```

After the microprocessor has executed this, (a) What locations will contain what new values? (b) What will be the stack pointer contents? (c) What will be the contents of ACCA and ACCB?

4. In this program segment:

```
VAL   FCB   $00,$7F
      LDS   VAL
      BSR   DELAY
```

assume the LDS instruction begins at location $0034. The subroutine DELAY is at address $0059. Give (a) the stack pointer contents after execution of the LDS instruction; (b) the program counter contents after fetching but before executing the BSR instruction; (c) the program counter contents after executing the BSR instruction.

5. For Exercise 4, after execution of the BSR instruction, give (a) the stack pointer contents; (b) the locations where the old program counter contents have been stored.

6. For this program segment:

```
ORG   $0
LDS   #$A0
JSR   $0180
```

give (a) the contents of the stack pointer before and after execution of the JSR instruction; (b) The value of old PCL and PCH and the locations where they are stored following the JSR instruction.

7. Assume the conditions left by Exercise 6. After the microprocessor has executed a RTS instruction, (a) What are the stack pointer contents? (b) What are the PC contents? (c) From what locations were the PC contents pulled? (d) What values are contained in these locations now?

8. For this program segment:

```
ORG   $50
JSR   BUMP
```

no LDS statement has been given. Suppose the stack pointer were loaded with the random value E0A1, a ROM address, and the middle of our seven-segment code table (Table 10.2.2). After execution of the JSR, would any values in the table be changed? If so, give the locations and their new contents. (b) When the subroutine BUMP has finished execution with the RTS instruction, will control be transferred back to the correct location in the calling program? If not, give the new program counter contents.

9. Refer to Example 9.4.4. Use BSR and RTS to create a 1-min delay subroutine, called WAITM. Modify appropriate lines of the blinking sign program, Figure 9.4.3, to use WAITM as a subroutine.

10. Modify the subroutine in Exercise 9 so that it saves all registers it uses. Write appropriate statements in the calling program that define temporary locations for the registers saved.

11. Refer to Figure 11.3.6 and suppose the instructions PSH A and PUL A were in inverse order in the subroutine. Trace the contents of the PC, the SP, and the stack locations from the BSR to the RTS. Would there be an error in the subroutine's return to the main program?

12. Modify the example of Figure 11.4.1 so that the value to be squared is passed via location XRL.

13. Modify the example of Figure 11.4.2 so that the subroutine returns the smallest value in ACCB and the length of the list minus one is in ACCA.

EXERCISES

Set B (answers not given)

1. Consider this program segment:

```
KEEPST  EQU  $___
STACKH  FCB  $__,$__
        LDS   STACKH
        INS
        STS   KEEPST
```

We wish to load the stack pointer with the value $00FF and to store it in location $00A0. (a) Fill in the preceding blanks so that this is accomplished. (b) What is the value of the stack pointer contents after the segment has been executed?

2. Consider this program segment:

```
LDS    #$E019
LDA A  #$9
PSH A
DEC A
PSH A
PSH A
```

After the microprocessor has executed this, (a) What locations will contain what new values? (b) What will be the contents of the stack pointer? (c) What will be contained in ACCA?

3. Given the look-up table of squares (Table 10.2.1) and this program segment:

```
LDS    #$96
PUL A
PUL B
ABA
STA A  $40
```

After the microprocessor has executed this, (a) What locations will contain what new values? (b) What will be the stack pointer contents? (c) What will be the contents of ACCA and ACCB?

4. In this program segment:

```
NUM  EQU  $01FF
     LDS   #NUM
     JSR   COUNT
```

Assume the LDS instruction begins at location $0079 and the subroutine COUNT begins at location $00A7. (a) Give the contents of the stack pointer after executing the LDS instruction; (b) Give the contents of the program counter after fetching but before executing the JSR instruction; (c) Give the contents of the program counter after executing the JSR instruction.

5. For Exercise 4, after execution of the JSR instruction, give (a) the stack pointer contents; (b) the contents of locations $01FF and $01FE.

6. For this program segment:

```
ORG   $70
LDS   #$0300
BSR   DELAY
```

give (a) the contents of the stack pointer before and after execution of the BSR instruction; (b) the value of old PCL and PCH and the locations where they are stored following the JSR instruction.

7. Assume the conditions left by the BSR instruction in Exercise 6. After the microprocessor has executed a RTS instruction, (a) What are the stack pointer contents? (b) What are the PC contents? (c) From what locations were the PC contents pulled? (d) What values are contained in those locations now?

8. For this program segment:

```
ORG   $100
JSR   $0160
```

no LDS statement has been given. Suppose the stack pointer were loaded with the random value $0102. (a) After execution of the JSR, what values in what locations will be changed? (b) Will control be transferred to the subroutine at location $0160? Explain.

9. Refer to Example 9.3.5, and use BSR and RTS to create a subroutine that causes a fixed 0.853-sec delay, called WINK. (Assume the Motorola D2 kit is to be used.) Modify appropriate lines of the MSGSUB program (Figure 11.3.5) to cause a 0.853-sec wait between characters.

10. Modify the subroutine in Exercise 9 so that it saves all registers it uses. Write appropriate statements in the calling program that define temporary locations for the registers saved.

11. Refer to Figure 11.3.6, and suppose, in place of the PSH A and PUL A instructions, there were two PSH A instructions. Trace the contents of the PC, the SP, and the stack locations from the BSR to the RTS. Would there be an error in the subroutine's return to the main program?

12. Modify the example of Figure 11.4.1 so that the value to be squared is passed via a memory location called NUM.

13. Modify the example of Figure 11.4.2 so that the smallest value is returned via a memory location called SMALST.

PROGRAMMING IDEAS

1. Write a program to evaluate $y = 3 + 4x^2$, using a subroutine called SQUARE to evaluate the square of x with a look-up table.

2. Write a program that steps through a list of ASCII characters and checks each for odd parity. If odd parity is not found, branch to a subroutine called ERROR (not defined here). The list is terminated by an ASCII blank. Use a subroutine called PARITY to determine the parity of each character.

3. Modify Programming Idea #2, Chapter 10, so that the hexadecimal-to-BCD conversion is done with a subroutine called HEXBCD.

4. Modify Programming Idea #9, Chapter 10, to use a delay subroutine called DELAY and a subroutine called GETCHAR to get the codes from the character table.

5. Build a table of squares using a subroutine called SQUARE to square a number by adding it to itself. Build the table by pushing the result of SQUARE onto the stack starting at location $00A0.
6. Refer to Figure 11.1.3, and write a subroutine for a three-level set of nested timing loops where each loop uses accumulator A as a counter. Save each value of accumulator A by pushing and pulling from the stack. Make this into a subroutine. The time for each loop should be variable and this data should be passed by the calling program. Show also the calling segment of the main program.

12 Interrupts

LEARNING OBJECTIVES

After completing this chapter, you should be able to:

1. Give a definition, explanation, or example for each of these: *polling, interrupt, servicing, interrupt service routine, hardware interrupt, software interrupt, active low, falling edge, rising edge, edge triggered, level sensitive, mask, interrupt mask bit, interrupt vector, program environment, breakpoint, interrupt input, interrupt output, wire-ORing,* PIA *interrupt flag bits,* PIA *mask bits,* PIA *edge control bit, prioritize.*
2. Explain the functions, priorities, and uses of the reset, nonmaskable interrupt, and interrupt request lines.
3. Explain how interrupt vectors are used to transfer control to the service routine.
4. Explain how the microprocessor saves and restores the program environment before and after servicing an interrupt.
5. Explain and use in programs the instructions SEI, CLI, SWI, WAI, and RTI.
6. Describe the interrupt and reset pins of the PIA and explain how they can be connected to the MPU and to peripheral devices.
7. Describe the bits of the PIA control registers and use them to configure the PIA in a given way or to poll a set of devices.
8. Describe the sequence of events during PIA interrupts, and determine the conditions necessary for an interrupt to happen.
9. Write routines for polling and prioritizing devices and setting up for interrupts.
10. Write interrupt service routines that include turning off the interrupt.

Most computers can do only one thing at a time. This might seem hard to believe if we see a large computer center with many terminals all in use at once and employees continuously feeding and retrieving stacks of printout and punched cards. But a computer is very fast. All the activities that are going on "take turns" in getting the computer's attention. You may have noticed that a large computer may be a bit slow to respond during hours of peak usage.

A microprocessor is somewhat slower than a large computer but is still fast compared with human physiological responses. We've seen that a single instruction requires only a few microseconds to be executed, and we learned to use timing loops when the microprocessor needs to be slowed down. So a microprocessor is capable of being responsible for the performance of many tasks at once, provided that we, the users, supply it with a mechanism of apportioning its time among them.

Recall the surveillance program of Chapter 9. The program causes the micro-processor to ask each device, one at a time, whether it needs service. This process is called **polling**. In the surveillance program the microprocessor polls the 3 security switches continuously. While the microprocessor is running this program, it can't do anything else. Perhaps there might be a burglary, a fire, or a power failure on the average of once every 6 months. For the microprocessor to do nothing but poll the security switches all this time is inefficient. If we programmed a personal computer to monitor the security switches, we'd also want to use it for things other than for a burglary, fire, or power failure.

We can compare the polling process of the surveillance program with the situation of a schoolteacher in a classroom constantly inquiring whether there was a fire, and at the same time being unable to teach. Instead, we know that school functions proceed unless the fire alarm rings, and then the teachers and students go outside.

Instead of the microprocessor continually asking whether there is a burglary, fire, or power failure, we'd like these outside events to tell the microprocessor when and only when one of them was occurring and needed attention. In this chapter we'll discuss some ways of doing this.

12.1 INTERRUPT FEATURES OF THE 6800

The 6800 has the equivalent of "fire alarms," called **interrupts**, which allow for a temporary suspension of a computer's executing program so that it can deal with a higher-priority task. The computer **services** the interrupt by transferring control to a program, called an **interrupt service routine**, written especially for the situation that caused the interrupt. After servicing the interrupt, the computer restores control to the interrupted program at the point where it was interrupted.

We distinguish between **hardware interrupts**, which are caused by signals from external devices (such as a smoke alarm), and **software interrupts**, which are caused by instructions in a program.

Hardware Interrupts of the 6800

External devices can interrupt the 6800 MPU by means of three input pins. We haven't talked about the pins of the 6800 for awhile. Figure 12.1.1 shows once again a diagram of the 6800 and its pins. In Chapter 1 we covered all the pins of the

FIGURE 12.1.1   Pin-Out of the 6800 Showing Interrupt Lines

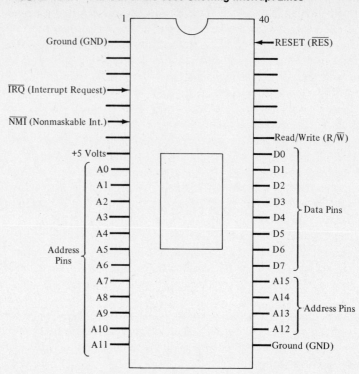

address bus and the data bus and a few of the control bus (ground, power, read/write). Now we're going to cover three more pins in the control bus: the interrupt pins.

The interrupt pins are called RESET ($\overline{\text{RES}}$), Nonmaskable Interrupt ($\overline{\text{NMI}}$), and Interrupt Request ($\overline{\text{IRQ}}$). Their abbreviations all have bars across them: $\overline{\text{IRQ}}$, $\overline{\text{NMI}}$, $\overline{\text{RES}}$. We read these, for example, "IRQ-bar," or "IRQ-not." A bar is placed over a symbol when that signal is **active low**, meaning that the function is performed when the line is at a low voltage and not when the line is at high voltage. Thus most of the time the $\overline{\text{IRQ}}$, $\overline{\text{NMI}}$, and $\overline{\text{RES}}$ lines would be high (inactive). For one of them to interrupt the MPU, its line must fall lów (active).

Throughout this chapter we'll adopt the convention of using the bar notation $\overline{\text{RES}}$, $\overline{\text{NMI}}$, and $\overline{\text{IRQ}}$ when talking about the pins (or lines) themselves. And we'll find it convenient to omit the bars (RES, NMI, IRQ) when talking about the corresponding interrupt.

The RESET pin is designed to be used by the microprocessor system, whereas the Interrupt Request and Nonmaskable Interrupt pins represent two lower priority levels of interrupt that can be used by the programmer. To illustrate priority levels, let's look at three common interrupting devices you might have in the house: the doorbell, the telephone, and a smoke alarm. Assuming you don't know who is on the other end of either, the doorbell and the telephone probably have about equal priority. If you were talking on the telephone and the doorbell rang, you'd have to decide whether to ignore the doorbell or answer it and vice versa. But if you were in the midst of answering the telephone or the doorbell and the fire alarm rang, you wouldn't ignore it. The fire alarm has higher priority than the doorbell or the telephone. You might disable the telephone and the doorbell temporarily to keep them from interrupting you while doing some important work. But you wouldn't disable the smoke alarm. Like these common devices, microprocessor interrupts can have different priority levels, too.

The RESET ($\overline{\text{RES}}$) line has the highest priority. Its function is for power-on initialization. When a microprocessor is first turned on, its program counter contains a random value. To execute its monitor program, the MPU's program counter must contain the starting address of the monitor program. Normally, a Reset button is wired to the $\overline{\text{RES}}$ line of the 6800. Pressing the Reset button pulls $\overline{\text{RES}}$ low and forces the starting address of the monitor program into the program counter. Then the microprocessor can execute the monitor program and we can communicate with the microprocessor via the keyboard and display. Also, often when executing a program on a microcomputer we end up in a continuous loop, either by accident or design. If you've been using either the Motorola D2 or the Heathkit trainer, you know how to get out of this situation: press the Reset button, and the display indicates that the monitor has regained control. This works because the Reset button is wired to the $\overline{\text{RES}}$ line of the 6800. Pressing Reset pulls that line low and activates the RESET pin, which in turn causes control to be transferred to the monitor program. RESET takes precedence over all other interrupts.

The chief difference between IRQ and NMI is whether or not they can be masked. When we **mask** an interrupt, we prevent it from happening. An executive can mask telephone interrupts by having a secretary hold all calls so that the executive doesn't hear the telephone. Similarly, we can mask the IRQ and prevent it from reaching the MPU. Just as we would never want to mask the smoke alarm, the nonmaskable interrupt, as its name implies, can't be masked. This difference lets us select an appropriate interrupt line according to what priority we place on an interrupting device. In a home computer system we might wire the $\overline{\text{NMI}}$ to the fire alarm and the $\overline{\text{IRQ}}$ to a less urgent function; say, a sensor that detected when the plants needed watering. In situations where priorities aren't so clearly defined, the $\overline{\text{IRQ}}$ line is usually reserved for programmer use so that the option of masking or not masking is available. For instance, the Motorola D2 uses the $\overline{\text{NMI}}$ for its E (escape) and N (single-step) functions and saves the $\overline{\text{IRQ}}$ for the user. The Heathkit trainer doesn't use either the $\overline{\text{NMI}}$ or the $\overline{\text{IRQ}}$ in its system; both may be used by the programmer.

Another difference between IRQ and NMI is in the way each is recognized by the MPU. Both are active low, but in the case of NMI it's the transition from high to low and not merely the state of being low that triggers the interrupt. Figure 12.1.2 illustrates this transition, called the **falling edge**. (The opposite of falling edge is the **rising edge**, which is a transition from low to high, also shown in Figure 12.1.2.)

FIGURE 12.1.2   NMI Is an Edge-Triggered Interrupt, While IRQ Is Level Sensitive

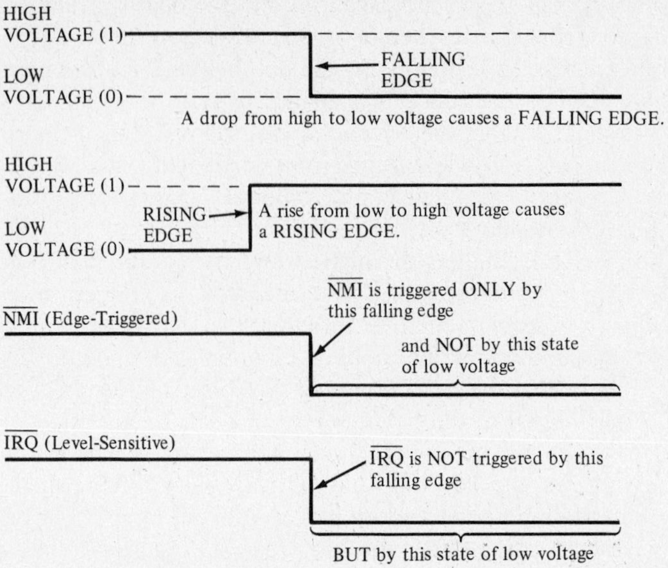

When a response is triggered by either the rising or the falling edge, we say that it is **edge-triggered**. Thus NMI is an edge-triggered interrupt. The MPU recognizes the NMI on the falling edge only. The NMI line might stay low for a time, but the MPU wouldn't recognize it more than once. Note that this prevents the NMI from interrupting itself. For the MPU to recognize the NMI a second time, the NMI line must go high and then low again.

In contrast with NMI, IRQ is **level-sensitive**, meaning that the MPU will respond when the line is at the appropriate level (high or low voltage). Because IRQ is active low, the MPU will respond when the IRQ line is at a low voltage. Just as an alarm will keep ringing until we turn it off, an IRQ will keep signaling the MPU as long as its line is low. To keep the IRQ from interrupting itself, the MPU "turns it off" by masking it against further IRQs.

But how do we and the MPU mask interrupts?

The Interrupt Mask Bit

The status register, diagrammed in Chapter 5, is shown once more in Figure 12.1.3. The **interrupt mask bit** (I), bit 4, is the only one we haven't already discussed. When this bit is set, the IRQ signal (but not the RES or the NMI) can't interrupt the MPU until the I bit is cleared.

Both the user and the microprocessor can control the interrupt mask bit. The two instructions, SEI (Set Interrupt Mask) and CLI (Clear Interrupt Mask) allow the user to determine the condition of this bit. The microprocessor controls the bit by

FIGURE 12.1.3   The Condition Code (Status) Register Featuring the Interrupt Mask

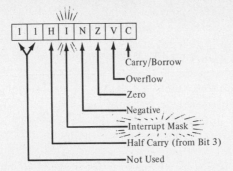

setting it *after* having received an interrupt signal but *before* starting to implement the interrupt service routine, in order to prevent further maskable interrupts from interrupting the microprocessor when it is already servicing an interrupt. Thus the IRQ is prevented from interrupting itself, because the microprocessor automatically sets the interrupt mask after it receives the IRQ. However, the NMI may interrupt the IRQ while the IRQ service routine is in progress. More about that later.

If we, the users, want to allow further interrupts while one is being serviced, we can countermand the microprocessor's setting of the I bit just by putting a CLI in our interrupt service routine.

But how does the microprocessor get to the interrupt service routines?

The Interrupt Vectors

The highest locations in a microcomputer's addressable memory are assigned to the **interrupt vectors**, which are locations assigned to interrupts and containing the starting address of their service routines. There are two vectors for each interrupt in the 6800: one for the low and one for the high-order byte of the address of its service routine. The actual values of the addresses assigned to the vectors depend on the particular microcomputer and its highest available address. Figure 12.1.4 shows the assignment of interrupt vectors for the 6800. The 6800 has four interrupts and each

FIGURE 12.1.4   Interrupt Vectors of the 6800 MPU Are Placed at the Eight Highest Available Addresses

Highest Address −7	IRQH	Interrupt Request
Highest Address −6	IRQL	
Highest Address −5	SWIH	Software Interrupt
Highest Address −4	SWIL	
Highest Address −3	NMIH	Nonmaskable Interrupt
Highest Address −2	NMIL	
Highest Address −1	RESH	RESET
Highest Address	RESL	

needs two addresses for its vector. So the highest eight addresses that are available are assigned to the interrupt vectors. We see from the figure that the RESET vector is at the highest two memory locations. The next is NMI, then SWI, Software Interrupt (which we'll be discussing a little later), then IRQ. These vectors are hardware characteristics of the 6800. When, for instance, the $\overline{\text{RES}}$ line goes low, the microprocessor will always go to the two highest memory locations and load the program counter with the contents of these locations. There is nothing the user can do to change the location of these interrupt vectors.

Why should the interrupt vectors be placed at the highest memory locations? To answer this, let's consider the memory assignments of a typical microprocessor system.

Figure 12.1.5 shows typical memory assignments that are generally used in microprocessor systems. RAM is usually placed at lowest memory so that the direct addressing mode can be used. ROM is usually placed at highest memory, and I/O is put somewhere in the middle. This leaves room for all three areas. Using the top 8 bytes of available memory for the interrupt vectors puts them at the top of the ROM area, so that the contents of these vectors can be part of the system's ROM.

Figure 12.1.6 compares the memory allocations of two real microprocessor systems: the Motorola D2 and the Heathkit trainer. First, we see that both follow the general scheme of Figure 12.1.5 but are quite different from each other. Because its highest available memory is $E3FF, the Motorola D2's interrupt vectors are assigned to $E3F8 through $E3FF. The Heathkit trainer's highest available address is $FFFF, so its interrupt vectors are from $FFF8 through $FFFF.

The location of the interrupt vectors is part of the hardware of the microprocessor, but the *contents* of the interrupt vectors are determined by the system designer and incorporated into the system's ROM. When a system ROM is being prepared, the person preparing the ROM loads the interrupt vectors with the appropriate addresses for each service routine. Usually, one or more of the interrupts (such as the IRQ) are being reserved for the user. For these, the designer of course

FIGURE 12.1.5 Typical Memory Assignments for a 6800 System

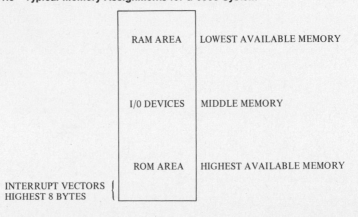

FIGURE 12.1.6 Comparison of Memory Maps of Two Microprocessor Systems

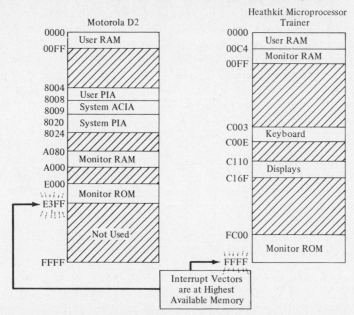

has no way of knowing the future address of the future user's future interrupt service routine. So the designer places a "dummy" address in each user interrupt vector. This gives the user a handle on the interrupt vector so that the new interrupt service routine can be pointed to. The user can place his or her routine at the dummy address, or point to still another location by using a jump instruction.

EXAMPLE 12.1.1

A designer is preparing a monitor ROM for a microcomputer whose highest memory location is $FFFF. The RESET service routine starts at location $E072 and the NMI service routine starts at $F1A0. The SWI service routine starts at $F37D. The IRQ is being saved for user implementation and its vector should contain $00FD. (a) What values should be placed in ROM in locations $FFF8 through $FFFF? (b) Later, a user of the system has written an IRQ service routine that begins at location $0B02. What addresses should be loaded with what contents so that when the IRQ line goes low control is transferred to location $0B02?

Solution

(a) We load the high-order byte of each service routine's starting address into the lower of the two bytes of its interrupt vector and the low-order byte of the starting address into the next byte of the interrupt vector. Thus $FFFE (RESH) should be loaded with $E0 and $FFFF should be loaded with $72, and so on. (b) $FFF8 and

$FFF9 will contain $00 and $FD, respectively. When the microprocessor's $\overline{\text{IRQ}}$ line goes low, the program counter will be loaded with $00FD, the predetermined starting address of the IRQ service routine. To start the execution of the service routine at $0B02, the first instruction starting at $00FD (the dummy address) should be a jump to $0B02 (7E 0B 02).

Answer: (a) ($FFF8)=00; ($FFF9)=$FD; ($FFFA)=$F3; ($FFFB)=$7D; ($FFFC)=$F1; ($FFFD)=$A0; ($FFFE)=$E0; ($FFFF)=$72. (b) ($00FD)=$7E (JMP); ($00FE)=$0B; ($00FF)=$02

Figure 12.1.7 shows how the transfer of control would take place using the dummy address of Example 12.1.1. In fact, the Heathkit Microprocessor Trainer's interrupt vectors all contain dummy addresses except for the RESET vector. The dummy addresses are all in the monitor RAM area.

EXAMPLE 12.1.2

In the Heathkit Microprocessor Trainer the locations contain these contents: ($FFF8)=$00; ($FFF9)=$F7; ($FFFA)=$00; ($FFFB)=$F4; ($FFFC)=$00; ($FFFD)=$F0; ($FFFE)=$FC; ($FFFF)=$00. (a) What is the starting address of the RESET service routine? (b) What are the dummy addresses for the other service routines?

Solution

We line these addresses up with their vector assignments in Figure 12.1.4. (a) The RESET vector is at highest memory ($FFFE and $FFFF), so the address of its

FIGURE 12.1.7 Transfer of Control when Interrupt Vector Contains a "Dummy" Address

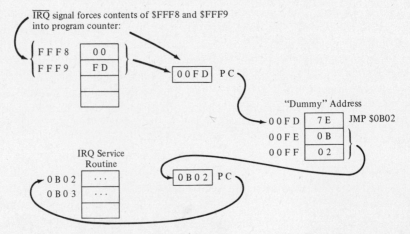

routine is the contents of these locations: $FC00. (b) We find the dummy addresses in the same way.

Answer: (a) RES: $FC00. (b) NMI: $00F0; SWI: $00F4; IRQ: $00F7

Next, we'll look at the details of how interrupts take place.

12.2 IMPLEMENTATION OF THE 6800's INTERRUPTS

We've seen what's built into the 6800 in terms of interrupt capability. Now we'll look at how interrupts occur.

Part of the definition of interrupt requires that the interrupted program be restored at the point where it was interrupted. The 6800's interrupt structure does this, and next we'll see how.

Saving Program Environment

When it gets a subroutine call, the microprocessor automatically saves the program counter contents. Because we, the users, have the option of placing the subroutine call wherever we like at a fixed point in the program, it's up to us to make sure that the calling program's register contents aren't destroyed by the subroutine. In subroutine calls only the program counter contents are the micro-processor's responsibility. But with an interrupt, we have a different situation. Whereas a subroutine call happens at a definite point in a program, an interrupt can occur at any point. Even if we pushed all the register contents onto the stack between every instruction (a ridiculous idea!), an interrupt might occur *after* an instruction but *before* we pushed the registers.

The contents of all the registers except for the stack pointer make up the **program environment**. When the microprocessor receives any interrupt except RESET, it saves the program environment by pushing the current register contents onto the stack. Figure 12.2.1 shows the order of pushing. The registers that have to be pushed are the program counter (2 bytes), the index register (2 bytes), ACCA (1 byte), ACCB (1 byte) and the status register (1 byte): 7 bytes in all to be pushed onto the stack. So the stack pointer contents will always be 7 less right after an interrupt. In the example of Figure 12.2.1 the stack pointer contents were $00FF before the interrupt and $00F8 after.

EXAMPLE 12.2.1

Suppose the registers have these contents: (ACCA)=$AA, (ACCB)=$BB, (XR)= $EEFF, (PC)=$0042, (CC)=$C1, (SP)=$07E0. Now an interrupt occurs. (a) What

FIGURE 12.2.1 An Interrupt Causes the Register Contents to Be Pushed onto the Stack in a Definite Order

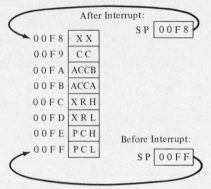

memory locations will have what new contents as a result of saving the program environment? (b) What will the new stack pointer contents be?

Solution

Before the interrupt, (SP)=\$07E0, so the program environment will be pushed onto the stack starting with this address. We look at Figure 12.2.1 to get the order: (\$07E0)=\$42, (\$07DF)=\$00, (\$07DE)=\$FF, (\$07DD)=\$EE, (\$07DC)=\$AA,

FIGURE 12.2.2 To Save the Program Environment During an Interrupt, the Microprocessor Pushes the Register Contents onto the Stack

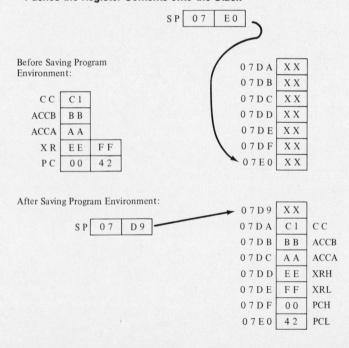

($07DB)=$BB, ($07DA)=$C1. The new stack pointer contents will be 7 less than they were before the interrupt.

Answer: (a) See preceding solution. (b) (SP)=$07D9

Figure 12.2.2 illustrates the stack contents before and after the interrupt of Example 12.2.1. All hardware and software interrupts *except* RESET save the program environment. RESET doesn't save anything, and there's no reason that it should. We press Reset to get the monitor started after powering up and before that the registers only contained garbage anyway. Another reason we press Reset is to get control back from "who knows where" to the monitor. In that case we never *want* to get back to where we were before we pressed Reset!

Next, we'll look at the special instructions dealing with interrupts.

Interrupt-Related Instructions

Table 12.2.1 shows the 6800's interrupt-related instructions. We've already mentioned the two instructions that control the interrupt mask bit of the status register: SEI and CLI.

We've also discussed SWI, Software Interrupt. Looking at its instruction information sheet, we note first that it takes 12 clock cycles to execute. When we next see all that it has to do, it's not surprising that it takes so long. The SWI does the following: (1) increments the program counter contents; (2) saves the program environment; (3) sets the interrupt mask bit; and (4) transfers control to the contents of the SWI interrupt vectors.

The major difference between SWI and a hardware interrupt is that we can put a SWI at a definite point in a program, whereas a hardware interrupt happens at any indefinite point. In the course of debugging a program we find it useful to place breakpoints in the program. A **breakpoint** is a point in a program where the MPU stops executing. The user would like to examine the contents of key registers and memory locations at a breakpoint for possible clues as to why the program might not be working. The SWI is useful for implementing breakpoints, for which the

TABLE 12.2.1 Interrupt-Related Instructions

Mnemonic	Name	Addressing Mode	Function
SEI	SET INTERRUPT MASK	INH	Sets I of status reg.
CLI	CLEAR INTERRUPT MASK	INH	Clears I of status reg.
SWI	SOFTWARE INTERRUPT	INH	Saves program environment Transfers control to address found in Locations FFFA & FFFB
WAI	WAIT FOR INTERRUPT	INH	Saves program environment Waits until interrupt occurs
RTI	RETURN FROM INTERRUPT	INH	Restores program environment to condition before interrupt Transfers control to (PC) contents before interrupt

monitors for both the Motorola D2 and Heathkit trainer use the SWI. The SWI is inserted where the user wishes to put a breakpoint. When the MPU encounters the SWI, it stops executing the program and pushes all the register contents onto the stack before going to the SWI vectors. Then the monitor can pull the register contents, displaying them to the user upon command via the function keys. In addition to using the SWI for implementing breakpoints, the writer of the Motorola D2 monitor used the SWI instruction to terminate user programs by having the SWI interrupt vectors point to an entry address to the monitor.

The Wait for Interrupt (WAI) is one we haven't mentioned yet, though the Heathkit trainer uses it to terminate programs. Looking at its instruction information sheet, we see that it: (1) increments the program counter contents; (2) saves the program environment; and (3) suspends execution of the program. At this point, the WAI command does just what its name says: It waits for an interrupt. Any of the three hardware interrupts will do:

RESET: If you've used the Heathkit trainer, you know that after executing a program that's terminated by WAI, the next step normally is to press Reset to get back to the monitor.

Nonmaskable Interrupt: If the microprocessor receives an $\overline{\text{NMI}}$ signal while WAI is in progress, it first sets the interrupt mask, then proceeds directly to the NMI interrupt vectors. It doesn't save the program environment, because the WAI already did that.

Interrupt Request: If the microprocessor receives an $\overline{\text{IRQ}}$ signal while WAI is in progress, it first examines the I bit to see whether the interrupt is permitted. If the I bit is set, the IRQ won't be implemented. In that case the microprocessor keeps on waiting until I is cleared or until it receives a $\overline{\text{RES}}$ or $\overline{\text{NMI}}$ signal. If, however, the I bit is clear, the microprocessor first sets the interrupt mask and then proceeds to the IRQ interrupt vectors. Again, because the program environment has already been saved by WAI, the IRQ doesn't save it again.

The advantage to using the WAI instruction is that by saving the registers it saves some time when an interrupt occurs. We see that the WAI takes 9 clock cycles to increment the PC contents and to save the program environment. In some cases this might be a critical amount of time.

Return from Interrupt, RTI, is analogous to RTS. Its object is to put things back the way they were before the interrupt. It restores the program environment by pulling it from the stack. Control is transferred back to the point in the program where it was interrupted, because the PC contents are restored. There is no separate activity to set or clear the interrupt mask bit, because when the status register contents are restored the I bit will have the condition it had before the interrupt. Just as RTS is always the last instruction in a subroutine, RTI is always the last instruction in an interrupt service routine.

EXAMPLE 12.2.2

Assume the conditions left by the interrupt of Example 12.2.1. The interrupt service routine is executed until the RTI instruction is encountered. After execution of the

RTI, state (a) the contents of all the registers and (b) the contents of locations $07DA through $07E0.

Solution

(a) Looking at the instruction information sheet, we see that the register contents are pulled in reverse order from that in which they were pushed. So incrementing the stack pointer to $07DA and pulling gives the contents of CC, and so on. At the end of pulling the registers the stack pointer will contain a value 7 greater than it contained before the RTS: $07D9 + $0007 = $07E0. (b) Because pulling from the stack doesn't remove values from the stack, locations $07DA through $07E0 have the same contents they had before the RTI.

Answer: (a) (CC) = $C1, (ACCB) = $BB, (ACCA) = $AA, (XR) = $EEFF, (PC) = $0042. (b) The same as before the RTI

Figure 12.2.3 illustrates the RTI instruction for the conditions of Example 12.2.2. We see that, like the RTS instruction, RTI puts things back almost the way they were before the interrupt—almost but not quite. The register values have been restored, and we note that because the status register is restored, the contents of the I bit (0, in this case) are the same as before the interrupt. The PC is loaded with the right value to resume the interrupted program. But as with the RTS instruction, the contents of the memory locations in the stack haven't been restored to the values they had before the interrupt. The stack locations still contain the saved register contents. We can look in the stack to see what the register values were before the interrupt; this is handy for implementing breakpoints and examining registers.

FIGURE 12.2.3 The RTI Causes the Program Environment to Be Restored by Pulling from the Stack

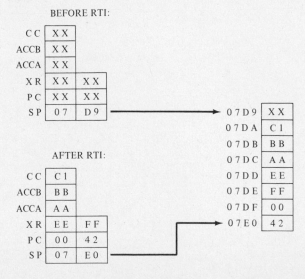

Another factor that isn't the same as before the interrupt is *time*. When a program that contains timing loops is interrupted, there's no way to put back the lost time. In a program where timing is critical, we should make sure that no interrupts can happen.

Summary

Figures 12.2.4 and 12.2.5 summarize the hardware and software interrupt sequences. We see that there are differences among them. The NMI and IRQ sequences cause the microprocessor to finish executing its current instruction before proceeding with the rest of the interrupt sequence. This is necessary if the registers are to be saved in an orderly fashion. We should note at this point that these sequences are also considered as "instructions" in that they have to be finished before another interrupt can occur. For instance, suppose the IRQ sequence were being executed. Now suppose that another IRQ occurs just as the box called "stack

FIGURE 12.2.4 Hardware Interrupt Sequences

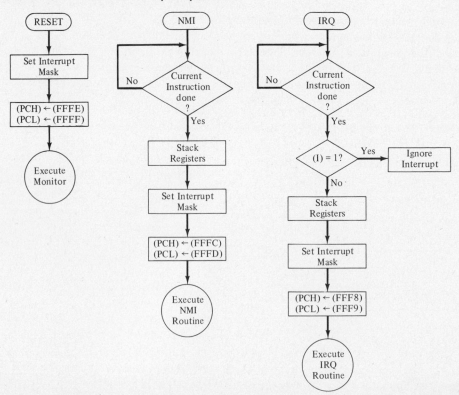

FIGURE 12.2.5 Software Interrupt Sequences

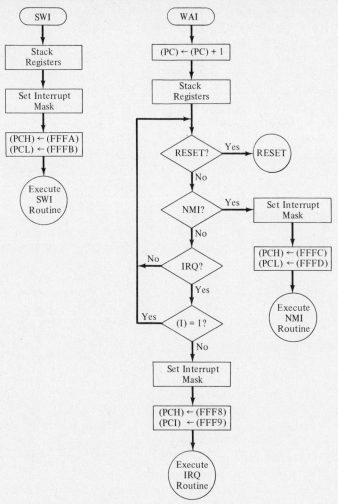

registers" is in the middle of being executed. The hardware of the 6800 is constructed so that the MPU must finish the whole interrupt sequence before recognizing another interrupt. In this case it would ignore the second IRQ because the routine had set the interrupt mask. We see that this is an automatic way to prevent the level-sensitive IRQ from interrupting itself before getting a chance to set the interrupt mask.

Let's consider the analogous situation with NMI. Suppose the NMI sequence is executed and the MPU is down to the "stack registers" box. Now suppose another NMI occurs. The MPU must finish the whole NMI sequence, through loading the program counter. But then the second NMI will be recognized, even though the interrupt mask had been set (this only prevents IRQs). The second NMI will cause another execution of the NMI service routine. But because the PC had been loaded previously with the address of the first NMI service routine, control will be smoothly transferred to the first NMI routine when the second NMI is finished.

With the RESET, it doesn't matter whether or not the current instruction is finished since we're not saving the register contents. With the SWI and WAI, the current instruction will obviously be finished before these are encountered in the program. In all cases the interrupt mask is set to prevent the interrupt from being interrupted by an IRQ.

We've looked at interrupts from the standpoint of the microprocessor: the "interruptee." Next we'll see interrupts from the standpoint of the peripheral devices: the "interrupters."

12.3 INTERRUPTS AND THE PIA

We've seen that the PIA can act as "go-between" for the MPU and one or more peripheral devices. This applies to interrupts, too. The PIA can receive interrupts from peripheral devices, passing them along to the MPU in an orderly way. First, we'll see what pins on the PIA have to do with interrupts.

Interrupt Pins of the PIA

The pins of the PIA were shown in Chapter 5 (Figure 5.1.2) with emphasis on the data lines. This diagram is shown again here in Figure 12.3.1. Now we'll be concerned with seven additional lines, indicated on the figure.

The PIA has two kinds of interrupt pins. Its **interrupt input pins** allow it to receive interrupts from peripherals, whereas its **interrupt output pins** pass an interrupt to the MPU. (Recall that the MPU has only interrupt inputs.) The PIA communicates with peripheral devices regarding interrupts by means of its control lines CA1, CA2, CB1, and CB2. As we might guess, A and B refer to the A and B sides of the PIA. Lines CA1 and CB1 are always interrupt inputs. Lines CA2 and CB2 have several uses, the simplest of which are as interrupt inputs such as CA1 and CB1. In this chapter we'll be using CA2 and CB2 only as interrupt inputs.

The PIA uses its interrupt outputs $\overline{\text{IRQA}}$ and $\overline{\text{IRQB}}$ to communicate with the MPU. A "low" on $\overline{\text{IRQA}}$ means that side A of the PIA is requesting an interrupt; a "low" on $\overline{\text{IRQB}}$ means that side B is requesting an interrupt.

The $\overline{\text{RES}}$ line is usually connected to the Reset button of the system (along with the $\overline{\text{RES}}$ line of the MPU). So when the MPU is reset, the PIA is reset also. Because the RESET automatically clears all registers of the PIA, it's important that the PIA gets reconfigured. This is done just by configuring the PIA as part of the RESET service routine.

FIGURE 12.3.1   More Pins of the PIA

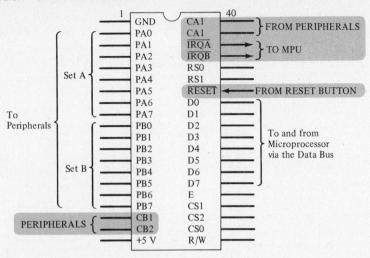

The PIA's two interrupt outputs, $\overline{\text{IRQA}}$ and $\overline{\text{IRQB}}$, can be connected to the MPU's two interrupt inputs $\overline{\text{IRQ}}$ and $\overline{\text{NMI}}$ in any configuration. If both $\overline{\text{IRQ}}$ and $\overline{\text{NMI}}$ are available to the user, we can connect one of the PIA's outputs to each. If the $\overline{\text{NMI}}$ is used by the system and only $\overline{\text{IRQ}}$ is left for the user, we can connect both $\overline{\text{IRQA}}$ and $\overline{\text{IRQB}}$ to the MPU's $\overline{\text{IRQ}}$ line.

Figure 12.3.2 shows one of the many possible configurations of peripherals, PIA, and MPU for a simple case where all four control lines are interrupt inputs to the PIA. In the figure $\overline{\text{IRQA}}$ and $\overline{\text{IRQB}}$ are wired together and connected to the MPU's $\overline{\text{IRQ}}$ input pin. This is called **wire-ORing** because wiring them together causes a signal on the MPU's input line if *either $\overline{\text{IRQA}}$ or $\overline{\text{IRQB}}$* becomes low. A dot is used on a wiring diagram to mean a connection, but that connection isn't always a wire-OR. In Figure 12.3.2, connection A, two lines connected to one, is a wire-OR. But connection B, one line connected to two, is just a connection and not a wire-OR.

In Figure 12.3.2 a different interrupting device is shown connected to each of lines CA1, CA2, CB1, and CB2. For the devices connected to side A the PIA passes the interrupt along to the MPU's $\overline{\text{IRQ}}$ line via $\overline{\text{IRQA}}$. Similarly if a device on side B interrupts the PIA, the MPU's $\overline{\text{IRQ}}$ line will get the interrupt via $\overline{\text{IRQB}}$.

In the setup shown any one of four possible devices can end up generating a single interrupt on the MPU's $\overline{\text{IRQ}}$ line. The MPU must have some way of knowing which device needs service so that it can call on the right service routine. Also, the priority of the devices has to be established in case more than one interrupt occurs at the same time. To see how these problems are solved, first, we should look again at the PIA's control register.

FIGURE 12.3.2   A Possible Configuration of PIA, MPU, and Peripheral Devices

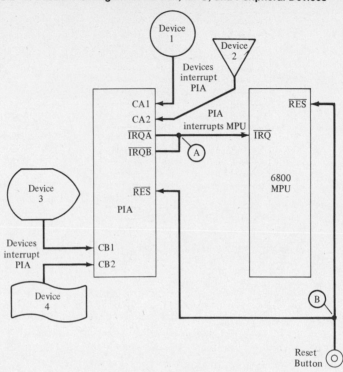

The PIA Control Register Revisited

Figure 12.3.3 shows a diagram of control register A. CRA and CRB are nearly the same, and for our present purposes, what we say for CRA goes for CRB, too.

So far, we've dealt only with bit 2 of the control register. Bit 2 lets us select between DRA and DDRA. Bit 2 is shaded in Figure 12.3.3 to indicate that we've covered this bit already. After bit 2 we look next at bit 5, which lets us decide how to use line CA2. For discussions now, we'll want to consider the simplest case, where CA2 behaves the same way as CA1: as an interrupt input. To select this function for CA2, we store a 0 in bit 5 of CRA. Now, whatever we say for CA1 goes for CA2, too.

Bits 6 and 7 are the **interrupt flag bits**. Bit 7 is automatically set if there is an interrupt input to the PIA on line CA1. So if device 1 (Figure 12.3.2) interrupted the PIA, bit 7 would be set. Bit 6 is automatically set if there is an interrupt input on line CA2. Thus if device 2 interrupted the PIA, bit 6 would be set. These two flags tell which device has caused the interrupt. The only way bits 6 and 7 of the PIA's control register can get set is by CA1 and CA2; the MPU can't set them. The MPU can, however, cause bits 6 and 7 of CRA to be cleared, by reading the PIA's DRA.

FIGURE 12.3.3 The PIA Control Register (CRA)

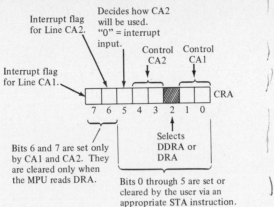

More about that later. Right now it's important to realize that the user can't store data in CRA bits 6 and 7.

The user can, however, store data in bits 0–5. Of these, we've covered bit 2 already, and bit 5 we've just agreed to clear to 0. So now we need to learn how to use bits 0, 1, 3, and 4. Because we've made CA2 behave like CA1, its two control bits (3 and 4) will be used in the same way as bits 0 and 1. Thus by learning to use bits 0 and 1, we'll have learned how to use bits 3 and 4, too.

Figure 12.3.4 shows the CA1 and CA2 control bits: 0, 1, 3, and 4. The simplest are the **mask bits**, which allow or disallow the PIA to interrupt the microprocessor. These are bit 0 for line CA1 and bit 3 for line CA2. If bits 0 and 3 are clear, then the PIA is not allowed to interrupt the MPU even though CA1 and/or CA2 might have set one or both of the PIA's interrupt flag bits.

We should explain the difference among the PIA's interrupt flag bits, its interrupt masks, and the interrupt mask in the MPU's status register. The interrupt flag bits get set whenever a device interrupts the PIA. (Devices are always allowed to interrupt the PIA.) If the interrupt masks of the PIA are set, the PIA is allowed to pass an interrupt on to the MPU. If the interrupt mask in the MPU's status register is set, then the MPU won't recognize the PIA's interrupt. Note that the PIA's and MPU's mask bits have opposite configurations: a 1 in the PIA's mask bit enables the interrupt, but a 1 in the MPU's mask bit disables the interrupts. We can illustrate this with an example.

Case 1: A call comes in to a business office and the secretary answers it. But the executive had left orders not to be interrupted by the telephone. So the secretary doesn't ring the executive. The call is masked at the first line of defense: the secretary. Now suppose that an interrupt comes into the PIA on CA1 and the PIA "answers" it (bit 7, CA1's interrupt flag bit, gets set). But the user had left orders that the MPU wasn't to be interrupted by CA1 (by putting a 0 in CA1's mask bit, bit 0 of CRA). So, the PIA doesn't pass CA1's interrupt on to the MPU. The interrupt is masked at the first line of defense: the PIA's interrupt mask.

FIGURE 12.3.4   CA1 and CA2 Control Bits

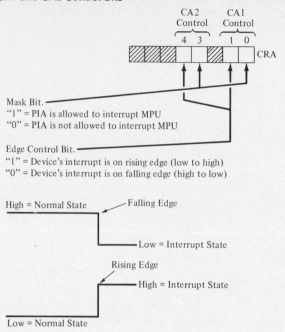

Mask Bit.
"1" = PIA is allowed to interrupt MPU
"0" = PIA is not allowed to interrupt MPU

Edge Control Bit.
"1" = Device's interrupt is on rising edge (low to high)
"0" = Device's interrupt is on falling edge (high to low)

Case 2: A call comes in to a business office and the secretary answers it. The secretary, this time, is allowed to interrupt the executive with the telephone. So the secretary rings the executive. However, the executive is unable to answer the phone, because someone important is in the office. Thus the call is masked at the second line of defense: the executive. Now suppose that an interrupt comes into the PIA on CA1 and the PIA answers it (bit 7, CA1's interrupt flag bit, gets set.) CA1, this time, is allowed to interrupt the MPU (there is a 1 in CA1's mask bit, bit 0 of CRA). So the PIA sends the interrupt to the MPU. However, the MPU is unable to receive the interrupt because there is a 1 in the I bit of its status register. Thus the interrupt is masked at the second line of defense: the MPU's interrupt mask.

Case 3: A call comes in to a business office, the secretary answers it, is allowed to interrupt the executive, rings the executive, and the executive answers. The call went through, because it wasn't masked at any point in the sequence. Now suppose that an interrupt comes to the PIA on CA1, bit 7 of CRA gets set, the PIA is allowed to interrupt the MPU (bit 0 of CRA is set). The MPU's I bit is clear, so the MPU receives the interrupt. The interrupt went through, because it wasn't masked at any point in the sequence.

In summary, interrupts that are masked in the PIA are never sent to the MPU. Interrupts that are not masked in the PIA but that are masked in the MPU are sent to the MPU but not received by it. Interrupts that are masked neither in the PIA nor in the MPU are received by the MPU. But in all cases the PIA's interrupt flag bit is set when a device sends an interrupt to the PIA.

Bits 1 and 4, the **edge control bits**, make it easier to use different kinds of peripheral devices. The $\overline{\text{IRQ}}$ line on the 6800 MPU is active low, but there are some peripheral devices whose interrupt signals are active high. All the PIA's interrupts are edge-triggered. The edge control bit lets us adjust the PIA so that it can accept either a falling edge (low to high) or a rising edge (high to low) as an interrupt input. When the edge control bit contains a 0, the PIA will expect the device's interrupt to occur on the falling edge of line CA1 (or CA2). When the edge control bit contains a 1, the PIA will expect the device's interrupt to occur on the rising edge of line CA1 (or CA2).

EXAMPLE 12.3.1

State what conditions would be established in the PIA by pressing the reset button.

Solution

Reset clears all the PIA registers, including the control registers. To see what effect this has, we look at each control bit one at a time. Bits 6 and 7: Placing a 0 in each of these bits clears the interrupt flags. Bit 5: Placing a 0 in bit 5 of CRA and CRB configures CA2 and CB2 as interrupt inputs. Bit 4: CA2 and CB2 interrupt inputs are on falling edge. Bit 3: CA2 and CB2 interrupts disabled. Bit 2: DDRA/DDRB, and not DRA/DRB, is addressed. Bit 1: CA1 and CB1 interrupt inputs are on falling edge. Bit 0: CA1 and CB1 interrupts disabled.

Note that when all interrupts are disabled, as they are here, the rest of the information really isn't needed. If there can be no interrupt, it is a moot point to say whether it would have been on the rising or falling edge, and so on. Disabling the interrupts on Reset allows the RESET service routine to be executed without interruption.

Reset clears all PIA registers, so DDRA/DDRB will contain all zeros, meaning that both sides are all inputs.

Answer: Interrupt flags cleared; CA2 and CB2 configured as interrupt inputs; all interrupts are on falling edge; DDRA/DDRB is addressed; all interrupts are disabled. Both sides configured as all inputs.

EXAMPLE 12.3.2

Write a program segment to configure CRA for these conditions: CA2 is interrupt input; CA2 interrupts enabled; CA2 interrupts on falling edge; address DRA; CA1 interrupts disabled. Express the control word in binary representation.

Solution

We locate each bit of CRA and determine what its contents should be. Bits 6 and 7 won't be affected by this operation, so it doesn't matter what we try to store in them (we'll choose zeros). And bit 5 we know will be 0 to define CA2 as an interrupt input. To enable CA2 interrupts, we need to store a 1 in CA2's interrupt mask (bit

3). To define a CA2 interrupt as the falling edge, we store a 0 in CA2's edge control bit (bit 4). To address DRA, we store a 1 in bit 2. To disable CA1 interrupts, we store a 0 in CA1's interrupt mask bit (bit 0). Finally, if CA1 is disabled, it doesn't matter what we store in CA1's edge control bit (bit 1), so we'll choose 0. We use the symbol "%" to mean binary representation in assembly language. Now our control word is %00001100.

Answer:

```
LDA A   #%00001100
STA A   CRA
```

In cases where we're interested in the contents of individual bits, it sometimes makes for a clearer program to express a control word in binary rather than in hexadecimal.

Next, we'll look at the sequencing that takes place during an interrupt.

Sequence of Events During PIA Interrupts

When a device interrupts the PIA, the following occur: (1) The PIA sets the flag bit (6 or 7) in the control register. (2) The PIA examines an appropriate mask bit (0 or 3) to see if the interrupt is enabled. (3) If the interrupt is enabled, the PIA causes one of its $\overline{IRQ}$ lines (A or B) to go low.

At this point, it's up to the MPU to see whether it will accept the interrupt. If the PIA's $\overline{IRQA}$ and/or $\overline{IRQB}$ lines are connected to the MPU's $\overline{NMI}$ input, there is no problem: the MPU will accept the interrupt. But if $\overline{IRQA}$ and/or $\overline{IRQB}$ are connected to the MPU's $\overline{IRQ}$ input, the MPU first examines its own interrupt mask (I). If I is clear, then the MPU will accept the interrupt and transfer control to the interrupt service routine. If I is set, the MPU will ignore the interrupt.

Servicing a PIA interrupt doesn't automatically clear the PIA's interrupt flag bits (control register bits 6 and 7). If one or both of these bits is set, the corresponding PIA $\overline{IRQ}$ line continues to be active low. To turn off the interrupt, an interrupt service routine written for a PIA interrupt should always contain an instruction to read the PIA's data register. To see why, recall that in the previous section we said that the MPU cannot write a 1 into the PIA's interrupt flag bits (6 and 7), and the only way that the MPU can clear these bits is by reading the appropriate data register. Thus the instruction LDA A DRA clears bits 6 and 7 in CRA, and LDA A DRB clears CRB bits 6 and 7. Once these are clear, the PIA's $\overline{IRQ}$ lines go high, removing the interrupt input to the MPU. But the MPU continues to service the interrupt.

Why clear the interrupt flag bits at all? If these aren't cleared, the corresponding $\overline{IRQ}$ line (A or B) will continue to be active low. This won't interfere with the MPU's execution of the interrupt service routine, but it will cause the interrupt to occur again each time control is returned to the interrupted program. To understand why, recall that when the RTI statement is executed at the end of the interrupt service routine, all the register contents from the interrupted program are pulled from the stack and control is transferred back to the interrupted program. Note that the old status register would have contained a 0 in the I bit (interrupts enabled), or else an IRQ couldn't have happened in the first place. If the $\overline{\text{IRQ}}$ line is still high, the interrupt will occur again, and again and again each time the RTI is executed. To keep out of such an infinite loop, we need to clear the interrupt flag bits.

Figure 12.3.5 shows an example of a simple setup. We have a smoke alarm, and no other devices, connected to the PIA. The smoke alarm is connected through CA1, and its interrupt happens on the rising edge. Its interrupt is enabled. The PIA's $\overline{\text{IRQA}}$ output line is connected to the MPU's $\overline{\text{IRQ}}$ input line.

At (1) the smoke alarm detects smoke. At (2) it sends an interrupt to the PIA by putting CA1 high. (The PIA expects this because CA1's edge bit contains a 1 meaning an interrupt on the rising edge.) At (3) the PIA sets bit 7 of CRA high (this bit is the interrupt flag for CA1). Next, the PIA examines the mask bit for CA1 (bit 0) to see whether this interrupt is enabled (4). At (5) the PIA finds that the interrupt is enabled. At (6) the PIA signals the interrupt by dropping $\overline{\text{IRQA}}$ low, which of course pulls the MPU's $\overline{\text{IRQ}}$ line low. At (7) the MPU examines its I status bit, finds it clear, and initiates the IRQ service routine. At (8) the MPU reads from DRA via LDA A DRA, which was part of the service routine. At (9) the interrupt flag is cleared when the MPU reads DRA. At (10) the absence of a 1 in the interrupt flag bit causes $\overline{\text{IRQA}}$ to go high and remove the interrupt.

Notice that no data was transferred during this interrupt. With a smoke alarm, the fact that there is an interrupt at all is data enough. But even though there was no data transferred, we still had to read from DRA in order to clear the interrupt flag.

EXAMPLE 12.3.3

Assume the setup of Figure 12.3.2, where IRQA and IRQB are both wired to the MPU's IRQ line. The control registers have these contents

(CRA)=0001 1101
(CRB)=0000 0110

Assume the MPU's interrupt mask is clear, and suppose each device sends a low signal to the PIA by having its line (CA1, CA2, CB1, and CB2) fall from high to low. State, for each (a) whether an interrupt would occur; (b) the contents of CRA and CRB immediately after the PIA receives the interrupt.

Solution

(a) For an interrupt to occur, two facts must be true: the interrupt must be enabled and the device must be sending an interrupt in the first place. First, let's see whether any interrupts are disabled (a 0 in the interrupt mask bit). Sure enough, side B's interrupts are disabled, because we find zeros in the CB1 and CB2 interrupt mask

FIGURE 12.3.5 Sequence During PIA Interrupt

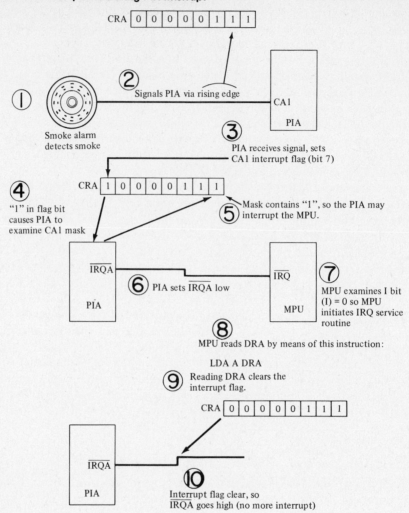

bits (bits 0 and 3). Devices 3 and 4, regardless of what they are sending, can't cause the PIA to interrupt the MPU. Side A, however, is enabled (CRA bits 0 and 3 are set).

Next, let's see whether the devices on side A are sending interrupt signals. Looking in the edge control bits, we find a 1 in the CA2 bit, meaning that the PIA expects an interrupt from CA2 on the rising edge. Since CA2 sent a falling edge, the PIA won't interpret it as an interrupt. But there is a 0 in CA1's edge control bit, so the PIA will interpret its falling edge as an interrupt. Thus device 1 is the only one that will cause an interrupt under these conditions.

(b) If the PIA receives an interrupt from a device, it will set that interrupt flag, *regardless of whether or not the interrupt is allowed*. If the interrupt is allowed, the $\overline{IRQ}$ line will go low; otherwise the $\overline{IRQ}$ line stays high. On side A, device 1 is sending an interrupt, so bit 7 will be set (and $\overline{IRQA}$ will go low). Device 2 isn't sending an interrupt, so bit 6 is clear. On side B, CB1's edge control bit contains a 1, so device 3 isn't sending an interrupt; CRB bit 7 is clear. CB2's edge control bit contains a 0, thus device 4 is sending an interrupt, and bit 6 of CRB will be set. (Since this interrupt is disabled, $\overline{IRQB}$ will remain high.)

Answer: (a) Only device 1 will cause an interrupt. (b) Device 1: (CRA)=%1001 1101. Device 2: (CRA)=%0001 1101. Device 3: (CRB)=%0000 0110. Device 4: (CRB)=%0101 0110

12.4 USING INTERRUPTS

Now that we've seen something about how interrupts work, we'll look at some examples for using them.

Polling and Prioritizing

Consider the setup of Figure 12.3.2. We mentioned that, with four devices possibly generating a single interrupt, the MPU must have some way of telling which device caused the interrupt and also some way of **prioritizing**: assigning priorities to the interrupting devices.

Where more than one device can interrupt, we still have to poll the devices to find out which one needs service. Note, however, that we only poll the devices *if* there is an interrupt. The arrangement of bits in the PIA's control registers makes it easy to tell which device caused an interrupt. We can detect a 1 in bit 7 by reading the control register and then using BMI or BPL. And we can detect a 1 in bit 6 by shifting left and using BMI or BPL. We establish priority by the order of polling: the highest priority first.

EXAMPLE 12.4.1

For the setup of Figure 12.3.2, suppose we have four interrupting devices, having these requirements:

DEVICE	PRIORITY	SUBROUTINE
Smoke alarm	1	FIRE
Burglar alarm	2	BURG
Power failure	3	POWR
Moisture detector	4	WATER

Write a polling routine that will establish these priorities (select the line where each device will be connected also) and branch to the appropriate subroutine for each device.

Solution

We establish priorities by the order of polling. The easiest interrupt bit to detect is bit 7 in either control register, so the priority 1 device should be connected to either CA1 or CB1. We'll connect the smoke alarm as device 1, the burglar alarm as device 2, the power failure as device 3, and the moisture detector as device 4. The routine:

```
LDA A   CRA     GET INTERRUPT FLAGS
BMI     FIRE    BIT 7 SET? GO TO FIRE
ASL A           NO, TEST BURGLAR ALARM
BMI     BURG    BIT 6 SET? GO TO BURG
LDA A   CRB     NO, TEST POWER FAILURE
BMI     POWR    BIT 7 SET? GO TO POWR
BRA     WATER   NO, MUST BE DRY PLANTS
```

Answer: See preceding solution.

Setting up for Interrupts

Just writing an interrupt service routine isn't all we have to do for our interrupt to be implemented. We have to program the microprocessor and the PIA so that they expect the interrupt and know how to handle it. This means (1) making the connection between the dummy address left for us by the monitor and the real starting address of our service routine; (2) configuring the PIA for our system; and (3) enabling the MPU's interrupts.

EXAMPLE 12.4.2

Write a routine that will set up the microprocessor and the PIA to use the setup of Example 12.4.1 on the IRQ line of a system where the dummy address provided is $A000. The interrupt service routine is to begin at location $6000. All devices except the power failure switch interrupt on the rising edge. Configure the PIA data lines for all outputs.

Solution

First, we disable the MPU's interrupts until we can get the system configured for them. Then we configure the PIA's control registers in the usual way and enable the interrupts.

```
SEI             DISABLE INTERRUPTS
CLR     CRA     ADDRESS DDRA
LDA A   #$FF    READY TO CONFIGURE ALL OUTPUTS
STA A   DDRA    SIDE A ALL OUTPUTS
CLR     CRB     ADDRESS DDRB
STA A   DDRB    SIDE B ALL OUTPUTS
```

```
LDA A   #%00011111   SIDE A DEVICES ALL RISING EDGE
STA A   CRA          AND INTERRUPTS ENABLED
LDA A   #%00011101   CB1 FALLING EDGE, CB2 RISING
STA A   CRB          AND INTERRUPTS ENABLED
CLI                  ENABLE MPU INTERRUPTS
```

Next, put a jump instruction in the dummy address:

```
ORG   $A000   START AT DUMMY ADDRESS
JMP   #$6000  GO TO INTERRUPT SERVICE ADDRESS
```

Answer: See preceding solution.

Because there is no input data other than the actual interrupts themselves, all the data lines can be configured as outputs (to be used perhaps by the interrupt service routine). Next, we'll consider an interrupt where there is actual data transferred.

Interrupt with Transfer of Data

A keyboard is a typical example of an interrupting device that has data to transfer.

EXAMPLE 12.4.3

We have connected an ASCII keyboard to $\overline{CA1}$ of the PIA. Whenever a key is pressed, an interrupt is generated through $\overline{IRQ}$ and DRA contains the ASCII equivalent of the key character. Each time a character is input, we wish to store it in a memory buffer that starts at location $A005. Upon receipt of an ASCII carriage return ($0D), the characters should be stored at the beginning of the buffer again. Write the setup and interrupt service routines. Assume the interrupt service routine is to be placed in ROM in the true IRQ interrupt vector.

Solution

The setup routine needs to configure side A only.

```
SETUP   SEI                    DISABLE MPU INTERRUPTS
        CLR    CRA             ADDRESS DDRA
        CLR    DDRA            SET SIDE A ALL INPUTS
        LDA A  #%00000101      ENABLE PIA INTERRUPTS, ADDRESS DRA,
        STA A  CRA             AND CONFIGURE FALLING EDGE
;INITIALIZE BUFFER POINTER
INIT    LDX    #$A005          POINT TO START OF BUFFER
        STX    POINTR          SAVE START OF BUFFER
        CLR    MRKR            CLEAR END MARKER
        CLI                    ENABLE MPU INTERRUPTS
;NOW WAIT FOR END OF LINE
WAIT    LDA A  MRKR            DONE WITH LINE?
        BEQ    WAIT            NOT YET
        SEI                    YES, DISABLE MPU INTERRUPTS
        BRA    INIT            AND GO REINITIALIZE
```

The service routine:

```
GETCHR   LDA A   DRA       GET ASCII CHARACTER
         CPA     #$0D      IS IT A CARRIAGE RETURN?
         BNE     STORE     NO, GO STORE IT
         INC     MRKR      INDICATE END OF LINE
STORE    LDX     POINTR    POINT TO BUFFER LOCATION
         STA A   0, X      PUT CHARACTER INTO BUFFER
         INX               POINT TO NEXT LOCATION
         STX     POINTR    KEEP YOUR PLACE FOR NEXT INT
         RTI               RETURN TO MAIN PROGRAM
```

Answer: See preceding program segments.

We've seen just a few examples of how interrupts can be used. There are many other possibilities, depending on the particular situation. More advanced texts may cover more sophisticated uses of the control lines of the PIA.

REVIEW QUESTIONS

1. Can most computers do more than one thing at a time? Explain.
2. What is **polling**? Give an example.
3. What is an interrupt? What does it mean to **service** the interrupt? What is an **interrupt service routine**?
4. What is the difference between **hardware interrupts** and **software interrupts**?
5. What are the 6800's three interrupt pins? What do the bars over their symbols mean?
6. What does it mean to **mask** an interrupt? Which of the 6800's interrupts can be masked?
7. What is a **falling edge** and a **rising edge**? What is meant by **edge-triggered**? Which 6800 interrupt is edge triggered?
8. What is meant by **level-sensitive**? Which 6800 interrupt is level-sensitive?
9. What is the 6800's **interrupt mask bit**? Where is it located, and what is it used for? How can the user control it?
10. What are **interrupt vectors**? What interrupt vectors does the 6800 have, and where are they located? Explain the location of interrupt vectors relative to microcomputers' memory maps.
11. How are the contents of the interrupt vectors determined? How is an interrupt vector reserved for the user? How does the user cause the interrupt vector to point to his/her service routine?
12. What is the microprocessor's **program environment**? How is the program environment saved during an interrupt?
13. Explain how to relate the contents of the stack locations with the register contents when these are saved during an interrupt.
14. Does RESET save the register contents? Explain.
15. What are the instructions SEI and CLI used for?
16. What is the SWI instruction? How is it different from a hardware interrupt? What is it frequently used for in microcomputers?

17. What is the WAI instruction? What does it do? What are the three ways a microcomputer can exit the WAI state?
18. What is the RTI instruction? Explain what happens to the stack contents and the register contents after execution of RTI. Does RTI put everything back the way it was before the interrupt? Explain.
19. Which interrupts require the microprocessor to finish the current instruction before servicing?
20. Which interrupts set the interrupt mask before servicing?
21. Which interrupts examine the interrupt mask before servicing?
22. Which interrupts increment the program counter before servicing?
23. Describe what happens if an NMI interrupts an IRQ in progress.
24. Name and describe the interrupt pins of the PIA. Which are interrupt inputs, and which are interrupt outputs?
25. What is the PIA's RESET line connected to? What happens when it is activated?
26. Describe some of the ways we can connect IRQA, IRQB, IRQ, and NMI.
27. What is bit 5 of the PIA control register used for? What value will it contain in this chapter?
28. What are the **interrupt flag bits**? How are they set? How can they be cleared?
29. What are the **control bits** for CA1 and CA2?
30. What are the PIA's **mask bits**? What is the meaning of a 1 or a 0 in a mask bit? Explain the difference among the PIA's interrupt flag bits, the PIA's mask bits, and the MPU's mask bit.
31. What are the PIA's **edge control bits**? How do we use them?
32. Explain how to tell what conditions would be established in the PIA by looking at the contents of the control registers.
33. Explain how to configure the PIA for a given set of interrupt conditions.
34. What are the conditions of the PIA after a RESET?
35. Why must the interrupt flag bits be cleared during a PIA interrupt service routine? What instruction accomplishes this?
36. Explain why it was necessary to read DRA in Figure 12.3.5 even though no data was transferred.
37. Explain how to tell whether an interrupt can occur by looking at the control register contents.
38. When several devices can interrupt, how do we poll and prioritize them?
39. What three things must we do to set up the MPU and the PIA for an interrupt? Explain how to write such a routine.
40. Explain how the routine of Example 12.4.3 works.

EXERCISES

SET A (answers at back of book)

1. We wish to prepare a monitor ROM. The RESET routine begins at $F2C8. The NMI routine begins at $FA32. The SWI and IRQ vectors are to be reserved for the user and should contain $00F2 and $00F6. $FFFF is the highest address available for this

system. (a) What should be the contents of ROM locations $FFF8 through $FFFF? (b) If, later, a user wrote an IRQ service routine, what should be the contents of what locations if the service routine started at location $A730?

2. In the Heathkit trainer, these locations contain these contents: ($FFF8)=$E0; ($FFF9) =$14; ($FFFA)=$E0; ($FFFB)=$32; ($FFFC)=$E0; ($FFFD)=$19; ($FFFE)=$E0; ($FFFF)=$8D. (a) What are the starting addresses of the RES, NMI, SWI, and IRQ service routines? (b) Although all are ROM locations, one of them—the IRQ—is a dummy address, to reserve this interrupt for the user. The contents of $E014 through $E018 are FE (LDX) A0 00 6E (JMP, indexed) 00. What is the true starting address of the IRQ service routine? Explain how the transfer of control takes place.

3. An interrupt has just occurred. The memory locations now have the contents: ($00F0) =$F0, ($00F1)=$23, ($00F2)=$4A, ($00F3)=$00, ($00F4)=$67, ($00F5)=$B3, ($00F6)=$E2. The stack pointer contents are now $00EF. What were the contents of all the registers (including the stack pointer) just before the interrupt?

4. The microprocessor encounters an RTI instruction. Before the RTI was executed, the stack pointer contents were $00E0, and the locations had these contents: ($00E0)= $E0; ($00E1)=$E1; ($00E2)=$E2; ($00E3)=$E3; ($00E4)=$E4; ($00E5)=$E5; ($00E6)=$E6; ($00E7)=$E7; ($00E8)=$00E8; ($E9)=$E9. What will be the register contents (including the stack pointer) after executing the RTI?

5. For this program segment:

```
LDA A   %00001111
STA A   CRA
```

State the effect of each control bit contents on the status of the PIA.

6. Write a program segment that will configure the PIA for these conditions: CA2 used as interrupt input; interrupts allowed for both CA1 and CA2; CA1 interrupts on rising edge, CA2 on falling edge; address DRA.

7. Assume the setup of Figure 12.3.2, but with $\overline{\text{IRQA}}$ wired to the MPU's $\overline{\text{IRQ}}$ line and with $\overline{\text{IRQB}}$ wired to the MPU's $\overline{\text{NMI}}$ line. For these contents of the control registers:

```
(CRA)=%0000 0111
(CRB)=%0000 1100
```

Assume the MPU's interrupt mask is set, and suppose each device sends a high signal to the PIA. State, for each device (a) whether an interrupt would occur and (b) the contents of CRA and CRB immediately after the PIA receives the interrupt.

8. We wish to use side A of the PIA to handle a smoke alarm and an ASCII keyboard, with the smoke alarm having higher priority than the keyboard. (a) To which control line should each be connected? (b) Write a polling routine with FIRE and DATA the names of the interrupt service routines.

9. Write a routine that will configure the PIA and set up for interrupts given the conditions of Exercise 8. Side A's data lines are to be all inputs. The dummy address for the IRQ is $00F2, and the polling routine starts at $C072. Both devices interrupt on the falling edge.

10. Write an interrupt service routine for the setup of Exercises 8 and 9 that reads a word input into DRA and stores it in a location called BUFFER. The routine should allow the fire alarm to interrupt it.

EXERCISES

SET B (answers not given)

1. (a) In a system where $FFFF is the highest address, what should locations $FFF8 through $FFFF contain in a ROM if the NMI, SWI, and IRQ vectors are all to be reserved for the user and the RESET service routine starts at location $E374? The dummy addresses of the NMI, SWI, and IRQ vectors are $00E2, $00E6, and $00EA, respectively. (b) A user has placed an NMI service routine at location $0172. What addresses should be loaded with what contents so that if the $\overline{\text{NMI}}$ line were to go low, control would be transferred to $0172?

2. Suppose we find the following contents in memory locations in a microcomputer system: ($FFF8)=$00; ($FFF9)=$E0; ($FFFA)=$00; ($FFFB)=$E6; ($FFFC)=$F2; ($FFFD)=$00; ($FFFE)=$F0; ($FFFF)=$60. (a) What are the starting addresses of RES, NMI, SWI, and IRQ? (b) Which of these are likely to be dummy addresses? Why?

3. Before an interrupt occurs, the registers have these contents: (PC)=$0045; (XR)= $0005; (ACCA)=$90; (ACCB)=$75; (CC)=$D0. (SP)=$00D7. (a) What locations will contain what new contents as a result of saving the program environment on receiving an interrupt? (b) What will the new stack pointer contents be after saving the environment?

4. After the execution of an RTI instruction, the registers have these contents: (CC)=$CC, (ACCB)=$BB, (ACCA)=$AA, (XR)=$DDEE, (PC)=$0055, (SP)=$00C4. Give the stack locations where these values are stored.

5. For this program segment

```
LDA A   #%11010100
STA A   CRA
```

State the effect of the contents of each control register bit on the status of the PIA.

6. Write a program segment that will configure the PIA for these conditions: CA2 is interrupt input; both CA1 and CA2 interrupts are on rising edge; interrupts from CA1 are allowed but not from CA2; address DRA.

7. Assume the setup of Figure 12.3.2, with both $\overline{\text{IRQA}}$ and $\overline{\text{IRQB}}$ connected to the MPU's $\overline{\text{NMI}}$ line. Assume these contents of control registers:

```
(CRA)=%00010101
(CRB)=%00001110
```

Assume the MPU's interrupt mask is set and each device sends these signals: device 1: low; device 2: high; device 3: low; device 4: high.
State (a) whether an interrupt would occur for each device and (b) the contents of CRA and CRB immediately after the PIA received the interrupt.

8. We have both $\overline{\text{IRQ}}$ and $\overline{\text{NMI}}$ available for use. We wish to connect a smoke alarm, a burglar alarm, and a telephone answering device to the PIA. The smoke alarm should have highest priority, followed by the burglar alarm. Both should be able to interrupt the telephone answering routine. (a) Suggest a configuration of devices, PIA, and MPU. (b) Write a polling routine where FIRE, BURGL and ANSWR are the names of the appropriate routines.

9. Write a routine that will configure the PIA for the setup in Exercise 8. Side A's data lines are to be all inputs and side B, all outputs. The dummy addresses are $A006 for the IRQ and $A008 for the NMI. All devices interrupt on the falling edge.

10. Write an interrupt service routine for ANSWR that activates a tape recorder by outputting a 1 in DB0. The routine should allow the fire and burglar alarms to interrupt it. The presence of the telephone message is indicated by the appropriate interrupt flag being set. The tape recorder should be turned off when the message is over.

PROGRAMMING IDEAS

1. We wish to count the number of people going through a revolving door. An electric eye causes a falling edge on its line, attached to one of the PIA control lines (your choice) when a person walks through its beam. Write a routine to set up for the interrupt, and write an interrupt service routine that increments a counter whenever the interrupt occurs. Allow for more than 256 people to go through the door.
2. For #1 we wish to terminate the count after a 6-hr period and display the count. Another PIA control line is attached to a timer, which interrupts on the rising edge at the end of 6 hr. At this time, branch to a subroutine DISPLY.
3. We can make a clock by connecting a 60 Hz AC line to one of the PIA's control lines. Every time the AC line interrupts, 1/60 of a second has elapsed. Write an interrupt service routine that has a fractional seconds counter, a seconds counter, a minutes counter, and an hours counter. Each time the interrupt occurs, the fractional seconds counter should be incremented. When the fractional seconds counter reaches decimal 60, it should be zeroed and the seconds counter incremented, and so on through the minutes and hours counter. When the hours counter reaches 12, it too should be zeroed. Write also the routine to set up for the interrupt.
4. One of the PIA's control lines is connected to a thermostat. When the thermostat is turned on, it goes from low to high voltage. Write an interrupt service routine that logs the amount of time the thermostat is on. Use the MPU's IRQ line, which is level-sensitive. Note that as long as the thermostat is on, the interrupt service routine can be executed and reexecuted until the thermostat is turned off. Write also the routine that sets up for the interrupts.

13 Serial Input/Output

LEARNING OBJECTIVES

After completing this chapter, you should be able to:

1. Give a definition, explanation, or example for each of these: *parallel I/O, serial I/O, serial input port, serial output port, synchronous, asynchronous, bit time, baud rate, frame, start bit, stop bit, mark, space, noise spike, glitch, Asynchronous Communications Interface Adapter (ACIA), Transmit Data Register (TDR), shift register, Receive Data Register (RDR), ACIA status register, ACIA control register, counter divide select bits, word select bits.*
2. Convert among bit time, baud rate, character time, and character rate, given any one of these and the number of bits per character.
3. Illustrate the serial ASCII character format.
4. Illustrate and use in programs the instructions ROL and ROR.
5. Explain how to transmit a character longer than 8 bits.
6. Use the PIA to input and output serial data.
7. Explain how to minimize errors due to noise or glitches.
8. Explain the functions of the Rx Data, Tx Data, IRQ, Rx CLK, and Tx CLK pins of the ACIA.
9. Explain how bit synchronization is done in the ACIA with an external clock.
10. List and explain the functions of bits 0 to 1 and 4 to 7 of the ACIA's status register and state the conditions present, given a specific status register contents.
11. List and explain the functions of all bits of the ACIA's control register except bits 5 and 6, and state the control word for a specific set of conditions.
12. Write program segments that address the ACIA's registers.
13. Write polling routines for simple I/O configurations containing the ACIA, PIA, and MPU.
14. Write simple receiving and transmitting routines.

So far, most of the input/output operations we've talked about have dealt with **parallel I/O**, meaning the transmission of a group of bits (usually a byte) simultaneously. In this chapter we'll introduce **serial I/O**, meaning the transmission of a group of bits one bit at a time.

Without knowing it, we *have* done a little serial I/O. Any application where we manipulate the contents of a single bit is serial I/O. The blinking sign program is a simple example. We receive the visual information "sign on" and "sign off" serially. If desired, we could program the blinking sign to send a message in Morse code, a familiar way of sending a message serially.

A **serial input port** is a single conductor (wire) over which serial data is input to the MPU from a peripheral device. A **serial output port** is a wire for outputting serial data from the MPU to a peripheral device. The major advantage to serial I/O is that it uses fewer wires than parallel I/O. To send ASCII characters serially, we need only one wire, whereas to send them in parallel we need at least seven wires (eight, with parity). By cutting down the number of wires, we simplify the system, reduce the number of physical parts that can break, lower the cost, and reduce the possibility of picking up random noise. A disadvantage of serial over parallel I/O is that serial I/O takes longer, because we must transmit a byte of data 1 bit at a time instead of all at once. For transmitting over long distances, such as by telephone or telegraph, serial is often our only choice.

To a user the most obvious application of serial I/O is in transmitting coded characters, such as ASCII. So in this chapter we'll be discussing mostly serial transmission of ASCII characters. First, we need to see how to modify an ASCII character so that we can send and receive it serially.

13.1 ASYNCHRONOUS SERIAL DATA

We can transmit serial ASCII characters **synchronously** by taking the same amount of time to transmit each character, with no time lapses in between characters. Synchronous data transfers might be done if blocks of data were to be moved from one place to another—say, from the computer's memory to magnetic disk storage or vice versa. But most serial transmission is **asynchronous**, meaning that indefinite periods of time may lapse between transmission of characters. A person typing into a terminal doesn't type at a constant rate. You might stop to think or to scratch your head or whatever. In asynchronous data transfer each ASCII character has to be a complete, recognizable entity.

Next, we'll see how that's accomplished.

Timing

We may represent a serial ASCII character as a series of current pulses that can be translated into 1's and 0's (high and low voltages). Figure 13.1.1 shows the ASCII character X ($58) depicted graphically as high and low voltages. The bits are transmitted with the LSB first, so on Figure 13.1.1 time increases from right to left. A transition from a 0 to a 1 or from 1 to 0 seems easy to detect. But what about a

FIGURE 13.1.1 An ASCII Character Can Be Expressed as a Series of High and Low Voltages

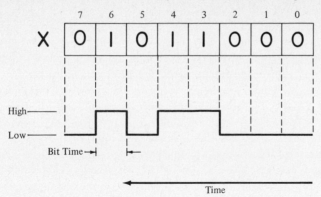

transition from a 0 to a 0 or a 1 to a 1? In Figure 13.1.1, for instance, there are three 0's and two 1's in a row. How does the microprocessor "know" that these are not just one low and one high voltage?

Bits transmitted in parallel can be identified by their physical locations. For example, for a byte of parallel data being transmitted on the data bus, we'd find the contents of bit 0 on line 0 of the data bus; the contents of bit 7 on line 7, and so on. But in serial data transmission there's no such thing as the physical location of a bit. Bits that are transmitted one at a time over a wire have to be defined in terms of **bit time**, the amount of time each spends going past a certain point along a wire.

We can choose among a number of standard bit times for a particular application. The bit time depends on the number of bits per second, called the **baud rate**, that we select. The bit time is the reciprocal of the baud rate. Some common available baud rates and their corresponding bit times are shown in Table 13.1.1.

Next, we'll see how to define the beginning and end of a character.

TABLE 13.1.1 Some Common Baud Rates and Bit Times

Baud Rate	Bit Time
110	9.09 msec
150	6.67 msec
300	3.33 msec
600	1.67 msec
1200	0.833 msec
2400	0.417 msec
4800	0.208 msec
9600	0.104 msec
12000	0.0833 msec
19200	0.0521 msec

Character Format

So that the beginning and end of an ASCII character are well defined, we **frame** the character with one **start bit** (a low voltage) at the beginning of the character, and one or more **stop bits** (a high voltage) at the end of the character. The character itself is transmitted starting with the least significant bit.

When no characters are being transmitted, the data line contains a high voltage, called a **mark**. To signal the beginning of a character, the line drops to low, called a **space**. A low voltage for 1 bit time is the start bit. Next come the bits of the ASCII character, then bit 7, and then the line goes high for the stop bit or bits. If no further characters are transmitted, the line stays high (mark). Figure 13.1.2 illustrates this formatting.

Another useful measure of transmission speed is the **character rate**, the number of characters per second. Its reciprocal is the **character time**. To calculate the character rate from the baud rate, we need to know how many bits are in a character. We see from Figure 13.1.2 that a character with 1 stop bit contains 10 bits per character, and a character with 2 stop bits contains 11 bits per character. If we know the baud rate and the number of stop bits, we can calculate the character rate.

EXAMPLE 13.1.1

For a format having 1 start and 2 stop bits plus an 8-bit ASCII character and transmitted at 1200 baud, calculate (a) the bit time; (b) the character rate; and (c) the character time.

Solution

(a) The bit time is just the reciprocal of the baud rate: $1/(1200 \text{ bits/sec}) = 0.833$ msec/bit. (b) With 2 stop bits, there are 11 bits per character. Then,

$$1200 \text{ bits/sec}/(11 \text{ bits/char}) = 109 \text{ chars/sec}$$

(c) The character time is just the reciprocal of the character rate:

$$1/(109 \text{ chars/sec}) = 9.17 \text{ msec/char}$$

FIGURE 13.1.2 ASCII Character Formatting

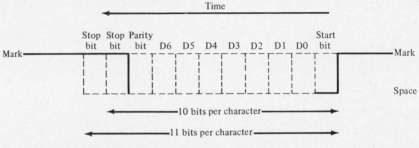

Character Time = (bits/char)(bit time)

Answer: (a) 0.833 msec/bit; (b) 109 chars/sec; (c) 9.17 msec/char

Next, we'll look at some ways of changing parallel to serial I/O.

13.2 SERIAL DATA WITH A PIA

We can set up a PIA to handle serial data. To do this, we'd assign one of the PIA's data lines as input and one as output. To send an ASCII character, we could shift the 8-bit ASCII character 1 bit to the right 8 times and send each bit out one at a time on the output data line. To receive an ASCII character, we could do the opposite: read each bit one at a time and shift it in to the left until we had a complete character. To get the right baud rate, we'd put in a delay loop for the exact bit time each time we send or receive a bit. The only difficulty we see is with the character length. With 1 start bit and 1 or 2 stop bits, we'll have a character that's longer than a byte. How can we transmit an 11-bit character when our registers are only 8 bits wide?

We can piece on a few extra bits by making use of the carry bit. To do this, we need to introduce two new instructions.

The Rotate Instructions

Related closely to the shift instructions are the rotate instructions, ROL—rotate left—and ROR—rotate right. Looking at the instruction information sheet for ROL, we see that it shifts all bits one place left. So far, it's like the ASL instruction. Unlike the ASL instruction, ROL loads bit 0 with the contents of the carry bit instead of always with zero. Like the ASL instruction, ROL loads the carry bit with the contents of bit 7. For ROR we have the same situation in the opposite direction.

Figure 13.2.1 illustrates the instructions ROL and ROR. When we rotate the number 1100 1100 one place left, bit 0 of the result will contain whatever was contained in the carry bit (0, in this case), and the carry bit will contain whatever was in bit 7 (1, in this case). Rotating the resulting number right gives us the original number again. We can't do this with ASL and LSR, because LSR always puts a zero, and not the contents of the carry bit, into bit 7 of the result.

EXAMPLE 13.2.1

Give the contents of accumulator A and of the carry bit after executing these program segments:

```
(a)  SEC              (b)  SEC
     LDA A   #$8A          LDA A   #$8A
     ROL A                 ASL A
     ROR A                 LSR A
```

FIGURE 13.2.1   The Rotate Instructions ROL and ROR

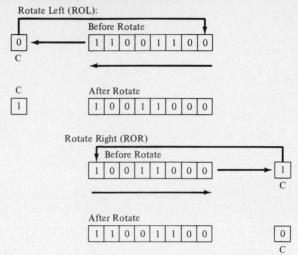

Rotate Left (ROL):

Rotate Right (ROR)

Solution

(a) We start with this situation:

          ACCA   C

     1 0 0 0 1 0 1 0   1

After the ROL A, bit 0 will contain the contents of C (a 1) and C will contain the contents of bit 7 (a 1).

          ACCA   C

     0 0 0 1 0 1 0 1   1

After the ROR A, bit 7 will contain the contents of C (a 1) and C gets the contents of bit 0 (a 1).

          ACCA   C

     1 0 0 0 1 0 1 0   1

The original conditions have been restored.

(b) Here, we start with the same situation:

          ACCA   C

     1 0 0 0 1 0 1 0   1

After the ASL A, bit 0 will contain a 0 and C gets the contents of bit 7 (a 1).

          ACCA   C

     0 0 0 1 0 1 0 0   1

After the LSR, bit 7 will contain a 0 and C gets the contents of bit 0 (a 0).

      ACCA   C

 0 0 0 0   1 0 1 0   0

Answer: (a) (ACCA)=$8A; (C)=1. (b) (ACCA)=$0A; (C)=0

In the example both ACCA and C recovered their initial values when ROR and ROL were used; not so with ASL and LSR. The ROL and ROR instructions provide us with a way of "extending" our 8-bit word to 9 bits.

EXAMPLE 13.2.2

We have configured the PIA so that DA0 is a serial output port. Write a program segment that will output the 9-bit word 111100010 serially through DA0 starting with the LSB.

Solution

We can construct a 9-bit word by using an accumulator plus the carry bit, with (C)=LSB. Then, we'll have this situation:

      ACCA   C

    1111   0001   0

To set (C)=0, we use CLC. Next, we must put each bit, starting with the LSB, into bit 0 of ACCA and then store ACCA in DRA to output the bit value. To get (C) into ACCA, we do a ROL A:

      ACCA   C

    1110   0010   1

After storing this value in DRA we can rotate right and store in DRA 8 times.

Answer

```
      CLC            CLEAR CARRY FOR LSB OF 9-BIT WORD
      LDA B   #$9    LOAD COUNTER FOR 9 BITS
      LDA A   #$F1   GET 8 MSB'S OF WORD
      ROL A          PUT LSB INTO BIT 0
OUT   STA A   DRA    OUTPUT THE BIT
      ROR A          NEXT BIT
      DEC B          DECREMENT COUNTER
      BNE     OUT    STILL MORE BITS? OUTPUT ANOTHER
```

The preceding program segment would output the bits very fast. To output at a specific baud rate, we would have to put in a delay loop for the exact bit time.

Next, we'll look at a program that outputs and inputs ASCII characters using a PIA.

A Serial Output Routine

We have configured the PIA so that DA0 is a serial output port and DA7, a serial input port. We wish to connect the PIA to a CRT terminal for transmission at 1200 baud with 1 start and 1 stop bit.

Figure 13.2.2 lists a subroutine that takes an ASCII character from a location, OUTBUF, and outputs it serially through DA0 to the CRT terminal at 1200 baud. With the examples we've had so far, it shouldn't be too difficult to see how this subroutine does it. We assume the PIA would have been configured by some other subroutine and the labels would have been established by the calling program.

In lines 9 through 11 we put a start bit of 0 into bit 0 of the ASCII character, as we did in Example 13.2.2. Next, in line 12, we load a bit counter with 10 (8 bits for the ASCII character plus 1 start and 1 stop bit). The loop to output the character starts at OUT. After outputting the bit, we branch to the subroutine DELAY, which

FIGURE 13.2.2   Serial Output via PIA

```
OUTCHR
M6800 ASSEMBLER LISTING VERSION 1.6     13 DEC 80 19:48   PAGE    2
SEROUT   DAT    13 DEC 80 19:47

                          3 ;THIS SUBROUTINE TAKES AN ASCII CHARACTER FROM LOCATION OUTBUF
                          4 ;AND OUTPUTS IT SERIALLY THROUGH DA0 TO CRT TERMINAL AT 1200 BAUD
                          5 ;WITH ONE START AND ONE STOP BIT
A302             6 OUTBUF   EQU      $A302
8020             7 DRA      EQU      $8020
0A00             8 DELAY    EQU      $0A00
0000 0C          9 CHROUT   CLC                       SET START BIT TO ZERO
0001 B6 A3 02   10          LDA A    OUTBUF           GET ASCII CHARACTER
0004 49         11          ROL A                     PUT START BIT IN BIT 0
0005 86 0A      12          LDA B    #10              LOAD COUNTER WITH BITCOUNT 10
0007 B7 80 20   13 OUT      STA A    DRA              OUTPUT THE BIT
000A BD 0A 00   14          JSR      DELAY            DELAY 0.833 MSEC FOR 1200 BAUD
000D 46         15          ROR A                     PUT NEXT BIT INTO BIT 0
000E 0D         16          SEC                       SET CARRY FOR STOP BIT IN MSB
000F 5A         17          DEC B                     DECREMENT BITCOUNT
0010 26 F5      18          BNE      OUT              STILL MORE BITS? OUTPUT ANOTHER
0012 39         19          RTS                       NO, RETURN
0013            20          END

NO STATEMENTS FLAGGED

CROSS-REFERENCE TABLE

CHROUT      0000      9
DELAY       0A00      8      14
DRA         8020      7      13
OUT         0007     13      18
OUTBUF      A302      6      10
```

gives us a bit time of 0.833 msec (1200 baud). In line 15 we rotate the next bit into position.

To add the stop bit (a 1) at the end of the ASCII character, we set the carry and rotate the 1 into the MSB of the ASCII character. Line 16 sets the carry so that a 1 will always be shifted in on the left each time the ROR A is executed. We only care about the bit right after the last bit in the ASCII character, but filling the rest of the word with 1's does no harm. The loop will be executed until all 10 bits have been output; then control is returned to the calling program.

A Serial Input Routine

Serial input is a bit trickier than serial output. In output the microprocessor is in control of when the data gets sent out. But in input the peripheral device is in control. The microprocessor can't input any data if there is no data to input; therefore its first problem is detecting the presence of data. The second is determining whether or not the data is valid. There are two sources of invalid data.

The first source comes from the fact that wires can, and do, pick up extraneous noise from outside, causing a **noise spike** or **glitch** of very short duration. The microprocessor must distinguish between a glitch and a valid signal, and time is the key. A signal that stays around for a whole bit time is probably valid, whereas a signal that goes away long before the bit time is over is a glitch. Figure 13.2.3 shows the difference between a glitch and a valid signal.

The second source of invalid data comes from the fact that the edges of the signals aren't so nice and sharp as we've been drawing them. A real signal's edges slope, because it takes a finite amount of time for the line to rise from low to high or

FIGURE 13.2.3   Reading Data at the Center of the Bit Helps to Ensure Valid Input Data

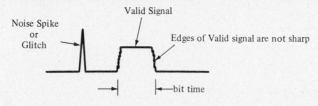
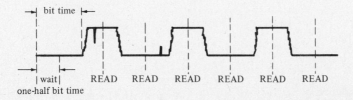

fall from high to low, and the edges themselves may be ragged because of glitches. Thus reading a signal right at the beginning might result in an error if the signal hadn't established its voltage at that time. To minimize error, we should give the signal a chance to settle down and establish its value. We can do this by reading at the center of the bit instead of at the beginning. We might still get an error from a glitch, but only if it happened exactly at the center of the bit. To read an ASCII character at the center of each bit, we'd first wait half a bit time to synchronize further bit times from the middle of 1 bit to the middle of the next. Figure 13.2.3 illustrates this problem.

FIGURE 13.2.4 Serial Input via PIA

```
INCHR
M6800 ASSEMBLER LISTING VERSION 1.6      13 DEC 80 19:41   PAGE      2
SERIN   DAT      13 DEC 80 19:40

                              3 ;THIS SUBROUTINE RECEIVES AN ASCII
                              4 ;CHARACTER INPUT SERIALLY VIA
                              5 ;DA7 AT 1200 BAUD WITH ONE START
                              6 ;AND ONE STOP BIT. THE CHARACTER
                              7 ;IS STORED IN LOCATION INBUF.
                              8 ;THE ROUTINE CHECKS THE STOP BIT
                              9 ;AND BRANCHES TO SUBROUTINE ERROR IF NOT 1.
      8020          10 DRA      EQU     $8020
      A076          11 HAFDLY   EQU     $A076
      A0A1          12 DELAY    EQU     $A0A1
      E538          13 INBUF    EQU     $E538
      0F34          14 ERROR    EQU     $0F34
      0000          15         ORG     $0F00
      0F00 B6 80 20 16 CHARIN  LDA A   DRA      GET INPUT PORT
      0F03 2B FB    17         BMI     CHARIN   STILL A MARK?
      0F05 BD A0 76 18         JSR     HAFDLY   WAIT ONE-HALF BIT TIME
      0F08 C6 08    19         LDA B   #$8      BITCOUNT FOR ASCII CHARACTER
      0F0A BD A0 A1 20 INPUT   JSR     DELAY    WAIT ONE BIT TIME
      0F0D 79 80 20 21         ROL     DRA      ROTATE DA7 INTO CARRY
      0F10 46       22         ROR A            NOW ROTATE IT FROM CARRY INTO CHAR
      0F11 5A       23         DEC B            DECREMENT BIT COUNT
      0F12 26 F6    24         BNE     INPUT    STILL MORE BITS? GET ANOTHER
      0F14 B7 E5 38 25         STA A.  INBUF    NO, DONE. STORE IN INBUF
      0F17 BD A0 A1 26         JSR     DELAY    DONE WITH CHAR, WAIT 1 BIT TIME
      0F1A B6 80 20 27         LDA A   DRA      GET STOP BIT
      0F1D 2A 15    28         BPL     ERROR    IF NOT A 1, FRAMING ERROR
      0F1F 39       29         RTS              OTHERWISE RETURN
      0F20          30         END

NO STATEMENTS FLAGGED

CROSS-REFERENCE TABLE

CHARIN    0F00      16    17
DELAY     A0A1      12    20    26
DRA       8020      10    16    2127
ERROR     0F34      14    28
HAFDLY    A076      11    18
INBUF     E538      13    25
INPUT     0F0A      20    24
```

Figure 13.2.4 lists a subroutine that receives an ASCII character input serially on DA7 for the same setup as the input program of Figure 13.2.2. The character is stored in location INBUF and the stop bit is checked. If there is no stop bit, control is transferred to subroutine ERROR. A mistake in the number of stop bits is called a **framing error**. When a framing error occurs, the receiver can ask for the message to be repeated.

In lines 16 and 17 the microprocessor is waiting for input data. As long as the data line contains a mark (high), there is no data. When the line falls low (a space, or start bit), this means that data is coming. In line 18 the subroutine HAFDLY causes a delay of one-half the bit time so that the readings are centered on the bits. In line 19 a bit counter is loaded with 8. At line 20 the input loop starts by waiting until the center of the bit. Then line 21 rotates the input bit (DA7) into the carry. Line 22 rotates the data from the carry into accumulator A. The first bit (the LSB) of the ASCII character will go into the MSB of accumulator A. But by the time we have been through the loop 8 times, the LSB will have been rotated into bit 0 where it belongs.

Next, we'll see that there's a special chip for serial I/O.

13.3 INTRODUCING THE ACIA

The **Asynchronous Communications Interface Adapter**, or **ACIA**, is a chip that provides a serial connection between the MPU and peripherals. Besides converting between parallel and serial I/O, the ACIA lets us select parity, transmission rate, and number of stop bits. It also detects parity and framing errors.

Figure 13.3.1 is a diagram of the ACIA, showing some of its pins. Of these, we'll be discussing only a few now. The data lines D0 through D7 carry parallel data to and from the microprocessor. The pin labeled "Rx Data" is called the Received

FIGURE 13.3.1 Pins of the ACIA

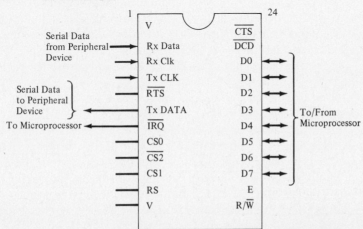

Data Line and is a serial input port to the ACIA from a serial device. The pin labeled "Tx Data" is called the Transmitted Data Line and is a serial output port from the ACIA to a serial device. The IRQ line gives the ACIA a mechanism for interrupting the microprocessor.

The two clock pins, Rx CLK and Tx CLK, are inputs from an external clock and are used by the ACIA to synchronize the data bits. Next, we'll see how this is done.

Timing in the ACIA

We haven't talked much about clocks and timing so far. But timing is particularly important in transmitting serial data, because time is the only dimension we have. The ACIA is set up to receive an external clock frequency that's a multiple of 64, 16, or 1 times the baud rate; 16 is the most commonly used multiple. For instance, the ACIA used in the cassette interface of the Motorola D2 Evaluation Kit runs at an external clock frequency of 4800 baud, which is 16 times its transmission rate of 300 baud.

Why is some multiple of the baud rate used, rather than the baud rate itself? To answer this, we recall from the previous section the necessity for reading the bits in the middle of the bit time rather than at the beginning to minimize error. When we used the PIA for serial I/O, we had to program this error minimization. But the ACIA does that for us.

The ACIA samples the start bit several times to make sure that it's valid. Then it reads the middle of each data bit. The ACIA reads on the rising edge of the external clock. The number of times it reads the start bit depends on what multiple of the baud rate we have chosen. It reads half the multiplicity plus one. For example, for a multiplicity of 16 it reads $16/2 + 1 = 9$ times; for a multiplicity of 64 it reads $64/2 + 1 = 33$ times.

Figure 13.3.2 shows a timing diagram for a multiplicity of 16. This is usually referred to as "divide by 16" or $\div 16$. This might seem confusing at first, but looking at the figure we see that it effectively divides the bit into 16 parts.

Let's take a typical situation and follow it through. Suppose there has been no transmission for a time, and there has been a high, or mark, on the line. The ACIA has been reading on the rising edge of each clock pulse and getting a 1 each time, so it does nothing.

Suddenly, the line drops from high to low, indicating a start bit. The next time the ACIA reads, it gets a 0. (Notice that the ACIA doesn't detect the 0 as soon as it appears, because it only reads on the rising edge of the clock.) After that, data is read on each rising edge for eight readings, or half of the start bit. If the ninth reading is also zero, the start bit is valid. To read the first data bit, the ACIA will read the data on the sixteenth rising edge, starting with this ninth reading.

By dividing the bit into small parts and sampling the start bit many times, we prevent glitches from looking like start bits. And the more parts we divide the bit

FIGURE 13.3.2 Bit Synchronization with External Clock Frequency 16×Baud Rate

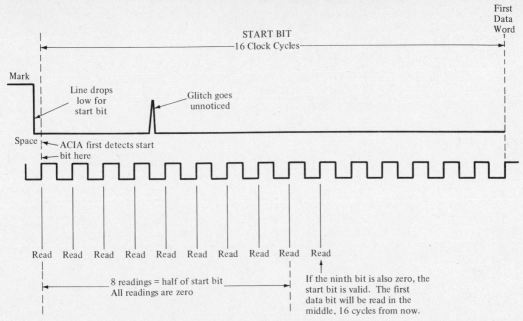

into, the more accurately we can locate its center. Recall that the ACIA detects the start bit only on the rising edge of the clock. The more rising edges we have, the sooner the ACIA will read the start.

The pins Rx CLK and Tx CLK are inputs to the ACIA from the external clock. Rx CLK is used to time the bits received; Tx CLK is used to time the bits transmitted. But both get their inputs from the same clock. The clock may be derived from the microprocessor's clock, or it may be a separate clock.

Registers of the ACIA

There are four. Two deal with data and two, with status and control. The **Transmit Data Register (TDR)** is a write-only 8-bit **shift register** that takes a byte of parallel data from the MPU and shifts it out serially. The **Receive Data Register (RDR)** is a read-only 8-bit shift register that collects and shifts in 8 bits of serial data from a peripheral and passes it to the MPU as parallel data.

Figure 13.3.3 illustrates the functions of the transmit data register and the receive data register.

The **Status Register (SR)** is an 8-bit register in the ACIA that is read-only by the MPU (or the user). That is, we can examine it but we can't change its contents. Figure 13.3.4 shows the bits of the ACIA's status register. Of these, we'll only be discussing bits 0, 1, 4, 5, 6, and 7 now.

FIGURE 13.3.3   The ACIA's RDR Converts Serial to Parallel Data, and the TDR Converts Parallel to Serial

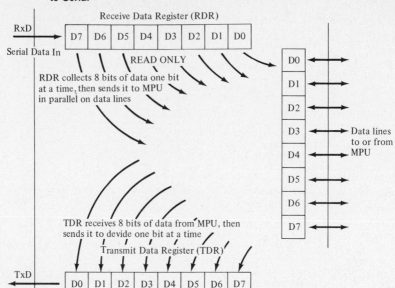

Bit 0, Receive Data Register Full (RDRF), contains a 1 when the ACIA has received 8 bits of data from a peripheral device. When this happens, it means that the ACIA has collected a byte of data for the MPU's data bus, and the MPU should read it. If additional data is input into the ACIA's RDR before the MPU reads it, some data will be lost. To prevent this, the ACIA sets bit 7 (IRQ) of its status register and doesn't clear it until the MPU reads the RDR.

Bit 1, Transmit Data Register Empty (TDRE), is the equivalent of bit 0 for output. Bit 1 contains a 1 when the ACIA has sent all the bits in the TDR to the peripheral device. This means that the MPU should store another byte of data in the

FIGURE 13.3.4   The ACIA's Status Register

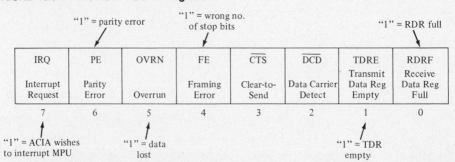

TDR. In this case also the IRQ bit (bit 7) gets set. When the MPU stores more data, bit 7 is cleared.

Bits 4, 5, and 6 are error-message bits. Bit 4 is set if there was a framing error, meaning a mistake in the number of stop bits. Bit 5, Overrun, is set if some data is lost because it wasn't read before new data was received. Bit 6, Parity Error (PE), is set if the parity of the transmitted character doesn't agree with the parity that has been established.

Bit 7, Interrupt Request (IRQ) is set when the ACIA wishes to interrupt the MPU. When this bit is set, the $\overline{\text{IRQ}}$ output line can go low and interrupt the MPU if the interrupt is enabled (more about that later.)

EXAMPLE 13.3.1

What conditions are present in the ACIA if the status register contains $92?

Solution

We write the word in binary and compare its bit values with the functions on Figure 13.3.4.

%1001 0010

Bit 7 set means that the ACIA wishes to interrupt the MPU. Bits 6 and 5 we pass over; bit 4 set means there is a framing error; bits 3 and 2 we pass over; bit 1 set means that the transmit data register is empty (which caused bit 7 to be set).

Answer: The ACIA is in the interrupt state, there is a framing error, and the TDR is empty.

The **Control Register (CR)** is an 8-bit register in the ACIA that determines division of external clock, number of data bits, parity, transmitter control, and interrupts enabled. The control register is write only. That is, we can write into it but we can't read from it. Figure 13.3.5 shows the control register and its bits. Unlike the PIA's control register, where each bit had a separate function, many of the ACIA's control bits function as groups of two or three. Table 13.3.1 lists the bit patterns for the functions controlled by bits 0 and 1 and by bits 2, 3, and 4. We won't be discussing bits 5 and 6 right now.

Bits 0 and 1 are the **counter divide select** bits, which let us select the divide ratio for the external clock. The values of 0 and 0 for a "divide by one" aren't used

FIGURE 13.3.5 The ACIA's Control Register

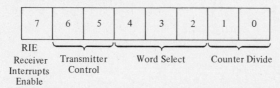

TABLE 13.3.1   Bit Patterns for Groups in Control Register

			Counter Divide Select Bits	
			1	0
	DIVIDE BY 1		0	0
	DIVIDE BY 16		0	1
	DIVIDE BY 64		1	0
	MASTER RESET		1	1

No. of Data Bits	Parity Bit	No. of Stop Bits	Word Select Bits		
			4	3	2
7	Even	2	0	0	0
7	Odd	2	0	0	1
7	Even	1	0	1	0
7	Odd	1	0	1	1
8	None	2	1	0	0
8	None	1	1	0	1
8	Even	1	1	1	0
8	Odd	1	1	1	1

much. If the baud rate is divided only by one, then we don't have the mechanism for multiple reads of the start bit and for centering the readings. The values of 1 and 1 are for the master reset. As seen from Figure 13.3.1, the ACIA has no RESET pin and has to be reset with software. Master reset clears the status register and initializes the received and transmitter. Resetting the ACIA is usually part of the RESET interrupt service routine and must be done before setting the clock divide ratio.

Bits 2, 3, and 4 are the **word select bits**. Here we can choose our word length, parity, and number of stop bits by selecting the appropriate bit pattern for our application.

Finally, bit 7 is the Receiver Interrupt Enable (RIE). If it is set, then interrupts are enabled when bit 7 of the status register is set.

EXAMPLE 13.3.2

What is the control word for this set of conditions: interrupts enabled; 7 data bits; even parity; 2 stop bits; divide by 16?

Solution

First, to enable interrupts we store a 1 in bit 7. Bits 5 and 6 will not be used and will be loaded with zeros. To get the bit pattern for 2, 3, and 4, we look at Table 13.3.1. For 7 data bits, even parity, and 2 stop bits we find the pattern 000. Next, the pattern for bits 0 and 1 is 01 for divide by 16.

Answer: %1000 0001, or $81

EXAMPLE 13.3.3

What conditions are specified by the control word $9E?

Solution

First, we write the word in binary: %1001 1110. Next, bit 7 set means interrupts enabled. We pass over bits 5 and 6; the bit pattern 111 for bits 2, 3, and 4 means an 8-bit word, odd parity, 1 stop bit. The bit pattern 10 on bits 1 and 0 means divide by 64.

Answer: Interrupts enabled, 8-bit word, odd parity, 1 stop bit, divide by 64.

Addressing the ACIA's Registers

If we look at the memory map of Figure 12.1.6, we see that the Motorola D2 places its ACIA at addresses $8008 and $8009, indicating that the four registers of the ACIA somehow have to share two addresses. This is reasonable, because we know that a similar situation exists in the PIA, where the data and data direction registers share the same address.

The system designer has the option of placing the ACIA at any two convenient consecutive addresses. The lower of the two is shared by the control and status registers. The control register is write only, so by writing into the common address (as with a STA instruction), we automatically address the control register. And if we read from the common address (as with a LDA instruction), we automatically address the status register. Note that we can never examine the control register to see what we've stored in it. Also, we can't change the contents of the status register because we can't write in it.

The higher of the two ACIA addresses is shared by the two data registers, the RDR and TDR. We have the same situation here as before. Writing into that address (as with a STA instruction) automatically addresses the TDR, and reading from that address (as with a LDA instruction) automatically addresses the RDR.

EXAMPLE 13.3.4

Write a program segment that first resets the ACIA of the Motorola D2, then sets it for interrupts disabled, 7 data bits, 2 stop bits, odd parity, and divide by 16. Then read the RDR.

Solution

The address of SR/CR is $8008, and TDR/RDR is $8009. So we make labels. To reset the ACIA, bits 0 and 1 must be set, and that's all we want to do, so that control word is %00000011, or $03. We figure out the next control word in the usual way

(%00000101, or $05). To read the RDR, we load an accumulator with the contents of RDR's address.

Answer

```
ACIACR   EQU   $8008
RDR      EQU   $8009
         LDA A  #$03     READY TO RESET ACIA
         STA A  ACIACR   RESET ACIA
         LDA A  #$05     DISABLE INTS, 7 DATA BITS, ODD PARITY,
         STA A  ACIACR   2 STOP BITS, AND DIVIDE BY 16
         LDA A  RDR      READ THE DATA REGISTER
```

Next, we'll look at some specific examples for using the ACIA.

13.4 USING THE ACIA

Like the PIA, the ACIA can be used in a number of ways. We could use an ACIA to interface the MPU with a CRT terminal, a printer, a teletype, or a modem (a device that provides a telephone connection between a computer and a remote terminal). The Motorola D2 uses an ACIA to interface the MPU with a cassette tape recorder so that programs can be stored on tape and reloaded into memory when desired.

A Simple Configuration

Figure 13.4.1 shows one of many possible configurations of MPU, ACIA, and PIA. We see that both the ACIA and the PIA can now interrupt the MPU. When an

FIGURE 13.4.1 A Possible Configuration of ACIA, PIA, and MPU

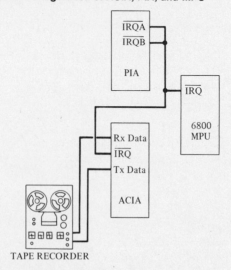

interrupt occurs, the MPU must poll the PIA and the ACIA to see which caused the interrupt. We know how to poll the PIA: examine bits 6 and 7 of the PIA's control register. To poll the ACIA, we examine bit 7 of the ACIA's status register, which will be set if the ACIA caused the interrupt. If the ACIA caused the interrupt, next the MPU must find out whether it is to transmit or receive data. If bit 0 of the ACIA's status register is set, then the MPU is to receive data by reading the RDR. If bit 1 of the status register is set, the MPU is to transmit data by storing a word in the TDR.

EXAMPLE 13.4.1

For a system configured as in Figure 13.4.1, the PIA is at addresses $7000, $7001, $7002, and $7003. The ACIA is at addresses $9000 and $9001. Write a polling routine that transfers control to a subroutine TRANS if the MPU is to transmit data, to RECV if the MPU is to receive data, and PIASRV if the interrupt came from the PIA. The ACIA is to have highest priority.

Solution

If the ACIA is to have highest priority, we poll it first. We assume that there are only two main sources of interrupt: the PIA and the ACIA. If the ACIA didn't interrupt, then the PIA must have. If bit 7 of the status register (address $9000) is set, then the ACIA caused the interrupt; if clear, we branch to PIASRV. Next, we look at bit 0 of the status register by shifting that bit right into the carry. If the carry is set, we branch to RECV. If clear, we assume that the interrupt came from the transmit data register.

Answer:

```
POLL   LDA A   $9000    GET ACIA SR CONTENTS
       BPL     PIASRV   NOT ACIA; MUST BE PIA
       LSR A            SHIFT BIT 0 INTO CARRY
       BCS     RECV     GO RECEIVE DATA
       BRA     TRANS    MUST BE TRANS INTERRUPT
```

A typical transmit sequence would have the microprocessor make sure that the TDR is empty by examining bit 1 of the status register. If bit 1 were clear the microprocessor would wait until it were set, then get the new data word and store it in the TDR. Then it would return to the calling program.

EXAMPLE 13.4.2

Write a subroutine called TRANS that checks to see whether the TDR is empty and, if it is, gets a byte of data from location TRNBUF, stores it in the TDR, and returns to the main program.

Solution

To see whether the TDR is empty, we read the status register and examine bit 1 by shifting or rotating twice into the carry. We keep examining this bit until it is set, then store the value.

Answer:

```
TRANS   LDA A   ACIASR   GET CONTENTS OF STATUS REGISTER
        ROR A            SHIFT BIT 0 RIGHT INTO CARRY
        ROR A            SHIFT BIT 1 RIGHT INTO CARRY
        BCC     TRANS    NOT EMPTY YET? WAIT
        LDA A   TRNBUF   GET NEW DATA WORD
        STA A   TDR      PUT IT IN TDR
        RTS              AND RETURN
```

Once the microprocessor stores the data word in the TDR, the ACIA will output the bits serially without any more attention from the MPU. The external clock will make sure that the bits are sent out. That's why we can just store the byte and continue with what we're doing.

Receiving data, as seen in Section 13.2, is slightly more involved than transmitting, especially when we use an ACIA. A routine to receive data would check the 3 error bits of the status register to make sure they were clear before reading the RDR.

EXAMPLE 13.4.3

Write a subroutine called RECV that first waits until the RDR is full. Then it should check the 3 error status bits. If PE is set, it should branch to subroutine PARERR. If overrun is set, branch to OVRN. If FE is set, branch to FERR. If these bits are all clear, read the data word and store it in RECBUF.

Solution

To see whether RDR is full, we check bit 0 by shifting right into the carry. We can check the error bits by shifting 1, 2, and 3 bits left, using ROL or ASL, and checking bit 7 each time. For example, to check bit 6, we shift 1 bit left; if bit 7 gets set, then 6 contained a 1.

Answer:

```
RECV     LDA A   ACIASR   GET CONTENTS OF STATUS REGISTER
         ROR A            SHIFT BIT 0 INTO CARRY
         BCC     RECV     RDR NOT FULL YET? WAIT
ERRCHK   LDA A   ACIASR   GET SR AGAIN FOR ERROR CHECK
         ROL A            SHIFT LEFT 1 BIT
         BMI     PARERR   BIT 6 SET? PARITY ERROR
         ROL A            SHIFT LEFT AGAIN
         BMI     OVRN     BIT 5 SET? OVERRUN
         ROL A            SHIFT LEFT ONE MORE TIME
```

```
BMI     FERR      BIT 4 SET? FRAMING ERROR
LDA A   RDR       NO ERRORS; RECEIVE DATA
STA A   RECBUF    STORE IT IN RECBUF
RTS               AND RETURN
```

A Sample Dump Routine

A transfer of a block of data from the microcomputer's memory to a peripheral is called a **dump** or **punch**. If we are willing to devote the microprocessor solely to this activity for the duration of the dump, we don't need to use interrupts. For example, the Motorola D2 dumps from memory to a cassette tape recorder without using interrupts.

Figure 13.4.2 is a flowchart and Figure 13.4.3 is a sample program to dump the contents of memory onto tape via an ACIA. The block can be of indefinite length. The user places the starting address of the data into $1000 and $1001 manually and the ending address into $1002 and $1003. We want to put $AA at the beginning of the dump as a control word and $FF at the end. Control should be returned to the monitor at address $E019 when the dump is complete.

Lines 3 through 12 explain the program and establish labels. Lines 13 and 14 reset the ACIA so that it can be configured. Line 15 points to the start of the block of data. Line 16 increments the contents of location $1003, which is the low-order byte of the ending address. We want to terminate when the index register points to the last address plus one. Lines 17 and 18 configure the ACIA as described. Lines 19 through 24 punch $AA and wait for it to be transmitted. The data itself is transferred with the loop from lines 25 through 33. Then lines 34 through 39 punch $FF at the end.

A Sample Load Routine

A transfer of a block of data from a peripheral device to the microcomputer's memory is called a **load**. As with the dump, we can load without using interrupts if the microprocessor devotes full time to the task.

Figure 13.4.4 shows a flowchart for a program to load memory with the contents of a cassette tape. The user puts the starting address into locations $1004 and $1005. The microprocessor looks for $AA to indicate the start of the data and for $FF to indicate the end.

Figure 13.4.5 lists the load program. This program is very simple. It ignores the error flags of the status register, but we could add subroutines to check these. In both the dump and load programs the return to monitor tells us that the transfer has been completed. Then we have to turn off the tape recorder ourselves. We could make the programs more sophisticated by turning the recorder on and off under program control.

FIGURE 13.4.2   General Flowchart for Dump Program

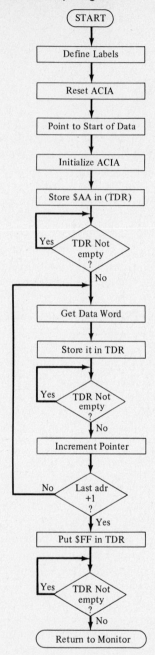

FIGURE 13.4.3 Dump Memory Contents onto Tape

DUMP
M6800 ASSEMBLER LISTING VERSION 1.6   13 DEC 80 19:18   PAGE   2
DUMP   DAT   13 DEC 80 19:17

```
                  3 ;THIS PROGRAM DUMPS A BLOCK OF DATA ONTO CASSETTE TAPE
                  4 ;USER LOADS STARTING ADDRESS OF DATA INTO $1000 AND $1001
                  5 ;AND ENDING ADDRESS OF DATA INTO $1002 AND $1003
8008              6 ACIACR EQU    $8008
8008              7 ACIASR EQU    ACIACR
8009              8 RDR    EQU    $8009
8009              9 TDR    EQU    RDR
E08D             10 MON    EQU    $E019
1000             11 BEGIN  EQU    $1000
1002             12 FINI   EQU    $1002
0000 86 03       13        LDA A  #$03        READY TO RESET ACIA
0002 B7 80 08    14        STA A  ACIACR      RESET ACIA
0005 FE 10 00    15        LDX    BEGIN       POINT TO START OF DATA BLOCK
0008 7C 10 03    16        INC    $1003       END POINTER TO LAST ADDR+1
000B 96 0D       17        LDA A  %00001101   READY TO CONFIG ACIA DISABLE INTERRUPTS,
000D B7 80 08    18        STA A  ACIACR      7 DATA BITS, ODD PARITY, DIVIDE BY 16
0010 86 AA       19        LDA A  #$AA        READY TO SEND START WORD
0012 B7 80 09    20        STA A  TDR         PUT IT INTO TDR
0015 B6 80 08    21 WAITD  LDA A  ACIASR      GET STATUS REG CONTENTS
0018 46          22        ROR A              PUT BIT 0 INTO CARRY
0019 46          23        ROR A              PUT BIT 1 INTO CARRY
001A 24 F9       24        BCC    WAITD       STILL TRANSMITTING BITS?
001C A6 00       25 GETD   LDA A  0,X         GET DATA BYTE
001E B7 80 09    26        STA A  TDR         PUT IT INTO TDR
0021 B6 80 08    27 WAIT2  LDA A  ACIASR      GET STATUS REG CONTENTS
0024 46          28        ROR A              PUT BIT 0 INTO CARRY
0025 46          29        ROR A              PUT BIT 1 INTO CARRY
0026 24 F9       30        BCC    WAIT2       STILL TRANSMITTING BITS?
0028 08          31        INX                NO, POINT TO NEXT DATA ENTRY
0029 BC 10 03    32        CPX    FINI        COMPARE WITH END ADDRESS
002C 26 EE       33        BNE    GETD        STILL DATA TO DUMP?
002E 86 FF       34        LDA A  #$FF        NO, READY TO SEND END CHARACTER
0030 B7 80 09    35        STA A  TDR         PUT FF IN TDR
0033 B6 80 08    36 WAIT3  LDA A  ACIASR      GET STATUS REG CONTENTS
0036 46          37        ROR A              PUT BIT 0 INTO CARRY
0037 46          38        ROR A              PUT BIT 1 INTO CARRY
0038 24 F9       39        BCC    WAIT3       STILL TRANSMITTING BITS?
003A 7E E0 8D    40        JMP    MON         NO, DONE
003D             41        END
```

NO STATEMENTS FLAGGED

CROSS-REFERENCE TABLE

ACIACR	8008	6	7	14	18
ACIASR	8008	7	21	27	36
BEGIN	1000	11	15		
FINI	1002	12	32		
GETD	001C	25	33		
MON	E08D	10	40		
RDR	8009	8	9		
TDR	8009	9	20	26	35
WAIT2	0021	27	30		
WAIT3	0033	36	39		
WAITD	0015	21	24		

FIGURE 13.4.4 Flowchart for Load Program

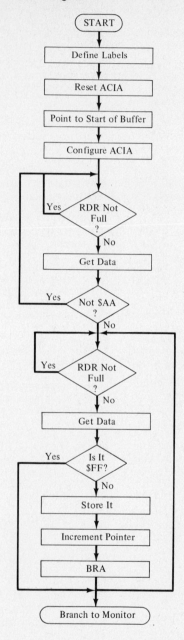

FIGURE 13.4.5   Load Memory from Tape

LOAD
M6800 ASSEMBLER LISTING VERSION 1.6   13 DEC 80 19:37   PAGE   2
LOAD   DAT   13 DEC 80 19:36

```
                    3 ;THIS PROGRAM LOADS A BLOCK OF DATA INTO MEMORY FROM
                    4 ;CASSETTE TAPE. USER LOADS STARTING ADDRESS OF DATA INTO
                    5 ;$1004 AND $1005. CONTROL IS RETURNED TO MONITOR WHEN FINISHED
1004                6 START    EQU     $1004
8008                7 ACIACR   EQU     $8008
8008                8 ACIASR   EQU     ACIACR
8009                9 RDR      EQU     $8009
8009               10 TDR      EQU     RDR
E019               11 MON      EQU     $E019
0000 86 03         12          LDA A  #$03          READY TO RESET ACIA
0002 B7 80 08      13          STA A   ACIACR       RESET ACIA
0005 FE 10 04      14          LDX     START        LOAD STARTING ADDRESS
0008 96 0D         15          LDA A  %00001101     READY TO CONFIG ACIA: DISABLE INTERRUPTS,
000A B7 80 08      16          STA A   ACIACR       7 DATA BITS, ODD PARITY, DIVIDE BY 16
000D B6 80 08      17 WAITL    LDA A   ACIASR       GET STATUS REGISTER
0010 46            18          ROR A                SHIFT BIT 0 INTO CARRY
0011 24 FA         19          BCC     WAITL        NOT READY TO READ?
0013 B6 80 09      20          LDA A   RDR          NO, GET DATA
0016 81 AA         21          CMP A  #$AA          IS IT THE START CONTROL WORD?
0018 26 F3         22          BNE     WAITL        NO, KEEP LOOKING
001A B6 80 08      23 WAIT1    LDA A   ACIASR       YES, GET SR
001D 46            24          ROR A                SHIFT BIT 0 INTO CARRY
001E 24 FA         25          BCC     WAIT1        NOT READY TO READ?
0020 B6 80 09      26          LDA A   RDR          NO, GET DATA
0023 81 FF         27          CMP A  #$FF          IS IT THE END CONTROL WORD?
0025 27 05         28          BEQ     DONE         YES, DONE
0027 A7 00         29          STA A   0,X          NO, STORE IN BUFFER
0029 08            30          INX                  INCREMENT POINTER
002A 20 EE         31          BRA     WAIT1        NEXT WORD
002C 7E E0 19      32 DONE     JMP     MON          BRANCH TO MONITOR
002F               33          END
```

NO STATEMENTS FLAGGED

CROSS-REFERENCE TABLE

ACIACR	8008	7	8	13	16
ACIASR	8008	8	17	23	
DONE	002C	32	28		
MON	E019	11	32		
RDR	8009	9	10	20	26
START	1004	6	14		
TDR	8009	10			
WAIT1	001A	23	25	31	
WAITL	000D	17	19	22	

In this chapter we've touched on a few, but not all, applications of the ACIA. More advanced texts will discuss the modem control aspects of the ACIA.

In the next chapter we'll look at still more I/O concepts.

REVIEW QUESTIONS

1. Explain the difference between **serial** and **parallel I/O**. Give a familiar simple example of serial I/O.
2. What is a **serial input** and a **serial output port**? What are their advantages over parallel I/O ports? What is the major disadvantage of serial I/O?
3. Explain the difference between **synchronous** and **asynchronous** serial data transmission. What is the major requirement in asynchronous transmission?
4. Illustrate with a sketch how we represent a serial ASCII character as a series of high and low voltages.
5. What are **bit time** and **baud rate**? How do we convert between them? Why do we need them?
6. What are **start** and **stop bits**? How do we use these to **frame** an ASCII character? Sketch an ASCII character that has 1 start bit and 2 stop bits.
7. How do we calculate the **character time** and **character rate**?
8. Explain how to use the ROL and ROR instructions. How are they different from the ASL and LSR instructions? How are they similar?
9. Explain how to use the rotate instructions to extend a serial ASCII character from 8 to 11 bits.
10. Which is more complex, serial input or output? Explain.
11. What is a **noise spike**? What is another name for it? How can it cause errors in transmission?
12. Why do we try to read each bit somewhere in the middle rather than near either edge?
13. Explain how to do serial I/O using a PIA.
14. What is an **ACIA**? What is its function?
15. Explain the functions of the ACIA pins Tx Data, Rx Data, IRQ, Tx CLK, and Rx CLK.
16. What is the relationship of the external clock frequency and the baud rate? Explain how the ACIA uses this relationship to synchronize serial bits.
17. What is a **shift register**? Illustrate the functions of the **transmit data register** and the **receive data register**. Can we read and write in either of these? Explain.
18. What are the ACIA's **status register** and **control register**? Can we read and write in either of these? Explain.
19. Define and explain all bits of the ACIA's status register except for bits 2 and 3. Explain how to interpret a specific status word.
20. Which are the control register's **counter divide select bits**? How do we use them?
21. Which are the control register's **word select bits**? What functions can we select using these, and how do we know what values to place in them?
22. What is the RIE bit? What is it used for?
23. Explain how to derive a control word for a given set of specifications.
24. Explain how the four ACIA registers share two addresses. How do we know which register we are addressing?

25. How do we poll the ACIA? How do we know whether the ACIA is ready to receive or to transmit?
26. Explain how to write a typical transmit and receive sequence.
27. How do we reset the ACIA? Why do we need to do this?
28. Explain the sample dump and load routines (Figures 13.4.3 and 13.4.5).

EXERCISES

Set A (answers at back of book)

1. For an ASCII character with 1 stop bit and a rate of 300 baud, calculate (a) the bit time; (b) the character rate; (c) the character time.
2. Give the contents of location WORD and the carry bit after these program segments are executed:

```
(a)  CLC            (b)  CLC
     LDA A  #$F0         LDA A #$F0
     STA A  WORD         STA A WORD
     ROR    WORD         ASL  WORD
     ROL    WORD         LSR  WORD
```

3. We have configured the PIA so that DA0 is a serial output port. Write a program segment that will output the 9-bit word 111100000 serially through DA0 starting with the MSB.
4. Modify the program of Figure 13.2.2 for 2 stop bits. Show only the statements that are new or changed.
5. In the program of Figure 13.2.4 we wish to check the parity of the input ASCII character using a subroutine PARCHK that takes a value in accumulator A and checks its parity. Insert statements with appropriate line numbers to accomplish this.
6. What conditions are present in the ACIA if the status register contains $C1?
7. What is the control word for these conditions: interrupts disabled; 8-bit data word; odd parity; 1 stop bit; divide by 64?
8. What conditions are specified by the control word $11?
9. Write a program segment that resets the ACIA, configures it for interrupts enabled, 7 data bits, 1 stop bit, even parity, and divide by 16. Then write $FF into the TDR. The ACIA's addresses are $C002 and $C003.
10. We have connected two ACIAs to a MPU's $\overline{IRQ}$ line. ACIA 1 is at $8000 and $8001 and ACIA 2 is at $8002 and $8003. ACIA 1 is connected to a receive-only device for emergency messages. ACIA 2 is connected to a CRT terminal. Write a polling routine with ACIA 1 having top priority. Branch to EMERG if there is an emergency message. Otherwise branch to TRANS or RECV if the interrupt resulted from the CRT terminal trying to transmit or receive.
11. Write a subroutine RECV for a no-parity situation. Ignore the parity error bit. If there is a framing error, branch to FRAMER. If there is an overrun, branch to OVERUN. Otherwise read the data register and store the word in $0100. Wait for one more data word, read it, and store it in $0101.

EXERCISES

Set B (answers not given)

1. For an ASCII character with 2 stop bits and a rate of 600 baud, calculate (a) the bit time; (b) the character rate; and (c) the character time.

2. Give the contents of accumulator B and the carry bit after each of these program segments is executed:

   (a)   SEC   (b)   SEC
         LDA B   LDA B # $FF
         ASL B   LDA B # $FF
         LSR B   ROR B
         ROL B

3. We have configured the PIA so that DA0 is a serial output port. Write a program segment that will output the 9-bit word 001111001 serially through DA0 starting with the LSB.

4. How would the program of Figure 13.2.2 be modified for a baud rate of 300?

5. Modify the program of Figure 13.2.4 for 2 stop bits. Show only the lines that have changed.

6. What conditions are present in the ACIA if the status register contains $10?

7. What is the control word for these conditions: interrupts enabled; 7-bit data word; odd parity; 1 stop bit; divide by 16?

8. What conditions are specified by the control word $8D?

9. Write a program segment that resets the ACIA, then configures it for interrupts disabled, 8-bit word, no parity, 2 stop bits, and divide by 64. Then read from the RDR. The ACIA's addresses are $A000 and $A001.

10. We have connected a PIA and an ACIA to a MPU. The PIA is at $9000, $9001, $9003, and $9004. The ACIA is at $A020 and $A021. Side A of the PIA is connected to a smoke alarm and has top priority. The ACIA is connected to a tape recorder and has next priority. Side B of the PIA is connected to a thermostat and has lowest priority. Write a polling routine that branches to FIRE, RECV, TRANS, or THERM if the appropriate device caused the interrupt.

11. Write a subroutine TRANS that checks to see whether the TDR is empty and, if it is, gets a byte of data from $A000 and stores it in the TDR. Repeat for 1 more byte of data and store it in $A000, then return.

PROGRAMMING IDEAS

1. With the PIA configured so that DA0 is a serial output port and DA7 a serial input port, write a program to output a block of data starting at location $A000 and ending at location $A0FF. The conditions are 300 baud, 2 stop bits. You may branch to undefined subroutines for timing delays and for configuring the PIA. Assume the block of data is to be moved all at once without using interrupts.

2. With the PIA configured as in (1), write a program to input a block of data and store it in memory starting at $A000. The end of the data is marked by $FF. Check each character for a framing error and branch to subroutine ERR if there is one. Assume the same conditions as in (1).

3. Write a program that initializes the ACIA for 7 bits of data, odd parity, and 2 stop bits, with divide by 16, disable interrupts. Transmit a block of data stored in locations $A000 through $A0AA.

4. We wish to receive a block of data 1 byte at a time, using interrupts to indicate that each byte is ready to be read by the MPU. There are $20 pieces of data, which are to be stored starting at location $9000. Write an interrupt service routine that will accomplish this. Disable MPU interrupts while this routine is in progress and enable them at the end. The calling program stores the starting address of the storage buffer in the index register.

5. The dump program of Figure 13.4.3 has a few primitive aspects. First, having only one control character at the beginning and at the end might cause errors later in loading if the actual data were AA or FF. Second, cassette tape usually contains some "leader" at the beginning that doesn't accept data. Write a dump program that punches 25 zeros at the beginning of the tape to get past the leader, then places double control characters at the beginning and at the end of the data. The program should compute the length of the block and use a counter to determine when to terminate.

6. Write a load program to input the tape produced by the dump program of (5). The microprocessor should expect two $AA's in a row and two $FF's in a row for the beginning and end of the file. Store the data beginning at $A000. Check each character for parity, framing, and overrun errors, and branch to subroutine ERR if one is found. Assume the same character format as in Figure 13.4.5.

7. Another primitive aspect of the dump and load programs of Figures 13.4.3 and 13.4.5 is that we must manually turn off the tape recorder when the dump or load is finished. Suppose we use a PIA in addition to the ACIA and we have wired DA7 to the motor control of the tape recorder so that a 0 in DA7 means "recorder on" and a 1 means "recorder off." Modify the dump program so that at the beginning the recorder is turned on and at the end it is turned off.

8. For the same conditions as in (7), and with DA6 wired to an LED, write a load program [or modify that of (6)] that turns the recorder on at the beginning and off at the end or if there is a parity, framing, or overrun error. If there is an error, the LED should be lit.

14 Introduction to System Configuration

LEARNING OBJECTIVES

After completing this chapter, you should be able to:

1. Give a definition, explanation, or example for each of these: *configure, two-state logic, binary logic, digital logic, logical operation, logic circuit, logic gate, NOT function, NOT gate, invert, inverter, OR gate, OR function, NOR function, NOR gate, exclusive-OR function, exclusive-OR gate, AND function, AND gate, strip, masking, mask, NAND function, NAND gate, three-state buffer, high impedance state, chip select, address decoding, register select, system layout worksheet, full decoding.*
2. State and illustrate with diagrams how to make these connections among the MPU and RAM, ROM, PIA, ACIA, and clock: power and ground, clock, read/write, data lines, interrupts, lower address lines.
3. Interpret logic diagrams in terms of input and output, and interpret and use the 6800's logic instructions.
4. Use the OR and AND instructions to strip or to restore bits.
5. Use the BIT instruction to test single bits in I/O programs.
6. Explain what happens during the high and low edges of the Phase 1 and Phase 2 clock signals.
7. Explain the MPU's VMA pin, and how to connect it and the Phase 2 clock to devices.
8. Devise an address decoding scheme for a system, and interpret an existing one.

We've seen some of the building blocks of a microprocessor system: the MPU, RAM, ROM, the ACIA, and the PIA. To make a system out of these components,

FIGURE 14.1.1 Pin Assignments

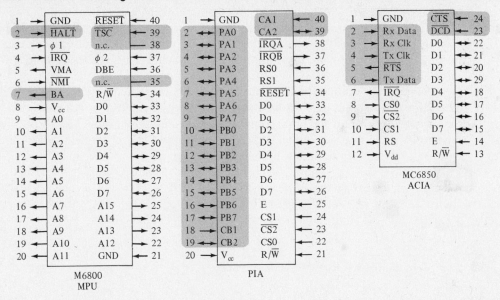

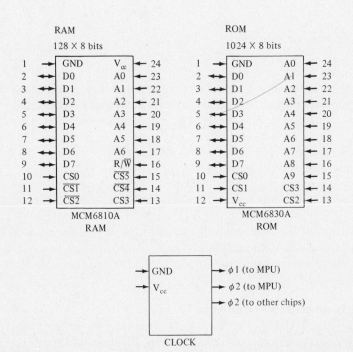

we have to connect them correctly, along with a clock to provide timing. Many books have been written about microprocessor interfacing and system design, and a detailed discussion of these is beyond the scope and intent of this book. However, in this chapter we'll attempt to introduce some of the considerations involved in making connections among these hardware components. Then readers can refer to more advanced texts fortified by a little prior knowledge.

Suppose we want to build a microprocessor system that has an MPU, three 128×8-bit RAMs, one 1024×8-bit ROM, two PIAs, one ACIA, and a clock. Each device has a set of pins for input/output, control, and power. Somehow these pins have to be wired into the system. When we **configure** a microprocessor system, we decide exactly how all devices will be wired together.

First, we have to know what pins we have to work with. We've seen pin diagrams of the MPU, the PIA, and the ACIA earlier. For convenience, these are shown side by side in Figure 14.1.1, along with a 128×8-bit RAM chip, a 1024×8-bit ROM chip, and a clock, which we haven't seen before.

14.1 THE SIMPLER PIN ASSIGNMENTS

As in several previous instances, our task won't seem so formidable if we can simplify it by eliminating some of the pins and first making those pin assignments that are the most straightforward.

Unused Pins on the MPU

The shaded pins on the MPU diagram of Figure 14.1.1 are pins that we won't be using in this chapter. Pin 2, $\overline{\text{HALT}}$, causes the microprocessor to finish executing the current instruction and stop. This input is sometimes used in microcomputer systems as a debugging tool and would be attached to some external control if it were used. In many applications $\overline{\text{HALT}}$ isn't needed, and in that case we want to wire it so that the MPU won't be halted. Because $\overline{\text{HALT}}$ is active low, wiring this pin permanently to +5 V (volts) will prevent it from becoming active.

We won't be using pin 39 (TSC) either, so we'll connect it to +5 V, too. Pin 7, which we're also not using, doesn't need to be connected to anything since it's an output.

Pins 35 and 38 are labeled n.c., which means "not connected." These are extra pins in the DIP for which no use was found, or whose function is reserved for other versions of the microprocessor.

Pins Connected to Peripherals

In previous chapters we covered lines of the PIA and ACIA that are connected to peripheral devices. So we won't need to discuss them further here. The shaded pins on the PIA and ACIA diagrams of Figure 14.1.1 are those that are connected to peripheral devices.

Next, we might take the approach of looking for pins that have the same name or function on each chip and of connecting them together.

Power and Ground

We see that all six devices have at least 1 pin called "GND" (ground) and one called V (voltage). This we expect, because without a power and a ground connection, an electrical device won't work. Figure 14.1.2 shows the power and ground connections between the devices in our system and a 5-V power supply. The small numbers are the pin numbers for the devices.

FIGURE 14.1.2 Power and Ground Connections in System

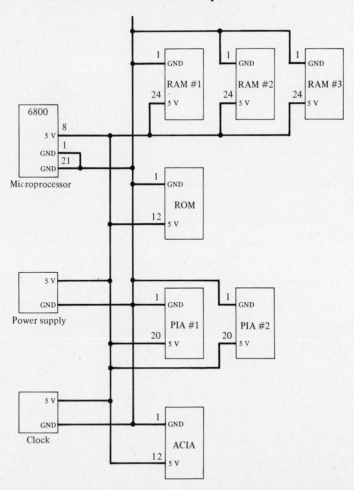

Interrupts

We know that the MPU has three interrupt inputs: $\overline{\text{RESET}}$, $\overline{\text{NMI}}$, and $\overline{\text{IRQ}}$. First, let's consider the reset. We know that the PIA has a $\overline{\text{RESET}}$ that is connected, along with the MPU's $\overline{\text{RESET}}$ pin, to an external push-button switch. We also know that the ACIA has no $\overline{\text{RESET}}$ pin but is reset in software. Looking at the diagrams for the RAM and ROM chips, we don't find any $\overline{\text{RESET}}$ pins for them either. Memory chips have a much simpler (but just as important) function than the PIA or ACIA: to store data. Memory chips don't have any other registers besides memory locations, and we certainly don't want to zero those every time we press Reset. So we'll have connections only between the $\overline{\text{RESET}}$ lines of the MPU and of the two PIA's.

We know that the MPU, the PIA, and ACIA all have interrupt lines. Looking at the RAM and ROM diagrams, we don't find any interrupt lines on them. These memory chips can't interrupt the MPU. So the interrupt connections are fairly simple. Figure 14.1.3 shows our interrupt connections. We've chosen to connect $\overline{\text{IRQB}}$ of PIA #2 to the MPU's $\overline{\text{NMI}}$ pin and all other interrupts, to the MPU's IRQ pin.

Clock Connections

We find two clock inputs to the MPU: $\phi 1$ (pin 3) and $\phi 2$ (pin 37). The clock itself has outputs labeled $\phi 1$ (to MPU), $\phi 2$ (to MPU), and $\phi 2$ (to other chips). We don't find any pins labeled as clock inputs on the other chips, thus we'll have to

FIGURE 14.1.3 Interrupt Connections for the System

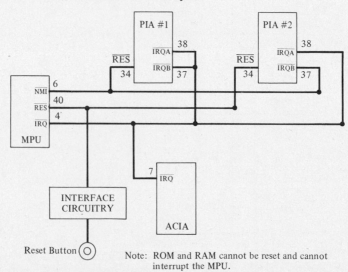

Note: ROM and RAM cannot be reset and cannot interrupt the MPU.

FIGURE 14.1.4   Connections Between MPU and Clock

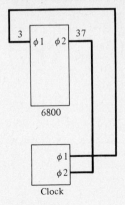

leave the clock output $\phi2$ (to other chips) for a bit later. Figure 14.1.4 shows the connections between the MPU and the clock.

Read/Write

We find a $R/\overline{W}$ pin on every chip but ROM. We recall from Chapter 1 that the $R/\overline{W}$, READ/$\overline{WRITE}$, pin is high when the MPU is reading and low when it is writing. In ROM there is no possibility of writing into it, so this pin isn't needed. For all of the others we connect their $R/\overline{W}$ inputs to the $R/\overline{W}$ output of the MPU.

Data Lines

All chips have data lines D0 through D7. This is expected, because the object of computing is to exchange and process data. We know that all of the data lines are connected through the data bus. Figure 14.1.5 shows the data bus and READ/$\overline{WRITE}$ line connections.

Lower Address Lines

We find address lines A0 through A6 on the RAM chip and address lines A0 through A9 on the ROM chip. The PIA and ACIA don't have any address lines at all. We can connect the MPU's address lines A0 through A6 to the RAM chips and A0 through A9, to the ROM chip. Figure 14.1.6 shows the MPU's lower address lines connected to RAM and ROM. Why different numbers of lines for RAM and ROM? Why don't the PIA and the ACIA have address lines? And what happens to the rest of the MPU's address lines?

FIGURE 14.1.5   Data Bus and R/$\overline{\text{W}}$ Connections

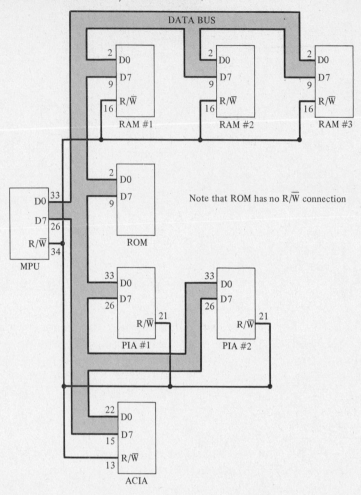

First, we recall that a memory chip is a matrix of bits that are located by row and column. The RAM chips we have chosen are 128×8 bits, meaning of course 128 bytes of storage, or $80 bytes. Each RAM chip has a built-in mechanism for locating a particular byte within its matrix. To give 128 possible combinations, we need 7 bits, or 7 address lines (A0–A6). All we have to do is to connect these to the MPU's equivalent address lines, and the RAM chip will do the rest.

Similarly, our ROM is 1024×8 bits, or 1024 bytes. To give 1024 combinations, we need 10 bits, or 10 address lines (A0–A9). Given those lines, the ROM chip will automatically locate a single byte within its matrix.

We've connected the same lower address lines to all the RAM chips and the ROM chip (which has one more address line than the RAM chip). Later on, we'll

FIGURE 14.1.6 Connecting the MPU's Lower Address Lines to RAM and ROM

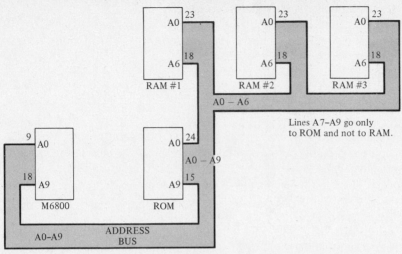

use the higher address lines to assign each device an exclusive block of memory that belongs to it only. This is how we separate the memory chips so that they don't all respond to the same value on the lower address lines.

The PIA and ACIA have no address lines because they don't need them. Instead of a matrix of memory locations, each PIA has only four meaningful addresses, and each ACIA has only two. We'll see a little later how we take care of these. As with RAM and ROM, we use the higher address lines to assign each PIA and the ACIA its own exclusive block of memory.

We've run out of obvious connections to make, but we've taken care of quite a few pins. Before we can see how to connect the remaining pins, we need to look at logical operations.

14.2 LOGICAL OPERATIONS

By now we're used to letting a binary number mean whatever we choose it to mean. In **two-state**, or **binary, logic**, the values 1 and 0 take on the meanings "true" and "false." In Chapter 7 we learned some arithmetic operations using 1's and 0's as numbers and saw that these operations could be described with truth tables.

Just as binary arithmetic consists of a set of variables (0 and 1) and a series of arithmetic operations, binary logic (also known as **digital logic**) consists of a set of variables (0 and 1) and a series of logical operations. A **logical operation** is one that treats the two variables 0 and 1 as false and true rather than as the numbers 0 and 1. Logical operations are implemented electronically with **logic circuits**. A logic circuit that has one or more inputs and only one output is a **logic gate**. In what follows, we'll denote logical input variables by A, B, C, D and output variables by the letters

X and Y. Just as we have symbols to describe arithmetic operations ($+$, $-$, and so on) there are symbols for each logical operation.

We'll look at each logical operation, its truth table, and the symbol for its gate. In addition, some logical operations have microprocessor instructions to carry out their functions, which we'll be looking at, too.

The NOT Function

The simplest logical operation is the **NOT function**. Its gate is called a **NOT gate** or, more commonly, an **inverter**. To **invert** means to reverse the value of a bit. An inverter is a gate with only one input and one output, and its output is always the opposite of its input. That is, if its input is 1 (true), the output is 0 (false) and vice versa. We realize that in digital logic circuits a 1 also means "high voltage" and a 0 "low voltage."

Figure 14.2.1 shows the symbol for the inverter, or NOT function, and its truth table. The NOT function is also expressed as an equation, which we read "X equals A-bar (or A-not or not-A)."

The 6800 instruction that performs the logical NOT function is one we've seen already: Complement (COM), which forms the 1's complement of a number.

The OR Function

An **OR gate**, like the remainder of the logical gates, may have more than one input but only one output. In the **OR function** the output is true if any one of the inputs is true. Here we can illustrate the OR function with a lamp, a battery, and 2 switches connected in parallel. Figure 14.2.2 shows that if either switch A OR switch B, or both, are closed, the lamp will light. Shown also on the figure is a two-input OR gate and its truth table. We see that for two inputs there are four possible combinations, and of those four only one (both inputs 0) gives an output of 0. Shown also is the equation for this function. The symbol $+$ (plus sign) stands for the

FIGURE 14.2.1 NOT Gate Symbol and Truth Tables

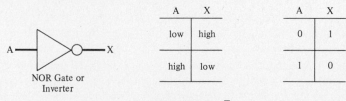

A	X
low	high
high	low

A	X
0	1
1	0

NOR Gate or Inverter

EQUATION: $X = \overline{A}$

Microprocessor Instruction: COM (Complement)

FIGURE 14.2.2   OR Gate Symbol, Illustration and Truth Tables

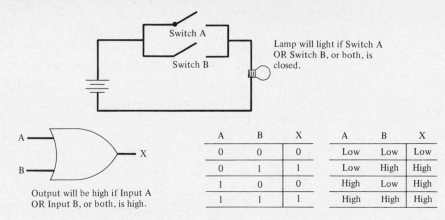

A	B	X
0	0	0
0	1	1
1	0	0
1	1	1

A	B	X
Low	Low	Low
Low	High	High
High	Low	High
High	High	High

Output will be high if Input A OR Input B, or both, is high.

Low output results only when both inputs are low.

EQUATION: A + B = X

Microprocessor Instruction: ORA, Inclusive OR

OR function. We read this equation "A OR B equals X" (with a verbal emphasis on the OR).

Figure 14.2.2 shows a two-input OR gate, but we can have any number of inputs. For any number of n inputs, the number of possible combinations of course is 2^n. No matter how many inputs we have, only the case where all inputs are zero will give us an output of 0. All other combinations give an output of 1.

EXAMPLE 14.2.1

For the following diagram state (a) the output if all inputs are zeros and (b) what combination of inputs will give an output of zero?

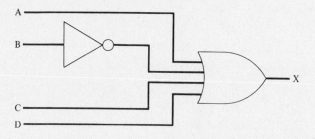

Solution

Here we have a four-input OR gate with an inverter in input B. If all inputs are 0, input B will be inverted to a 1 before going through the OR gate, and one 1 is all we need to give an output of 1. (b) To get an output of 0, all inputs to the OR gate must be 0, so input B has to be a 1.

Answer: (a) 1; (b) A=0, B=1, C=0, D=0

The 6800 instruction that performs the OR function is ORA, Inclusive OR (why this is called "inclusive" OR will be apparent shortly). Looking at ORA's instruction information sheet, we see that it performs a logical OR, bit by bit, of 2 numbers.

EXAMPLE 14.2.2

What will be the contents of accumulator A after the execution of this program segment:

```
LDA  A  #$09
ORA  NUM
```

(a) if (NUM)=$00; (b) if (NUM)=$FF; (c) if (NUM)=$30.

Solution

To OR 2 hexadecimal numbers, we write them in binary and OR each bit individually.

(a)	0000	1000	Any bit that contains a 1 for either input
	0000	0000	will contain a 1 in the result.
	0000	1000	
(b)	0000	1000	
	1111	1111	
	1111	1111	
(c)	0000	1000	
	0011	0000	
	0011	1000	

Answer: (a) $09; (b) $FF; (c) $39

In (a) of the preceding example ORing the number with all zeros gave us the original number. In (b) ORing it with all 1's gave us all 1's. A useful feature of the OR function is: *ORing a bit with zero lets that bit retain its value; ORing it with one sets it to one.* This is useful if we want to change part of a number but not all of it. For instance, converting a BCD number to its ASCII equivalent involves setting bits 4 and 5 of the number so that the MSD is $3.

FIGURE 14.2.3   NOR Gate Symbol and Truth Tables

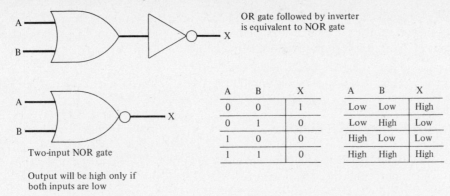

OR gate followed by inverter
is equivalent to NOR gate

Two-input NOR gate

Output will be high only if
both inputs are low

EQUATION: $X = \overline{A + B}$

A	B	X
0	0	1
0	1	0
1	0	0
1	1	0

A	B	X
Low	Low	High
Low	High	Low
High	Low	Low
High	High	High

Part (c) of the previous example converts the BCD number $09 to its ASCII equivalent by ORing it with $30. All bits except 4 and 5 retain their original value; 4 and 5 are set to 1's.

The NOR Function

Inverting the result of an OR operation gives us the equivalent of a **NOR function**, where all inputs must be low to get a high output.

Figure 14.2.3 shows a two-input **NOR gate**. The little circle, or "bubble" is used here, as it is in the inverter, to mean "not," or "invert." To do the NOR operation, we first OR the values, then invert that result. The equation is read as "X equals NOT A OR B."

There is no 6800 instruction that performs the NOR function. But we could accomplish a NOR by using the ORA followed by COM.

EXAMPLE 14.2.3

For the following diagram, state (a) the output if all inputs are 0; and (b) the inputs necessary to get an output of 1.

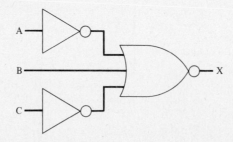

Solution

(a) We perform the OR function first and then invert it. Inverting A and C to 1's gives the OR result of 1, and inverting that gives a 0 for the total result. (b) To get an output of 1, all inputs to the NOR gate must be 0. So A and C must be 1.

Answer: (a) 0; (b) A=1, B=0, C=1

The Exclusive OR Function

The **exclusive OR (XOR) function** gives an output of 1 only if an odd number of 1's are input; otherwise the output is 0. So for half the combinations the output will be 1, and for the other half the output will be 0.

Figure 14.2.4 shows a a two-input **exclusive OR gate** and its truth table. We read the equation "X equals A exclusive OR B." The symbol $\oplus$ stands for the exclusive OR function. The last entry in the truth table—two 1 inputs—is excluded from having an output of 1. Now we see why OR is called "*in*clusive OR."

There is a microprocessor instruction EOR, Exclusive OR. Turning to its instruction information sheet, we see that it performs the exclusive OR function bit by bit on 2 numbers.

EXAMPLE 14.2.4

State the contents of accumulator A after executing this program segment (a) if (FROG)=$00; (b) if (FROG)=$FF; (c) if (FROG)=$A5.

```
LDA  A  #$A5
EOR  A  FROG
```

Solution

First, write each pair of numbers in binary. This time, two 1's will result in a 0.

(a)   1010   0101
       0000   0000
      —————————
       1010   0101   The same result as for inclusive OR.

FIGURE 14.2.4   Exclusive OR Gate Symbol, Illustration and Truth Tables

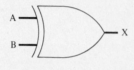

A	B	X
0	0	0
0	1	1
1	0	1
1	1	0

A	B	X
Low	Low	Low
Low	High	High
High	Low	High
High	High	Low

EQUATION: X = A $\oplus$ B

Microprocessor Instruction: EOR, Exclusive Or

(b)   1010   0101
       1111   1111
       ――――――――――
       0101   1010   The ones complement of $A5.

(c)   1010   0101
       1010   0101
       ――――――――――
       0000   0000   All bits are cleared.

Answer: (a) $A5; (b) $5A; (c) 00

We see that XORing a bit with 0 lets it retain its original value, as in the OR function. XORing a bit with 1 complements (inverts) the bit, instead of always setting it as with the OR function. And XORing a number with itself zeros it.

The AND Function

In the **AND function** the output is 1 only if all inputs are 1. We can illustrate the AND function with a lamp, a battery, and 2 switches, this time connected in series. We see in Figure 14.2.5 that switch A AND switch B must be closed for the lamp to light. The figure also shows a two-input **AND gate**, its truth table, and equation. We read the equation "A AND B equals X," with emphasis on the AND to distinguish it from *and* meaning "plus." Note that ANDing and adding are different operations.

FIGURE 14.2.5   AND Gate Symbol, Illustration and Truth Tables

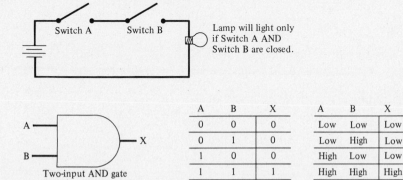

A	B	X		A	B	X
0	0	0		Low	Low	Low
0	1	0		Low	High	Low
1	0	0		High	Low	Low
1	1	1		High	High	High

Two-input AND gate

EQUATION: A · B = X

Microprocessor Insturction: AND, logical AND

EXAMPLE 14.2.5

For the following diagram state (a) the output if all inputs are 0; (b) the output if all inputs are 1; and (c) the inputs necessary for an output of 1.

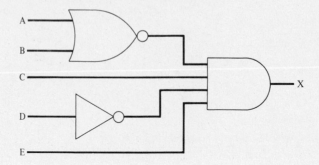

Solution

All inputs to the AND gate must be 1 for the output to be 1. (a) If any input to the AND gate is 0 the output is 0; (b) if all inputs are 1, then some of the inputs to the AND gate will be 0 and the output will be 0; (c) for all inputs to the AND gate to be 1, inputs A, B, and D must be 0.

Answer: (a) 0; (b) 0; (c) A=0, B=0, C=1, D=0, E=1

The microprocessor instruction AND, called logical AND, ANDs 2 numbers bit by bit.

EXAMPLE 14.2.6

For this program segment:

```
LDA A   #$35
AND A   GNARF
```

state the contents of accumulator A after execution if (a) (GNARF)=$00; (b) (GNARF)=$FF; (c) (GNARF)=$0F.

Solution

We write out each pair of numbers in binary and AND each bit.

	(a) 0011 0101	(b) 0011 0101	(c) 0011 0101
	0000 0000	1111 1111	0000 1111
	0000 0000	0011 0101	0000 0101

Answer: (a) 00; (b) $35; (c) $05

Here we see that ANDing a bit with 0 zeros the bit, and ANDing a bit with 1 lets it retain its value. Thus we may **strip** (change to 0) a number of some of its "1" bits as in (c). Here, we stripped the most significant hexadecimal digit of its "1" bits by ANDing that digit with all zeros. We let the least significant digit retain its value by ANDing with all 1's. This is useful for converting an ASCII character to its BCD equivalent, the reverse of the process we saw using the OR function where the BCD number was converted to its ASCII equivalent. To strip a number of some of its bits, we protect the part we want to keep. This process is called **masking**. Webster's definition of *mask* is "to cover for protection." In our specific situation a **mask** is a bit pattern that isolates one or more bits from a group of bits (usually a byte). In Example 14.2.6(c), the number $0F is a mask because it isolates the four LSBs from the four MSBs.

Related to the AND instruction is BIT, Bit Test. Looking at its instruction information sheet, we see that it performs the logical AND of 2 numbers and sets or clears the N and Z status bits but doesn't change the values of either operand. We recall a similar situation with the CMP instruction, which subtracts 2 numbers and affects the status register but not the operands.

The BIT instruction is useful when we want to test single bits. Up to now, we used shift and rotate instructions to test single bits. A useful alternative is the BIT instruction.

EXAMPLE 14.2.7

In Example 13.4.2 (Chapter 13) we used a rotate instruction twice to test the contents of bit 1, TDRF. Write a program segment using BIT that accomplishes the same thing.

Solution

We wish to isolate bit 1 from the rest, and if it is a 1 we want to transmit a word. ANDing the contents of the accumulator with a mask that contains a 1 in bit 1 and 0's everywhere else ($02) will do the job. Here's how that works:

XXXX	XXXX	The unknown contents of ACCA
0000	0010	
(0000	00X0)	The effective result (not stored in ACCA)

We recall that ANDing a bit with a 1 lets it retain its original value. So if bit 1 contained a 1 in the original number, it will still contain a 1, giving a nonzero result. If bit 1 contained a 0 in the original number, then the result will be 0 and the Z status bit will be set.

Answer

```
BIT A   #$02   MASK TDRF BIT
BEQ     TRANS  NOT EMPTY YET?   WAIT
```

FIGURE 14.2.6 NAND Gate Symbol, Illustration and Truth Tables

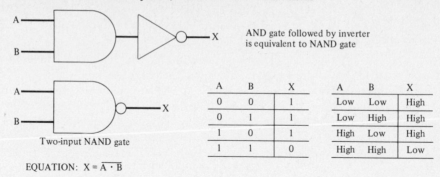

AND gate followed by inverter
is equivalent to NAND gate

Two-input NAND gate

A	B	X
0	0	1
0	1	1
1	0	1
1	1	0

A	B	X
Low	Low	High
Low	High	High
High	Low	High
High	High	Low

EQUATION: $X = \overline{A \cdot B}$

Here, we were able to use one less instruction to test this bit. And of course the farther away from either end of the word the bit we want to test is, the more instructions we will save.

The NAND Function

Inverting the result of an AND operation gives us the equivalent of a **NAND function**, where all inputs must be high to give a low output.

Figure 14.2.6 shows a two-input **NAND gate**, its truth tables, and its equation, which we read "X equals NOT (A AND B)." As in the NOR function, the ANDing is done before the NOTing.

There isn't any microprocessor instruction for NAND. But we could program the NAND function by using the AND followed by COM.

EXAMPLE 14.2.8

In the following diagram state (a) the output if all inputs are 0; (b) the output if all inputs are 1; (c) the inputs necessary for an output of 0.

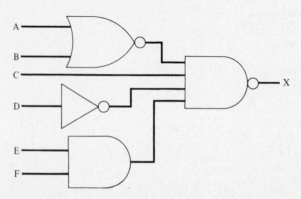

Solution

(a) If any one input to the NAND gate is 0, the output is 1. (b) If all inputs are 1, then A, B, and D cause an input of 0 and the output will be 1. (c) For the output to be 0, all inputs to the NAND gate have to be 1.

Answer: (a) 1; (b) 1; (c) A=0, B=0, C=1, D=0, E=1, F=1

This covers all the logical functions we'll need. The logical instructions are summarized in Table 14.2.1.

TABLE 14.2.1   6800 Logical Instructions

Mnemonic	Name	Function
COM	COMPLEMENT	Performs logical NOT (INVERT) on each bit of operand
ORA	INCLUSIVE OR	Performs logical OR of two 8-bit numbers
EOR	EXCLUSIVE OR	Performs XOR of two 8-bit numbers
AND	LOGICAL AND	Performs logical AND of two 8-bit numbers
BIT	BIT TEST	Performs logical AND of two 8-bit numbers, but does not change either operand

14.3 THE REMAINING CONNECTIONS

Let's take stock of what pins are left to connect. On the MPU, we have only pin 5 (VMA), pin 36 (DBE), and the address lines. On the PIA we have pins 18, 19, 21 to 25, 35, and 36. On the ACIA we have pins 8 to 11 and 14. On RAM we have pins 10 to 15; on ROM we have pins 10, 11, 13, and 14. On the clock we still have to connect the $\phi2$ (to other chips). Figure 14.3.1 shows what pins we still have to connect.

Believe it or not, a single purpose lies behind the way we connect all the rest of the pins, that is, to make sure that each device—memory, ACIA, or PIA—accesses the data bus when and only when it is supposed to. "When it is supposed to" actually has three facets. First, a unique address should ensure that only one piece of data gets transferred. When the MPU reads, for instance, the ACIA's status register, no other device should be able to put data onto the data bus. Second, data should get onto the data bus in accordance with the microcomputer's timing requirements. Third, data should get onto the data bus only if it has somewhere to go. That is, if there is a valid address on the address bus.

Three-State Buffers

Imagine a railroad system that had only one railroad track connected to many sidings, each containing a train with its engine running. If we let all the trains onto

FIGURE 14.3.1 Pins Not Yet Accounted For

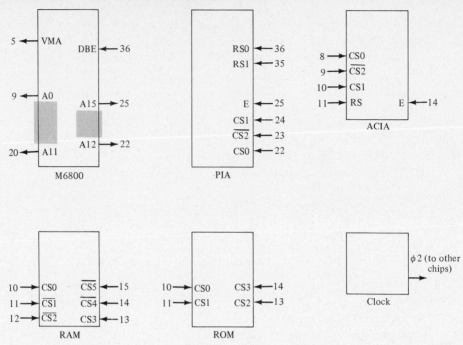

the track at once, the situation would be impossible. Instead, we'd have a controlled switch at each siding so that only one train at a time could get onto the track.

We have the same situation with the data bus. The various devices—RAM, ROM, the PIA, the ACIA—are all ready to get onto the same data bus at once. If we let them, the situation would be just as impossible (though maybe not potentially as destructive) as if we let all the trains onto the track at once. Instead, we have a controlled switch at each device so that only one at a time can get onto the data bus.

When we connect two inverters so that the output from one is the input to the other, we have a noninverting amplifier or **buffer**. The word *noninverting* means that the output has the same value (1 or 0, high or low) as the input value. The word *amplifier* means that the number of devices that can be serviced is increased. The more devices we attach to the data bus, the more buffering we need.

A two-state buffer has one input and one output. But a **three-state buffer** has two inputs and one output. Besides the data input, there is an enable/disable input. So there are three possible states for the buffer: 1, 0, or disabled. We can compare this situation with an electric light, where there are also three possibilities: on, off, or unplugged. When a lamp is unplugged, it doesn't matter whether the switch is on or off. The lamp is disconnected from the electrical circuit. Similarly, when the three-state buffer is disabled, it doesn't matter whether it contains a 1 or a 0. The buffer is disconnected from the circuit. We call this state the **high impedance state**

FIGURE 14.3.2   Two- and Three-State Noninverting Buffers

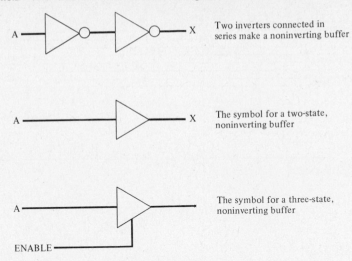

Two inverters connected in series make a noninverting buffer

The symbol for a two-state, noninverting buffer

The symbol for a three-state, noninverting buffer

(also referred to as disabled, disconnected, or floating). Figure 14.3.2 shows the symbols for a noninverting two-state and a three-state buffer.

We can buy packages of three-state buffers in DIPs. These are also called bus extenders, bus drivers, or line drivers. However, most RAMs and ROMs have their own built-in three-state buffers. Figure 14.3.3 shows a set of 8 three-state buffers placed in a RAM chip. In a way the situation is like a set of racehorses at the starting gate. The horses are prevented from entering the track as long as the gate is closed. When it's appropriate for them to enter the track, a control switch opens all the gates at once and the horses are able to get onto the track. In the same way, when the three-state buffers are disabled, the data from RAM is prevented from entering the data bus. When it's appropriate for the data to enter the data bus (that is, when the MPU wishes to read one of the RAM locations), the buffers are enabled and the data gets onto the data bus. At this time all other devices' three-state buffers would be disabled.

But how does each device's set of three-state buffers get enabled or disabled?

Chip Selects

The three-state buffers in RAM, ROM, the PIA, and the ACIA are enabled by one or more pins on each chip. These pins, called **chip selects** (CS), are active when the MPU is addressing that chip. For the chip's three-state buffers to be enabled, all its chip selects must be in their active states.

Let's look back at Figure 14.1.1 to see how many and what kind of chip selects are available on each. The PIA has three: CS0 (pin 22), active high; CS1 (pin 24),

FIGURE 14.3.3 Three-State Buffers Make Sure That Only One Device at a Time Gets onto the Date Bus

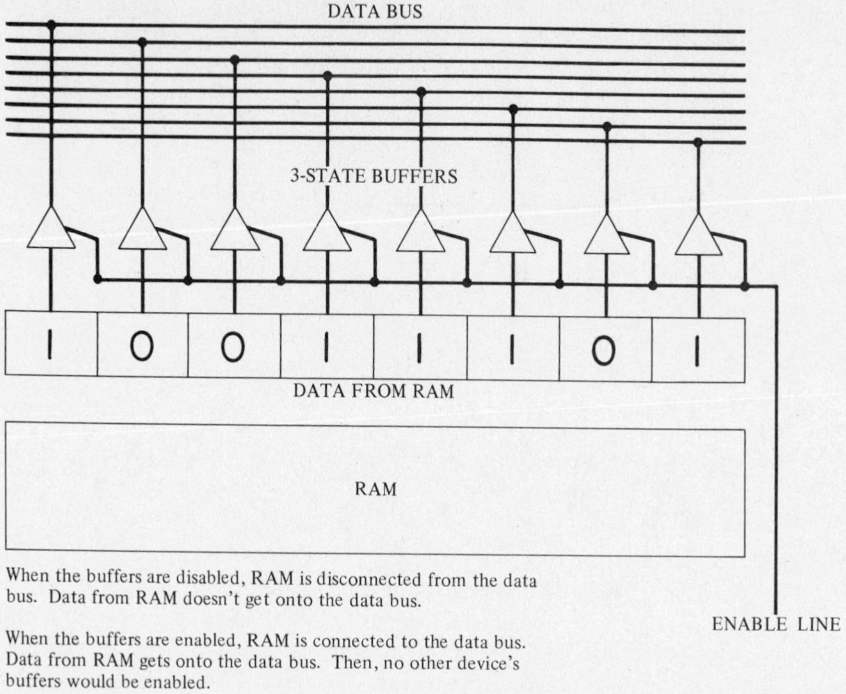
DATA BUS
3-STATE BUFFERS
1 0 0 1 1 1 0 1
DATA FROM RAM
RAM
When the buffers are disabled, RAM is disconnected from the data bus. Data from RAM doesn't get onto the data bus.
When the buffers are enabled, RAM is connected to the data bus. Data from RAM gets onto the data bus. Then, no other device's buffers would be enabled.
ENABLE LINE

active high; and CS2 (pin 23), active low. For the PIA's three-state buffers to be enabled, CS0 and CS1 must be high and CS2 low, all at the same time.

The ACIA has the same set of chip selects as the PIA. The RAM chip has six chip selects, two active high (CS0 and CS3), and four active low (CS1, 2, 4, and 5). The ROM chip has only four, all programmable by the user as to high or low active state. When the ROM is prepared, the designer would decide at that time which would be active high and which active low.

These inputs receive combined outputs from the MPU's address lines and VMA, plus the $\phi 2$ clock signal. Next, we'll see how the clock enters into the picture.

Timing

We've talked a little about clocks and timing. Actually, there isn't just one clock signal, but two. The phase 1 ($\phi 1$) clock signal is received only by the MPU and not by the other devices. Phase 2 ($\phi 2$) has two signals: one for the MPU and one for the other devices. The two $\phi 2$ signals provide the same timing. Two are needed so that each can be compatible with its device type.

FIGURE 14.3.4 Timing of First Instruction Cycle

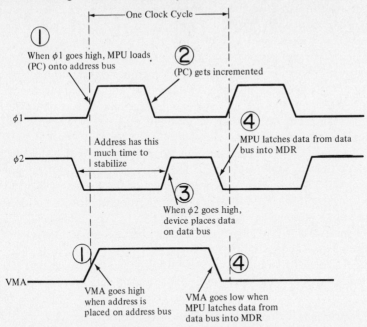

When we say "$\phi 2$," we mean both phase 2 signals. The relationship between $\phi 1$ and $\phi 2$ is shown in Figure 14.3.4. Note that both $\phi 1$ and $\phi 2$ have high pulses within the other clock signal's low pulse. This is to allow the address and data lines to stabilize, as we'll soon see.

Figure 14.3.4 shows the timing of the first instruction cycle. No matter what the instruction is, the activity during the first cycle is always to fetch the OP code from the program address. At (1) $\phi 1$ goes high, and the MPU places the contents of the program counter onto the address bus. At the same time, VMA (Valid Memory Address) goes high, meaning that there is a valid address on the address bus. The device (in this case, RAM) does nothing because at this point $\phi 2$ is low. At (2) the contents of the program counter are incremented. Still RAM does nothing, until (3) when $\phi 2$ goes high. Then RAM puts its data onto the data bus. The way the clock signals are arranged gives the address the longest possible time—from (1) to (3)—to stabilize.

When $\phi 2$ goes low at (4), the MPU reads the data from the data bus and latches it into its MDR. Here, the data bus has had a chance to stabilize between (3) and (4). When the MPU reads the data, VMA goes low, meaning that the address bus no longer contains a valid address.

We can notice a few facts from the figure. First, we see that the MPU reacts to both the $\phi 1$ and $\phi 2$ clock signals. (Now we see why we connected both of them to the MPU in Section 14.1.) Next, we see that the device that's being addressed reacts only when $\phi2$ goes high. If the device is to release its data to the data bus, the device's three-state buffers must be enabled by a high on $\phi2$. Third, we see that VMA goes high when there is a valid address on the address bus. We want our device to respond only when the address is valid, so we should use this signal to enable the device's three-state buffers, too.

When might the address not be valid? Sometimes during the execute phase of an instruction, the MPU is doing internal operations and not addressing memory at all. In that case there would still be an address on the address bus (left over from the previous operation), but it wouldn't be valid. In this case VMA goes low and we want all devices to be disabled.

The PIA and the ACIA each have an Enable (E) pin, which does just what it says: a high on that pin enables the chip. The enable is similar to a chip select. If we AND the $\phi2$ and VMA signals and connect them to the E pins of the PIA and the ACIA, we'll make sure that these devices won't respond unless the address is valid AND the $\phi2$ clock signal goes high.

The memory chips don't have any E pins, but we can connect the VMA $\phi2$ signal to one of their chip selects.

Normally, the DBE input pin on the MPU is connected to the $\phi2$ clock input. DBE, Data Bus Enable, is the three-state enable for the data bus. If it's low, the data

FIGURE 14.3.5 ϕ**2-VMA Connections Among MPU and Devices**

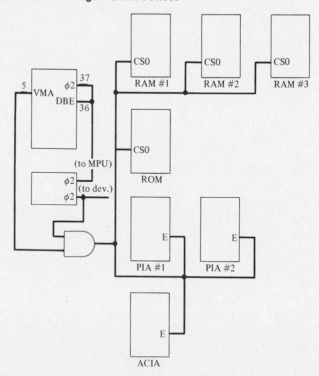

bus is in the high impedance state. For a data transfer to take place between the MPU and a device, of course the data bus has to be enabled. Wiring DBE to $\phi2$ will make sure that it is enabled when $\phi2$ is high. Once the data bus is enabled, its direction depends on the R/$\overline{\text{W}}$ line: if R/$\overline{\text{W}}$ is high, the MPU is reading; if low, writing.

Figure 14.3.5 shows the connections we've just talked about. All we have left now are a few chip selects and address lines, which we'll discuss next.

14.4 ADDRESS DECODING

By **address decoding**, we mean the process by which the MPU's address lines are connected to the select lines of devices so that each device has a unique set of addresses. This can be done using logic gates. All the logic gates we represented as symbols in Section 14.2 have real physical counterparts. If we look at the circuit board of any microprocessor system, we see some integrated circuits that aren't the MPU, PIA, ACIA, RAM, or ROM. Many of these are logic gates.

We can buy just about any kind of logic gate. These are usually packaged several gates to a DIP, unless the gate has a large number of inputs. For instance, one type of IC contains 3 three-input NOR gates in a 14-pin DIP. Another contains 4 two-input NAND gates per 14-pin DIP. Still another contains 1 eight-input NAND gate, and so on. In Section 14.3 we used one logic gate already in our system design—We ANDed VMA with phase 2. To implement this in hardware, we'd use one gate in a package of several two-input AND gates.

The task that remains for us is to connect the MPU's address lines to the remaining chip selects and register selects of the devices. First, let's talk about the register selects.

Register Selects

The **register select** pins are used, as the name implies, to select a particular register on a device where more than one register can be addressed. The PIA has two: RS0 and RS1. The ACIA has one: RS.

Earlier we said that on RAM and ROM the lower address lines are used by the chip to locate an address on that chip. Similarly, the lowest address lines A0 and A1 are used by the PIA and ACIA to locate an address (in this case, a register) on that chip. We connect these address lines to the register select lines on each device.

Figure 14.4.1 shows truth tables for the register select lines. The ACIA's is simple: a low on RS selects the control/status pair, and a high, the RDR/TDR pair. We recall that one of the pair is selected, depending on the condition of the R/$\overline{\text{W}}$ line. The ACIA's RS pin is connected to address line A0.

FIGURE 14.4.1 Truth Tables for Register Selects

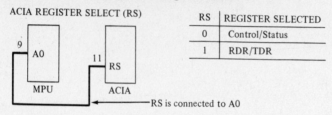

ACIA REGISTER SELECT (RS)

RS	REGISTER SELECTED
0	Control/Status
1	RDR/TDR

RS is connected to A0

PIA REGISTER SELECTS (RS0, RS1)

RS1 selects the side: 0 = Side A, 1 = Side B
RS0 selects the register: 0 = DDR/DR, 1 = CR

RS1	RS0	REGISTER SELECTED
0	0	DDRA/DRA
0	1	CRA
1	0	DDRB/DRB
1	1	CRB

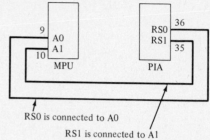

RS0 is connected to A0

RS1 is connected to A1

EXAMPLE 14.4.1

What ACIA register is selected if (a) A0 and $R/\overline{W}$ are both low; (b) if A0 and $R/\overline{W}$ are both high?

Solution

(a) Looking at Figure 14.4.1, we find that 0 on A0 means a 0 on RS, which selects the control/status pair. If $R/\overline{W}$ is low, this means that the MPU is writing, so the control register is addressed. (b) A high on A0 means a 1 on RS, selecting the RDR/TDR pair. $R/\overline{W}$ high means that the MPU is reading, so RDR is being addressed.

Answer: (a) control register; (b) RDR

For the PIA we have six registers to select among: three from each side. RS1, connected to address line A1, selects the side. If RS1 is low, side A is selected, and if high, side B. RS0, connected to address line A0, selects the register or register combination. If RS0 is low, the DDR/DR combination is selected; if high, CR. We recall that DDR or DR are selected from the pair by the contents of bit 2 of the control register.

EXAMPLE 14.4.2

What PIA register or register pair is being selected if (a) A0 and A1 are both low; (b) A0 and A1 are both high?

Solution

(a) A0 and A1 both low means RS1 and RS0 are both low: DRA/DDRA. (b) A0 and A1 both high means RS1 and RS0 are both high: CRB.

Answer: (a) DRA/DDRA; (b) CRB

Now, all that remains is to connect the rest of the chip selects to the address lines. First, we should think about where we want each device to reside in memory.

Assigning Addresses

We use these guidelines for assigning addresses to the devices:

ROM: Highest memory (so as to include interrupt vectors)
ACIA/PIA: Middle memory
RAM: Lowest memory (to use direct addressing mode)

Our ROM chip occupies 1024 addresses ($0400), so to put it at highest memory we assign it $FC00 through FFFF. We'll arbitrarily assign PIA #1 to addresses $0800 through $0803, PIA #2 to $0C00 through $0C03, and the ACIA to $0400 and $0401. We have three RAM chips, each worth $80 locations. We'll put RAM #1 at lowest addresses: $0000 through $007F. RAM #2 gets $0080 through $00FF, and RAM #3 will occupy $0100 through $017F.

Now, we're ready to start assigning the address lines.

Using Worksheets

In configuring a system, we find it convenient to use a system layout worksheet, shown in Figure 14.4.2.

First, write in each device, grouping the device types together. All RAMs are the same device type; all ROMs too (if we had more than one ROM). The PIA and the ACIA are considered to be the same device type, because they have the same set of RS lines.

Next, place Xs in all the address squares that are used to select an address within a device. This will be A0 through A6 for the RAMs, A0 through A9 for the ROM, A0 through A1 for the PIA, and A0 for the ACIA.

Next, fill in the assigned addresses.

Figure 14.4.3 shows the worksheet filled in thus far.

FIGURE 14.4.2 System Layout Work Sheet

| SYSTEM LAYOUT WORK SHEET | | | | | | | | | | | | | | | | | | |
| DEVICE | MPU ADDRESS LINES (A0 – A15) | | | | | | | | | | | | | | | | ADDRESS | |
	15	14	13	12	11	10	9	8	7	6	5	4	3	2	1	0	FROM	TO
RAM #1																		
RAM #2																		
RAM #3																		
ROM																		
ACIA																		
PIA #1																		
PIA #2																		

FIGURE 14.4.3 System Layout Work Sheet

| DEVICE | MPU ADDRESS LINES (A0 – A15) | | | | | | | | | | | | | | | | ADDRESS | |
	15	14	13	12	11	10	9	8	7	6	5	4	3	2	1	0	FROM	TO
RAM #1										X	X	X	X	X	X	X	0000	007F
RAM #2										X	X	X	X	X	X	X	0080	00FF
RAM #3										X	X	X	X	X	X	X	0100	017F
ROM							X	X	X	X	X	X	X	X	X	X	FC00	FFFF
ACIA																X	0400	0401
PIA #1															X	X	0800	0803
PIA #2															X	X	0C00	0C03

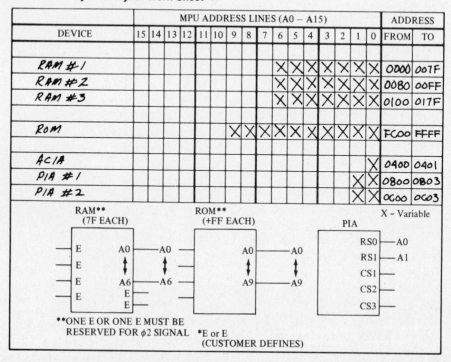

RAM** (7F EACH)   ROM** (+FF EACH)   X – Variable   PIA

**ONE E OR ONE E MUST BE RESERVED FOR φ2 SIGNAL   *E or E (CUSTOMER DEFINES)

FIGURE 14.4.4 System Layout Work Sheet

SYSTEM LAYOUT WORK SHEET

DEVICE	15	14	13	12	11	10	9	8	7	6	5	4	3	2	1	0	ADDRESS FROM	ADDRESS TO
RAM #1	0	0	0	0	0	0	0	0	0	X	X	X	X	X	X	X	0000	007F
RAM #2	0	0	0	0	0	0	0	0	1	X	X	X	X	X	X	X	0080	00FF
RAM #3	0	0	0	0	0	0	0	1	0	X	X	X	X	X	X	X	0100	017F
ROM	1	1	1	1	1	1	X	X	X	X	X	X	X	X	X	X	FC00	FFFF
ACIA	0	0	0	0	0	1	0	0	0	0	0	0	0	0	0	X	0400	0401
PIA #1	0	0	0	0	1	0	0	0	0	0	0	0	0	0	X	X	0800	0803
PIA #2	0	0	0	0	1	1	0	0	0	0	0	0	0	0	X	X	0C00	0C03

DEVICE	15	14	13	12	11	10	9	8	7	6	5	4	3	2	1	0	ADDRESS FROM	ADDRESS TO

(MPU ADDRESS LINES (A0 – A15))

X - Variable

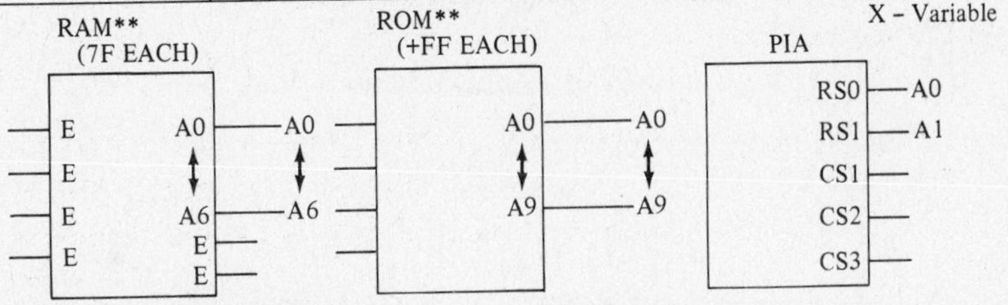
RAM**
(7F EACH)
E
E
E
E
A0
A6
E
E
A0
A6
ROM**
(+FF EACH)
A0
A9
A0
A9
PIA
RS0
A0
RS1
A1
CS1
CS2
CS3

**ONE E OR ONE E MUST BE RESERVED FOR $\phi 2$ SIGNAL

*E or E (CUSTOMER DEFINES)

Next, put values into the remaining address boxes to correspond to the device's highest assigned address. Figure 14.4.4 shows the finished worksheets.

The next step is to connect the address lines to the chip selects so that the addresses we've assigned will be implemented.

Connecting the Address Lines

We'll connect the address lines to the chip selects using logic gates. There are many ways of doing this. Figuring out an address decoding scheme for each device type is easy and fun.

EXAMPLE 14.4.3

Devise an address decoding scheme for the three RAM chips according to the values on Figure 14.4.4.

Solution

First, we take stock of the chip selects we have: four active low (CS1, 2, 4, and 5) and one active high (CS3). Next, we look at the address lines of the three RAM chips to see which are the same: Lines 15 through 9 all contain zeros. We could OR these all together into one or more active low chip selects for each chip. There are many ways we could do this. Let's OR A15 through A13 together into CS1 and A12 through A9, into CS2.

Now we have two active low chip selects (CS4, CS5) and one active high (CS3). Lines A8 and A7 have different combinations for the three chips. A7 and A8 are both 0 for RAM #1, so we could connect them to both of RAM #1's active low chip selects (CS4, CS5). We don't need CS3 of RAM #1, so we can just tie it permanently to 5 V. For RAM #2 A8 is 0 and A7 is 1. So we can connect A8 to both active low chip selects (CS4 and CS5) and A7, to the active high chip select (CS3). For RAM #3, A8 is 1, so we connect it to CS3. And A7 is 0, so we connect it to both CS4 and CS5.

Figure 14.4.5 shows a diagram of this scheme.

Answer: OR A15 through A13 to CS1; OR A12 through A9 to CS2; connect A8 to CS4 of RAMs #1 and #2, A8 to CS3 of RAM #3, A7 to CS5 of RAMs #1 and #2, A7 to CS3 of RAM #2. CS4 to CS5 on RAMs #2 and #3 and CS3 to 5 V on RAM #1.

Once we've got a decoding scheme, we should check it to be sure that it really does what we want it to do.

FIGURE 14.4.5 Sample Address Decoding Scheme for RAMs

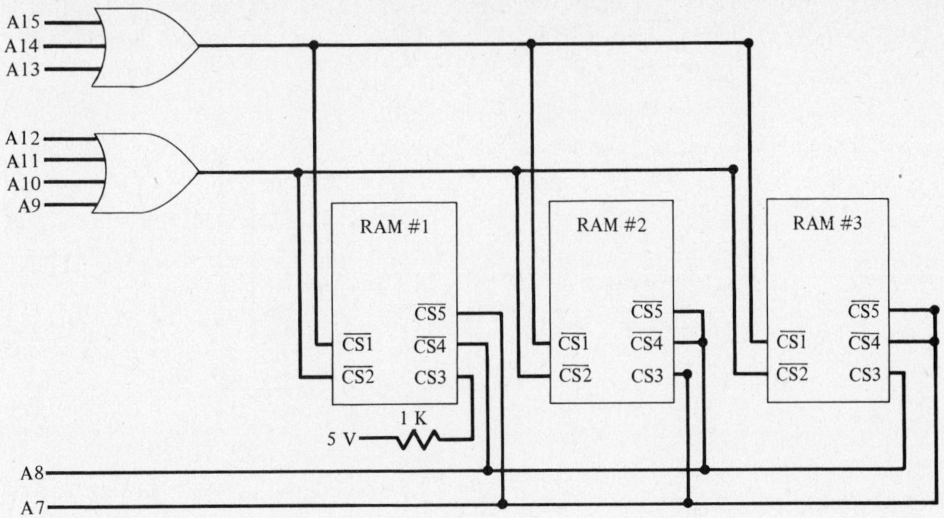

EXAMPLE 14.4.4

State whether any devices in Figure 14.4.5 would be selected by each of these addresses. If a device is selected, state which one. (a) $0048; (b) $FFC5; (c) $8002; (d) $00A0; (e) $C001; (f) $013C; (g) $A001.

Solution

We ignore the seven LSBs, because these aren't part of the decoding scheme. We write each number in binary, then apply its address line values to the diagram of Figure 14.4.5.

(a)	0000	0000	0	RAM #1 is selected
(b)	1111	1111	1	None are selected
(c)	1000	0000	0	None are selected
(d)	0000	0000	1	RAM #2 is selected
(e)	1100	0000	0	None are selected
(f)	0000	0001	0	RAM #3 is selected
(g)	1010	0000	0	None are selected

Answer: See preceding solution.

In the previous example we wanted to make sure that: (1) an address in each of the assigned RAM areas did in fact select the correct RAM chip and (2) an address

FIGURE 14.4.6   A Decoding Scheme for ROM

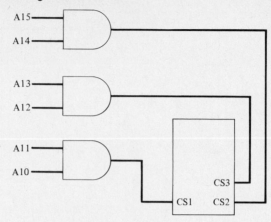

FIGURE 14.4.7   Decoding Scheme for ACIA and PIAs

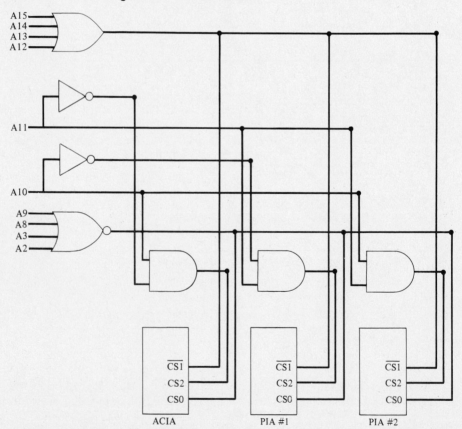

FIGURE 14.4.8 System Layout Work Sheet

DEVICE	15	14	13	12	11	10	9	8	7	6	5	4	3	2	1	0	FROM	TO
RAM #1	0	0						0	0	X	X	X	X	X	X	X	0000	007F
RAM #2	0	0						0	1	X	X	X	X	X	X	X	0080	00FF
RAM #3	0	0						1	0	X	X	X	X	X	X	X	0100	017F
ROM	1	1	1	1			X	X	X	X	X	X	X	X	X	X	F000	F3FF
ACIA	0	1											1			X	4004	4005
PIA #1	0	1										1			X	X	4008	400B
PIA #2	0	1									1				X	X	4010	4013

The table above is titled "SYSTEM LAYOUT WORK SHEET" with column span "MPU ADDRESS LINES (A0 – A15)" over columns 15–0 and "ADDRESS" over FROM/TO.

DEVICE	15	14	13	12	11	10	9	8	7	6	5	4	3	2	1	0	FROM	TO

Column span: "MPU ADDRESS LINES (A0 – A15)" and "ADDRESS".

RAM** (7F EACH)

```
— E      A0 — A0
— E      ↕     ↕
— E      A6 — A6
— E      E
         E
```

ROM** (+FF EACH)

```
         A0 — A0
         ↕     ↕
         A9 — A9
```

PIA

```
RSO — A0
RS1 — A1
CS1 —
CS2 —
CS3 —
```

X – Variable

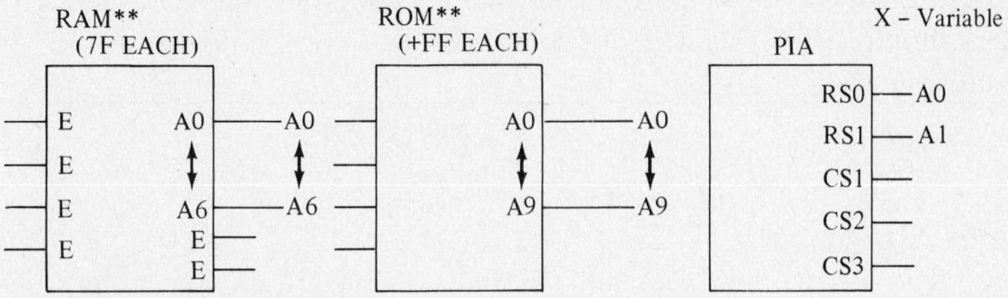

**ONE E OR ONE E MUST BE RESERVED FOR φ2 SIGNAL   *E or E (CUSTOMER DEFINES)

reserved for ROM, the PIAs, or the ACIA did NOT select a RAM chip. All these conditions were satisfied.

Figures 14.4.6 and 14.4.7 show decoding schemes for ROM and for the PIAs and ACIA. The reader should study these diagrams and verify that they are correct.

Some Simplifications

In our scheme the RAM and ROM chips are **fully decoded**, meaning that every address line is connected to them. However, looking at the worksheet and the diagram, we see that the ACIA and the PIA aren't fully decoded. Address lines 4 to 7 aren't connected to them.

EXAMPLE 14.4.5

Give the range of addresses that will select the ACIA according to the diagram of Figure 14.4.7.

Solution

Because lines 4 through 7 aren't connected to the ACIA, it doesn't matter whether these lines contain a 0 or a 1. So the range would be from the address where lines 4 through 7 all contained 0's (0400) to the address where lines 4 through 7 all contained 1's and line 0 was a 1 (04F1)

Answer: $0400 to $04F1

As long as the devices don't interfere with each other, they don't have to be fully decoded. If we're not using all portions of memory, as we aren't here, we can get away with connecting fewer address lines and using fewer logic gates.

Figure 14.4.8 shows a worksheet with a configuration that isn't fully decoded. Readers should study this worksheet and verify that each device would be selected to the exclusion of all the others.

REVIEW QUESTIONS

1. What does it mean to **configure** a microprocessor system?
2. How do we connect the power and ground pins of the devices?
3. What interrupt connections are made in the system? What clock connections are made to the MPU?

4. How are the $\overline{\text{READ}/\text{WRITE}}$ and data lines connected?

5. How many address lines does the sample RAM chip have? the ROM? Why do they have different numbers of address lines? What does the chip do with the address lines? Why don't the ACIA and PIA have address lines?

6. What is **two-state logic**? (What is another word for it?)

7. What is a **logical operation**, a **logic circuit**, and a **logic gate**? How do we express the inputs and outputs of a logic gate?

8. What is a **NOT function**? What is another name for it? Sketch a **NOT gate**. What is the 6800 instruction for NOT?

9. What is an **OR function**? Sketch a two-input **OR gate** and its truth table. What is the symbol for OR?

10. What is the 6800 instruction for OR? What does it do? How can we use the OR instruction to set some bits, and not others, of a byte?

11. What is a **NOR function**? Sketch a two-input **NOR gate** and its truth table. Is there a 6800 instruction for NOR?

12. What is an **exclusive OR** function? Sketch a two-input **exclusive OR gate** and its truth table. Show how it is different from inclusive OR. What is the 6800 instruction for exclusive OR? How can we complement or zero a number using this instruction?

13. What is an **AND function**? Sketch a two-input **AND gate** and its truth table. What is the symbol for AND?

14. What is the 6800 instruction for AND? How can we use the AND instruction to **strip** bits from a number? What is **masking**? a **mask**? Give an example.

15. What is the BIT instruction? How is it like the AND instruction, and how is it different? What is it used for? Give an example.

16. What is a **NAND function**? Sketch a two-input **NAND gate** and its truth table. Is there a 6800 instruction for NAND?

17. What is the purpose that underlies connecting the remaining pins of the devices?

18. What is a **three-state buffer**? Why do we need them? Sketch the symbol for a three-state buffer. What are the three states called?

19. What are **chip selects**? How do they relate to a chip's three-state buffers? Are they active high or active low? Explain.

20. What happens at the beginning of an instruction when the phase 1 clock signal goes high? when it goes low? How about the phase 2 clock signal? Which controls the MPU? the other devices?

21. What is the VMA pin of the MPU? When is it high? When is it low? How do we connect it to the devices? Explain.

22. What is the enable pin of the PIA and ACIA for? What do we usually connect to it?

23. What is the DBE pin of the MPU? How is it connected? Why?

24. What is **address decoding**? How can we use logic gates to decode addresses?

25. What are **register select** pins? How many does the ACIA have? the PIA? What address lines are they connected to? How do their contents determine which register is selected?

26. Explain how we begin assigning addresses to devices. How do we use a system layout worksheet to begin decoding addresses?

27. How do we construct an address decoding scheme? How do we verify that it will work?

28. What do we mean by **fully decoded**? Does an address always have to be fully decoded? Explain.

EXERCISES

Set A (answers at back of book)

1. For Diagram 1A state (a) the output of all inputs are 0; (b) the output if all inputs are 1; (c) the inputs necessary to give an output of 0.

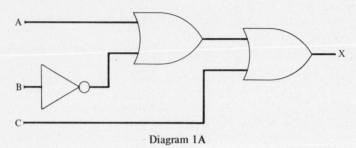

Diagram 1A

2. What will be the contents of accumulator A after the execution of this program segment:

```
LDA A  GOOP
ORA    #$0F
```

(a) if (GOOP)=$F0; (b) if (GOOP)=$40; (c) if (GOOP)=$65

3. What value should be ORed with the BCD number 07 to change it to its ASCII equivalent? Could more than one number be used? Explain.

4. For Diagram 2A state (a) the output if all inputs are 1; (b) the output if all inputs are 0; (c) the inputs necessary to give an output of 1.

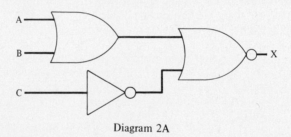

Diagram 2A

5. For this program segment:

```
LDA A  #$7B
EOR A  ——
```

what hexadecimal number should be put in the blank space to (a) zero accumulator A; (b) ones complement accumulator A; (c) ones complement bits 0 to 3 and leave bits 4 to 7 unchanged?

6. Modify Example 13.4.3 (Chapter 13) by using BIT to test RDRFD and the error bits.

7. For diagram 3A state (a) the output if all inputs are 0's; (b) the output if all inputs are 1's; (c) the inputs necessary for the output to be 0.

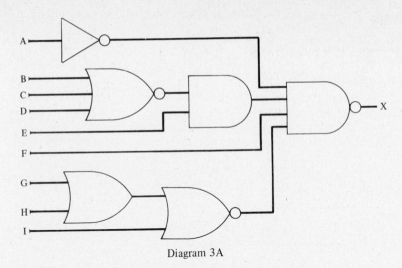

Diagram 3A

8. What ACIA register is selected if A0 is low and R/$\overline{W}$ is high?
9. What PIA register or register pair is being selected if A0 is high and A1 is low?
10. Refer to the diagram of Figure 14.4.6, and state whether the ROM would be selected for these addresses: (a) $FF00; (b) $FFF0; (c) $FD17; (d) $FF82.
11. For the decoding scheme of Figure 14.4.7, state which device on that figure, if any, would be selected by each of these addresses: (a) $0D03; (b) $0801; (c) $0C03; (d) $03FF.
12. Give the range of addresses that will select PIA #1 according to the diagram of Figure 14.4.7.

EXERCISES

Set B (answers not given)

1. For Diagram 1B state (a) the output if all inputs are 0; (b) the output if all inputs are 1; (c) the inputs necessary to give an output of 0.

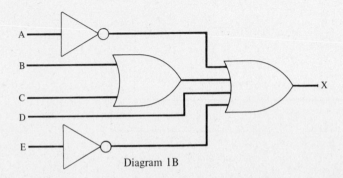

Diagram 1B

2. What will be the contents of accumulator B after the execution of this program segment:

```
CLR B
ORA B   NERF
```

   (a) if (NERF)=$00; (b) if (NERF)=$FF; (c) if (NERF)=$1A

3. (a) What hexadecimal number should be ORed with an ASCII value to set the parity bit? (b) Can we clear the parity bit by ORing? Explain.

4. For Diagram 2B state (a) the output if all inputs are 1; (b) the output if all inputs are 0; (c) the inputs necessary to give an output of 0.

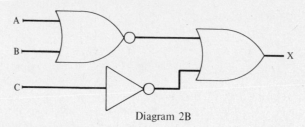

Diagram 2B

5. For this program segment:

```
LDA A   FLUB
XOR A   #$37
```

   what would be the contents of accumulator A after executing if (a) (FLUB)=$FF; (b) (FLUB)=$37; (c) (FLUB)=$C8?

6. Modify the dump program (Chapter 13) of Figure 13.4.3 so that the TDR bit is checked, using the Bit Test (BIT) instruction. List only those lines that are changed.

7. In Diagram 3B state (a) the output if all inputs are 0's; (b) the output if all inputs are 1's; (c) the inputs necessary for the output to be 0.

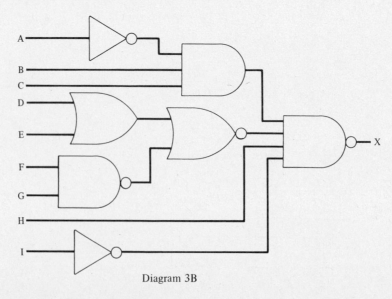

Diagram 3B

8. What ACIA register is selected if A0 is high and R/$\overline{\text{W}}$ is low?
9. What PIA register or register pair is being selected if A0 is low and A1 is high?
10. Refer to the diagram of Figure 14.4.6, and state whether the ROM would be selected for these addresses: (a) $EFF0; (b) $F800; (c) $FE9D; (d) $F0FF.
11. For the decoding scheme of Figure 14.4.7, state which device on that figure, if any, would be selected by each of these addresses: (a) $0400; (b) $E003; (c) $0CF0. (d) $0AF3.
12. Give the range of addresses that will select PIA #2 according to the diagram of Figure 14.4.7.

DESIGN IDEAS

1. Design a system that has two 128×8-bit RAMs, one 1024×8-bit ROM, one PIA, and one ACIA. The RAM should start at address 0000. The PIA should start at address $2004, with the ACIA immediately following it. The last address of ROM should be $08FF. You may determine the condition (active high or low) of the ROM chip selects.
2. Design a system that has four RAMs, two ROMs, three PIAs, and two ACIAs. Two of the RAMs are for use by the system's monitor and should be placed directly below ROM in memory. You may determine the addresses and the condition of the ROM chip selects.
3. Design a system that has three RAMs, one PIA, one ACIA, and one 2048×8-bit ROM. The ROM has 11 address lines, 8 data lines, and one user-programmable chip select. You may determine the addresses and the condition of the ROM chip select.

APPENDIX A
Definition
of the Executable
Instructions

A.1 Nomenclature

The following nomenclature is used in the subsequent definitions.

(a) *Operators*
    ( ) = a location
    ← = is transferred to
    ↑ = "is pulled from stack"
    ↓ = "is pushed"
    · = Boolean AND
    = Boolean (Inclusive) OR
    ⊕ = Exclusive OR
    ≈ = Boolean NOT

(b) *Registers in the MPU*
    ACCA = Accumulator A
    ACCB = Accumulator B
    ACCX = Accumulator ACCA or ACCB
    CC   = Condition codes register
    IX   = Index register, 16 bits
    IXH = Index register, higher order 8 bits
    IXL = Index register, lower order 8 bits
    PC   = Program counter, 16 bits

Reprinted in part from the M6800 Programming Reference Manual by permission of Motorola, Inc.

PCH = Program counter, higher order 8 bits
PCL = Program counter, lower order 8 bits
SP = Stack pointer
SPH = Stack pointer high
SPL = Stack pointer low

(c) *Memory and Addressing*

M = A memory location (one byte)

M+1 = The byte of memory at 0001 plus the address of the memory location indicated by "M."

Rel = Relative address (i.e., the two's complement number stored in the second byte of machine code corresponding to a branch instruction).

(d) *Bits 0 thru 5 of the Condition Codes Register*

C = Carry —borrow   bit —0
V = Two's complement overflow indicator   bit —1
Z = Zero indicator   bit —2
N = Negative indicator   bit —3
I = Interrupt mask   bit —4
H = Half carry   bit —5

(e) *Status of Individual Bits BEFORE Execution of an Instruction*

An = Bit n of ACCA $(n = 7, 6, 5, \ldots, 0)$
Bn = Bit n of ACCB $(n = 7, 6, 5, \ldots, 0)$
IXHn = Bit n of IXH $(n = 7, 6, 5, \ldots, 0)$
IXLn = Bit n of IXL $(n = 7, 6, 5, \ldots, 0)$
Mn = Bit n of M $(n = 7, 6, 5, \ldots, 0)$
SPHn = Bit n of SPH $(n = 7, 6, 5, \ldots, 0)$
SPLn = Bit n of SPL $(n = 7, 6, 5, \ldots, 0)$
Xn = Bit n of ACCX $(n = 7, 6, 5, \ldots, 0)$

(f) *Status of Individual Bits of the RESULT of Execution of an Instruction*

(i) For 8-bit Results

Rn = Bit n of the result $(n = 7, 6, 5, \ldots, 0)$

This applies to instructions which provide a result contained in a single byte of memory or in an 8-bit register.

(ii) For 16-bit Results

RHn = Bit n of the more significant byte of the result $(n = 7, 6, 5, \ldots, 0)$

RLn = Bit n of the less significant byte of the result $(n = 7, 6, 5, \ldots, 0)$

This applies to instructions which provide a result contained in two consecutive bytes of memory or in a 16-bit register.

A.2 Executable Instructions (definition of)

Detailed definitions of the 72 executable instructions of the source language are provided on the following pages.

Add Accumulator B to Accumulator A

ABA

Operation: $(ACCA) \leftarrow (ACCA) + (ACCB)$

Description: Add the contents of ACCB to the contents of ACCA and store the result in ACCA. The contents of ACCB are unchanged.

Condition Codes: H: Set if there was a carry from bit 3; cleared otherwise.

                  I: Not affected.

                  N: Set if the result is negative; cleared otherwise.

                  Z: Set if the result is zero; cleared otherwise.

                  V: Set if there was two's complement overflow as a result of the operation; cleared otherwise.

                  C: Set if there was a carry from the most significant bit of the result; cleared otherwise.

Addressing Modes, Execution Time, and Machine Code (hexadecimal)

Addressing Modes	Execution Time (No. of cycles)	Number of bytes of machine code	Machine Code HEX.
Inherent	2	1	1B

ADC

Operation: $(ACCX) \leftarrow (ACCX) + (M) + (C)$

Description: Add together the contents of the carry bit, the contents of a memory location, and the contents of an accumulator.

Condition Codes: Store the result in the accumulator.

H: Set if there was a carry from bit 3; cleared otherwise.

I: Not affected.

N: Set if the result is negative.

Z: Set if the result is zero.

V: Set if there was two's complement overflow as a result of the operation; cleared otherwise.

C: Set if there was a carry from the most significant bit of the result; cleared otherwise.

Addressing Modes, Execution Time, and Machine Code (hexadecimal)
(DUAL OPERAND)

Addressing Modes	Execution Time (No. of cycles)	Number of bytes of machine code	Machine Code HEX.
A IMM	2	2	89
A DIR	3	2	99
A EXT	4	3	B9
A IND	5	2	A9
B IMM	2	2	C9
B DIR	3	2	D9
B EXT	4	3	F9
B IND	5	2	E9

Add Without Carry

Operation: $(ACCX) \leftarrow (ACCX) + (M)$

Description: Add the contents of a memory location to the contents of an accumulator, and place the result in the accumulator.

Condition Codes: H: Set if there was a carry from bit 3.

                  I: Not affected.

                  N: Set if the result is negative; cleared otherwise.

                  Z: Set if the result is zero; cleared otherwise.

                  V: Set if there was two's complement overflow as a result of the operation; cleared otherwise.

                  C: Set if there was a carry from the most significant bit of the result; cleared otherwise.

Addressing Modes, Execution Time, and Machine Code (hexadecimal)

(DUAL OPERAND)

Addressing Modes	Execution Time (No. of cycles)	Number of bytes of machine code	Machine Code HEX.
A IMM	2	2	8B
A DIR	3	2	9B
A EXT	4	3	BB
A IND	5	2	AB
B IMM	2	2	CB
B DIR	3	2	DB
B EXT	4	3	FB
B IND	5	2	EB

AND

Operation: $(ACCX) \leftarrow (ACCX) \cdot (M)$

Description: Performs logical "AND" between the contents of ACCX and the contents of M and places the result in ACCX. (Each bit of ACCX after the operation will be the logical "AND" of the corresponding bits of M and of ACCX before the operation.)

Condition Codes:
- H: Not affected.
- I: Not affected.
- N: Set if most significant bit of the result is set; cleared otherwise.
- Z: Set if all bits of the result are cleared; cleared otherwise.
- V: Cleared.
- C: Not affected.

Addressing Modes, Execution Time, and Machine Code (hexadecimal)

Addressing Modes	Execution Time (No. of cycles)	Number of bytes of machine code	Machine Code HEX.
A IMM	2	2	84
A DIR	3	2	94
A EXT	4	3	B4
A IND	5	2	A4
B IMM	2	2	C4
B DIR	3	2	D4
B EXT	4	3	F4
B IND	5	2	E4

Arithmetic Shift Left

Operation:

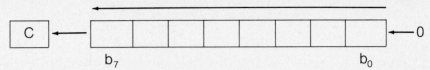

b_7 b_0

Description: Shift all bits of the ACCX or M one place to the left. Bit 0 is loaded with a zero. The C bit is loaded from the most significant bit of ACCX or M.

Condition Codes: H: Not affected.

                       I: Not affected.

                      N: Set if the result is negative; cleared otherwise.

                      Z: Set if the result is zero; cleared otherwise.

                      V: Set if the shift caused a change in sign of the operand.

                      C: Set if, before the operation, the most significant bit of the ACCX or M was set; cleared otherwise.

Addressing Modes, Execution Time, and Machine Code (hexadecimal)

Addressing Modes	Execution Time (No. of cycles)	Number of bytes of machine code	Machine Code
			HEX.
A	2	1	48
B	2	1	58
EXT	6	3	78
IND	7	2	68

ASR

Operation:

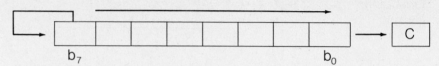

b_7 b_0

Description: Shift all bits of ACCX or M one place to the right. Bit 7 is held constant. Bit 0 is loaded into the C bit.

Condition Codes:
H: Not affected.
I: Not affected.
N: Set if the most significant bit of the result is set; cleared otherwise.
Z: Set if all bits of the result are cleared; cleared otherwise.
V: Set if, after the completion of the shift operation, EITHER (N is set and C is cleared) OR (N is cleared and C is set); cleared otherwise.
C: Set if, before the operation, the least significant bit of the ACCX or M was set; cleared otherwise.

Addressing Modes, Execution Time, and Machine Code (hexadecimal)

Addressing Modes	Execution Time (No. of cycles)	Number of bytes of machine code	Machine Code HEX.
A	2	1	47
B	2	1	57
EXT	6	3	77
IND	7	2	67

Branch if Carry Clear

Operation: $(PC) \leftarrow (PC) + REL$ if $(C) = 0$

Description: Test the state of the C bit and cause a branch if C is clear. See BRA instruction for further details of the execution of the branch.

Condition Codes: Not affected.

Addressing Modes, Execution Time, and Machine Code (hexadecimal)

Addressing Modes	Execution Time (No. of cycles)	Number of bytes of machine code	Machine Code HEX.
REL	4	2	24

BCS

Branch if Carry Set

Operation: $(PC) \leftarrow (PC) + REL$ if $(C) = 1$

Description: Test the state of the C bit and cause a branch if C is set.
                See BRA instruction for further details of the execution of the
                branch.

Condition Codes: Not affected.

Addressing Modes, Execution Time, and Machine Code (hexadecimal)

Addressing Modes	Execution Time (No. of cycles)	Number of bytes of machine code	Machine Code
			HEX.
REL	4	2	25

Branch if Greater than or Equal to Zero

Operation: $(PC) \leftarrow (PC) + REL$ if $(N) \oplus (V) = 0$

i.e., if $(ACCX) \geqslant (M)$

(Two's complement numbers)

Description: Cause a branch if (N is set and V is set) OR (N is clear and V is clear).

If the BGE instruction is executed immediately after execution of any of the instructions CBA, CMP, SBA, or SUB, the branch will occur if and only if the two's complement number represented by the minuend (i.e., ACCX) was greater than or equal to the two's complement number represented by the subtrahend (i.e., M).

See BRA instruction for details of the branch.

Condition Codes: Not affected.

Addressing Modes, Execution Time, and Machine Code (hexadecimal)

Addressing Modes	Execution Time (No. of cycles)	Number of bytes of machine code	Machine Code HEX.
REL	4	2	2C

BGT

Operation: $(PC) \leftarrow (PC) + REL$ if $(Z) \odot [(N) \oplus (V)] = 0$

i.e. if $(ACCX) > (M)$

(Two's complement numbers)

Description: Cause a branch if [Z is clear] AND [(N is set and V is set) OR (N is clear and V is clear)].

If the BGT instruction is executed immediately after execution of any of the instructions CBA, CMP, SBA, or SUB, the branch will occur if and only if the two's complement number represented by the minuend (i.e., ACCX) was greater than the two's complement number represented by the subtrahend (i.e., M).

See BRA instruction for details of the branch.

Condition Codes: Not affected.

Addressing Modes, Execution Time, and Machine Code (hexadecimal)

Addressing Modes	Execution Time (No. of cycles)	Number of bytes of machine code	Machine Code HEX
REL	4	2	2E

Branch if Equal

Operation: $(PC) \leftarrow (PC) + REL$ if $(Z) = 1$

Description: Test the state of the Z bit and cause a branch if the Z bit is set. See BRA instruction for further details of the execution of the branch.

Condition Codes: Not affected.

Addressing Modes, Execution Time, and Machine Code (hexadecimal)

Addressing Modes	Execution Time (No. of cycles)	Number of bytes of machine code	Machine Code HEX
REL	4	2	27

BIT

Operation: (ACCX)·(M)

Description: Perform the logical "AND" comparison of the contents of ACCX and the contents of M and modify condition codes accordingly. Neither the contents of ACCX or M operands are affected. (Each bit of the result of the "AND" would be the logical "AND" of the corresponding bits of M and ACCX.)

Condition Codes: H: Not affected.

                 I: Not affected.

                 N: Set if the most significant bit of the result of the "AND" would be set; cleared otherwise.

                 Z: Set if all bits of the result of the "AND" would be cleared; cleared otherwise.

                 V: Cleared.

                 C: Not affected.

Addressing Modes, Execution Time, and Machine Code (hexadecimal)

Addressing Modes	Execution Time (No. of cycles)	Number of bytes of machine code	Machine Code HEX.
A IMM	2	2	85
A DIR	3	2	95
A EXT	4	3	B5
A IND	5	2	A5
B IMM	2	2	C5
B DIR	3	2	D5
B EXT	4	3	F5
B IND	5	2	E5

Branch if Less than or Equal to Zero **BLE**

Operation: $(PC) \leftarrow (PC) + REL$ if $(Z) \odot [(N) \oplus (V)] = 1$

i.e., if $(ACCX) \leqslant (M)$

(Two's complement numbers)

Description: Cause a branch if [Z is set] OR [(N is set and V is clear) OR (N is clear and V is set)].

If the BLE instruction is executed immediately after execution of any of the instructions CBA, CMP, SBA, or SUB, the branch will occur if and only if the two's complement number represented by the minuend (i.e. ACCX) was less then or equal to the two's complement number represented by the subtrahend (i.e. M).

See BRA instruction for details of the branch.

Condition Codes: Not affected.

Addressing Modes, Execution Time, and Machine Code (hexadecimal)

Addressing Modes	Execution Time (No. of cycles)	Number of bytes of machine code	Machine Code HEX.
REL	4	2	2F

BHI

Operation: $(PC) \leftarrow (PC) + REL$ if $(C) \cdot (Z) = 0$

                                       i.e., if $(ACCX) > (M)$

                                  (Unsigned binary numbers)

Description: Cause a branch if (C is clear) AND (Z is clear).
If the BHI instruction is executed immediately after execution of any of the instructions CBA, CMP, SBA, or SUB, the branch will occur if and only if the unsigned binary number represented by the minuend (i.e. ACCX) was greater than the unsigned binary number represented by the subtrahend (i.e. M).
See BRA instruction for details of the execution of the branch.

Condition Codes: Not affected.

Addressing Modes, Execution Time, and Machine Code (hexadecimal)

Addressing Modes	Execution Time (No. of cycles)	Number of bytes of machine code	Machine Code HEX.
REL	4	2	22

Branch if Less than Zero

Operation: $PC \leftarrow (PC) + REL$ if $(N) \oplus (V) = 1$

i.e., if $(ACCX) < (M)$

(Two's complement numbers)

Description: Cause a branch if (N is set and V is clear) OR (N is clear and V is set).

If the BLT instruction is executed immediately after execution of any of the instructions CBA, CMP, SBA, or SUB, the branch will occur if and only if the two's complement number represented by the minuend (i.e., ACCX) was less than the two's complement number represented by the subtrahend (i.e., M).

See BRA instruction for details of the branch.

Condition Codes: Not affected.

Addressing Modes, Execution Time, and Machine Code (hexadecimal)

Addressing Modes	Execution Time (No. of cycles)	Number of bytes of machine code	Machine Code HEX.
REL	4	2	2D

BLS

Branch if Lower or Same

Operation: $(PC) \leftarrow (PC) + REL$ if $(C) \odot (Z) = 1$

i.e., if $(ACCX) \leqslant (M)$

(unsigned binary numbers)

Description: Cause a branch if (C is set) OR (Z is set).

If the BLS instruction is executed immediately after execution of any of the instructions CBA, CMP, SBA, or SUB, the branch will occur if and only if the unsigned binary number represented by the minuend (i.e., ACCX) was less than or equal to the unsigned binary number represented by the subtrahend (i.e., M).

See BRA instruction for details of the execution of the branch.

Condition Codes: Not affected.

Addressing Modes, Execution Time, and Machine Code (hexadecimal)

Addressing Modes	Execution Time (No. of cycles)	Number of bytes of machine code	Machine Code HEX.
REL	4	2	23

Branch if Minus

Operation: $(PC) \leftarrow (PC) + REL$ if $(N) = 1$

Description: Tests the state of the N bit and causes a branch if N is set.
                    See BRA instruction for details of the execution of the branch.

Condition Codes: Not affected.

Addressing Modes, Execution Time, and Machine Code (hexadecimal)

Addressing Modes	Execution Time (No. of cycles)	Number of bytes of machine code	Machine Code
			HEX.
REL	4	2	2B

BNE

Branch if Not Equal

Operation: $(PC) \leftarrow (PC) + REL$ if $(Z) = 0$

Description: Test the state of the Z bit and cause a branch if the Z bit is clear. See BRA instruction for details of the execution of the branch.

Condition Codes: Not affected.

Addressing Modes, Execution Time, and Machine Code (hexadecimal)

Addressing Modes	Execution Time (No. of cycles)	Number of bytes of machine code	Machine Code
			Hex.
REL	4	2	26

Branch if Plus

Operation: $(PC) \leftarrow (PC) + REL$ if $(N) = 0$

Description: Test the state of the N bit and cause a branch if N is clear.
See BRA instruction for details of the execution of the branch.

Condition Codes: Not affected.

Addressing Modes, Execution Time, and Machine Code (hexadecimal)

Addressing Modes	Execution Time (No. of cycles)	Number of bytes of machine code	Machine Code HEX.
REL	4	2	2A

BRA

Operation: $(PC) \leftarrow (PC) + REL$

Description: Transfer control to an address computed by adding a 1-byte signed displacement, REL, to the contents of the program counter. A sign extension is performed on REL prior to the addition.

Note: In assembly language, an instruction using the relative addressing mode specifies the location where control is to be transferred as either a numerical or symbolic absolute address. The assembler then computes the relative address.

Condition Codes: Not affected.

Addressing Modes, Execution Time, and Machine Code (hexadecimal)

Addressing Modes	Execution Time (No. of cycles)	Number of bytes of machine code	Machine Code
			HEX.
REL	4	2	20

Branch to Subroutine

Operation:

$$\downarrow (PCL)$$
$$(SP) \leftarrow (SP) - 0001$$
$$\downarrow (PCH)$$
$$(SP) \leftarrow (SP) - 0001$$
$$(PC) \leftarrow (PC) + REL$$

Description: The program counter contents are pushed onto the stack, 1 byte at a time, starting with the least significant byte. The stack pointer contents are incremented after each push. Then control is transferred to the subroutine by adding the relative address to the program counter contents and placing the result in the program counter.

Condition Codes: Not affected.

Addressing Modes, Execution Time, and Machine Code (hexadecimal)

Addressing Modes	Execution Time (No. of cycles)	Number of bytes of machine code	Machine Code HEX.
REL	8	2	8D

BRANCH TO SUBROUTINE EXAMPLE

		Memory Location	Machine Code (Hex)	Assembler Language		
				Label	Operator	Operand
A. *Before*						
(PC)	←	$1000	8D		BSR	CHARLI
		$1001	50			
(SP)	←	$EFFF				
B. *After*						
(PC)	←	$1052	**	CHARLI	***	*****
(SP)	←	$EFFD				
		$EFFE	10			
		$EFFF	02			

BVC

Branch if Overflow Clear

Operation: $(PC) \leftarrow (PC) + REL$ if $(V) = 0$

Description: Test the state of the V bit and cause a branch if the V bit is clear. See BRA instruction for details of the execution of the branch.

Condition Codes: Not affected.

Addressing Modes, Execution Time, and Machine Code (hexadecimal)

Addressing Modes	Execution Time (No. of cycles)	Number of bytes of machine code	Machine Code HEX.
REL	4	2	28

Branch if Overflow Set

BVS

Operation: $(PC) \leftarrow (PC) + REL$ if $(V) = 1$

Description: Test the state of the V bit and cause a branch if the V bit is set.
See BRA instruction for details of the execution of the branch.

Condition Codes: Not affected.

Addressing Modes, Execution Time, and Machine Code (hexadecimal)

Addressing Modes	Execution Time (No. of cycles)	Number of bytes of machine code	Machine Code HEX.
REL	4	2	29

CBA

Compare Accumulators

Operation: $(ACCA) - (ACCB)$

Description: Compare the contents of ACCA and the contents of ACCB and set the condition codes, which may be used for arithmetic and logical conditional branches. Both operands are unaffected.

Condition Codes: H: Not affected.

                      I: Not affected.

                     N: Set if the result is negative; cleared otherwise.

                     Z: Set if the result is zero; cleared otherwise.

                     V: Set if the subtraction would cause two's complement overflow; cleared otherwise.

                     C: Set if the subtraction would require a borrow into the most significant bit of the result; clear otherwise.

Addressing Modes, Execution Time, and Machine Code (hexadecimal)

Addressing Modes	Execution Time (No. of cycles)	Number of bytes of machine code	Machine Code
			HEX.
INHERENT	2	1	11

Clear Carry

CLC

Operation: C bit ← 0
Description: Clear the carry bit in the processor condition codes register.
Condition Codes: H: Not affected.
                  I: Not affected.
                  N: Not affected.
                  Z: Not affected.
                  V: Not affected.
                  C: Cleared.

Addressing Modes, Execution Time, and Machine Code (hexadecimal)

Addressing Modes	Execution Time (No. of cycles)	Number of bytes of machine code	Machine Code HEX.
INHERENT	2	1	0C

CLI

Clear Interrupt Mask

Operation: I bit ← 0

Description: Clear the interrupt mask bit in the processor condition codes register. This enables the microprocessor to service an interrupt from a peripheral device if signalled by a high state of the "Interrupt Request" control input.

Condition Codes:
H: Not affected.
I: Cleared.
N: Not affected.
Z: Not affected.
V: Not affected.
C: Not affected.

Addressing Modes, Execution Time, and Machine Code (hexadecimal)

Addressing Modes	Execution Time (No. of cycles)	Number of bytes of machine code	Machine Code HEX.
INHERENT	2	1	0E

Clear

Operation: (ACCX) ← 00
or: (M) ← 00
Description: The contents of ACCX or M are replaced with zeros.
Condition Codes: H: Not affected.
                 I: Not affected.
                 N: Cleared.
                 Z: Set.
                 V: Cleared.
                 C: Cleared.

Addressing Modes, Execution Time, and Machine Code (hexadecimal)

Addressing Modes	Execution Time (No. of cycles)	Number of bytes of machine code	Machine Code HEX.
A	2	1	4F
B	2	1	5F
EXT	6	3	7F
IND	7	2	6F

CLV

Operation: V bit ← 0

Description: Clear the two's complement overflow bit in the processor condition codes register.

Condition Codes: H: Not affected.
                I: Not affected.
                N: Not affected.
                Z: Not affected.
                V: Cleared.
                C: Not affected.

Addressing Modes, Execution Time, and Machine Code (hexadecimal)

Addressing Modes	Execution Time (No. of cycles)	Number of bytes of machine code	Machine Code HEX.
INHERENT	2	1	0A

Compare

CMP

Operation: $(ACCX) - (M)$

Description: Compare the contents of ACCX and the contents of M and determine the condition codes, which may be used subsequently for controlling conditional branching. Both operands are unaffected.

Condition Codes:
- H: Not affected.
- I: Not affected.
- N: Set if the result is negative; cleared otherwise.
- Z: Set if the result is zero; cleared otherwise.
- V: Set if the subtraction would cause two's complement overflow; cleared otherwise.
- C: Carry is set if the unsigned value of the contents of memory is larger than the unsigned value of the accumulator; reset otherwise.

Addressing Modes, Execution Time, and Machine Code (hexadecimal)

(DUAL OPERAND)

Addressing Modes	Execution Time (No. of cycles)	Number of bytes of machine code	Machine Code HEX.
A IMM	2	2	81
A DIR	3	2	91
A EXT	4	3	B1
A IND	5	2	A1
B IMM	2	2	C1
B DIR	3	2	D1
B EXT	4	3	F1
B IND	5	2	E1

COM

Complement

Operation: $(ACCX) \leftarrow \approx (ACCX) = FF - (ACCX)$

or: $(M) \leftarrow \approx (M) = FF - (M)$

Description: Replace the contents of ACCX or M with its one's complement. (Each bit of the contents of ACCX or M is inverted.)

Condition Codes: H: Not affected.

                  I: Not affected.

                  N: Set if the result is negative; cleared otherwise.

                  Z: Set if the result is zero; cleared otherwise.

                  V: Cleared.

                  C: Set.

Addressing Modes, Execution Time, and Machine Code (hexadecimal)

Addressing Modes	Execution Time (No. of cycles)	Number of bytes of machine code	Machine Code HEX.
A	2	1	43
B	2	1	53
EXT	6	3	73
IND	7	2	63

Compare Index Register **CPX**

Operation: $(IXL) - (M+1)$
$(IXH) - (M)$

Description: Compare the most significant byte of (IX) with the contents of M specified by the program, and compare the least significant byte of (IX) with the contents of one plus the address specified by the program. Compare by subtracting as above, and set or reset Z. The operands remain unchanged.

The N and V bits, though determined by this operation, are not intended for conditional branching.

The C bit is not affected by this operation.

Condition Codes:
H: Not affected.
I: Not affected.
N: Set if the most significant bit of the result of the subtraction from the more significant byte of the index register would be set; cleared otherwise.
Z: Set if all bits of the results of both subtractions would be cleared; cleared otherwise.
V: Set if the subtraction from the more significant byte of the index register would cause two's complement overflow; cleared otherwise.
C: Not affected.

Addressing Modes, Execution Time, and Machine Code (hexadecimal)

Addressing Modes	Execution Time (No. of cycles)	Number of bytes of machine code	Machine Code HEX.
IMM	3	3	8C
DIR	4	2	9C
EXT	5	3	BC
IND	6	2	AC

DAA

Decimal Adjust ACCA

Operation: Add hexadecimal numbers 00, 06, 60, or 66 to ACCA, and also set the carry bit, if indicated by the following table:

State of C-bit before DAA (Col. 1)	Upper Half-byte (bits 4–7) (Col. 2)	Initial Half-carry H-bit (Col. 3)	Lower to ACCA (bits 0–3) (Col. 4)	Number Added by DAA (Col. 5)	State of C-bit after DAA (Col. 6)
0	0–9	0	0–9	00	0
0	0–8	0	A–F	06	0
0	0–9	1	0–3	06	0
0	A–F	0	0–9	60	1
0	9–F	0	A–F	66	1
0	A–F	1	0–3	66	1
1	0–2	0	0–9	60	1
1	0–2	0	A–F	66	1
1	0–3	1	0–3	66	1

Note: Columns (1) through (4) of the above table represent all possible cases which can result from any of the operations ABA, ADD, or ADC, with initial carry either set or clear, applied to two binary-coded-decimal operands. The table shows hexadecimal values.

Description: If the contents of ACCA and the state of the carry-borrow bit C and the half-carry bit H are all the result of applying any of the operations ABA, ADD, or ADC to binary-coded-decimal operands, with or without an initial carry, the DAA operation will function as follows.

Subject to the above condition, the DAA operation will adjust the contents of ACCA and the C bit to represent the correct binary-coded-decimal sum and the correct state of the carry.

Condition Codes: H: Not affected.
I: Not affected.
N: Set if bit 7 of the result is set; cleared otherwise.
Z: Set if the result is zero; cleared otherwise.
V: Not defined.
C: Set or reset according to the same rule as if the DAA and an immediately preceding ABA, ADD, or ADC were replaced by a hypothetical binary-coded-decimal addition.

Addressing Modes, Execution Time, and Machine Code (hexadecimal)

Addressing Modes	Execution Time (No. of cycles)	Number of bytes of machine code	Machine Code
			HEX.
INHERENT	2	1	19

DEC

Operation: $(ACCX) \leftarrow (ACCX) - 01$
or: $(M) \leftarrow (M) - 01$
Description: Subtract one from the contents of ACCX or M.
Condition Codes: H: Not affected.
                  I: Not affected.
                  N: Set if the result is negative; cleared otherwise.
                  Z: Set if the result is zero; cleared otherwise.
                  V: Set if there was two's complement overflow as a result of the operation; cleared otherwise. Two's complement overflow occurs if and only if (ACCX) or (M) was 80 before the operation.
                  C: Not affected.

Addressing Modes, Execution Time, and Machine Code (hexadecimal)

Addressing Modes	Execution Time (No. of cycles)	Number of bytes of machine code	Machine Code HEX.
A	2	1	4A
B	2	1	5A
EXT	6	3	7A
IND	7	2	6A

Decrement Stack Pointer

Operation: (SP) ← (SP) − 0001
Description: Subtract one from the stack pointer contents.
Condition Codes: Not affected.

Addressing Modes, Execution Time, and Machine Code (hexadecimal)

Addressing Modes	Execution Time (No. of cycles)	Number of bytes of machine code	Machine Code HEX.
INHERENT	4	1	34

DEX

Decrement Index Register

Operation: $(IX) \leftarrow (IX) - 0001$

Description: Subtract one from the index register contents.

Only the Z bit is set or reset according to the result of this operation.

Condition Codes: H: Not affected.
- I: Not affected.
- N: Not affected.
- Z: Set if the result is zero; cleared otherwise.
- V: Not affected.
- C: Not affected.

Addressing Modes, Execution Time, and Machine Code (hexadecimal)

Addressing Modes	Execution Time (No. of cycles)	Number of bytes of machine code	Machine Code HEX.
INHERENT	4	1	09

Exclusive OR

Operation: $(ACCX) \leftarrow (ACCX) \oplus (M)$

Description: Perform logical "EXCLUSIVE OR" between the contents of ACCX and the contents of M, and place the result in ACCX. (Each bit of ACCX after the operation will be the logical "EXCLUSIVE OR" of the corresponding bit of M and ACCX before the operation.)

Condition Codes: H: Not affected.
                     I: Not affected.
                    N: Set if most significant bit of the result is set; cleared otherwise.
                    Z: Set if all bits of the result are cleared; cleared otherwise.
                    V: Cleared.
                    C: Not affected.

Addressing Modes, Execution Time, and Machine Code (hexadecimal)

Addressing Modes	Execution Time (No. of cycles)	Number of bytes of machine code	Machine Code HEX.
A IMM	2	2	88
A DIR	3	2	98
A EXT	4	3	B8
A IND	5	2	A8
B IMM	2	2	C8
B DIR	3	2	D8
B EXT	4	3	F8
B IND	5	2	E8

INC

Increment

Operation: $(ACCX) \leftarrow (ACCX) + 01$
or: $(M) \leftarrow (M) + 01$
Description: Add one to the contents of ACCX or M.
Condition Codes: H: Not affected.
                 I: Not affected.
                N: Set if the result is negative; cleared otherwise.
                Z: Set if the result is zero; cleared otherwise.
                V: Set if there was two's complement overflow as a result of the operation; cleared otherwise. Two's complement overflow will occur if and only if (ACCX) or (M) was 7F before the operation.
                C: Not affected.

Addressing Modes, Execution Time, and Machine Code (hexadecimal)

Addressing Modes	Execution Time (No. of cycles)	Number of bytes of machine code	Machine Code HEX.
A	2	1	4C
B	2	1	5C
EXT	6	3	7C
IND	7	2	6C

Increment Stack Pointer

Operation: $(SP) \leftarrow (SP) + 0001$

Description: Add one to the stack pointer contents.

Condition Codes: Not affected.

Addressing Modes, Execution Time, and Machine Code (hexadecimal)

Addressing Modes	Execution Time (No. of cycles)	Number of bytes of machine code	Machine Code
			HEX.
INHERENT	4	1	31

INX

Operation: $(IX) \leftarrow (IX) + 0001$

Description: Add one to the index register contents.

Only the Z bit is set or reset according to the result of this operation.

Condition Codes: H: Not affected.

                 I: Not affected.

                 N: Not affected.

                 Z: Set if the result is zero; cleared otherwise.

                 V: Not affected.

                 C: Not affected.

Addressing Modes, Execution Time, and Machine Code (hexadecimal)

Addressing Modes	Execution Time (No. of cycles)	Number of bytes of machine code	Machine Code HEX.
INHERENT	4	1	08

Jump

JMP

Operation: (PC) ← Absolute address

Description: Transfer control unconditionally to an absolute address according to the rules of extended or indexed addressing. In extended addressing the absolute address occupies 2 bytes following the JMP OP code.

Condition Codes: Not affected.

Addressing Modes, Execution Time, and Machine Code (hexadecimal)

Addressing Modes	Execution Time (No. of cycles)	Number of bytes of machine code	Machine Code
			HEX.
EXT	3	3	7E
IND	4	2	6E

JSR

Operation:

$$\downarrow (PCL)$$
$$(SP) \leftarrow (SP) - 0001$$
$$\downarrow (PCH)$$
$$(SP) \leftarrow (SP) - 0001$$
$$(PC) \leftarrow \text{numerical address}$$

Description: The program counter contents are pushed onto the stack, 1 byte at a time, starting with the least significant byte. The stack pointer contents are incremented after each push. Then control is transferred to the address specified by the program, following the rules of extended or indexed addressing.

Condition Codes: Not affected.

Addressing Modes, Execution Time, and Machine Code (hexadecimal)

Addressing Modes	Execution Time (No. of cycles)	Number of bytes of machine code	Machine Code HEX.
EXT	9	3	BD
IND	8	2	AD

JUMP TO SUBROUTINE EXAMPLE (extended mode)

		Memory Location	Machine Code (Hex)	Assembler Language Label	Operator	Operand
A. *Before:*						
PC	→	$0FFF	BD		JSR	CHARLI
		$1000	20			
		$1001	77			
SP	←	$EFFF				
B. *After:*						
PC	→	$2077	**	CHARLI	***	*****
SP	→	$EFFD				
		$EFFE	10			
		$EFFF	02			

Load Accumulator

Operation: $(ACCX) \leftarrow (M)$

Description: The contents of a memory location are placed in (loaded into) the accumulator.

Condition Codes:
H: Not affected.
I: Not affected.
N: Set if the number loaded is negative; cleared otherwise.
Z: Set if the number loaded is zero; cleared otherwise.
V: Cleared.
C: Not affected.

Addressing Modes, Execution Time, and Machine Code (hexadecimal)

(DUAL OPERAND)

Addressing Modes	Execution Time (No. of cycles)	Number of bytes of machine code	Machine Code HEX.
A IMM	2	2	86
A DIR	3	2	96
A EXT	4	3	B6
A IND	5	2	A6
B IMM	2	2	C6
B DIR	3	2	D6
B EXT	4	3	F6
B IND	5	2	E6

LDS

Operation: (SPH) ← (M)

(SPL) ← (M + 1)

Description: Load the more significant byte of the stack pointer from the byte of memory at the address specified by the program, and load the less significant byte of the stack pointer from the next byte of memory, at one plus the address specified by the program.

Condition Codes: H: Not affected.

I: Not affected.

N: Set if the 16-bit number loaded is negative; cleared otherwise.

Z: Set if the number loaded is zero; cleared otherwise.

V: Cleared.

C: Not affected.

Addressing Modes, Execution Time, and Machine Code (hexadecimal)

Addressing Modes	Execution Time (No. of cycles)	Number of bytes of machine code	Machine Code
			HEX.
IMM	3	3	8E
DIR	4	2	9E
EXT	5	3	BE
IND	6	2	AE

Load Index Register

Operation: $(IXH) \leftarrow (M)$
                           $(IXL) \leftarrow (M+1)$

Description: Load the more significant byte of the index register from the byte of memory at the address specified by the program, and load the less significant byte of the index register from the next byte of memory, at one plus the address specified by the program.

Condition Codes: H: Not affected.
                      I: Not affected.
                      N: Set if the 16-bit number loaded is negative; cleared otherwise.
                      Z: Set if the number loaded is zero; cleared otherwise.
                      V: Cleared.
                      C: Not affected.

Addressing Modes, Execution Time, and Machine Code (hexadecimal)

Addressing Modes	Execution Time (No. of cycles)	Number of bytes of machine code	Machine Code HEX.
IMM	3	3	CE
DIR	4	2	DE
EXT	5	3	FE
IND	6	2	EE

LSR

Operation:

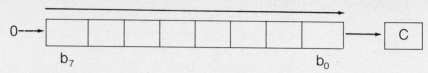

$$0 \longrightarrow \boxed{ \ \ \ \ \ \ \ \ \ \ \ \ \ \ } \longrightarrow \boxed{C}$$

b_7 b_0

Description: Shift all bits of ACCX or M one place to the right. Bit 7 is loaded with a zero. The C bit is loaded from the least significant bit of ACCX or M.

Condition Codes: H: Not affected.

                      I: Not affected.

                      N: Cleared.

                      Z: Set if the result is zero; cleared otherwise.

                      V: Set if the operation sets C; cleared otherwise.

                      C: Set if, before the operation, the least significant bit of the ACCX or M was set; cleared otherwise.

Addressing Modes, Execution Time, and Machine Code (hexadecimal)

Addressing Modes	Execution Time (No. of cycles)	Number of bytes of machine code	Machine Code HEX.
A	2	1	44
B	2	1	54
EXT	6	3	74
IND	7	2	64

Negate

Operation: $(ACCX) \leftarrow -(ACCX) = 00 - (ACCX)$
or: $(M) \leftarrow -(M) = 00 - (M)$
Description: Replace the contents of ACCX or M with its two's complement. Note that 80 is left unchanged.
Condition Codes: H: Not affected.
                  I: Not affected.
                  N: Set if the result is negative; cleared otherwise.
                  Z: Set if the result is zero; cleared otherwise.
                  V: Set if there would be two's complement overflow as a result of the implied subtraction from zero; this will occur if and only if the contents of ACCX or M is 80.
                  C: Set if there would be a borrow in the implied subtraction from zero; the C bit will be set in all cases except when the contents of ACCX or M is 00.

Addressing Modes, Execution Time, and Machine Code (hexadecimal)

Addressing Modes	Execution Time (No. of cycles)	Number of bytes of machine code	Machine Code HEX.
A	2	1	40
B	2	1	50
EXT	6	3	70
IND	7	2	60

NOP

Description: This is a single-word instruction which causes only the program counter to be incremented. No other registers are affected.

Condition Codes: Not affected.

Addressing Modes, Execution Time, and Machine Code (hexadecimal)

Addressing Modes	Execution Time (No. of cycles)	Number of bytes of machine code	Machine Code
			HEX.
INHERENT	2	1	01

Inclusive OR

Operation: $(ACCX) \leftarrow (ACCX) \quad (M)$

Description: Perform logical "OR" between the contents of ACCX and the contents of M and places the result in ACCX. (Each bit of ACCX after the operation will be the logical "OR" of the corresponding bits of M and of ACCX before the operation).

Condition Codes: H: Not affected.
I: Not affected.
N: Set if most significant bit of the result is set; cleared otherwise.
Z: Set if all bits of the result are cleared; cleared otherwise.
V: Cleared.
C: Not affected.

Addressing Modes, Execution Time, and Machine Code (hexadecimal)

(DUAL OPERAND)

Addressing Modes	Execution Time (No. of cycles)	Number of bytes of machine code	Machine Code HEX.
A IMM	2	2	8A
A DIR	3	2	9A
A EXT	4	3	BA
A IND	5	2	AA
B IMM	2	2	CA
B DIR	3	2	DA
B EXT	4	3	FA
B IND	5	2	EA

PSH

Operation: ↓ (ACCX)

(SP) ← (SP) − 0001

Description: Store the contents of ACCX in the stack at the address contained in the stack pointer. Then decrement the contents of the stack pointer.

Condition Codes: Not affected.

Addressing Modes, Execution Time, and Machine Code (hexadecimal)

Addressing Modes	Execution Time (No. of cycles)	Number of bytes of machine code	Machine Code HEX.
A	4	1	36
B	4	1	37

Pull Data from Stack

Operation: $(SP) \leftarrow (SP) + 0001$
$\uparrow (ACCX)$

Description: Increment the stack pointer contents. Then load ACCX from the address contained in the stack pointer.

Condition Codes: Not affected.

Addressing Modes, Execution Time, and Machine Code (hexadecimal)

Addressing Modes	Execution Time (No. of cycles)	Number of bytes of machine code	Machine Code HEX.
A	4	1	32
B	4	1	33

ROL

Operation:

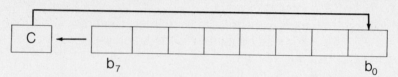

$$b_7 \qquad\qquad\qquad\qquad\qquad b_0$$

Description: Shift all bits of ACCX or M one place to the left. Bit 0 is loaded from the C bit. The C bit is loaded from the most significant bit of ACCX or M.

Condition Codes: H: Not affected.

I: Not affected.

N: Set if the result is negative; cleared otherwise.

Z: Set if the result is zero; cleared otherwise.

V: Set if the operation causes a change in sign; cleared otherwise.

C: Set if, before the operation, the most significant bit of the ACCX or M was set; cleared otherwise.

Addressing Modes, Execution Time, and Machine Code (hexadecimal)

Addressing Modes	Execution Time (No. of cycles)	Number of bytes of machine code	Machine Code HEX.
A	2	1	49
B	2	1	59
EXT	6	3	79
IND	7	2	69

Operation:

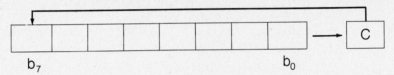

b_7 b_0

Description: Shift all bits of ACCX or M one place to the right. Bit 7 is loaded from the C bit. The C bit is loaded from the least significant bit of ACCX or M.

Condition Codes: H: Not affected.

                    I: Not affected.

                    N: Set if the result is negative; cleared otherwise.

                    Z: Set if the result is zero; cleared otherwise.

                    V: Set if, after the completion of the operation, EITHER (N is set and C is cleared) OR (N is cleared and C is set); cleared otherwise.

                    C: Set if, before the operation, the least significant bit of the ACCX or M was set; cleared otherwise.

Addressing Modes, Execution Time, and Machine Code (hexadecimal)

Addressing Modes	Execution Time (No. of cycles)	Number of bytes of machine code	Machine Code HEX.
A	2	1	46
B	2	1	56
EXT	6	3	76
IND	7	2	66

RTI

Operation: $(SP) \leftarrow (SP) + 0001 , \uparrow CC$
$(SP) \leftarrow (SP) + 0001 , \uparrow ACCB$
$(SP) \leftarrow (SP) + 0001 , \uparrow ACCA$
$(SP) \leftarrow (SP) + 0001 , \uparrow IXH$
$(SP) \leftarrow (SP) + 0001 , \uparrow IXL$
$(SP) \leftarrow (SP) + 0001 , \uparrow PCH$
$(SP) \leftarrow (SP) + 0001 , \uparrow PCL$

Description: Restore the CC, ACCB, ACCA, IX, and PC contents by pulling from the stack in the order shown. Increment the stack pointer contents before each pull.

Condition Codes: Restored to the states pulled from the stack.

Addressing Modes, Execution Time, and Machine Code (hexadecimal)

Addressing Modes	Execution Time (No. of cycles)	Number of bytes of machine code	Machine Code HEX.
INHERENT	10	1	3B

RETURN FROM INTERRUPT EXAMPLE

		Memory Location	Machine Code (Hex)	Assembler Language		
				Label	Operator	Operand
A. *Before*						
PC	→	$D066	3B		RTI	
SP	→	$EFF8				
		$EFF9	11HINZVC	(binary)		
		$EFFA	12			
		$EFFB	34			
		$EFFC	56			
		$EFFD	78			
		$EFFE	55			
		$EFFF	67			

B. *After*

PC	→	$5567	**		***	*****
		$EFF8				
		$EFF9	11HINZVC	(binary)		
		$EFFA	12			
		$EFFB	34			
		$EFFC	56			
		$EFFD	78			
		$EFFE	55			
SP	→	$EFFF	67			

CC = HINZVC (binary)

ACCB = 12 (Hex)   IXH = 56 (Hex)
ACCA = 34 (Hex)   IXL = 78 (Hex)

RTS

Operation: $(SP) \leftarrow (SP) + 0001$
                           $\uparrow (PCH)$
                           $(SP) \leftarrow (SP) + 0001$
                           $\uparrow (PCL)$

Description: The program counter contents are restored by pulling 2 bytes from the stack and storing them in the program counter, high-order byte first. The stack pointer contents are incremented before each pull.

Condition Codes: Not affected.

Addressing Modes, Execution Time, and Machine Code (hexadecimal)

Addressing Modes	Execution Time (No. of cycles)	Number of bytes of machine code	Machine Code HEX.
INHERENT	5	1	39

RETURN FROM SUBROUTINE EXAMPLE

	Memory Location	Machine Code (Hex)	Assembler Language		
			Label	Operator	Operand
A. *Before*					
PC	$30A2	39		RTS	
SP	$EFFD				
	$EFFE	10			
	$EFFF	02			
B. *After*					
PC	$1002	**		***	*****
	$EFFD				
	$EFFE	10			
SP	$EFFF	02			

Subtract Accumulators

SBA

Operation: $(ACCA) \leftarrow (ACCA) - (ACCB)$

Description: Subtract the contents of ACCB from the contents of ACCA and place the result in ACCA. The contents of ACCB are not affected.

Condition Codes: H: Not affected.

I: Not affected.

N: Set if the result is negative; cleared otherwise.

Z: Set if the result is zero; cleared otherwise.

V: Set if there was two's complement overflow as a result of the operation.

C: Carry is set if the absolute value of accumulator B plus previous carry is larger than the absolute value of accumulator A; reset otherwise.

Addressing Modes, Execution Time, and Machine Code (hexadecimal)

Addressing Modes	Execution Time (No. of cycles)	Number of bytes of machine code	Machine Code
			HEX.
INHERENT	2	1	10

SBC

Subtract with Carry

Operation: $(ACCX) \leftarrow (ACCX) - (M) - (C)$

Description: Subtract the contents of M and C from the contents of ACCX and place the result in ACCX.

Condition Codes:
H: Not affected.
I: Not affected.
N: Set if the result is negative; cleared otherwise.
Z: Set if the result is zero; cleared otherwise.
V: Set if there was two's complement overflow as a result of the operation; cleared otherwise.
C: Carry is set if the absolute value of the contents of memory plus previous carry is larger than the absolute value of the accumulator; reset otherwise.

Addressing Modes, Execution Time, and Machine Code (hexadecimal)

(DUAL OPERAND)

Addressing Modes	Execution Time (No. of cycles)	Number of bytes of machine code	Machine Code HEX.
A IMM	2	2	82
A DIR	3	2	92
A EXT	4	3	B2
A IND	5	2	A2
B IMM	2	2	C2
B DIR	3	2	D2
B EXT	4	3	F2
B IND	5	2	E2

Set Carry

Operation: C bit ← 1

Description: Sets the carry bit in the processor condition codes register.

Condition Codes: H: Not affected.

                           I: Not affected.

                           N: Not affected.

                           Z: Not affected.

                           V: Not affected.

                           C: Set.

Addressing Modes, Execution Time, and Machine Code (hexadecimal)

Addressing Modes	Execution Time (No. of cycles)	Number of bytes of machine code	Machine Code HEX.
INHERENT	2	1	0D

SEI

Operation: I bit ← 1

Description: Set the interrupt mask bit in the processor condition codes register. The microprocessor is inhibited from servicing an interrupt from a peripheral device, and will continue with execution of the instructions of the program, until the interrupt mask bit has been cleared.

Condition Codes: H: Not affected.
I: Set.
N: Not affected.
Z: Not affected.
V: Not affected.
C: Not affected.

Addressing Modes, Execution Time, and Machine Code (hexadecimal)

Addressing Modes	Execution Time (No. of cycles)	Number of bytes of machine code	Machine Code
			HEX.
INHERENT	2	1	0F

Set Two's Complement Overflow Bit

Operation: V bit ← 1

Description: Set the two's complement overflow bit in the processor condition codes register.

Condition Codes: H: Not affected.
                   I: Not affected.
                   N: Not affected.
                   Z: Not affected.
                   V: Set.
                   C: Not affected.

Addressing Modes, Execution Time, and Machine Code (hexadecimal)

Addressing Modes	Execution Time (No. of cycles)	Number of bytes of machine code	Machine Code HEX.
INHERENT	2	1	0B

STA

Operation: (M) ← (ACCX)

Description: Store (copy) the contents of an accumulator in a memory location. (The contents of the accumulator are unchanged.)

Condition Codes: H: Not affected.

I: Not affected.

N: Set if the number stored is negative; cleared otherwise.

Z: Set if the number stored is zero; cleared otherwise.

V: Cleared.

C: Not affected.

Addressing Modes, Execution Time, and Machine Code (hexadecimal)

Addressing Modes	Execution Time (No. of cycles)	Number of bytes of machine code	Machine Code HEX.
A DIR	4	2	97
A EXT	5	3	B7
A IND	6	2	A7
B DIR	4	2	D7
B EXT	5	3	F7
B IND	6	2	E7

Store Stack Pointer

Operation: $(M) \leftarrow (SPH)$
                        $(M+1) \leftarrow (SPL)$

Description: Store the more significant byte of the stack pointer in memory at the address specified by the program, and store the less significant byte of the stack pointer at the next location in memory, at one plus the address specified by the program.

Condition Codes: H: Not affected.
                      I: Not affected.
                      N: Set if the 16-bit number stored is negative; cleared otherwise.
                      Z: Set if the number stored is zero; cleared otherwise.
                      V: Cleared.
                      C: Not affected.

Addressing Modes, Execution Time, and Machine Code (hexadecimal)

Addressing Modes	Execution Time (No. of cycles)	Number of bytes of machine code	Machine Code
			HEX.
DIR	5	2	9F
EXT	6	3	BF
IND	7	2	AF

STX

Store Index Register

Operation: $(M) \leftarrow (IXH)$

$(M+1) \leftarrow (IXL)$

Description: Store the more significant byte of the index register in memory at the address specified by the program, and store the less significant byte of the index register at the next location in memory (at one plus the address specified by the program).

Condition Codes: H: Not affected.

              I: Not affected.

              N: Set if the 16-bit number stored is negative; cleared otherwise.

              Z: Set if the number stored is zero; cleared otherwise.

              V: Cleared.

              C: Not affected.

Addressing Modes, Execution Time, and Machine Code (hexadecimal)

Addressing Modes	Execution Time (No. of cycles)	Number of bytes of machine code	Machine Code HEX.
DIR	5	2	DF
EXT	6	3	FF
IND	7	2	EF

Subtract

Operation: $(ACCX) \leftarrow (ACCX) - (M)$

Description: Subtract the contents of M from the contents of ACCX and place the result in ACCX.

Condition Codes: H: Not affected.

I: Not affected.

N: Set if the result is negative.

Z: Set if the result is zero.

V: Set if there was two's complement overflow as a result of the operation; cleared otherwise.

C: Set if the absolute value of the contents of memory is larger than the absolute value of the accumulator; reset otherwise.

Addressing Modes, Execution Time, and Machine Code (hexadecimal)

(DUAL OPERAND)

Addressing Modes	Execution Time (No. of cycles)	Number of bytes of machine code	Machine Code HEX.
A IMM	2	2	80
A DIR	3	2	90
A EXT	4	3	B0
A IND	5	2	A0
B IMM	2	2	C0
B DIR	3	2	D0
B EXT	4	3	F0
B IND	5	2	E0

SWI

Operation:

$$\downarrow (PCL), (SP) \leftarrow (SP) - 0001$$
$$\downarrow (PCH), (SP) \leftarrow (SP) - 0001$$
$$\downarrow (IXL), (SP) \leftarrow (SP) - 0001$$
$$\downarrow (IXH), (SP) \leftarrow (SP) - 0001$$
$$\downarrow (ACCA), (SP) \leftarrow (SP) - 0001$$
$$\downarrow (ACCB), (SP) \leftarrow (SP) - 0001$$
$$\downarrow (CC), (SP) \leftarrow (SP) - 0001$$
$$I \leftarrow 1$$
$$(PCH) \leftarrow (n - 0005)$$
$$(PCL) \leftarrow (n - 0004)$$

Description: Save the program environment by pushing the contents of the PC, IX, ACCA, and ACCB onto the stack in the order shown above. Decrement the stack pointer contents after each push. Then set the interrupt mask bit. Transfer control to the service routine by loading the program counter with the contents of the SWI interrupt vector at addresses $n - 0004$ and $n - 0005$, where n is the highest available address.

Condition Codes: H: Not affected.
       I: Set.
      N: Not affected.
      Z: Not affected.
      V: Not affected.
      C: Not affected.

Addressing Modes, Execution Time, and Machine Code (hexadecimal)

Addressing Modes	Execution Time (No. of cycles)	Number of bytes of machine code	Machine Code HEX.
INHERENT	12	1	3F

SOFTWARE INTERRUPT EXAMPLE

A. *Before:*

CC = HINZVC (binary)
ACCB = 12 (Hex)   IXH = 56 (Hex)
ACCA = 34 (Hex)   IXL = 78 (Hex)

		Memory Location	Machine Code (Hex)	Assembler Language		
				Label	Operator	Operand
PC	→	$5566	3F		SWI	
SP	→	$EFFF				
		$FFFA	D0			
		$FFFB	55			

B. *After:*

		Memory Location	Machine Code (Hex)			
PC	→	$D055				
SP	→	$EFF8				
		$EFF9	11HINZVC	(binary)		
		$EFFA	12			
		$EFFB	34			
		$EFFC	56			
		$EFFD	78			
		$EFFE	55			
		$EFFF	67			

Note: This example assumes that FFFF is the memory location addressed when all lines of the address bus go to the high state.

TAB

Transfer from Accumulator A to Accumulator B

Operation: (ACCB) ← (ACCA)

Description: Move the contents of ACCA to ACCB. The former contents of ACCB are lost. The contents of ACCA are not changed.

Condition Codes: H: Not affected.
                     I: Not affected.
                     N: Set if the number moved is negative; cleared otherwise.
                     Z: Set if the number moved is zero; cleared otherwise.
                     V: Cleared.
                     C: Not affected.

Addressing Modes, Execution Time, and Machine Code (hexadecimal)

Addressing Modes	Execution Time (No. of cycles)	Number of bytes of machine code	Machine Code HEX.
INHERENT	2	1	16

Transfer from Accumulator A
to Processor Condition Codes Register

Operation: (CC) ← (ACCA)

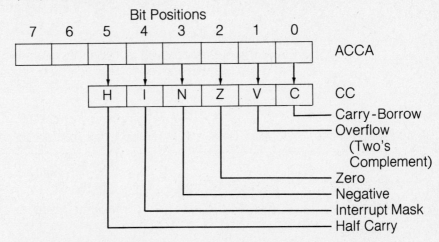

Bit Positions

Description: Transfer the contents of bit positions 0 thru 5 of accumulator A to the corresponding bit positions of the processor condition codes register. The contents of accumulator A remain unchanged.

Condition Codes: Set or reset according to the contents of the respective bits 0 thru 5 of accumulator A.

Addressing Modes, Execution Time, and Machine Code (hexadecimal)

Addressing Modes	Execution Time (No. of cycles)	Number of bytes of machine code	Machine Code
			HEX.
INHERENT	2	1	06

TBA

Transfer from Accumulator B to Accumulator A

Operation: (ACCA) ← (ACCB)

Description: Move the contents of ACCB to ACCA. The former contents of ACCA are lost. The contents of ACCB are not changed.

Condition Codes: H: Not affected.

I: Not affected.

N: Set if the number moved is negative; cleared otherwise.

Z: Set if the number moved is zero; cleared otherwise.

V: Cleared.

C: Not affected.

Addressing Modes, Execution Time, and Machine Code (hexadecimal)

Addressing Modes	Execution Time (No. of cycles)	Number of bytes of machine code	Machine Code HEX.
INHERENT	2	1	17

Transfer from Processor Condition Codes Register to Accumulator A

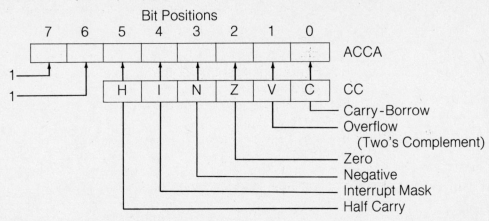

TPA

Operation: $(ACCA) \leftarrow (CC)$

Bit Positions

| 7 | 6 | 5 | 4 | 3 | 2 | 1 | 0 |

ACCA

| | | H | I | N | Z | V | C | CC

Carry-Borrow
Overflow
    (Two's Complement)
Zero
Negative
Interrupt Mask
Half Carry

Description: Transfer the contents of the processor condition codes register to corresponding bit positions 0 thru 5 of accumulator A. Bit positions 6 and 7 of accumulator A are set (i.e., go to the "1" state). The processor condition codes register remains unchanged.

Condition Codes: Not affected.

Addressing Modes, Execution Time, and Machine Code (hexadecimal)

Addressing Modes	Execution Time (No. of cycles)	Number of bytes of machine code	Machine Code
			HEX.
INHERENT	2	1	07

TST

Operation: $(ACCX) - 00$

                          $(M) - 00$

Description: Set condition codes N and Z according to the contents of ACCX or M.

Condition Codes: H: Not affected.

                       I: Not affected.

                       N: Set if most significant bit of the contents of ACCX or M is set; cleared otherwise.

                       Z: Set if all bits of the contents of ACCX or M are cleared; cleared otherwise.

                       V: Cleared.

                       C: Cleared.

Addressing Modes, Execution Time, and Machine Code (hexadecimal)

Addressing Modes	Execution Time (No. of cycles)	Number of bytes of machine code	Machine Code HEX.
A	2	1	4D
B	2	1	5D
EXT	6	3	7D
IND	7	2	6D

Transfer from Stack Pointer to Index Register **TSX**

Operation: $(IX) \leftarrow (SP) + 0001$

Description: Load the index register with one plus the contents of the stack pointer. The contents of the stack pointer remain unchanged.

Condition Codes: Not affected.

Addressing Modes, Execution Time, and Machine Code (hexadecimal)

Addressing Modes	Execution Time (No. of cycles)	Number of bytes of machine code	Machine Code HEX.
INHERENT	4	1	30

TXS

Transfer from Index Register to Stack Pointer

Operation: $(SP) \leftarrow (IX) - 0001$

Description: Load the stack pointer with the contents of the index register, minus one. The contents of the index register remain unchanged.

Condition Codes: Not affected.

Addressing Modes, Execution Time, and Machine Code (hexadecimal)

Addressing Modes	Execution Time (No. of cycles)	Number of bytes of machine code	Machine Code HEX.
INHERENT	4	1	35

Wait for Interrupt

Operation:

$\downarrow (PCL), (SP) \leftarrow (SP) - 0001$
$\downarrow (PCH), (SP) \leftarrow (SP) - 0001$
$\downarrow (IXL), (SP) \leftarrow (SP) - 0001$
$\downarrow (IXH), (SP) \leftarrow (SP) - 0001$
$\downarrow (ACCA), (SP) \leftarrow (SP) - 0001$
$\downarrow (ACCB), (SP) \leftarrow (SP) - 0001$
$\downarrow (CC), (SP) \leftarrow (SP) - 0001$

Description: Save the program environment by pushing the contents of the PC, IX, ACCA, ACCB, and CC onto the stack in the order shown above. Decrement the stack pointer after each push. Suspend execution of the program until an interrupt occurs.

When an interrupt does occur, check the I bit. If set, continue waiting until clear. When the I bit is clear, set it and transfer control to the location whose address is contained in the vector of the particular interrupt.

Condition Codes: H: Not affected.
I: Not affected until an interrupt request signal is detected on the interrupt request control line. When the interrupt request is received the I bit is set and further execution takes place, provided the I bit was initially clear.
N: Not affected.
Z: Not affected.
V: Not affected.
C: Not affected.

Addressing Modes, Execution Time, and Machine Code (hexadecimal)

Addressing Modes	Execution Time (No. of cycles)	Number of bytes of machine code	Machine Code HEX.
INHERENT	9	1	3E

TABLE A-1. Addressing Formats (1)

Addressing Mode of Second Operand	First Operand	
	Accumulator A	Accumulator B
IMMediate	CCC A #number CCC A # symbol CCC A #expression CCC A #'C	CCC B #number CCC B #symbol CCC B #expression CCC B #'C
DIRect or EXTended	CCC A number CCC A symbol CCC A expression	CCC B number CCC B symbol CCC B expression
INDexed	CCC A X CCC Z ,X CCC A number,X CCC A symbol,X CCC A expression,X	CCC B X CCC B ,X CCC B number,X CCC B symbol,X CCC B expression,X

Notes: 1. CCC = mnemonic operator of source instruction.

2. "symbol" may be the special symbol "*".

3. "expression" may contain the special symbol "*".

4. space may be omitted before A or B.

Applicable to the following source instructions:

ADC ADD AND BIT CMP
EOR LDA ORA SBC SUB

*Special symbol indicating program counter.

TABLE A-2. Addressing Formats (2)

Addressing Mode of Second Operand	First Operand	
	Accumulator A	Accumulator B
DIRect or EXTended	STA A number STA A symbol STA A expression	STA B number STA B symbol STA B expression
INDexed	STA A X STA A ,X STA A number,X STA A symbol,X STA A expression,X	STA B X STA B ,X STA B number,X STA B symbol,X STA B expression,X

Notes: 1. "symbol" may be the special symbol "*".

2. "expression" may contain the special symbol "*".

3. Space may be omitted before A or B.

Applicable to the source instruction:

STA

*Special symbol indicating program counter.

TABLE A-3. Addressing Formats (3)

Operand or Addressing Mode	Formats
Accumulator A	CCC A
Accumulator B	CCC B
EXTended	CCC number CCC symbol CCC expression
INDexed	CCC X CCC ,X CCC number,X CCC symbol,X CCC expression,X

Notes: 1. CCC = mnemonic operator of source instruction.

2. "symbol" may be the special symbol "*".

3. "expression" may contain the special symbol "*".

4. Space may be omitted before A or B.

Applicable to the following source instructions:

ASL   ASR   CLR   COM   DEC   INC
LSR   NEG   ROL   ROR   TST

*Special symbol indicating program counter.

TABLE A-4. Addressing Formats (4)

Operand	Formats
Accumulator A	CCC A
Accumulator B	CCC B

Notes: 1. CCC = mnemonic operator of source instruction.

2. Space may be omitted before A or B.

Applicable to the following source instructions:

PSH   PUL

TABLE A-5. Addressing Formats (5)

Addressing Mode	Formats
IMMediate	CCC #number CCC #symbol CCC #expression CCC #'C
DIRect or EXTended	CCC number CCC symbol CCC expression
INDexed	CCC X CCC ,X CCC number,X CCC symbol,X CCC expression,X

Notes: 1. CCC = mnemonic operator of source instruction.

2. "symbol" may be the special symbol "*".

3. "expression" may contain the special symbol "*".

Applicable to the following source instructions:

CPX   LDS   LDX

*Special symbol indicating program counter.

TABLE A-6. Addressing Formats (6)

Addressing Mode	Formats
DIRect or EXTended	CCC number CCC symbol CCC expression
INDexed	CCC X CCC ,X CCC number,X CCC symbol,X CCC expression,X

Notes: 1. CCC = mnemonic operator of source instruction.

2. "symbol" may be the special symbol "*".

3. "expression" may contain the special symbol "*".

Applicable to the following source instructions:

STS   STX

*Special symbol indicating program counter.

TABLE A-7. Addressing Formats (7)

Addressing Mode	Formats
EXTended	CCC number CCC symbol CCC expression
INDexed	CCC X CCC ,X CCC number,X CCC symbol,X CCC expression,X

Notes: 1. CCC = mnemonic operator of source instruction.

2. "symbol" may be the special symbol "*".

3. "expression" may contain the special symbol "*".

Applicable to the following source instructions:

JMP   JSR

*Special symbol indicating program counter.

TABLE A-8. Addressing Formats (8)

Addressing Mode	Formats
RELative	CCC number CCC symbol CCC expression

Notes: 1. CCC = mnemonic operator of source instruction.

2. "symbol" may be the special symbol "*".

3. "expression" may contain the special symbol "*".

Applicable to the following source instructions:

BCC BCS BEQ BGE BGT BHI BLE BLS
BLT BMI BNE BPL BRA BSR BVC BVS

*Special symbol indicating program counter.

APPENDIX B
M6800
Cross Assembler
Reference Manual

Reprinted by permission of Motorola, Inc.

CHAPTER 1

INTRODUCTION

1.1   GENERAL

The M68SAM Cross Assembler is a program that processes source
program statements written in M6800 Assembly Language. The Cross
Assembler translates these source statements into object programs
compatible with the M68EML Simulator or the EXORciser loader, and
produces a listing of the source program.

1.2   M68SAM CROSS ASSEMBLY LANGUAGE

The symbolic language used to code source programs to be processed
by the assembler is called the M68SAM Cross Assembly Language.
The language is a collection of mnemonic symbols representing:

. Operations

- M6800 machine-instruction operation codes

- Cross Assembler directives

. Symbolic names (labels)

. Operators

. Special symbols

1.2.1   Machine Operation Codes

The assembly language provides mnemonic machine-instruction operation
codes for all machine instructions in the M6800 instruction set. The M6800
instructions are described in detail in the M6800 Programming Manual.

1.2.2   Directives

The assembly language also contains mnemonic directives which specify
auxiliary actions to be performed by the assembler. Directives are not
always translated to machine language. (Directives are described in
Chapter 3 and a summary of directives is included in Appendix C.)

1.3   M68SAM CROSS ASSEMBLER

The M68SAM Cross Assembler translates source statements written in
M68SAM Cross Assembly Language into machine language, assigns storage
locations to instructions and data, and performs auxiliary assembler
actions designated by the programmer.

1.3.1   Assembler Aims

The two basic aims of the M68SAM Cross Assembler are:

. To provide the programmer with the means to
   translate his source coding into object code
   that is in the format required by the M68EML
   Simulator or an EXORciser-compatible loader.

. To provide a printed listing containing the
   source language input, assembler object code,
   and additional information (such as error codes,
   if any) useful to the programmer in analyzing
   his program.

1.3.2   Assembler Processing

The assembler reads the source program twice: first, to develop
the symbol tables; second, to assemble the object program with reference
to the symbol tables developed in pass one. During the pass two, the
object code and the assembly listing are generated. Each source language
line is processed before the next line is read.

As each line is processed, the assembler examines the location,
operation, and operand fields. The operation code table is scanned for
a match with the operation field. If a standard machine operation code
is being processed, the proper data is inserted into the object code.
If a directive is specified, the proper action is taken. The object
code and the assembly listing are formed for output, with any detected
actual or potential errors flagged before the line containing the error
is printed.

1.3.3   Assembler Features

Assembler directives assist the programmer:

. In controlling the assembler output.

. In defining data and symbols.

. In allocating storage.

Refer to Chapter 3 for mnemonic operation codes for these functions.

CHAPTER 2

CODING M6800 ASSEMBLY LANGUAGE PROGRAMS

2.1 SOURCE STATEMENT FORMAT

Programs written in assembly language consist of a sequence of source statements. Each source statement consists of a sequence of ASCII characters. Refer to Appendix A for a listing of the supported ASCII character set.

Each source statement may include up to five fields:

. Sequence number

. Label (or "*" implying a comment)

. Operation

. Operand

. Comment

2.1.1 Sequence Numbers

The sequence number field is an option provided as a programmer convenience. The sequence number field starts at the beginning of a source line and consists of up to five decimal digits (the value must be less than 65,536). Sequence numbers must be followed by a space.

Although sequence numbers are optional, they must be consistently used or not used for an entire program. If the first source statement includes a sequence number, then every succeeding statement must also include a sequence number. If the first source statement is unnumbered, then no other statement may be numbered.

2.1.2 Label Field

The label field occurs directly after the sequence number field (if there is one) or as the first field of a source line. The label field may take one of the following forms:

(1) An asterisk (*) as the first character indicates that the rest of the source line is a comment and should be ignored (except for listing purposes) by the assembler.

(2) A blank (b̸) as the first character indicates that the label field is empty (the line is not a comment and does not have a label).

(3) A symbol.

The attributes of a symbol are:

. consists of 1 to 6 characters

. valid characters in a symbol are A-Z and 0-9.

. the first character of a symbol must be alphabetic.

. the symbols "A", "B", and "X" are special symbols
  used by the assembler and should never be used in the
  label field.

A symbol may occur only once in the label field. If a symbol
does occur in more than one label field, then each reference to that
symbol will cause an error.

A label (symbol in the label field) is normally assigned the
value of the program location counter of the first byte of the instruction
or data being assembled.

The EQU directive requires a label which is not assigned the value
of the program counter. Refer to the EQU description in Chapter 3.

Some directives must not have a label in the label field. These
directives include: ORG, NAM, END, OPT, PAGE, and SPC.

Each symbol in a program is allocated a 4 word block in the symbol
table.

2.1.3   Operation Field

The operation field occurs directly after the label field in an
assembly language source statement. This field consists of an operation
code of three or four characters.

Entries in the operation code field may be one of two types:

. machine mnemonic operation code - these correspond
  directly to M6800 machine instructions. This operation code field includes the "A" or "B" character
  for the "dual" or "accumulator" addressing modes.
  For compatibility with other M6800 assemblers, a
  space may separate the operator from the accumulator
  designation (i.e. LDA A is the same as LDAA).

. directive - special operation codes known to the
  assembler which control the assembly process rather
  than being translated directly to machine language.

The assembler first searches for operation codes in the table of
machine operation codes and directives. If not found, an error message
is printed.

2.1.4   Operand Field

Interpretation of the operand field is dependent on the operation
field. For the M6800 machine instructions, the operand field must specify
the addressing mode. The operand field formats and the corresponding
addressing modes are as follows:

Operand Format		M6800 Machine Instruction Addressing Mode
no operand	-	inherent and accumulator
< expression >	-	direct, extended or relative (direct will be used if possible)
# < expression >	-	immediate
< expression >,X	-	indexed

Addressing modes and expressions are described in the M6800 Programming Manual. For directives calls, the operand can take on other forms. Directives are described in Chapter 3.

2.1.5   Comment Field

The last field of an M6800 assembly language source statement is the comment field. This field is optional and is ignored by the assembler except for being included in the listing. The comment field is separated from the operand field (or the operator field if there is no operand) by one or more blanks and may consist of any ASCII character. This field is important in documenting the operation of a program.

2.2   EXPRESSIONS

An expression is a combination of symbols and/or numbers separated by one of the arithmetic operators (+, -, *, or 1).

The assembler evaluates expressions algebraically from left to right without parenthetical grouping. There is no precedence hierarchy among the arithmetic operators. A fractional result, or immediate result obtained during the evaluation of an expression will be truncated to an integer value.

NUMBERS:

Decimal: < number >

Hexidecimal: $< number >   or   < number > H

         (first digit in latter case must be 0-9)

Octal: @< number >   or   < number >0   or   < number >Q

Binary: %< number >   or   < number >B

ASCII Literal:

' < character >   (apostrophe followed by an ASCII character)

The result is the numeric value for the ASCII character.

```
00010                           NAM    CNSTNT
00020            *
00030            *            PROGRAM TO ILLUSTRATE CONSTANTS
00040            *


00060 0000 0008          FDB    %1000     BINARY
00070 0002 0200          FDB    @1000     OCTAL
00080 0004 03E8          FDB    1000      DECIMAL
00090 0006 1000          FDB    $1000     HEXADECIMAL
00100 0008 0008          FDB    1000B     BINARY
00110 000A 0200          FDB    10000     OCTAL
00120 000C 0200          FDB    1000Q     OCTAL
00130 000E 1000          FDB    1000H     HEXADECIMAL
00140 0010 58            FCB    'X
00150                    END
```

2.3   SYMBOL

A symbol in an expression is similar to a symbol in the label field except that the value of the symbol is referenced instead of defined. The special symbol "*" is recognized by the assembler as the value of the current location counter (first byte of an instruction) when used in the context of a symbol.

A 16-bit integer value is associated with each symbol. This value is used in place of the symbol during algebraic manipulations.

The M68SAM Cross Assembler is a two-pass assembler. The symbol table is built on the first pass. Object records and listing are produced on the second pass. Certain expressions cannot be fully evaluated during the first pass because they may contain (forward) references to symbols which have not yet been defined. In some cases, a symbol may not be defined before being used in the second pass. Since the assembler cannot evaluate such symbols, these cases are treated as errors. Only one level of forward referencing is allowed.

2.4   M6800 ADDRESSING MODES

2.4.1   Inherent And Accumulator Addressing Mode

The M6800 includes some instructions which require only an operation code byte. These self-contained instructions employ inherent or accumulator addressing and do not require the operand field when written in the M68SAM Cross Assembly language.

2.4.2   Immediate Addressing Mode

Immediate addressing refers to the use of one or two bytes immediately following the instruction operation code as the instruction operand. Immediate addressing is selected by preceding the operand field in the source line with the character "#". The expression following the "#" may require one or two bytes, depending on the instruction.

2.4.3   Relative Addressing Mode

Relative addressing is used by the branch instructions. Branches can be made only within the range -126 to 129 relative to the first byte of the branch instruction:

$$(PC+2)-128 \leq D \leq (PC+2)+127$$

PC = address of first byte of branch instruction

D = address of the destination of the branch

The actual branch offset in the second byte of the branch instruction is the two's complement representation of the difference between the location of the byte immediately following the branch instruction and the location of the destination.

2.4.4   Indexed Addressing Mode

Indexed addresses are relative to the M6800 index register. The address is calculated at the time of instruction execution by adding the one-byte displacement in the second instruction byte to the current contents of the 16-bit X register. Since no sign extension is performed, the offset cannot be negative.

Indexed addressing is normally indicated by the characters ",X" following the expression in the operand field. (Special cases of ",X" or "X" alone are the same as "Ø,X".)

2.4.5   Direct And Extended Addressing Mode

Direct and extended addressing utilize one (direct) or two (extended) bytes to form the address of the operand desired. Direct addressing is limited to the first 256 bytes of memory, Ø-255. Direct and extended addressing are selected by simply putting an expression in the operand field of the source line. Direct addressing is used if possible. An error results if a directly-addressable variable is referenced before it is defined in a source program since this can cause a phasing error. To avoid phasing problems, directly addressable variables should always be defined before any reference to the variable.

2.5   ASSEMBLER OUTPUT

Assembler outputs include an assembly listing and an object program.

2.5.1   Assembly Listing

The assembly listing includes the source program as well as additional information generated by the assembler. Most lines in the listing correspond directly to a source statement. Lines which do not correspond directly to a source line include:

. page header lines

. error lines (see Appendix D for a listing of error numbers)

. expansion lines for the FCC, FDB, FCB directives

Most listing lines follow the standard format shown in the following table.

TABLE 2-1. Standard Format

(Special cases may not use exactly the same format)

COLUMN	CONTENTS
1 - 5	Source Line # - 5 digit decimal counter kept by assembler
7 - 10	Current Location Counter Value (in hex)

TABLE 2-1. Standard Format (Continued)

COLUMN	CONTENTS
12 - 13	Machine Operation Code (hex)
15 - 16	First Byte of Operand (hex)
17 - 18	Second Byte of Operand (if there is one)
20 - 25	Label Field
27 - 31	Operation Field
34 - 41	Operand Field (longer operand extends into comment field)
43 - Last Column	Comment Field

2.5.2   OBJECT PROGRAM

A detailed description of the object format is included in Appendix E.

CHAPTER 3

ASSEMBLER DIRECTIVES

3.1 INTRODUCTION

Assembler directives (or pseudo-ops) are instructions to the assembler rather than instructions to be directly translated into object code. This section describes the directives recognized by the M68SAM Cross Assembler.

In Table 3-1, directives are grouped by function performed. Detailed descriptions of each directive are arranged alphabetically.

TABLE 3-1 M68SAM Cross Assembler Directives

DIRECTIVE	FUNCTION
ASSEMBLY CONTROL	
NAM	Program Name
ORG	Origin
END	Program End
SYMBOL DEFINITION	
EQU	Assign Permanent Value
DATA DEFINITION/ STORAGE ALLOCATION	
FCC	Character String Data
FCB	One Byte Data
FDB	Double Byte Data
RMB	Reserve Memory Bytes
LISTING CONTROL	
PAGE	Top of Page
SPC	Skip "n" Lines
OPT DB8	Octal Display Base
OPT DB10	Decimal Display Base
OPT DB16	Hexadecimal Display Base (Selected by Default)
OPT LIST	Selects Listing of the Assembly (Selected by Default)
OPT NOLIST	Suppresses the Printing of the Assembly Listing

3.2 END

FORMAT: END

DESCRIPTION: The END directive indicates to the assembler that the source is finished. Subsequent source statements are ignored. The END directive encountered at the end of the first pass through the source program causes the assembler to start the second pass.

3.3 EQU - Equate Symbol Value

FORMAT: <label> EQU <expression> [<comments>]

DESCRIPTION: The EQU directive assigns the value of the expression in the operand field to the symbol in the label field. The label and expression follow the rules given in a previous section. Note that EQU is one operator that assigns a value other than the program location counter to the label. The program location counter is not affected by this directive. The label and operand fields are both required and the label cannot be defined anywhere else in the program.

The expression in the operand field of an EQU cannot include a symbol that is undefined or not yet defined (no forward references are allowed).

```
00010                     NAM      EQU
00020            *
00030            *     PROGRAM TO ILLUSTRATE USE OF THE EQU
00040            *     DIRECTIVE
00050            *


00070 0000 0064  LABEL1 RMB       100
00080      0032  LABEL2 EQU       LABEL1+50    LABEL2 ASSIGNED VALUE DE
00090      0032  LABEL3 EQU       LABEL2
00100 0064 96 32         LDA A    LABEL2
00110 0066 D6 32         LDA B    LABEL3
00120                    END
```

3.4   FCB - Form Constant Byte

FORMAT: [<label>]   FCB

$$\left\{ \begin{matrix} \left\{ \begin{matrix} <expr> \\ <null> \end{matrix} \right\} , & \left[\begin{matrix} <expr> \\ , \end{matrix} \right. , & \left. \begin{matrix} 00 \\ 0 \end{matrix} \right] & [<expr>] \\ <expr> & & & \end{matrix} \right\}$$

<comments>

DESCRIPTION: The FCB directive may have one or more operands, separated
by commas. An 8-bit unsigned binary number corresponding
to the value of each operand is stored in a byte of the
object program. If there is more than one operand, they
are stored in successive bytes. The operand field may
contain the actual value (decimal, hexadecimal, octal or
binary). Alternatively, the operand may be a symbol or
an expression which can be assigned a numerical value
by the assembler.

An FCB directive followed by one or more null operands
separated by commas will store zeros for the null operands.


```
00010                          NAM    FCB
00020              *
00030              *    PROGRAM TO ILLUSTRATE USE OF FORM
00040              *    CONSTANT BYTE DIRECTIVE
00050              *



00070 0000 FF                  FCB    $FF
00080 0001 00    LABEL         FCB    ,$F,23
      0002 0F
      0003 17
00090 0004 02                  FCB    %010    LABEL+1
00100                          END
```

3.5   FCC - Form Constant Character

FORMAT: [<label>]   FCC

$$\left\{ \begin{array}{l} \text{d} \quad <\text{ASCII string}> \quad \text{d} \\ <\text{decimal number}> , \quad <\text{ASCII string}> \end{array} \right\}$$

< comments >

NOTE: 1. "d" is any non-numeric character (used as a delimeter).

2. ASCII string may not include a carriage return.

DESCRIPTION: The FCC directive translates strings of characters into their 7-bit ASCII codes. Any of the characters which correspond to ASCII hexadecimal codes 20 (SP) through 5F (__) can be processed by this directive.

1. Count, comma, text. Where the count specifies how many ASCII characters to generate and the text begins following the first comma of the operand. Should the count be longer than the text, spaces will be inserted to fill the count. Maximum count is 255.

2. Text enclosed between identical delimiters, each being any single character. (If the delimiters are numbers, the text must not begin with a comma.)

If the string in the operand comprises more than one character, the ASCII codes corresponding to the successive characters are entered into successive bytes of memory.

```
00010                          NAM  FCC
00020                 *
00030                 *        PROGRAM TO ILLUSTRATE USE
00035                 *        OF FCC DIRECTIVE
00040                 *


00060  0000  54      MSC1      FCC    /TEXT/
       0001  45
       0002  58
       0003  54
00070  0004  54      MSC2      FCC    9,TEXT
       0005  45
       0006  58
       0007  54
       0008  20
       0009  20
       000A  20
       000B  20
       000C  20
00080  000D  4D                FCC    ?MORE TEXT?
       000E  4F
       000F  52
       0010  45
       0011  20
       0012  54
       0013  45
       0014  58
       0015  54
00090                          END
```

FORMAT: $\langle label \rangle$ FDB

$$\left\{ \begin{array}{l} \left. \begin{array}{l} \langle expr \rangle , \\ \langle null \rangle , \end{array} \right\} \quad \left[\begin{array}{l} \langle expr \rangle , \\ , \end{array} \right]_{0}^{00} \left[\langle expr \rangle \right] \\[2em] \langle expr \rangle \\[1em] \langle comments \rangle \end{array} \right\}$$

DESCRIPTION: The FDB directive may have one or more operands separated by commas. The 16-bit unsigned binary number corresponding to the value of each operand is stored in two bytes of the object program. If there is more than one operand, they are stored in successive bytes. The operand field may contain the actual value (decimal, hexadecimal, octal or binary). Alternatively, the operand may be a symbol or an expression which can be assigned a numerical value by the assembler.

An FDB directive followed by one or more null operands separated by commas will store zeros for the null operands. The label is optional.

```
00010                          NAM    FDB
00020              *
00030              *           PROGRAM TO ILLUSTRATE USE OF
00035              *           FORM DOUBLE
00040              *           BYTE CONSTANT DIRECTIVE
00050              *



00070 0000 0002                FDB    2
00080 0002 0000 LABEL          FDB    ,$F,$FF,$FFF,,$FFFF
      0004 000F
      0006 00FF
      0008 0FFF
      000A 0000
      000C FFFF
00090 000E 000C                FDB    LABEL+10,LABEL+5,LABEL
      0010 0007
      0012 0002
00100                          END
```

3.7   NAM – Program Name .

FORMAT: NAM   < program name >   [< comments >]

DESCRIPTION: The NAM directive must be the first statement of a
              M68SAM Cross Assembler source program. The NAM
              directive does not allow a label, but it does require
              an operand -- a program name (one-six characters).

3.8   OPT – Output Option

FORMAT: OPT   < option >   [, < option >]

DESCRIPTION: The "OPT" directive is used to give the programmer
              optional control of the format of assembler output.
              The "OPT" directive is not translated into machine
              code.

              No label may be used with the "OPT" directive.

              The options are written in the operand field following
              the directive, and are separated by commas.

              If options are selected in the middle of an assembly
              they are not altered at the beginning of pass two.

              The available options are:

OPTION	MEANING
DB8	Octal display base
DB10	Decimal display base
DB16	Hexadecimal display base (selected by default)
LIST	Selects listing of the assembly (selected by default)
NOLIST	Suppresses the printing of the assembly listing.

505

```
00010                        NAM    OPT
00020              *
00030              *         PROGRAM TO ILLUSTRATE USE OF THE
00035              *         OPTION
00040              *         DIRECTIVE
00050


00070                        OPT    DB8    OUTPUT IN OCTAL
00080  000000 007            FCB    7,8,9,10,11
       000001 010
       000002 011
       000003 012
       000004 013
00090                        OPT    DB10   OUTPUT IN DECIMAL
00100  00005 007             FCB    7,8,9,10,11
       00006 008
       00007 009
       00008 010
       00009 011
00110                        OPT    DB16   OUTPUT IN HEXADECIMAL
00120  000A 07               FCB    7,8,9,10,11
       000B 08
       000C 09
       000D 0A
       000E 0B
00130                        END
```

3.9   ORG – Origin

FORMAT: ORG < expression >   [< comments >]

DESCRIPTION: The ORG directive changes the program counter to the value specified by the expression in its operand field. Subsequent statements are assigned memory locations starting with the new program counter value. If no ORG is specified, the program counter is initialized with a value of 0. The ORG directive may not include a label.

```
00010                     NAM    ORG
00020           *
00030           *         PROGRAM TO ILLUSTRATE USE OF THE ORIGIN
00040           *         DIRECTIVE
00050           *


00070 0000 0001  BILL     RMB    1          PC STARTS AT ZERO
00080      0001  JOHN     EQU    *
00090 0020                ORG    $20        PC SET TO HEX 20
00100 0020 000A           RMB    10
00110 0001                ORG    JOHN       PC SET TO VALUE OF JOHN
00120 0001 000A           RMB    10
00130                     END
```

3.10 PAGE — Top of Page

FORMAT: PAGE

DESCRIPTION: The PAGE directive causes the assembler to advance the paper to the top of the next page. The PAGE directive does not appear on the program listing. No label or operand is used, and no machine code results. Its presence is shown by a missing assembly line number in the listing.

3.11 RMB — Reserve Memory Bytes

FORMAT: $\left[<\text{label}>\right]$ RMB $<\text{expression}>$ $\left[<\text{comments}>\right]$

DESCRIPTION: The RMB directive causes the location counter to be increased by the value of the operand field. This reserves a block of memory whose length is equal to the value of the operand field. The operand field may contain the actual number (decimal, hexadecimal, octal or binary) equal to the number of bytes to be reserved. Alternatively, the operand may be a symbol or an expression which can be assigned a numerical value by the assembler.

The block of memory which is reserved by the RMB directive is unchanged by that directive.

```
00010              NAM    RMB
00020        *
00030        *     PROGRAM TO ILLUSTRATE USE OF THE RESERVE
00040        *     MEMORY BYTE DIRECTIVE
00050        *


00070 0000 0001  CLAB1    RMB    1          1 BYTE RESERVED FOR CLAB1
00080 0001 0002  CLAB2    RMB    2          2 BYTES RESERVED FOR CLAB2
00090 0003 0003           RMB    *-CLAB1    EXPRESSION DETERMINES SIZE
00100                     END
```

3.12   SPC - Space

FORMAT: SPC   <expression>

DESCRIPTION: The SPC directive provides n vertical spaces for
formatting the program listing. It does not itself
appear in the listing. The number of lines to be left
blank is stated by an operand in the operand field.
Its presence is shown by a missing assembly listing
line number.

The operand would normally contain the actual number
(decimal, hexadecimal, octal or binary) equal to the
number of lines to be left blank. A symbol or an
expression is also allowed.

When the SPC directive causes the listing to cross
page boundaries, only those blank lines required to
get to the top of the next page will be generated.

CHAPTER 4

M68SAM CROSS ASSEMBLER INSTALLATION

The M68SAM Cross Assembler is written in ANSI FORTRAN and is designed to be both portable and machine independent. All of the non-standard FORTRAN functions have been isolated and identified as such. This Cross Assembler is logically structured for overlays for those cases where memory requirements are critical. Program parameters such as the length of the print line, the number of lines per page, and the input/output assignments are easily modified.

4.1   INSTALLATION

Install the M68SAM Cross Assembler on a given computer in accordance with the following procedures:

a. Modify the machine dependent routines.

NOTE

For most common computers, step a. has already been done by Motorola.

b. Compile and link edit (create a load module).

c. Supply the necessary job control statements to assign the input/output devices and to invoke execution.

4.2   MACHINE DEPENDENT PROGRAMS

Internal documentation is included with every subroutine in the M68SAM Cross Assembler. This documentation consists of program identification, revision level, date of last revision, revisions, function of the subroutine, the contents of each subroutine argument before and after subroutine execution, and computer dependency information. The second statement of each program identifies the program as being machine dependent or independent. If "ALL" appears in the "CMP:" field, then the routine is machine independent. The "CMP:" field identifies the machine dependent routines by identifying the computer for which they were specifically written. The routines that may require modification are described in Table 4-1.

4.3   OVERLAYS

The M68SAM Cross Assembler is logically structured for overlays. A "root" section and three segments can be easily defined as shown in Figure 4-1.

TABLE 4-1. MACHINE DEPENDENT PROGRAMS

PROGRAM NAME	PROGRAM DESCRIPTION
MPAM	Main program of the Cross Assembler. The "PROGRAM" statement, if required, may need to be modified.
MPADBK	Data block for labeled common. Logical unit assignments and program statements are initialized.

	VARIABLE	FUNCTION
	LULT	Logical unit of list device
	LUER	Logical unit of error reporting device
	LUSI	Logical unit of source input device
	LUOT	Logical unit of object tape output
	IPGLOL	Length of list line (maximum = 121)
	IPGLEN	Number of lines per printed page

PROGRAM NAME	PROGRAM DESCRIPTION
MPARSI	Routine which opens, closes, rewinds, and reads records from the source input file. Records are read in 80A1 format into array ISIBUF
MPUCVC	Converts a character in A1 format to its ASCII equivalent characters right justified, zero-filled.
MPUTRA	Translates a character from the machine character set into its ASCII equivalent character. It is an optional subroutine and is used only on those computers using other than ASCII character set.
MPUCA1	Converts an array of ASCII characters right justified, one per word to their equivalent code for the computer's character set in an A1 format.

TABLE 4-1. MACHINE DEPENDENT PROGRAMS (CONTINUED)

PROGRAM NAME	PROGRAM DESCRIPTION
MPUCA2	Converts an array of ASCII characters right justified, two per word to their equivalent code for the computer's character set in an A2 format.
MPUAND	Performs the Boolean AND function on the two operands passed as subroutine arguements.
MPUIOR	Performs the Boolean inclusive OR function on the two operands passed as routine arguements.

The calls to subroutines (segments), MPAM1, MPAM2, and MPAM3 all occur in subroutine MPAMØ which is located in the root section. It may be necessary to modify routines MPAM, MPAMØ, MPAM1, MPAM2, and MPAM3 in order to define the above overlay layout and to add calls (in MPAMØ) to the overlay processor to load each of the segments.

4.4   SYMBOL TABLE

The user defined symbols in an M6800 source program are stored in four-word blocks in the ISYM array. The first three words of each block contain the symbol (two ASCII words per block--right justified). The fourth word is the value of the symbol. The first 13 words of the symbol are predefined with the reserved symbols A, B, and X for the M6800 register.

To increase or decrease the size of the symbol table, make the following changes:

a. Modify the common statements which declare that variable ISIM is an array in programs MPAM, MPADBK, MPAFSY, MPASSY, and MPAM3.

b. Set the value of LSYM to the new length of ISYM in the block data program MPADBK.

c. Adjust the size of array KCOMON in program MPAM to reflect the change in size of ISYM. Variable KCOMON is dimensioned to the entire size of common and equivalent to the first word of common.

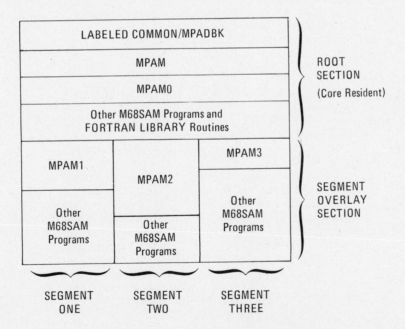

FIGURE 4-1. Overlay Map

CHARACTER SET

The character set recognized by the Motorola M68SAM Cross Assembler is a subset of ASCII (American Standard Code for Information Interchange, 1968). The ASCII Code is shown in the following figure. The following characters are recognized by the assembler.

1. The upper case letters A through Z

2. The integers 0 through 9

3. Four arithmetic operators: + - * /

4. Characters used as special prefixes:

   # (pounds sign) specifies the immediate mode of addressing
   $ (dollar sign) specifies a hexadecimal number
   @ (commercial at) specifies an octal number
   % (percent) specifies a binary number
   ' (apostrophe) specifies an ASCII literal character

5. Characters used as special suffixes:

   B (letter B) specifies a binary number
   H (letter H) specifies a hexadecimal number
   O (letter O) specifies an octal number
   Q (letter Q) specifies an octal number

6. Two separating characters:

   SPACE
   , (comma)

7. A comment in a source statement may include any characters with ASCII hexadecimal values from 20 (SP) through 5F (_).

8. In addition to the above, the assembler has the capability of reading strings of characters and of entering the corresponding 7-bit ASCII code into specified locations in the memory. This capability is provided by the assembler directive FCC (see Chapter 3). Any characters corresponding to ASCII hexadecimal values 20 (SP) through 5F (_) can be processed. This kind of processing can also be done, for a single ASCII character, by using the immediate mode of addressing with an operand in the form " 'C ". All such character conversions result in the most significant bit being reset to zero.

BITS 4 thru 6 —	0	1	2	3	4	5	6	7
0	NUL	DLE	SP	0	@	P		p
1	SOH	DC1	!	1	A	Q	a	q
2	STX	DC2	"	2	B	R	b	r
3	ETX	DC3	#	3	C	S	c	s
4	EOT	DC4	$	4	D	T	d	t
5	ENQ	NAK	%	5	E	U	e	u
6	ACK	SYN	&	6	F	V	f	v
7	BEL	ETB	'	7	G	W	g	w
8	BS	CAN	(	8	H	X	h	x
9	HT	EM	)	9	I	Y	i	y
A	LF	SUB	*	:	J	Z	j	z
B	VT	ESC	+	;	K	[	k	{
C	FF	FS	,	<	L	/	l	/
D	CR	GS	-	=	M	]	m	}
E	SO	RS	.	>	N	⟨	n	≈
F	SI	US	/	?	O	—	o	DEL

BITS 0 thru 3

FIGURE A-1 ASCII Code

SUMMARY OF M6800 INSTRUCTIONS

	(Dual Operand)	ACCX	Immediate	Direct	Extended	Indexed	Inherent	Relative
ABA		•	•	•	•	•	2	•
ADC	x	•	2	3	4	5	•	•
ADD	x	•	2	3	4	5	•	•
AND	x	•	2	3	4	5	•	•
ASL		2	•	•	6	7	•	•
ASR		2	•	•	6	7	•	•
BCC		•	•	•	•	•	•	4
BCS		•	•	•	•	•	•	4
BEA		•	•	•	•	•	•	4
BGE		•	•	•	•	•	•	4
BGT		•	•	•	•	•	•	4
BHI		•	•	•	•	•	•	4
BIT	x	•	2	3	4	5	•	•
BLE		•	•	•	•	•	•	4
BLS		•	•	•	•	•	•	4
BLT		•	•	•	•	•	•	4
BMI		•	•	•	•	•	•	4
BNE		•	•	•	•	•	•	4
BPL		•	•	•	•	•	•	4
BRA		•	•	•	•	•	•	4
BSR		•	•	•	•	•	•	8
BVC		•	•	•	•	•	•	4
BVS		•	•	•	•	•	•	4
CBA		•	•	•	•	•	2	•
CLC		•	•	•	•	•	2	•
CLI		•	•	•	•	•	2	•
CLR		2	•	•	6	7	•	•
CLV		•	•	•	•	•	2	•
CMP	x	•	2	3	4	5	•	•
COM		2	•	•	6	7	•	•
CPX		•	3	4	5	6	•	•
DAA		•	•	•	•	•	2	•
DEC		2	•	•	6	7	•	•
DES		•	•	•	•	•	4	•
DEX		•	•	•	•	•	4	•
EOR	x	•	2	3	4	5	•	•

	(Dual Operand)	ACCX	Immediate	Direct	Extended	Indexed	Inherent
INC		2	•	•	6	7	•
INS		•	•	•	•	•	4
INX		•	•	•	•	•	4
JMP		•	•	•	3	4	•
JSR		•	•	•	9	8	•
LDA	x	•	2	3	4	5	•
LDS		•	3	4	5	6	•
LDX		•	3	4	5	6	•
LSR		2	•	•	6	7	•
NEG		2	•	•	6	7	•
NOP		•	•	•	•	•	2
ORA	x	•	2	3	4	5	•
PSH		4	•	•	•	•	•
PUL		4	•	•	•	•	•
ROL		2	•	•	6	7	•
ROR		2	•	•	6	7	•
RTI		•	•	•	•	•	10
RTS		•	•	•	•	•	5
SBA		•	•	•	•	•	2
SBC	x	•	2	3	4	5	•
SEC		•	•	•	•	•	2
SEI		•	•	•	•	•	2
SEV		•	•	•	•	•	2
STA	x	•	•	4	5	6	•
STS		•	•	5	6	7	•
STX		•	•	5	6	7	•
SUB	x	•	2	3	4	5	•
SWI		•	•	•	•	•	12
TAB		•	•	•	•	•	2
TAP		•	•	•	•	•	2
TBA		•	•	•	•	•	2
TPA		•	•	•	•	•	2
TST		2	•	•	6	7	•
TSX		•	•	•	•	•	4
TXS		•	•	•	•	•	4
WAI		•	•	•	•	•	9

NOTE: Interrupt time is 12 cycles from the end of the instruction being executed, except following a WAI instruction. Then it is 4 cycles.

INSTRUCTION ADDRESSING MODES AND EXECUTION TIMES
(TIMES IN MACHINE CYCLES)

TABLE 3 — ACCUMULATOR AND MEMORY INSTRUCTIONS

OPERATIONS	MNEMONIC	IMMED OP	~	=	DIRECT OP	~	=	INDEX OP	~	=	EXTND OP	~	=	IMPLIED OP	~	=	BOOLEAN/ARITHMETIC OPERATION (All register labels refer to contents)	H	I	N	Z	V	C
Add	ADDA	8B	2	2	9B	3	2	AB	5	2	BB	4	3				A + M → A	↕	●	↕	↕	↕	↕
	ADDB	CB	2	2	DB	3	2	EB	5	2	FB	4	3				B + M → B	↕	●	↕	↕	↕	↕
Add Acmltrs	ABA													1B	2	1	A + B → A	↕	●	↕	↕	↕	↕
Add with Carry	ADCA	89	2	2	99	3	2	A9	5	2	B9	4	3				A + M + C → A	↕	●	↕	↕	↕	↕
	ADCB	C9	2	2	D9	3	2	E9	5	2	F9	4	3				B + M + C → B	↕	●	↕	↕	↕	↕
And	ANDA	84	2	2	94	3	2	A4	5	2	B4	4	3				A · M → A	●	●	↕	↕	R	●
	ANDB	C4	2	2	D4	3	2	E4	5	2	F4	4	3				B · M → B	●	●	↕	↕	R	●
Bit Test	BITA	85	2	2	95	3	2	A5	5	2	B5	4	3				A · M	●	●	↕	↕	R	●
	BITB	C5	2	2	D5	3	2	E5	5	2	F5	4	3				B · M	●	●	↕	↕	R	●
Clear	CLR							6F	7	2	7F	6	3				00 → M	●	●	R	S	R	R
	CLRA													4F	2	1	00 → A	●	●	R	S	R	R
	CLRB													5F	2	1	00 → B	●	●	R	S	R	R
Compare	CMPA	81	2	2	91	3	2	A1	5	2	B1	4	3				A − M	●	●	↕	↕	↕	↕
	CMPB	C1	2	2	D1	3	2	E1	5	2	F1	4	3				B − M	●	●	↕	↕	↕	↕
Compare Acmltrs	CBA													11	2	1	A − B	●	●	↕	↕	↕	↕
Complement, 1's	COM							63	7	2	73	6	3				$\overline{M}$ → M	●	●	↕	↕	R	S
	COMA													43	2	1	$\overline{A}$ → A	●	●	↕	↕	R	S
	COMB													53	2	1	$\overline{B}$ → B	●	●	↕	↕	R	S
Complement, 2's	NEG							60	7	2	70	6	3				00 − M → M	●	●	↕	↕	①	②
(Negate)	NEGA													40	2	1	00 − A → A	●	●	↕	↕	①	②
	NEGB													50	2	1	00 − B → B	●	●	↕	↕	①	②
Decimal Adjust, A	DAA													19	2	1	Converts Binary Add. of BCD Characters into BCD Format	●	●	↕	↕	↕	③
Decrement	DEC							6A	7	2	7A	6	3				M − 1 → M	●	●	↕	↕	④	●
	DECA													4A	2	1	A − 1 → A	●	●	↕	↕	④	●
	DECB													5A	2	1	B − 1 → B	●	●	↕	↕	④	●
Exclusive OR	EORA	88	2	2	98	3	2	A8	5	2	B8	4	3				A ⊕ M → A	●	●	↕	↕	R	●
	EORB	C8	2	2	D8	3	2	E8	5	2	F8	4	3				B ⊕ M → B	●	●	↕	↕	R	●
Increment	INC							6C	7	2	7C	6	3				M + 1 → M	●	●	↕	↕	⑤	●
	INCA													4C	2	1	A + 1 → A	●	●	↕	↕	⑤	●
	INCB													5C	2	1	B + 1 → B	●	●	↕	↕	⑤	●
Load Acmltr	LDAA	86	2	2	96	3	2	A6	5	2	B6	4	3				M → A	●	●	↕	↕	R	●
	LDAB	C6	2	2	D6	3	2	E6	5	2	F6	4	3				M → B	●	●	↕	↕	R	●
Or, Inclusive	ORAA	8A	2	2	9A	3	2	AA	5	2	BA	4	3				A + M → A	●	●	↕	↕	R	●
	ORAB	CA	2	2	DA	3	2	EA	5	2	FA	4	3				B + M → B	●	●	↕	↕	R	●
Push Data	PSHA													36	4	1	A → M$_{SP}$, SP − 1 → SP	●	●	●	●	●	●
	PSHB													37	4	1	B → M$_{SP}$, SP − 1 → SP	●	●	●	●	●	●
Pull Data	PULA													32	4	1	SP + 1 → SP, M$_{SP}$ → A	●	●	●	●	●	●
	PULB													33	4	1	SP + 1 → SP, M$_{SP}$ → B	●	●	●	●	●	●
Rotate Left	ROL							69	7	2	79	6	3				M	●	●	↕	↕	⑥	↕
	ROLA													49	2	1	A	●	●	↕	↕	⑥	↕
	ROLB													59	2	1	B	●	●	↕	↕	⑥	↕
Rotate Right	ROR							66	7	2	76	6	3				M	●	●	↕	↕	⑥	↕
	RORA													46	2	1	A	●	●	↕	↕	⑥	↕
	RORB													56	2	1	B	●	●	↕	↕	⑥	↕
Shift Left, Arithmetic	ASL							68	7	2	78	6	3				M	●	●	↕	↕	⑥	↕
	ASLA													48	2	1	A	●	●	↕	↕	⑥	↕
	ASLB													58	2	1	B	●	●	↕	↕	⑥	↕
Shift Right, Arithmetic	ASR							67	7	2	77	6	3				M	●	●	↕	↕	⑥	↕
	ASRA													47	2	1	A	●	●	↕	↕	⑥	↕
	ASRB													57	2	1	B	●	●	↕	↕	⑥	↕
Shift Right, Logic	LSR							64	7	2	74	6	3				M	●	●	R	↕	⑥	↕
	LSRA													44	2	1	A	●	●	R	↕	⑥	↕
	LSRB													54	2	1	B	●	●	R	↕	⑥	↕
Store Acmltr.	STAA				97	4	2	A7	6	2	B7	5	3				A → M	●	●	↕	↕	R	●
	STAB				D7	4	2	E7	6	2	F7	5	3				B → M	●	●	↕	↕	R	●
Subtract	SUBA	80	2	2	90	3	2	A0	5	2	B0	4	3				A − M → A	●	●	↕	↕	↕	↕
	SUBB	C0	2	2	D0	3	2	E0	5	2	F0	4	3				B − M → B	●	●	↕	↕	↕	↕
Subtract Acmltrs.	SBA													10	2	1	A − B → A	●	●	↕	↕	↕	↕
Subtr. with Carry	SBCA	82	2	2	92	3	2	A2	5	2	B2	4	3				A − M − C → A	●	●	↕	↕	↕	↕
	SBCB	C2	2	2	D2	3	2	E2	5	2	F2	4	3				B − M − C → B	●	●	↕	↕	↕	↕
Transfer Acmltrs	TAB													16	2	1	A → B	●	●	↕	↕	R	●
	TBA													17	2	1	B → A	●	●	↕	↕	R	●
Test, Zero or Minus	TST							6D	7	2	7D	6	3				M − 00	●	●	↕	↕	R	R
	TSTA													4D	2	1	A − 00	●	●	↕	↕	R	R
	TSTB													5D	2	1	B − 00	●	●	↕	↕	R	R

Rotate Left:
C ← ☐ ← [☐☐☐☐☐☐☐☐] ← b7 ... b0

Rotate Right:
☐ → [☐☐☐☐☐☐☐☐] → ☐ C, b7 ... b0

Shift Left, Arithmetic:
☐ ← [☐☐☐☐☐☐☐☐] ← 0, C b7 ... b0

Shift Right, Arithmetic:
[☐☐☐☐☐☐☐☐] → ☐ C, b7 ... b0

Shift Right, Logic:
0 → [☐☐☐☐☐☐☐☐] → ☐ C, b7 ... b0

H	I	N	Z	V	C

LEGEND:

OP   Operation Code (Hexadecimal);
~   Number of MPU Cycles;
=   Number of Program Bytes;
+   Arithmetic Plus;
−   Arithmetic Minus;
·   Boolean AND;
M$_{SP}$ Contents of memory location pointed to be Stack Pointer;

+   Boolean Inclusive OR;
⊙   Boolean Exclusive OR;
$\overline{M}$ Complement of M;
→   Transfer Into;
0   Bit = Zero;
00   Byte = Zero;

CONDITION CODE SYMBOLS:

H   Half-carry from bit 3;
I   Interrupt mask
N   Negative (sign bit)
Z   Zero (byte)
V   Overflow, 2's complement
C   Carry from bit 7
R   Reset Always
S   Set Always
↕   Test and set if true, cleared otherwise
●   Not Affected

Note — Accumulator addressing mode instructions are included in the column for IMPLIED addressing

APPENDIX C

DIRECTIVE SUMMARY

DIRECTIVE	FUNCTION
ASSEMBLY CONTROL	
NAM	Program Name
ORG	Origin
END	Program End
SYMBOL DEFINITION	
EQU	Assign Permanent Value
DATA DEFINITION/ STORAGE ALLOCATION	
FCC	Character String Data
FCB	One Byte Data
FDB	Double Byte Data
RMB	Reserve Memory Bytes
LISTING CONTROL	
PAGE	Top of Page
SPC	Skip "n" Lines
OPT DB8	Octal Display Base
OPT DB10	Decimal Display Base
OPT DB16	Hexadecimal Display Base (selected by default)
OPT LIST	Selects Listing of the Assembly (selected by default)
OPT NOLIST	Suppresses the Printing of the Assembly Listing

APPENDIX D

ASSEMBLER ERROR MESSAGES

201 NAM DIRECTIVE ERROR
MESSAGE: ****ERROR 201 AAAAAA
MEANING: THE NAM DIRECTIVE IS NOT THE FIRST SOURCE
STATEMENT, IT IS MISSING, OR IT OCCURS
MORE THAN ONCE IN THE SAME SOURCE PROGRAM.

202 LABEL OR OPCODE ERROR
MESSAGE: ****ERROR 202 AAAAAA
MEANING: THE LABEL OR OPCODE SYMBOL DOES NOT BEGIN
WITH AN ALPHABETIC CHARACTER.

203 STATEMENT ERROR
MESSAGE: ****ERROR 203 AAAAAA
MEANING: THE STATEMENT IS BLANK OR ONLY CONTAINS A
LABEL.

204 SYNTAX ERROR
MESSAGE: ****ERROR 204 AAAAAA
MEANING: THE STATEMENT IS SYNTACTICALLY INCORRECT.

205 LABEL ERROR
MESSAGE: ****ERROR 205 AAAAAA
MEANING: THE STATEMENT LABEL FIELD IS NOT TERMINATED
WITH A SPACE.

206 REDEFINED SYMBOL
MESSAGE: ****ERROR 206 AAAAAA
MEANING: THE SYMBOL HAS PREVIOUSLY BEEN DEFINED.
THE FIRST VALUE IS IN SYMBOL TABLE.

207 UNDEFINED OPCODE
MESSAGE: ****ERROR 207 AAAAAA
MEANING: THE SYMBOL IN THE OPCODE FIELD IS NOT A
VALID OPCODE MNEMONIC OR DIRECTIVE.

208 BRANCH ERROR
MESSAGE: ****ERROR 208 AAAAAA
MEANING: THE BRANCH COUNT IS BEYOND THE RELATIVE
BYTE'S RANGE. THE ALLOWABLE RANGE IS:
$(*+2)-128 < D < (*+2)+127$
WHERE: *=ADDRESS OF THE FIRST BYTE OF THE
BRANCH INSTRUCTION
D=ADDRESS OF THE DESTINATION OF
THE BRANCH INSTRUCTION.

209   ILLEGAL ADDRESS MODE
MESSAGE: ****ERROR 209 AAAAAA
MEANING: THE MODE OF ADDRESSING IS NOT ALLOWED WITH
THE OPCODE TYPE.

210   BYTE OVERFLOW
MESSAGE: ****ERROR 210 AAAAAA
MEANING: AN EXPRESSION CONVERTED TO A VALUE GREATER
THAN 255 (DECIMAL). THIS ERROR ALSO OCCURS
ON COMPUTER SYSTEMS HAVING WORD LENGTHS OF
16 BITS WHEN USING NEGATIVE OPERANDS IN
THE IMMEDIATE ADDRESSING MODE. EXAMPLE:
    LDA A   #-5   ; CAUSES ERROR 210
THE ERROR MAY BE AVOIDED BY USING THE 8
BIT TWO'S COMPLEMENT OF THE NUMBER.
EXAMPLE:
    LDA A   #$FB   ; ASSEMBLES OK

211   UNDEFINED SYMBOL
MESSAGE: ****ERROR 211 AAAAAA
MEANING: THE SYMBOL DOES NOT APPEAR IN A LABEL
FIELD.

212   DIRECTIVE OPERAND ERROR
MESSAGE: ****ERROR 212 AAAAAA
MEANING: SYNTAX ERROR IN THE OPERAND FIELD OF A
DIRECTIVE.

213   EQU DIRECTIVE SYNTAX ERROR
MESSAGE: ****ERROR 213 AAAAAA
MEANING: THE STRUCTURE OF THE EQU DIRECTIVE IS
SYNTACTICALLY INCORRECT OR IT HAS NO LABEL.

214   FCB DIRECTIVE SYNTAX ERROR
MESSAGE: ****ERROR 214 AAAAAA
MEANING: THE STRUCTURE OF THE FCB DIRECTIVE IS
SYNTACTICALLY INCORRECT.

215   FDB DIRECTIVE SYNTAX ERROR
MESSAGE: ****ERROR 215 AAAAAA
MEANING: THE STRUCTURE OF THE FDB DIRECTIVE IS
SYNTACTICALLY INCORRECT.

216   DIRECTIVE OPERAND ERROR
MESSAGE: ****ERROR 216 AAAAAA
MEANING: THE DIRECTIVE'S OPERAND FIELD IS IN ERROR.

217   OPT DIRECTIVE ERROR
MESSAGE: ****ERROR 217 AAAAAA

MEANING: THE STRUCTURE OF THE OPT DIRECTIVE IS
SYNTACTICALLY INCORRECT OR THE OPTION IS
UNDEFINED

218   ADDRESS BEYOND THE MACHINE FILE BOUNDS
MESSAGE: ****ERROR 218 AAAAAA
MEANING: AN ADDRESS WAS GENERATED WHICH LIES
OUTSIDE THE MEMORY BOUNDS AS DEFINED BY
THE VIRTUAL MACHINE FILE. TO EXTEND THE
LAST ADDREESS (LWA) OF THE MACHINE (MF
FILE) RUN THE MPBVM PROGRAM. ENTER
''LWLWA'' WHERE LWA IS THE NEW LAST WORD
ADDRESS. THE SYSTEM WILL PROMPT THE USER
FOR THE NAME OF THE MF FILE.

220   PHASING ERROR
MESSAGE: ****ERROR 220 AAAAAA
MEANING: THE VALUE OF THE P COUNTER DURING PASS 1
AND PASS 2 FOR THE SAME INSTRUCTION IS
DIFFERENT.

221   SYMBOL TABLE OVERFLOW
MESSAGE: ****ERROR 221 AAAAAA
MEANING: THE SYMBOL TABLE HAS OVERFLOWED. THE NEW
SYMBOL WAS NOT STORED AND ALL REFERENCES
TO IT WILL BE FLAGGED AS AN ERROR.

222   SYNTAX ERROR IN THE SYMBOL
MESSAGE: ****ERROR 222 AAAAAA
MEANING: THE ONE-CHARACTER SYMBOLS A, B, AND X
CANNOT BE USED FOR USER-DEFINED SYMBOLS.
THEIR USE IS RESTRICTED FOR REFERENCES
TO THE ACCUMULATORS (A & B) AND TO THE
INDEX REGISTER (X). ERROR 222 ALSO FLAGS
ALL SOURCE STATEMENTS CONTAINING A
SYMBOL THAT HAS BEEN REDEFINED.

223   THE DIRECTIVE CANNOT HAVE A LABEL
MESSAGE: ****ERROR 223 AAAAAA
MEANING: THE DIRECTIVE CANNOT HAVE A LABEL. THE
LABEL FIELD MUST BE EMPTY (BLANK).

224   ERROR IN USING THE OPTION DIRECTIVES OTAPE OR
MEMORY
MESSAGE: ****ERROR 224 AAAAAA
MEANING: THE OTAPE=FILENAME OR MEMORY=FILENAME IS
NOT THE FILENAME USED ON THE 1ST
OCCURRENCE OF THE OPTION OR THE OPTION
WAS NOMEMORY AND A FILENAME WAS SPECIFIED.

ABSOLUTE OBJECT RECORD FORMAT

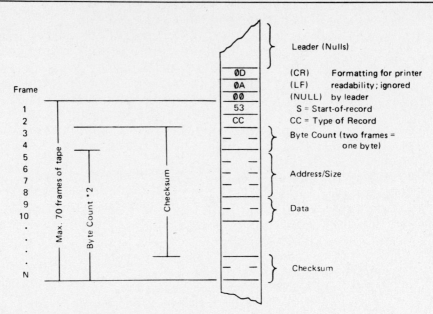

Frames 3 through N are hexadecimal digits (in 7-bit ASCII) which are converted to BCD. Two BCD digits are combined to make one 8-bit byte.

The checksum is the one's complement of the summation of 8-bit bytes.

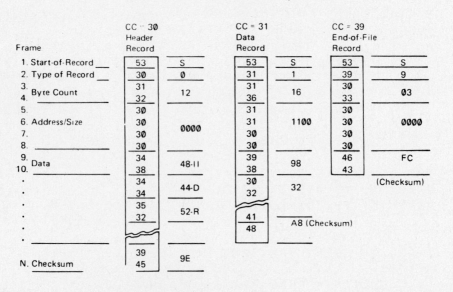

APPENDIX F

SAMPLE PROGRAM

An example of an M6800 source program, its assembly listing and object code output follows.

```
 NAM PGM
* REVISION 00
 ORG 256
COUNT EQU @3  @ INDICATES OCTAL VALUE
START LDS #STACK INZ STACK POINTER
 LDX ADDR
 LDA B  #COUNT IMMEDIATE ADDRESSING
BACK LDA A 10 DIRECT ADDRESSING
 CMP A 2,X INDEXED ADDRESSING
 BEQ FOUND RELATIVE ADDRESSING
 DEX IMPLIED ADDRESSING
 DEC B  ACCUMULATOR ONLY ADDRESSING
 BNE BACK
 WAI  WAIT FOR INTERRUPT
 SPC 1
FOUND JSR SUBRTN    JUMP TO SUBROUTINE
 JMP START EXTENDED ADDRESSING
* COMMENT STATEMENT NOTE TRUNCATION 01234567890123456789
SUBRTN TAB COMMENT FIELD TRUNCATION0123456789
 ORA A BYTE    SET MOST SIGNIFICANT BIT
 RTS  RETURN FROM SUBROUTINE
 SPC 2
 RMB 20 SCRATCH AREA FOR STACK
STACK RMB 1 START OF STACK
BYTE FCB $80 FORM CONSTANT BYTE
  FCB $10,$4  $ INDICATES HEXADECIMAL
ADDR FDB DATA FORM CONSTANT DOUBLE BYTE
DATA FCC 'SET' FORM CONSTANT DATA STRING (ASCII)
 END
```

M68SAM IS THE PROPERTY OF MOTOROLA SPD, INC.
COPYRIGHT 1974 TO 1976 BY MOTOROLA INC

MOTOROLA M6800 CROSS ASSEMBLER, RELEASE 1.3

```
00001                    NAM     PGM
00002                * REVISION 00
00003 0100               ORG     256
00004      0003  COUNT   EQU     @3          @ INDICATES OCTAL VALUE
00005 0100 8E 0132 START LDS     #STACK      INZ STACK POINTER
00006 0103 FE 0136       LDX     ADDR
00007 0106 C6 03         LDA B   #COUNT      IMMEDIATE ADDRESSING
00008 0108 96 0A   BACK  LDA A   10          DIRECT ADDRESSING
00009 010A A1 02         CMP A   2,X         INDEXED ADDRESSING
00010 010C 27 05         BEQ     FOUND       RELATIVE ADDRESSING
00011 010E 09            DEX                 IMPLIED ADDRESSING
00012 010F 5A            DEC B               ACCUMULATOR ONLY ADDRESSING
00013 0110 26 F6         BNE     BACK
00014 0112 3E            WAI                 WAIT FOR INTERRUPT

00016 0113 BD 0119 FOUND JSR     SUBRTN      JUMP TO SUBROUTINE
00017 0116 7E 0100       JMP     START       EXTENDED ADDRESSING
00018                * COMMENT STATEMENT NOTE TRUNCATION 0123456789012345
00019 0119 16    SUBRTN  TAB                 COMMENT FIELD TRUNCATION01234
00020 011A BA 0133       ORA A   BYTE        SET MOST SIGNIFICANT BIT
00021 011D 39            RTS                 RETURN FROM SUBROUTINE


00023 011E 0014          RMB     20          SCRATCH AREA FOR STACK
00024 0132 0001   STACK  RMB     1           START OF STACK
00025 0133 80     BYTE   FCB     $80         FORM CONSTANT BYTE
00026 0134 10            FCB     $10,$4      $ INDICATES HEXADECIMAL
      0135 04
00027 0136 0138   ADDR   FDB     DATA        FORM CONSTANT DOUBLE BYTE
00028 0138 53     DATA   FCC     'SET'       FORM CONSTANT DATA STRING (AS
      0139 45
      013A 54
00029                    END
```

SYMBOL TABLE

```
COUNT  0003  START  0100  BACK   0108  FOUND  0113  SUBRTN 0119
STACK  0132  BYTE   0133  ADDR   0136  DATA   0138
```

S0060000484452B
S11301008E0132FE0136C603960AA1022705095A5A
S1110110026F63EBD01197E810016BA013339F0
S10B01338010040138534554O7
S9030000FC

Chapter 2

1. Eight
2. a. $(2 \times 10^1) + (5 \times 10^0)$
   b. $(9 \times 10^5) + (9 \times 10^4) + (9 \times 10^3) + (9 \times 10^2) + (9 \times 10^1) + (9 \times 10^0)$
   c. (4×10^0)
3. a. 65,536 values   b. 16 Mbytes
4. $1 \times 2^7 + 0 \times 2^6 + 0 \times 2^5 + 1 \times 2^4 + 1 \times 2^3 + 1 \times 2^2 + 1 \times 2^1 + 1 \times 2^0$
5. a. 0–7   b. 0–15   c. 0–63   d. 0–1023   e. 0–255
6. a. 14   b. 8   c. 13
7. a. 1000 1100   b. 0000 1000   c. 0010 0101
   d. 1101 1111   e. 1010 1010
8. a. 7   b. 42   c. 204   d. 24   e. 255
9. a. 0000 1000   b. 0010 0001   c. 0001 0011
   d. 1101 1110   e. 0100 0101
10. Bit 0 (the LSB)
11. a. 0100 1001 0110   b. 0111 1000
    c. 0101 0010 1000 0000
12. a. 15   b. 876   c. 49
13. a. 21   b. 2166   c. 73 (All are larger than those of Ex. 12)
14. (b) and (c), because they contain bit patterns not allowed in BCD
15. a. 0100 0100   b. 0100 1101
16. a. 0010 0000 1001   b. 0010 0101 0011
17. a. 2C   b. FADE   c. D0
18. a. 0001 1010   b. 0100 0000 1011 1101   c. 0000 1111
19. a. 243   b. 10,823   c. 10
20. a. FF   b. 53   c. 278

21. **a.** 0010 0100 0011   **b.** 0001 0000 1000 0010 0011
    c. 0001 0000
22. **a.** 183   **b.** 0001 1000 0011   **c.** B7
23. **a.** 0001 1100 1000   **b.** 0100 0101 0110   **c.** 1C8
24. **a.** 1110 1010   **b.** 234   **c.** 0010 0011 0100
25. **a.** 67   **b.** 0100 0011   **c.** 43
26. 1000 0000 0000 0000; −32,768; 8000
27. 9C, negative; 1100 1111, negative
28. 1000 0101; 85 in hexadecimal

Chapter 3

1. The numerical value for z is the largest; for A, the smallest.
2. $, 2, 5, 9, C, J, R
3. Each lower case letter has the same least significant digit as its upper case counterpart. Upper case letters have 4 or 5 as their most significant digit, whereas lower case letters have 6 or 7.
4. TESTING: 1,2,3,4
5. 57, 48, 41, 54, 27, 53, 20, 55, 50, 2C, 20, 44, 4F, 43, 3F
6. **a.** D7, 48, 41, D4, 27, 53, A0, 55, 50, AC, A0, 44, CF, C3, 3F
   b. 57, C8, C1, 54, A7, D3, 20, D5, D0, 2C, 20, C4, 4F, 43, BF
7. (b), (d), and (f)
8. **a.** Bits 0, 1, 2, 3, 4, and 6
   b. FF and A0
   c. 80 and 8F (Other values are possible for (b) and (c).)
9. **a.** 92   **b.** 0A   **c.** 02   **d.** 01
   e. 90   **f.** 88   **g.** 00
10. **a.** Bedroom light, coffee pot, and living room light on; bathroom thermostat to 68; window shades up
    b. bathroom light, clock radio, and living room light on; bathroom thermostat to 55; window shades up
    c. bedroom light, TV, bathroom light, living room light on; bathroom thermostat to 55; window shades down
11. **a.** Decimal equivalent 214; hexadecimal equivalent B6; (no BCD interpretation possible) ASCII numeral 6 with odd parity; for Figure 3.2.3, bedroom light, TV, bathroom light, living room light on, bathroom thermostat to 68, window shades up; OP code for load accumulator A with contents of a memory location
    b. Hexadecimal equivalent 73; binary 0111 0011; decimal equivalent 55; as BCD number, 73; for Figure 3.2.3, TV, clock radio, and living room light on; bathroom thermostat to 68, window shades up, no OP code listed.

12. B6, OP code; B6, high-order byte of address; 00, low-order byte of address; B0, OP code; B0, high-order byte of address; 00, low-order byte of address; B7, OP code; B7, high-order byte of address; 00, low-order byte of address; 3E, OP code. Data addresses: 1A, 3F, and 25 are all numerical data.

Chapter 4

1. a. Clear: H, N; Set: I, Z, V, C b. Clear: All
   c. Clear: I; Set: H, N, Z, V, C
2. a. E6 b. C8 c. FB
3. a. Add accumulator B to accumulator A:

   $$(ACCA) \leftarrow (ACCA) + (ACCB)$$

   b. Decrement:

   $$(ACCX) \leftarrow (ACCX) - 01 \text{ or } (M) \leftarrow (M) - 01$$

   c. Subtract: $(ACCX) \leftarrow (ACCX) - (M)$
   d. Transfer from accumulator A to accumulator B:

   $$(ACCB) \leftarrow (ACCA)$$

4. a. "Add the contents of accumulator A to the contents of accumulator B, and place the results in accumulator A."

   Sources: ACCA and ACCB
   Destination: ACCA

   b. "Subtract one from the contents of the accumulator, and place the result in the accumulator."

   Source: ACCX
   Destination: ACCX

   or: "Subtract one from the contents of a memory location, and place the result in that memory location."

   Source: M
   Destination: M

   c. "Subtract the contents of a memory location from the contents of the accumulator, and place the result in the accumulator."

   Sources: ACCX, M
   Destination: ACCX

   d. "Place the contents of accumulator A into accumulator B."

   Source: ACCA
   Destination: ACCB

5. a. "The contents of location $0054 are subtracted from the contents of accumulator B, and the result is placed in accumulator B."

b. "Accumulator B gets the contents of location $2054."

c. "One is subtracted from the contents of accumulator B, and the result placed in accumulator B."

d. "The contents of accumulator A are added to the contents of location $0015, and the result is placed in accumulator A."

6. a. SUB B   b. LDA B   c. DEC B   d. ADD A

7. a. (ACCB) ← (ACCA)
   b. ($00A3) ← (ACCA)
   c. (ACCA) ← (ACCA) + (ACCB)
   d. ($0053) ← ($0053) − 01

8. a. TAB   b. STA A   c. ABA   d. DEC

9. a. C: set if there is a carry; Z: set if result is zero; N: set if result is negative.

b. C: not affected; Z: set if result is zero; N: set if result is negative.

c. C: set if there was a borrow; Z: set if result is zero; N: set if result is negative.

d. C: not affected; Z: set if number transferred is zero; N: set if number transferred is negative.

10. C5

11. a. immediate   b. extended or direct
    c. extended   d. inherent

12. a. LDA B #$F0; machine code: C6 (IMM)

b. STA A $00A3; machine code: B7(EXT), 97(DIR)

c. LDA A $1200; machine code: B6

d. TAB; machine code: 16

13. a. immediate   b. extended   c. inherent

14. START   LDA B $0000   Put contents of $0000 into ACCB
            STA B $00F0   Put contents of ACCB into $00F0
            WAI   Wait

The value D0 would be input into location $0000.

15. 0200   D6 00   START   LDA B $0000   Put ($0000) into ACCB
    0202   D7 F0   STA B $00F0   Put (ACCB) into $00F0
    0204   3E   WAI   Wait

16. 0000   96 34   START   LDA A $0034   Get contents of $0034
    0002   B0 01 52   SUB A   Sub ($0152) from (ACCA)
    0005   97 35   STA A $0035   Put answer in $0035
    0007   3E   WAI   Wait

17. 0100   86 32   START   LDA A   #$32   Put $32 in ACCA
    0102   C6 10   LDA B   #$10   Put $10 in ACCB
    0104   1B   ABA   Add (ACCA) to (ACCB)
    0105   97 73   STA A $0073   Put result in $0073
    0107   3E   WAI   Wait

18. 0020   86 FF   START   LDA A   #$FF   Put $FF into ACCA
    0022   4A   DEC A   Subtract one from it
    0023   16   TAB   Put result in ACCB
    0024   F7 02 30   STA B $0230   Put result in $0230
    0027   3E   WAI   Wait

Chapter 5

1. a. 1100 1011 ($CB)   b. 0101 0010 ($52)
2. a. 1001 1110 ($9E)   b. 0001 1111 ($1F)
3. $F8
4. Inputs: 0,2,3; the rest outputs
5. a. (bit 2) = 1; DRA   c. (bit 2) = 1; DRA
   b. (bit 2) = 1; DRA   d. (bit 2) = 0; DDRA
6. a. (CRA) = $04
   b. (CRB) = $00
7. ($8021) = $00; ($8023) = $04
8. (Bit 2) of both CRs is 0, so we are addressing DDRs.
   Side A: Lines 0, 3, 6, and 7 are output; the rest are input.
   Side B: Lines 4 and 5 are output; the rest are input.
9. To address DDRs: ($8021) = $00, ($8023) = $00
   To configure DDRs: ($8020) = $F0, ($8022) = $55
10. To address DRs: ($8021) = $04, ($8023) = $04
    To load DRs: ($8020) = $77 ($8022) = $90
11. On side A nothing will be output because DRA is configured for all inputs. On side B $90 will be output because DRB is configured for all outputs.
12. 0 = $3F; 1 = $06; 2 = $5B; 3 = $4F
13. a. $61   b. $0C;   c. $47   d. $41

Chapter 6

1. a.

SEQ.	LABEL	OP'N.	OPERAND	COMMENT
000		NAM	TIMES3	
010	;THIS PROGRAM MULTIPLIES A NUMBER BY 3 BY ADDING IT TO ITSELF			
020	;TWICE. THE NUMBER IS IN LOCATION $00F0.			
030		LDA A	$00F0	GET THE NUMBER
040		ADD A	$00F0	ADD IT TO ITSELF
050		ADD A	$00F0	ADD IT TO ITSELF AGAIN
060		STA A	$00F1	PUT THE ANSWER INTO LOCATION 00F1
070		WAI		WAIT
080		END		

b.

SEQ.	LABEL	OP'N	OPERAND	COMMENT
000		NAM	SBTRCT	
010	;THIS PROGRAM SUBTRACTS ONE NUMBER FROM ANOTHER			
115		ORG	$0200	
020		LDA B	$0100	GET MINUEND

```
030          SUB B   $0101      SUBTRACT SUBTRAHEND FROM MINUEND
040          STA B   $102       STORE RESULT IN LOCATION 0102
050          WAI                WAIT
060          END
```

c.

```
100          NAM     EQUATN
110    ;THIS PROGRAM EVALUATES THE EQUATION NUM2 = 2(NUM1+1).
120    NUM1  EQU     $0000
130    NUM2  EQU     $0001
140          ORG     $0010
150          LDA A   NUM1       GET VALUE OF NUM1
160          INC A              ADD ONE TO IT
170          TAB                PUT RESULT INTO ACCB
180          ABA                NOW ADD (NUM1+1) TO ITSELF
190          STA A   NUM2       AND PUT THE END RESULT INTO NUM2
200          WAI                WAIT
210          END
```

d.

```
100          NAM     SWAP
110    ;THIS PROGRAM SWAPS THE CONTENTS OF ACCA AND ACCB
120    TEMP  EQU     $0040
130          ORG     $0010
140          STA A   TEMP       SAVE CONTENTS OF ACCA IN TEMP
150          TBA                MOVE CONTENTS OF ACCB TO ACCA
160          LDA B   TEMP       NOW RETRIEVE ORIG. (ACCA)
170          WAI                WAIT
180          END
```

2. NAM; $8005; $8004; DRA; CRA; FF; STA A; LDA A; CRA; 00; DRA; END.

3.
```
155    DIGIT   EQU     $0300
157            ORG     $0010
210    GETDIG  LDA A   DIGIT      GET 7-SEGMENT CODE
```

4. a. mnemonic in label field
   b. NAM must not have a label
   c. label in operation field
   d. typing error: LDB instead of LDA B
   e. O (oh) instead of 0 (zero) in number
   f. label must not begin with a numeral
   g. $ omitted from hexadecimal number
   h. typing error: $ instead of

5.
```
a. 210            LDA A   #$FF      READY TO SET ALL OUTPUTS
b. 100            NAM     PROGRM
c. 010    HERE    STA A   PLACE
d. 020            LDA B   #$02      PUT 2 INTO ACCB
e. 000            CLR     $8005     CLEAR CRA
f. 150    TIMES2  LDA A   MULT      GET THE MULTIPLICAND
g. 220            INC     $00FF     INCREMENT LOCATION 00FF
h. 130    ;THIS IS A COMMENT
```

Chapter 7

1. **a.** 0011 1100, carry out $=1$ **b.** 1111 1110, carry out $=0$
   c. 1100 0001, carry out $=0$ **d.** 0111 1110, carry out $=1$
2. **a.** $06, carry out $=1$ **b.** $EADB, carry out $=1$
   c. $C3, carry out $=0$ **d.** $336D, carry out $=1$
3. Exercise 1: a and d. Exercise 2: a, b, and d
4. **a.** 0000 0001. Verification: 0000 0001 + 1111 1111 = 0000 0000, with a carry of 1.
   b. 1000 1000. Verification: 1000 1000 + 0111 1000 = 0000 0000, with a carry of 1.
   c. 0101 1101. Verification: 0101 1101 + 1010 0011 = 0000 0000, with a carry of 1.
   d. 1000 0000. Verification: 1000 0000 + 1000 0000 = 0000 0000, with a carry of 1.
5. **a.** $CC. Verification: CC + 34 = 00, with a carry of 1.
   b. $5313. Verification: $5313 + $ACED = 0000, with a carry of 1.
   c. $83. Verification: 83 + 7D = 00, with a carry of 1.
   d. $FFF1. Verification: FFF1 + 000F = 0000, with a carry of 1.
6. $CE: sixteens complement = $32. The binary equivalent of $CE = 1100 1110. The twos complement of 1100 1110 is 0011 0010, which is $32 in hexadecimal.
7. **a.** 4C − 1B = 4C + E5 = 31   **b.** D8 − A1 = D8 + 5F = 37
   c. ACDC − 1212 = ACDC + EDEE = 9ACA   **d.** F1F0 − A127 = F1F0 + 5ED9 = 50C9.
8. **a.** 1100 0110   **b.** 0111 0100   **c.** 7B   **d.** 86
9. **a.** − 42   **b.** + 57   **c.** + 64   **d.** − 18
10. **a.** binary 0011 0001, decimal + 49
    b. hexadecimal $F2, decimal − 14
    c. binary 0011 0110, decimal + 54
    d. hexadecimal $B9FD, decimal − 17923
11. c
12. **a.** (C) = 0, (V) = 0   **b.** (C) = 1, (V) = 1
    c. (C) = 0, (V) = 1   **d.** (C) = 0, (V) = 0
13. **a.** $FF   **b.** (N) = 1, (Z) = 0, (V) = 0, (C) = 0
14. **a.** (1)$00   **b.** (N) = 0, (Z) = 1, (V) = 0, (C) = 1
15. **a.** Result: $BB. (N) = 1, (Z) = 0, (V) = 0, (C) = 1
    b. Result: $DC. (N) = 1, (Z) = 0, (V) = 0, (C) = 0
    c. Result: $69. (N) = 0, (Z) = 0, (V) = 0, (C) = 1
16. **a.** 0111 0101   **b.** 0001 0111, with a carry of 1
    c. 0110 0101, with a carry of 1
    d. 0010 0100, with a carry of 1
17. (ACCA) = 46

Chapter 8

1. **a.** $0019 **b.** $000B **c.** $0029
2. **a.** before, $0105; after, $00F6 **b.** before, $00F9; after, $0101
3. $0012: $00; $0013: $05
4. Only JMP could be used, because the range is beyond the -128 to $+127$ locations of the BRA instruction.
5. a, b, c
6. b, c, g
7. BCS. The condition would be set up by the addition.
8. BEQ. We would use LDA A (or LDA B) DRA to set up the condition.
9.

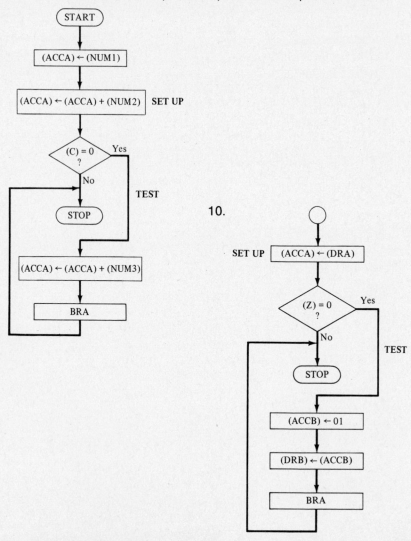

10.

11.

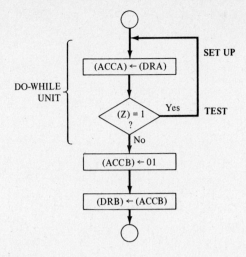

Chapter 9

1. **a.** yes **b.** yes **c.** no

2.
```
300   START   LDA A   DRA
310           CMP A   COMB
330           BNE     START   IF NOT EQUAL, KEEP LOOKING
```

3. **a.** yes; (ACCA) = $46 **b.** yes; (ACCA) = $40, (NUM1) = $20.
   c. yes; (ACCB) = 0

4.
```
250           ASL A   SHIFT UNTIL WE GET DA2
251           ASL A
252           ASL A
253           ASL A
254           ASL A
255           ASL A   DA2    SHOULD BE IN CARRY NOW
256           BCS     POWR   IF THIS ONE, BRANCH TO POWR
257           ASL A   DA1    SHOULD BE IN CARRY NOW
258           BCS     FIRE   IF SET, BRANCH TO FIRE
259           BRA     BURG   MUST BE BURG THEN
```

5.
```
230   CHECK   LDA A   DRA    GET INPUT FROM DRA
235           COM A          COMPLEMENT IT
240           BEQ     CHECK  IF ZERO, KEEP CHECKING
```

6. **a.** $80 = 128 (decimal). Then, 12.000 μsec/pass × 128 passes = 1536 + 4 =
   1540 μsec.
   b. From 0 to 0 is 256 passes.

   12.000 μsec/pass × 256 passes = 3072 + 4 = 3076 μsec.

7. **a.** LDA A (Ext.): 4 cycles × 2.000 μsec/cycle = 8.000 μsec
   b. DEC (Ext.): 6 cycles × 2.000 μsec/cycle = 12.00 μsec
   c. LSR A: 2 cycles × 2.000 μsec/cycle = 4.000 μsec

8. $0A00 = 2560 passes. 2560 passes × 8 cycles/pass × 1.627 μsec/cycle =
   33320.96 μsec, or about 33.3 msec

9. Cycle time $= 1/$clock frequency $= 1$ sec$/10^6$ cycles $= 1.000 \times 10^{-6}$ sec, or 1.000 μsec

10. We want half the number of passes: 32,768 (decimal). This is $8000. Then, the only change is one line:

220 START LDX #$8000 INITIALIZE COUNTER IN XR

11. INC (EXT)   6 cycles
    BNE   4 cycles
    TOTAL   10 cycles (iterative part of loop)

    10 cycles/pass $\times$ 256 passes $=$ 2560 cycles

    Initialization (CLR) (Ext.) $=$ 6 cycles
                          TOTAL   2566 cycles

    2566 cycles $\times$ 2.000 μsec/cycle $=$ 5132 μsec $=$ 5.132 msec

12. No. of passes $= (8.000 \times 105 \ \mu$sec$)/(16.27 \ \mu$sec/pass$)$

    $= 49170.2$, which we round to 49171.

    Convert 49171 (decimal) to hexadecimal: $C013

    Check delay time:

    Iterative: 49171 passes $\times$ 10 cycles/pass $=$ 491,710 cycles

    Initialization: LDX (IMM)   3 cycles
                   COM (EXT)   6 cycles
                   BRA   4 cycles
                TOTAL 491,723 cycles

    Execution time $=$ 491,723 $\times$ 1.627 μsec/cycle $=$ 800033 μsec, or 0.800033 sec (close enough).
    Answer: $C013

13. $A3D7 $= 41943$ (dec.) passes through inner loop. Then, 41943 passes $\times$ 8 cycles/pass $=$ 335,544 cycles for the inner loop. Adding 9 cycles for the three instructions of the outer loop gives 335,553 cycles/pass for the outer loop. $7F $= 127$ (dec.) passes through outer loop. Then, 127 passes $\times$ 335,553 cycles/pass $\times$ 2.000 μsec/cycle $=$ 67.1106 sec (1.119 min).

14. For a 4-minute delay, we run a 1-sec delay 240 times ($F0 for outer loop counter). To adjust the inner loop to 1 sec:

    $10^6 \ \mu$sec$/(1.627 \ \mu$sec/cycle$) =$ 614,628 cycles

    Less LDX (imm.) -3 cycles
    Less DEC A -2 cycles
    Less BNE -4 cycles

    TOTAL   614,619 cycles left for inner loop

For the inner loop, we use the loop of Example 9.4.3:

```
        LDX   #VAL
TICK    NOP
        DEX
        BNE   TICK
```

This loop takes 10 cycles for the iterative part.

Then, 614,619 cycles/(10 cycles/pass) = 61,461.9 passes, which we round to 61,462.

Inner loop counter value: decimal 61,462 equals $F016.

Answer: Inner loop counter, $F016; outer loop counter, $F0.

15. To delay for an hour, we need to go through our 4-min routine 15 times. So our third level loop needs to have its counter (ACCB, in this case) loaded with $0F.

Here's the program segment:

```
        LDA B   #$F       LOAD LOOP3 COUNTER WITH 15
LOOP3   LDA A   #$F0      INIT COUNTER FOR LOOP2
LOOP2   LDX     #$F016    INITIALIZE LOOP1 FOR 1 SEC
LOOP1   NOP               DELAY AN EXTRA 2 CYCLES IN LOOP1
        DEX               DECREMENT LOOP1 COUNTER
        BNE     LOOP 1    STILL MORE TO GO FOR 1 SEC?
        DEC A             NO, DECREMENT LOOP2 COUNTER
        BNE     LOOP2     STILL MORE TO GO FOR 4 MIN?
        DEC B             NO, DECREMENT LOOP3 COUNTER
        BNE     LOOP3     STILL MORE TO GO FOR 1 HR?
```

Chapter 10

1. a. $0020; b. yes

2.
```
LDX     #$A0
STA B   $13,X
```

3.
```
LDX     #$30
ADD A   $10,X
```

4. a. $24 b. $64 c. $64 d. $79

5. a. no b. yes c. no

6. a.
```
LDX     #$4
LDA A   $96,X
```
b.
```
LDX     #$96
LDA A   $6,X
```
c.
```
LDX     #$96
LDA A   $3,X
```
d.
```
LDX     #$0
LDA A   $9F,X
```

7. a. $FF04; b. $03A7; c. $0065; d. $3140

8. a. 290 LDA A $B0; b. 330 LDA A $AB,X;

   c. 290 LDA A $C0 and 330 LDA A $42,X

9. PROGRAM A: 120 START LDX #$1001 POINT TO START OF LIST
                  150   CPX #$1022 MORE LOCATIONS TO CLEAR?

   PROGRAM B: 120 START LDX #$1021
                              CPX #$1000 MORE LOCATIONS TO CLEAR?

10. 120 START LDX #$11 NUMBER OF ITEMS ON LIST
    DELETE LINE 150
    130 ZAP   CLR $DF,X

11. PROGRAM A: 160 MOVIT LDA A $20,X GET A VALUE
                170   STA A $0,X STORE IT IN NEW LOCATION
                180   CMP A #$0D COMPARE WITH ASCII OR

    PROGRAM B: 150 MOVIT LDA A $20,X GET A VALUE
                160   CMP A #$0D IS IT A CR?
                180   STA A $0,X NO, STORE IT IN NEW LIST

12. a. DGTBL: 00; TEMPXR: 0006, 0007; INIT: 0020
    b. DGTBL: 1003; TEMPXR: 1000, 1001; INIT: 0010

13. 195 DGTBL FCB $0B,$EF,$06,$3F,$63,$EF,$63,$EF,$40,$EF,$21,$EF
    390   CPX   #$CC   COMPARE WITH LAST ENTRY + 1

    195 DGTBL FCB $40,$EF,$63,$EF,$63,$EF,$06,$EF,$0B,$EF

14. 290 START   LDX   #$A   LOAD XR WITH LENGTH OF TABLE
    300 GETLTR LDA A $BF,X GET CODE VALUE FROM TABLE
    380   DEX AND POINT TO NEXT ENTRY ON TABLE
    DELETE LINE 390

15. (a) if (RUNT) is less than (NEWNUM), the branch is taken and the swap not performed. (If (RUNT) is equal to (NEWNUM), the swap will be performed, but we wouldn't notice.) The result would be that the smallest SIGNED number would appear at the top of the list. (b) if (RUNT) is greater than (NEWNUM), the branch is taken and the swap not performed. So if (RUNT) is less than or equal to (NEWNUM), the swap is performed. The result would be that the largest SIGNED number would appear at the top of the list.

16. a.   Replace BLS with BHI
    b.

    150 DONE   FCB $A0,$00   SAVE END ADDRESS
    158 XRL   FCB $10
    180 LOOK   DEX   POINT TO NEWNUM

    c.   Delete 150

    175   CMP A #$0D   IS IT A CR
    176   BEQ   OUTCOD YES, CHECK LF
    275 OUTCOD LDA A $1,X   GET NEXT LOCATION
    276   CMP A #$0A   IS IT LF?
    277   BNE   LOOK   NO, KEEP LOOKING

17. 140 DONE   FCB $A0,$00
    160 XRL   FCB $10
    190 LOOK   DEX

18. a.   Yes. ASCII characters with no parity increase numerically in alphabetical order.
    b. and c. No. In each case a 1 in bit 7 would throw the numerical order off. Before searching the list, the program must clear the parity bit to 0. This could be done by shifting the character one bit left, clearing the carry bit, and shifting one bit right.

Chapter 11

1. ($A0D0) = $01; ($A0D1) = $F2; ($AA00) = $01; ($AA01) = $F1
2. a. ($00EE) = $00; ($00ED) = $00; ($00EC) = $FF
    b. (SP) = ($00EB)   c. (ACCA) = $00; (ACCB) = $FF

3. **a.** ($00F2) = $F0 **b.** (SP) = $00F2 **c.** (ACCA) = $F0; (ACCB) = $F1

4. **a.** LDS uses the extended mode, so the contents of VAL, defined by the FCB directive, are loaded into SP. (SP) = $007F.

   b. LDS takes 3 bytes and BSR takes two. So (PC) = $0039.

   c. (PC) = $0059

5. **a.** $007D **b.** ($007E) = (PCH); ($007F) = PCL

6. **a.** (SP) before JSR = $00A0; after, $009E

   b. old (PCL) = $06, stored in $00A0; old (PCH) = $00, stored in $009F

7. **a.** (SP) = $00A0 **b.** (PC) = $0006

   c. From locations $00A0 and $009F

   d. They still have the same contents: ($009F) = $00; ($00A0) = $06.

8. **a.** No; ROM addresses cannot be written into.

   b. No; (PC) = $1808.

9. The subroutine:

```
WAITM    LDA A    #$3C      INITIALIZE OUTER LOOP COUNTER
OUTRLP   LDX      #$F423    INITIALIZE INNER LOOP COUNTER
INRLP    DEX                DECREMENT INNER LOOP COUNTER
         BNE      INRLP     STILL MORE TO GO FOR 1 SEC?
         DEC A              NO, DECREMENT OUTER LOOP COUNTER
         BNE      OUTRLP    STILL MORE TO GO FOR 1 MIN?
         RTS                NO, RETURN TO CALLING PROGRAM
```

The calling program:

```
CONT   BSR   WAITM   DELAY 1 MINUTE
```

10. The subroutine:

```
WAITM    PSH A              SAVE USER ACCA CONTENTS
         STX      TEMPX     SAVE USER XR CONTENTS
         LDA A    #$3C      INITIALIZE OUTER LOOP COUNTER
OUTRLP   LDX      #$F423    INITIALIZE INNER LOOP COUNTER
INRLP    DEX                DECREMENT INNER LOOP COUNTER
         BNE      INRLP     STILL MORE TO GO FOR 1 SEC?
         DEC A              NO, DECREMENT OUTER LOOP COUNTER
         BNE      OUTRLP    STILL MORE TO GO FOR 4 MIN?
         PUL A    TEMPA     NO, RESTORE USER ACCA CONTENTS
         LDX      TEMPXR    AND USER XR CONTENTS
         RTS                RETURN TO CALLING PROGRAM
```

This statement would have to be in calling program:

```
TEMPXR   RMB   2   SAVE 2 BYTES FOR TEMP XR STORAGE
```

11. The SP is loaded with $00FF, so at (1), PCL ($05) is pushed onto the stack at location $00FF, and (SP) is decremented. At (2), PCH ($00) is pushed onto the stack at location $00FE, and (SP) is decremented to $00FD. At (3), the address of CONFIG (whatever it is) is loaded into PC for the transfer of control. Then (SP) = $00FD.

   Next, the PUL A (4) increments (SP) to $00FE and pulls $00 from the stack into accumulator A. Then, at (5), the value $00 is pushed onto the stack at location $00FE and the stack pointer decremented to $00FD.

   Next, the RTS increments SP to $00FF and pulls $0005 into the PC. Answer: No error would be caused this time.

12. We add a line to the calling program:

```
LDA A   #VBL   PUT VARIABLE INTO ACCA
STA A   XRL    PUT IT IN XRL
```

The subroutine:

```
SQRSUB  LDX  XRH   POIINT TO SQUARE
```

13.

```
            LDA A   LENGTH   GO GET LENGTH              }  main
            DEC A            SUBTRACT ONE FROM LENGTH   }  program
   _ _ _ _ _ _ _ _ _
SMLSUB      LDA B   0,X      GET RUNT                   }
            CMP B   0,X      COMPARE IT TO RUNT         }  subroutine
   _ _ _ _ _ _ _ _ _
            LDA B   0,X      REPLACE RUNT WITH NEWNUM
NOSWP       DEC A            DECREMENT LIST LENGTH
```

Chapter 12

1. a. ($FFF8) = $00; ($FFF9) = $F6; ($FFFA) = $00; ($FFFB) = $F2; ($FFFC) = $FA; ($FFFD) = $32; ($FFFE) = $F2; ($FFFF) = $C8.
   b. $00F6. Locations $00F6, $00F7, and $00F8 should contain 7E A7 C0, a JMP to location $A7C0.

2. a. (RES) = $E08D; NMI = $E019; SWI = $E032; IRQ = $E014.
   b. The true address of IRQ is $A000. The index register is loaded with $A000. The JMP, indexed with an offset of 0, loads the PC with $A000.

3. (CC) = $F0; (ACCB) = $23; (ACCA) = $4A; (XR) = $0067; (PC) = $B3E2, (SP) = $00F6

4. (CC) = $E1; (ACCB) = $E2; (ACCA) = $E3; (XR) = $E4E5; (PC) = $E6E7; (SP) = $00E7

5. Bits 6 and 7, no effect; Bit 5: CA2 is interrupt input. Bit 4: CA2 interrupts on falling edge. Bit 3: CA2 interrupts enabled. Bit 2: DRA will be addressed. Bit 1: CA1 interrupts on rising edge. Bit 0: CA1 interrupts enabled.

6.
```
LDA A   %00001111
STA A   CRA
```

7. a. Because the MPU's interrupt mask is set, no interrupts will occur for any devices wired to IRQ (the side A devices), so no interrupts for devices 1 or 2. For side B CB1's mask bit contains a 0, so no interrupt will occur for device 3 no matter what it is sending. CB2's mask bit is set so its interrupt is allowed. But its edge bit contains a 0, meaning that its interrupt occurs on the falling edge. So no interrupt will occur for device 4. Answer: No interrupts will occur for any device.
   b. We look for a low-to-high transition in the edge control bits, which is a 1. In side A, CA1 has such a transition so its interrupt flag bit (bit 7) will be set. CA2's interrupt flag bit will be clear. In side B, CB2 has a high-to-low transition, so its interrupt flag bit (bit 6) will not be set. CB1's interrupt flag bit

will be clear. Answer: Device 1: %1000 0111; Device 2: %0000 0111; Device 3: %0000 1100; Device 4: %0000 1100

8. a.   Smoke alarm to CA1, keyboard to CA2.

   b.

```
LDA A  CRA   GET INTERRUPT FLAGS
BMI    FIRE  BIT 7 SET, GO TO FIRE
BRA    DATA  MUST BE KEYBOARD
```

9.
```
SEI    #            SET MPU INTERRUPT MASK
LDX    #$C072       STORE INTERRUPT SERVICE ADDRESS
STA A  $00F2        IN DUMMY
CLR    CRA          ADDRESS DDRA
CLR    DDRA         SIDE A ALL INPUTS
LDA A  #%00001101   ADDRESS DRA, ENABLE INTERRUPTS
STA A  CRA          AND SET FALLING EDGE FOR BOTH
CLI                 ENABLE MPU INTERRUPTS
```

10.
```
CLI                 ENABLE FIRE INTERRUPT
LDA A  DRA          GET INPUT DATA
STA A  BUFFER       STORE IT IN BUFFER
RTI                 AND RETURN
```

Chapter 13

1. a. $1/(300 \text{ bits}/\text{sec}) = 3.33 \text{ msec}/\text{bit}$
   b. $300 \text{ bits}/\text{sec}/(10 \text{ bits}/\text{char}) = 30 \text{ chars}/\text{sec}$
   c. $1/(30 \text{ chars}/\text{sec}) = 33.3 \text{ msec}/\text{char}$

2. a. (WORD) = $F0; (C) = 0
   b. (WORD) = $70;

3.
```
       SEC                SET CARRY FOR MSB OF 9-BIT WORD
       LDA B  #$9          LOAD COUNTER FOR 9 BITS
       LDA A  #$E0         GET 8 LSB'S OF WORD
OUT    STA A  DRA          OUTPUT THE BIT
       ROL A               NEXT BIT
       DEC B               DECREMENT COUNTER
       BNE    OUT          STILL MORE BITS? OUTPUT ANOTHER
```

4.
```
12     LDA B  #11          LOAD COUNTER WITH BITCOUNT 11
```

5.
```
245    LDA A  INBUF        GET ASCII CHARACTER
247    BSR    PARCHK       GO CHECK PARITY
```

6. Interrupt condition; parity error; RDR full.

7. %00011110, or $1E.

8. Interrupts disabled, 8-bit data word, no parity, 2 stop bits, divide by 16.

9.

```
ACIACR  EQU    $C002
TDR     EQU    $C003
        LDA A  #$03          READY TO RESET ACIA
        STA A  ACIACR        RESET ACIA
        LDA A  %10001001     CONFIG ACIA FOR 7 DATA BITS,
        STA A  ACIACR        EVEN PARITY, AND DIVIDE BY 16
        LDA A  #$FF          READY TO WRITE FF
        STA A  TDR           WRITE FF INTO TDR
```

10.

```
POLL    LDA A  $8000         GET ACIA 1 SR
        BMI    EMERG         BIT 7 SET? EMERGENCY MESSAGE
        LDA A  $8002         GET ACIA 2 SR MUST BE CRT
        ROR A                PUT BIT 0 INTO CARRY
        BCS    RECV          RDR FULL? GO TO RECV
        BRA    TRANS         MUST BE TDR
```

11.

```
RECV    LDX    #$0100        POINT TO FIRST ADDRESS
GETSR   LDA A  ACIASR        GET STATUS REG
        ROR A                SHIFT BIT 0 INTO CARRY
        BCC    RECV          RDR NOT FULL YET? WAIT
        LDA A  ACIASR        GET STATUS REG FOR ERROR CHECK
        ROL A                SKIP PARITY ERROR BIT
        ROL A                PUT OVERRUN IN BIT 7
        BMI    OVRRUN        IF SET, GO TO OVERRUN
        ROL A                PUT FE IN BIT 7
        BMI    FRAMER        IF SET, GO TO FRAMER
        LDA A  RDR           GET DATA WORD
        STA A  0,X           STORE IT
        INX                  POINT TO NEXT STORAGE LOCATION
        CPX    #$0102        COMPARE WITH LAST ADR + 1
        BNE    GETSR         ONE MORE TO GO?
        RTS                  NO, RETURN
```

Chapter 14

1. a. 1   b. 1   c. A = 0, B = 1, C = 0
2. a. $FF   b. $4F   c. $6F
3. The numbers $30, $37, $36, $35, $34, $33, $32, and $31 would all work. Bits 0, 1, and 2 of the word are "don't cares" because they contain 1's in the original number.
4. a. 0   b. 0   c. A = 0, B = 0, C = 1
5. a. $7B   b. $FF   c. $0F
6.

```
RECV    LDA A  ACIASR        GET CONTENTS OF STATUS REG
        BIT    #%00000001    TEST RDRF
        BEQ    RECV          RDR NOT FULL YET? WAIT
        BIT    #%01000000    TEST PARITY
        BNE    PARERR        BIT 6 SET? PARITY ERROR
```

```
BIT     #%00100000    TEST OVERRUN
BNE     OVRN          BIT 5 SET? OVERRUN
BIT     #%00010000    TEST FRAMING ERROR
BNE     FERR          BIT 4 SET? FRAMING ERRORS
```

7. **a.** 1 **b.** 1 **c.** A = 0, B = 0, C = 0, D = 0, E = 1, F = 1, G = 0, H = 0, I = 0
8. The status register
9. CRA
10. **a.** yes **b.** yes **c.** yes **d.** yes
11. **a.** none **b.** PIA #1 **c.** PIA #2 **d.** none
12. $0800 to $08F3

APPENDIX D
Some Characteristics
of the MC68000
16-Bit Microprocessor

Reprinted from the *MC68000 16 Bit Microprocessor User's Manual* by permission of Motorola, Inc.

CHAPTER 1
GENERAL DESCRIPTION

1.0 INTRODUCTION

This section contains a general description of the MC68000 Microprocessor.

1.1 OVERVIEW

Advances in semiconductor technology have provided the capability to place on a single silicon chip a microprocessor at least an order of magnitude higher in performance and circuit complexity than has been previously available. The MC68000 is the first of a family of such VLSI microprocessors from Motorola. It combines state-of-the-art technology and advanced circuit design techniques with computer sciences to achieve an architecturally advanced 16-bit microprocessor. The high density of active elements coupled with an order of magnitude increase in performance over the original MC6800 is the direct result of significant advances in semiconductor technology. Advances such as dry plasma etching, projection printing, and HMOS (high-density, short-channel MOS) circuit design techniques shown in figure 1-1 have provided a sound technological base that has allowed Motorola's system engineers, computer scientists and marketing engineers a large degree of innovative freedom. The goals of applying this innovative freedom to microprocessors are to make the microprocessor easy to use, more reliable and more flexible for applications, while maximizing performance.

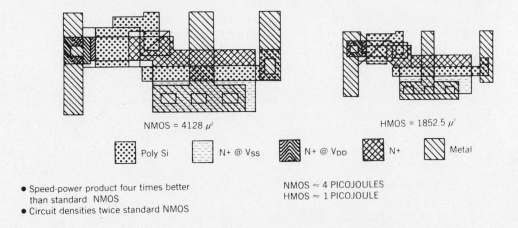

NMOS = 4128 μ^2 HMOS = 1852.5 μ^2

Poly Si   N+ @ V$_{SS}$ N+ @ V$_{DD}$ N+   Metal

- Speed-power product four times better than standard NMOS
- Circuit densities twice standard NMOS

NMOS ≈ 4 PICOJOULES
HMOS ≈ 1 PICOJOULE

Figure 1-1. HMOS Circuit Design Techniques

The resources available to the MC68000 user consist of the following:

32-bit data and address registers

16 megabyte direct addressing range

56 powerful instruction types

Operations on five main data types

Memory mapped I/O

14 addressing modes

Particular emphasis has been given to the architecture to make it regular with respect to the registers, instructions (including all addressing modes), and data types. A consistent structure makes the architecture easy to learn and program, and, in the process, reduces both the time required to write programs and the space required to store programs. The net result is a great reduction in the cost and risk of developing software.

High systems throughput (up to an aggregate of two million instruction and data word transfers per second) is achieved even with readily available standard product memories with comparatively slow access times. The design flexibility of the data bus allows the mixing of slow and fast memories or peripherals with the processor, automatically optimizing the transfer rate on every access to keep the system operating at peak efficiency.

The hardware design of the CPU was heavily influenced by advances made in software technology. High-level language compilers as well as code produced from high-level languages must run efficiently on the new generation 16-bit and 32-bit microprocessors. The MC68000 supports high-level languages with its consistent architecture, multiple registers and stacks, large addressing range and high level language oriented instructions (LINK, UNLK, CHK, etc.). Also, operating systems for controlling the software operating environment of the MC68000 are supported by privileged instructions, memory management, a powerful vectored multi-level interrupt and trap structure, and specific instructions (MOVEP, MOVEM, TRAP, etc.).

The processor also provides both hardware and software interlocks for multiprocessor systems. The MC68000 contains bus arbitration logic for a shared bus and shared memory environment (shared with other MC68000 processors, DMA devices, etc.). Multiprocessor systems are also supported with software instructions (TAS — test and set operand). The MC68000 offers the maximum flexibility for microprocessor-based multiprocessor systems.

Advanced architecture processors must not only offer efficient solutions to large complex problems but must be able to handle the small, simple problems with proportional efficiency. The MC68000 has been designed to offer the maximum in performance and versatility to solve simple and complex problems efficiently.

As shown in figure 1-2, the MC68000 offers seventeen 32-bit registers in addition to the 32-bit program counter and 16-bit status register. The first eight registers (D0-D7) are used as data registers for byte (8-bit), word (16-bit) and long word (32-bit) data operations. The second set of seven registers (A0-A6) and the system stack pointer (A7) may be used as software stack pointers and base address registers. In addition, these registers may be used for word and long word address operations. All of the seventeen registers may be used as index registers.

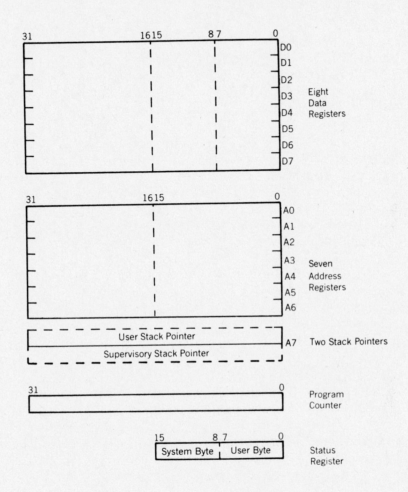

Figure 1-2. Programming Model

The 24-bit address bus provides a memory addressing range of more than 16 megabytes (actually 16,777,216 bytes). This large range of addressing capability, coupled with a memory management unit, allows large, modular programs to be developed and operated without resorting to cumbersome and time consuming software bookkeeping and paging techniques.

The status register, shown in figure 1-3, contains the interrupt mask (8 levels available) as well as the condition codes; overflow (V), zero (Z), negative (N), carry (C), and extend (X). Additional status bits indicate that the processor is in a trace (T) mode and/or in a supervisor (S) state. Ample space remains in the status register for future extensions of the MC68000 family.

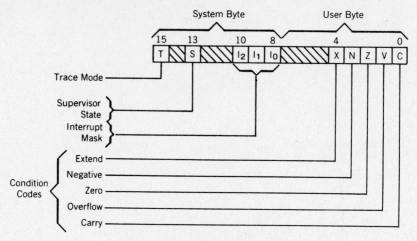

Figure 1-3. Status Register

Five basic data types are supported. These data types are:
- Bits
- BCD digits (4-bits)
- Bytes (8-bits)
- Words (16-bits)
- Long words (32-bits)

In addition, operations on other data types such as memory addresses, status word data, etc. are provided for in the instruction set.

The 14 flexible addressing modes, shown in table 1-1 include six basic types:
- Register Direct
- Register Indirect
- Absolute
- Immediate
- Program Counter Relative
- Implied

Included in the register indirect addressing modes is the capability to do post-incrementing, predecrementing, offsetting and indexing. Program counter relative mode can also be modified via indexing and offsetting.

548

Table 1-1. Data Addressing Modes

Mode	Generation
Register Direct Addressing Data Register Direct Address Register Direct	EA = Dn EA = An
Absolute Data Addressing Absolute Short Absolute Long	EA = (Next Word) EA = (Next Two Words)
Program Counter Relative Addressing Relative with Offset Relative with Index and Offset	EA = (PC) + d_{16} EA = (PC) + (Xn) + d_8
Register Indirect Addressing Register Indirect Postincrement Register Indirect Predecrement Register Indirect Register Indirect With Offset Indexed Register Indirect With Offset	EA = (An) EA = (An), An ← An + N An ← An – N, EA = (An) EA = (An) + d_{16} EA = (An) + (Xn) + d_8
Immediate Data Addressing Immediate Quick Immediate	DATA = Next Word(s) Inherent Data
Implied Addressing Implied Register	EA = SR, USP, SP, PC

NOTES:

EA = Effective Address
An = Address Register
Dn = Data Register
Xn = Address or Data Register used as Index Register
SR = Status Register
PC = Program Counter

d_8 = Eight-bit Offset (displacement)
d_{16} = Sixteen-bit Offset (displacement)
N = 1 for Byte, 2 for Words and 4 for Long Words
( ) = Contents of
← = Replaces

The MC68000 instruction set is shown in table 1-2. Some additional instructions are variations, or subsets of these and they appear in table 1-3. Special emphasis has been given to the instruction set's support of structured high-level languages to facilitate ease of programming. Each instruction, with few exceptions, operates on bytes, words, and long words and most instructions can use any of the 14 addressing modes. Combining instruction types, data types, and addressing modes, over 1000 useful instructions are provided. These instructions include signed and unsigned multiply and divide, "quick" arithmetic operations, BCD arithmetic and expanded operations (through traps). Additionally, its highly-symmetric, proprietary microcoded structure provides a sound, flexible base for the future.

Table 1-2. Instruction Set

Mnemonic	Description
ABCD	Add Decimal with Extend
ADD	Add
AND	Logical And
ASL	Arithmetic Shift Left
ASR	Arithmetic Shift Right
B_{cc}	Branch Conditionally
BCHG	Bit Test and Change
BCLR	Bit Test and Clear
BRA	Branch Always
BSET	Bit Test and Set
BSR	Branch to Subroutine
BTST	Bit Test
CHK	Check Register Against Bounds
CLR	Clear Operand
CMP	Compare
DB_{cc}	Test Cond., Decrement and Branch
DIVS	Signed Divide
DIVU	Unsigned Divide
EOR	Exclusive Or
EXG	Exchange Registers
EXT	Sign Extend
JMP	Jump
JSR	Jump to Subroutine
LEA	Load Effective Address
LINK	Link Stack
LSL	Logical Shift Left
LSR	Logical Shift Right
MOVE	Move
MOVEM	Move Multiple Registers
MOVEP	Move Peripheral Data
MULS	Signed Multiply
MULU	Unsigned Multiply
NBCD	Negate Decimal with Extend
NEG	Negate
NOP	No Operation
NOT	One's Complement
OR	Logical Or
PEA	Push Effective Address
RESET	Reset External Devices
ROL	Rotate Left without Extend
ROR	Rotate Right without Extend
ROXL	Rotate Left with Extend
ROXR	Rotate Right with Extend
RTE	Return from Exception
RTR	Return and Restore
RTS	Return from Subroutine

Table 1-2. Instruction Set (continued)

Mnemonic	Description
SBCD	Subtract Decimal with Extend
Scc	Set Conditional
STOP	Stop
SUB	Subtract
SWAP	Swap Data Register Halves
TAS	Test and Set Operand
TRAP	Trap
TRAPV	Trap on Overflow
TST	Test
UNLK	Unlink

Table 1-3. Variations of Instruction Types

Instruction Type	Variation	Description
ADD	ADD	Add
	ADDA	Add Address
	ADDQ	Add Quick
	ADDI	Add Immediate
	ADDX	Add with Extend
AND	AND	Logical And
	ANDI	And Immediate
CMP	CMP	Compare
	CMPA	Compare Address
	CMPM	Compare Memory
	CMPI	Compare Immediate
EOR	EOR	Exclusive Or
	EORI	Exclusive Or Immediate
MOVE	MOVE	Move
	MOVEA	Move Address
	MOVEQ	Move Quick
	MOVE from SR	Move from Status Register
	MOVE to SR	Move to Status Register
	MOVE to CCR	Move to Condition Codes
	MOVE to USP	Move to User Stack Pointer
NEG	NEG	Negate
	NEGX	Negate with Extend
OR	OR	Logical Or
	ORI	Or Immediate
SUB	SUB	Subtract
	SUBA	Subtract Address
	SUBI	Subtract Immediate
	SUBQ	Subtract Quick
	SUBX	Subtract with Extend

CHAPTER 2
DATA ORGANIZATION AND
ADDRESSING CAPABILITIES

2.0 INTRODUCTION

This section describes the data organization and addressing capabilities of the MC68000.

2.1 OPERAND SIZE

Operand sizes are defined as follows: a byte equals 8 bits, a word equals 16 bits, and a long word equals 32 bits. The operand size for each instruction is either explicitly encoded in the instruction or implicitly defined by the instruction operation. All explicit instructions support byte, word or long word operands. Implicit instructions support some subset of all three sizes.

2.2 DATA ORGANIZATION IN REGISTERS

The eight data registers support data operands of 1, 8, 16, or 32 bits. The seven address registers together with the active stack pointer support address operands of 32 bits.

2.2.1 DATA REGISTERS. Each data register is 32 bits wide. Byte operands occupy the low order 8 bits, word operands the low order 16 bits, and long word operands the entire 32 bits. The least significant bit is addressed as bit zero; the most significant bit is addressed as bit 31.

When a data register is used as either a source or destination operand, only the appropriate low order portion is changed; the remaining high-order portion is neither used nor changed.

2.2.2 ADDRESS REGISTERS. Each address register and the stack pointer is 32 bits wide and holds a full 32 bit address. Address registers do not support byte sized operands. Therefore, when an address register is used as a source operand, either the low order word or the entire long word operand is used pending upon the operation size. When an address register is used as the destination operand, the entire register is affected regardless of the operation size. If the operation size is word, any other operands are sign extended to 32 bits before the operation is performed.

affected regardless of the operation size. If the operation size is word, any other operands are sign extended to 32 bits before the operation is performed.

2.3 DATA ORGANIZATION IN MEMORY

Bytes are individually addressable with the high order byte having an even address the same as the word as shown in figure 2-1. The low order byte has an odd address that is one count higher than the word address. Instructions and multibyte data are accessed only on word (even byte) boundaries. If a long word datum is located at address n (n even), then the second word of that datum is located at address n + 2.

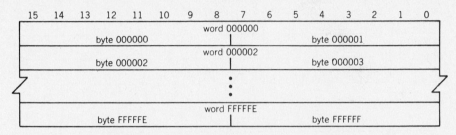

Figure 2-1. Word Organization In Memory

The data types supported by the MC68000 are: bit data, integer data of 8, 16, and 32 bits, 32-bit addresses and binary coded decimal data. Each of these data types is put in memory as shown in figure 2-2.

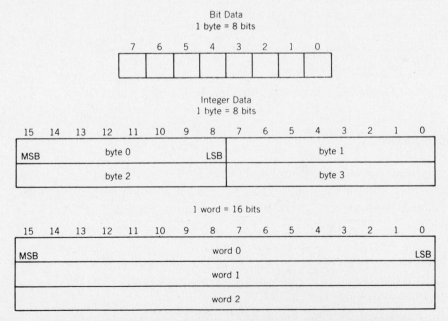

Figure 2-2. Data Organization In Memory (Sheet 1 Of 2)

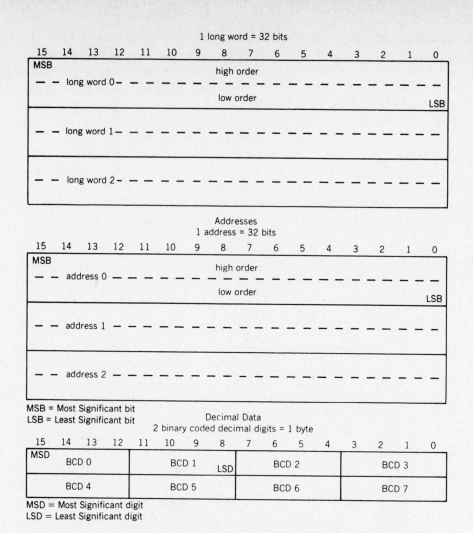

MSB = Most Significant bit
LSB = Least Significant bit

MSD = Most Significant digit
LSD = Least Significant digit

Figure 2-2. Data Organization In Memory (Sheet 2 Of 2)

2.4 ADDRESSING

Instructions for the MC68000 contain two kinds of information: the type of function to be performed, and the location of the operand(s) on which to perform that function. The methods used to locate (address) the operand(s) are explained in the following paragraphs.

Instructions specify an operand location in one of three ways:

Register Specification — the number of the register is given in the register field of the instruction.

Effective Address — use of the different effective address modes.

Implicit Reference — the definition of certain instructions implies the use of specific registers.

2.5 INSTRUCTION FORMAT

Instructions are from one to five words in length as shown in figure 2-3. The length of the instruction and the operation to be performed is specified by the first word of the instruction which is called the operation word. The remaining words further specify the operands. These words are either immediate operands or extensions to the effective address mode specified in the operation word.

15	14	13	12	11	10	9	8	7	6	5	4	3	2	1	0
Operation Word (first word specifies operation and modes)														
Immediate operand (if any, one or two words)														
Source effective address extension (if any, one or two words)														
Destination effective address extension (if any, one or two words)														

Figure 2-3. Instruction Format

2.6 PROGRAM/DATA REFERENCES

The MC68000 separates memory references into two classes: program references, and data references. Program references, as the name implies, are references to that section of memory that contains the program being executed. Data references refer to that section of memory that contains data. Generally, operand reads are from the data space. All operand writes are to the data space.

2.7 REGISTER NOTATION

Appendix B contains a definition of the register transfer language (RTL) used in describing instruction operations. The RTL description of registers identifies the registers as follows:

An — address register (n specifies the register number)   CCR — condition code half of the status register

Dn — data register (n specifies the register number)   SP — the active stack pointer (either user or supervisor)

Rn — any register, address or data (n specifies the register number)   USP — user stack pointer

                             SSP — supervisor stack pointer

PC — program counter   d — displacement value

SR — status register   N — operand size in bytes (1, 2, 4)

2.8 ADDRESS REGISTER INDIRECT NOTATION

When an address register is used to point to a memory location, the addressing mode is called address register indirect. The term indirect is used because the operation of the instruction is not directed to the address register itself, but to the memory location pointed to by the address register. The RTL symbol for the indirect mode is an address register designation followed by an at symbol (@). The notation A4@ indicates that the content of address register four points to the memory location that will be used as the operand.

2.9 REGISTER SPECIFICATION

The register field within an instruction specifies the register to be used. Other fields within the instruction specify whether the register selected is an address or data register and how the register is to be used.

2.10 EFFECTIVE ADDRESS

Most instructions specify the location of an operand by using the effective address field in the operation word. For example, figure 2-4 shows the general format of the single effective address instruction operation word. The effective address is composed of two 3-bit fields: the mode field, and the register field. The value in the mode field selects the different address modes. The register field contains the number of a register.

The effective address field may require additional information to fully specify the operand. This additional information, called the effective address extension, is contained in a following word or words and is considered part of the instruction as shown in figure 2-3. The effective address modes are grouped into three categories: register direct, memory addressing, and special.

15	14	13	12	11	10	9	8	7	6	5	4	3	2	1	0
										Effective Address					
X	X	X	X	X	X	X	X	X	X	Mode			Register		

Figure 2-4. Single-Effective-Address-Instruction Operation Word—General Format

2.10.1 REGISTER DIRECT MODES. These effective addressing modes specify that the operand is in one of the 16 multifunction registers.

2.10.1.1 Data Register Direct. The operand is in the data register specified by the effective address register field.

    Generation: EA = Dn
    RTL Notation: Dn
    Mode: 000
    Register: n

Data Register Dn

Operand

2.10.1.2 Address Register Direct. The operand is in the address register specified by the effective address register field.

    Generation: EA = An

    RTL Notation: An

    Mode: 001

    Register: n

Address Register An

Operand

2.10.2 MEMORY ADDRESS MODES. These effective addressing modes specify that the operand is in memory and provide the specific address of the operand.

2.10.2.1 Address Register Indirect. The address of the operand is in the address register specified by the register field. The reference is classified as a data reference with the exception of the jump and jump to subroutine instructions.

    Generation: EA = (An)

    RTL Notation: An@

    Mode: 010

    Register: n

Address Register An

Memory Address

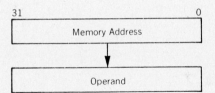

2.10.2.2 Address Register Indirect With Postincrement. The address of the operand is in the address register specified by the register field. After the operand address is used, it is incremented by one, two, or four depending upon whether the size of the operand is byte, word, or long word. If the address register is the stack pointer and the operand size is byte, the address is incremented by two rather than one to keep the stack pointer on a word boundary. The reference is classified as a data reference.

    Generation: EA = (An)
                     An = An + N

    RTL Notation: An@+

    Mode: 011

    Register: n

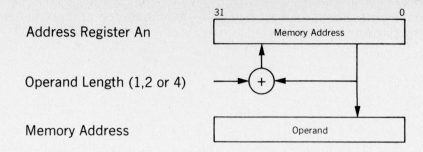

Address Register An

Operand Length (1,2 or 4)

Memory Address

2.10.2.3 Address Register Indirect With Predecrement.

The address of the operand is in the address register specified by the register field. Before the operand address is used, it is decremented by one, two, or four depending upon whether the operand size is byte, word, or long word. If the address register is the stack pointer and the operand size is byte, the address is decremented by two rather than one to keep the stack pointer on a word boundary. The reference is classified as a data reference.

Generation: An = An – N
                EA = (An)

RTL Notation: An@–

Mode: 100

Register: n

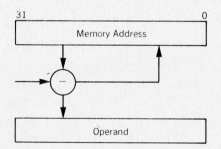

Address Register An

Operand Length (1,2 or 4)

Memory Address

2.10.2.4 Address Register Indirect With Displacement.

This address mode requires one word of extension. The address of the operand is the sum of the address in the address register and the sign-extended 16-bit displacement integer in the extension word. The reference is classified as a data reference with the exception of the jump and jump to subroutine instructions.

Generation: EA = (An) + d

RTL Notation: An@(d)

Mode: 101

Register: n

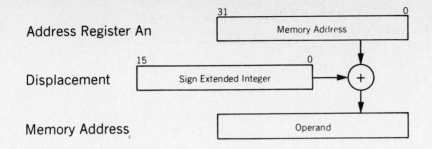

Address Register An

Displacement

Memory Address

2.10.2.5 Address Register Indirect With Index.
This address mode requires one word of extension formatted as shown below.

15	14	13	12	11	10	9	8	7	6	5	4	3	2	1	0
D/A		Register		W/L	0	0	0				Displacement Integer				

Bit 15 —
    Index register indicator
    0 — data register
    1 — address register

Bits 14 through 12 —
    Index register number

Bit 11 —
    Index Size
    0 — sign-extended, low order integer in index register
    1 — long value in index register

The address of the operand is the sum of the address in the address register, the sign-extended displacement integer in the low order eight bits of the extension word, and the contents of the index register. The reference is classified as a data reference with the exception of the jump and jump to subroutine instructions.

Generation: EA = (An) + (Ri) + d

RTL Notation: An@(d, Ri.W)
                    An@(d, Ri.L)

Mode: 110

Register: n

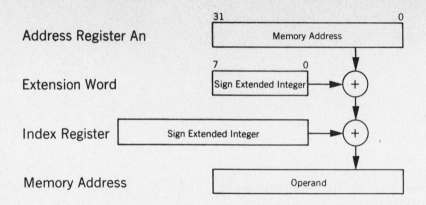

Address Register An

Extension Word

Index Register

Memory Address

2.10.3 SPECIAL ADDRESS MODES.
The special address modes use the effective address register field to specify the special addressing mode instead of a register number.

2.10.3.1 Absolute Short Address.
This address mode requires one word of extension. The address of the operand is in the extension word. The 16-bit address is sign extended before it is used. The reference is classified as a data reference with the exception of the jump and jump to subroutine instructions.

Generation: EA given
RTL Notation: xxx.W
Mode: 111
Register: 000

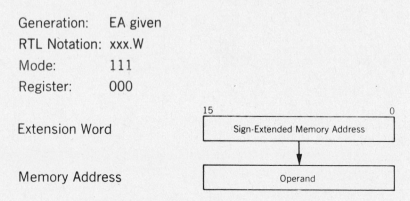

Extension Word

Memory Address

2.10.3.2 Absolute Long Address.
This address requires two words of extension. The address of the operand is developed by the concatenation of the extension words. The high-order part of the address is the first extension word; the low order part of the address is the second extension word. The reference is classified as a data reference with the exception of the jump and jump to subroutine instructions.

Generation: EA given
RTL Notation: xxx.L
Mode: 111
Register: 001

First Extension Word

Second Extension Word

Memory Address

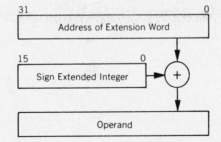

2.10.3.3 Program Counter With Displacement.
This address mode requires one word of extension. The address of the operand is the sum of the address in the program counter and the sign-extended 16-bit displacement integer in the extension word. The value in the program counter is the address of the extension word. The reference is classified as a program reference.

Generation: EA = (PC) + d
RTL Notation: PC@(d)
Mode: 111
Register: 010

Program Counter

Extension Word

Memory Address

2.10.3.4 Program Counter With Index.
This address mode requires one word of extension formatted as shown below.

15	14	13	12	11	10	9	8	7	6	5	4	3	2	1	0
D/A	Register			W/L	0	0	0	Displacement Integer							

561

Bit 15 —
    Index register indicator
    0 — data register
    1 — address register
Bits 14 through 12 —
    Index register number
Bit 11 —

    Index size
    0 — sign-extended, low order word integer in index register
    1 — long value in index register

The address is the sum of the address in the program counter, the sign-extended displacement integer in the lower eight bits of the extension word, and the contents of the index register. The value in the program counter is the address of the extension word. This reference is classified as a program reference.

Generation: EA = (PC) + (Ri) + d

RTL Notation: PC@(d, Ri.W)
                     PC@(d, Ri.L)

Mode: 111

Register: 011

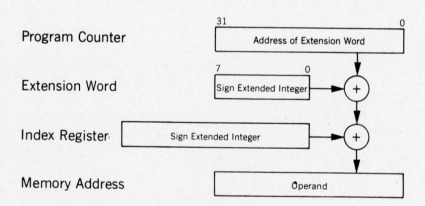

2.10.3.5 Immediate Data.   This address mode requires either one or two words of extension depending on the size of the operation.

    Byte operation — operand is low order byte of extension word

    Word operation — operand is extension word

    Long word operation — operand is in the two extension words, high order 16-bits are in the first extension word, low order 16 bits are in the second extension word.

Generation: Operand given

RTL Notation: #xxxx

Mode: 111

Register: 100

The extension word formats are shown below:

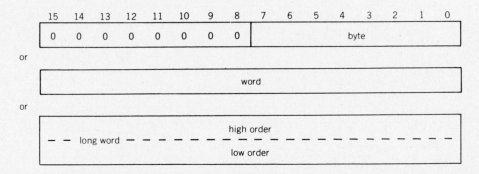

2.10.3.6 Condition Codes Or Status Register.
A selected set of instructions may reference the status register by means of the effective address field. These are:

ANDI to CCR	EORI to CCR	ORI to CCR
ANDI to SR	EORI to SR	ORI to SR

RTL Notation: CCR or SR

Mode: 111

Register: 100

2.10.4 EFFECTIVE ADDRESS ENCODING SUMMARY.
Table 2-1 is a summary of the effective addressing modes discussed in the previous paragraphs.

Table 2-1. Effective Address Encoding Summary

Addressing Mode	Mode	Register
Data Register Direct	000	register number
Address Register Direct	001	register number
Address Register Indirect	010	register number
Address Register Indirect with Postincrement	011	register number
Address Register Indirect with Predecrement	100	register number
Address Register Indirect with Displacement	101	register number
Address Register Indirect with Index	110	register number
Absolute Short	111	000
Absolute Long	111	001
Program Counter with Displacement	111	010
Program Counter with Index	111	011
Immediate or Status Register	111	100

2.11 IMPLICIT REFERENCE

Some instructions make implicit reference to the program counter (PC), the system stack pointer (SP), the supervisor stack pointer (SSP), the user stack pointer (USP), or the status register (SR). Table 2-2 provides a list of these instructions and the registers implied.

Table 2-2. Implicit Instruction Reference Summary

Instruction	Implied Register(s)
Branch Conditional (B$_{cc}$), Branch Always (BRA)	PC
Branch to Subroutine (BSR)	PC, SP
Check Register against Bounds (CHK)	SSP, SR
Test Condition , Decrement and Branch (DB$_{cc}$)	PC
Signed Divide (DIVS)	SSP, SR
Unsigned Divide (DIVU)	SSP, SR
Jump (JMP)	PC
Jump to Subroutine (JSR)	PC, SP
Link and Allocate (LINK)	SP
Move Condition Codes (MOVE CCR)	SR
Move Status Register (MOVE SR)	SR
Move User Stack Pointer (MOVE USP)	USP
Push Effective Address (PEA)	SP
Return from Exception (RTE)	PC, SP, SR
Return and Restore Condition Codes (RTR)	PC, SP, SR
Return from Subroutine (RTS)	PC, SP
Trap (TRAP)	SSP, SR
Trap on Overflow (TRAPV)	SSP, SR
Unlink (UNLK)	SP

2.12 STACKS AND QUEUES

In addition to supporting the array data structure with the index addressing mode, the MC68000 also supports stack and queue data structures with the address register indirect postincrement and predecrement addressing modes. A stack is a last-in-first-out (LIFO) list, a queue is a first-in-first-out (FIFO) list. When data is added to a stack or queue, it is "pushed" onto the structure; when it is removed, it is "pulled" from the structure.

The system stack is used implicitly by many instructions; user stacks and queues may be created and maintained through the addressing modes.

2.12.1 SYSTEM STACK. Address register seven (A7) is the system stack pointer (SP). The system stack pointer is either the supervisor stack pointer (SSP) or the user stack pointer (USP), depending on the state of the S-bit in the status register. If the S-bit indicates supervisor state the SSP is the active system stack pointer, and the USP cannot be referenced as an address register. If the S-bit indicates user state, the USP is the active system stack pointer, and the SSP cannot be referenced. Each system stack fills from high memory to low memory. The address mode SP@– creates a new item on the active system stack, and the address mode SP@+ deletes an item from the active system stack.

The program counter is saved on the active system stack on subroutine calls, and restored from the active system stack on returns. On the other hand, both the program counter and the status register are saved on the supervisor stack during the processing of traps and interrupts. Thus, the correct execution of the supervisor state code is not dependent on the behavior of user code and user programs may use the user stack pointer arbitrarily.

In order to keep data on the system stack aligned properly, data entry on the stack is restricted so that data is always put in the stack on a word boundary. Thus byte data is pushed on or pulled from the system stack in the high order half of the word; the lower half is unchanged.

2.12.2 USER STACKS. User stacks can be implemented and manipulated by employing the address register indirect with postincrement and predecrement addressing modes. Using an address register (one of A0 through A6), the user may implement stacks which are filled either from high memory to low memory, or vice versa. The important things to remember are:

— using predecrement, the register is decremented before its contents are used as the pointer into the stack,

— using postincrement, the register is incremented after its contents are used as the pointer into the stack,

— byte data must be put on the stack in pairs when mixed with word or long data so that the stack will not get misaligned when the data is retrieved. Word and long accesses must be on word boundary (even) addresses.

Stack growth from high to low memory is implemented with

An@– to push data on the stack,
An@+ to pull data from the stack.

After either a push or a pull operation, register An points to the last (top) item on the stack. This is illustrated as:

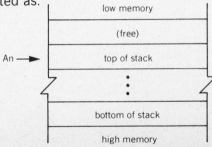

565

Stack growth from low to high memory is implemented with

An@+ to push data on the stack,
An@- to pull data from the stack.

After either a push or a pull operation, register An points to the next available space on the stack. This is illustrated as:

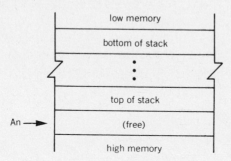

2.12.3 QUEUES. User queues can be implemented and manipulated with the address register indirect with postincrement or predecrement addressing modes. Using a pair of address registers (two of A0 through A6), the user may implement queues which are filled either from high memory to low memory, or vice versa. Because queues are pushed from one end and pulled from the other, two registers are used: the put and get pointers.

Queue growth from low to high memory is implemented with

Aput@+ to put data into the queue,
Aget@+ to get data from the queue.

After a put operation, the put address register points to the next available space in the queue and the unchanged get address register points to the next item to remove from the queue. After a get operation, the get address register points to the next item to remove from the queue and the unchanged put address register points to the next available space in the queue. This is illustrated as:

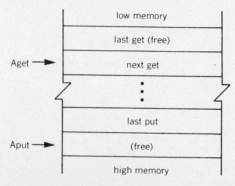

If the queue is to be implemented as a circular buffer, the address register should be checked and, if necessary, adjusted before the put or get operation is performed. The address register is adjusted by subtracting the buffer length (in bytes).

Queue growth from high to low memory is implemented with

Aput@– to put data into the queue,
Aget@– to get data from the queue.

After a put operation, the put address register points to the last item put in the queue, and the unchanged get address register points to the last item removed from the queue. After a get operation, the get address register points to the last item removed from the queue and the unchanged put address register points to the last item put in the queue. This is illustrated as:

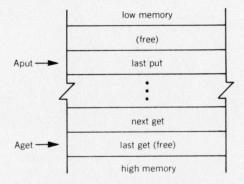

If the queue is to be implemented as a circular buffer, the get or put operation should be performed first, and then the address register should be checked and, if necessary, adjusted. The address register is adjusted by adding the buffer length (in bytes).

CHAPTER 3
INSTRUCTION SET SUMMARY

3.0 INTRODUCTION

This chapter contains an overview of the form and structure of the MC68000 instruction set. The instructions form a set of tools that include all the machine functions to perform the following operations:

Data Movement
Integer Arithmetic
Logical
Shift and Rotate
Bit Manipulation
Binary Coded Decimal
Program Control
System Control

The complete range of instruction capabilities combined with the flexible addressing modes described in Chapter 2 provide a very flexible base for program development. Detailed information about each instruction is given in Appendix B.

3.1 DATA MOVEMENT OPERATIONS

The basic method of data acquisition (transfer and storage) is provided by the move (MOVE) instruction. The move instruction and the effective addressing modes allow both address and data manipulation. Data move instructions allow byte, word, and long word operands to be transferred from memory to memory, memory to register, register to memory, and register to register. Address move instructions allow word and long word operand transfers and ensure that only legal address manipulations are executed. In addition to the general move instruction there are several special data movement instructions: move multiple registers (MOVEM), move peripheral data (MOVEP), exchange registers (EXG), load effective address (LEA), push effective address (PEA), link stack (LINK), unlink stack (UNLK), and move quick (MOVEQ). Table 3-1 is a summary of the data movement operations.

Table 3-1. Data Movement Operations

Instruction	Operand Size	Operation
EXG	32	Rx ⟶ Ry
LEA	32	EA ⟶ An
LINK	—	An ⟶ SP@− SP ⟶ An SP + d ⟶ SP
MOVE	8, 16, 32	(EA)s ⟶ EAd
MOVEM	16, 32	(EA) ⟶ An, Dn An, Dn ⟶ EA
MOVEP	16, 32	(EA) ⟶ Dn Dn ⟶ EA
MOVEQ	8	#xxx ⟶ Dn
PEA	32	EA ⟶ SP@−
SWAP	32	Dn [31:16]⟷Dn [15:0]
UNLK	—	An ⟶ SP SP @+ ⟶ An

Notes:
s = source
d = destination
[ ] = bit numbers

3.2 INTEGER ARITHMETIC OPERATIONS

The arithmetic operations include the four basic operations of add (ADD), subtract (SUB), multiply (MUL), and divide (DIV) as well as arithmetic compare (CMP), clear (CLR), and negate (NEG). The add and subtract instructions are available for both address and data operations, with data operations accepting all operand sizes. Address operations are limited to legal address size operands (16 or 32 bits). Data, address, and memory compare operations are also available. The clear and negate instructions may be used on all sizes of data operands.

The multiply and divide operations are available for signed and unsigned operands using word multiply to produce a long product, and a long word dividend with word divisor to produce a word quotient with a word remainder.

Multiprecision and mixed size arithmetic can be accomplished using a set of extended instructions. These instructions are: add extended (ADDX), subtract extended (SUBX), sign extend (EXT), and negate binary with extend (NEGX).

A test operand (TST) instruction that will set the condition codes as a result of a compare of the operand with zero is also available. Test and set (TAS) is a synchronization instruction useful in multiprocessor systems. Table 3-2 is a summary of the integer arithmetic operations.

Table 3-2. Integer Arithmetic Operations

Instruction	Operand Size	Operation
ADD	8, 16, 32	Dn + (EA) → Dn
		(EA) + Dn → EA
		(EA) + #xxx → EA
	16, 32	An + (EA) → An
ADDX	8, 16, 32	Dx + Dy + X → Dx
	16, 32	Ax@- Ay@- + X → Ax@
CLR	8, 16, 32	0 → EA
CMP	8, 16, 32	Dn - (EA)
		(EA) - #xxx
		Ax@+ - Ay@+
	16, 32	An - (EA)
DIVS	32 ÷ 16	Dn/(EA) → Dn
DIVU	32 ÷ 16	Dn/(EA) → Dn
EXT	8 → 16	$(Dn)_8 \to Dn_{16}$
	16 → 32	$(Dn)_{16} \to Dn_{32}$
MULS	16 * 16 → 32	Dn * (EA) → Dn
MULU	16 * 16 → 32	Dn * (EA) → Dn
NEG	8, 16, 32	0 - (EA) → EA
NEGX	8, 16, 32	0 - (EA) - X → EA
SUB	8, 16, 32	Dn - (EA) → Dn
		(EA) - Dn → EA
		(EA) - #xxx → EA
	16, 32	An - (EA) → An
SUBX	8, 16, 32	Dx - Dy - X → Dx
		Ax@- - Ay@- - X → Ax@
TAS	8	(EA) - 0, 1 → EA[7]
TST	8, 16, 32	(EA) - 0

Note:
  [ ] = bit number

3.3 LOGICAL OPERATIONS

Logical operation instructions AND, OR, EOR, and NOT are available for all sizes of integer data operands. A similar set of immediate instructions (ANDI, ORI, and EORI) provide these logical operations with all sizes of immediate data. Table 3-3 is a summary of the logical operations.

3.4 SHIFT AND ROTATE OPERATIONS

Shift operations in both directions are provided by the arithmetic instructions ASR and ASL and logical shift instructions LSR and LSL. The rotate instructions (with and without extend) available are ROXR, ROXL, ROR, and ROL. All shift and rotate operations can be performed in either registers or memory. Register shifts and rotates support all operand sizes and allow a shift count specified in the instruction of one to eight bits, or 0 to 63 bits specified in a data register.

Memory shifts and rotates are for word operands only and allow only single-bit shifts or rotates.

Table 3-4 is a summary of the shift and rotate operations.

Table 3-3. Logical Operations

Instruction	Operand Size	Operation
AND	8, 16, 32	Dn ∧ (EA) → Dn (EA) ∧ Dn → EA (EA) ∧ #xxx → EA
OR	8, 16, 32	Dn v (EA) → Dn (EA) v Dn → EA (EA) v #xxx → EA
EOR	8, 16, 32	(EA) ⊕ Dy → EA (EA) ⊕ #xxx → EA
NOT	8, 16, 32	~(EA) → EA

Note:
  ~ = invert

Table 3-4. Shift and Rotate Operations

Instruction	Operand Size	Operation
ASL	8, 16, 32	
ASR	8, 16, 32	
LSL	8, 16, 32	
LSR	8, 16, 32	
ROL	8, 16, 32	
ROR	8, 16, 32	
ROXL	8, 16, 32	
ROXR	8, 16, 32	

3.5 BIT MANIPULATION OPERATIONS

Bit manipulation operations are accomplished using the following instructions: bit test (BTST), bit test and set (BSET), bit test and clear (BCLR), and bit test and change (BCHG). Table 3-5 is a summary of the bit manipulation operations.

Table 3-5. Bit Manipulation Operations

Instruction	Operand Size	Operation
BTST	8, 32	$\sim$ bit of (EA) $\rightarrow$ Z
BSET	8, 32	$\sim$ bit of (EA) $\rightarrow$ Z 1 $\rightarrow$ bit of EA
BCLR	8, 32	$\sim$ bit of (EA) $\rightarrow$ Z 0 $\rightarrow$ bit of EA
BCHG	8, 32	$\sim$ bit of (EA) $\rightarrow$ Z $\sim$ bit of (EA) $\rightarrow$ bit of EA

3.6 BINARY CODED DECIMAL OPERATIONS

Multiprecision arithmetic operations on binary coded decimal numbers are accomplished using the following instructions: add decimal with extend (ABCD), subtract decimal with extend (SBCD), and negate decimal with extend (NBCD). Table 3-6 is a summary of the binary coded decimal operations.

Table 3-6. Binary Coded Decimal Operations

Instruction	Operand Size	Operation
ABCD	8	$Dx_{10} + Dy_{10} + X \rightarrow Dx$ $Ax@-_{10} + Ay@-_{10} + X \rightarrow Ax@$
SBCD	8	$Dx_{10} - Dy_{10} - X \rightarrow Dx$ $Ax@-_{10} - Ay@-_{10} - X \rightarrow Ax@$
NBCD	8	$0 - (EA)_{10} - X \rightarrow EA$

3.7 PROGRAM CONTROL OPERATIONS

Program control operations are accomplished using a series of conditional and unconditional branch instructions and return instructions. These instructions are summarized in table 3-7.

The conditional instructions provide setting and branching for the following conditions:

CC — carry clear
CS — carry set
EQ — equal
F — never true
GE — greater or equal
GT — greater than
HI — high
LE — less or equal
LS — low or same
LT — less than
MI — minus
NE — not equal
PL — plus
T — always true
VC — no overflow
VS — overflow

Table 3-7. Program Control Operations

Instruction	Operation
Conditional	
B$_{CC}$	Branch conditionally (14 conditions) 8- and 16-bit displacement
DB$_{CC}$	Test condition, decrement and branch. 16-bit displacement
S$_{CC}$	Set byte conditionally (16 conditions)
Unconditional	
BRA	Branch always 8- and 16-bit displacement
BSR	Branch to subroutine 8- and 16-bit displacement
JMP	Jump
JSR	Jump to subroutine
Returns	
RTR	Return and restore condition codes
RTS	Return from subroutine

3.8 SYSTEM CONTROL OPERATIONS

System control operations are accomplished by using privileged instructions, trap generating instructions, and instructions that use or modify the status register. These instructions are summarized in table 3-8.

Table 3-8. System Control Operations

Instruction	Operation
Privileged	
RESET	Reset external devices
RTE	Return from exception
STOP	Stop program execution
ORI to SR	Logical OR to status register
MOVE USP	Move user stack pointer
ANDI to SR	Logical AND to status register
EORI to SR	Logical EOR to status register
MOVE EA to SR	Load new status register
Trap Generating	
TRAP	Trap
TRAPV	Trap on overflow
CHK	Check register against bounds
Status Register	
ANDI to CCR	Logical AND to condition codes
EORI to CCR	Logical EOR to condition codes
MOVE EA to CCR	Load new condition codes
ORI to CCR	Logical OR to condition codes
MOVE SR to EA	Store status register

CHAPTER 4
SIGNAL AND BUS OPERATION DESCRIPTION

4.0 INTRODUCTION

This chapter contains a brief description of the input and output signals. A discussion of bus operation during the various machine cycles and operations is also given.

4.1 SIGNAL DESCRIPTION

The input and output signals can be functionally organized into the groups shown in figure 4-1. The following paragraphs provide a brief description of the signals and also a reference (if applicable) to other chapters that contain more detail about the function being performed.

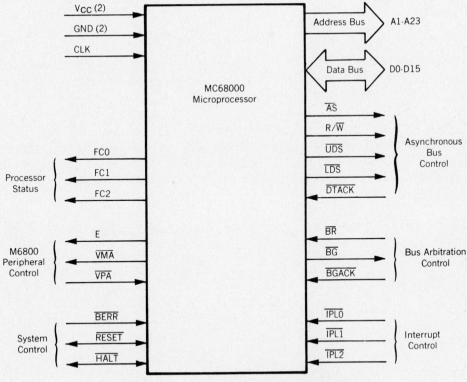

Figure 4-1. Input and Output Signals

4.1.1 ADDRESS BUS (A1 THROUGH A23). This 23-bit, unidirectional, three-state bus is capable of addressing 8 megawords of data. It provides the address for bus operation during all cycles except interrupt cycles. During interrupt cycles, address lines A1, A2, and A3 provide information about what level interrupt is being serviced while address lines A4 through A23 are all set to a logic high.

4.1.2 DATA BUS (D0 THROUGH D15). This 16-bit, bidirectional, three-state bus is the general purpose data path. It can transfer and accept data in either word or byte length. During an interrupt acknowledge cycle, the external device supplies the vector number on data lines D0 through D7.

4.1.3 ASYNCHRONOUS BUS CONTROL. Asynchronous data transfers are handled using the following control signals: address strobe, read/write, upper and lower data strobes, and data transfer acknowledge. These signals are explained in the following paragraphs.

4.1.3.1 Address Strobe ($\overline{\text{AS}}$). This signal indicates that there is a valid address on the address bus.

4.1.3.2 Read/Write (R/$\overline{\text{W}}$). This signal defines the data bus transfer as a read or write cycle. The R/$\overline{\text{W}}$ signal also works in conjunction with the upper and lower data strobes as explained in the following paragraph.

4.1.3.3 Upper And Lower Data Strobes ($\overline{\text{UDS}}$, $\overline{\text{LDS}}$). These signals control the data on the data bus as shown in table 4-1. When the R/$\overline{\text{W}}$ line is high, the processor will read from the data bus as indicated. When the R/$\overline{\text{W}}$ line is low, the processor will write to the data bus as shown.

Table 4-1. Data Strobe Control of Data Bus

$\overline{\text{UDS}}$	$\overline{\text{LDS}}$	R/$\overline{\text{W}}$	D8-D15	D0-D7
High	High	—	No valid data	No valid data
Low	Low	High	Valid data bits 8-15	Valid data bits 0-7
High	Low	High	No valid data	Valid data bits 0-7
Low	High	High	Valid data bits 8-15	No valid data
Low	Low	Low	Valid data bits 8-15	Valid data bits 0-7
High	Low	Low	Valid data bits 0-7*	Valid data bits 0-7
Low	High	Low	Valid data bits 8-15	Valid data bits 8-15*

*These conditions are a result of current implementation and may not appear on future devices.

4.1.3.4 Data Transfer Acknowledge ($\overline{\text{DTACK}}$). This input indicates that the data transfer is completed. When the processor recognizes $\overline{\text{DTACK}}$ during a read cycle, data is latched and the bus cycle terminated. When $\overline{\text{DTACK}}$ is recognized during a write cycle, the bus cycle is terminated.

4.1.4 BUS ARBITRATION CONTROL. These three signals form a bus arbitration circuit to determine which device will be the bus master device. Refer to paragraph 4.2.2 for a detailed description.

4.1.4.1 Bus Request ($\overline{\text{BR}}$). This input is wire ORed with all other devices that could be bus masters. This input indicates to the processor that some other device desires to become the bus master.

4.1.4.2 Bus Grant ($\overline{\text{BG}}$). This output indicates to all other potential bus master devices that the processor will release bus control at the end of the current bus cycle.

4.1.4.3 Bus Grant Acknowledge ($\overline{\text{BGACK}}$). This input indicates that some other device has become the bus master. This signal cannot be asserted until the following four conditions are met:

1. a bus grant has been received

2. address strobe is inactive which indicates that the microprocessor is not using the bus

3. data transfer acknowledge is inactive which indicates that either memory or the peripherals are not using the bus

4. bus grant acknowledge is inactive which indicates that no other device is still claiming bus mastership.

4.1.5 INTERRUPT CONTROL ($\overline{\text{IPL0}}$, $\overline{\text{IPL1}}$, $\overline{\text{IPL2}}$). These input pins indicate the encoded priority level of the device requesting an interrupt. Level seven is the highest priority while level zero indicates that no interrupts are requested. The least significant bit is contained in $\overline{\text{IPL0}}$ and the most significant bit is contained in $\overline{\text{IPL2}}$. Refer to Chapter 5 for details on interrupt operation.

4.1.6 SYSTEM CONTROL. The system control inputs are used to either reset or halt the processor and to indicate to the processor that bus errors have occurred. The three system control inputs are explained in the following paragraphs.

577

4.1.6.1 Bus Error (BERR).   This input informs the processor that there is a problem with the cycle currently being executed. Problems may be a result of:

1. nonresponding devices
2. interrupt vector number acquisition failure
3. illegal access request as determined by a memory management unit
4. other application dependent errors.

The bus error signal interacts with the halt signal to determine if exception processing should be performed or the current bus cycle should be retried.

Refer to paragraph 4.2.3 for additional information about the interaction of the bus error and halt signals.

4.1.6.2 Reset (RESET).   This bidirectional signal line acts to reset (initiate a system initialization sequence) the processor in response to an external reset signal. An internally generated reset (result of a RESET instruction) causes all external devices to be reset and the internal state of the processor is not affected. A total system reset (processor and external devices) is the result of external halt and reset signals applied at the same time. Refer to paragraph 4.2.4 for additional information about reset operation.

4.1.6.3 Halt (HALT).   When this bidirectional line is driven by an external device, it will cause the processor to stop at the completion of the current bus cycle. When the processor has been halted using this input, all control signals are inactive and all three-state lines are put in their high impedance state. Refer to paragraph 4.2.3 for additional information about the interaction between the halt and bus error signals.

When the processor has stopped executing instructions, such as in a double bus fault condition, the halt line is driven by the processor to indicate to external devices that the processor has stopped.

4.1.7 M6800 PERIPHERAL CONTROL.   These control signals are used to allow the interfacing of synchronous M6800 peripheral devices with the asynchronous MC68000. These signals are explained in the following paragraphs.

4.1.7.1 Enable (E). This signal is the standard enable signal common to all M6800 type peripheral devices. The period for this output is ten MC68000 clock periods (six clocks low; four clocks high).

4.1.7.2 Valid Peripheral Address ($\overline{\text{VPA}}$). This input indicates that the device or region addressed is a M6800 family device and that data transfer should coincide with the enable (E) signal. This input also indicates that the processor should use automatic vectoring for an interrupt. Refer to Chapter 6.

4.1.7.3 Valid Memory Address ($\overline{\text{VMA}}$). This output is used to indicate to M6800 peripheral devices that there is a valid address on the address bus and the processor is synchronized to enable. This signal only responds to a valid peripheral address ($\overline{\text{VPA}}$) input which indicates that the peripheral is a M6800 family device.

4.1.8 PROCESSOR STATUS (FC0, FC1, FC2). These function code outputs indicate the mode (user or supervisor) and the cycle type currently being executed as shown in table 4-2. The information indicated by the function code outputs is valid whenever address strobe ($\overline{\text{AS}}$) is active.

Table 4-2. Function Code Outputs

FC2	FC1	FC0	Cycle Type
Low	Low	Low	(Undefined, Reserved)
Low	Low	High	User Data
Low	High	Low	User Program
Low	High	High	(Undefined, Reserved)
High	Low	Low	(Undefined, Reserved)
High	Low	High	Supervisor Data
High	High	Low	Supervisor Program
High	High	High	Interrupt Acknowledge

4.1.9 CLOCK (CLK). The clock input is a TTL compatible signal that is internally buffered for development of the internal clocks needed by the processor. The clock input shall be a constant frequency.

4.1.10 SIGNAL SUMMARY.   Table 4-3 is a summary of all the signals discussed in the previous paragraphs.

Table 4-3. Signal Summary

Signal Name	Mnemonic	Input/Output	Active State	Three State
Address Bus	A1-A23	output	high	yes
Data Bus	D0-D15	input/output	high	yes
Address Strobe	$\overline{AS}$	output	low	yes
Read/Write	R/$\overline{W}$	output	read-high write-low	yes
Upper and Lower Data Strobes	$\overline{UDS}$, $\overline{LDS}$	output	low	yes
Data Transfer Acknowledge	$\overline{DTACK}$	input	low	no
Bus Request	$\overline{BR}$	input	low	no
Bus Grant	$\overline{BG}$	output	low	no
Bus Grant Acknowledge	$\overline{BGACK}$	input	low	no
Interrupt Priority Level	$\overline{IPL0}$, $\overline{IPL1}$, $\overline{IPL2}$	input	low	no
Bus Error	$\overline{BERR}$	input	low	no
Reset	$\overline{RESET}$	input/output	low	no*
Halt	$\overline{HALT}$	input/output	low	no*
Enable	E	output	high	no
Valid Memory Address	$\overline{VMA}$	output	low	yes
Valid Peripheral Address	$\overline{VPA}$	input	low	no
Function Code Output	FC0, FC1, FC2	output	high	yes
Clock	CLK	input	high	no
Power Input	V_{CC}	Input	—	—
Ground	GND	Input	—	—

*open drain

4.2 BUS OPERATION

The following paragraphs explain control signal and bus operation during data transfer operations, bus arbitration, bus error and halt conditions, and reset operation.

4.2.1 DATA TRANSFER OPERATIONS.   Transfer of data between devices involves the following leads:

- Address Bus A1 through A23
- Data Bus D0 through D15
- Control Signals

The address and data buses are separate parallel buses used to transfer data using an asynchronous bus structure. In all cycles, the bus master assumes responsibility for deskewing all signals it issues at both the start and end of a cycle. In addition, the bus

APPENDIX A
CONDITION CODES COMPUTATION

A.0 INTRODUCTION

This appendix provides a discussion of how the condition codes were developed, the meanings of each bit, how they are computed, and how they are represented in the instruction set details.

Two criteria were used in developing the condition codes:

Consistency — across instruction, uses, and instances

Meaningful results — no change unless it provides useful information

The consistency across instructions means that instructions which are special cases of more general instructions affect the condition codes in the same way. Consistency across instances means that if an instruction ever affects a condition code, it will always affect that condition code. Consistency across uses means that whether the condition codes were set by a compare, test, or move instruction, the conditional instructions test the same situation. The tests used for the conditional instructions and the code computations are given in paragraph A.4.

A.1 CONDITION CODE REGISTER.

The condition code register portion of the status register contains five bits:

N — Negative
Z — Zero
V — Overflow
C — Carry
X — Extend

The first four bits are true condition code bits in that they reflect the condition of the result of a processor operation. The X-bit is an operand for multiprecision computations. The carry bit (C) and the multiprecision operand extend bit (X) are separate in the MC68000 to simplify the programming model.

A.2 CONDITION CODE REGISTER NOTATION

In the instruction set details given in Appendix B, the description of the effect on the condition codes is given in the following form:

Condition Codes:

X	N	Z	V	C

where:

N (negative)   set if the most significant bit of the result is set. Cleared otherwise.

Z (zero)   set if the result equals zero. Cleared otherwise.

V (overflow)   set if there was an arithmetic overflow. This implies that the result is not representable in the operand size. Cleared otherwise.

C (carry)   set if a carry is generated out of the most significant bit of the operands for an addition. Also set if a borrow is generated in a subtraction. Cleared otherwise.

X (extend)   transparent to data movement. When affected, it is set the same as the C-bit.

The notational convention that appears in the representation of the condition code register is:

*   set according to the result of the operation

—   not affected by the operation

0   cleared

1   set

U   undefined after the operation

A.3 CONDITION CODE COMPUTATION

Most operations take a source operand and a destination operand, compute, and store the result in the destination location. Unary operations take a destination operand, compute, and store the result in the destination location. Table A-1 details how each instruction sets the condition codes.

Table A-1. Condition Code Computations

Operations	X	N	Z	V	C	Special Definition
ABCD	*	U	?	U	?	C = Decimal Carry $Z = Z \cdot R_m \cdot \ldots \cdot \overline{R_0}$
ADD, ADDI, ADDQ	*	*	*	?	?	$V = S_m \cdot D_m \cdot \overline{R_m} + \overline{S_m} \cdot \overline{D_m} \cdot R_m$ $C = S_m \cdot D_m + \overline{R_m} \cdot D_m + S_m \cdot \overline{R_m}$
ADDX	*	*	?	?	?	$V = S_m \cdot D_m \cdot \overline{R_m} + \overline{S_m} \cdot \overline{D_m} \cdot R_m$ $C = S_m \cdot D_m + \overline{R_m} \cdot D_m + S_m \cdot \overline{R_m}$ $Z = Z \cdot \overline{R_m} \cdot \ldots \cdot \overline{R_0}$
AND, ANDI, EOR, EORI, MOVEQ, MOVE, OR, ORI, CLR, EXT NOT, TAS, TST	—	*	*	0	0	
CHK	—	*	U	U	U	
SUB, SUBI SUBQ	*	*	*	?	?	$V = \overline{S_m} \cdot D_m \cdot \overline{R_m} + S_m \cdot \overline{D_m} \cdot R_m$ $C = S_m \cdot \overline{D_m} + R_m \cdot \overline{D_m} + S_m \cdot R_m$
SUBX	*	*	?	?	?	$V = \overline{S_m} \cdot D_m \cdot \overline{R_m} + S_m \cdot \overline{D_m} \cdot R_m$ $C = S_m \cdot \overline{D_m} + R_m \cdot \overline{D_m} + S_m \cdot R_m$ $Z = Z \cdot R_m \cdot \ldots \cdot \overline{R_0}$
CMP, CMPI, CMPM	—	*	*	?	?	$V = \overline{S_m} \cdot D_m \cdot \overline{R_m} + S_m \cdot \overline{D_m} \cdot R_m$ $C = S_m \cdot \overline{D_m} + R_m \cdot \overline{D_m} + S_m \cdot R_m$
DIVS, DIVU	—	*	*	?	0	V = Division Overflow
MULS, MULU	—	*	*	0	0	
SBCD, NBCD	*	U	?	U	?	C = Decimal Borrow $Z = Z \cdot \overline{R_m} \cdot \ldots \cdot \overline{R_0}$
NEG	*	*	*	?	?	$V = D_m \cdot R_m,\ C = D_m + R_m$
NEGX	*	*	?	?	?	$V = D_m \cdot R_m,\ C = D_m + R_m$ $Z = Z \cdot \overline{R_m} \cdot \ldots \cdot \overline{R_0}$
BTST, BCHG, BSET, BCLR	—	—	?	—	—	$Z = \overline{D_n}$
ASL	*	*	*	?	?	$V = D_m \cdot (\overline{D_{m-1}} + \ldots + \overline{D_{m-r}})$ $\quad + \overline{D_m} \cdot (D_{m-1} + \ldots + D_{m-r})$ $C = D_{m-r+1}$
ASL (r = 0)	—	*	*	0	0	
LSL, ROXL	*	*	*	0	?	$C = D_{m-r+1}$
LSR (r = 0)	—	*	*	0	0	
ROXL (r = 0)	—	*	*	0	?	$C = X$
ROL	—	*	*	0	?	$C = D_{m-r+1}$
ROL (r = 0)	—	*	*	0	0	
ASR, LSR, ROXR	*	*	*	0	?	$C = D_{r-1}$
ASR, LSR (r = 0)	—	*	*	0	0	
ROXR (r = 0)	—	*	*	0	?	$C = X$
ROR	—	*	*	0	?	$C = D_{r-1}$
ROR (r = 0)	—	*	*	0	0	

— Not affected
U Undefined
? Other — see Special Definition

* General Case:
$X = C$
$N = R_m$
$Z = \overline{R_m} \cdot \ldots \cdot \overline{R_0}$

Sm — Source operand most significant bit
Dm — Destination operand most significant bit
Rm — Result bit most significant bit
n — bit number
r — shift amount

A.4 CONDITIONAL TESTS

Table A-2 lists the condition names, encodings, and tests for the conditional branch and set instructions. The test associated with each condition is a logical formula based on the current state of the condition codes. If this formula evaluates to 1, the condition succeeds, or is true. If the formula evaluates to 0, the condition is unsuccessful, or false. For example, the T condition always succeeds, while the EQ condition succeeds only if the Z bit is currently set in the condition codes.

Table A-2. Conditional Tests

Mnemonic	Condition	Encoding	Test
T	true	0000	1
F	false	0001	0
HI	high	0010	$\overline{C} \cdot \overline{Z}$
LS	low or same	0011	$C + Z$
CC	carry clear	0100	$\overline{C}$
CS	carry set	0101	C
NE	not equal	0110	$\overline{Z}$
EQ	equal	0111	Z
VC	overflow clear	1000	$\overline{V}$
VS	overflow set	1001	V
PL	plus	1010	$\overline{N}$
MI	minus	1011	N
GE	greater or equal	1100	$N \cdot V + \overline{N} \cdot \overline{V}$
LT	less than	1101	$N \cdot \overline{V} + \overline{N} \cdot V$
GT	greater than	1110	$N \cdot V \cdot \overline{Z} + \overline{N} \cdot \overline{V} \cdot \overline{Z}$
LE	less or equal	1111	$Z + N \cdot \overline{V} + \overline{N} \cdot V$

APPENDIX C
INSTRUCTION FORMAT SUMMARY

C.0 INTRODUCTION

This appendix provides a summary of the first word in each instruction of the instruction set. Table C-1 is an operation code (op-code) map which illustrates how bits 15 through 12 are used to specify the operations. The remaining paragraph groups the instructions according to the op-code map.

Table C-1. Operation Code Map

Bits 15 thru 12	Operation
0000	Bit Manipulation/MOVEP/Immediate
0001	Move Byte
0010	Move Long
0011	Move Word
0100	Miscellaneous
0101	ADDQ/SUBQ/S_{CC}/DB$_{CC}$
0110	B$_{CC}$
0111	MOVEQ
1000	OR/DIV/SBCD
1001	SUB/SUBX
1010	(Unassigned)
1011	CMP/EOR
1100	AND/MUL/ABCD/EXG
1101	ADD/ADDX
1110	Shift/Rotate
1111	(Unassigned)

C.1 BIT MANIPULATION, MOVE PERIPHERAL, IMMEDIATE INSTRUCTIONS

Dynamic Bit

15	14	13	12	11	10	9	8	7	6	5	4	3	2	1	0
0	0	0	0	Register			1	Type		Effective Address					

Static Bit

15	14	13	12	11	10	9	8	7	6	5	4	3	2	1	0
0	0	0	0	1	0	0	0	Type		Effective Address					

Bit Type Codes: TST = 00, CHG = 01, CLR = 10, SET = 11

MOVEP

15	14	13	12	11	10	9	8	7	6	5	4	3	2	1	0
0	0	0	0	Register			Op-Mode			0	0	1	Register		

OR Immediate

15	14	13	12	11	10	9	8	7	6	5	4	3	2	1	0
0	0	0	0	0	0	0	0	Size		Effective Address					

AND Immediate

15	14	13	12	11	10	9	8	7	6	5	4	3	2	1	0
0	0	0	0	0	0	1	0	Size		Effective Address					

SUB Immediate

15	14	13	12	11	10	9	8	7	6	5	4	3	2	1	0
0	0	0	0	0	1	0	0	Size		Effective Address					

ADD Immediate

15	14	13	12	11	10	9	8	7	6	5	4	3	2	1	0
0	0	0	0	0	1	1	0	Size		Effective Address					

EOR Immediate

15	14	13	12	11	10	9	8	7	6	5	4	3	2	1	0
0	0	0	0	1	0	1	0	Size		Effective Address					

CMP Immediate

15	14	13	12	11	10	9	8	7	6	5	4	3	2	1	0
0	0	0	0	1	1	0	0	Size		Effective Address					

C.2 MOVE BYTE INSTRUCTION

MOVE Byte

15	14	13	12	11	10	9	8	7	6	5	4	3	2	1	0
0	0	0	1	Destination Register		Mode				Source Mode			Register		

C.3 MOVE LONG INSTRUCTION

MOVE Long

15	14	13	12	11	10	9	8	7	6	5	4	3	2	1	0
0	0	1	0	Destination Register		Mode				Source Mode			Register		

C.4 MOVE WORD INSTRUCTION

MOVE Word

15	14	13	12	11	10	9	8	7	6	5	4	3	2	1	0
0	0	1	1	Destination Register		Mode				Source Mode			Register		

C.5 MISCELLANEOUS INSTRUCTIONS

NEGX

15	14	13	12	11	10	9	8	7	6	5	4	3	2	1	0
0	1	0	0	0	0	0	0	Size		Effective Address					

MOVE from SR

15	14	13	12	11	10	9	8	7	6	5	4	3	2	1	0
0	1	0	0	0	0	0	0	1	1	Effective Address					

CLR

15	14	13	12	11	10	9	8	7	6	5	4	3	2	1	0
0	1	0	0	0	0	1	0	Size		Effective Address					

NEG

15	14	13	12	11	10	9	8	7	6	5	4	3	2	1	0
0	1	0	0	0	1	0	0	Size		Effective Address					

MOVE to CCR

15	14	13	12	11	10	9	8	7	6	5	4	3	2	1	0
0	1	0	0	0	1	0	0	1	1	Effective Address					

NOT

15	14	13	12	11	10	9	8	7	6	5	4	3	2	1	0
0	1	0	0	0	1	1	0	Size		Effective Address					

MOVE to SR

15	14	13	12	11	10	9	8	7	6	5	4	3	2	1	0
0	1	0	0	0	1	1	0	1	1	Effective Address					

NBCD

15	14	13	12	11	10	9	8	7	6	5	4	3	2	1	0
0	1	0	0	1	0	0	0	0	0	Effective Address					

PEA

15	14	13	12	11	10	9	8	7	6	5	4	3	2	1	0
0	1	0	0	1	0	0	0	0	1	Effective Address					

SWAP

15	14	13	12	11	10	9	8	7	6	5	4	3	2	1	0
0	1	0	0	1	0	0	0	0	1	0	0	0	Register		

MOVEM Registers to EA

15	14	13	12	11	10	9	8	7	6	5	4	3	2	1	0
0	1	0	0	1	0	0	0	1	Sz	Effective Address					

EXTW

15	14	13	12	11	10	9	8	7	6	5	4	3	2	1	0
0	1	0	0	1	0	0	0	1	0	0	0	0	Register		

EXTL

15	14	13	12	11	10	9	8	7	6	5	4	3	2	1	0
0	1	0	0	1	0	0	0	1	1	0	0	0	Register		

TST

15	14	13	12	11	10	9	8	7	6	5	4	3	2	1	0
0	1	0	0	1	0	1	0	Size		Effective Address					

TAS

15	14	13	12	11	10	9	8	7	6	5	4	3	2	1	0
0	1	0	0	1	0	1	0	1	1	Effective Address					

MOVEM EA to Registers

15	14	13	12	11	10	9	8	7	6	5	4	3	2	1	0
0	1	0	0	1	1	0	0	1	Sz	Effective Address					

TRAP

15	14	13	12	11	10	9	8	7	6	5	4	3	2	1	0
0	1	0	0	1	1	1	0	0	1	0	0	Vector			

LINK

15	14	13	12	11	10	9	8	7	6	5	4	3	2	1	0
0	1	0	0	1	1	1	0	0	1	0	1	0	Register		

UNLK

15	14	13	12	11	10	9	8	7	6	5	4	3	2	1	0
0	1	0	0	1	1	1	0	0	1	0	1	1	Register		

MOVE to USP

15	14	13	12	11	10	9	8	7	6	5	4	3	2	1	0
0	1	0	0	1	1	1	0	0	1	1	0	0	Register		

MOVE from USP

15	14	13	12	11	10	9	8	7	6	5	4	3	2	1	0
0	1	0	0	1	1	1	0	0	1	1	0	1	Register		

RESET

15	14	13	12	11	10	9	8	7	6	5	4	3	2	1	0
0	1	0	0	1	1	1	0	0	1	1	1	0	0	0	0

NOP

15	14	13	12	11	10	9	8	7	6	5	4	3	2	1	0
0	1	0	0	1	1	1	0	0	1	1	1	0	0	0	1

STOP

15	14	13	12	11	10	9	8	7	6	5	4	3	2	1	0
0	1	0	0	1	1	1	0	0	1	1	1	0	0	1	0

RTE

15	14	13	12	11	10	9	8	7	6	5	4	3	2	1	0
0	1	0	0	1	1	1	0	0	1	1	1	0	0	1	1

RTS

15	14	13	12	11	10	9	8	7	6	5	4	3	2	1	0
0	1	0	0	1	1	1	0	0	1	1	1	0	1	0	1

TRAPV

15	14	13	12	11	10	9	8	7	6	5	4	3	2	1	0
0	1	0	0	1	1	1	0	0	1	1	1	0	1	1	0

RTR

15	14	13	12	11	10	9	8	7	6	5	4	3	2	1	0
0	1	0	0	1	1	1	0	0	1	1	1	0	1	1	1

JSR

15	14	13	12	11	10	9	8	7	6	5	4	3	2	1	0
0	1	0	0	1	1	1	0	1	0	Effective Address					

JMP

15	14	13	12	11	10	9	8	7	6	5	4	3	2	1	0
0	1	0	0	1	1	1	0	1	1	Effective Address					

CHK

15	14	13	12	11	10	9	8	7	6	5	4	3	2	1	0
0	1	0	0	Register			1	1	0	Effective Address					

LEA

15	14	13	12	11	10	9	8	7	6	5	4	3	2	1	0
0	1	0	0	Register			1	1	1	Effective Address					

C.6 ADD QUICK, SUBTRACT QUICK, SET CONDITIONALLY, DECREMENT INSTRUCTIONS

ADDQ

15	14	13	12	11	10	9	8	7	6	5	4	3	2	1	0
0	1	0	1	Data			0	Size		Effective Address					

SUBQ

15	14	13	12	11	10	9	8	7	6	5	4	3	2	1	0
0	1	0	1	Data			1	Size		Effective Address					

Scc

15	14	13	12	11	10	9	8	7	6	5	4	3	2	1	0
0	1	0	1	Condition				1	1	Effective Address					

DB_{CC}

15	14	13	12	11	10	9	8	7	6	5	4	3	2	1	0
0	1	0	1	Condition				1	1	0	0	1	Register		

C.7 BRANCH CONDITIONALLY INSTRUCTION

B_{CC}

15	14	13	12	11	10	9	8	7	6	5	4	3	2	1	0
0	1	1	0	Condition				8-bit Displacement							

C.8 MOVE QUICK INSTRUCTION

MOVEQ

15	14	13	12	11	10	9	8	7	6	5	4	3	2	1	0
0	1	1	1	Register			0	Data							

C.9 OR, DIVIDE, SUBTRACT DECIMAL INSTRUCTIONS

OR

15	14	13	12	11	10	9	8	7	6	5	4	3	2	1	0
1	0	0	0	Register			Op-Mode			Effective Address					

DIVU

15	14	13	12	11	10	9	8	7	6	5	4	3	2	1	0
1	0	0	0	Register			0	1	1	Effective Address					

DIVS

15	14	13	12	11	10	9	8	7	6	5	4	3	2	1	0
1	0	0	0	Register			1	1	1	Effective Address					

SBCD

15	14	13	12	11	10	9	8	7	6	5	4	3	2	1	0
1	0	0	0	Destination Register			1	0	0	0	0	R/M	Source Register		

R/M (register/memory): register – register = 0, memory – memory = 1

C.10 SUBTRACT, SUBTRACT EXTENDED INSTRUCTIONS

SUB

15	14	13	12	11	10	9	8	7	6	5	4	3	2	1	0
1	0	0	1	Register			Op-Mode			Effective Address					

SUBX

15	14	13	12	11	10	9	8	7	6	5	4	3	2	1	0
1	0	0	1	Destination Register			1	Size		0	0	R/M	Source Register		

R/M (register/memory): register– register = 0, memory – memory = 1

C.11 COMPARE, EXCLUSIVE OR INSTRUCTIONS

CMP

15	14	13	12	11	10	9	8	7	6	5	4	3	2	1	0
1	0	1	1	Register			Op-Mode			Effective Address					

CMPM

15	14	13	12	11	10	9	8	7	6	5	4	3	2	1	0
1	0	1	1	Register			1	Size		0	0	1	Register		

EOR

15	14	13	12	11	10	9	8	7	6	5	4	3	2	1	0
1	0	1	1	Register			1	Size		Effective Address					

C.12 AND, MULTIPLY, ADD DECIMAL, EXCHANGE INSTRUCTIONS

AND

15	14	13	12	11	10	9	8	7	6	5	4	3	2	1	0
1	1	0	0	Register			Op-Mode			Effective Address					

MULU

15	14	13	12	11	10	9	8	7	6	5	4	3	2	1	0
1	1	0	0	Register			0	1	1	Effective Address					

MULS

15	14	13	12	11	10	9	8	7	6	5	4	3	2	1	0
1	1	0	0	Register			1	1	1	Effective Address					

ABCD

15	14	13	12	11	10	9	8	7	6	5	4	3	2	1	0
1	1	0	0	Destination Register			1	0	0	0	0	R/M	Source Register		

R/M (register/memory): register – register = 0, memory – memory = 1

EXGD

15	14	13	12	11	10	9	8	7	6	5	4	3	2	1	0
1	1	0	0	Data Register			1	0	1	0	0	0	Data Register		

EXGA

15	14	13	12	11	10	9	8	7	6	5	4	3	2	1	0
1	1	0	0	Address Register			1	0	1	0	0	1	Address Register		

EXGM

15	14	13	12	11	10	9	8	7	6	5	4	3	2	1	0
1	1	0	0	Data Register			1	1	0	0	0	1	Address Register		

C.13 ADD, ADD EXTENDED INSTRUCTIONS

ADD

15	14	13	12	11	10	9	8	7	6	5	4	3	2	1	0
1	1	0	1	Register			Op-Mode			Effective Address					

ADDX

15	14	13	12	11	10	9	8	7	6	5	4	3	2	1	0
1	1	0	1	Destination Register			1	Size		0	0	R/M	Source Register		

R/M (register/memory): register – register = 0, memory – memory = 1

C.14 SHIFT/ROTATE INSTRUCTIONS

Data Register Shifts

15	14	13	12	11	10	9	8	7	6	5	4	3	2	1	0
1	1	1	0	Count/ Register			d	Size		i/r	Type		Register		

Memory Shifts

15	14	13	12	11	10	9	8	7	6	5	4	3	2	1	0
1	1	1	0	0	Type		d	1	1	Effective Address					

Shift Type Codes: AS = 00, LS = 01, ROX = 10, RO = 11
d (direction): Right = 0, Left = 1
i/r (count source): Immediate Count = 0, Register Count = 1

APPENDIX E
PINOUT DIAGRAM

E.0 INTRODUCTION

This appendix contains a pinout diagram of the MC68000. Refer to figure E-1.

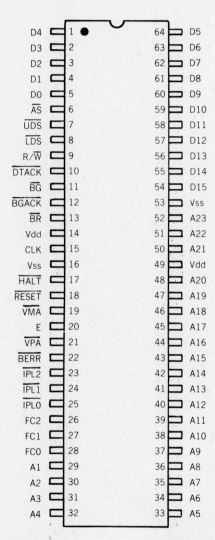

Figure E-1. Pinout Diagram

GLOSSARY

Absolute address: A number that specifies the address of a location in memory, as opposed to a relative address, which specifies a displacement.

Accumulator: A working register.

ACIA: (*See* Asynchronous Communications Interface Adapter)

Active low: A designation meaning that the function is performed when the appropriate line or signal is at low voltage and not when the line is at high voltage.

Address: A number that identifies a single location in memory.

Address bus: A bus that transmits an address and lets the MPU select an individual location in memory.

Address decoding: The process by which the MPU's address lines are connected to the select lines of devices so that each device has a unique set of addresses.

Addressing mode: Method of specifying exactly how the operand of an instruction identifies the data.

Address word: A set of bits used to determine an address.

Algorithm: A series of logical steps to be followed sequentially in order to solve a problem or perform a task.

ALU: (*See* Arithmetic and Logic Unit)

American Standard Code for Information Interchange (*See* ASCII)

AND function: A logic function where the output is 1 only if all the inputs are 1.

AND gate: A logic gate for the AND function.

Architecture: A description of a microprocessor system's hardware parts, how they are connected, and how they communicate with each other.

Arithmetic and Logic Unit (ALU): That part of a CPU that performs arithmetic and logical operations and executes data transfers.

ASCII: American Standard Code for Information Interchange. A 7-bit character code.

Assembler: A program that translates an assembly language program into a machine language program.

Assembler directive: An instruction to the assembler, not translated into machine code.

Assembling: Translating an assembly language program into a machine language program.

Assembly (symbolic) language: A language in which symbols are used instead of numbers to represent OP codes and operands.

Asynchronous: Indefinite periods of time may lapse between transmission of pieces of data.

Asynchronous Communications Interface Adapter (ACIA):   A chip that provides a serial connection between the MPU and peripherals.

Base: A number used as reference for constructing a number system.

Base complement: In any base number system, 2 numbers that add up to 0 with a carry of 1 are defined as base complements of one another.

Base sixteen: Number system having sixteen digits, 0–9 and A–F.

Base ten: Number system having ten digits, 0–9 (decimal system).

Base two: Number system having two digits, 0–1.

Baud rate: Bits per second (the reciprocal of bit time).

BCD: (*See* Binary Coded Decimal)

Bidirectional: Data can flow in one of two directions.

Binary: Having two states.

Binary Coded Decimal (BCD):   A number system in which a set of 4 bits represents 1 decimal digit.

Binary logic: A system of data manipulation using a set of variables (1 and 0) and a series of logical operations.

Binary representation: Base 2 number system.

Bit: A binary digit.

Bit time: The amount of time to transmit a single bit.

Block diagram: A graphic description of individual parts of a system and how they interact.

Breakpoint: A point in a program where the MPU stops executing.

Buffer: A device that increases the number of other devices that can be serviced.

Bus: A set of wires used to transmit information among two or more devices.

Byte: A set of 8 bits.

Call: To transfer control from a main program to a subroutine.

Calling instructions: Instructions that call a subroutine.

Calling program: A main program that calls a subroutine.

Carry: A digit that has a nonzero value when the sum of two or more digits equals or exceeds the base of the number system.

Carry status bit (C):   Bit 0 in the 6800's status register; set if the result of an ALU operation is a number too large to be contained in the 8-bit data word.

Central Processor Unit (CPU):   (*See* Processor)

Character code: A code in which a binary number represents a character.

Character rate: The number of characters transmitted per second.

Character time: The amount of time to transmit a single character (the reciprocal of character rate).

Chip: (*See* Integrated Circuit)

Chip Select (CS):   A pin that, when active, lets a chip access the data bus. A chip select is active when the MPU is addressing that chip.

Cleared: Contents set to zero.

Clock: A device that produces a series of regular pulses that synchronize the operations within a microcomputer.

Clock cycle: The interval between successive positive or negative transitions in a clock pulse.

Clock frequency: The reciprocal of cycle time; or, the number of clock cycles per second.

Comment field: Field in an assembly language program that contains a comment.

Computer: A machine that processes data.

Computer program: A series of instructions that direct a computer to perform a specific task.

Condition Code (CC) register: A 1-byte register whose individual bits contain information about conditions in the microcomputer.

Conditional branch: A point in a flowchart that contains a decision box; the flowchart branches in one of two directions, depending on a certain condition.

Conditional transfer of control: A transfer of control that takes place only if a specific condition is satisfied.

Configure (a system):   To design a scheme of connecting a MPU to other devices in a system.

Configure (PIA):   To set the peripheral data lines of the PIA to be inputs or outputs.

Connection box: A circular flowchart element used for connecting one segment of a flowchart to another segment (used when lack of space dictates continuation of a flowchart onto another page).

Control bus: A bus that transmits control signals.

Control character: A character that performs a function without resulting in anything being typed.

Control register (ACIA):   An 8-bit write-only register in the ACIA that determines division of external clock, number of data bits, parity, transmitter control, and interrupts enable.

Control register (PIA):   A register in the PIA that allows the user to choose among a variety of functions. There are two control registers: one for side A (CRA) and one for side B (CRB).

Control unit: That part of the CPU that directs the fetching and executing of instructions, by providing timing and control signals.

Control word: A word stored in a location used for control.

Counter divide select: A set of 2 bits (0 and 1) in the ACIA's control register, used to select the divide ratio for the external clock.

Counting loop: A loop that is iterated a definite number of times.

Cross assembler: An assembler that assembles a program to be run on another computer.

Cycle time: The time it takes a microcomputer to complete one clock cycle.

Data address: An address whose location contains the value (the data) to be operated on by the program.

Data bus: A bus that transmits data into and out of MPU.

Data Direction Register (DDR) for PIA: A register in the PIA whose contents determines whether each bit in the corresponding data register will be used for input (0) or output (1). There are two DDRs; one for side A (DDRA) and one for side B (DDRB).

Data Register (DR) for PIA: (*See* Peripheral data register)

Data word: A set of bits corresponding to the number of data lines.

Decision box: A diamond-shaped flowchart element having one input and two possible outputs: "yes" and "no," depending on whether or not some predetermined condition is true or false.

Decode: To interpret an instruction.

Delay routine: A routine used in any program where a specific time delay is desired.

Destination: In a data transfer, the final location of the data.

Digit: A nonnegative integer smaller than the base of the number system.

Digital logic: (*See* Binary logic)

DIP: (*See* Dual In-line Package)

Direct addressing mode: An addressing mode in which the data to be processed is in a memory location identified by a 1-byte address, which is the low-order byte of a zero page operand.

Don't care: A bit whose value doesn't matter (usually because the bit isn't connected).

Double-precision arithmetic: Arithmetic using two computer words to represent one number.

DO-WHILE unit: (*See* Loop)

Dual In-line Package (DIP): A type of IC packaging having two parallel rows of pins.

Dump (punch): To transfer a block of data from a microcomputer's memory to a peripheral.

EAROM: (*See* Electrically Alterable Read Only Memory)

Edge control bit (of PIA): Bits 1 and 4 of the PIA's control register. When set, these bits cause the PIA to expect an interrupt on the rising edge; otherwise, the PIA expects the interrupt on the falling edge.

Edge-triggered: A response triggered by either the rising or the falling edge and not by the level.

Editor: A program that allows the user to correct or modify text.

Electrically Alterable Read-Only Memory (EAROM): A type of Read-Only Memory that can be both programmed and erased with electrical stimuli.

Element: A box representing a specific step in a flowchart.

EPROM: (*See* Erasable Programmable Read Only Memory)

Erasable Programmable Read-Only Memory (EPROM): A type of Read-Only Memory that can be erased by applying ultraviolet light, and then reprogrammed.

Even parity: Having an even number of "1" bits.

Exclusive OR (XOR) function: A logic function that gives an output of 1 only if an odd number of 1's are input.

Exclusive OR (XOR) gate: A logic gate for the exclusive OR function.

Execute: To carry out the instructions in a computer program.

Extended addressing mode: An addressing mode in which the data to be processed is in a memory location identified by a 2-byte address (the operand).

Falling edge: A transition from high to low voltage.

Fetch: The reading of an instruction by a computer.

Field: A column in an assembly language program.

Fifteens complement: When expressed in base sixteen, 2 numbers are fifteens complements of one another if their sum is all F's.

Flip-flop: An electronic switch that can have one of two states.

Flowchart: A graphical representation of an algorithm.

Frame: To place start and stop bits around a serially transmitted character.

Framing error: A mistake in the number of stop bits.

Full adder: A device that adds 3 single-digit inputs and produces 2 outputs (sum and carry).

Fully decoded: Every address line is used in connecting a device.

Garbage: Data that has no meaning in the present context.

General register transfer notation: Register transfer notation, using the general terms M and X for memory and accumulator.

Glitch (noise spike):   Extraneous noise picked up on a wire.

Half-carry status bit (H):   Bit 5 of the 6800's status register; set if there is a carry from the least significant nibble during an addition.

Hand-assembling: The process of translating an assembly language program into a machine language program by hand rather than by an assembler.

Hand-coding: (*See* Hand-assembling)

Hardware: The physical parts of a computer.

Hardware interrupt: An interrupt caused by an external device connected to one of the MPU's interrupt pins.

Hexadecimal: Base sixteen number system.

Hexadecimal digit: A digit in base sixteen.

Hexadecimal representation: The name for the base sixteen number system, in which a set of 4 binary digits is equivalent to 1 hexadecimal digit.

High impedance state: A state in which a device is disabled or disconnected from the circuit.

High-order byte: The leftmost byte, or leftmost 2 hexadecimal digits.

High (voltage):   Around 5 V.

IC: (*See* Integrated Circuit)

IF-THEN-ELSE unit: A flowchart segment that contains a decision box and its alternative task boxes. That is, IF the condition is true, THEN do something; otherwise (ELSE) do something else.

Immediate addressing mode: An addressing mode in which the data to be processed is the operand that follows immediately after the OP code.

Immediate operand: The number that follows the OP code in the immediate addressing mode.

Increment: To increase by a small amount (one, for the 6800).

Indexed addressing mode: An addressing mode where the address of the operand is computed by adding an offset to the index register contents.

Index register: A register whose contents are used in computing an indexed address. The 6800's index register is 2 bytes long.

Inherent addressing mode: An addressing mode in which either the data to be processed is found in an internal register or there is no data.

Input: Data given to the microprocessor.

Input/Output (I/O): The link between the microprocessor and the outside world.

Input/Output port: The place where data comes into and goes out of a device.

Instruction: A statement that tells the microprocessor what to do. Consists of an operation plus one or more operands.

Instruction code: (*See* Operation Code)

Instruction Register (IR): A 1-byte register that holds the OP code temporarily until it can be interpreted.

Instruction set: A set of operations and OP codes characteristic of a specific microprocessor.

Interface circuitry: An assembly of electrical circuit elements that provide the necessary connection between a microcomputer and an external device.

Integrated Circuit (IC): A piece of silicon that has several electronic parts on it (a complete circuit).

Internal bus: A set of conductors within the MPU over which signals are exchanged among its components.

Interrupt: A temporary suspension of a computer's executing program so that it can deal with a higher-priority task.

Interrupt flag bits (of PIA): Bits 6 and 7 of the PIA's control register; bit 7 is set if an interrupt occurs on CA1. Bit 6 is set if an interrupt occurs on CA2.

Interrupt input pin (of PIA): A pin through which the PIA may receive an interrupt from a peripheral device.

Interrupt mask bit: Bit 4 of the 6800's status register. When this bit is set, the IRQ signal (but not the RES or NMI) is prevented from interrupting the MPU.

Interrupt output pin (of PIA): A pin through which the PIA may pass an interrupt to the MPU.

Interrupt service routine: A routine to be executed in the event of an interrupt.

Interrupt vectors: Locations assigned to interrupts, containing the starting address of their service routines.

Invert: To reverse the value of a bit.

Inverter (NOT gate): A gate or device with one input and one output. The output always has the opposite state to the input.

I/O: (*See* Input/Output)

I/O port: (*See* Input/Output Port)

Iterative portion of loop: The part of a loop that is repeated.

Kilobyte (kbyte):   1024 bytes.

Label: A group of 1 to 6 alphanumeric characters, of which the first must be alphabetic, used to identify a program name, statement, or memory location.

Label field: A field in an assembly language program that may contain a label, be empty, or contain a comment.

Large-Scale Integration (LSI):   The technology enabling more and more electronic parts to be put onto smaller and smaller chips.

Least Significant Digit (LSD):   The rightmost digit in a number.

LED: (*See* Light-Emitting Diode)

Level-sensitive: A response triggered by the level (high or low voltage) of a line, and not by the edge.

LIFO: Last-In-First-Out.

Light-Emitting Diode (LED):   A small device (a diode) that produces a red light when turned on.

Line number: A number used for identifying or locating a line in a program.

Listing: A document that shows a side-by-side comparison of the assembly language program and the machine language program resulting from it.

Load: To copy a number from a memory location into a register; or to transfer a block of data from a peripheral device to the microcomputer's memory.

Logical operation: An operation that treats the two variables 1 and 0 as true and false rather than as the numbers "1" and "0."

Logic circuit: The electronic implementation of a logical operation.

Logic gate: A logic circuit that has one or more inputs and only one output.

Look-up table: A table that contains two equivalent sets of values stored side by side so that any one of them can be retrieved at will.

Loop (DO-WHILE unit):   A program or flowchart structure that causes certain operations to be performed over and over until some end condition is reached.

Loop counter: A device used to keep track of the number of times through a loop.

Low (voltage):   Around 0 V.

Low-order byte: The rightmost byte, or 2 hexadecimal digits.

LSD: (*See* Least Significant Digit)

LSI: (*See* Large-Scale Integration)

Machine code: Binary or hexadecimal numbers used to convey instructions to a microprocessor (a "machine").

Machine language: Binary or hexadecimal numbers used to convey instructions to a microprocessor (a machine).

MAR: (*See* Memory Address Register)

Mark: A high voltage on a serial data line that denotes no characters are being transmitted.

Mask: A bit pattern that isolates one or more bits from a group.

Mask bit (of PIA):   Bits 0 and 3 of the PIA's control register. If bit 0 is set, the PIA is not allowed to pass along a CA1 interrupt to the MPU. If bit 3 is set, the PIA is not allowed to pass along a CA2 interrupt to the MPU.

Masking: Protection of part of a set of bits prior to an operation.

MDR: (*See* Memory Data Register)

Megabyte (mbyte): 1,048,576 bytes.

Memory: A set of physical locations that can contain numbers.

Memory Address Register (MAR): A 2-byte register, not accessible to the user, that the MPU uses to hold temporarily an address that has been fetched from memory.

Memory Data Register (MDR): A 1-byte register, not accessible to the user, that the MPU uses to store data temporarily.

Memory-mapped I/O: Input and output devices are assigned specific addresses in memory to be read from (input) or written to (output).

Microcomputer: A microprocessor plus memory and I/O.

Micro instruction: A single instruction in a microprogram.

Microprocessor (MPU): A single small device that performs the functions of a CPU. The MPU contains the calculating, decoding, and decision-making parts of a computer on a single chip.

Microprocessor system: A microprocessor plus other devices needed to do a specific task.

Microprogram: A set of micro instructions for the hardware operations needed to execute an instruction.

Mnemonic: A group of letters (usually three, sometimes four) that symbolize an instruction.

Monitor: A program with which the user can communicate with a microprocessor through I/O. The monitor also lets the user run programs, examine and change the contents of registers and memory locations, and examine the status of the processor.

Most Significant Digit (MSD): The leftmost digit in a number.

MPU: (*See* Microprocessor)

MSD: (*See* Most Significant Digit)

NAND function: A function that inverts the result of the AND operation.

NAND gate: A logic gate for the NAND function.

Negative status bit (N): Bit 3 in the 6800's status register; set if bit 7 of the result is set after an ALU operation.

Negative transition: A change from a high to a low voltage.

Nested loops: Loops within loops.

Nested subroutines: Subroutines within subroutines.

Nibble: Half a byte (4 bits).

Nines complement: When expressed in the decimal system, 2 numbers are nines complements of one another when their sum is all nines.

Noise spike: (*See* Glitch)

Nonvolatile memory: A type of memory where data is retained even when the power is shut off.

NOR function: A function that inverts the result of an OR operation.

NOR gate: The logic gate for the NOR function.

NOT function: A logic function that reverses the input value.

NOT gate: (*See* Inverter)

Object code: The hexadecimal or binary numbers contained in an object program.

Object program: The machine language program resulting from the assembling of a source program.

Odd parity: Having an odd number of "1" bits.

Offset: An 8-bit unsigned number that, when added to the index register contents, gives an indexed address.

Ones complement: When expressed in binary, 2 numbers are ones complements of one another if their sum is all 1's. The ones complement of a binary number may also be obtained by reversing the value of each bit.

OP code: (*See* Operation code)

Operand: The quantity that is operated on. (The object of the instruction.)

Operand field: Field in an assembly language program that contains the operand.

Operation: That part of an instruction that tells what to do. (The verb of the instruction.)

Operation code (OP code): A binary or hexadecimal number that serves as a code for a particular operation.

Operation field: Field in an assembly language program that contains the operation; that is, a mnemonic or assembler directive.

OR function: A logic function where the output is true if any one of its inputs is true.

OR gate: A logic gate for the OR function.

Output: Data from the microprocessor.

Overflow: A condition resulting from the addition of signed numbers where the result exceeds the range of signed numbers allowed by the number of digits available.

Overflow status bit (V): Bit 1 of the 6800's status register; set if an overflow occurs as a result of an arithmetic operation.

Page zero addressing: (*See* Direct addressing)

Parallel I/O: The transmission of a group of bits (usually a byte) simultaneously.

Parameters: Data passed between a subroutine and a calling program.

Parity bit: The bit that is used to adjust the parity of a binary number (bit 7 in ASCII code).

Passing parameters: Giving data to and getting data from subroutines.

Peripheral: A unit of processing equipment external to the CPU, such as a keypad, display, or printer.

Peripheral data pins (for PIA): Pins for sending or receiving data to or from peripheral devices.

Peripheral data register (for PIA): Also called Data Register (DR). A register in the PIA that holds the current data to be input to output from the PIA. There are two data registers, for side A (DRA) and side B (DRB), respectively.

Peripheral Interface Adapter (PIA): A device that interfaces with a peripheral under direction from the CPU.

PIA: (*See* Peripheral Interface Adapter)

Pin: A connector in a DIP by which the device may be connected to other devices.

Pin-out: A diagram showing the pins of an IC and what they represent.

Polling: To interrogate each I/O device to determine whether or not it needs service.

Positional notation: A system of notation where the number is represented as a sum of individual digits multiplied by exponentials (of the base) that represent their positional values.

Positive transition: A change from a low to a high voltage.

Prioritize: To assign priorities to interrupting devices.

Processor: That part of a computer that fetches, decodes, and executes instructions; it contains the control, calculating, and decision-making sections of a computer.

Program address: An address whose location contains a word that is part of a program instruction.

Program control: Control of a computer's actions by means of a series of instructions in a computer program.

Program Counter (PC):   A 2-byte register that holds the address of the next location whose contents are to be fetched.

Program environment: The contents of all registers except for the stack pointer.

Programmable Read-Only Memory (PROM):   A type of Read Only Memory that is programmable by the user.

PROM: (*See* Programmable Read-Only Memory)

Pulling from the stack: Copying the top value from a microprocessor's stack.

Punch: (*See* Dump)

Pushing onto the stack: Storing a value in the top memory location of a microprocessor's stack.

Radix: (*See* Base)

RAM: (*See* Random Access Memory)

Random Access Memory (RAM):   A type of memory in which any individual location may be accessed directly. Usually Read/Write Memory.

RDR: (*See* Receive Data Register)

Read: To nondestructively copy a number from one location to another.

Read-Only Memory (ROM):   A type of memory having only read capabilities.

Read/Write memory: A type of memory that has both read and write capabilities.

Receive Data Register (RDR):   A read-only 8-bit shift register in the ACIA that collects and shifts in 8 bits of serial data from a peripheral and passes it to the MPU as parallel data.

Register: A physical location that can contain a binary value.

Register select: A pin used to select a register on a device that has more than one register.

Register transfer notation: Shorthand notation describing an instruction in terms of data transfer among registers and memory locations.

Relative address: A signed displacement that is added to the current program counter contents. The result of the addition is placed back in the program counter to effect a transfer of control.

Relative addressing mode: An addressing mode where the OP code is followed by a 1-byte relative address.

Resident assembler: An assembler that resides on the same computer on which it will be run.

Return: To transfer control from a subroutine to the calling program.

Return instruction: An instruction that causes a return.

Rising edge: A transition from low to high voltage.

ROM: (*See* Read-Only Memory)

Routine: A program segment that performs a specialized task and can be part of a larger program.

Sensing loop: A loop whose terminal condition is caused by an external event.

Sequence field: Field in an assembly language program that contains line numbers if they are used.

Serial: One bit at a time.

Serial input port: A single conductor over which serial data is input to the MPU from a peripheral device.

Serial I/O: The transmission of a group of bits one bit at a time.

Serial output port: A wire for outputting serial data from the MPU to a peripheral device.

Service (of an interrupt): To transfer control to the interrupt service routine.

Set: The contents are set to one.

Seven-segment display: A device having seven bar-shaped segments composed of LEDs. When all segments are turned on, a figure "8" is displayed. Numerals and some characters are formed by selectively lighting segments of the display.

Shift register: A register in which a word of data may be shifted to the right or to the left.

Sign bit: The most significant bit in a signed binary number.

Signed binary number: A binary number that can be specified either as positive or negative.

Sign extension: Filling out the 8 more significant bits with all 0's (00 in hexadecimal) if the number is positive, and with all 1's (FF in hexadecimal) if the number is negative.

Software: Computer programs.

Software aid: (*See* Utility program)

Software interrupt: An interrupt caused by an instruction in a program.

Source: In a data transfer, the location where the data originates.

Source code: The specific symbols in a source program.

Source program: An assembly language program.

Space: A low voltage that signals the beginning of a serial character.

Specific register transfer notation: Register transfer notation using specific symbols for memory locations and registers.

Stack: A set of contiguous memory locations used in Last-In-First-Out (LIFO) fashion.

Stack pointer: A register (2 bytes, for the 6800) in the CPU whose contents determine the location where data is to be pushed onto the stack.

Start bit: A low voltage at the beginning of a serial character.

Status register: (*See* Condition code register)

Status register of ACIA: An 8-bit read-only register in the ACIA that gives the status of various conditions in the ACIA.

Stop bit: A high voltage that denotes the end of a serial character.

Store: To copy a number from a register into a memory location.

Subroutine: A routine that causes the microprocessor to return to the main program automatically at the point of departure.

Symbolic language: (*See* Assembly language)

Synchronous: Taking the same amount of time to transmit each piece of data, with no time lapses in between.

Table: A systematic arrangement of data in rows and columns for ready reference.

Task box: A flowchart element that contains an operation.

Tens complement: Base complement in the decimal system.

Terminal box: A flowchart element that shows where the flowchart starts or stops.

Three-state buffer: A buffer that has three possible states: 1, 0, and disabled (high impedance).

Timing loop: A loop whose purpose is to provide a time delay.

Toggle: To reverse the state of a bit or switch.

Two-state logic: (*See* Binary logic)

Transfer of control: A departure from the normal sequential execution of instructions to a new specific location.

Transmit Data Register (TDR):   A write-only 8-bit shift register in the ACIA. The TDR takes a byte of parallel data from the MPU and shifts it out serially.

Triple precision arithmetic: Arithmetic involving 3-byte numbers.

Truth table: A table that gives the outputs for all possible inputs to a system.

Twos complement: Base complement in the binary system.

Unconditional transfer of control: A transfer of control that takes place always; no decision is involved.

Unidirectional: Data may flow in one direction only.

Unsigned binary number: A binary number whose sign is not specified.

Utility program: Program that helps the user in program (or text) writing.

Variable data: Data whose value may vary from one time to the next.

Volatile memory: A type of memory where data stored is retained only as long as power is supplied.

Wire-OR: Wiring two inputs to a single pin so that either one will activate the pin.

Word: A set of bits of varying length, usually multiples of four or eight.

Word select bits: Bits 2, 3, and 4 of the ACIA's control register. The user may select word length, parity, and number of stop bits with the bit pattern in the word select bits.

Working register: A register in which various operations may be performed on the contents and the results accumulated.

Write: To store a number destructively in a location.

Zero status bit (Z):   Bit 2 in the 6800's status register; set if the result of an ALU operation is zero.

Index